CONTENTS

INTRODUCTION *By Lindy Zesch*	vii
HIGHLIGHTS 1961-1993 *32 Years in the American Theatre*	ix
USING THIS BOOK	xv
THEATRES	xvii
THEATRE PROFILES	1
THEATRE CHRONOLOGY	178
REGIONAL INDEX	180
INDEX OF NAMES	182
INDEX OF TITLES	210
ABOUT TCG	220

THEATRE PROFILES 11

THEATRE PROFILES 11

THE ILLUSTRATED GUIDE
TO AMERICA'S NONPROFIT
PROFESSIONAL THEATRE

EDITED BY STEVEN SAMUELS

THEATRE COMMUNICATIONS GROUP
NEW YORK • 1994

Theatre Profiles 11 and TCG's other resource publications are supported, in part, by a generous grant from the Andrew W. Mellon Foundation.

TCG also gratefully acknowledges the support of American Express Company, Ameritech Foundation, ARCO Foundation, AT&T Foundation, The Coca-Cola Company, Consolidated Edison Company of New York, Council of Literary Magazines and Presses, The Nathan Cummings Foundation, Dayton Hudson Foundation, 1st Nationwide Bank, Ford Foundation, The Hyde and Watson Foundation, The James Irvine Foundation, Jerome Foundation, Metropolitan Life Foundation, National Broadcasting Company, Inc., National Endowment for the Arts, New York City Department of Cultural Affairs, New York State Council on the Arts, The New York Times Company Foundation, The Pew Charitable Trusts, Philip Morris Companies Inc., The Rockefeller Foundation, The Scherman Foundation, The Shubert Foundation, The Audrey Skirball-Kenis Theatre, Inc., United States Information Agency, Lila Wallace-Reader's Digest Fund.

Copyright © 1994 by Theatre Communications Group, Inc., 355 Lexington Ave., New York, NY 10017.

All rights reserved. Except for brief passages quoted in newspaper, magazine, radio or television reviews, no part of this book may be reproduced in any form or by any means, electronic or mechanical, including photocopying or recording, or by an information storage and retrieval system, without permission in writing from the publisher.

TCG would like to thank the following staff members and individuals who helped with the massive job of preparing this volume: Stephanie Coen, Gretchen Griffin, Sheela Kangal, Julie Kramer, Linda MacColl, Gillian Richards and Lisa Yoffee.

Design and composition by Dushan and Peter Lukic

ISBN 1-55936-077-1

First Edition, March 1994

On the cover: McCarter Theatre Center for the Performing Arts. Frances McDormand in Three Sisters. Photo by T. Charles Erickson.

Frontis: The Shakespeare Theatre. Top to bottom: Floyd King, Sabrina Le Beauf and Melissa Gallagher in As You Like It. Photo by Joan Marcus.

INTRODUCTION
By Lindy Zesch

The nonprofit professional theatre movement swept the country in the early 1960s, inspired by the existence of a few pioneering theatres scattered in cities like Houston, San Francisco and Washington, D.C., and by the growing Off-Broadway movement in New York. The movement reached its peak in the 1970s; by then, the landscape was covered from coast to coast, and theatres had even sprung up in Alaska and Hawaii. For the first time in history, Americans had access to homegrown professional theatre, not just amateur theatre and touring Broadway road shows.

The 238 theatres profiled in this 1991-93 edition of *Theatre Profiles* are located in 131 communities across the country, representing 39 states and the District of Columbia. They reflect a wide artistic, cultural and geographical scope, including theatres that specialize in classics, new plays and musicals; companies that focus on theatre for young audiences, ethnically specific work, as well as more wide-ranging, eclectic repertoires; and ensembles that experiment with new forms and techniques that will inform and affect the work of the future.

Each of the theatres in this book is professional, meeting basic eligibility requirements to become a constituent of Theatre Communications Group, the national organization for the American theatre.

In TCG's most recent annual survey of the finances and productivity of the field, *Theatre Facts 92*, the 182 participating theatres constituted a $366-million national enterprise, played to a total attendance of more than 16 million, presented 46,184 performances of more than 2,300 productions and employed more than 27,600 actors, directors, designers, playwrights, administrators and technicians all across the country.

The survey revealed that the lingering recession continued to take a heavy toll on the nonprofit professional theatres, which were extremely vulnerable to the economic downturn in the overall marketplace. Nearly half the survey universe ended the year with operating deficits, and four theatres were forced to cease operations in 1991-92.

Through increasingly sophisticated marketing techniques, combined with some financially motivated programming choices, the theatres managed to sustain attendance levels, but touring of productions declined sharply, and cutbacks affected such developmental activities as workshops, staged readings and other ancillary programs. Many theatres were also forced to cut salaries, reduce full-time staffs, or make do with diminished artistic resources to make ends meet.

Reductions in state and federal government grants, along with a first-time decline in support from the business community, impacted contributed income levels. While strong growth in donations from individuals and foundation grants improved the otherwise bleak statistics, total contributed income did not manage to keep pace with inflation, and expenses grew considerably faster than income.

Although the arts continued to experience attacks from conservatives in Congress and right-wing religious groups that began in 1990, the election of Bill Clinton as President and his public statements in support of the arts offered new hope for the future of the National Endowment for the Arts. In the fall of 1993, arts advocates—and the theatre community in particular—were ecstatic with the appointment of actress Jane Alexander, the first professional artist to head the NEA.

In spite of the economic and political issues that confronted the American theatre throughout the past two seasons, there were many extraordinary achievements, including Pulitzer Prizes awarded to works of epic scope that commenced life at nonprofit theatres and were further developed at other theatres before moving on to the commercial marketplace of

Broadway: Robert Schenkkan's six-hour play, *The Kentucky Cycle*, which premiered at Seattle's Intiman Theatre and received a second production at the Mark Taper Forum in Los Angeles; and Tony Kushner's *Angels in America: Millennium Approaches*, the first half of his two-part epic, which began life at San Francisco's Eureka Theatre prior to productions at the Mark Taper Forum and London's National Theatre. Works of such scale belie the economic troubles of the field and suggest that artistic imperatives drive theatres even in difficult times.

Anna Deavere Smith's stunningly provocative one-woman show, *Fires in the Mirror*, opened at the New York Shakespeare Festival and demonstrated once again theatre's unique ability to address social issues in ways the media and politicians often fail to do. Through her unique form of cultural journalism, Smith created a piece of pure theatre that enabled audiences to confront the explosive issues surrounding events in the Crown Heights section of Brooklyn that polarized the Jewish and African-American communities, and revealed the diverse views that can divide our multicultural society.

Other trends in the field include expanded efforts to engage in international exchange with theatre colleagues and companies around the globe, continued creation of new companies that will eventually join the roster of theatres listed in future volumes of this series, a growing interest in collaborative work and coproductions, and increased cultural diversity on stages across the country, reflecting our nation's changing demographics.

This edition of *Theatre Profiles* is the eleventh in a biennial series that now encompasses twenty-two seasons since the first volume appeared in 1973, covering the 1971-73 seasons. Taken in its entirety the series constitutes an extraordinary history of an unprecedented artistic movement.

—Lindy Zesch
December 1993

HIGHLIGHTS 1961-1993
32 Years in the American Theatre

Although the early sixties were a turning point in the American theatre, the seeds of three alternatives to Broadway's commercial activities had been planted prior to 1960. The Off-Broadway movement, which had been established with the success of several companies including an early nonprofit theatre—Circle in the Square (founded 1951)—faced escalating costs, prompting the rise of what inevitably became known as Off-*Off* Broadway. This energetic offshoot encompassed the efforts of such pioneering groups as The Living Theatre (1951) and Caffe Cino (1958). Elsewhere in the U.S., what was coming to be known as the "regional theatre movement" had taken hold in such cities as Cleveland (The Cleveland Play House, 1915), Chicago (Goodman Theatre, 1925), Abingdon, Va. (Robert Porterfield's Barter Theatre, 1933), Houston (Alley Theatre, 1947), Dallas (Margo Jones's Theatre 47, 1947), Washington, D.C. (Arena Stage, 1950) and San Francisco (Actors Workshop, 1952).

In addition to these regional or resident theatres, a number of Shakespeare festivals dotted the American landscape, including the Oregon Shakespeare Festival in Ashland (1935), Old Globe Theatre in San Diego (1937), New York Shakespeare Festival (1954) and American Shakespeare Theatre in Stratford, Conn. (1955). It was from these roots—the early regional companies along with a vital Off-Off Broadway movement—that the full-fledged non-commercial theatre sprang, spreading, through the seventies, to the furthest reaches of the nation.

1961—The Living Theatre presents Kenneth Brown's *The Brig*, following its influential 1959 production of Jack Gelber's *The Connection*. Tennessee Williams's last widely acclaimed play, *Night of the Iguana*, appears on Broadway. The Judson Poets' Theatre, under the direction of Al Carmines, opens in lower Manhattan's Judson Church. The Bread and Puppet Theatre is born in New York with a production of *Totentanz*. Ford Foundation trustees appropriate an initial $9 million to begin "strengthening the position of resident theatre in the U.S." along with $244,000 for the establishment of Theatre Communications Group. In addition, Ford vice president for the humanities and arts W. McNeil Lowry engages Danny Newman, through TCG, as a sub-scription consultant, sparking enormous audience growth throughout the nation.

1962—Edward Albee's *Who's Afraid of Virginia Woolf?* opens on Broadway, directed by Alan Schneider. New York Shakespeare Festival's 2,300-seat, open-air Delacorte Theatre opens in Central Park. Arthur Kopit's *Oh Dad, Poor Dad . . .* premieres Off Broadway. Ellen Stewart creates Cafe La MaMa Off-Off Broadway, beginning with Tennessee Williams's *One Arm*. The Great Lakes Shakespeare Festival opens in Cleveland.

1963—The Guthrie Theater, the first institutional theatre in the U.S. built solely with community support and dedicated to a classical repertoire, opens in Minneapolis with *Hamlet*. Joseph Chaikin, along with Peter Feldman and a group of artists, founds the Open Theatre in New York. The Seattle Repertory Theatre and Center Stage in Baltimore begin operations. Gilbert Moses and John O'Neal open the Free Southern Theatre at Mississippi's Tougaloo College, in response to the Civil Rights movement.

1964—The first two plays of budding playwright Sam Shepard, *Cowboy* and *Rock Garden*, are produced at New York's Theatre Genesis. The Lincoln Center Repertory Theatre is established with Elia Kazan and Robert Whitehead at the helm. The Phoenix and APA theatres merge, and for four years produce plays in repertory on Broadway. The recently founded American Place Theatre opens Off Broadway with a production of Robert Lowell's *The Old Glory*. Adrian Hall founds Trinity Repertory Company (originally Trinity Square Repertory Company) in Providence. Among other theatres to begin operation are Actors Theatre of Louisville and Hartford Stage Company. Ming Cho Lee designs sets for a production of *Electra* in Central Park, forging a new, sculptural design style. The Living Theatre begins two decades of exile in Europe and South America.

1965—San Francisco's American Conservatory Theatre, the first company to operate a professional conservatory, opens under the artistic direction of William Ball. Luis Valdez founds El Teatro Campesino to entertain California's striking farm workers. Robert Kalfin founds the Chelsea Theater Center in Manhattan. The O'Neill Theater Center holds its first National Playwrights' Conference in Waterford, Conn. President Lyndon B. Johnson signs legislation creating the National Endowment for the Arts. Long Wharf Theatre opens in New Haven.

1966—The Twentieth Century Fund publishes the first book to study in depth the subject of economics and the arts, *Performing Arts—The Economic Dilemma*, by William J. Baumol and William G. Bowen. The NEA receives its first funds from Congress: $2.5 million to be spread among all the arts throughout the country. Robert Brustein establishes the Yale Repertory Theatre, to operate in conjunction with the Yale School of

Drama. Jules Irving and Herbert Blau bring members of their Actors Workshop from San Francisco to found a new company at New York's Lincoln Center. Megan Terry's *Viet Rock* is born out of an Open Theatre workshop. Ronald Ribman's *Journey of the Fifth Horse*, featuring Dustin Hoffman, premieres at the American Place Theatre. The first League of Resident Theatres contract comes into being.

1967—Sir Tyrone Guthrie directs the *Oresteia* at the Guthrie, with designs by Tanya Moiseiwitsch. John Houseman's Theatre Group, in residence at UCLA since 1959, is invited to move into the Los Angeles Music Center and becomes the Mark Taper Forum; Gordon Davidson is appointed artistic director. Barbara Garson's *MacBird* is first performed at New York's Village Gate. Edward Albee's *A Delicate Balance* wins the Pulitzer Prize for Drama. The New York Shakespeare Festival moves into its new facility, the Public Theater on Lafayette Street, opening with the rock musical *Hair*. Richard Schechner founds The Performance Group in New York along Grotowski-inspired lines. The San Francisco Mime Troupe (founded in 1959 by Ronnie Davis) comes to national prominence with a cross-country tour of anti-war scenarios. Douglas Turner Ward, Robert Hooks and Gerald S. Krone found the Negro Ensemble Company in New York, opening with Peter Weiss's *Song of the Lusitanian Bogey*. Eugene Lee designs his first set for Trinity Repertory Company, *The Threepenny Opera*, beginning a long association with the theatre and with director Adrian Hall. A group of theatre artists, psychologists and social scientists found the National Theatre of the Deaf. Joe Cino commits suicide and Caffe Cino closes its doors.

1968—The Open Theatre presents Jean-Claude van Itallie's *The Serpent*, and The Performance Group opens *Dionysus in 69*. The Living Theatre returns to the U.S. briefly to present *Paradise Now* and *Frankenstein* at the Yale Repertory Theatre and the Brooklyn Academy of Music. *Hair* brings Broadway its first nude scene. The Arena Stage production of *The Great White Hope* opens on Broadway, winning the Pulitzer. Richard Foreman founds the Ontological-Hysteric Theatre.

1969—Gilbert Moses directs the Chelsea Theater Center production of Amiri Baraka's *Slave Ship* at the Brooklyn Academy of Music, with an elaborate environment designed by Eugene Lee. Robert Wilson founds the Byrd Hoffman School of Byrds. Marshall W. Mason, Lanford Wilson and colleagues found Circle Repertory Company in New York. Gerald Freedman's production of *The Taming of the Shrew* at the New York Shakespeare Festival uses American farce techniques inspired by Chaplin, Keaton and the like. Romanian director Andrei Serban arrives in the U.S. and begins directing at La MaMa. Broadway's ANTA Theatre hosts the first showcase of work from the nation's resident theatres, including the American Conservatory Theatre, the American Shakespeare Theatre, Trinity Repertory Company and the National Theatre of the Deaf.

1970—A collective of performing artists founds Mabou Mines, and Lee Breuer presents the first of his "Animations." Daniel Berrigan's *The Trial of the Catonsville Nine*, directed by Gordon Davidson, premieres at the Mark Taper Forum. Andre Gregory and his Manhattan Project premiere their landmark *Alice in Wonderland* in New York.

1971—Peter Brook and the Royal Shakespeare Company return to New York with their *Midsummer Night's Dream*. The Negro Ensemble Company produces *The River Niger* and takes it on tour. David Rabe's *The Basic Training of Pavlo Hummel* premieres at the New York Shakespeare Festival. Playwrights Horizons, dedicated to new work, is founded by Robert Moss in New York City. Lyn Austin founds the Music-Theatre Group/Lenox Arts Center in Massachusetts to nurture dynamic collaborations among music and theatre artists. The Rockefeller Foundation launches its Fellowships for American Playwrights program.

1972—In collaboration with composer Elizabeth Swados, Andrei Serban directs his adaptation of *Medea* at La MaMa, the first play in a classical trilogy that will later be presented collectively as *Fragments of a Trilogy*. John Houseman and Margot Harley found The Acting Company, a national touring theatre, with members of the first graduating class of the Juilliard School's Drama Division. A bill of four Beckett plays including *Krapp's Last Tape* and *Happy Days* opens at Lincoln Center, directed by Alan Schneider and featuring Hume Cronyn and Jessica Tandy. A Richard Foreman/Stanley Silverman collaboration entitled *Dr. Selavy's Magic Theatre* bows at Music-Theatre Group.

1973—Joseph Papp assumes direction of theatre at Lincoln Center. The Ridiculous Theatrical Company, founded by Charles Ludlam in 1967, presents *Camille* with Ludlam in the title role. *Candide*, directed by Hal Prince, premieres at the Chelsea Theater Center. Adrian Hall and Richard Cumming's *Feasting with Panthers* premieres at Trinity Repertory Company and is then televised nationally in the first season of WNET's "Theatre in America" series. Arena Stage is chosen by the U.S. State Department to be the first American company to tour the Soviet Union, and they take *Our Town* and *Inherit the Wind*. The Open Theatre disbands. TCG publishes the inaugural edition of *Theatre Profiles*, covering 89 theatres.

1974—*A Chorus Line* debuts at the New York Shakespeare Festival's Public Theater, after a long workshop period (later going on to Broadway and the 1976 Pulitzer). Liviu Ciulei directs his first play in the U.S., Buchner's *Leonce and Lena*, at Arena Stage. Miguel Pinero's *Short Eyes* opens at the Theatre at the Riverside Church. The Yale Repertory Theatre produces a musical version of Aristophanes' *The Frogs* in the university swimming pool.

1975—Edward Albee wins his second Pulitzer for *Seascape*. The New Federal Theatre production of Ntozake Shange's *For Colored Girls . . .* opens, then moves to the New York Shakespeare Festival. Gregory Mosher directs the world premiere of David Mamet's *American Buffalo* at the Goodman's Stage 2 in Chicago. The Los Angeles Actors' Theatre is founded by Ralph Waite. Richard Foreman directs *The Threepenny Opera* at Lincoln Center. Mabou Mines adapts and produces two Beckett works, *Cascando* and *The Lost Ones*, featuring music by Philip Glass.

1976—Robert Wilson's *Einstein on the Beach* premieres at France's Avignon Festival, and is subsequently produced at the Metropolitan Opera in New York. Lynne Meadow stages David Rudkin's *Ashes* at the Manhattan Theatre Club. *Annie* premieres at the Goodspeed Opera House in Connecticut. David Rabe's *Streamers* premieres at Long Wharf Theatre, directed by Mike Nichols. Fired after a controversial season at Trinity, Adrian Hall in turn fires his board of trustees and remains at the helm. Actors Theatre of Louisville, under the artistic direction of Jon Jory, presents its first Festival of New American Plays. The Alaska Repertory Theatre is founded and is the 50th state's first professional performing arts institution. TCG holds its first National Conference at Yale University, bringing the national nonprofit theatre community together for the first time.

1977—Richard Maltby, Jr. directs his Fats Waller revue, *Ain't Misbehavin'*, at Manhattan Theatre Club. Christopher Durang's *A History of the American Film* enjoys a triple opening at Arena Stage, the Mark Taper Forum and Hartford Stage Company. Michael Cristofer's *The Shadow Box*, born at the Mark Taper, wins the Pulitzer after a run on Broadway. Andrei Serban's production of Chekhov's *The Cherry Orchard* opens at Lincoln Center.

1978—The Oregon Shakespeare Festival completes the entire Shakespeare canon for the second time (having completed it once in 1959). The American Place Theatre inaugurates its Women's Project. Ernest Thompson's *On Golden Pond* bows at the Hudson Guild Theatre. D.L. Coburn's *The Gin Game*, which had premiered at American Theatre Arts in Los Angeles in a different production, wins the Pulitzer. *Zoot Suit* by Luis Valdez is produced at the Mark Taper. Sam Shepard's *Buried Child*, directed by Robert Woodruff, premieres at the Magic Theatre in San Francisco, forging an alliance between the writer, the director and the theatre. (The play will go on to net the Pulitzer the following season.) Arthur Kopit's *Wings* is produced at the Yale Repertory Theatre and moves on to Broadway.

1979—Mark Medoff's *Children of a Lesser God* premieres at the Mark Taper Forum under Gordon Davidson's direction. John Hirsch is hired by the Seattle Repertory Theatre as consulting artistic director. The BAM Theater Company, dedicated to a "company approach to the classics," opens at the Brooklyn Academy of Music under the direction of David Jones, but survives only two seasons. Lloyd Richards is appointed to head both the Yale Repertory Theatre and Yale School of Drama, and institutes a new play festival entitled Winterfest. Robert Brustein founds the American Repertory Theatre at Harvard University.

1980—Richmond Crinkley and an artistic directorate take over operation of the theatre at Lincoln Center and produce one season. Wilford Leach breathes new energy into Gilbert and Sullivan's *Pirates of Penzance*, and it soon transfers from the New York Shakespeare Festival's Delacorte Theater to Broadway. The Yale Repertory Theatre's production of Athol Fugard's *A Lesson from Aloes*, directed by the playwright, begins Fugard's fruitful association with Lloyd Richards and the theatre. Lanford Wilson's *Talley's Folly*, which originated at his theatrical "home base," Circle Repertory Company, under Marshall W. Mason's direction, wins the Pulitzer. The Denver Center Theatre Company is founded as a component of the Denver Center for the Performing Arts.

1981—Liviu Ciulei is appointed artistic director of the Guthrie and opens with an acclaimed production of *The Tempest*. The Phoenix Theatre closes after a number of moves around New York City. Tennessee Williams turns to the noncommercial theatre to premiere his *Something Cloudy, Something Clear* at New York's Cocteau Repertory, and his *A House Not Meant to Stand* at the Goodman Theatre. Charles Fuller's *A Soldier's Play* opens at the Negro Ensemble Company, going on to win the Pulitzer for 1982 and tour extensively. The Wooster Group's *Route 1 & 9* opens at New York's Performing Garage to a flurry of controversy over what some feel is its racist content. Bill Irwin brings his *The Regard of Flight* to the American Place Theatre after its appearance at the New Theatre Festival in Baltimore, introducing the "new vaudeville" movement.

1982—The Eureka Theatre Company in San Francisco commissions Emily Mann to write a play that is to become *Execution of Justice*. *Torch Song Trilogy*, born sequentially at La MaMa, lands on Broadway. *Little Shop of Horrors*, the Howard Ashman/Alan Menken musical based on a low-budget horror film, opens at New York's WPA Theatre.

1983—The Brooklyn Academy of Music holds its first Next Wave Festival, featuring Lee Breuer's *Gospel at Colonus* and *The Photographer*, a collaboration of David Gordon, JoAnne Akalaitis and Philip Glass. Marsha Norman's *'night, Mother*, first produced at the American Repertory Theatre, wins the Pulitzer. *In the Belly of the Beast*, adapted by Adrian Hall from Jack Henry Abbott's book, opens at Trinity Repertory Company. The Theatre Project Company of St. Louis stirs up the community and jeopardizes its state funding with a production of *Sister Mary Ignatius...* which some brand "anti-Catholic." *Sunday in the Park with George* begins life as a workshop production at Playwrights Horizons. Mabou Mines and Interart Theatre collaborate on a production of Franz Xaver Kroetz's *Through the Leaves*. Alan Schneider directs his last play in America, Pinter's *Other Places*, at the Manhattan Theatre Club. *The Ballad of Soapy Smith* by Michael Weller opens the Seattle Repertory Theatre's new Bagley Wright Theatre complex. Two productions from Chicago's Steppenwolf Theatre Company, *True West* and *And a Nightingale Sang...*, introduce New York audiences to the energetic "Steppenwolf style."

1984—The Goodman Theatre production of David Mamet's *Glengarry Glen Ross*, directed by Gregory Mosher, transfers to Broadway and wins the Pulitzer, while its production of *Hurlyburly*, directed by Mike Nichols, travels from the Goodman to Off

Broadway and Broadway. Berkeley Repertory Theatre, under newly appointed artistic director Sharon Ott, produces *Kingdom Come*, a drama about Norwegian pioneers in the Midwest, using black, Hispanic and Asian-American actors. Robert Wilson produces his first fullscale work in this country since *Einstein on the Beach*, *The CIVIL warS*, at the American Repertory Theatre. The first Olympic Arts Festival is held in Los Angeles, presenting such international artists as Ariane Mnouchkine's Theatre du Soleil, Pina Bausch's Wuppertaler Tanztheater, Tadashi Suzuki's SCOT Theatre and Giorgio Strehler's Piccolo Teatro. James Reston Jr.'s *Jonestown Express* premieres at Trinity Repertory Company. Peter Sellars is appointed artistic director of the American National Theatre at the Kennedy Center. Milwaukee Repertory Theater artistic director John Dillon stages *Death of a Salesman* in Japan with an all-Japanese cast. After several visa denials, Dario Fo is finally permitted into the U.S., not to perform but to attend the Broadway opening of his *Accidental Death of an Anarchist*, which originated at Arena Stage. *Garden of Earthly Delights* by Martha Clarke and Richard Peaslee premieres at Music-Theatre Group/Lenox Arts Center. *American Theatre*, a national monthly magazine, begins publication.

1985—The new Los Angeles Theatre Center opens its four-theatre performing arts facility, and the Alabama Shakespeare Festival's new $21.5 million theatre begins operation in Montgomery. Former Goodman artistic director Gregory Mosher is appointed artistic director and Bernard Gersten managing director of the new Lincoln Center Repertory Company. Liviu Ciulei resigns from the Guthrie, directing *A Midsummer Night's Dream* as his final production. He is succeeded by Garland Wright. *Big River*, the Roger Miller/William Hauptman musical developed at American Repertory Theatre and the La Jolla Playhouse, moves to Broadway in a production staged by Des McAnuff, salvaging an indifferent commercial season and sweeping the Tonys. Wooster Group member Spalding Gray continues his exploration of the autobiographical monologue with his most ambitious work, *Swimming to Cambodia*, taking it on national and international tour after performances in New York. Circle Repertory Company tours Japan with two productions, launching a ten-year project initiated by the Japan-United States Friendship Commission. The Joyce Theater inaugurates an annual American Theatre Exchange, inviting the Mark Taper Forum, the Yale Repertory Theatre and the Alley Theatre to bring productions to New York.

1986—After 20 years as general director of the company he founded, William Ball resigns from San Francisco's American Conservatory Theater and founding member/executive director Edward Hastings is appointed artistic director. Former Wisdom Bridge artistic director Robert Falls and Frank Galati are appointed artistic director and associate director, respectively, of Chicago's Goodman Theatre. Michael Kahn directs *Romeo and Juliet* for his inaugural production as artistic director of the Shakespeare Theatre at the Folger in Washington, D.C. The First National Hispanic Theatre Conference, a gathering of more than 150 Hispanic theatre organizations in the United States and Puerto Rico, convenes in San Antonio, Texas. INTAR Hispanic American Arts Center in New York celebrates its 20th anniversary with five specially commissioned plays. The First National Symposium on Non-Traditional Casting convenes in New York with over 500 in attendance. Lee Blessing's *A Walk in the Woods* is produced at Yale Repertory Theatre after having been developed at the O'Neill Theater Center's National Playwrights Conference, held annually in Waterford, Conn. The New York Shakespeare Festival brings attention to the AIDS crisis with its production of Larry Kramer's *The Normal Heart*. Crossroads Theatre Company in New Brunswick, N.J. premieres George C. Wolfe's *The Colored Museum* directed by company co-founder/co-artistic director L. Kenneth Richardson. Ping Chong's Fiji Company and Meredith Monk present *The Games* at the Brooklyn Academy of Music. Euripides' *Alcestis*, translated and adapted by Robert Wilson, is produced by the American Repertory Theatre in Cambridge, Massachusetts.

1987—August Wilson's *Fences*, originally produced at Yale Repertory Theatre and various other resident theatres across the country, arrives on Broadway and goes on to win the Pulitzer Prize. Exiled Soviet director Yuri Lyubimov makes his American debut at Washington, D.C.'s Arena Stage with an adaptation of Dostoevsky's *Crime and Punishment*. Peter Brook's nine-hour production of *The Mahabharata* is presented at the Los Angeles Festival and the Brooklyn Academy of Music's Next Wave Festival. Chicago's International Theatre Festival debuts. New York's Lincoln Center Theater presents Mbongeni Ngema's *Sarafina!*, a South African musical about Township school children. Alfred Uhry's *Driving Miss Daisy* premieres at New York's Playwrights Horizons, and goes on to win the 1988 Pulitzer Prize, receive national and international stage productions and become a successful film. Marshall W. Mason resigns from New York's Circle Repertory Company, where he is succeeded by co-founder Tanya Berezin. Garland Wright begins his tenure as artistic director of the Guthrie Theater in Minneapolis with *The Misanthrope*. New York Shakespeare Festival producer Joseph Papp announces an ambitious six-year plan to present all 36 Shakespeare plays with foremost American actors in leading roles.

1988—*The Artistic Home*, a landmark report on the series of nationwide meetings with artistic directors convened as part of TCG's National Artistic Agenda Project, is published. The Milwaukee Repertory Theater, Washington D.C.'s Arena Stage, Berkeley Repertory Theatre and StageWest of Springfield, Mass. bring acclaimed Japanese director Tadashi Suzuki to America to adapt and direct *The Tale of Lear* using actors from each theatre who had studied with Sukuzi in Japan. Three artistic directors—Mark Lamos of Hartford Stage Company, Nagle Jackson of the McCarter Theatre in Princeton, N.J. and Theodore Mann of New York's Circle in the Square—become the first Americans to direct Soviet companies in Soviet theatres. The First New York International Festival of the Arts, offering some 350 events in all arts disciplines, is held in New York. Eugene O'Neill's centenary is celebrated with commemorative productions in theatres across the country, including Yale Repertory Theatre's productions of *Ah, Wilderness* and *Long Day's Journey into Night* starring Jason Robards and Colleen Dewhurst. Chicago's Steppenwolf Company mounts the premiere stage version of John Steinbeck's *The Grapes of Wrath*, adapted and directed by Frank Galati. Founder Gregory A. Falls resigns as artistic director of A Contemporary Theatre in Seattle, where he is succeeded by Jeff Steitzer. David Henry Hwang's *M. Butterfly* opens on Broadway.

1989—PepsiCo's Summerfare, held annually at the State University of New York in Purchase, marks its 10th and final season with "Perestroika on Stage," hosting the Anatoly Vasiliev Theatre Company and Pushkin Theatre from the Soviet Union and Poland's Stary Theatre Company. Founding artistic director Mako resigns from East West Players in Los Angeles, the country's oldest Asian-American theatre, and Nobu McCarthy is named to succeed him. Theatre de la Jeune Lune in Minneapolis marks the 200th birthday of the French Revolution and its own 10th anniversary with the epic production, *1789—The French Revolution*. Cornerstone Theater, founded in 1986, mounts a controversial, racially mixed production of *Romeo and Juliet* in Port Gibson, Miss., employing actors from both the company and the community. *New Music*, an ambitious trilogy of plays by Reynolds Price, debuts at the Cleveland Play House under the guidance of recently appointed artistic director Josephine Abady. David Feldshuh's historical drama *Miss Evers' Boys* debuts at Baltimore's Center Stage. John Hirsch directs *Coriolanus* for the Old Globe Theatre in San Diego. The Hartford Stage Company presents Ibsen's complete *Peer Gynt* in a two-part, five-hour production. Wendy Wasserstein's *The Heidi Chronicles*, developed at Seattle Repertory Theatre and New York's Playwrights Horizons before moving to Broadway, is awarded the Pulitzer Prize. Adrian Hall, the first person to serve simultaneously as artistic head of two major institutions, steps down as head of the Dallas Theater Center and Trinity Repertory Company in Providence, R.I. Nikos Psacharopoulos, founder and artistic director of the Williamstown Theatre Festival since 1955, dies and is succeeded by Peter Hunt. Martin L. Platt, founder and artistic director of the Alabama Shakespeare Festival, resigns after 17 years and is succeeded by Kent Thompson. Gregory Boyd becomes artistic director of Houston's Alley Theatre and is succeeded at StageWest in Springfield, Mass. by Eric Hill. Vaclav Havel, banned in his native country since 1969 but sustained in this country at the New York Shakespeare Festival and Philadelphia's Wilma Theater, is elected President of Czechoslovakia.

1990—Sparked by exhibits of work by the late photographer Robert Mapplethorpe and visual artist Andres Serrano, Senator Jesse Helms and other conservative legislators and religious groups launch a campaign against federal funding of controversial art that threatens to cripple the National Endowment for the Arts and sets off an explosion of debate among artists and professionals across the country. August Wilson is awarded his second Pulitzer Prize for *The Piano Lesson*. John Guare's *Six Degrees of Separation* premieres at New York's Lincoln Center Theater. Director and actor Kenneth Leon is appointed artistic director of Atlanta's Alliance Theatre Company. Boston's Huntington Theatre presents the premiere of *O, Pioneers!*, adapted by Darrah Cloud from Willa Cather, which is later filmed for television's *Great Performances*. Julie Taymor and Elliot Goldenthal adapt Horacio Quiroga's *Juan Darien* for the Music-Theatre Group. Michael Greif—appointed with David Greenspan, George C. Wolfe and artistic associate JoAnne Akalaitis to a new artistic collective at the New York Shakespeare Festival—revives Sophie Treadwell's little-known 1928 feminist drama, *Machinal*. Playwright and director Emily Mann succeeds Nagle Jackson as artistic director of the McCarter Theatre in Princeton, N.J. Mary B. Robinson opens her debut season as artistic director of the Philadelphia Drama Guild with Athol Fugard's *Boesman and Lena*. Tony Kushner's two-part epic *Angels in America* is commissioned and produced by San Francisco's Eureka Theatre. Productions by Ingmar Bergman, Tadeusz Kantor's Cricot 2 company and the State Theatre of Lithuania enliven the second New York International Festival of the Arts. The New York Shakespeare Festival production of *A Chorus Line* ends the longest run in Broadway history after 6,137 performances. New York's Chelsea Stage, founded as the Hudson Guild Theatre in 1896, closes.

1991—George C. Wolfe's *Jelly's Last Jam*, written with Susan Birkenhead, debuts at the Mark Taper Forum in Los Angeles. South Coast Repertory commissions and premieres *Sight Unseen* by Donald Margulies. Robert Schenkkan's *The Kentucky Cycle* premieres at Seattle's Intiman Theatre Company; it later wins the Pulitzer Prize, the first play to receive the prize before being produced on Broadway. Ron Daniels' production of *Hamlet* is co-produced by the American Repertory Theatre in Massachusetts and the Pittsburgh Public Theater. The Los Angeles Theatre Center closes, declaring bankruptcy. *La Bête* by David Hirson opens on Broadway. New York Theatre Workshop debuts Caryl Churchill's *Mad Forest*. In the shadow of continuing battles over freedom of expression, the Idaho Shakespeare Festival cancels its production of *Spring Awakening* in fear of offending "community standards." A federal judge rules that the National Endowment for the Arts "anti-obscenity" clause (which was required to be signed by all 1990 grant recipients) is unconstitutional. Zelda Fichandler, founding artistic director of Washington, D.C.'s Arena Stage, retires after 40 years at its helm to become artistic director of New York's The Acting Company and is succeeded by Douglas C. Wager. Lloyd Richards completes his term as director of the Yale Repertory Theatre and Yale School of Drama in Connecticut and is succeeded by Stan Wojewodski Jr., whose artistic director position at Baltimore's Center Stage is filled by Irene Lewis. Joseph Papp, founder of the New York Shakespeare Festival, appoints JoAnne Akalaitis artistic director and dies within the year. Henry Woronicz succeeds Jerry Turner as artistic director of the Oregon Shakespeare Festival. André Bishop succeeds Gregory Mosher as artistic director of New York's Lincoln

Center Theater. Don Scardino succeeds Bishop at Playwrights Horizons. The arts community mourns the loss of actors Colleen Dewhurst and Mildred Dunnock; choreographer Martha Graham; and director William Ball, founder of San Francisco's American Conservatory Theater.

1992—Playwright and actor Anna Deavere Smith debuts her one-person, multi-character show about race, culture and identity, *Fires in the Mirror*, at the New York Shakespeare Festival. Marivaux's *The Triumph of Love*, directed and adapted by Stephen Wadsworth, opens at the McCarter Theatre in New Jersey and sets off a "rediscovery" of the 18th-century French playwright by theatres across the country. *The Baltimore Waltz*, Paula Vogel's response to the AIDS crisis, premieres at New York's Circle Repertory Company under the direction of Anne Bogart. Director Des McAnuff stages *The Who's Tommy* at the La Jolla Playhouse. Tony Kushner's *Angels in America: Part One, Millennium Approaches*, which began life at San Francisco's Eureka Theatre, and was further developed at the Mark Taper Forum in Los Angeles prior to its Broadway run, wins the Pulitzer Prize. John Frohnmayer resigns as chairman of the National Endowment for the Arts after two-and-a-half tumultuous years at its helm. Almost immediately, acting chairman Anne-Imelda Radice vetoes two National Council-supported grants, prompting two Endowment review panels (including the Theater Program solo theatre artists fellowships panel) to suspend deliberations. Stephen Sondheim and Wallace Stegner turn down the National Medal for the Arts. Four defunded performance artists who sued the Endowment—Karen Finley, Holly Hughes, Tim Miller and John Fleck—are vindicated when a federal judge rules that the NEA decency standard violated the First Amendment. Carey Perloff succeeds Edward Hastings as artistic director of the American Conservatory Theater in San Francisco and is succeeded at New York's Classic Stage Company by David Esbjornson. Libby Appel is appointed artistic director of the Indiana Repertory Theatre following the death of Tom Haas. Tim Bond succeeds founding artistic director Ruben Sierra at Seattle's Group Theatre. Founder Arthur Storch resigns from New York's Syracuse Stage and Tazewell Thompson is named to succeed him. Richard Hamburger is appointed artistic director of the Dallas Theater Center, and is succeeded at Maine's Portland Stage Company by Greg Leaming.

USING THIS BOOK

Hartford Stage. Frank Raiter, Timothy Barone, David Patrick Kelly and Joshua Donoghue in Tartuffe. Photo by T. Charles Erickson.

All the theatres included in *Theatre Profiles 11* are constituents of Theatre Communications Group, the national organization for the nonprofit professional theatre. Information was requested in the summer and fall of 1993. The text of this volume is based on the materials submitted by the 238 theatres included. The following notes provide a guide to the elements of the book.

Personnel
Each theatre's current artistic and managerial leaders are included. This information was updated through January 1, 1994. If there had been a change in the artistic leadership of the theatre within the past two seasons, the former artistic head is noted following the artistic statement, with an indication of the season(s) for which he or she was responsible.

Contact Information
The mailing address of each organization is included, which is not necessarily the address of the theatre. Telephone numbers are listed as business office "(bus.)", box office "(b.o.)" or "(fax)." An unlabeled number serves for both business and box office.

Founding Date and Founders
The founding date represents the beginning of public performances or, in a few cases, the conceptual or legal establishment of the organization. The names of all founders are listed under the date.

Season
The season information is included as a general guide to the annual performance dates of each theatre. The months listed indicate the opening and closing of each theatre's season. "Year-round" designates companies that perform continuously throughout the year; "variable" indicates irregular or varying schedules.

Facilities
The facilities are the theatre space(s) in which each company regularly performs. The seating capacity and type of stage are included for

each facility. The name of the space is provided if it differs from the organization's name. The information is current as of July 1993 and doesn't necessarily indicate the performance venues of the seasons highlighted in the book. The following terminology is used in describing each facility:

PROSCENIUM: The traditional, picture-window stage separated from the auditorium by a proscenium arch, so that the audience views the action from a single "fourth wall" perspective.

THRUST: All types of facilities wherein the stage juts into the audience and is thereby surrounded on three sides. A "modified thrust" or "modified proscenium" protrudes less, often utilizing a fan-shaped apron on which action can take place.

ARENA: Also called "theatre-in-the-round." The audience completely surrounds the stage.

FLEXIBLE: All types of theatre spaces which can be altered or converted from one category to another.

CABARET: A simple performance platform, with the audience usually seated at tables.

Finances

Operating expenses are included to provide a general sense of the overall size of each theatre's operation. Most often the financial figures are from calendar year 1992 or fiscal year 1992-93, the most recent year available at the time information was gathered for *Theatre Profiles*.

Actors' Equity Association Contracts

The following AEA abbreviations are used:

BAT:	Bay Area Theatre contract
CAT:	Chicago Area Theatre contract
COST:	Council on Stock Theatres contract
CORST:	Council on Resident Stock Theatres contract
LORT:	League of Resident Theatres contract
SPT:	Small Professional Theatre contract
TYA:	Theatre for Young Audiences contract
U/RTA:	University/Resident Theatre Association contract

The letters enclosed in parentheses following the contract abbreviations designate the contract type, based on the size of theatre and scale of payment. Please note that members of the League of Resident Theatres (LORT) also operate under agreements with the Society of Stage Directors and Choreographers (SSDC) and United Scenic Artists (USA), which are referenced to the LORT Equity contracts. For more specific information on these contracts, please contact the unions directly.

Artistic Director's Statement

All artistic heads were invited to submit a statement describing the artistic philosophy governing the work at their respective institutions from their personal perspectives. While all have been edited for style, every attempt has been made to retain the individuality of each statement.

Production Lists

Productions from the 1991-92 and the 1992-93 seasons (1992 and 1993 for theatres with summer operations) are listed, most often in the chronological order in which they were produced. The title of each production is immediately followed by the name of the playwright and, where applicable, the adapter, translator and/or source of literary adaptation if such information was provided by the theatre. In the case of musicals, all composers, librettists and lyricists are included. The director and set, lighting, costume and sound designers follow, designated by a letter in parentheses directly preceding the name—(D), (S), (L), (C), (SD). Musical directors (MD) and choreographers (CH) are included for musicals only; other personnel are excluded due to space limitations. Personnel who appear repeatedly in a single season are frequently summarized in a prefatory note.

Photographs

A photograph from one of each theatre's listed productions accompanies each entry. The photos help convey the range and diversity of production activity and were generally selected for clarity of image from those submitted for possible inclusion by the theatre. Actors' names are included in the caption when there are five or fewer actors pictured.

Regional Index

A geographical, state-by-state listing of every theatre is included to readily identify theatres by region.

Theatre Chronology

The "time line" history of the founding of the nonprofit professional theatres included in this volume is intended to demonstrate the growth pattern of the decentralized nonprofit professional theatre movement in the United States.

Name/Title Indices

Playwrights, composers, artistic and management heads, directors, designers and founders appear in the index of names. For convenience, a separate index includes titles of all dramatic works listed in this book.

THEATRES

Academy Theatre
A Contemporary Theatre
The Acting Company
Actor's Express
Actors Theatre of Louisville
Addison Centre Theatre
Alabama Shakespeare Festival
Alice B. Theatre
Alley Theatre
Alliance Theatre Company
American Conservatory Theater
American Inside Theatre
American Music Theater Festival
American Repertory Theatre
American Stage Festival
American Theatre Company
Antenna Theater
Arden Theatre Company
Arena Stage
Arizona Theatre Company
The Arkansas Arts Center
   Children's Theatre
Arkansas Repertory Theatre
ArtReach Touring Theatre
Asolo Theatre Company
A Traveling Jewish Theatre
Bailiwick Repertory
Barter Theatre
The Bathhouse Theatre
Bay Street Theatre Festival
Berkeley Repertory Theatre
Berkshire Theatre Festival
Bilingual Foundation of the Arts
Birmingham Children's Theatre
Blackfriars Theatre
Bloomsburg Theatre Ensemble
BoarsHead: Michigan Public
   Theater
Bristol Riverside Theatre
California Theatre Center
Capital Repertory Company
Center Stage
Center Theater
Cheltenham Center for the Arts
The Children's Theatre Company
Childsplay, Inc.
Child's Play Touring Theatre
Cincinnati Playhouse in the Park
Circle Repertory Company
CitiArts Theatre
City Theatre Company
Clarence Brown Theatre Company
Classic Stage Company (CSC)
The Cleveland Play House
Cleveland Public Theatre
Coconut Grove Playhouse
The Colony Studio Theatre
Cornerstone Theater Company
The Coterie
Court Theatre

Berkeley Repertory Theatre. James Carpenter and Andrew Mutnick in Mad Forest. Photo by Ken Friedman.

xviii THEATRES

Crossroads Theatre Company
Cumberland County Playhouse
Dallas Theater Center
David Gordon/Pick Up Company
Delaware Theatre Company
Dell'Arte Players Company
Denver Center Theatre Company
Detroit Repertory Theatre
El Teatro Campesino
Emmy Gifford Children's Theater
The Empty Space Theatre
En Garde Arts
Ensemble Theatre of Cincinnati
First Stage Milwaukee
Florida Studio Theatre
Ford's Theatre
Free Street Programs
Fulton Theatre Company
George Street Playhouse
Germinal Stage Denver
GeVa Theatre
Goodman Theatre
Goodspeed Opera House
Great American History Theatre
Great Lakes Theater Festival
The Group: Seattle's MultiCultural Theatre
The Guthrie Theater
Hangar Theatre
Hartford Stage Company
Hippodrome State Theatre
Honolulu Theatre for Youth
Horizon Theatre Company
Horse Cave Theatre
Huntington Theatre Company
Illinois Theatre Center
Illusion Theater
The Independent Eye
Indiana Repertory Theatre
INTAR Hispanic American Arts Center
Intiman Theatre Company
Irondale Ensemble Project
Jean Cocteau Repertory
Jewish Repertory Theatre
Jomandi Productions, Inc.
La Jolla Playhouse
La MaMa Experimental Theater Club
L. A. Theatre Works
Lincoln Center Theater
Live Oak Theatre
Living Stage Theatre Company
Long Wharf Theatre
Mabou Mines
Madison Repertory Theatre
Mad River Theater Works
Magic Theatre

Manhattan Theatre Club
Marin Theatre Company
Mark Taper Forum
McCarter Theatre Center for the Performing Arts
Merrimack Repertory Theatre
Mill Mountain Theatre
Milwaukee Chamber Theatre
Milwaukee Repertory Theater
Missouri Repertory Theatre
Mixed Blood Theatre Company
Music-Theatre Group
National Jewish Theater
Nebraska Theatre Caravan
New American Theater
New Dramatists
New Federal Theatre
New Jersey Shakespeare Festival
New Mexico Repertory Theatre
New Repertory Theatre
New Stage Theatre
New York Shakespeare Festival
New York State Theatre Institute
New York Theatre Workshop
Novel Stages
Oakland Ensemble Theatre
Odyssey Theatre Ensemble
Old Globe Theatre
Olney Theatre
Omaha Magic Theatre
O'Neill Theater Center
Ontological-Hysteric Theater
The Open Eye: New Stagings
Oregon Shakespeare Festival
Organic Theater Company
Pan Asian Repertory Theatre
PCPA Theaterfest
Pennsylvania Stage Company
Penumbra Theatre Company
The People's Light and Theatre Company
Perseverance Theatre
Philadelphia Drama Guild
Philadelphia Festival Theatre for New Plays
The Philadelphia Theatre Company
The Phoenix Theatre Company
Ping Chong and Company
Pioneer Theatre Company
Pittsburgh Public Theater
Playhouse on the Square
PlayMakers Repertory Company
The Playwrights' Center
Playwrights Horizons
The Pollard Theatre
Pope Theatre Company
Portland Repertory Theater
Portland Stage Company

The Purple Rose Theatre Company
Remains Theatre
Repertorio Español
The Repertory Theatre of St. Louis
Riverside Theatre
The Road Company
Roadside Theater
Roundabout Theatre Company
Round House Theatre
Sacramento Theatre Company
The Salt Lake Acting Company
San Diego Repertory Theatre
San Jose Repertory Theatre
Seattle Children's Theatre
Seattle Repertory Theatre
Second Stage Theatre
7 Stages
Shakespeare & Company
Shakespeare Repertory
Shakespeare Santa Cruz
The Shakespeare Tavern
The Shakespeare Theatre
Society Hill Playhouse
Source Theatre Company
South Coast Repertory
Stage One: The Louisville Children's Theatre
Stage West
StageWest
Stamford Theatre Works
Steppenwolf Theatre Company
St. Louis Black Repertory Company
Studio Arena Theatre
The Studio Theatre
Syracuse Stage
Tacoma Actors Guild
Tennessee Repertory Theatre
Thalia Spanish Theatre
Theater at Lime Kiln
The Theater at Monmouth
Theatre de la Jeune Lune
Theater Emory
Theatre for a New Audience
Theater for the New City
Theatre IV
Theatre in the Square
TheatreVirginia
TheatreWorks
Theatreworks/USA
Theatre X
Theatrical Outfit
Touchstone Theatre
Trinity Repertory Company
Unicorn Theatre
Utah Shakespearean Festival
Victory Gardens Theater
Vineyard Theatre
Virginia Stage Company
The Walnut Street Theatre Company

West Coast Ensemble
White River Theatre Festival
Williamstown Theatre Festival
The Wilma Theater
Wisdom Bridge Theatre
Women's Project & Productions
Woolly Mammoth Theatre Company
The Wooster Group
Worcester Foothills Theatre Company
Yale Repertory Theatre
Young Playwrights Inc.
Zachary Scott Theatre Center

THEATRE PROFILES 11

The Guthrie Theater. Stephen Pelinski in The Illusion. Photo by Michal Daniel.

Academy Theatre

FRANK WITTOW
Producing Artistic Director

LORENNE FEY
Managing Director

KATHERINE SPEAR
Board Chairman

501 Means St. NW
Atlanta, GA 30318
(404) 525-4111
(404) 688-8009 (fax)

FOUNDED 1956
Frank Wittow

SEASON
Sept.-June

FACILITIES
Seating Capacity: 75
Stage: flexible

FINANCES
July 1, 1992-June 30, 1993
Expenses: $220,000

CONTRACTS
AEA letter of agreement

The Academy Theatre is a professional company whose mission is to serve the community through interdependent programs: touring original, issue-oriented Theatre for Youth plays with themes of family, peer pressure, addiction and the environment throughout the Southeast; presenting and developing new plays by local and regional playwrights through classes, readings and a New Play Series that strives to provide Atlanta's audiences with fresh, stimulating theatrical experiences; facilitating Human Service Programs with disenfranchised populations that give participants such as inner-city youth, developmentally disabled adults and incarcerated adolescents an avenue to express creatively the issues that are relevant to their lives; and training a professional ensemble of actors, directors, playwrights and facilitators to fulfill the social and artistic needs of our community.
—*Frank Wittow*

PRODUCTIONS 1991-1992

Direction by Frank Wittow and lighting and sound design by Margaret S. Tucker unless otherwise noted.

Tiny Tim is Dead, Barbara Lebow; (S) Elliott Berman; (L) Jessica Coale; (C) Barbara Lebow; (SD) Tom Spock
State Prisoners, Ed Brock, Jr.; (S) Elliott Berman
Guest House, Randal Jackson; (S) Elliott Berman
Basic Needs, Sabina Angel; music: Klimchak; (S) Elliott Berman
Families, book, music and lyrics: company-developed
Family Rhyme-Time, Barbara Lebow
Masks, book, music and lyrics: company-developed; (D) Judith Shotwell
Images of Addiction: book, music and lyrics: company-developed

PRODUCTIONS 1992-93

Direction by Frank Wittow unless otherwise noted.

The Song of Grendelyn, Russell Davis
The Rainbow Gave You Birth, Victor M. Depta
Wasteland, company-developed; music and lyrics: Keena Rivers; (S) Stage Right; (MD) Keena Rivers
The Magic Fish, company-developed; (D) Barbara Lebow and Chris Curran; (C) Blanche Thompson
Words and Works of Dr. Martin Luther King, Jr., company-developed
Families, book, music and lyrics: company-developed
Masks, book, music and lyrics: company-developed; (D) Judith Shotwell
Images of Addiction, book, music and lyrics: company-developed

Academy Theatre. LaParee Young and Steven Pradia in *Tiny Tim is Dead*. Photo: Alan David.

A Contemporary Theatre

JEFF STEITZER
Artistic Director

SUSAN TRAPNELL MORITZ
Managing Director

PHIL C. SCHERMER
Producing Director

DOUGLAS E. NORBERG
Board Chairman

Box 19400
Seattle, WA 98109
(206) 285-3220 (bus.)
(206) 285-5110 (b.o.)
(206) 298-3100 (fax)

FOUNDED 1965
Gregory A. Falls

SEASON
May-Dec.

FACILITIES
Seating Capacity: 449
Stage: thrust

FINANCES
Jan. 1, 1992-Dec. 31, 1992
Expenses: $2,527,341

CONTRACTS
AEA LORT (C) and TYA

A Contemporary Theatre is dedicated to offering provocative, engaging and theatrical contemporary plays in productions that represent the most vibrant collaborations among actors, directors and designers that we can assemble. At ACT, the playwright is the predominant point of focus, with priority given to generating work through commissions to writers whose efforts we want to support on a long-term basis. ACT vigorously seeks out dramatists with lively, unique voices: playwrights whose work examines issues that are socially pertinent to our audience; whose writing appeals to the head, heart and soul; and whose aesthetic is informed by the imaginative possibilities that can occur only on

A CONTEMPORARY THEATRE

A Contemporary Theatre. Marianne Owen and Linda Emond in *Our Country's Good*. Photo: Chris Bennion.

the stage. Our professional theatre for young audiences, the Young ACT Company, is one year younger than our mainstage series. It has produced more than 30 plays, half of which were original scripts, performed for hundreds of thousands of young people throughout Washington State.
—*Jeff Steitzer*

PRODUCTIONS 1991

My Children! My Africa!, Athol Fugard; (D) Gary Gisselman; (S) Shelley Henze Schermer; (L) Phil C. Schermer; (C) Rose Pederson; (SD) Steven M. Klein

The Illusion, Pierre Corneille, adapt: Tony Kushner; (D) David Ira Goldstein; (S) Greg Lucas; (L) Rick Paulsen; (C) Gene Davis Buck; (SD) David Hunter Koch

Tears of Rage, Doris Baizley; (D) Steven Dietz; (S) Lori Sullivan Worthman; (L) Rick Paulsen; (C) Laura Crow; (SD) Steven M. Klein

Our Country's Good, adapt: Timberlake Wertenbaker, from Thomas Keneally; (D) Jeff Steitzer; (S) Michael Olich; (L) Peter Maradudin; (C) Michael Olich; (SD) Jim Ragland

Willi, adapt: John Pielmeier, from Willi Unsoeld; (D) David Ira Goldstein; (S) Scott Weldin; (L) Rick Paulsen; (C) Carolyn Keim

Halcyon Days, Steven Dietz; (D) Jeff Steitzer; (S) Vicki Smith; (L) Rick Paulsen; (C) Sam Fleming; (SD) Steven M. Klein

A Christmas Carol, adapt: Gregory A. Falls, from Charles Dickens; (D) David Ira Goldstein; (S) Bill Forrester; (L) Richard Hogle; (C) Nanrose Buchman

PRODUCTIONS 1992

Theatre of the Air, The Flying Karamazov Brothers; (D) The Flying Karamazov Brothers; (L) Peter Dansky

Banjo Dancing, Stephen Wade; (D) Milton Kramer

Trust, Steven Dietz; (D) Steven Dietz; (S) Michael Olich; (L) Rick Paulsen; (C) Carolyn Keim; (SD) Jim Ragland

Shadowlands, William Nicholson; (D) David Ira Goldstein; (S) Bill Forrester; (L) Don Darnutzer; (C) Rose Pederson; (SD) Steven M. Klein

The Revengers' Comedies, Parts I & II, Alan Ayckbourn; (D) Jeff Steitzer; (S) Shelley Henze Schermer; (L) Richard Hogle; (C) Jeanne Arnold; (SD) Steven M. Klein

Eleemosynary, Lee Blessing; (D) Laurence Ballard; (S) Scott Weldin; (L) Rick Paulsen; (C) Rose Pederson; (SD) David Hunter Koch

Sunsets and Glories, Peter Barnes; (D) Jeff Steitzer; (S) Charlene Hall; (L) Brenda Berry; (C) Rose Pederson; (SD) Todd Barton

A Christmas Carol, adapt: Gregory A. Falls, from Charles Dickens; (D) Laurence Ballard; (S) Bill Forrester; (L) Ashley York Kennedy; (C) Nanrose Buchman; (SD) Steven M. Klein

The Acting Company

ZELDA FICHANDLER
Artistic Director

MARGOT HARLEY
Executive Producer

JOHN MILLER-STEPHANY
Associate Producer

EDGAR LANSBURY
Board Chairman

JOAN M. WARBURG
Board President

Box 898, Times Square Station
New York, NY 10108
(212) 564-3510
(212) 714-2643 (fax)

FOUNDED 1972
John Houseman, Margot Harley

SEASON
Variable

FINANCES
July 1, 1991-June 30, 1992
Expenses: $2,138,000

CONTRACTS
AEA LORT (C) and (D)

Made up of a mix of young actors who have just completed their conservatory training and experienced professionals, the Acting Company has gathered itself around the idea of an ensemble that trains and performs and teaches together. The company regards the actor as the center of the theatre art: the greater the expressivity of the actor's instrument, and of the ensemble as a whole, the more profound the experience of the audience. In a country that has not significantly valued or provided for the development of the actor or supported the educative power of the theatre, the Acting Company fills an important niche. In the 1993-94 season, the company's 15-member touring ensemble will play in 40 cities and towns in 19 states on a stage specially designed to be carried from place to place. The actors and designers comprise an ethnic mosaic which reflects the audiences to whom the work is geared. As the Acting Company's artistic director, I hope to fulfill and extend the vision of Margot Harley and the late John Houseman, who founded the company in 1972.
—*Zelda Fichandler*

PRODUCTIONS 1991-1992

A Midsummer Night's Dream, William Shakespeare; (D) Joe Dowling; (S) Douglas Stein; (L) Allen Lee Hughes; (C) Catherine Zuber

Blood Knot, Athol Fugard; (D) Tazewell Thompson; (S) Douglas Stein; (L) Allen Lee Hughes; (C) Paul Tazewell; (SD) Susan R. White

Note: During its 1992-93 season, The Acting Company developed a long-range artistic and financial plan.

The Acting Company. Mark Stewart Guin and Terra Vandergaw in *A Midsummer Night's Dream*. Photo: Diane Gorodnitzki.

Actor's Express

CHRIS COLEMAN
Artistic Director

JENNIFER DEER
Managing Director

DEBORAH HUNTER
Board President

280 Elizabeth St., Suite C-101
Atlanta, GA 30307
(404) 221-0125 (bus.)
(404) 221-0831 (b.o.)

FOUNDED 1988
Chris Coleman, Harold Leaver

SEASON
Year-round

FACILITIES
Seating Capacity: 200
Stage: flexible

FINANCES
Sept. 1, 1992-Aug. 31, 1993
Expenses: $293,964

Actor's Express is a five-year-old theatre company based in Atlanta, Georgia. The range of our work is vast and eclectic (from Moss Hart to Calderón in a single season). We are a theatre of intuition and our goal is to produce plays that sweep us off our feet, fill us with a sense of wonder and leave us dizzy. A play, for us, is like a stick of dynamite that holds within it the possibility of exploding our preconceptions of ourselves and the world around us. The point of the work is not necessarily to "hold as 'twere the mirror up to nature," but to blast past our everyday routine and get to something bigger, cooler, funnier, scarier and deeper.
—*Chris Coleman*

PRODUCTIONS 1991-1992

Sets by Theo Harness, lighting by Tim Habeger and costumes by Tina Hightower unless otherwise noted.

The Harvey Milk Show, book and lyrics: Dan Pruitt; music: Patrick Hutchison; (D) and (CH) Stephen Petty; (L) Milton Sams; (MD) Walter Huff
Glengarry Glen Ross, David Mamet; (D) Luann Purcell; (L) Milton Sams

The Caucasian Chalk Circle, Bertolt Brecht, trans: Eric Bentley; (D) Chris Coleman; (S) Tim Habeger; (C) Joanna Schmink
Traps, Caryl Churchill; (D) Chris Coleman; (L) Milton Sams; (C) Joanna Schmink
Stand-Up Tragedy, Bill Cain; (D) Chris Coleman
Danny and the Deep Blue Sea, John Patrick Shanley; (D) Tim Habeger

PRODUCTIONS 1992-1993

Sets by Theo Harness and costumes by Tina Hightower unless otherwise noted.

The Harvey Milk Show, book and lyrics: Dan Pruitt; music: Patrick Hutchison; (D) and (CH) Stephen Petty; (L) Milton Sams; (MD) Michael Monroe
The Women, Clare Boothe Luce; (D) Stephen Petty; (L) Bridgett Beier; (C) Joanna Schmink
Passion, Peter Nichols; (D) Chris Coleman; (L) Tanya Tveit
Fool for Love, Sam Shepard; (D) Chris Coleman; (L) Bridgett Beier; (SD) Darren Law
You, The Night & The Music, company-developed; (D) Stephen Petty; (L) Bridgett Beier; (MD) Kevin Kemp

Actor's Express. Susie Spear in *Caucasian Chalk Circle*. Photo: David Zeiger.

Actors Theatre of Louisville

JON JORY
Producing Director

ALEXANDER SPEER
Executive Director

MARILEE HEBERT-SLATER
Associate Director

ROBERT O. COLLINS, JR.
Board President

316-320 West Main St.
Louisville, KY 40202-4218
(502) 584-1265 (bus.)
(502) 584-1205 (b.o.)
(502) 561-3300 (fax)

FOUNDED 1964
Ewel Cornett, Richard Block

SEASON
Sept.-June

FACILITIES
Pamela Brown Auditorium
Seating Capacity: 637
Stage: thrust

Victor Jory Theatre
Seating Capacity: 159
Stage: thrust

Downstairs at Actors
Seating Capacity: 100
Stage: cabaret

FINANCES
June 1, 1992-May 31, 1993
Expenses: $4,714,000

CONTRACTS
AEA LORT (B) and (D)

Actors Theatre of Louisville has four primary areas of emphasis which constitute an artistic policy. Central to our aesthetic is the discovery and development of a new generation of American playwrights. In the last 19 years, Actors Theatre has produced the work of more than 200 new writers. The Humana Festival of New American Plays is our major outlet for this work, strongly backed by a commissioning program. Our second area of emphasis is an interdisciplinary approach to the classical theatre, combining lectures, discussions, films and plays through the annual Classics in Context Festival. Working under a different umbrella theme each year, this festival provides new insights into the classical repertoire, both for our company and our resident audience. The Bingham Signature Shakespeare Series supplements programming by presenting one of the Bard's masterworks each season. In addition, since 1980, Actors Theatre has performed by invitation at festivals and theatres in 14 countries.
—*Jon Jory*

PRODUCTIONS 1991-1992

Sets by Paul Owen, lighting by Karl E. Haas and costumes by Laura Patterson unless otherwise noted.

Classics in Context Festival:
Tales From the Vienna Woods, Odon von Horvath, trans: Christopher Hampton; (D) Mladen Kiselov; (C) Marcia Dixcy
Love and Revolution, A Brecht Cabaret, performed by The Berliner Ensemble; (D) Dr. Rene Serge Mund; (MD) Karl-Heinz Nehring

Rock 'N' Roles From William Shakespeare, Jim Luigs; (D) Clinton Turner Davis; (L) Rob Dillard; (C) Kevin R. McLeod
The Mystery of Irma Vep, Charles Ludlam; (D) Jon Jory; (S) John Lee Beatty; (C) Lindsay W. Davis
Quartermaine's Terms, Simon Gray; (D) Steven D. Albrezzi; (L) Matthew J. Reinert
A Christmas Carol, adapt: Jon Jory and Marcia Dixcy, from Charles Dickens; (D) Frazier W. Marsh; (S) Elmon Webb and Virginia Dancy; (C) Lewis D. Rampino and Hollis Jenkins-Evans
The Gift of the Magi, book adapt, music and lyrics: Peter Ekstrom, from O. Henry; (D) Ron Nakahara; (L) Casey Clark; (C) Hollis Jenkins-Evans
Lettice and Lovage, Peter Shaffer; (D) Nagle Jackson
Prelude to a Kiss, Craig Lucas; (D) Bob Krakower
The Heidi Chronicles, Wendy Wasserstein; (D) Frazier W. Marsh

Humana Festival of New American Plays:
Hyaena, Ross MacLean; (D) Mladen Kiselov; (L) Mary Louise Geiger
D. Boone, Marsha Norman; (D) Gloria Muzio; (C) Pamela Scofield
The Old Lady's Guide to Survival, Mayo Simon; (D) Alan Mandell; (L) Mary Louise Geiger; (C) Hollis Jenkins-Evans
Bondage, David Henry Hwang; (D) Oskar Eustis; (L) Mary Louise Geiger
Devotees in the Garden of Love, Suzan-Lori Parks; (D) Oskar Eustis; (L) Mary Louise Geiger
Evelyn and the Polka King, book: John Olive; music: Carl Finch and Bob Lucas; lyrics: Bob Lucas; (D) Jeff Hooper; (C) Pamela Scofield
The Carving of Mount Rushmore, John Conklin; (D) and (S) John Conklin; (C) Pamela Scofield
Marisol, Jose Rivera; (D) Marcus Stern; (L) Mary Louise Geiger

Driving Miss Daisy, Alfred Uhry; (D) Ray Fry; (C) Hollis Jenkins-Evans
Antony and Cleopatra, William Shakespeare; (D) Jon Jory; (S) Ming Cho Lee; (L) Stephen Strawbridge; (C) Marcia Dixcy

PRODUCTIONS 1992-1993

Sets by Paul Owen, lighting by Karl E. Haas and costumes by Laura Patterson unless otherwise noted.

Classics in Context Festival:
Brief Lives, adapt: Patrick Garland, from John Aubrey; (D) Ray Fry; (C) Hollis Jenkins-Evans
The Beaux' Stratagem, George Farquhar; (D) Jon Jory; (S) Virginia Dancy and Elmon Webb
The Passion of Dracula, adapt: Bob Hall and David Richmond, from Bram Stoker; (D) Frazier W. Marsh
Give 'Em Hell, Harry!, Samuel Gallu; (D) Scott Zigler; (L) Rob Dillard; (C) Hollis Jenkins-Evans
Rock 'N' Roles From William Shakespeare, Jim Luigs; (D) Juliette Carrillo; (L) Rob Dillard; (C) Kevin R. McLeod
A Christmas Carol, adapt: Jon Jory and Marcia Dixcy, from Charles Dickens; (D) Larry Deckel; (S) Elmon Webb and Virginia Dancy; (C) Lewis D. Rampino and Hollis Jenkins-Evans
The Gift of the Magi, book adapt, music and lyrics: Peter Ekstrom, from O. Henry; (D) Frazier W. Marsh; (L) Casey Clark; (C) Hollis Jenkins-Evans
Picnic, William Inge; (D) Anne Bogart; (S) John Conklin; (L) Mimi Jordan Sherin

Humana Festival of New American Plays:
Stanton's Garage, Joan Ackermann; (D) Steven D. Albrezzi
Shooting Simone, Lynne Kaufmann; (D) Laszlo Marton
Jennine's Diary and *Watermelon Rinds*, Regina Taylor; (D) Novella Nelson; (L) Marcus Dilliard; (C) Toni-Leslie James
The Ice Fishing Play, Kevin Kling; (D) Michael Sommers; (C) Toni-Leslie James
Deadly Virtues, Brian Jucha; (D) Brian Jucha; (L) Marcus Dilliard
Keely and Du, Jane Martin; (D) Jon Jory; (L) Marcus Dilliard

Born Yesterday, Garson Kanin; (D) Ray Fry; (C) Hollis Jenkins-Evans
Suds, Melinda Gilb, Steve Gunderson and Bryan Scott; (D) Will Robertson; (MD) Tom Wojtas; (CH) Javier Velasco

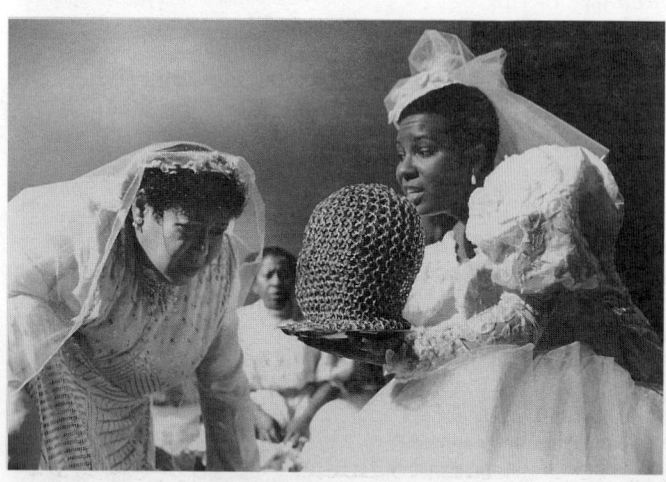

Actors Theatre of Louisville. Esther Scott, Margarette Robinson and Sandra Sydney in *Devotees in the Garden of Love*. Photo: Richard Trigg.

Addison Centre Theatre

KELLY COTTEN
Artistic Director
DAVID MINTON
Executive Director

SHAFI PAREKH
Board President

Box 933
Addison, TX 75001
(214) 788-3203 (bus.)
(214) 788-3200 (b.o.)
(214) 788-3206 (fax)

FOUNDED 1976
C.J. Webster, Frank Ford

SEASON
Year-round

FACILITIES
Mainstage
Seating Capacity: 200
Stage: flexible

Rehearsal/Education
Seating Capacity: 75
Stage: flexible

Old Stone Cottage
Seating Capacity: 50
Stage: flexible

FINANCES
Oct. 1, 1991-Sept. 30, 1992
Expenses: $522,100

CONTRACTS
AEA SPT

Addison Centre Theatre is a professional theatre committed to existential and social self-examination, and employing a design-based dramaturgy to explore and enliven the mysterious relationships between text, performance and audience. In 1992 the company expanded into a new, nationally acclaimed experimental facility, custom-designed to showcase our signature style of flexible environmental production. Always striving to be innovative and challenging, ACT produces a wide variety of material that ranges from populist to avant-garde: unusual new scripts by leading contemporary authors, bold reinterpretations of classic texts (including adaptations of nontheatrical works) and, finally, interdisciplinary and/or

Addison Centre Theatre. *The Three Cuckolds.* Photo: Susan Kandell.

cross-cultural collaborations with other artists and companies. The professional family of ACT is made up of a small staff and a core of affiliated artists. Through our work we hope to stimulate a positive and synergistic interchange of ideas and values between artists, audiences and our community.

—Kelly Cotten

PRODUCTIONS 1991-1992

Pick Up Ax, Anthony Clarvoe; (D) Lisa A. Tromovitch; (S) Robert J. Kruger; (L) Robert McVay; (C) Georgia Ford; (SD) Lamar Livingston

Holy Ghosts, Romulus Linney; (D) Kelly Cotten; (S) Kelly Cotten and Robert J. Kruger; (L) Robert J. Kruger; (C) Georgia Ford; (SD) Lamar Livingston

Henry VI, Parts 1-3, adapt: David Minton and Jillian Raye, from William Shakespeare; (D), (S) and (L) David Minton; (C) Christine Griswold

Endgame, Samuel Beckett; (D) Kelly Cotten; (S) Robert Winn; (L) Robert J. Kruger; (C) Georgia Ford; (SD) Bob Price

What Fools These Mortals Be, William Shakespeare, adapt: Fred Curchack; (D), (S), (L), (C) and (SD) Fred Curchack

The Illusion, Pierre Corneille, adapt: Tony Kushner; (D) Patrick Kelly; (S) Kelly Cotten; (L) Robert J. Kruger and Robert McVay; (C) Happy Yancey; (SD) Scott Miller

21A, Kevin Kling; (D) Ivan Klousia; (S) and (L) Russell H. Champa; (SD) Bruce DuBose

H.I.D., Howard Brenton; (D) Kelly Cotten; (S) and (L) Robert McVay; (C) Diana Figueroa-Story; (SD) Kelly Cotten

PRODUCTIONS 1992-1993

Oklahoma!, book adapt and lyrics: Oscar Hammerstein, II, from Lynn Riggs; music: Richard Rodgers; (D) Kelly Cotten; (S) Nelson Robinson; (L) Robert J. Kruger; (C) Bill Edwards; (MD) Jon Schweikhard; (CH) David Larsen; (SD) David Natinsky

Play With Repeats, Martin Crimp; (D) David Minton; (S) and (L) Robert Bessolo

Boy Meets Girl, Bella and Samuel Spewack; (D) Kelly Cotten; (S) Kateri M. Cale; (L) Russell H. Champa; (C) Georgia Wagenhurst; (SD) David Natinsky

The Three Cuckolds, Leon Katz, adapt: Bill Irwin with Michael Greif; (D) Raphael Parry; (S) Robert Winn; (L) Robert McVay; (C) Giva Taylor; (SD) Bruce Richardson

A Kind of Arden, Martin Crimp; (D) David Minton; (S) and (L) Robert Bessolo

Shakin' the Mess Outta Misery, Shay Youngblood; (D) Cecelia Flores; (S) Cheryl Denson; (L) Keith Buresh; (C) Happy Yancey; (SD) David Natinsky

The Glass Menagerie, Tennessee Williams; (D) Kelly Cotten; (S) Nelson Robinson; (L) Russell H. Champa; (C) Georgia Wagenhurst; (SD) Lamar Livingston

Alabama Shakespeare Festival

KENT THOMPSON
Artistic Director

TAYLOR DAWSON
Board Chairman

1 Festival Drive
Montgomery, AL 36117-4605
(205) 271-5300 (bus.)
(205) 271-5353, (800) 841-4ASF (b.o.)
(205) 271-5348 (fax)

FOUNDED 1972
Martin L. Platt

SEASON
Year-round

FACILITIES
Festival Stage
Seating Capacity: 750
Stage: proscenium-thrust

The Octagon
Seating Capacity: 225
Stage: flexible

FINANCES
Oct. 1, 1992-Sept. 30, 1993
Expenses: $5,757,500

CONTRACTS
AEA LORT (C) and (D)

Classical theatre is devoted to telling the greatest stories of humankind—Shakespeare being the most profound and enduring storyteller of all time. The Alabama Shakespeare Festival is dedicated to artistic excellence in the production and performance of classics and the best contemporary plays. ASF has initiated the Southern Writers Project to create and produce indigenous new plays which may ultimately become classics, and to reach and touch all the people of the region. ASF is committed to the challenge of repertory theatre created by a diverse ensemble of resident artists, and to diversity in programming, staffing and audiences. Fundamentally important to its mission are the MFA programs that develop new theatre professionals. As the State Theatre of Alabama, ASF also serves as a major educational resource and lifelong learning center for the Southeast. Its educational programs help develop in participants of all ages the capacity for language, thought and imagination—vital skills for all areas of our lives.

—Kent Thompson

PRODUCTIONS 1991-1992

Sound design by Kristen R. Kuipers.

Peter Pan, book: James M. Barrie; music: Mark Charlap; lyrics: Carolyn Leigh; (D) Kent Thompson; (S) Charles Caldwell; (L) Richard Moore; (C) Jeanne Button; (MD) William Henderson; (CH) Carol Delk Thompson

Alabama Shakespeare Festival. Herb Downer and Steven David Martin in *A Midsummer Night's Dream.* Photo: Scarsbrook/ASF.

The Misanthrope, Moliere; adapt: Neil Bartlett; (D) Vincent Murphy; (S) Leslie Taylor; (L) Terry Cermak; (C) Michael Krass

A Toby Show, Aurand Harris; (D) Carol Delk Thompson; (S) Charles Caldwell; (L) Terry Cermak; (C) Pamela Wallize; (MD) Ron Guthrie

The Little Foxes, Lillian Hellman; (D) Kent Thompson; (S) Paul Wonsek; (L) Terry Cermak; (C) Susan E. Mickey

Miss Evers' Boys, David Feldshuh; (D) Benny Sato Ambush; (S) Jefferson Sage; (L) Clifton Taylor; (C) Alvin Perry; (CH) Barbara Sullivan

King Lear, William Shakespeare; (D) Kent Thompson; (S) William Bloodgood; (L) Liz Lee; (C) Alan Armstrong

Arms and the Man, George Bernard Shaw; (D) Stephen Hollis; (S) Charles Caldwell; (L) Michael Rourke; (C) Susan Tsu

The Comedy of Errors, William Shakespeare; (D) Jared Sakren; (S) and (C) Charles Caldwell; (L) Liz Lee

Shadowlands, William Nicholson; (D) Charles Towers; (S) and (C) David Crank; (L) Michael Rourke

Lend Me a Tenor, Ken Ludwig; (D) Gavin Cameron Webb; (S) Jim Maronek; (L) Liz Lee; (C) Kristine Kearney; (MD) James Conely

Richard II, William Shakespeare; (D) Kent Thompson; (S) Charles Caldwell; (L) Michael Rourke; (C) Elizabeth Novak

Love Letters, A.R. Gurney, Jr.; (D) Steven David Martin; (S) David Crank; (L) Terry Cermak; (C) Pamela Wallize

PRODUCTIONS 1992-1993

Sound design by Kristen R. Kuipers.

Big River, book adapt: William Hauptman, from Mark Twain; music and lyrics: Roger Miller; (D) Kent Thompson; (S) Charles Caldwell; (L) William H. Grant, III; (C) Jeanne Button; (MD) Dennis West; (CH) Carol Delk Thompson

I Hate Hamlet, Paul Rudnick; (D) Steven David Martin; (S) Bennet Averyt; (L) Michael Rourke; (C) Pamela Wallize

Pinocchio, adapt: Arnold Wengrow, from Carlo Collodi; (D) Darwin Knight; (S) Charles Caldwell; (L) Terry Cermak; (C) Pamela Wallize

Our Town, Thornton Wilder; (D) Cynthia White; (S) Christopher Harrison; (L) Liz Lee; (C) Alvin Perry

A Raisin in the Sun, Lorraine Hansberry; (D) Edward G. Smith; (S) Charles Caldwell; (L) William H. Grant, III; (C) Mary Mease Warren

A Midsummer Night's Dream, William Shakespeare; (D) Carol Delk Thompson; (S) Marjorie Bradley Kellogg; (L) Liz Lee; (C) Susan E. Mickey

Heartbreak House, George Bernard Shaw; (D) Kent Thompson; (S) and (C) David Crank; (L) Terry Cermak

Henry IV, Part 1, William Shakespeare; (D) Kent Thompson; (S) and (C) Charles Caldwell; (L) Liz Lee

Blithe Spirit, Noel Coward; (D) Charles Newell; (S) Charles Kading; (L) Terry Cermak; (C) Elizabeth Novak

Dumas, John McNicholas; (D) Kent Thompson; (S) Richard Isackes; (L) Liz Lee; (C) Paul Tazewell

Henry IV, Part 2, William Shakespeare; (D) Stephen Hollis; (S) and (C) Charles Caldwell; (L) Terry Cermak

Alice B. Theatre

SUSAN FINQUE
Artistic Director

KAREN TAYLOR
Board President

1100 East Pike, The Third Floor
Seattle, WA 98122
(206) 322-5723 (bus.)
(206) 322-5423 (b.o.)
(206) 324-8124 (fax)

FOUNDED 1984
Rick Rankin

SEASON
Sept.-June

FACILITIES
Broadway Performance Hall
Seating Capacity: 298
Stage: proscenium

Theatre Off Jackson
Seating Capacity: 148
Stage: modified thrust

Pioneer Square Theatre
Seating Capacity: 225
Stage: modified proscenium

Little Theatre Off Broadway
Seating Capacity: 110
Stage: flexible

FINANCES
July 1, 1992-June 30, 1993
Expenses: $403,000

CONTRACTS
AEA SPT and SLEUTH

Alice B. Theatre: A Gay and Lesbian Theatre for All People is dedicated to producing professional theatre and cultural events that are racially and culturally diverse, have gender parity, and are offered in a spirit of integrity, creativity, social responsibility, adventure and excellence. We are not about doing community theatre where boys kiss boys and girls kiss girls. We're out to revolutionize the society that exists between performers and the public, and to produce work which is so undeniably original, provocative and fabulous that artists and audiences flock to us. Our programming includes productions on our main and alternative stages, touring, education and developmental workshops. We produce world-premiere projects each season and balance the production of the best contemporary scripts with the staging of irreverent treatments of classics, hosting the best lesbian and gay artists from all over the world and nurturing emerging artists. Alice is no longer the loud and insanely ambitious new kid on the block. We are a leader in the lesbian/gay theatre movement, and widely respected in the Seattle arts community as innovators, risk-takers and consummate professionals.

—Susan Finque

Note: During the 1991-92 season, Rick Rankin served as founding artistic director.

PRODUCTIONS 1991-1992

Meat My Beat/Latin Lezbo Comic, Albert Antonio Araiza and Monica Palacios; (L) Collier Woods

Alice B. Theatre. *Language of Love.* Photo: Chris Bennion.

Split Britches Meet Bloolips, *Belle Reprieve*, book: Lois Weaver, Peggy Shaw, Bette Bourne and Precious Pearl; Cassandra Monologue by Deb Margolin; music: Laka Daisical and Phil Booth; addtl lyrics: Paul Shaw; (D) Lois Weaver; (S) Nancy Bardawil and Matthew Owens; (C) Susan Young

The Holiday Survival Game Show, Peggy Platt, Rick Rankin and others; addtl material: Lisa Koch; music and lyrics: Lisa Koch, David Koch, Michelle Baudry, Chad Henry, Linda Schierman and Scott Warrender; (D) and (CH) Steve Tomkins; (S) Glynn Barlett; (L) Meg Fox; (C) Michelle Dunn; (MD) Troy Gordon

Breaking the Code, Hugh Whitemore; (D) Daniel Wilson; (S) Karen Gjelsteen; (L) Tim Saternow; (C) Anthony; (SD) Steven M. Klein

Grease, book, music and lyrics: Jim Jacobs and Warren Casey; (D) and (SD) Jillian Armenante; (S) Gary Smoot; (L) Gary Vaughn; (C) Michelle Dunn; (MD) Chris Jeffries; (CH) Mayme Paul-Thompson

Gay and Lesbian Theatre Festival:
Contents Under Pressure, Deb Parks-Satterfield with Susan Finque and ensemble; (D) and (CH) Susan Finque; (S) Jason Townley; (L) Collier Woods; (C) Abil Done; (SD) Steven M. Klein

Hidden History, adapt: Drew Emery and ensemble, from oral histories of Seattle's lesbian and gay elders; (D) Patricia Van Kirk; (S) Brendan Willis, with projections by Steve Barrett; (L) Collier Woods; (C) Abil Done; (SD) Steven M. Klein

PRODUCTIONS 1992-1993

Louisiana Purchase, Rick Rankin; addtl material from Chief Joseph (Nez Perce), Sojourner Truth, Yu Wang, Elizabeth Cady Stanton, Adolf Hitler and other sources; (D) Susan Finque; (S) Cory Walters; (L) Dan Corson; (C) Abil Done; (MD) Chris Jeffries; (CH) Kabby Mitchell, III; (SD) Steven M. Klein

The 1993 Holiday Survival Game Show, Peggy Platt and Beto Araiza; music: Lisa Koch with David Koch; lyrics: Lisa Koch; (D) Susan Finque; (S) Glynn Barlett; (L) Dan Corson; (C) Robert Kaiser; (MD) Troy Gordon; (CH) Jillian Armenante

The Baltimore Waltz, Paula Vogel; (D) Susan Finque; (S) Craig Labenz; (L) Patty Mathieu; (C) Ariana Casey; (SD) David Pascal

Language of Love, Drew Emery with Lewis Merkin; (D) Howie Seago; (S) Jennifer Lee; (L) Patty West; (C) Jim Westerland; (SD) David Pascal

Sub Rosa, book: Nikki Appino, Kristin Newbom and ensemble; music: Jim Ragland; lyrics: Nikki Appino, Kristin Newbom and Jim Ragland; (D) Nikki Appino and Kristin Newbom; (S) Dan Corson, with projections by Steve Barrett and Dan Saimo; (L) Dan Corson; (C) Abil Done; (MD) and (SD) Jim Ragland; (CH) Nikki Appino, Kristin Bewbom and ensemble

Gay and Lesbian Theatre Festival:
Brave New Smiles, The Five Lesbian Brothers
Dance Noise
The Deloatch Suite, Kabby Mitchell, III
Wade Madsen
Heat, Keith Hennessey
Lardo Weeping, Terry Galloway
White Disabled Talent, Greg Walloch
Bible Belt, Paul Bonin Rodriguez
Comedy On a Grand Scale, Four Big Girls
Knockin' Em Dead at the Limbo Lounge, Mark Findley
The Campers
Dark Fruit, Pomo Afro Homos; (D) Susan Finque; (L) Dan Corson

Alley Theatre

GREGORY BOYD
Artistic Director

MEREDITH J. LONG
Board Chairman

615 Texas Ave.
Houston, TX 77002
(713) 228-9341 (bus.)
(713) 228-8421 (b.o.)
(713) 222-6542 (fax)

FOUNDED 1947
Nina Vance

SEASON
Sept.-July

Alley Theatre. James Black and Peter Webster in *A Flea in Her Ear*. Photo: Jim Caldwell.

FACILITIES
Large Stage
Seating Capacity: 824
Stage: thrust

Hugo V. Neuhaus
Seating Capacity: 296
Stage: arena

FINANCES
July 1, 1992-June 30, 1993
Expenses: $6,200,000

CONTRACTS
AEA LORT (B) and (C)

The Alley Theatre, one of America's oldest resident theatres, produces a diverse repertoire of new plays, reinterpretations of classic plays, and new music-theatre works. Since 1989, the Alley has forged a mission to create for leading theatre artists from around the world a home where they can develop their work. The Alley is among the few American theatres with a resident acting company. Joining the resident company are associate artists Edward Albee, Jose Quintero, Frank Wildhorn and Robert Wilson. Alley productions have been seen throughout the United States and abroad. The Alley is also committed to educational and outreach programs, including community-based productions, the Rockwell Fund Studio and a professional internship program. To increase the intellectual discourse surrounding theatrical production, we sponsor an extensive series of pre- and postperformance discussions, symposiums and lectures.
—*Gregory Boyd*

PRODUCTIONS 1991-1992

Lighting by Howell Binkley and sound design by Joe Pino unless otherwise noted.

Le Cirque Invisible, Victoria Chaplin and Jean-Baptiste Thierree

Other People's Money, Jerry Sterner; (D) Michael Wilson; (S) Jay Michael Jagim; (L) Christina Giannelli; (C) Ainslie Bruneau; (SD) Kevin Dunayer

Calliope Jam, Christopher Baker; (D) Christopher Baker; (S) Lynda J. Kwallek; (L) Steffani Compton; (C) Martin E. Vreeland

A Flea in Her Ear, Georges Feydeau; adapt: Gregory Boyd; (D) Gregory Boyd; (S) Derek McLane; (C) David C. Woolard

A Christmas Carol, adapt: Michael Wilson, from Charles Dickens; (D) Michael Wilson; (S) Jay Michael Jagim; (C) Ainslie Bruneau

Marriage Play, Edward Albee; (D) Edward Albee; (S) and (C) Derek McLane

The Kiddie Pool, Michael Wilson; (D) Ron Link; (S) Yael Pardess; (C) David C. Woolard; (SD) Kevin Dunayer

Miss Evers' Boys, David Feldshuh; (D) Claude Purdy; (S) James D. Sandefur; (L) Christina Giannelli; (C) Donna M. Kress

American Vaudeville, book: Anne Bogart and Tina Landau; various composers and lyricists; (D) Anne Bogart; (S) Douglas Stein; (C) David C. Woolard; (MD) Ted Sperling

The Baltimore Waltz, Paula Vogel; (D) Anne Bogart; (S) Loy Arcenas; (L) Dennis Parichy; (C) Walker Hicklin; (SD) John Gromada

Forever Plaid, book: Stuart Ross; various composers and lyricists; (D) and (CH) Stuart Ross; (S) Neil Peter Jampolis; (L) Jane Reisman; (C) Debra Stein; (MD) James Raitt

PRODUCTIONS 1992-1993

One Flew Over the Cuckoo's Nest, adapt: Dale Wasserman, from Ken Kesey; (D) Gregory Boyd; (S) Richard H. Young; (C) Steffani Compton

The Front Page, Ben Hecht and Charles MacArthur; (D) Gregory Boyd; (S) Hugh Landwehr; (C) David C. Woolard

Danton's Death, Georg Buchner; trans: Robert Auletta; (D) and (S) Robert Wilson; (L) Stephen Strawbridge and Robert Wilson; (C) John Conklin

A Christmas Carol, adapt: Michael Wilson, from Charles Dickens; (D) Michael Wilson; (S) Jay Michael Jagim; (C) Ainslie Bruneau

Lips Together, Teeth Apart, Terrence McNally; (D) Michael Wilson; (S) Hugh Landwehr; (C) Steffani Compton

From the Mississippi Delta, Dr. Endesha Ida Mae Holland; (D) Seret Scott; (S) Jane LaMotte; (L) Ashley York Kennedy; (C) Lisa A. Vollrath; (SD) Jeff Ladman

Our Town, Thornton Wilder; (D) Jose Quintero; (S) and (L) Kevin Rigdon; (C) Noel Taylor; (SD) C.E. Slisky

Billy Bishop Goes to War, John Gray and Eric Peterson; (D) Gregory Boyd; (S) Robert N. Schmidt; (L) Christina Giannelli; (C) Steffani Compton; (SD) C.E. Slisky

Dracula, A Musical Nightmare, book adapt and lyrics: Douglas Johnson, from Bram Stoker; music: John Aschenbrenner; (D) Douglas Johnson; (S) Richard H. Young; (L) Mary Louise Geiger; (C) Susan Tsu; (MD) John Aschenbrenner; (CH) Chesley Krohn

Death and the Maiden, Ariel Dorfman; (D) Ken Grantham; (S) Robert N. Schmidt; (L) Noele Stollmack; (C) Steffani Compton; (SD) C.E. Slisky

Macbeth, William Shakespeare; (D) Gregory Boyd; (S) Vincent Mountain; (C) Judith Anne Dolan

Alliance Theatre Company

KENNETH LEON
Artistic Director

EDITH H. LOVE
Managing Director

ROBERT REISER
Board Chairman

Robert W. Woodruff Arts Center
1280 Peachtree St. NE
Atlanta, GA 30309
(404) 898-1132 (bus.)
(404) 892-2414 (b.o.)
(404) 898-9576 (fax)

FOUNDED 1968
Atlanta Arts Alliance

Alliance Theatre Company. Ben Halley, Jr. and Larry Golden in *Playland*. Photo: T. Charles Erickson.

SEASON
Sept.-May

FACILITIES
Memorial Arts Building
Seating Capacity: 784
Stage: proscenium

Studio Theatre
Seating Capacity: 200
Stage: flexible

14th Street Playhouse
Mainstage
Seating Capacity: 374
Stage: proscenium

Second Stage
Seating Capacity: 200
Stage: flexible

Stage 3
Seating Capacity: 75
Stage: flexible

FINANCES
Aug. 1, 1991-July 31, 1992
Expenses: $7,129,066

CONTRACTS
AEA LORT (B), (D) and TYA

As we approach the 21st century, it is imperative that the American theatre address those problems that face us as diverse people living in an increasingly shrinking world. Through the nurturing of artists, we are committed to touching the lives of the total community, regardless of race, creed, physical handicap, geographical barriers or economic status. The Alliance Theatre is dedicated to producing exciting, entertaining and evocative programs for a culturally diverse audience with a strong bond to our community.

—*Kenneth Leon*

PRODUCTIONS 1991-1992

Sets by Dex Edwards unless otherwise noted.

Other People's Money, Jerry Sterner; (D) Vincent Murphy; (S) Leslie Taylor; (L) Thomas C. Hase; (C) Jeff Cone; (SD) Brian Kettler

A Man For All Seasons, Robert Bolt; (D) Libby Appel; (S) Michael C. Smith; (L) Robert Peterson; (C) Susan E. Mickey

Club Magic, book: Sandra Deer; music: Dwight Andrews; lyrics: Dwight Andrews and Sandra Deer; (D) John Stephens; (L) Thomas C. Hase; (C) Judy Winograd; (MD) Dwight Andrews; (CH) Stephen Petty

Wenceslas Square, Larry Shue; (D) Richard E.T. White; (S) and (L) Linda Buchanan; (C) Yvonne Lee

A Christmas Carol, adapt: Sandra Deer, from Charles Dickens; (D) Kenneth Leon; (S) John Paoletti and Mary Griswold, with Dex Edwards; (L) William B. Duncan; (C) John Paoletti and Mary Griswold, with Jeff Cone

The Piano Lesson, August Wilson; (D) Kenneth Leon; (S) Marjorie Bradley Kellogg; (L) Ann G. Wrightson; (C) Judy Dearing

The Wind in the Willows, adapt: John Stephens, from Kenneth Grahame; (D) John Stevens; (L) Liz Lee; (C) Stephanie Kaskel

Ain't Misbehavin', conceived: Murray Horwitz and Richard Maltby, Jr.; music and lyrics: Fats Waller, et al; (D) and (CH) Arthur Faria; (S) and (L) Kent Dorsey; (C) Randy Barcelo

Ghosts, Henrik Ibsen; trans: Rick Davis and Brian Johnston; (D) Chris Coleman; (L) P. Hamilton Shinn; (C) Susan E. Mickey

Forever Plaid, book: Stuart Ross; various composers and lyricists; (D) and (CH) Stuart Ross; (S) Neil Peter Jampolis; (L) Jane Reisman; (C) Debra Stein; (MD) M. Michael Fauss; (SD) Marc Salzberg

PRODUCTIONS 1992-1993

Direction by Kenneth Leon, sets by Dex Edwards, lighting by Ann G. Wrightson and costumes by Susan E. Mickey unless otherwise noted.

Much Ado About Nothing, William Shakespeare; (D) Adrian Hall; (S) Eugene Lee; (L) Natasha Katz

Playland, Athol Fugard; (D) Athol Fugard; (S) and (C) Susan Hilferty; (L) Dennis Parichy; (SD) David Budries

Jax and the Graviteers, Brent Trammell and Dex Edwards; (D) Rosemary Newcott; (L) P. Hamilton Shinn; (C) Brent Trammell with Jeff Cone

Flyin' West, Pearl Cleage; (L) P. Hamilton Shinn; (C) Jeff Cone

A Christmas Carol, adapt: Sandra Deer, from Charles Dickens; (L) William B. Duncan; (C) Jeff Cone

A Streetcar Named Desire, Tennessee Williams; (S) Marjorie Bradley Kellogg; (C) Judy Dearing

The Last Fairytale, John Stephens; (D) John Stephens; (S) Rochelle Barker; (C) Jeff Cone

American Conservatory Theater. *The Learned Ladies*. Photos: Ken Friedman.

Once on This Island, book and lyrics: Lynn Ahrens; music: Stephen Flaherty; (D) and (CH) David H. Bell; (L) Diane Ferry Williams; (MD) M. Michael Fauss
Betrayal, Harold Pinter; (D) and (S) Michael Olich
So Long On Lonely Street, Sandra Deer; (D) Seret Scott; (L) Peter Maradudin

American Conservatory Theater

CAREY PERLOFF
Artistic Director

ALAN L. STEIN
Board President

30 Grant Ave., 6th Floor
San Francisco, CA 94108-5800
(415) 749-2200 (bus.)
(415) 749-2228 (b.o.)
(415) 834-3360 (fax)

FOUNDED 1965
William Ball

SEASON
Oct.-May

FACILITIES
Geary Theatre°
Seating Capacity: 1,038
Stage: proscenium

°*A.C.T. presently operates in various theatres as a result of the October 17, 1989 earthquake damage to the Geary Theatre. The theatres include: The Orpheum, Stage Door Theatre and Marines Memorial Theatre.*

FINANCES
June 1, 1992-May 31, 1993
Expenses: $9,400,000

CONTRACTS
AEA LORT (A)

ACT is an artist-driven theatre in which training and production are inextricably linked to create work that aspires to the highest standards of American performance. We believe that innovative productions of great works from the past help to expand our common contemporary experience. We are thus committed to the interaction of original and classical work, both on our stages and at the heart of our Conservatory. ACT seeks plays that are provocative, entertaining and theatrical, large in ideas and complex in vision. We are particularly interested in plays that explore the richness of language in a media-saturated age. As a theatre that is community-based but national in scope, we are committed to an audience and company that reflect the diversity of American society, and to work that helps connect us to cultures within and beyond our borders.

—*Carey Perloff*

Note: During the 1991-92 season, Edward Hastings served as artistic director.

PRODUCTIONS 1991-1992

Lighting by Derek Duarte and sound design by Stephen LeGrand unless otherwise noted.

Cat on a Hot Tin Roof, Tennessee Williams; (D) Warner Shook; (S) Joel Fontaine; (C) Sandra Woodall
The Piano Lesson, August Wilson; (D) Lloyd Richards; (S) E. David Cosier, Jr.; (L) Christopher Akerlind; (C) Constanza Romero; (SD) Tom Clark
Taking Steps, Alan Ayckbourn; (D) Richard E.T. White; (S) Joel Fontaine; (C) Christine Dougherty
A Christmas Carol, book adapt: Dennis Powers and Laird Williamson, from Charles Dickens; music: Lee Hoiby and Tim Weil; lyrics: Laird Williamson; (D) David Maier, after Laird Williamson; (S) Robert Blackman; (C) Robert Morgan; (MD) Scott DeTurk; (CH) Angene Feves and Susan Pilar
Some Enchanted Evening, music: Richard Rodgers; lyrics: Oscar Hammerstein, II; (D) Paul Blake; (MD) Harper Mackay
Cyrano de Bergerac, Edmond Rostand; trans: Brian Hooker; adapt: Dennis Powers; (D) Sabin Epstein; (S) Richard Seger; (C) Robert Fletcher
Charley's Aunt, Brandon Thomas; (D) Edward Hastings; (S) Joel Fontaine; (C) Gerard Howland
The Cocktail Hour, A.R. Gurney, Jr.; (D) Albert Takazauckas; (S) Steven Rubin; (C) David Draper
Good, C.P. Taylor; (D) John C. Fletcher; (S) Jeffrey Struckman; (L) Derek Duarte and Greg Sullivan; (C) Beaver Bauer

PRODUCTIONS 1992-1993

Sound design by Stephen LeGrand unless otherwise noted.

Creditors, August Strindberg; trans: Paul Walsh; (D) Carey Perloff; (S) Donald Eastman; (L) Frances Aronson; (C) Callie Floor
The Pope and the Witch, Dario Fo; trans: Joan Holden; (D) Richard Seyd; (S) and (L) Kent Dorsey; (C) Christine Dougherty
Miss Evers' Boys, David Feldshuh; (D) Benny Sato Ambush; (S) Jefferson Sage; (L) Clifton Taylor; (C) Alvin Perry
A Christmas Carol, adapt: Dennis Powers and Laird Williamson, from Charles Dickens; music: Lee Hoiby and Tim Weil; lyrics: Laird Williamson; (D) David Maier, after Laird Williamson; (S) Robert Blackman; (L) Derek Duarte; (C) Robert Morgan; (MD) Scott DeTurk; (CH) Angene Feves
Bon Appetit!, adapt: Mark Shulgasser, from Ruth Draper and Julia Child; music: Lee Hoiby; (D) Carey Perloff; (S) Donald Eastman; (L) Kent Dorsey; (C) Rita Riggs and Jean Putch; (MD) Todd Sisley
The Late Great Ladies of Blues & Jazz, adapt: Sandra Reaves; (D) Ricardo Khan; (L) Kent Dorsey; (C) Michael Hannah; (MD) Herschel Dwellingham
The Duchess of Malfi, John Webster; (D) Robert Woodruff; (S) George Tsypin; (L) James F. Ingalls; (C) Sandra Woodall; (SD) Bruce Odland
Antigone, Sophocles; trans and adapt: Timberlake Wertenbaker; (D) Carey Perloff; (S) Kate Edmunds; (L) Peter Maradudin; (C) Donna Zakowska
Dinner at Eight, George S. Kaufman and Edna Ferber; (D) Albert Takazauckas; (S) Barbara Mesney; (L) Kurt Landisman; (C) Deborah Nadoolman
The Learned Ladies, Moliere; trans and adapt: Freyda Thomas; (D) Richard Seyd; (S) Ralph Funicello; (L) Peter Maradudin; (C) Beaver Bauer

American Inside Theatre

MORRIGAN HURT
Artistic Director

MARK SIMPSON
Producing Director

MARQ STANKOWSKI
Board President

Box 217
Genesee Depot, WI 53127
(414) 968-4770 (bus.)
(414) 547-8333 (b.o.)
(414) 968-4555 (fax)

FOUNDED 1989
Morrigan Hurt

SEASON
Sept.-May

FACILITIES
Otteson
Seating Capacity: 240
Stage: flexible

Lunt/Fontanne
Seating Capacity: 285
Stage: proscenium

American Inside Theatre. Howard Friedland, Peter Reeves and David diFranceso in *True West*. Photo: Robert Smith.

Pabst
Seating Capacity: 1,350
Stage: proscenium

FINANCES
July 1, 1992-June 30, 1993
Expenses: $459,000

CONTRACTS
AEA SPT

American Inside Theatre started small and got bigger. We've had some exciting and foolish ideas that we'd rather not mention, but here are a few we're willing to admit to: a mission to produce works by American playwrights; development of new voices through our annual plays-in-progress series; commitment to nurture future theatre artists through our Young People's Conservatory workshop; extensive community and educational outreach programs, including frequent classroom visits and an ongoing relationship with the local Hispanic community; a close-knit resident ensemble of actors, designers and technicians; and in our spare time...spearheading the modest task of transforming Ten Chimneys, the 21-acre estate of Broadway greats Alfred Lunt and Lynn Fontanne, into a complete museum/theatre complex. This serves to keep us all pretty busy, and for the most part happy. Above all, we want to love this work we do, for as long as it lasts.

—*Morrigan Hurt*

PRODUCTIONS 1991-1992
Lighting by Andrew Meyers, costumes by Cecelia Mason and sound design by the directors and Randy Bobo unless otherwise noted.

The Glass Menagerie, Tennessee Williams; (D) Morrigan Hurt; (S) David Justin
Holiday, Philip Barry; (D) Ron Peluso; (S) Charles Erven
A Hatful of Rain, Michael Gazzo; (D) David Maier; (S) Charles Erven; (C) Mary Shissler
Crimes of the Heart, Beth Henley; (D) Amy Zeh; (S) Paul Gegenhuber
True West, Sam Shepard; (D) Mark Simpson

PRODUCTIONS 1992-1993
Lighting by Andrew Meyers, costumes by Cecelia Mason and sound design by the director and Randy Bobo unless otherwise noted.

I Hate Hamlet, Paul Rudnick; (D) Morrigan Hurt; (S) Rick Rasmussen
It's A Wonderful Life, adapt: company, from the original screenplay; (D) Ron Peluso; (S) Rick Rasmussen; (SD) Laura Gordon
K2, Patrick Meyers; (D) Morrigan Hurt; (S) David Justin
The Swan, Elizabeth Egloff; (D) Jon Kretzu; (S) Paul Gegenhuber
Broadway Bound, Neil Simon; (D) Mark Simpson; (S) Rick Rasmussen

American Music Theater Festival

MARJORIE SAMOFF
Producing Director

ERIC SALZMAN
Artistic Director

DONNA VIDAS POWELL
Managing Director

JAMES GINTY
Board Chairman

1835 Market St., 4th Floor
Philadelphia, PA 19103
(215) 557-9140 (bus.)
(215) 567-0670 (b.o.)
(215) 988-0798 (fax)

FOUNDED 1984
Marjorie Samoff, Eric Salzman, Ron Kaiserman

SEASON
Mar.-June

FACILITIES
Plays & Players Theatre
Seating Capacity: 324
Stage: proscenium

Zellerbach Theater at the Annenberg Center
Seating Capacity: 900
Stage: thrust

Walnut Street Theatre
Seating Capacity: 1,000
Stage: proscenium

FINANCES
Jan. 1, 1992-Dec. 31, 1992
Expenses: $2,000,000

CONTRACTS
AEA LORT (D) and letter of agreement

The American Music Theater Festival's mission is to develop, produce and present contemporary music-theatre in all its forms: musical comedy, music drama, opera and experimental works. We give priority to works that seek to break new ground and to redraw the boundaries that have traditionally separated opera and musical comedy. We support the develop-

American Music Theater Festival. Tiffani Barbour, Robert Christophe, David Hughes and Keith Robert Bennett in *Bobos*. Photo: Mark Garvin.

ment of creative artists over time, and provide opportunities for both established and emerging artists to take risks and gain mastery of the music-theatre form. Through coproductions and touring, we aim to bring our productions to national audiences. AMTF's program includes mainstage productions, workshops, readings, commissioning, outreach, a youth company and a resident developmental ensemble. Long-range, AMTF aims to create and disseminate a body of new music-theatre work that is a lasting contribution to our field, and to provide a creative environment in which artists of the highest caliber can find support for adventurous new work.
—Marjorie Samoff

PRODUCTIONS 1992

Sound design by Theatre Sound.

Amphigorey, book and lyrics: Edward Gorey; music: Peter Golub; (D) and (CH) Daniel Levans; (S) Edward Gorey; (L) Roger Morgan; (C) Ann Roth; (MD) Thomas Fay
Herringbone, book: Tom Cone; music: Skip Kennon; lyrics: Ellen Fitzhugh; (D) Kenneth Elliott; (S) Brian J. Whitehill; (L) Vivien Leone; (C) Debra Tennenbaum; (MD) Thomas Fay; (CH) Tee Scatuorchio
Tania, book and lyrics: Michael John LaChiusa; music: Anthony Davis; (D) Christopher Alden; (S) Paul Steinberg; (L) Robert Wierzel; (C) Gabriel Berry

PRODUCTIONS 1993

Bobos, book and lyrics: Ed Shockley; music: James McBride; (D) Bertin Rowser; (S) and (L) Mark Somerfield; (C) Felix E. Cochren; (MD) Steven Ford; (CH) Monica Johnson; (SD) Jim Badrak and Jim Brosseau
States of Independence, book and lyrics: Tina Landau; music: Ricky Ian Gordon; (D) Tina Landau; (S) James Schuette; (L) Natasha Katz; (C) Melina Root; (MD) Robert Kapilow; (SD) Eric Liljestrand
Stories from the Nerve Bible, book, music and lyrics: Laurie Anderson; (D) Laurie Anderson; (L) Michael Chybowski
Sheila's Day, book, music and lyrics: Duma Ndlovu; (D) Mbongeni Ngema; (S) Charles McClennahan; (L) Victor En Yu Tan; (C) Toni-Leslie James; (SD) Jim Badrak and Jim Brosseau

American Repertory Theatre

ROBERT BRUSTEIN
Artistic Director

ROBERT J. ORCHARD
Managing Director

RON DANIELS
Associate Artistic Director

PAUL A. BUTTENWIESER
Advisory Board Chair

Loeb Drama Center
64 Brattle St.
Cambridge, MA 02138
(617) 495-2668 (bus.)
(617) 547-8300 (b.o.)
(617) 495-1705 (fax)

FOUNDED 1979
Robert Brustein

SEASON
Year-round

FACILITIES
Loeb Drama Center
Seating Capacity: 556
Stage: flexible

Hasty Pudding Theatre
Seating Capacity: 353
Stage: proscenium

FINANCES
Aug. 1, 1991-July 31, 1992
Expenses: $5,948,263

CONTRACTS
AEA LORT (B)

The American Repertory Theatre, founded as a professional producing organization and a theatrical training conservatory, is one of a very few companies in this country with a resident acting ensemble performing in rotating repertory. The company has presented 95 productions, including more than 45 premieres, new translations and adaptations. Our productions, which have increasingly involved artists of national and international stature from a wide variety of disciplines, generally fall into three distinct categories: newly interpreted classical productions, new American plays, and neglected works of the past, frequently involving music. ART has toured extensively within this country (including an appearance at the 1984 Olympic Arts Festival in Los Angeles) and abroad, including performances in Tokyo, Madrid, Avignon, Paris, Venice, Edinburgh, Tel Aviv, Belgrade, London and Amsterdam. In 1987, the American Repertory Theatre Institute for Advanced Theatre Training at Harvard, currently directed by Ron Daniels, began formal instruction under the direction of Richard Riddell. ART received the 1985 Jujamcyn award and a special Tony award in 1986 for continued excellence in resident theatre.
—Robert Brustein

American Repertory Theatre. Margaret Gibson, Jack Willis, Gustave Johnson and Patti Allison in *Heartbreak House*. Photo: Richard Feldman.

PRODUCTIONS 1991-1992

Costumes by Catherine Zuber and sound design by Maribeth Back unless otherwise noted.

Hamlet, William Shakespeare; (D) Ron Daniels; (S) and (C) Antony MacDonald; (L) Frances Aronson
Misalliance, George Bernard Shaw; (D) David Wheeler; (S) Derek McLane; (L) Christopher Akerlind
The Seagull, Anton Chekhov; trans: George Calderon; adapt: Robert Brustein; (D) Ron Daniels; (S) Antony MacDonald; (L) James F. Ingalls
Media Amok, Christopher Durang; (D) Les Waters; (S) Bill Clarke; (L) John Ambrosone
Oleanna, David Mamet; (D) David Mamet; (S) Michael Merritt; (L) Kevin Rigdon; (C) Harriet Voyt
Hedda Gabler, Henrik Ibsen; trans: Edmund Gosse; adapt: Daniel Stern; (D) Adrian Hall; (S) Derek McLane; (L) Natasha Katz
The Servant of Two Masters, Carlo Goldoni; book adapt and lyrics: Shelley Berc and Andrei Belgrader; music: Rusty Magee; (D) Andrei Belgrader; (S) Anita Stewart; (L) Natasha Katz

PRODUCTIONS 1992-1993

Costumes by Catherine Zuber, lighting by John Ambrosone and sound design by Maribeth Back unless otherwise noted.

Black Snow, adapt: Keith Dewhurst, from Mikhail Bulgakov; (D) Richard Jones; (S) and (C) Antony MacDonald; (L) Scott Zielinski
Heartbreak House, George Bernard Shaw; (D) David Wheeler; (S) Derek McLane; (L) Howell Binkley
Dream of the Red Spider, Ronald Ribman; (D) Ron Daniels; (S) Riccardo Hernandez; (L) Frances Aronson
Silence, Cunning, Exile, Stuart Greenman; (D) Ron Daniels; (S) Christine Jones; (C) Karen Eister
The L.A. Plays, Han Ong; (D) Steve Maler; (S) Christine Jones; (C) Gail Buckley; (SD) Donald DiNicola
Orphee, adapt: Robert Brustein, from Jean Cocteau; music: Philip Glass; (D) Francesca Zambello; (S) Robert Israel; (L) Pat Collins; (MD) Martin Goldray

Those the River Keeps, David Rabe; (D) David Rabe; (S) Loren Sherman; (C) Gail Buckley
Cakewalk, Peter Feibleman; (D) Ron Daniels; (S) Tony Straiges; (L) Howell Binkley

American Stage Festival

MATTHEW PARENT
Producing Director

DAVID HENDERSON
General Manager

JAY DINKEL
Board President

Box 225
Milford, NH 03055-0225
(603) 673-4005 (bus.)
(603) 673-7515 (b.o.)
(603) 673-4792 (fax)

FOUNDED 1975
Terry C. Lorden

SEASON
May-Sept.

FACILITIES
Seating Capacity: 498
Stage: proscenium

FINANCES
Nov. 1, 1991-Oct. 31, 1992
Expenses: $739,548

CONTRACTS
AEA LORT (D)

One of the best things a theatre can do is to have an intimate dialogue with the audience it serves. The American Stage Festival celebrates the theatre with its community each summer in a festival environment. We are committed to programming that is rich, challenging and varied. We are also committed to superior production values, realizing that quality is paramount in the continuing development of our audience. We hear our audience, and we try to accommodate their cultural, entertainment and personal values. More importantly, we listen to our audience. And our audience listens to us. They have heard the voices of playwrights old and new and have allowed us to challenge their views and beliefs. The warm relationship between our audience and the Festival has also allowed the Festival to survive dire economic times and continue to flourish in a nonurban setting. Our theatre belongs to our community and is a testament to the community's desire to foster professional, invigorating and provocative theatrical entertainment.

—*Matthew Parent*

Note: During the 1991-92 season, Richard Rose served as artistic director.

PRODUCTIONS 1992

Shirley Valentine, Willy Russell; (D) Richard Rose; (S) Charles Morgan; (L) David Brown; (C) Jane Alois Stein
Jacques Brel is Alive and Well and Living in Paris, book adapt and lyrics: Eric Blau and Mort Shuman; music: Jacques Brel; (D) Robert Walsh; (S) Rob Odorisio; (L) and (SD) David A. Strang; (MD) Winston Clark; (CH) Marguerite Mathews
The Break, Jay MacNamee; (D) Peter Bennett; (S) Gary English; (L) Linda O'Brien; (C) Amanda J. Comer
The Children's Hour, Lillian Hellman; (D) Fontaine Syer; (S) Clifton Taylor; (L) Kendall Smith; (C) Amanda Aldridge
Malice Aforethought, Erik Jendresen; (D) Richard Rose; (S) Charles Morgan; (L) Clifton Taylor; (C) Laura Poole

PRODUCTIONS 1993

Little Shop of Horrors, book adapt and lyrics: Howard Ashman, from Charles Griffith; music: Alan Menken; (D) and (CH) Michael Oster; (S) Bill Savoy; (L) Betsy Adams; (C) Andrew Poleszak; (MD) Adam Levowitz; (SD) Barry Funderburg
Crimes of the Heart, Beth Henley; (D) Matthew Parent; (S) Charles Morgan; (L) John Gisondi; (C) Andrew Poleszak
Love Letters, A.R. Gurney, Jr.; (S) Richard Mason; (C) Karalee Dawn
The Country Girl, Clifford Odets; (D) and (S) Richard Mason; (L) Richard Harmon; (C) Betsy Adams; (SD) Andrew Poleszak
Broadway Bound, Neil Simon; (D) Matthew Parent; (S) and (L) John Gisondi; (C) Andrew Poleszak; (SD) Barry Funderburg

American Stage Festival. Susan Browning, Judith Hawking, Robert Walsh and Kathleen Mahony-Bennett in *The Children's Hour*. Photo: Michael Bettencourt.

American Theatre Company

KITTY ROBERTS
Producing Artistic Director

LINDA K. KIDD
Administrative Assistant

ROD EDWARDS
Board Chairman

Box 1265
Tulsa, OK 74101-1265
(918) 747-9494 (bus.)
(918) 596-7111 (b.o.)
(918) 584-0486 (fax)

FOUNDED 1970
Kitty Roberts

SEASON
Oct.-July

FACILITIES
Tulsa Performing Arts
John H. Williams Theatre
Seating Capacity: 420
Stage: proscenium

Tulsa Performing Arts
Studio I
Seating Capacity: 280
Stage: arena

Philbrook Museum of Art
Patti Johnson Wilson
Auditorium
Seating Capacity: 250
Stage: proscenium

FINANCES
July 1, 1993-June 30, 1994
Expenses: $312,000

CONTRACTS
AEA Guest Artist

Oklahoma's pioneer spirit arises from a life shared together at the edge of recent American history—the forced resettlement of Native Americans from 1820 on, the land rush by European settlers in 1889, statehood in 1907, the oil boom from 1912 to 1920, the Dust Bowl depression of the 1930s, the expansion of military bases during World War II, the energy crisis and oil embargo of 1973. As Tulsa's only resident professional theatre company, the American Theatre Company can persuade Oklahomans that their frontier

American Theatre Company. Karl Krause in *A Christmas Carol*. Photo: John McCormack.

viewpoint is mirrored in the traditions of world drama, and that their frontier voices can be expressed in a unique dramatic idiom. Therefore, our goal is to play a leading role in shaping a common public vision for the economic, political, educational, religious and artistic life of Oklahoma. American Theatre Company presents six mainstage productions, a summer show, a young people's theatre summer production and three Global Village Children's Theatre productions, as well as conducting ongoing educational outreach.

—*Kitty Roberts*

PRODUCTIONS 1991-92

Direction by Lori Bryant, sets by Ricky Green Newkirk, lighting by Richard Wilson and costumes by Randy Blair unless otherwise noted.

Corpse, Gerald Moon; (D)David Valla; (SD) David Bagsby
A Christmas Carol, book adapt: Robert L. Odle, from Charles Dickens; music: Richard Averill; lyrics: Richard Averill and Robert L. Odle; (S) Richard Ellis; (C) Pam Curtis and Randy Blair; (MD) Ted Auwen; (CH) David Rickel; (SD) John Jack
Ain't Misbehavin', conceived: Murray Horwitz and Richard Maltby, Jr.; music and lyrics: Fats Waller, et al; (D) Randy Blair; (S) Richard Ellis; (MD) Carl Curtis; (CH) David Rickel; (SD) Brett Jarvis

Other People's Money, Jerry Sterner; (D) Jim Runyan; (S) Richard Ellis; (SD) Irving Productions
Educating Rita, Willy Russell; (D) Tyrone Wilkerson
Annie, book: Thomas Meehan; music: Charles Strouse; lyrics: Martin Charnin; (D) Randy Blair; (C) Pam Curtis; (MD) Ted Auwen and Doug Smith; (CH) David Ricket
Don't Sleep Under the Mapou Tree, Greer Sucke; (S) Tad Townes; (L) Kevin Stretch; (C) Pam Curtis
The Dinosaur Play, Steve and Kathy Hotchner; (S) Lori Bryant; (C) Pam Curtis

PRODUCTIONS 1992-93

Sets by Richard Ellis, lighting by Tad Townes, costumes by Randy Blair and sound design by Irving Productions unless otherwise noted.

Little Shop of Horrors, book adapt and lyrics: Howard Ashman, from Charles Griffith; music: Alan Menken; (D) Randy Blair; (L) Richard Wilson; (MD) Joyce Shanks; (CH) David Rickel
A Christmas Carol, book adapt: Robert L. Odle, from Charles Dickens; music: Richard Averill; lyrics: Richard Averill and Robert L. Odle; (D) Jim Queen; (C) Pam Curtis andJo Wimer; (MD) Ted Auwen; (CH) David Rickel
From the Mississippi Delta, Dr. Endesha Ida Mae Holland; (D) Tyrone Wilkerson
The Miracle Worker, William Gibson; (D) Lori Bryant; (C) Pam Curtis
Lettice and Lovage, Peter Shaffer; (D) Jim Runyan; (S) Ricky Green Newkirk; (C) Pam Curtis
Greater Tuna, Jaston Williams, Joe Sears and Ed Howard; (D) Randy Blair; (S) Rick Hildebrant; (L) M. Spelvin
Anansi, adapt: Barbara Winther, from West African folk tales; (D) Ozella Mahone; (S) Randy Blair; (L) Rick Hildebrant
Golliwhoppers, Flora B. Atkin; (D) Ozella Mahone; (L) and (C) Rick Hildebrant

Antenna Theater

CHRIS HARDMAN
Artistic Director

CHRISTINE MURRAY
Administrative Director

DAVID SHICKELE
Board Chairman

Box 176
Sausalito, CA 94966
(415) 332-4862 (bus.)
(415) 331-8512 (b.o.)
(415) 332-4870 (fax)

FOUNDED 1980
Chris Hardman

SEASON
Variable

FINANCES
Jan. 1, 1992-Dec. 31, 1992
Expenses: $259,250

Since Antenna's founding, I have been called everything from an "enfant terrible" to a "savior" to a "saboteur" for my experiments with the mechanics of the audience/performance relationship. Antenna produces events that involve the audience in ways hitherto unexplored by traditional theatre. Receive, Transform, Transmit. These are the key elements of Antenna's work. We gather interviews and other input from our community; we transform it into theatre; and we then transmit it back to our audience via an experiential performance event. Our work often blends masks, puppetry, mime, dance, taped narratives and performance sculpture with new and emerging technologies. Antenna has pioneered new theatrical formats involving infrared transmitted sound, 3-D slides,

Antenna Theater. Taino Indians and Columbus Horse from *The Appearance of Civilization*. Photo: Ronald M. Davis

Walkmans, interactive radio, sensory-tripped animation, carnival elements and public-art projects. In the future, we plan to continue experimenting with performance formats, incorporating new multimedia technologies, blurring the lines between the theatre and its audience even more.

—*Chris Hardman*

PRODUCTIONS 1991-1992

Plays and direction by Chris Hardman, visual design by Ronald M. Davis and Chris Hardman, and sound design by David Torgersen unless otherwise noted.

Etiquette of the Undercaste
All You Can Eat; visual design: Ronald M. Davis
Caveat Emptor! Buyer Beware!; visual design: Ronald M. Davis

PRODUCTIONS 1992-1993

Plays and direction by Chris Hardman, visual design by Ronald M. Davis and Chris Hardman, and sound design by David Torgersen unless otherwise noted.

Eye To Eye; (D) Charles Queary
The Appearance of Civilization; (D) Tori Truss
Etiquette of the Undercaste

Arden Theatre Company

TERRENCE J. NOLEN
Producing Artistic Director

AARON POSNER
Artistic Director

AMY L. MURPHY
Managing Director

SHEILA KUTNER
Board President

Box 801
Philadelphia, PA 19105
(215) 829-8900
(215) 829-1735 (fax)

FOUNDED 1988
Terrence J. Nolen, Aaron Posner, Amy L. Murphy

SEASON
Sept.-May

FACILITIES
St. Stephen's Alley
Seating Capacity: 150-175
Stage: flexible

FINANCES
June 1, 1992-May 31, 1993
Expenses: $485,442

CONTRACTS
AEA letter of agreement

The Arden Theatre Company is dedicated to bringing to life the greatest stories by the greatest storytellers of all time. Since the greatest stories touch some essential part of the human experience, the *story itself* remains the primary focus of all our productions. The Arden will draw from any source which is inherently dramatic and theatrical—fiction, nonfiction, poetry, music and drama; adapting nondramatic writings to the stage is an important aspect of our work. These new texts create fascinating challenges which force us to create new theatrical language, establish new conventions, and continually reinvent and rediscover theatrical possibilities. The Arden stages works for the diverse Philadelphia community that arouse, provoke, illuminate and inspire. All our programs aim to enrich the lives of those living throughout our diverse community. Our commitment is *here*, with local students, actors, authors, artists and audiences.

—*Terrence J. Nolen, Aaron Posner*

PRODUCTIONS 1991-1992

Sound design by Connie Lockwood unless otherwise noted.

Talley's Folly, Lanford Wilson; (D) Aaron Posner; (S) Phillip A. Graneto; (L) Curt Senie; (C) Michele Osherow; (SD) Bob Perdick
Saint Joan, George Bernard Shaw; (D) Terrence J. Nolen; (S) David Slovic; (L) Ellen M. Owens; (C) Michele Osherow
The Brothers K., adapt: Terrence J. Nolen and Aaron Posner, from Fyodor Dostoevski; (D) Terrence J. Nolen and Aaron Posner; (S) David Slovic; (L) John Stephen Hoey; (C) Tracy E. D'Altilia
The Dragon, Yevgeny Shvartz; (D) Terrence J. Nolen; (S) and (C) Janet Cleveland; (L) Paul Richardson

Arden Theatre Company. Bekka Eaton and Tom Teti in *Talley's Folly*. Photo: Lisa Block.

PRODUCTIONS 1992-1993

Echoes of the Jazz Age, book adapt and lyrics: Aaron Posner, from Hemingway, Porter, Parker, Fitzgerald, Waller and White; music: Ricardo Martin; (D) Aaron Posner; (S) Patty Bennett; (L) John Stephen Hoey; (C) Mimi O'Donnell; (MD) Ricardo Martin
Change Partners & Dance, Dennis Raymond Smeal; (D) Terrence J. Nolen; (S) David Slovic; (L) Curt Senie; (C) Mimi O'Donnell; (SD) Connie Lockwood
The Tempest, William Shakespeare; (D) Aaron Posner and Mark Lord; (S) and (C) Hiroshi Iwasaki; (L) John Stephen Hoey; (SD) Jonathan Sher
Sweeney Todd, book adapt: Hugh Wheeler, from Christopher Bond; music and lyrics: Stephen Sondheim; (D) Terrence J. Nolen; (S) James F. Pyne, Jr.; (L) Deborah Peretz; (C) Marla Jurglanis; (MD) John Waldie

Arena Stage

DOUGLAS C. WAGER
Artistic Director

STEPHEN RICHARD
Executive Director

RILEY K. TEMPLE
Board President

6th and Maine Ave. SW
Washington, DC 20024
(202) 554-9066 (bus.)
(202) 488-3300 (b.o.)
(202) 488-4056 (fax)

FOUNDED 1950
Edward Mangum, Zelda Fichandler, Thomas C. Fichandler

SEASON
Sept.-June

FACILITIES
The Fichandler Stage
Seating Capacity: 818
Stage: arena

The Kreeger Theater
Seating Capacity: 514
Stage: thrust

The Old Vat Theater
Seating Capacity: 180
Stage: flexible

FINANCES
July 1, 1992-June 30, 1993
Expenses: $9,200,000

CONTRACTS
AEA LORT (B+) and (D)

Arena Stage enters its fifth decade, under new leadership, dedicated to its founding belief that true artistic excellence is achieved by means of a resident ensemble of actors, artists, craftspeople and administrators who collaborate in an evolutionary process from play to play, season after season. We are committed to enriching the imaginative and spiritual life of our audience. Our repertoire provides our community with an aggressively eclectic mix of classics and new works, musicals and culturally diverse offerings. The actor inhabits the epicenter of our work as a living instrument of human expressivity. Arena has expanded and reemphasized its longstanding commitment to encourage participation by people of color in every aspect of the theatre's life by establishing a comprehensive cultural diversity program which includes the Allen Lee Hughes Fellows Program for the training of ethnically diverse young people in artistic, technical and administrative areas. We seek to create a vibrant emotional and intellectual theatrical landscape that, through storytelling, probes the infinite mystery of the human experience.
—*Douglas C. Wager*

PRODUCTIONS 1991-1992

Sound design by Susan R. White unless otherwise noted.

The Time of your Life, William Saroyan; (D) and (S) Liviu Ciulei; (L) Nancy Schertler; (C) Marjorie Slaiman
Yerma, Federico Garcia Lorca; trans: W.S. Merwin; music: Fabian V. Obispo, Jr.; (D) Tazewell Thompson; (S) Loy Arcenas; (L) Nancy Schertler; (C) Paul Tazewell
A Wonderful Life, book adapt and lyrics: Sheldon Harnick, from the original screenplay; music: Joe Raposo; (D) Douglas C. Wager; (S) Thomas Lynch; (L) Allen Lee Hughes; (C) Jess Goldstein; (MD) Jeffrey Saver; (CH) Joey McKneely
Jar the Floor, Cheryl L. West; (D) Tazewell Thompson; (S) Thomas Lynch; (L) Christopher Townsend; (C) Betty Siegel
The School for Wives, Moliere; adapt: Neil Bartlett; (D) Kyle Donnelly; (S) Loy Arcenas; (L) Allen Lee Hughes; (C) Paul Tazewell
Trinidad Sisters, adapt: Mustapha Matura from Anton Chekhov; (D) Clinton Turner Davis; (S) Charles McClennahan; (L) Nancy Schertler; (C) Marjorie Slaiman
Mrs. Klein, Nicholas Wright; (D) Zelda Fichandler; (S) Douglas Stein; (L) Nancy Schertler; (C) Paul Tazewell
The Visit, Friedrich Durrenmatt; trans: Maurice Valency; (D) Douglas C. Wager; (S) Adrianne Lobel; (L) Nancy Schertler; (C) Marjorie Slaiman
The Father, August Strindberg, trans: John Osborne, and **The Stronger**, August Strindberg, trans: Laurence Maslon; (D) Douglas C. Wager (*The Father*); (D) Laurence Maslon (*The Stronger*); (S) Marina Draghici; (L) Kevin J. Lawson; (C) Marjorie Slaiman; (SD) Robin Heath

PRODUCTIONS 1992-1993

Sound design by Susan R. White unless otherwise noted.

Of Thee I Sing, book: George S. Kaufman and Morrie Ryskind; music: George Gershwin; lyrics: Ira Gershwin; (D) Douglas C. Wager; (S) Zack Brown; (L) Allen Lee Hughes; (C) Marjorie Slaiman; (MD) William Huckaby; (CH) Marcia Milgrom Dodge
The Way of the World, William Congreve; (D) Kyle Donnelly; (S) Loy Arcenas; (L) Allen Lee Hughes; (C) Paul Tazewell
The African Company Presents "Richard III", Carlyle Brown; (D) Tazewell Thompson; (S) Douglas Stein; (L) Allen Lee Hughes; (C) Paul Tazewell
Blood Knot, Athol Fugard (co-produced by the Acting Company); (D) Tazewell Thompson; (S) Douglas Stein; (L) Allen Lee Hughes; (C) Paul Tazewell
It's the Truth (If You Think it Is), Luigi Pirandello; trans: Laurence Maslon; (D) and (S) Liviu Ciulei; (L) Nancy Schertler; (C) Marina Draghici
Avner the Eccentric; (L) Jeff Norberry
Summer and Smoke, Tennessee Williams; (D) Kyle Donnelly; (S) Marina Draghici; (L) Nancy Schertler; (C) Marjorie Slaiman
The Brothers Karamazov, Paul Magid (co-produced by Seattle Repertory Theatre and The Flying Karamazov Brothers); music: Doug Wieselman and Gina Leishman; lyrics: Howard Patterson; (D) Daniel Sullivan; (S) Andrew Wood Boughton; (L) Allen Lee Hughes; (C) Caryn Neman; (MD) Doug Wieselman and Gina Leishman; (CH) Doug Elkins; (SD) Steven M. Klein and Susan R. White
The Skin of Our Teeth, Thornton Wilder; (D) Douglas C. Wager; (S) Thomas Lynch; (L) Nancy Schertler; (C) Paul Tazewell

New Voices for a New America:
Antigone in New York, Janusz Glowacki; trans: Joan Torres; (D) Laurence Maslon; (S) Katherine Jennings; (L) Christopher V. Lewton; (C) Marjorie Slaiman; (SD) Robin Heath
The America Play, Suzan-Lori Parks; (D) Peter Wallace; (S) Katherine Jennings; (L) Christopher V. Lewton; (C) Rachel V. Ivey; (SD) Robin Heath
East Texas Hot Links, Eugene Lee; (D) Clinton Turner Davis; (S) Katherine Jennings; (L) Christopher Driscoll; (C) Rachel V. Ivey; (SD) Robin Heath
A Small World, Mustapha Matura; (D) Kyle Donnelly; (S) Katherine Jennings; (L) Kim O. Ford; (C) Rachel V. Ivey; (SD) Robin Heath

Arena Stage. Pamela Nyberg in *Summer and Smoke*. Photo: Joan Marcus

15

Arizona Theatre Company

DAVID IRA GOLDSTEIN
Artistic Director

ROBERT ALPAUGH
Managing Director

MARY K. STERLING
Board Chairman

Box 1631
Tucson, AZ 85702
(602) 884-8210 (bus.)
(602) 622-2823 (b.o.)
(602) 628-9129 (fax)

808 North 1st St.
Phoenix, AZ 85004
(602) 234-2892 (bus.)
279-0534 (b.o.)
248-9234 (fax)

FOUNDED 1967
Sandy Rosenthal

SEASON
Oct.-June

FACILITIES
Temple of Music and Art
(Tucson)
Seating Capacity: 603
Stage: proscenium

Herberger Theater Center
(Phoenix)
Seating Capacity: 790
Stage: proscenium

FINANCES
July 1, 1992-June 30, 1993
Expenses: $3,345,967

CONTRACTS
AEA LORT (C)

Arizona Theatre Company seeks to honor the diversity, intelligence and good will of our audience through producing a wide-ranging repertoire of both new and classic works that are of relevance to the heart and mind. Now, in our 27th year, our unique two-city operation in Tucson and Phoenix gives us the opportunity to serve a broadly diverse audience. We feel that the generative spark of theatre is contained in the imagination of writers who find singular ways to tell us universal truths about the human experience. Whether in our mainstage season, through our commissions, in our outreach programming, through collaborations with other companies or through our New Play Reading Series, we seek to engage artists and staff of the highest caliber to bring those stories to life. We seek, in all our work, to be inclusive rather than exclusive; to serve as an essential educational resource for the people of Arizona; and to actively work to assure cultural diversity and wide public access in all our endeavors.
—*David Ira Goldstein*

Note: During the 1992-93 season, Robert Alpaugh served as acting artistic director.

PRODUCTIONS 1991-1992

She Stoops to Conquer, Oliver Goldsmith; (D) Edward Payson Call; (S) Greg Lucas; (L) Don Darnutzer; (C) Peggy Kellner; (SD) Brian Peterson

Ain't Misbehavin', conceived: Murray Horwitz and Richard Maltby, Jr.; music and lyrics: Fats Waller et al; (D) and (CH) Arthur Faria; (S) and (L) Kent Dorsey; (C) Bobby Culbert; (SD) Mark Micelli

Who's Afraid of Virginia Woolf?, Edward Albee; (D) Austin Pendleton; (S) Greg Lucas; (L) Tracy Odishaw; (C) Sigrid Insull; (SD) Brian Peterson

The Heidi Chronicles, Wendy Wasserstein; (D) David Ira Goldstein; (S) Jeff Thomson; (L) Don Darnutzer; (C) Rose Pederson; (SD) Steven M. Klein

Minor Demons, Bruce Graham; (D) Andrew J. Traister; (S) Greg Lucas; (L) Rick Paulsen; (C) Francis Kenny; (SD) Brian Peterson

Sea Marks, Gardner McKay; (D) Matthew Wiener; (S) Greg Lucas; (L) Tracy Odishaw; (C) Kish Finnegan; (SD) Brian Peterson

PRODUCTIONS 1992-1993

One Crazy Day or The Marriage of Figaro, trans and adapt: Roger Downey, from Pierre-Augustine de Beaumarchais; (D) David Ira Goldstein; (S) Greg Lucas; (L) Don Darnutzer; (C) David Kay Mickelsen; (SD) Steve Klein

The All Night Strut, Fran Charnas; various composers and lyricists; (D) David Ira Goldstein; (S) Greg Lucas; (L) Tracy Odishaw; (C) David Kay Mickelsen; (MD) Jerry Harkey; (CH) Steve Tomkins

Nora, Ingmar Bergman; trans: Frederick J. Marker; adapt from *A Doll House* by Henrik Ibsen; (D) Matthew Wiener; (S) Michael Miller; (L) Scott Zielinski; (C) Laura Crow; (SD) Dan Schreier

Fertility Rights, Michael Michaelian; (D) David Ira Goldstein; (S) Jeff Thomson; (L) Tracy Odishaw; (C) Rose Pederson; (SD) Eric Webster

M. Butterfly, David Henry Hwang; (D) Dennis Bigelow; (S) William Bloodgood; (L) Robert Peterson; (C) Deborah M. Dryden; (SD) David de Berry

Willi, John Pielmeier, adapt from Willi Unsoeld; (D) David Ira Goldstein; (S) Greg Lucas; (L) Rick Peterson; (C) Carolyn Keim

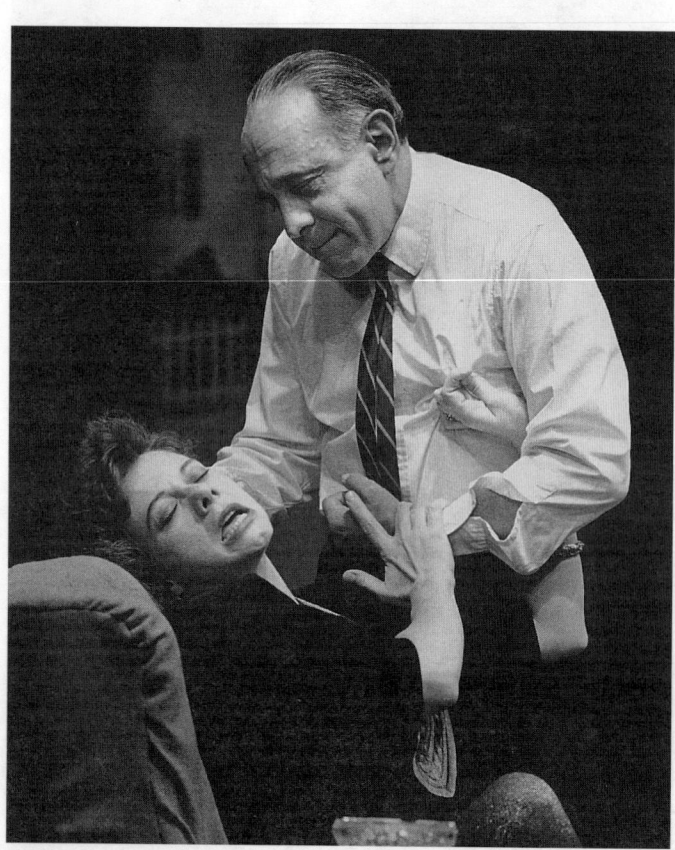

Arizona Theatre Company. Rondi Reed and George Morfogen in *Who's Afraid of Virginia Woolf?* Photo: Tim Fuller.

The Arkansas Arts Center Children's Theatre

BRADLEY D. ANDERSON
Artistic Director

P.J. POWERS
Theatre Administrative Manager

PHIL L. HERRINGTON
Board President

Box 2137
Little Rock, AR 72203
(501) 372-4000
(501) 375-8053 (fax)

FOUNDED 1963
Museum of Fine Arts, The Junior League of Little Rock, The Fine Arts Club

SEASON
Sept.-May

FACILITIES
The Arkansas Arts Center Theatre
Seating Capacity: 389
Stage: proscenium

The Arkansas Arts Center Theatre Studio
Seating Capacity: 200
Stage: flexible

The Arkansas Arts Center Children's Theatre. Donovan Suitt, Richard J. Sillen, Jr., Sarah Boss, Pamie Adam and Amber Minor in *Aladdin and the Wonderful Lamp*. Photo: Dixie Knight.

FINANCES
July 1, 1992-June 30, 1993
Expenses: $372,027

The Arkansas Arts Center Children's Theatre exists to provide high-quality theatre experiences for young people and their families. We provide a master/apprentice education where children work alongside professional actors, all sharing in the common goal of excellence. Our best work can be experienced on at least three distinct levels: For the young child there is simply a great story and lots of sensory pleasure; the older child enjoys more of the subtleties in the language and in the art form; adults appreciate the more sophisticated humor or irony and see the symbolism that moves beyond the immediate story to the world at large. A dedicated ensemble of actors, directors and designers produce a mainstage season, three touring productions and an experimental lab studio, and teach in an intensive summer theatre academy that brings children into direct working contact with the creative process. We attempt to educate young audiences through artistic observations of the human condition, while trying to heighten the quality of theatre experiences for children.
—*Bradley D. Anderson*

PRODUCTIONS 1991-1992

Music by Lori Loree and costumes by Mark Hughes unless otherwise noted.

The Ugly Duckling, adapt: Alan Keith Smith, from Hans Christian Andersen; (D) Bradley D. Anderson; (S) James E. Lyden; (L) Richard J. Sillen, Jr.
The Secret Garden, adapt: Thomas W. Olson, from Frances Hodgson Burnett; (D) and (L) Alan Keith Smith; (S) Laura Hohanshelt and Mike Pittman; (SD) Brett A. Nicholson
The Toymaker's Apprentice, book: Martin McGeachy; lyrics: Lori Loree and P.J. Powers; (D) Bradley D. Anderson; (S) Alan Keith Smith; (L) Kathy Gray; (MD) Lori Loree; (CH) Pamie Adam
The Jungle Book, adapt: Alan Keith Smith, from Rudyard Kipling; (D) and (S) Alan Keith Smith; (L) Charles R. Kaiser
The Witch of Blackbird Pond, adapt: Thomas W. Olson, from Elizabeth George Speare; (D) Bradley D. Anderson; (L) Charles R. Kaiser; (SD) Brett A. Nicholson
Aladdin and the Wonderful Lamp, adapt: Timothy Mason, from *1,001 Nights*; (D) and (S) Alan Keith Smith; (L) Charles R. Kaiser; (SD) Brett A. Nicholson
Giants: Myths and Legends, Alan Keith Smith; (D) Debbie Weber; (S) Alan Keith Smith
Sleeping Beauty, adapt: P.J. Powers, from Charles Perrault; (D) and (S) Bradley D. Anderson
The Ugly Duckling, adapt: Alan Keith Smith, from Hans Christian Andersen; (D) and (S) Bradley D. Anderson

PRODUCTIONS 1992-1993

Music by Lori Loree and costumes by Mark Hughes unless otherwise noted.

The World of Mother Goose, adapt: Bradley D. Anderson; (S) Pamie Adam; (L) Chris Davis
Hurricane Dreams: The Voyages of Christopher Columbus, Alan Keith Smith; (D) Bradley D. Anderson; (S) Alan Keith Smith; (L) Chris Davis; (SD) Brett A. Nicholson
Sleeping Beauty, adapt: P.J. Powers, from Charles Perrault; (D) Bradley D. Anderson; (S) Mary Alyce Hare; (L) Alan Keith Smith
Madeline and the Gypsies, adapt: John Clark Donahue, from Ludwig Bemelmans; (D) Debbie Weber; (S) Alan Keith Smith; (C) Chris Davis
Heidi, adapt: Thomas W. Olson, from Johanna Spyri; (D) Bradley D. Anderson; (S) Pamie Adam; (L) Chris Davis; (SD) Brett A. Nicholson
Pinocchio, adapt: Alan Keith Smith, from Carlo Collodi; (D) Alan Keith Smith; (S) Pamie Adam; (L) Chris Davis
The Princess and the Pea, adapt: P.J. Powers, from Hans Christian Andersen; (D) Debbie Weber; (S) Jimi Brewi
Jack Frost, Alan Keith Smith; (D) Debbie Weber; (S) Pamie Adam
The Jungle Book: Tales from Peace Rock, adapt: Alan Keith Smith, from Rudyard Kipling; (D) and (S) Alan Keith Smith

Arkansas Repertory Theatre

CLIFF FANNIN BAKER
Producing Artistic Director

H. MAURICE MITCHELL
Board Chairman

Box 110
Little Rock, AR 72203
(501) 378-0445 (bus.)
(501) 378-0405 (b.o.)
(501) 378-0012 (fax)

FOUNDED 1976
Cliff Fannin Baker

SEASON
Sept.-May

FACILITIES
MainStage Theatre
Seating Capacity: 354
Stage: proscenium

SecondStage Theatre
Seating Capacity: 99
Stage: flexible

Arkansas Repertory Theatre. Robert Ginnaven and Melanie Johnson in *God's Country*. Photo: Barry Arthur.

FINANCES
July 1, 1992-June 30, 1993
Expenses: $1,130,000

CONTRACTS
AEA letter of agreement

Arkansas Rep's 17th season is hallmarked by the diversity of our audiences and our outreach goals, while exhibiting a prevailing interest in contemporary scripts and American playwrights. Our mission at the Rep has remained a constant: to provoke, educate and entertain our audiences while providing meaningful experiences for the professional artistic company. The Rep is still best described as "emerging." We moved into a new performing arts center in 1988, and we operate under a letter of agreement with Actors' Equity Association. Our subscription base has doubled in the past few years, our company is growing and our programming is challenging both artists and audiences. We are proud of the theatre's regional reputation and local impact. Our programs include an eight-play mainstage season, selected second-stage productions, play readings and "Talkbacks," a professional intern program, a 14-year-old arts-in-education program and a six-state regional tour.
—*Cliff Fannin Baker*

PRODUCTIONS 1991-1992

Direction by Cliff Fannin Baker, sets by Mike Nichols, lighting by Ken White and sound design by Chip Salerno unless otherwise noted.

Lend Me a Tenor, Ken Ludwig; (D) Charlie Hensley; (C) Marianne Custer
God's Country, Steven Dietz; (C) Joan Wilson
Into the Woods, book: James Lapine; music and lyrics: Stephen Sondheim; (C) Yslan Hicks; (MD) Mark Janas; (CH) Debbie Wools Rawn and Jana Beard Stodola
The All Night Strut, Fran Charnas; various composers and lyricists; (D) Steve Tomkins; (C) Yslan Hicks; (MD) Darcy Danielson
Hannah Davis, Leslie Lee; (D) James B. Nicola; (S) Llewellyn Harrison; (C) Connie Fails
Fran & Brian, James McLure; (C) Connie Fails
The Widow's Best Friend, Randy Hall; (S) Bart Healy, adapted by Mike Nichols; (C) Bradford Wood and Gregory Polk
Godspell, book: John Michael Tebelak; music and lyrics: Stephen Schwartz; (D) Ken McCulough; (C) Mark Hughes; (MD) Mark Janas; (CH) Ann Halligan-Donahue
Beirut, Alan Browne; (D) Brad Mooy; (S) Mike Nichols; (L) Stephen Pax; (C) Joan Wilson; (SD) Catherine Tarbox
Judevine, David Budbill; (D) Brad Mooy; (L) Stephen Pax
Bed, Jim Cartwright; (D) Brad Mooy; (S) Mike Nichols; (C) Joan Wilson

PRODUCTIONS 1992-1993

Direction by Cliff Fannin Baker, sets by Mike Nichols, lighting by Ken White, costumes by Don Bolinger and sound design by Chip Salerno unless otherwise noted.

Smoke on the Mountain, Constance Ray; (D) Alan Bailey
Patio/Porch, Jack Heifner
A...My Name is Alice, conceived: Joan Micklin Silver and Julianne Boyd; various composers and lyricists; (MD) Mark Janas; (CH) Janet Younts
The Glass Menagerie, Tennessee Williams
Radio Gals, book, music and lyrics: Mike Craver and Mark Hardwick; (C) Yslan Hicks; (MD) Mark Hardwick
I Hate Hamlet, Paul Rudnick; (D) Brad Mooy; (C) Yslan Hicks
Blues in the Night, conceived: Sheldon Epps; various composers and lyricists; (D) Brad Mooy; (MD) Mark Janas; (CH) Ron J. Hutchins
Shakin' the Mess Outta Misery, Shay Youngblood; (D) Fred Scarborough
Reckless, Craig Lucas; (D) Brad Mooy; (L) Michael D. Klima
Six Women with Brain Death or Expiring Minds Want to Know, book: Cheryl Benge, Christy Brandt, Rosanna E. Coppedge, Valerie Fagan, Ross Freese, Mark Houston, Sandee Johnson and Peggy Pharr Wilson; music and lyrics: Mark Houston; (D) Brad Mooy; (MD) Ruth Hooper; (CH) Tanya Simpson

ArtReach Touring Theatre

KATHRYN SCHULTZ MILLER
Artistic Director

ANDI GUESS
Business Manager

ROBERT J. BONINI
Board Chairman

3074 Madison Road
Cincinnati, OH 45209
(513) 871-2300
(513) 871-2501 (fax)

FOUNDED 1976
Kathryn Schultz Miller, Barry I. Miller

SEASON
Year-round

FINANCES
July 1, 1992-June 30, 1993
Expenses: $453,000

ArtReach's artistic mission is simple and clear: to present intelligent well-crafted work that touches the hearts and minds of our young audiences. We emphasize carefully structured plots with fully developed characters that offer our actors the opportunity to express themselves fully. Each script must inspire thought and understanding. In these past years we have presented works that inspire the young mind to consider the courage of Amelia Earhart, the tragedy of the Cherokees' lost homeland, and the meaning of the words "truth" and "justice" in the telling of King Arthur's mythic life. We have found that the youngest child will respond in a surprisingly mature way to serious subjects presented with honesty and purpose. These are the kinds of experiences that contribute to the intellectual and artistic sensitivity each child will carry through life. We remain dedicated to this very important work.
— *Kathryn Schultz Miller*

PRODUCTIONS 1991-1992

Plays and adaptations by Kathryn Schultz Miller, direction and sets by Dahn Schwarz, lighting by Ron Shaw, costumes by Kathie Brookfield and sound design by Andrew Durbin unless otherwise noted.

Young Cherokee
Trail of Tears
The Sword in the Stone; (D) Eric Weisheit
The Knights of the Round Table; (D) Eric Weisheit
The Legend of Sleepy Hollow, from Washington Irving; (D) Shelley Weisheit

PRODUCTIONS 1992-1993

Plays and adaptations by Kathryn Schultz Miller, direction and sets by Dahn Schwarz, lighting by Ron Shaw, costumes by Kathie Brookfield and sound design by Andrew Durbin unless otherwise noted.

ArtReach Touring Theatre. Eddie Wilder, Kathryn Slyker and Derek Anthony in *The Time Machine*. Photo: Barry J. Miller.

The Time Machine, from H.G. Wells; (D) Mary Sutton; (C) Sharon Foster; (SD) John McDaniel
Amelia Earhart; (D) Julie Beckman; (S) Dahn Schwarz and Michael Blankenship; (C) Sharon Foster; (SD) John McDaniel
Young Cherokee
Trail of Tears
The Sword in the Stone; (D) Eric Weisheit

Asolo Theatre Company

MARGARET BOOKER
Artistic Director

LINDA DiGABRIELE
Administrative Director

JOHN D. WELCH
Board President

Asolo Center for the Performing Arts
555 North Tamiami Trail
Sarasota, FL 34243
(813) 351-9010 (bus.)
(813) 351-8000 (b.o.)
(813) 351-5796 (fax)

FOUNDED 1960
Eberle Thomas, Robert Strane, Richard G. Fallon, Arthur Dorlag

SEASON
Oct.-July

FACILITIES
Mainstage
Seating Capacity: 499
Stage: proscenium

Second Stage
Seating Capacity: 175
Stage: flexible

FINANCES
July 1, 1992-June 30, 1993
Expenses: $4,059,636

CONTRACTS
AEA LORT (C)

The Asolo Theatre Company's artistic goal is to provide a nurturing and challenging environment for theatre artists to create innovative work for an intergenerational and culturally diverse audience. Florida's oldest nonprofit professional theatre, Asolo presents classics with freshness and new vision, develops new musical theatre, and premieres plays with dedication and respect for the playwright's art. Asolo's Access to the Arts Program works extensively within the school system and the community to introduce new programming and encourage participation in the theatre's activities.
—Margaret Booker

PRODUCTIONS 1991-1992

Direction by Margaret Booker unless otherwise noted.

Svengali, book adapt: Gregory Boyd, from George DuMaurier; music: Frank Wildhorn; lyrics: Frank Wildhorn, Gregory Boyd and John Bettis; (D) Gregory Boyd; (S) Jerome Sirlin; (L) Howell Binkley; (C) V. Jane Suttell; (MD) Douglas Besterman; (SD) Karl Richardson
Lost Electra, Bruce E. Rodgers; (S) David Potts; (L) Robert Wierzel; (C) Susan Tsu; (SD) David Smith
My Three Angels, Bella Spewack and Samuel Spewack; (D) Worth Gardner; (S) Paul Shortt; (L) Kirk Bookman; (C) Howard Tsvi Kaplan; (SD) Bert Taylor
Remembrance, Graham Reid; (D) Terence Lamude; (S) Robert Klingelhoefer; (L) John McLain; (C) Howard Tsvi Kaplan; (SD) Tom Gould
The Man of Mode, Sir George Etherege; (D) Anthony Cornish; (S) Ken Foy; (L) Norbert Kolb; (C) Howard Tsvi Kaplan; (SD) Bert Taylor
Odd Jobs, Frank Moher; (S) Robert Dahlstrom; (L) Jim Sale; (C) Robert Dahlstrom; (SD) Seth Cooper
Fences, August Wilson; (D) Oz Scott; (S) G.W. Mercier; (L) Victor En Yu Tan; (C) Judy Dearing; (SD) Bert Taylor
Sons of Don Juan, John PiRoman; (S) James Morgan; (L) Robert Wierzel; (C) Laura Crow; (SD) Bert Taylor

PRODUCTIONS 1992-1993

Direction by Margaret Booker unless otherwise noted.

Real Women Have Curves, Josefina Lopez; (S) James Morgan; (L) Robert Wierzel; (C) Tina Cantu Navarro; (SD) Bert Taylor

Asolo Theatre Company. Murphy Geyer and Jane Gabbert in *Lost Electra*. Photo: Lawrence C. Vaughn.

The Substance of Fire, Jon Robin Baitz; (D) Jay Broad; (S) R. Michael Miller; (L) Victor En Yu Tan; (C) Howard Tsvi Kaplan; (SD) Bert Taylor
Centerburg Tales, adapt: Bruce E. Rodgers, from Robert McCloskey; (S) David Potts; (L) Donald Holder; (C) Barbra Kravitz; (SD) Dan Schreier
Sweet & Hot, conceived: Julianne Boyd; music: Harold Arlen; various lyricists; (D) Julianne Boyd; (S) Ken Foy; (L) Natasha Katz; (C) David C. Woolard; (MD) William Foster McDaniel; (CH) Hope Clarke; (SD) Karl Richardson
Nora, adapt: Ingmar Bergman, from Henrik Ibsen; trans: Frederick J. Marker and Lise-Lone Marker; (S) Alexander Okun; (L) James Sale; (C) John Carver Sullivan
Lips Together, Teeth Apart, Terrence McNally; (D) Terence Lamude; (S) Eldon Elder; (L) John McLain; (C) Howard Tsvi Kaplan; (SD) Bert Taylor
Legacies, Kermit Frazier; (S) G.W. Mercier; (L) Robert Wierzel; (C) Judy Dearing; (SD) Baikida Carroll
Love Letters, A.R. Gurney, Jr.; (D) Pamela Berlin; (S) Robert Klingelhoefer; (L) Victor En Yu Tan; (C) Vicki Holden

A Traveling Jewish Theatre

COREY FISCHER, NAOMI NEWMAN, ALBERT GREENBERG, HELEN STOLTZFUS
Artistic Ensemble

JAMES A. KLEINMANN
Managing Director

EVAN MENDELSON
Board President

Box 421985
San Francisco, CA 94142-1985
(415) 399-1809
(415) 399-1844 (fax)

FOUNDED 1978
Corey Fischer, Naomi Newman, Albert Greenberg

SEASON
Oct.-Apr.

FACILITIES
Life on the Water
Seating Capacity: 200
Stage: flexible

Magic Theatre
Seating Capacity: 150
Stage: proscenium

FINANCES
July 1, 1992-June 30, 1993
Expenses: $300,000

A Traveling Jewish Theatre. John O'Neal and Naoimi Newman in *Crossing the Broken Bridge.* Photo: Margaret Benes Miller.

CONTRACTS
AEA BAT

A Traveling Jewish Theatre was born out of a desire to create a theatre that would give contemporary form to unexplored areas of Jewish imagination, culture and history. While our works often have their point of departure in Jewish experience, they are performed for audiences of widely diverse backgrounds. Since 1978 we have created over a dozen original works of theatre whose subjects range from the legends of Hasidism to the challenge of intermarriage, from the Middle East crisis to African-American/Jewish relations, and from the healing nature of storytelling to the reclamation of women's wisdom. We use music, masks, puppets, bare stages, naked faces, English, Yiddish, Hebrew, Ladino, silence and sound as tools to share what we feel needs to be shared. Now celebrating our 15th season, we have toured our productions to regional theatres, international theatre festivals, universities and community centers throughout the United States, Canada, Europe and Israel.

—*Corey Fischer*

PRODUCTIONS 1991-1992

Sometimes We Need a Story More Than Food, Corey Fischer; (D) Helen Stoltzfus
Blonde Like You, Albert Greenberg; (D) Stephen Rappaport
Snake Talk, Naomi Newman; (D) Martha Boesing
Crossing the Broken Bridge, Naomi Newman and John O'Neal; (D) Steven Kent
Dance of Exile, Naomi Newman, Albert Greenberg and Corey Fischer; (D) Helen Stoltzfus and Naomi Newman

PRODUCTIONS 1992-1993

14 Years in One Night: A Retrospective, company-developed; (D) Naomi Newman and Helen Stoltzfus
Crossing the Broken Bridge, Naomi Newman and John O'Neal; (D) Steven Kent
Sometimes We Need a Story More Than Food, Corey Fischer; (D) Helen Stoltzfus
Snake Talk, Naomi Newman; (D) Martha Boesing

Bailiwick Repertory

DAVID ZAK
Executive Director

STEVEN DECKER
General Manager

RANDY TALCOTT
Board President

1225 West Belmont
Chicago, IL 60657
(312) 883-1090 (bus.)
(312) 327-5252 (b.o.)
(312) 327-1404 (fax)

FOUNDED 1982
Phebe Bohart, Cheri Epping, David Pearson, David Zak, Larry Wyatt, Michael P. O'Brien, Linda Leveque

SEASON
Year-round

FACILITIES
Theatre Building
Seating Capacity: 148
Stage: thrust
Jane Adams Hull House
Seating Capacity: 140
Stage: thrust

FINANCES
July 1, 1992-June 30, 1993
Expenses: $491,965

CONTRACTS
AEA CAT

Bailiwick Repertory is dedicated to achieving the vision of gifted directors in productions of the best classical, contemporary and newly commissioned work by making the director the fulcrum of the artistic process. It is the only theatre in the Midwest to present 52 weeks of theatre a year in a repertory format, ranging from classics like Shaw and Brecht to the newest trends in musicals and performance art. Its diverse programming includes the Mainstage Series (classics), New Directions Series (new works and new formats), Directors Festival (directors' one-act showcase) and Pride Performance Series (gay and lesbian works). In its first 11 seasons, the company earned 74 Joseph Jefferson award recommendations and citations in every category, including production, performance, new work and design. The seven shows recommended as outstanding productions—*Threepenny Opera*, *Animal Farm*, *The Count of Monte Cristo*, *Ourselves Alone*, *Incorruptible*, *The Lisbon Traviata* and *Execution of Justice*—represent the wide range of Bailiwick's interests.

—*David Zak*

PRODUCTIONS 1991-1992

Lighting by Benjamin A. Solotaire and costumes by Nanette Acosta unless otherwise noted.

Bailiwick Repertory. *A Preliminary Inquiry into the Methods Used to Create and Maintain a Segregated Society.* Photo: Roger Lewin/Jennifer Girard Studio.

The Lisbon Traviata, Terrence McNally; (D) Judy O'Malley; (S) Richard Penrod and Jacqueline Penrod; (L) Tom Fleming; (C) Daryl Stone

Alfred Stieglitz Loves O'Keeffe, Lanie Robertson; (D) Judy O'Malley; (S) Daniel Ostling; (C) Dawn Dewitt; (SD) Jeff Applebaum

The Count of Monte Cristo, adapt: Jeff Casazza and David Zak, from Alexander Dumas; (D) David Zak; (S) Bruce Bergner

Light in Love, Christopher Cartmill; (D) Jessica Donnelly, David Zak and Christopher Cartmill; (S) Philip Nolan; (SD) Christopher Cartmill

At Long Last Leo, Mark Stein; (D) Judy O'Malley; (S) Mark Netherland; (SD) Galen G. Ramsey

The Carrott Carrot and Other Proclivities, Richard Kalinski; (D) Molly Burns; (S) Phillip Jay Hickox; (C) Jackie Melissas

Daystar, adapt: Walter Miller, from Medieval Miracle Plays; (D) Kristen Gehring; (S) Bruce Bergner; (L) Steven Vitarelli; (C) David Clark

Laughing Wild, Christopher Durang; (D) David Bontumasti; (S) Mark Netherland; (C) Shifra Werch

Pride Series:
Sets by Carl Forsberg, lighting by John Narun, costumes by Nick Harris and sound design by Loretta Cattani.

Connections of the Heart, book and lyrics: Paula Berg; music: Diane Laffey and Paula Berg; (D) and (CH) Liz Pazik; (MD) Laurie Lee Moses

Comrades and Lovers, Jonathan Ned Katz; (D) Patrick Trettenero

Trafficking in Broken Hearts, Edwin Sanchez; (D) Ralph Flores

Hannah Free, Claudia Allen; (D) Laurie Attea

Flesh and Blood, Colin Thomas; (D) David Dillon

Lust and Pity, Hilary Sloan; (D) Shifra Werch

Directors Festival 1992:
Various playwrights; various directors.

PRODUCTIONS 1992-1993

Sets by Robert A. Knuth and lighting by John Narun unless otherwise noted.

A Preliminary Inquiry Into the Methods Used to Create and Maintain a Segregated Society, adapt: Clay Shirky, from Amnesty International and police reports, political speeches and rap music lyrics; (D) Clay Shirky and Tanya White; (S) and (L) Clay Shirky

Light in Love and *Light in the Heart of the Dragon*, Christopher Cartmill; (D) David Zak; (C) Darice DaMata-Geiger; (SD) Christopher Cartmill

Party, David Dillon; (D) David Dillon; (C) Kevin Peterson

Saint Joan, George Bernard Shaw; (D) Roger Smart

Saint Joan of the Stockyards, Bertolt Brecht; trans: Frank Jones; music: Christopher Moore; (D) David Zak; (C) Kevin Peterson; (MD) Christopher Moore; (CH) Angela Allyn

The Rose Tattoo, Tennessee Williams; (D) Cecilie Keenan; (S) Alan Donahue; (L) Julio Pedota; (C) Mara Blumenfeld; (SD) Larry Mohl

Falling in Love Again, a holiday cabaret with Craig Figtree and Steve Carson

Pride Series:
Sets by Robert A. Knuth, lighting by John Narun and costumes by Kevin Peterson unless otherwise noted.

Son of Fire, book, music and lyrics: Christopher Moore; (D) David Zak; (C) U-Tate; (MD) Dan Stetzel; (CH) Angela Allyn

Oh, Holy Allen Ginsberg: Oh, Holy Shit Sweet Jesus Tantric Buddha Dharma Road, Nicholas A. Patricca; (D) Steve Scott

Her Aching Heart, Byrony Lavery; (D) Beverly Brumm; (SD) Warren Kaplan

The Expense of Spirit, Michael Barto; (D) Michael Barto

Small Domestic Acts, Joan Lipkin; (D) Beverly Brumm

The Harvey Milk Show, book and lyrics: Dan Pruitt; music: Patrick Hutchison; (D) Matt Callahan; (MD) Dan Stetzel; (CH) Bobby Dewitt

Directors Festival 1993:
Various playwrights; various directors.

Barter Theatre. Emily Loesser and Pamela Stewart in *The Miracle Worker*.

Barter Theatre

RICHARD ROSE
Producing Artistic Director

PEARL HAYTER
Business Manager

FILLMORE McPHERSON
Board President

Box 867
Abingdon, VA 24210-0867
(703) 628-2281 (bus.)
(703) 628-3991 (b.o.)
(703) 628-4551 (fax)

FOUNDED 1933
Robert Porterfield

SEASON
Apr.-Nov.

FACILITIES
Seating Capacity: 402
Stage: proscenium

Barter Playhouse
Seating Capacity: 150
Stage: thrust

FINANCES
Jan. 1, 1992-Dec. 31, 1992
Expenses: $1,138,598

CONTRACTS
AEA LORT (D)

Barter Theatre, the State Theatre of Virginia, is one of America's oldest, longest-running professional resident theatre companies. Founded by visionary Robert Porterfield, the theatre had its beginnings during the Great Depression, opening its doors with the motto "With vegetables you cannot sell, you can buy a good laugh." Since that time, the list of Barter's alumni reads like a who's who of American theatre. The theatre artists at Barter are dedicated to the following aims: to encourage the betterment of the human spirit and the enrichment of the human soul, whether through laughter, tears or just a smile; to challenge the thoughts of intelligent people and to reflect honest society through experience both familiar and foreign to everyday life; to bring insight to the hidden and depth of meaning to the obvious through the use of images and visual stimulation; and, ultimately, to touch the hearts, to challenge the minds and to reach into the depth of the souls of all who enter Barter's doors, young and old alike.

—*Richard Rose*

Note: During the 1991-92 season, Rex Partington served as artistic director/producer.

PRODUCTIONS 1992

Lighting by William J. Sauerbrey, III and sound design by Tony Partington.

The Corn is Green, Emlyn Williams; (D) Rex Partington; (S) Parmalee Welles; (C) Pamela Hale

Quilters, Molly Newman and Barbara Damashek; (D) Dorothy Marie Robinson; (C) Pamela Hale

As You Like It, William Shakespeare; (D) Shepard Sobel; (S) Robert Joel Schwartz; (C) Barbara A. Bell

Everybody Loves Opal, John Patrick; (D) Ken Costigan; (S) Daniel Ettinger; (C) Veronica Worts

Peg of My Heart, J. Hartley Manners; (D) Ken Costigan; (S) Daniel Ettinger; (C) Veronica Worts

The Mystery of Irma Vep, Charles Ludlam; (D) John Briggs; (S) Daniel Ettinger; (C) Howard Tsvi Kaplan

First Light:
Direction, sets and lighting by John Hardy, music and musical direction by Logan Brown, and costumes by Stacy Riley.

The Lion, the Witch and the Wardrobe, adapt: Don Quinn, from C.S. Lewis

The Wind in the Willows, adapt: Joseph Baldwin, from Kenneth Grahame

PRODUCTIONS 1993

The Miracle Worker, William Gibson; (D) Richard Rose; (S) Gary English; (L) Kendall Smith; (C) Amanda Aldridge

Lend Me a Tenor, Ken Ludwig; (D) Peter Bennett; (S) and (L) Daniel Ettinger; (C) Lynda L. Salsbury

The Cocktail Hour, A.R. Gurney, Jr.; (D) Ken Costigan; (S) Dale F. Jordan; (L) William J. Sauerbrey, III; (C) Amanda Aldridge

A Funny Thing Happened on the Way to the Forum, book: Burt Shevelove and Larry Gelbart; music and lyrics: Stephen Sondheim; (D) Daniel Schay; (S) Gary English; (L) Clifton Taylor; (C) Kevin Pothier; (MD) Winston Clark; (CH) Amanda Aldridge; (SD) Don Tindall

Kuru, John Manheimer; (D) Richard Rose; (S) and (L) Clifton Taylor; (C) Mary Myers; (SD) Don Tindall

Other People's Money, Jerry Sterner; (D) Michael Mederios; (S) Daniel Ettinger; (L) William J. Sauerbrey, III; (C) Amanda Aldridge

Dracula, adapt: Richard Rose, from Bram Stoker; (D) Richard Rose; (S) Charles Morgan; (L) Kendall Smith; (C) Amanda Aldridge

Nunsense, book, music and lyrics: Dan Goggin; (D) and (CH) Nancy Carroll; (S) Janie Fleigel; (L) William J. Sauerbrey, III; (C) Kim Oathaut; (MD) Logan Brown

Frankie and Johnny in the Clair de Lune, Terrence McNally; (D) John Hardy; (S) Janie Fleigel; (L) William J. Sauerbrey, III; (C) Kim Oathaut; (SD) Don Tindall

First Light:
Direction by Gail Katz, choreography by Amanda Aldridge and costumes by Wayne Hilton unless otherwise noted.

The Emperor's New Clothes, adapt: Judith Baker Kase; (D) John Hardy

Step on a Crack, Susan Zeder

Whispers of the Olde World, John Hardy; (D) John Hardy

Wiley and the Hairy Man, Susan Zeder

Androcles and the Lion, adapt: Aurand Harris

The Bathhouse Theatre. Hillary Spector in *The Skin of Our Teeth*. Photo: Fred Andrews.

The Bathhouse Theatre

ARNE ZASLOVE
Artistic Director

PHIL PETERS
Managing Director

KATHLEEN SOUTHWICK
Board President

7312 West Greenlake Drive N
Seattle, WA 98103
(206) 783-0053 (bus.)
(206) 524-9108 (b.o.)
(206) 784-3966 (fax)

FOUNDED 1980
Arne Zaslove, Mary-Claire Burke

SEASON
Year-round

FACILITIES
Seating Capacity: 174
Stage: 3/4 thrust

FINANCES
Jan. 1, 1992-Dec. 31, 1992
Expenses: $993,000

CONTRACTS
AEA SPT

Storytelling has, throughout time, been a method of self-examination and self-revelation. The community is purged of its ills by the shaman/actor/artist/healer. At the Bathhouse, we see ourselves as being in a position to create change: to change the awareness of individuals so that they assume responsibility for making the earth safer, healthier and more balanced. The cornerstone of our approach is the performing ensemble, in the classical European tradition. Through that medium, we explore material that asks the fundamental questions and touches the human spirit directly–sometimes in classics of world stage literature, sometimes in pieces we have woven together ourselves from elements of popular American culture. Theatre must regulate and reflect, monitor and maintain a healthy balance. Theatre can improve the weather of the soul.

—*Arne Zaslove*

PRODUCTIONS 1992

Sets by Kathryn Rathke and sound design by Eric Chappelle.

The Imaginary Invalid, Moliere; trans: Arne Zaslove and K.C. Brown; (D) Arne Zaslove; (L) Richard Hogle; (C) Mark Mitchell
Sometimes We Need a Story More Than Food, Corey Fischer (co-produced by A Traveling Jewish Theatre); (D) Helen Stoltzfus; (L) Kathrine Mattson
The Hostage, Brendan Behan; (D) Mark Samuels; (L) Judy Wolcott; (C) Deborah Skorstad
Love's Labour's Lost, William Shakespeare; (D) Arne Zaslove; (L) Judy Wolcott; (C) Sherry Lyon
A Legend of St. Nickolas, book and lyrics: Arne Zaslove; music: Robert Davidson; (D) Arne Zaslove; (L) Richard Hogle; (C) Sherry Lyon; (MD) Robert Davidson

PRODUCTIONS 1993

Direction by Arne Zaslove, costumes by Sherry Lyon and sound design by Eric Chappelle unless otherwise noted.

The Skin of Our Teeth, Thornton Wilder; (S) Kathryn Rathke; (L) Richard Hogle
The Mousetrap, Agatha Christie; (D) Allen Galli; (S) Judith Cullen; (L) Judy Wolcott
Romeo and Juliet, William Shakespeare; (S) Jeff Frkonja; (L) Meg Fox
The Golem, Claire Vardiel; (S) Kathryn Rathke; (L) Judy Wolcott; (C) Deborah Skorstad

Bay Street Theatre Festival

SYBIL CHRISTOPHER, EMMA WALTON
Co-Artistic Directors

MATTHEW B. BRUFFEE
Managing Director

ANA DANIEL
Acting Board Chair

Box 810
Sag Harbor, NY 11963
(516) 725-0818 (bus.)
(516) 725-1108 (b.o.)
(516) 725-0906 (fax)

FOUNDED 1992
Sybil Christopher, Stephen Hamilton, Emma Walton

SEASON
Mar.-Dec.

FACILITIES
Seating Capacity: 299
Stage: thrust

FINANCES
Jan. 1, 1992-Dec. 31, 1992
Expenses: $634,999

CONTRACTS
AEA SPT

Bay Street Theatre Festival's mission is to create an artistic haven where an extended family of established and emerging artists may flourish in an atmosphere free from commercial pressures. Bay Street is a true festival in that it celebrates theatre through a variety of supportive programs, including a mainstage season of adventurous, high-quality productions; a developmental reading series to discover and explore new work; a Master's Lecture Series and an Apprenticeship/Intern Program to inspire future theatre artists; lighthearted weekend cabarets; and an Educational Outreach Program to nurture tomorrow's audiences and encourage a sense of wonder in the children of our community. It is our commitment to exercise fiscal responsibility so that our work may be defined by our imagination and not our resources, and to provide a gathering point for artists and audiences alike, sharing a collective theatrical experience which speaks to the head, heart, soul (and funny bone!) of our eclectic community.
—*Sybil Christopher, Ella Walton*

PRODUCTIONS 1992

Direction by Christopher A. Smith, sets by Tony Walton, lighting by Michael Lincoln, costumes by Sharon Sprague and sound design by Randy Freed unless otherwise noted.

Men's Lives, adapt: Joe Pintauro, from Peter Matthiessen
Three Hotels, Jon Robin Baitz; (D) Joe Mantello; (S) Loy Arcenas
Inspecting Carol, Daniel Sullivan and the Seattle Repertory Resident Acting Company

PRODUCTIONS 1993

Lighting by Michael Lincoln and sound design by Randy Freed unless otherwise noted.

Full Gallop: An Evening with Diana Vreeland, adapt: Mark Hampton and Mary-Louise Wilson, from Diana Vreeland and George Plimpton; (D) Richard Mogavero; (S), (L) and (C) Michael Sharp
Alone at the Beach, Richard Dresser; (D) Susann Brinkley; (S) Sharon Sprague
Desdemona, Paula Vogel; (D) Gloria Muzio; (S) Derek McLane; (C) Jess Goldstein
Men's Lives, adapt: Joe Pintauro, from Peter Matthiessen; (D) Christopher A. Smith; (S) Tony Walton; (C) Sharon Sprague

Berkeley Repertory Theatre

SHARON OTT
Artistic Director

SUSAN MEDAK
Managing Director

ANTHONY TACCONE
Associate Artistic Director

CAROLE B. BERG
Board President

2025 Addison St.
Berkeley, CA 94704
(510) 204-8901 (bus.)
(510) 845-4700 (b.o.)
(510) 841-7711 (fax)

FOUNDED 1968
Michael W. Leibert

Bay Street Theatre Festival. Alan North and Jay Patterson in *Men's Lives*. Photo: Renate Pfeiderer.

BERKELEY REPERTORY THEATRE

Berkeley Repertory Theatre. Bruce Beatty, Adriane Lenox and Stephen Burks in *Spunk*. Photo: Ken Friedman.

SEASON
Sept.-July

FACILITIES
Mark Taper Mainstage
Seating Capacity: 401
Stage: flexible

FINANCES
Sept. 1, 1992-Aug. 31, 1993
Expenses: $3,947,000

CONTRACTS
AEA LORT (B)

Berkeley Repertory Theatre is dedicated to an ensemble of first-rate artists—including actors, playwrights, directors, artisans and designers. We intend the theatre to be a place where plays are created, not just produced, communicating a distinct attitude about the world of the play and about the world around us. Our repertoire includes plays chosen from the major classical and contemporary dramatic literatures, specifically works that emphasize the cultural richness that makes American art so dynamic and vital. We will involve dramatists, either as playwrights-in-residence or on commission, in the development of original pieces. It is our intention to view the works of the past through the eyes of the present; even when a play is chosen from the classical repertoire, it will be given the focus and attention of a new play. We will also research and produce classical works that are outside the Anglo-European repertoire. As a regional resource, we will continue to expand our TEAM program for young audiences, augmenting the Student Matinee Program and school touring productions.
—*Sharon Ott*

PRODUCTIONS 1991-1992

Sound design by Stephen LeGrand unless otherwise noted.

Major Barbara, George Bernard Shaw; (D) Anthony Taccone; (S) Kate Edmunds; (L) Kent Dorsey; (C) Candice Donnelly
Spunk, adapt: George C. Wolfe, from Zora Neale Hurston; music: Chic Street Man; (D) George C. Wolfe; (S) Loy Arcenas; (L) Donald Holder; (C) Toni-Leslie James; (CH) Hope Clarke
McTeague: A Tale of San Francisco, adapt: Neal Bell, from Frank Norris; (D) Sharon Ott; (S) George Tsypin; (L) James F. Ingalls; (C) Lydia Tanji
The Importance of Being Earnest, Oscar Wilde; (D) Richard E.T. White; (S) Kent Dorsey; (L) Peter Maradudin; (C) Rose Pederson
Woody Guthrie's American Song, book: Peter Glazer; music and lyrics: Woody Guthrie; (D) Peter Glazer; (S) Philipp Jung; (L) Derek Duarte; (C) Susan Snowden; (MD) Tony Marcus
Dream of a Common Language, Heather McDonald; (D) Sharon Ott; (S) Kate Edmunds; (L) Kent Dorsey; (C) Susan Hilferty; (SD) David Torgersen
The Convict's Return, Geoff Hoyle; (D) Anthony Taccone; (S) Kate Edmunds; (L) Kent Dorsey; (C) Susan Hilferty

PRODUCTIONS 1992-1993

Speed-the-Plow, David Mamet; (D) Richard E.T. White; (S) and (L) Kent Dorsey; (C) Christine Dougherty; (SD) Stephen LeGrand
Mad Forest, Caryl Churchill; (D) Mark Wing-Davey; (S) and (C) Marina Draghici; (L) Peter Maradudin; (SD) Mark Bennett
Volpone, Ben Jonson; adapt: Joan Holden; (D) Anthony Taccone; (S) and (L) Kent Dorsey; (C) Gabriel Berry; (SD) Stephen LeGrand and Eric Drew Feldman
The Lady from the Sea, Henrik Ibsen; trans: Gerry Bamman and Irene B. Berman; (D) Sharon Ott; (S) Kate Edmunds; (L) Peter Maradudin; (C) Deborah M. Dryden; (SD) Chris Poole and Stephen LeGrand
Private Lives, Noel Coward; (D) Sharon Ott; (S) Kate Edmunds; (L) Paulie Jenkins; (C) Toni-Leslie James; (SD) Matthew Spiro
Dragonwings, Laurence Yep; (D) Phyllis S.K. Look; (S) Joseph D. Dodd; (L) David K.H. Elliott; (C) Lydia Tanji; (SD) Scott Koue
Mother Jones: The Most Dangerous Woman in America, created and performed: Ronnie Gilbert; music and lyrics: Si Kahn; (D) Timothy Near; (S) Kent Dorsey; (L) David K.H. Elliott; (C) Christine Dougherty; (MD) Jeff Langley; (SD) Stephen LeGrand

Berkshire Theatre Festival

JULIANNE BOYD
Artistic Director

CHUCK STILL
Managing Director

JANE P. FITZPATRICK
Board President

Box 797
Stockbridge, MA 01262
(413) 298-5536 (bus.)
(413) 298-5576 (b.o.)
(413) 298-3368 (fax)

FOUNDED 1928
Three Arts Society

SEASON
June-Aug.

FACILITIES
Mainstage
Seating Capacity: 427
Stage: proscenium

Berkshire Theatre Festival. Jacquey Maltby, Terry Burrell and Monica Pege in *Sweet & Hot*. Photo: T. Charles Erickson.

Unicorn Theatre
Seating Capacity: 100
Stage: thrust

Children's Theatre
Seating Capacity: 100
Stage: arena

FINANCES
Sept. 1, 1992-Aug. 31, 1993
Expenses: $1,119,603

CONTRACTS
AEA LORT (B)

From its inception 65 years ago, the Berkshire Theatre Festival's mission has been threefold: to present thought-provoking professional entertainment to its audiences; to offer established and emerging actors, directors, designers and playwrights the opportunity to work in a relaxed and supportive environment; and to provide quality educational programs to aspiring theatre artists. To that end, BTF supports three stages: our Playhouse, presenting Equity productions of new works as well as outstanding contemporary plays and lesser-known American classics; the Unicorn Theatre, where the main focus is on fostering early- to mid-career directors who wish to experiment with a specific vision and/or style; and the Children's Theatre in the tent, where our acting interns perform in plays by local students enrolled in our Young American Playwrights Program. This year BTF has begun expanding its season by presenting a December holiday show, staged readings and actors' classes throughout the year.
—*Julianne Boyd*

Note: During the 1991-92 season, Richard Dunlap served as artistic director.

PRODUCTIONS 1992

Lighting by Kenneth Posner and sound design by Timothy J. Anderson unless otherwise noted.

Ain't Misbehavin', conceived: Murray Horwitz and Richard Maltby, Jr.; music and lyrics: Fats Waller, et al; (D) and (CH) Marcia Milgrom Dodge; (S) James Noone; (C) Michael Krass; (MD) Neal Tate
Quartermaine's Terms, Simon Gray; (D) Gordon Edelstein; (S) Hugh Landwehr; (C) David Murin; (SD) John Gromada
The Cocktail Hour, A.R. Gurney, Jr.; (D) Terry Schreiber; (S) R. Michael Miller; (C) Gregg Barnes

Charley's Aunt, Brandon Thomas; (D) Richard Dunlap; (S) John Falabella; (C) Gail Brassard

PRODUCTIONS 1993

Sweet & Hot, conceived: Julianne Boyd; music: Harold Arlen; various lyricists; (D) Julianne Boyd; (S) Ken Foy; (L) Howell Binkley; (C) David C. Woolard; (MD) Danny Holgate; (CH) Hope Clarke; (SD) Timothy J. Anderson
Camping with Henry and Tom, Mark St. Germain; (D) Paul Lazarus; (S) James Leonard Joy; (L) Donald Holder; (C) Candice Donnelly; (SD) Timothy J. Anderson
Breaking the Code, Hugh Whitemore; (D) Melvin Bernhardt; (L) Kenneth Posner; (SD) John Gromada
Blithe Spirit, Noel Coward; (D) Gordon Edelstein; (S) Hugh Landwehr; (L) Kenneth Posner; (C) Jess Goldstein; (SD) John Gromada

Bilingual Foundation of the Arts

MARGARITA GALBAN
Artistic Director

CARMEN ZAPATA
President/Producing Director

JIM PAYNE
Managing Director

AL MEJIA
Board Chairman

421 North Ave. 19
Los Angeles, CA 90031
(213) 225-4044
(213) 225-1250 (fax)

FOUNDED 1973
Margarita Galban, Estela Scarlata, Carmen Zapata

SEASON
Year-round

FACILITIES
Little Theatre
Seating Capacity: 99
Stage: thrust

Los Angeles Theatre Center—Tom Bradley Theatre
Seating Capacity: 499
Stage: thrust

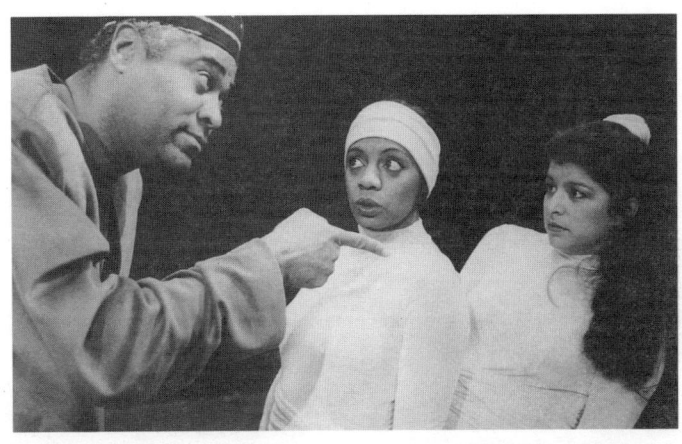

Bilingual Foundation of the Arts. Charles Dumas, Novel Sholars and Teresa Velarde in B/C Historia.

Stage Theatre 3
Seating Capacity: 299
Stage: thrust

FINANCES
Jan. 1, 1992-Dec. 31, 1992
Expenses: $723,661

CONTRACTS
AEA TYA and CAT (B) and (D), and 99-seat theatre plan

BFA presents classic and contemporary Hispanic drama from across the Americas and around the world, bringing to life the best plays written in the Spanish language and those written in English that reflect Hispanic history, traditions and cultures. BFA is a literature-based theatre with a commitment to quality translations and adaptations, providing access through language–an artistic doorway through which the rich diversity of Hispanic dramatic literature may be experienced by people of all cultures and preserved for future generations. Over and above its special interests, BFA's first priority is the art of theatre. Its bilingual productions provide a professional laboratory wherein Hispanic theatre artists acquire advanced linguistic and interpretive skills. Its staged readings of new work create a forum for artistic exploration and allow Hispanic playwrights to cultivate their craft. Its theatre-in-education programs help to develop future audiences through appreciation for the artform.
—*Margarita Galban*

PRODUCTIONS 1991-1992

Direction by Margarita Galban, sets and sound design by Estela Scarlata and lighting by Robert Fromer unless otherwise noted.

Made in Lanus, Nelly Fernandez Tiscornia; trans: Margarita Stocker (to English); (C) Julie-Ann Agosto
Women Without Men, Edward Gallardo; trans: Margarita Stocker (to Spanish); (D) Charles Bazaldua; (C) Julie-Ann Agosto
Lorca: Child of the Moon, trans: Michael Dewell and Carmen Zapata; adapt: Margarita Galban, from Federico Garcia Lorca; music: Ian Krouse; (C) Richard Smart; (MD) Ian Krouse; (CH) Mari Sandoval; (SD) All Music
Los de Abajo, Mariano Azuela; trans: Ruben Garfias (to English); adapt: Margarita Galban; (C) Estela Scarlata

PRODUCTIONS 1992-1993

Direction by Margarita Galban, sets and sound design by Estela Scarlata and lighting by Robert Fromer unless otherwise noted.

La Falsa Cronica de Juana la Loca, Miguel Sabido; trans: Margarita Stocker (to English); (C) Richard Smart
My Visits with MGM, Edit Villarreal; trans: Lina Montalvo (to Spanish); (D) Jose Cruz Gonzalez; (C) Gabriel Espinoza; (SD) Mark Friedman
La Celestina, Fernando de Rojas; trans: Margarita Stocker (to English); adapt: Margarita Galban; (C) Richard Smart
B/C Historia, C. Bernard Jackson; (D) C. Bernard Jackson; (C) Richard Smart; (SD) Jon Gottlieb
Contrabando, Victor Hugo Rascon Banda; trans: Ruben Garfias (to English); (C) Estela Scarlata; (SD) Jon Gottlieb
Fuente Ovejuna, Lope de Vega; adapt: Margarita Galban and Lina Montalvo

Birmingham Children's Theatre

JAMES W. RYE
Managing Director

CHARLES D. PERRY, JR.
Board President

Box 1362
Birmingham, AL 35201
(205) 324-0470

FOUNDED 1947
Junior League of Birmingham

SEASON
Sept.-May

FACILITIES
Birmingham-Jefferson Civic Center Theatre
Seating Capacity: 1,072
Stage: flexible

Birmingham-Jefferson Civic Center Theatre Lab
Seating Capacity: 250
Stage: flexible

FINANCES
July 1, 1992-June 30, 1993
Expenses: $925,000

Since 1981, Birmingham Children's Theatre has commissioned 21 new scripts, including original stories, musicals, adaptations and plays on historic topics. We continue to discover new voices among playwrights and to encourage established playwrights to experiment with new directions in dramatic literature for youth. In addition to the slate of 500 performances which we present annually, our Academy of Performing Arts workshops offer classes in acting, creative dramatics, musical theatre and movement for children aged 7 to 17. In presenting performances, we take special pride in the fact that we take no shortcuts in terms of production values. Our design team presents a constantly evolving vision which never ceases to thrill and delight our audiences. We have never accepted the concept that children's theatre is less provocative than other forms of theatre; our shows consistently reflect our commitment to quality and innovation through productions which challenge, stimulate and entertain young audiences.

—*James W. Rye*

PRODUCTIONS 1991-1992

Sets and lighting by T. Gary Weatherly and costumes by Jeffrey Todhunter unless otherwise noted.

Foxfire, Hume Cronyn and Susan Cooper; (D) Roy R. Hudson
Hansel and Gretel, adapt: Moses Goldberg, from The Brothers Grimm; (D) Jeanmarie Collins; (S) Vernon Push
Santa's Adventure in the Merrywood Mega Mall, Betty Pewitt and Jean Pierce; (D) Jeanmarie Collins; (S) Vernon Push
The Princess and the Pea, adapt: Paul Lavrakas, from Hans Christian Andersen; (D) Charles Burr; (C) Deborah Fleischman
Ama and the White Crane, Maureen A. O'Toole; (D) Edward Journey; (C) Deborah Fleischman
White Sails, Dark Seas: The Voyages of Columbus, Paul Lavrakas; (D) Kim Peter Kovac; (C) Deborah Fleischman
Cinderella, adapt: Bix Doughty, from Charles Perrault; (D) Michael Flowers; (C) Deborah Fleischman; (SD) Jay Tumminello
A Christmas Carol, adapt: Darwin Reid Payne, from Charles Dickens; (D) Roy R. Hudson; (SD) Ted Clark

PRODUCTIONS 1992-1993

Sets and lighting by T. Gary Weatherly and costumes by Jeffrey Todhunter unless otherwise noted.

Romeo and Juliet, William Shakespeare; (D) Edward Journey; (SD) Joe Zellner
Little Red Riding Hood and *Three Little Pigs*, book and lyrics: Moses Goldberg; music: Ewel Cornett; (D) Jeanmarie Collins; (S) Vernon Push
Aesop's Fables, adapt: Jeanmarie Collins; (D) Jeanmarie Collins; (S) Vernon Push
The Wind in the Willows, adapt: Michael Price Nelson, from Kenneth Grahame; (D) Charles Burr; (C) Deborah Fleischman
The Emperor's New Clothes, adapt: Michael Price Nelson, from Hans Christian Andersen; (D) Edward Journey; (C) Deborah Fleischman; (SD) Joe Zellner
Annie Oakley & Buffalo Bill, book and lyrics: Joan Shepard and Evan Thompson; music: John Clifton; (D) Michael Flowers; (C) Deborah Fleischman; (MD) Michael Flowers and Ruth Ammons Henry
The Best Christmas Pageant Ever, adapt: Barbara Robinson; (D) and (S) Roy R. Hudson

Birmingham Children's Theatre. Andrew Richards, Kitty Clarke and Eric Tichenor in *Ama and the White Crane*. Photo: Bruce Southerland.

Blackfriars Theatre

RALPH ELIAS
Artistic Director

ALLISON BRENNAN
Producer

DAN HALLECK
Managing Director

RONALD L. STYN
Board President

Box 126957
San Diego, CA 92112-6957
(619) 232-4088

FOUNDED 1982
Kim McCallum, Lisa Rigdon

SEASON
Sept.-June

FACILITIES
Bristol Court Playhouse (through 1992)
Seating Capacity: 78
Stage: proscenium

FINANCES
July 1, 1992-June 30, 1993
Expenses: $250,000

CONTRACTS
AEA SPT

Blackfriars Theatre seeks to present plays that explore the human condition by exposing conflicts and characters that have an archetypal or mythic dimension, even when this dimension exists beneath the surface of a contemporary, seemingly "mundane" setting. Our primary focus in production is on the soundness and integrity of the actor's process as the key to achieving the highly detailed performance which transports an audience. Blackfriars has developed a small resident company of actors and designers dedicated to working together on an ongoing basis to achieve a higher quality of ensemble production. However, casting and design assignments are not exclusively limited to company artists. Innovative set design and closely integrated sound and lighting elements have also become characteristic of Blackfriars stagings. Our Community Collaborations Program provides administrative

Blackfriars Theatre. Linda Libby in *The Unseen Hand*. Photo: Kim Blackford.

and technical support in co-productions with emerging multicultural and educational organizations.
—*Ralph Elias*

PRODUCTIONS 1991-1992

State of the Art Heart, book and lyrics: Ron Covington and Tonis Thomas; music: Ron Covington; (D) Anasa Briggs-Graves; (S), (L) and (SD) Steven Steppe; (C) Bunny Mitchell; (MD) Ron Covington; (CH) Donald Nathaniel Robinson
Abundance, Beth Henley; (D) Ralph Elias; (S) Beeb Salzer; (L) James A. Roth; (C) Clare Henkel; (SD) Lawrence Czoka
More of the Laughing Buddha Wholistik Radio Theatre, Todd Blakesley and Burnham Joiner; (D) Todd Blakesley; (S) Paul J. Kruse; (L) Rodger Henderson; (SD) Burnham Joiner
The Puppetmaster of Lodz, Gilles Segal; trans: Sara O'Connor; (D) Ralph Elias; (S) and (C) Beeb Salzer; (L) James A. Roth; (SD) Lawrence Czoka
Getting Around, adapt: Ralph Elias, from Arthur Schnitzler; trans: Chrissy Vogele and Ralph Elias; (D) Ralph Elias; (S) John Blunt; (L) Debra Marks; (C) Stacey Rae; (SD) Lawrence Czoka

PRODUCTIONS 1992-1993

The Toilet and *Dutchman*, LeRoi Jones (Amiri Baraka) (co-produced by Grassroots Theater); (D) and (S) Keith Geller and Eric Wallach; (L) Peter Smith; (C) Patrick Lathrop
The Importance of Being Earnest, Oscar Wilde; (D) Ralph Elias; (S) Beeb Salzer; (L) James A. Roth; (C) Stacey Rae; (SD) Lawrence Czoka
The Unseen Hand, Sam Shepard; (D) Ralph Elias; (S) John Blunt; (L) James A. Roth; (C) Stacey Rae; (SD) Lawrence Czoka

Bloomsburg Theatre Ensemble

GERARD STROPNICKY
Ensemble Director

STEVE BEVANS
Administrative Director

CAROL RHEAM
Board President

Box 66
Bloomsburg, PA 17815
(717) 784-5530 (bus.)
(717) 784-8181 (b.o.)
(717) 784-4912 (fax)

FOUNDED 1978
Ensemble

SEASON
Oct.-June

FACILITIES
Alvina Krause Theatre
Seating Capacity: 369
Stage: proscenium

FINANCES
Sept. 1, 1992-Aug. 31, 1993
Expenses: $530,000

Bloomsburg Theatre Ensemble believes that theatre must be an essential component of community life—just like a library, a school, a church or a hospital. It remains in a rural region because it needs a home where dialogue with an audience is possible and where its impact on the community is positive and demonstrable. Programs include an artistically adventurous and deliberately eclectic mainstage season presented in the Alvina Krause Theatre (named for the acting teacher who was the guiding spirit behind the founding of the company); a statewide Theatre in the Classroom tour; and the BTE Theatre School. As members of one of the nation's few true resident ensembles, BTE's eight artists are empowered with responsibility for the decisions that determine their artistic destiny. BTE has toured internationally, explored intercultural collaborations and earned a reputation for excellence. It has helped provide the national definition of the community-centered professional theatre company.
—*Gerard Stropnicky*

Note: During the 1991-92 and 1992-93 seasons, Leigh Strimbeck served as ensemble director.

PRODUCTIONS 1991-1992

Costumes by David Smith unless otherwise noted.

The Taming of the Shrew, William Shakespeare; adapt: Gerard Stropnicky; (D) Gerard Stropnicky; (S) James Bazewicz; (L) Richard Latta
A Christmas Carol, adapt: Julia Flood, from Charles Dickens; (D) Julia Flood; (S) Drew Miller; (L) Douglas Cox
The Guardsman, Ferenc Molnar; trans: Frank Marcus; (D) Gerard Stropnicky; (S) James Bazewicz; (L) A.C. Hickox
Daytrips, Jo Carson; (D) Leigh Strimbeck; (S) Robert Katkowsky; (L) Judith Daitsman
Women of Bakkhos, Euripides; trans: Robert Bagg; (D) Whit MacLaughlin; (S) and (C) Nephelie Andonyadis; (L) Geoff Korf
Along the Susquehanna, company-developed; (D) Gerard Stropnicky and Laurie McCants

Bloomsburg Theatre Ensemble. Leigh Strimbeck, A. Elizabeth Dowd, Meg Boscov, James Goode and David Moreland in *The Guardsman*. Photo: Marlin Wagner.

PRODUCTIONS 1992-1993

Of Thee I Sing, book: George S. Kaufman and Morrie Ryskind; music: George Gershwin; lyrics: Ira Gershwin; (D) David Moreland; (S) Robert Katkowsky; (L) Richard Latta; (C) Kathleen Egan; (MD) William Decker; (CH) Stephanie Farenwald

Alice's Adventures in Wonderland, adapt: Laurie McCants, from Lewis Carroll; (D) Laurie McCants; (S) and (C) F. Elaine Williams; (L) Mary Louise Geiger; (SD) Kyle Gann

The Glass Menagerie, Tennessee Williams; (D) Martin Shell; (S) James Bazewicz; (L) Richard Latta; (C) Sharon S.Q. Campbell

Mrs. Warren's Profession, George Bernard Shaw; (D) Gerard Stropnicky; (S) James Bazewicz; (L) Richard Latta; (C) Elly Van Horne

The Visit, Friedrich Durrenmatt; trans: Patrick Bowles; (D) Mark Ramont; (S) and (C) Nephelie Andonyadis; (L) Geoff Korf

The Mystery of Irma Vep, Charles Ludlam; (D) A. Elizabeth Dowd; (S) Stephen A. Kaelin; (L) Barry Demansky; (C) April Bevans

Under African Skies, adapt: James Goode and David Moreland, from African folk tales; (D) Mapopa Mtonga, James Goode and David Moreland

BoarsHead: Michigan Public Theater

JOHN PEAKES
Artistic Director

JUDITH L. GENTRY
Managing Director

WILLIAM P. WEINER
Board Chairperson

425 South Grand Ave.
Lansing, MI 48933
(517) 484-7800 (bus.)
(517) 484-7805 (b.o.)

FOUNDED 1966
Richard Thomsen, John Peakes

SEASON
Sept.-May

FACILITIES
Seating Capacity: 249
Stage: thrust

FINANCES
June 1, 1991-May 31, 1992
Expenses: $425,660

CONTRACTS
AEA SPT

BoarsHead: Michigan Public Theater is a center for theatre in its region. Our goal is the presentation of high-standard professional theatre chosen from the classic and modern repertoires. BoarsHead has a strong commitment to the staging of new plays, and its support of emerging playwrights is manifest in its seasons. The resident company remains dedicated to the idea of an expanding theatre, reaching into both the community and the state. Plays tour statewide, new pieces are developed by area writers, and designs are commissioned from area artists. The effort to involve new audiences is central. The theatre exists for the company as well, providing time and space for artists' individual growth and development. Our focus remains the audience. Productions must be accessible, must address the concerns of the time and then, hopefully, remain with our audiences beyond the moment.
—*John Peakes*

PRODUCTIONS 1991-1992

Eleemosynary, Lee Blessing; (D) Judith L. Gentry; (S) Fred Engelgau; (L) Rick Knapp; (C) Barbara Channer Thomsen

Fiddler on the Roof, book adapt: Joseph Stein, from Sholom Aleichem; music: Jerry Bock; lyrics: Sheldon Harnick; (D) Kristine Thatcher; (S) and (L) Gordon R. Phetteplace; (C) Charlotte Deardorff; (MD) John Dale Smith; (CH) Jerome Robbins, reproduced by Donnell A. Henton

Handy Dandy, William Gibson; (D) Judith L. Gentry; (S) Fred Engelgau; (L) Stephen R. Carns; (C) Barbara Channer Thomsen; (SD) Scott Thompson

The Mousetrap, Agatha Christie; (D) John Peakes; (S) Gordon R. Phetteplace; (L) Rick Knapp; (C) Kelly A. Rinne; (SD) Scott Thompson

BoarsHead: Michigan Public Theater. Caitlin Hart and Kate Konigisor in *Eleemosynary*. Photo: Connie Peakes.

The Mystery of Irma Vep, Charles Ludlam; (D) John Peakes; (S) Gordon R. Phetteplace; (L) Stephen R. Carns; (C) Kelly A. Rinne; (SD) Scott Thompson

PRODUCTIONS 1992-1993

Other People's Money, Jerry Sterner; (D) Judith L. Gentry; (S) Tim Stapleton; (L) Gordon R. Phetteplace; (C) Ann Kessler

Inspecting Carol, Daniel Sullivan and the Seattle Repertory Resident Acting Company; (D) John Peakes; (S) Tim Stapleton; (L) Gordon R. Phetteplace; (C) Ann Kessler

Shirley Valentine, Willy Russell; (D) Judith L. Gentry; (S) Gordon R. Phetteplace; (L) Sandy Thomley; (C) Barbara Channer Thomsen

The Hostage, Brendan Behan; (D) Jon Baisch; (S) Linda Janosko; (L) Gayla A. Madsen; (C) Gretel Geist

Waiting for Godot, Samuel Beckett; (D) Gus Kaikkonen; (S) Fred Engelgau; (L) Sandy Thomley; (C) Barbara Channer Thomsen

You Can't Take It With You, George S. Kaufman and Moss Hart; (D) John Peakes; (S) Gordon R. Phetteplace; (L) Sandy Thomley; (C) Ann Kessler

Bristol Riverside Theatre

SUSAN D. ATKINSON
Producing Artistic Director

CAROL MIGNONI FERGUSON
Board President

Box 1250
Bristol, PA 19007
(215) 785-6664 (bus.)
(215) 788-7827 (b.o.)

FOUNDED 1987
Susan D. Atkinson, Robert K. O'Neill

SEASON
Sept.-May

FACILITIES
Mainstage
Seating Capacity: 302
Stage: proscenium

Showroom
Seating Capacity: 80
Stage: flexible

FINANCES
Sept. 1, 1992-Aug. 31, 1993
Expenses: $547,309

CONTRACTS
AEA letter of agreement

Bristol Riverside Theatre is a professional, nonprofit theatre company dedicated to freshly interpreting vintage plays, musicals and classics and to developing new plays and playwrights. Our goal is to fully cultivate the artistic merits of each work and to share with our audiences the excitement of a new approach or the discovery of an unearthed treasure. Our primary concern is maintaining artistic integrity and pursuing excellence in our efforts to affirm the rich cultural heritage of Bucks County and the entire region, the legacy of theatre, the betterment of the quality of life and the sharing of high-quality, affordable entertainment.

—*Susan D. Atkinson*

PRODUCTIONS 1991-1992

Sets by Bart Healy, lighting by Robert A. Thorpe and costumes by Bradford Wood and Gregory A. Poplyk unless otherwise noted.

Murrow, Michael Hickey; (D) Susan D. Atkinson; (S) Robert Getty; (SD) David Miers
You Can't Take It With You, George S. Kaufman and Moss Hart; (D) Barbara McCulloh; (S) Lewis Folden; (L) Scott Pinkney
The Widow's Best Friend, Randy Hall; (D) Cliff Fannin Baker
The Brothers Booth!, W. Stuart McDowell; (D) Tom Bullard; (L) Scott Pinkney; (SD) Deena Kaye
Two by Two, book adapt: Peter Stone, from Clifford Odets; music: Richard Rodgers; lyrics: Martin Charnin; (D) and (MD) Keith Alan Baker; (C) Gregory A. Poplyk

PRODUCTIONS 1992-1993

Sets by Bart Healy, lighting by Robert A. Thorpe and costumes by Patricia Briggs unless otherwise noted.

Lend Me a Tenor, Ken Ludwig; (D) Keith Baker; (C) Gregory A. Poplyk
The Price, Arthur Miller; (D) Susan D. Atkinson
Greater Tuna, Jaston Williams, Joe Sears and Ed Howard; (D) Susan D. Atkinson; (C) Dawna Gregory
Macbett, Eugene Ionesco; trans: Charles Marowitz; (D) Keith Baker; (S) Robert A. Thorpe; (L) Scott Pinkney; (SD) Christopher Peraino
The Rothschilds; book adapt: Sherman Yellen, from Frederick Morton; music: Jerry Bock; lyrics: Sheldon Harnick; (D) Richard Edelman; (L) James E. Streeter; (MD) Edward Keith; (CH) Jonathan Cerullo

Bristol Riverside Theatre. Jill Brennan, Greg Wood and Barbara McCulloh in *Macbett*. Photo: Sue Callan.

California Theatre Center

GAYLE CORNELISON
General Director

SUSAN EARLE
Administrative Director

CHRIS McCOMB
Board President

Box 2007
Sunnyvale, CA 94087
(408) 245-2979 (bus.)
(408) 245-2978 (b.o.)
(408) 245-0235 (fax)

FOUNDED 1976
Gayle Cornelison

SEASON
Sept.-Aug.

FACILITIES
Sunnyvale Performing Arts Center
Seating Capacity: 200
Stage: proscenium

FINANCES
July 1, 1991-June 30, 1992
Expenses: $930,000

CONTRACTS
AEA Guest Artist

The California Theatre Center is a company with three major programs: a resident company that performs primarily for students and families from October to May; a resident company that performs primarily for adults in the summer; and touring companies that perform regionally, nationally and internationally. The performing artist is the focal point of CTC. Since our society fails to recognize the value of performers, it is essential that their worth be fully appreciated in our theatre. We attempt to provide the performing artist with the best possible environment so that he or she can be as creative as possible. At CTC we believe it is important for us to think of excellence as a process rather than a product. Our company strives toward the goal of outstanding theatre. As we grow and mature our concern is with the future, not the past. What we are attempting in the present is always far more exciting than our past successes. We are passionately driven by our search for excellence.

—*Gayle Cornelison*

PRODUCTIONS 1991-1992

Lighting by Bill M. Rupel and costumes by Jane Lambert unless otherwise noted.

What Part Will I Play, Mary Hall Surface; (D) and (S) Holly Cornelison; (C) Kate Heine; (SD) Mary Hall Surface
Sleeping Beauty, adapt: Gayle Cornelison, from The Brothers Grimm; (D) Sam Beverage; (S) Paul G. Vallerga; (SD) Clayton Doherty
Christopher Columbus, Will Huddleston; (D) Lynne A. Pace; (S) Paul G. Vallerga; (SD) Lynne A. Pace and Patricia A. Mudd
The Elves and the Shoemaker, adapt: Gayle Cornelison, from The Brothers Grimm; (D) and (SD) Will Huddleston; (S) Paul G. Vallerga; (C) Colleen Troy Lewis
A Christmas Carol, adapt: Mary Hall Surface, from Charles Dickens; (D) and (SD) Gayle Cornelison; (S) Michael Cook
Santa's Secret, Clayton Doherty and Mary Gibboney; (D) Cameron Mattox; (S) Paul G. Vallerga; (C) Colleen Troy Lewis; (SD) Brian Bennett

CALIFORNIA THEATRE CENTER

California Theatre Center. Conrad Cimarra, Robert Greene and Lisa Mallette in *The Ugly Duckling*. Photo: Marcia Lepler.

Tom Sawyer, adapt: Gayle Cornelison, from Mark Twain; (D) Gayle Cornelison; (S) Patricia A. Mudd; (C) A. James Hawkins; (SD) Lynne A. Pace
Beauty and the Beast, adapt: Gayle Cornelison, from Mme. Le Prince de Beaumont; (D) and (SD) Mary Hall Surface; (S) Paul G. Vallerga; (C) Colleen Troy Lewis
The Snow Queen, book and lyrics: James Keller, from Hans Christian Andersen; music: Thomas Tierney; (D) Albert Takazauckas; (S) Dawn Swiderski; (L) Kurt Landisman; (MD) Michael Horsley; (SD) Ron Mitchell
The Ugly Duckling, book adapt and lyrics: Gayle Cornelison, from Hans Christian Andersen; music: Brian Bennett; (D) Will Huddleston; (S) Michael Cook; (C) Colleen Troy Lewis
The Dream of Aladdin, Brian Kral; (D) Gayle Cornelison; (S) Paul G. Vallerga
Charlotte's Web, adapt: Joseph Robinette, from E.B. White; (D) Will Huddleston; (S) Michael Cook; (C) A. James Hawkins; (SD) Patricia A. Mudd
Two Men on a Roof, Nino D. Introna and Giacomo Ravicchio; (D) Goran Sarring; (S) Andrew Jones
Imagine, Clayton Doherty; (D) Will Huddleston; (S) Michael Essad; (C) Colleen Troy Lewis
Love's Labour's Lost, William Shakespeare; (D) and (SD) Will Huddleston; (S) Peter-Tolin Baker; (L) Mary Kathryn Farrow; (C) Colleen Troy Lewis

The Comedy of Errors, William Shakespeare; (D) Gayle Cornelison; (S) Peter-Tolin Baker; (L) Mary Kathryn Farrow
Dracula, adapt: Gayle Cornelison, from Bram Stoker; (D) Gayle Cornelison; (S) Peter-Tolin Baker; (L) Mary Kathryn Farrow
Mass Appeal, Bill C. Davis; (D) Brian Kral; (S) Peter-Tolin Baker; (L) Mary Kathryn Farrow; (C) Holly Cornelison

PRODUCTIONS 1992-1993

Sets by Paul G. Vallerga, lighting by Mary Farrow and costumes by Colleen Troy Lewis unless otherwise noted.

The Great War of Rikki-Tikki-Tavi, book adapt: Alexander Ivanov and Alexander Mikhailov, from Rudyard Kipling; music: Boris Kiseljov; lyrics: Olga Muratova; (D) Alexander Mikhailov; (S) and (C) Irina Tkachenko; (CH) Vera Lesnichaja
Charlotte's Web, adapt: Joseph Robinette, from E.B. White; (D) Will Huddleston; (S) Michael Cook; (L) Bill M. Rupel; (C) A. James Hawkins; (SD) Patricia A. Mudd
The Ugly Duckling, book adapt and lyrics: Gayle Cornelison, from Hans Christian Andersen; music: Brian Bennett; (D) Will Huddleston; (S) Michael Cook; (L) Bill M. Rupel
Jamie 22, Gayle Cornelison; (D) Will Huddleston; (L) Paul G. Vallerga; (SD) Jeffra Cook
I Don't Want to Go to Bed, Gayle Cornelison; (D) and (SD) Holly Cornelison; (S) Mary Kathryn Farrow

The Elves and the Shoemaker, adapt: Gayle Cornelison, from The Brothers Grimm; (D) and (SD) Bruce Merrill; (L) Paul G. Vallerga
A Little Princess, adapt: Gayle Cornelison, from Frances Hodgson Burnett; (D) Gayle Cornelison; (SD) Holly Cornelison
Tales of Brer Rabbit, adapt: Gayle Cornelison, from Joel Chandler Harris; (D) Gayle Cornelison; (C) Jane Lambert
A Midsummer Night's Dream, William Shakespeare; adapt: Gayle Cornelison and Kit Wilder; (D) and (SD) Kit Wilder; (C) Jane Lambert
Imagine, Clayton Doherty; (D) Will Huddleston; (S) Michael Essad
A Perfect Balance, Mary Hall Surface; (D) and (SD) Mary Hall Surface; (S) and (C) Kevin Reese
The Reluctant Dragon, adapt: Mary Hall Surface, from Kenneth Grahame; (D) Mary Hall Surface; (S) Peter-Tolin Baker; (SD) Robert Goldstein
Most Valuable Player, Mary Hall Surface and original cast; (D) Will Huddleston; (C) Jane Lambert; (SD) Kevin Reese
Alice in Wonderland, adapt: Mary Hall Surface, from Lewis Carroll; (D) Will Huddleston; (S) Michael Cook; (L) Paul G. Vallerga; (C) Jane Lambert
The Miracle Worker, William Gibson; (D) Gayle Cornelison
The Frog Prince, adapt: Gayle Cornelison, from The Brothers Grimm; (D) and (SD) Bruce Merrill; (S) Peter-Tolin Baker; (C) Jane Lambert; (CH) Sarah Huff Walker
Stop the World—I Want to Get Off, book, music and lyrics: Anthony Newley and Leslie Bricusse; (D) Will Huddleston; (S) Peter-Tolin Baker; (MD) Michael Horsley
Arms and the Man, George Bernard Shaw; (D) Gayle Cornelison; (S) Peter-Tolin Baker
The Taming of the Shrew, William Shakespeare; (D) Graham Whitehead; (S) Peter-Tolin Baker; (C) Jane Lambert
Romeo and Juliet, William Shakespeare; (D) Alexander Mikhailov; (S) Peter-Tolin Baker; (C) Jane Lambert

Capital Repertory Company

BRUCE BOUCHARD
Artistic Director

PETER CLOUGH
Producing Director

Box 399
Albany, NY 12201-0399
(518) 462-4531 (bus.)
(518) 462-4534 (b.o.)
(518) 465-0213 (fax)

FOUNDED 1980
Michael Van Landingham, Oakley Hall, III

SEASON
Oct.-June

FACILITIES
Market Theatre
Seating Capacity: 254
Stage: thrust

FINANCES
July 1, 1991-June 30, 1992
Expenses: $1,372,000

CONTRACTS
AEA LORT (D)

The worlds we make onstage are reflective of and instructive to the world in which we live. As the very act of looking at artwork is the act of education, we seek to turn the unconscious and mysterious inside out, in works of intellectual and emotional integrity. Our aim is to inspire re-vision of our selves and our community. Our work is contemporary: We present premieres, second productions of new works and texts largely unfamiliar to our audience. Our productions of modern and traditional classics highlight aspects of these plays which address current conditions and beg reexamination of both the factual shape of history and the human event of history-making. As we enter our second decade, we point with pride to a long-term association with a body of artists who return to Capital Rep as "artistic home" to stretch and refine their craft.

—Bruce Bouchard

PRODUCTIONS 1991-1992

The House of Blue Leaves, John Guare; (D) Michael J. Hume; (S) Donald Eastman; (L) Kenneth Posner; (C) Lynda L. Salsbury; (SD) David Wiggall

Remembrance, Graham Reid; (D) Bruce Bouchard; (S) Rick Dennis; (L) Brian MacDevitt; (C) Martha Hally; (SD) David Wiggall

Peacetime, Elaine Berman; (D) Pamela Berlin; (S) Edward Gianfrancesco; (L) Craig Evans; (C) Mimi Maxmen; (SD) David Wiggall

How I Got That Story, Amlin Gray; (D) Mark Dalton; (S) Teal Usher; (L) David Wiggall; (C) James Scott; (SD) Andrew Luft

The Sum of Us, David Stevens; (D) Jamie Brown; (S) James Noone; (L) Phil Monat; (C) Randall E. Klein; (SD) James Wildman

Broadway Bound, Neil Simon; (D) John Pynchon Holms; (S) David Gallo; (L) David Wiggall; (C) Lynda L. Salsbury; (SD) Tom Gould

PRODUCTIONS 1992-1993

Lips Together, Teeth Apart, Terrence McNally; (D) Bruce Bouchard; (S) James Noone; (L) Brian MacDevitt; (C) Martha Hally; (SD) David Wiggall

Absurd Person Singular, Alan Ayckbourn; (D) John Pynchon Holms; (S) David Gallo; (L) David Wiggall; (C) Lynda L. Salsbury; (SD) Tom Gould

The Substance of Fire, Jon Robin Baitz; (D) Gideon Y. Schein; (S) Richard Hoover; (L) Jeanne G. Koenig; (C) Melissa Toth; (SD) David Wiggall

Shirley Valentine, Willy Russell; (D) Pamela Berlin; (S) and (C) G.W. Mercier; (L) Jackie Manassee; (SD) David Wiggall

Cat on a Hot Tin Roof, Tennessee Williams; (D) Bruce Bouchard; (S) Keith Henery; (L) and (SD) David A. Strang; (C) Polly Byers

I Do! I Do!, book adapt and lyrics: Tom Jones, from Jan de Hartog; music: Harvey Schmidt; (D) and (CH) David Holdgrive; (S) James Noone; (L) Tom Sturge; (C) Lynda L. Salsbury; (MD) Garth Roberts

Center Stage. Stephen Markle, Cherry Jones and James J. Lawless in *A Moon for the Misbegotten*. Photo: Richard Anderson.

Center Stage

IRENE LEWIS
Artistic Director

PETER W. CULMAN
Managing Director

NANCY K. ROCHE
Board President

700 North Calvert St.
Baltimore, MD 21202
(410) 685-3200 (bus.)
(410) 332-0033 (b.o.)
(410) 539-3912 (fax)

FOUNDED 1963
Community Arts Committee

SEASON
Oct.-June

FACILITIES
The Pearlstone Theater
Seating Capacity: 541
Stage: thrust

The Head Theater
Seating Capacity: 150-350
Stage: flexible

FINANCES
July 1, 1991-June 30, 1992
Expenses: $3,775,000

CONTRACTS
AEA LORT (B) and (C)

As the artistic director of Center Stage, I am interested in investigating the spirit of the great works of dramatic literature through highly theatrical productions of the classics, supplemented by daring and innovative new voices in contemporary playwriting. I hope to enlist a diverse and inquisitive audience that embraces works that are literate, intellectually challenging, bold and often disturbing. Happily, Center Stage is one theatre with two performance spaces, allowing us to suit the project to the venue, the idea to the space. Its endowment enables us to remain somewhat aggressive (even in this difficult climate) in the area of artist compensation and the commissioning of new projects. This flexibility ideally will offer some welcome relief from the situation in which the demands of traditional season selection (e.g., balanced subscription offerings) become *de facto* artistic policy.
—*Irene Lewis*

PRODUCTIONS 1991-1992

The Queen and the Rebels, Ugo Betti; trans: Rick Davis and Brian Johnston; adapt: Jackson Phippin; (D) Irene Lewis; (S) Christopher Barreca; (L) Stephen Strawbridge; (C) Catherine Zuber; (SD) Janet Kalas

My Children! My Africa!, Athol Fugard; (D) Lisa Peterson; (S) Derek McLane; (L) Peter Kaczorowski; (C) Catherine Zuber; (SD) Mark Bennett and JR Conklin

A Doll House, Henrik Ibsen; trans: Rick Davis and Brian Johnston; adapt: Jackson Phippin; (D) Jackson Phippin; (S) Tony Straiges; (L) Stephen Strawbridge; (C) Catherine Zuber; (SD) Dan Schreier

Pericles, Prince of Tyre, William Shakespeare; (D) Irene Lewis; (S) John Conklin; (L) Pat Collins; (C) Susan Hilferty; (SD) Mark McCoin

Capital Repertory Company. Claywood Sempliner and Lee Brock in *Lips Together, Teeth Apart*. Photo: Joe Schuyler.

Police Boys, Marion Isaac McClinton; (D) Marion Isaac McClinton; (S) Donald Eastman; (L) James F. Ingalls; (C) Paul Tazewell; (SD) Mark Bennett
The Baltimore Waltz, Paula Vogel; (D) Michael Greif; (S) Donald Eastman; (L) James F. Ingalls; (C) Paul Tazewell; (SD) Mark Bennett
The Misanthrope, Moliere; trans: Richard Wilbur; (D) Irene Lewis; (S) Kate Edmunds; (L) Pat Collins; (C) Catherine Zuber; (SD) Jeremy Grody

PRODUCTIONS 1992-1993

The Servant of Two Masters, Carlo Goldoni; trans: Tom Cone; (D) Irene Lewis; (S) Christopher Barreca; (L) Jennifer Tipton; (C) Catherine Zuber; (SD) John Gromada
T Bone N Weasel, Jon Klein; (D) Jackson Phippin; (S) Neil Patel; (L) Peter Kaczorowski; (C) Linda Fisher; (SD) Janet Kalas
A Moon for the Misbegotten, Eugene O'Neill; (D) Lisa Peterson; (S) Kate Edmunds; (L) Pat Collins; (C) Paul Tazewell; (SD) Mark Bennett
Escape from Happiness, George F. Walker; (D) Irene Lewis; (S) Michael Yeargan; (L) Stephen Strawbridge; (C) Jess Goldstein; (SD) Janet Kalas
Lady Day at Emerson's Bar and Grill, Lanie Robertson; (D) George Faison; (S) Christopher Barreca; (L) Tom Sturge; (C) Toni-Leslie James; (SD) JR Conklin
Arms and the Man, George Bernard Shaw; (D) Irene Lewis; (S) John Conklin; (L) Pat Collins; (C) Candice Donnelly; (SD) Mark Bennett

Center Theater. JoAnn Carney, Dan LaMorte and Gus Buktenica in *Hapgood*. Photo: Ricardo Garza.

Center Theater

DAN LAMORTE
Artistic Director

RJ COLEMAN
General Manager

DIANE TUSCHER-ANCEDE
Board President

1346 West Devon Ave.
Chicago, IL 60660
(312) 508-0200 (bus.)
(312) 508-5422 (b.o.)
(312) 508-9584 (fax)

FOUNDED 1984
Dan LaMorte, Dale Calandra, Marc Vann, Carole Gutierrez, Eileen Manganaro

SEASON
Sept.-July

FACILITIES
Mainstage
Seating Capacity: 99
Stage: thrust

Studio
Seating Capacity: 30
Stage: flexible

FINANCES
Sept. 1, 1991-Aug. 31, 1992
Expenses: $318,429

CONTRACTS
AEA CAT

Center Theater was built from values inspired by its own training program for theatre artists. The Training Center for the Working Actor created an environment in which actors can receive a coherent and unified, lifelong approach to the art and science of acting. New programs exist for playwrights and directors, and will soon exist for designers and administrators. Dedication to exploring the freedom of art and to taking the risk of creating new forms of theatre is the primary objective. The Center Theater Ensemble is committed to this philosophy and presents diverse works exploring new and established materials in original, bold and imaginative productions that truthfully give the play to the audience. To inspire new audiences, the theatre has developed ArtsReach, an educational touring program that conducts workshops and residencies, and forms partnerships. Center Theater provides an artistic home, and pursues this value through its Ensemble, Training Center and ArtsReach programs to inspire atists and audiences alike.

—*Dan LaMorte*

PRODUCTIONS 1991-1992

Lighting by Chris Phillips, costumes by Lynn Sandberg and sound design by Joe Cerqua unless otherwise noted.

Hapgood, Tom Stoppard; (D) Mary Zimmerman; (S) Rob Hamilton; (SD) Eric Huffman
Inside George, Dan LaMorte; (D) Kevin Rigdon; (S) Daniel Ostling; (C) Dawn Dewitt
Kingdom of Earth, Tennessee Williams; (D) Dale Calandra; (S) Brett A. Snodgrass
Abundance, Beth Henley; (D) Dan LaMorte; (S) Kurt Sharp
Through the Leaves, Franz Xaver Kroetz; adapt: Norbert Ruebsaat; (D) Dan LaMorte and Claus Koenig; (S) and (C) Brett A. Snodgrass; (L) Kelly Heligas
Bobby Gould in Hell, David Mamet; (D) Marc Rosenbush; (S), (L) and (C) Brett A. Snodgrass

PRODUCTIONS 1992-1993

Sets by Rob Hamilton, lighting by Chris Phillips, costumes by Lynn Sandberg and sound design by Joe Cerqua unless otherwise noted.

Control Freaks, Beth Henley; (D) Beth Henley
archy & mehitabel, book adapt: Joe Darion and Mel Brooks, from Don Marquis; music: George Kleinsinger; lyrics: Joe Darion; (D) Dale Calandra; (L) Tom Fleming; (MD) Mark Elliott; (CH) David Puszh
Life During Wartime, Keith Reddin (co-produced by Wisdom Bridge Theatre); (D) Michael Maggio; (SD) Joe Cerqua and Michael Bodeen
Katzelmacher, Rainer Werner Fassbinder; trans: Denis Calandra; (D) Dan LaMorte; (S) Kurt Sharp
Law/Order, Elizabeth Shepherd; (D) Randi Collins Hard; (S) Thom Bumblauskas; (L) Michael Jon Burris; (SD) Tim Schirmer

Cheltenham Center for the Arts

KEN MARINI
Artistic Director

SHIRLEY M. TRAUGER
Executive Director

BERNARD S. BERGMAN
Board President

439 Ashbourne Road
Cheltenham, PA 19012
(215) 379-4660 (bus.)
(215) 379-4027 (b.o.)

FOUNDED 1940
Gladys Wagner

SEASON
Sept.-June

FACILITIES
Bernard H. Berger Theater
Seating Capacity: 140
Stage: proscenium

FINANCES
June 1, 1992-May 31, 1993
Expenses: $225,633

CONTRACTS
AEA SPT

The Cheltenham Center for the Arts is a theatre and visual arts center formed to promote the practice and appreciation of contemporary art. This vision encompasses a wide variety of ideas

Cheltenham Center for the Arts. Drew Ebersole and Larry Attile in *Catch!* Photo: Baruch Schwartz.

and voices—voices that speak of the complexity of our reality, that imagine the possibilities of the future and remind us of our history. To realize our aims, we are currently pursuing three ways of creating theatre. First of all, we produce what we call "created works"—original theatre pieces that are created with the artists of our theatre. Second, we produce distinctive new plays brought to us by playwrights from across the country. Third, we produce proven works of the best contemporary playwrights. For us the theatre is a meeting house where people come to dream and wonder, to examine and question—a safe place where new or different views are experienced and understood.

—*Ken Marini*

PRODUCTIONS 1991-1992

The Wonderful Ice Cream Suit, Ray Bradbury; (D) Ken Marini; (S), (L) and (SD) Robert Smythe; (C) M. Michael Montgomery

Serenading Louie, Lanford Wilson; (D) Alex Dmitriev; (S) David P. Gordon; (L) Marc S. Goldberg; (C) Barbara Beccio; (SD) Robert D. Biasetti

Catch!, Jason Katims; (D) Lynn M. Thomson; (S) David P. Gordon; (L) Mark Andrew; (C) M. Michael Montgomery; (SD) Charles Brastow

A Distant Mirror, Robert Smythe; (D) Ken Marini; (S) and (L) Mark Somerfield; (C) Marla Jurglanis; (SD) Adam Wenick

All My Sons, Arthur Miller; (D) Ken Marini; (S) David P. Gordon; (L) Ellen Owen; (C) M. Michael Montgomery; (SD) Charles Brastow

PRODUCTIONS 1992-1993

Sets by David P. Gordon, costumes by M. Michael Montgomery and sound design by Bob Perdick unless otherwise noted.

A Life in the Theatre, David Mamet; (D) Ken Marini; (L) Adam Macks

Hearts Beating Faster, Ralph Pape; (D) Ken Marini; (L) Adam Macks; (SD) Charles Brastow

Reckless, Craig Lucas; (D) Harriet Power; (L) Rebecca G. Frederick

Tough Love, Nancy Bagshow-Reasoner; (D) Paul Meshejian; (L) Deborah Peretz

The Children's Theatre Company

JON CRANNEY
Executive Producer

**GARY GISSELMAN,
WENDY LEHR**
Associate Artistic Directors

**KENNETH F. GOLDSTEIN,
EMMANUEL J. OTIS**
Board Co-Chairmen

2400 Third Ave. S
Minneapolis, MN 55404
(612) 874-0500 (bus.)
(612) 874-0400 (b.o.)
(612) 874-8119 (fax)

FOUNDED 1961
Beth Linnerson

SEASON
Sept.-June

FACILITIES
Mainstage
Seating Capacity: 746
Stage: proscenium

Studio Theatre
Seating Capacity: 150
Stage: flexible

FINANCES
July 1, 1992-June 30, 1993
Expenses: $5,649,522

CONTRACTS
AEA Guest Artist

The Children's Theatre Company is dedicated to the creation and presentation of new adaptations and original plays for young people and families, inspired by classic and contemporary sources. A rotating repertory season of six mainstage productions comprises full-scale musicals, children's classics and literary dramas, created by CTC's resident artists and artisans (80 full-time staff), who are complemented by numerous guest artists. National touring and international cultural exchanges enhance CTC's understanding of and its influence within the world theatre community. CTC also provides classroom/workshop training for children and adolescents, as well as intern-apprentice positions for young adults, culminating in appropriate performance opportunities with CTC's resident company. To maintain an artistic sanctuary and wellspring that is resourceful, responsive and responsible, and to provide an honest, reverent, relevant and challenging artistic experience for artist and audience is the legacy and continuing quest of the Children's Theatre Company.

—*Jon Cranney*

PRODUCTIONS 1991-1992

Musical direction by Victor Zupanc and sound design by Scott W. Edwards unless otherwise noted.

A Wrinkle in Time, adapt: Marjorie Bradley Kellogg, from Madeleine L'Engle; (D) Gary Gisselman; (S) Marjorie Bradley Kellogg; (L) Kirk Bookman; (C) William Schroder

The Children's Theatre Company. *On the Wings of the Hummingbird: Tales of Trinidad*. Photo: Cheryl Walsh-Bellville.

On the Wings of the Hummingbird: Tales of Trinidad, Beverly Smith-Dawson; music: "Bongo-Jerie"; lyrics: Beverly Smith-Dawson and "Bongo-Jerie"; (D) Richard D. Thompson; (S) Steven Kennedy; (L) Kirk Bookman; (C) Ricia Birturk; (CH) Marvette Knight; (SD) Victor Zupanc

The Canterville Ghost, adapt: Marisha Chamberlain, from Oscar Wilde; (D) Jon Cranney; (S) Jim Guenther; (L) Charles D. Craun; (C) David Kay Mickelsen

The Little Match Girl, adapt: John Clark Donahue, from Hans Christian Andersen; (D) Wendy Lehr; (S) Jack Barkla; (L) Michael Murnane; (C) Gene Davis Buck; (SD) Robert Jorissen

Merry Christmas, Strega Nona, book adapt: Thomas W. Olson, from Tomie de Paola; music: Alan Shorter; lyrics: Thomas W. Olson and Alan Shorter; (D) Gary Gisselman; (S) Steven Kennedy; (L) Barry Browning; (C) Tomie de Paola; (MD) Anita Ruth

Ramona Quimby, adapt: Len Jenkin, from Beverly Cleary; (D) Jon Cranney; (S) Stephen Quinn; (L) Robert Wierzel; (C) David Kay Mickelsen

Our Town, Thornton Wilder; (D) Gary Gisselman; (S) Carey W. Thornton; (L) Robert Wierzel; (C) David Kay Mickelsen

Beauty and the Beast, adapt: Constance Congdon, from Mme. Le Prince de Beaumont; (D) Wendy Lehr; (S) and (C) Desmond Heeley; (L) Duane M. Schuler

PRODUCTIONS 1992-1993

Musical direction by Victor Zupanc and sound design by Scott W. Edwards unless otherwise noted.

Treasure Island, adapt: Frederick Gaines, from Robert Louis Stevenson; (D) Gary Gisselman; (S) Greg Lucas; (L) Don Darnutzer; (C) David Kay Mickelsen

Mr. Popper's Penguins, book adapt and lyrics: Timothy Mason, from Richard and Florence Atwater; music: Mel Marvin; (D) Jon Cranney; (S) Jim Guenther; (L) Don Darnutzer; (C) David Kay Mickelsen; (MD) Anita Ruth; (CH) Vance Holmes; (SD) Andrew Mayer

The Jungle Book, adapt: Thomas W. Olson, from Rudyard Kipling; (D) Wendy Lehr; (S) and (C) Maggie Belle Calin; (L) Charles D. Craun

The Velveteen Rabbit, adapt: Thomas W. Olson, from Margery Williams; (D) Jon Cranney; (S) Tom Butsch; (L) Dawn Chiang; (C) Gene Davis Buck

Beatrix Potter's Christmas, Thomas W. Olson; (D) Myron Johnson; (S) Laura Mohanshelt, after Jack Barkla; (L) Michael Murnane; (C) Christopher Beesley

The Miser, Moliere; adapt: Gary Gisselman; (D) Gary Gisselman; (S) Vicki Smith; (L) Charles D. Craun; (C) David Kay Mickelsen; (SD) Reid Rejsa

The Wonderful World of Oz, adapt: Thomas W. Olson, from L. Frank Baum; (D) Gary Gisselman; (S) Tom Butsch; (L) Charles D. Craun; (C) William Schroder

The 500 Hats of Bartholomew Cubbins, book adapt and lyrics: Timothy Mason, from Dr. Seuss; music: Hiram Titus; (D) Jon Cranney and Wendy Lehr; (S) Jack Barkla; (L) Marcus Dilliard; (C) Judith Cooper; (SD) Reid Rejsa

Childsplay, Inc.

DAVID SAAR
Artistic Director

GARY BACAL
Managing Director

KAREN FISCH
Board Chair

Box 517
Tempe, AZ 85280
(602) 350-8101 (bus.)
(602) 350-8112 (b.o.)
(602) 350-8584 (fax)

FOUNDED 1977
David Saar

SEASON
Sept.-May

FACILITIES
Tempe Performing Arts Center
Seating Capacity: 150
Stage: flexible

Herberger Theater Center
Seating Capacity: 300
Stage: proscenium

Scottsdale Center for the Arts
Seating Capacity: 800
Stage: proscenium

FINANCES
July 1, 1992-June 30, 1993
Expenses: $587,158

Childsplay was founded by a group of artists who were in love with the process of theatre and convinced that it could make a difference in the lives of young people. We exist to create theatre so strikingly original in form or content, or both, that it instills in young people an enduring awe, love and respect for the medium. In so doing we work to preserve imagination and wonder, those hallmarks of childhood which are the keys to our future. It is vital that our audiences be exposed to theatre which entertains, but also challenges and provokes, providing insights which can impact and influence "real-life" problems and possibilities. Our search for material leads us to new interpretations of classic literature, ongoing commissions of new works by regional, national and international playwrights, and company-developed explorations.
—*David Saar*

PRODUCTIONS 1991-1992

Direction by David Saar, sets by Jeff Thomson and costumes by Susan Johnson-Hood unless otherwise noted.

Childsplay, Inc. Jere Luisi and Richard Trujillo in *Noodle Doodle Box*. Photo: Hal Martin Fogel.

The Reluctant Dragon, adapt: Mary Hall Surface, from Kenneth Grahame; (S) Greg Lucas; (L) Marc Riske

Through the Looking Glass, book adapt and music: Ross Care, from Lewis Carroll; lyrics: Charles Leayman; (D) and (CH) Michael Barnard; (L) Luetta Newnam and Jon Gentry; (C) Rebecca Akins; (MD) Craig Bohmler

The Velveteen Rabbit, adapt: B. Burgess Clark, from Margery Williams; (L) Marc Riske; (C) Rebecca Akins

Noodle Doodle Box, trans and adapt: Anita and Alex Page, from Paul Maar; (L) and (C) Jeff Thomson; (SD) Allen Lea

Montana Molly and the Peppermint Kid, book: Monica Long Ross; music and lyrics: Alan Ruch; (S) Greg Lucas; (L) Marc Riske; (MD) Alan Ruch; (CH) Michael Barnard

Most Valuable Player, Mary Hall Surface and the original California Theater Center company; (L) Luetta Newnam; (SD) Bryn Pryor

PRODUCTIONS 1992-1993

Direction by David Saar, sets by Jeff Thomson and costumes by Susan Johnson-Hood unless otherwise noted.

The Nightingale, adapt: Tom Poole, from Hans Christian Andersen; (L) Marc Riske

Noodle Doodle Box, trans and adapt: Anita and Alex Page, from Paul Maar; (L) Jeff Thomson; (SD) Allen Lea

Montana Molly and the Peppermint Kid, book: Monica Long Ross; music and lyrics: Alan Ruch; (D) Debra K. Stevens; (S) Greg Lucas; (MD) Alan Ruch; (CH) Michael Barnard

The Velveteen Rabbit, adapt: B. Burgess Clark, from Margery Williams; (L) Marc Riske; (C) Rebecca Akins

Tales of the Grotesque, adapt: Eberle Thomas, from Edgar Allan Poe; (D) and (L) Jon Gentry; (S) Jere Luisi; (C) Gro Johre; (SD) Allen Lea

Phoebe Joins the Circus, book: Monica Long Ross; music and lyrics: Alan Ruch; (D) Michael Barnard; (S) Greg Lucas; (L) Luetta Newnam; (MD) Alan Ruch; (CH) David Barker

The Yellow Boat, book: David Saar; music and lyrics: Alan Ruch; (D) and (CH) Carol North Evans; (S) Greg Lucas; (L) Amarante L. Lucero; (MD) Alan Ruch

Bocon!, Lisa Loomer; (L) Marc Riske; (SD) Allen Lea

Child's Play Touring Theatre

VICTOR PODAGROSI
Artistic Director

JUNE PODAGROSI
Executive Director

JOAN MAZZONELLI
Board President

2650 West Belden Ave.,
2nd Floor
Chicago, IL 60647
(312) 235-8911
(312) 235-5478 (fax)

FOUNDED 1979
June Podagrosi,
Victor Podagrosi

SEASON
Year-round

FINANCES
Sept. 1, 1992-Aug. 31, 1993
Expenses: $557,280

Child's Play Touring Theatre is a professional theatre for young audiences, dedicated to performing stories and poems written by children. Every year we present works by hundreds of young poets, essayists and short-story writers, discovering exciting theatre in their imaginations. As the raw material for theatre, we find literature written by children to be technically demanding and artistically satisfying. Children create delightfully bizarre characters and unusual plot twists; their writing can also display startling candor and sharp insight when they address social issues and private concerns. We believe that every theatre dedicated to serving children has a part in shaping the audiences of the future. Child's Play takes that goal one step further–we're working to inspire the artists of the future. As writers, children have a unique voice that should be heard. Child's Play Touring Theatre provides a stage where that voice can be shared, examined and treasured.
—*Victor Podagrosi*

PRODUCTIONS 1991-1992

All productions company-developed. Direction by Victor Podagrosi, sets by Jeff Richmond and Michael Thomas, and costumes by Barbara Niederer.

Do the Write Thing!
Writing Is...Child's Play
New Voices
Me, a Scientist?
Animal Tales and Dinosaur Scales
The Christmas that Almost Wasn't

PRODUCTIONS 1992-1993

All productions company-developed. Direction by Victor Podagrosi, sets by Jeff Richmond and Michael Thomas, and costumes by Barbara Niederer.

Do the Write Thing!
Writing Is...Child's Play
New Voices
Kids for President!
Animal Tales and Dinosaur Scales
The Christmas that Almost Wasn't

Cincinnati Playhouse in the Park

EDWARD STERN
Producing Artistic Director

BUZZ WARD
Executive Director

STONA J. FITCH
Board President

Box 6537
Cincinnati, OH 45206
(513) 345-2242 (bus.)
(513) 421-3888 (b.o.)
(513) 345-2254 (fax)

FOUNDED 1960
Community members

SEASON
Sept.-July

FACILITIES
Robert S. Marx Theatre
Seating Capacity: 629
Stage: thrust

Thompson Shelterhouse Theatre
Seating Capacity: 220
Stage: thrust

FINANCES
Sept. 1, 1991-Aug. 31, 1992
Expenses: $4,459,293

CONTRACTS
AEA LORT (B) and (D)

For 33 years Cincinnati Playhouse has continued to be the standard for theatrical excellence in this region. Under its new producing artistic director, the Playhouse continues to present a deliberately eclectic mixture of plays while recommitting itself both to new plays and to the broadening of its present audience. The annual Lois and Richard Rosenthal New Play Prize provides special underwriting to secure the best new American works for the Playhouse. In addition to our 10-play season (five shows in our Thompson Shelterhouse Theatre, five in our Robert S. Marx Theatre) and a nonsubscriber production of *A Christmas Carol*, the Playhouse books in approximately six shows a year to tour throughout the region's school systems. The shows are selected to celebrate the cultural diversity found within our community.
—*Edward Stern*

PRODUCTIONS 1991-1992

Lighting by Kirk Bookman and sound design by David Smith unless otherwise noted.

Our Town, Thornton Wilder; (D) Jay E. Raphael; (S) Joseph P. Tilford; (C) Elizabeth Covey

Speed-the-Plow, David Mamet; (D) Jay E. Raphael; (S) G.W. Mercier; (L) Jackie Manassee; (C) Jan Finnell

A Christmas Carol, adapt: Howard Dallin, from Charles Dickens; (D) Howard Dallin; (S) James Leonard Joy; (C) David Murin

Japango, Richard Epp; (D) Kent Stephens; (S) Victor A. Becker; (C) Susan E. Mickey

From the Mississippi Delta, Dr. Endesha Ida Mae Holland; (D) Oz Scott; (S) and (C) G.W. Mercier

Child's Play Touring Theatre. Janet Brooks, Eric Traynor and Laura Novak Mead in The Christmas that Almost Wasn't. *Photo: Tom Lindfors.*

Cincinnati Playhouse in the Park. Ebony Jo-Ann and Kim Brockington in *From the Mississippi Delta*. Photo: Sandy Underwood.

Billy Bishop Goes to War, John Gray and Eric Peterson; (D) Howard Dallin; (S) Lori Sullivan Worthman; (C) Delmar L. Rinehart, Jr.
The Cocktail Hour, A.R. Gurney, Jr.; (D) Christopher Ashley; (S) James Leonard Joy; (C) Lisa Molyneux
Perfect For You, Doll, Steven Sater; (D) Beth Schachter; (S) and (C) Craig Clipper; (L) Victor En Yu Tan
Hot 'n Cole, conceived: David Holdgrive, Mark Waldrop and George Kramer; music and lyrics: Cole Porter; (D) and (CH) David Holdgrive; (S) James Leonard Joy; (C) Mariann Verheyen; (MD) George Kramer
Lady Day at Emerson's Bar and Grill, Lanie Robertson; (D) Jonathan Wilson; (S) Joseph P. Tilford

PRODUCTIONS 1992-1993

Lighting by Kirk Bookman and sound design by David Smith unless otherwise noted.

"Master Harold"...and the boys, Athol Fugard; (D) Stephen Hollis; (S) and (C) David Crank
The House of Blue Leaves, John Guare; (D) Edward Stern; (S) David Potts; (C) Michael Krass
Shirley Valentine, Willy Russell; (D) Linda Atkinson; (S) Robert Barnett; (L) Jeff Gress; (C) Lisa Molyneux
A Christmas Carol, adapt: Howard Dallin, from Charles Dickens; (D) Howard Dallin; (S) James Leonard Joy; (C) David Murin
Our Country's Good, adapt: Timberlake Wertenbaker, from Thomas Keneally; (D) Edward Stern; (S) Andrew Jackness and David Crank; (L) Christopher Akerlind; (C) Candice Donnelly and Elizabeth Hope Clancy
Scotland Road, Jeffrey Hatcher; (D) Edward Stern; (S) Karen TenEyck; (C) Delmar L. Rinehart, Jr.
The Immigrant, Mark Harelik; (D) Charles Towers; (S) Bill Clarke; (L) Nancy Schertler; (C) Candice Cain
Separation, Tom Kempinski; (D) Susan Kerner; (S) Ursula Belden; (L) Jeff Gress; (C) D. Bartlett Blair
A Moon for the Misbegotten, Eugene O'Neill; (D) Amy Saltz; (S) John Ezell; (L) Jackie Manassee; (C) D. Bartlett Blair
Smoke on the Mountain, Constance Ray; (D) Alan Bailey; (S) Peter Harrison; (L) Victor En Yu Tan; (C) Don Bolinger
Ain't Misbehavin', conceived: Murray Horwitz and Richard Maltby, Jr.; music and lyrics: Fats Waller, et al; (D) and (CH) Carl Jablonski; (S) and (C) Eduardo Sicangco; (MD) Kevin Toney

Circle Repertory Company

TANYA BEREZIN
Artistic Director

ABIGAIL EVANS
Managing Director

JOHN A. LACK
Board Chairman

632 Broadway, 6th Floor
New York, NY 10012
(212) 505-6010 (bus.)
(212) 924-7100 (b.o.)
(212) 505-8520 (fax)

FOUNDED 1969
Lanford Wilson, Robert Thirkield, Marshall W. Mason, Tanya Berezin

SEASON
Sept.-June

FACILITIES
Seating Capacity: 160
Stage: flexible

FINANCES
July 1, 1992-June 30, 1993
Expenses: $2,200,000

CONTRACTS
AEA Off Broadway

Circle Repertory Company comprises a family of more than 200 theatre artists who share a commitment to excellence and a vision of truth and humanity in the theatre. Now in its third decade, Circle Rep has become a national resource of new plays, producing more than a hundred that have subsequently been presented at scores of professional theatres in all 50 states and many foreign countries. Dedicated to developing American works for the stage, Circle Rep continues to expand its body of work to include a multiplicity of American voices and world visions. Our developmental process, which includes a writers and directors lab, as well as three series of staged readings, allows us to challenge our mature theatre artists to explore new areas of their art while proceeding with an active search for new talent. It is this collaboration by an ensemble of artists to create a vibrant and vital theatrical experience that has become the source of growth and creative achievement for the company over the last two decades.
—*Tanya Berezin*

PRODUCTIONS 1991-1992

Lighting by Dennis Parichy unless otherwise noted.

Babylon Gardens, Timothy Mason; (D) Joe Mantello; (S) Loy Arcenas; (L) Dennis Parichy and Michael J. Baldassari; (C) Toni-Leslie James; (SD) Scott Lehrer

Circle Repertory Company. Richard Thompson, Cherry Jones and Joe Mantello in *The Baltimore Waltz*. Photo: Gerry Goodstein.

The Rose Quartet, Thomas Cumella; (D) Tee Scatuorchio; (S) Loren Sherman; (C) Thomas L. Keller; (SD) Stewart Werner and Chuck London
The Baltimore Waltz, Paula Vogel; (D) Anne Bogart; (S) Loy Arcenas; (C) Walker Hicklin; (SD) John Gromada
Empty Hearts, John Bishop; (D) John Bishop; (S) John Lee Beatty; (C) Ann Roth and Bridget Kelly; (SD) Stewart Werner and Chuck London

PRODUCTIONS 1992-1993

Sound design by Chuck London and Stewart Werner unless otherwise noted.

The Destiny of Me, Larry Kramer; (D) Marshall W. Mason; (S) John Lee Beatty; (L) Dennis Parichy; (C) Melina Root
Orpheus in Love, libretto: Craig Lucas; music: Gerald Busby; (D) Kirsten Sanderson; (S) Derek McLane; (L) Debra J. Kletter; (C) Walker Hicklin; (MD) Charles Prince
Redwood Curtain, Lanford Wilson; (D) Marshall W. Mason; (S) John Lee Beatty; (L) Dennis Parichy; (C) Laura Crow
Three Hotels, Jon Robin Baitz; (D) Joe Mantello; (S) Loy Arcenas; (L) Brian MacDevitt; (C) Jess Goldstein; (SD) Scott Lehrer
And Baby Makes Seven, Paula Vogel; (D) Calvin Skaggs; (S) Derek McLane; (L) Peter Kaczorowski; (C) Walker Hicklin; (SD) Donna Riley

CitiArts Theatre

RICHARD H. ELLIOTT
Artistic Director

ANDREW F. HOLTZ
Managing Director

PHILLIP ARNOLD
Board President

1950 Parkside Drive, MS/15
Concord, CA 94519
(510) 671-3065 (bus.)
(510) 671-3388 (b.o.)
(510) 676-5726 (fax)

FOUNDED 1974
City of Concord

SEASON
Year-round

FACILITIES
Willows Theatre
Seating Capacity: 203
Stage: proscenium

Gasoline Alley Theatre
Seating Capacity: 150
Stage: flexible

Maggie Crum Theatre
Seating Capacity: 154
Stage: thrust

Studio Theatre
Seating Capacity: 100
Stage: flexible

FINANCES
July 1, 1992-June 30, 1993
Expenses: $966,800

CONTRACTS
AEA BAT

CitiArts Theatre produces small-scale, popular plays and musicals that are new, contemporary or rarely produced. CitiArts is committed to the development and production of new works and to the continued advancement of the professional actor. CitiArts strives to perpetuate the artform of live theatre by creating relationships with playwrights, designers and other theatre artists whose work will make a mark on generations to come.
—*Richard H. Elliott*

PRODUCTIONS 1991-1992

Lighting by Chris Guptill and costumes by Loren Tripp unless otherwise noted.

Grease, book, music and lyrics: Jim Jacobs and Warren Casey; (D) Andrew F. Holtz; (S) Eric Sinkkonen; (MD) Nick DiScala; (CH) Renee Pulliam; (SD) Jack McKie
The Lilies of the Field, adapt: F. Andrew Leslie, from William E. Barrett; (D) Richard H. Elliott; (S) Birch Thomas

CitiArts Theatre. Michael Page and Maura Vaughn in *The Lilies of the Field*. Photo: Judy Lepire.

Sing For Your Supper, music: Richard Rodgers; lyrics: Oscar Hammerstein, II; (D) and (CH) John Staniunas; (S) Karl Rawicz; (C) Magrita Klassen; (MD) Michael Horsley; (SD) Jack McKie
Crossing Delancey, Susan Sandler; (D) Fred Williams; (S) Peter-Tolin Baker; (L) Ellen Shireman
Smoke on the Mountain, Constance Ray; (D) Richard H. Elliott and Andrew F. Holtz; (S) Peter-Tolin Baker; (L) Kristi Zufall
The Sea Horse, Edward J. Moore; (D) Richard H. Elliott; (S) Loren Tripp; (SD) Brett Burnes

PRODUCTIONS 1992-1993

Lighting by Chris Guptill unless otherwise noted.

Arsenic and Old Lace, Joseph Kesselring; (D) Richard H. Elliott; (S) Loren Tripp; (L) Ellen Shireman; (C) Chriss Zaida; (SD) Andrew F. Holtz and Brett Burnes
Goblin Market, book adapt and lyrics: Polly Pen and Peggy Harmon, from Christina Rossetti; music: Polly Pen(D) Andrew F. Holtz; (S) Karl Rawicz; (C) Chriss Zaida; (CH) John Butterfield
Dearly Departed, David Bottrell and Jessie Jones; (D) Richard H. Elliott; (S) Eric Sinkkonen; (L) Ellen Shireman; (C) Chriss Zaida; (SD) Andrew F. Holtz and Brett Burnes

Nunsense, book, music and lyrics: Dan Goggin; (D) Richard H. Elliott; (S) Jennifer Varbalow; (L) Kristi Zufall; (C) C.E. Haynes; (MD) John Tuttle; (CH) Eduardo Armendizo
The Valentine Touch, book: Jack Wrangler; music: Bob Haber; lyrics: Hal Hackady; (D) and (CH) Neal Kenyon; (S) Jeff Rowlings; (C) George Pereira; (MD) Andrew F. Holtz; (SD) Jack McKie
Love Letters, A.R. Gurney, Jr.; (D) Dan Cawthon; (S) Robert Webb
Alabama Rain, Heather McCutchen; (D) Richard H. Elliott; (S) Kate Boyd; (C) T.J. Wilcock
Gunmetal Blues, book: Scott Wentworth; music: Craig Bohmler; lyrics: Marion Adler; (D) Davis Hall; (S) Eduardo Sicangco; (MD) Craig Bohmler
Grover, Randy Hall; (D) Cliff Fannin Baker; (S) Peter-Tolin Baker; (L) Ellen Shireman; (C) Magrita Klassen; (SD) Ron Mitchell
Closer Than Ever, conceived: Steven Scott Smith; music: David Shire; lyrics: Richard Maltby, Jr.; (D) Andrew F. Holtz; (S) Robert Webb; (C) Karen Lim; (MD) Peter Maleitzky; (CH) Renee Pulliam

City Theatre Company

MARC MASTERSON
Producing Director

CHRISTINE D. ISHAM
Director of Strategic Development

ROBERT M. FRANKEL
Board President

57 South 13th St.
Pittsburgh, PA 15203
(412) 431-4400 (bus.)
(412) 431-CITY, 431-4900 (b.o.)
(412) 431-5535 (fax)

FOUNDED 1973
City of Pittsburgh

SEASON
Sept.-May

FACILITIES
City Theatre
Seating Capacity: 275
Stage: flexible

City Theatre Lab
Seating Capacity: 99
Stage: flexible

FINANCES
July 1, 1992-June 30, 1993
Expenses: $998,000

CONTRACTS
AEA SPT

City Theatre's mission is to develop and produce plays of substance and ideas that are relevant to diverse, contemporary audiences. Its vision is to establish a community of talented and dedicated artists who collaborate in an environment which nurtures the development of challenging plays. The company firmly believes in the importance of taking artistic risks while striving for excellence. In addition, City Theatre is committed to developing an audience representative of the community in which the theatre exists, while providing the means for enhancing theatre appreciation through comprehensive education and outreach programs. As the company enters the 1993-94 season, there is a particular focus on developing unique programs—consistent with its mission—for middle and high school age audiences.

—*Marc Masterson*

PRODUCTIONS 1991-1992

Sets by Tony Ferrieri, costumes by Lorraine Venberg and sound design by Michael P. Albert unless otherwise noted.

Bricklayers, Elvira J. DiPaolo; (D) Larry John Meyers; (L) Cindy Limauro
Act Without Words I and II, Samuel Beckett; (D) Marc Masterson; (L) Bob Steinbeck
Tuesday, Jewel Walker; (D) Jewel Walker; (L) Bob Steinbeck
Miss Evers' Boys, David Feldshuh; (D) Jacqueline Yancey; (L) William O'Donnell
Seventy Scenes of Halloween, Jeffrey M. Jones; (D) Jed Allen Harris; (S) Anne Thompson; (L) R.C. Baker
Our Country's Good, adapt: Timberlake Wertenbaker, from Thomas Keneally; (D) Marc Masterson; (L) William O'Donnell

PRODUCTIONS 1992-1993

Sets by Tony Ferrieri, costumes by Lorraine Venberg and sound design by Richard Norwood unless otherwise noted.

Cabaret Verboten, conceived and adapt: Jeremy Lawrence; trans: Kathleen L. Komar, Peter Jelavich and Laurence Senelick; various composers and lyricists; (D) Jeremy Lawrence; (S) Charles McCarry; (L) R.C. Baker; (MD) Nathan Hurwitz; (CH) Tome Cousin; (SD) Michael P. Albert
Holiday Memories, adapt: Russell Vandenbroucke, from Truman Capote; (D) Susan V. Booth; (L) William O'Donnell; (C) Kim Brown
The Baltimore Waltz, Paula Vogel; (D) Jed Allen Harris; (L) Norman Russell
Evelyn and the Polka King, John Olive; music: Carl Finch and Bob Lucas; lyrics: Bob Lucas; (D) Marc Masterson; (L) William O'Donnell; (MD) Bob Lucas
Temptation, Vaclav Havel; trans: Marie Winn; (D) Mladen Kiselov; (S) Cletus Anderson; (L) William O'Donnell
The Man Who Lived Underground, adapt: Marc Masterson and Don Marshall, from Richard Wright; (D) Marc Masterson; (L) Richard Norwood; (C) Angela M. Vesco; (SD) Jack Etheridge

Clarence Brown Theatre Company

THOMAS P. COOKE
Artistic Director

MARGARET FERGUSON
General Manager

ROBERT C. PARROTT
Board Chairperson

206 McClung Tower
Knoxville, TN 37996
(615) 974-6011 (bus.)
(615) 974-5161 (b.o.)
(615) 974-8546 (fax)

FOUNDED 1974
Anthony Quayle, Ralph G. Allen

SEASON
Sept.-June

FACILITIES
Clarence Brown Theatre
Seating Capacity: 600
Stage: proscenium

Clarence Brown Theatre Lab
Seating Capacity: 125
Stage: thrust

Carousel Theatre
Seating Capacity: 350
Stage: flexible

FINANCES
July 1, 1991-June 30, 1992
Expenses: $618,354

CONTRACTS
AEA LORT (D)

The Clarence Brown Theatre Company is the professional component of the theatre program of the University of Tennessee and is intended to provide the university community and the American southeast region with theatre of the highest caliber. The company has a distinguished tradition of presenting the finest professional theatre and is committed to the development of new plays. It has brought to regional audiences such performances as Anthony Quayle in *Macbeth*, Simon Ward in Isherwood's *A Meeting by the River*, and Zoe Caldwell and Dame Judith Anderson in *Medea*. During the past four seasons, the company has participated in the development of an International Theatre Research Center at UT.

—*Thomas P. Cooke*

PRODUCTIONS 1991-1992

Sets by Jim Moran, lighting by John Horner, costumes by Marianne Custer and sound design by David Emberton unless otherwise noted.

When the Nightingale Sings, book and lyrics: Joyce Carol Thomas; music: Steven Roberts; (D) Stan Brown; (MD) Paul Jones; (CH) Sian Edwards
I'm Not Rappaport, Herb Gardner; (D) Richard Jennings; (L) Jim Moran; (C) Kendra Johnson
Les Liaisons Dangereuses, adapt: Christopher Hampton, from Choderlos de Laclos; (D) Albert J. Harris

City Theatre Company. Larry John Meyers and Martin Giles in *Temptation*.
Photo: Suellen Fitzsimmons.

Clarence Brown Theatre Company. Pamela J. Hurley, Robert Hock, Barry Mulholland, Kelly Woodruff and Catharine Curzon in *A Man for All Seasons*.

PRODUCTIONS 1992-1993

Lighting by John Horner, costumes by Bill Black and sound design by David Emberton unless otherwise noted.

A Man For All Seasons, Robert Bolt; (D) Albert J. Harris; (S) William J. Windsor
Man and Superman, George Bernard Shaw; (D) Thomas P. Cooke; (S) Robert Cothran
Driving Miss Daisy, Alfred Uhry; (D) Robert Mashburn; (S) Jim Moran; (L) L.J. DeCuir; (C) Marianne Custer

Classic Stage Company (CSC)

(Formerly CSC Repertory Ltd.)

DAVID ESBJORNSON
Artistic Director

PATRICIA TAYLOR
Managing Director

TURNER P. SMITH
Board President

136 East 13th St.
New York, NY 10003
(212) 477-5808 (bus.)
(212) 677-4210 (b.o.)
(212) 477-7504 (fax)

FOUNDED 1967
Christopher Martin

SEASON
Sept.-May

FACILITIES
CSC Theatre
Seating Capacity: 180
Stage: flexible

FINANCES
July 1, 1991-June 30, 1992
Expenses: $672,753

CONTRACTS
AEA letter of agreement

Classic Stage Company exists to discover and reinterpret classical dramatic literature and to bring it innovatively to the stage. Located in New York City's East Village, CSC is committed to a theatre of language, theatricality and relevant subject matter. We actively encourage contemporary American playwrights from a variety of cultural backgrounds to create new translations and adaptations of classic plays, which we develop through our Classic Contenders readings and workshops. City Stages for City Students offers free matinees to New York City students, and our new Classic Adventures series draws young audiences to CSC's mainstage classics.

—*David Esbjornson*

Note: During the 1991-92 season, Carey Perloff served as artistic director.

PRODUCTIONS 1991-1992

Bon Appetit!, adapt: Mark Shulgasser, from Ruth Draper and Julia Child; music: Lee Hoiby; (D) Carey Perloff; (S) Donald Eastman; (L) Mary Louise Geiger; (C) Rita Riggs and Jean Putch
Cabaret Verboten, conceived and adapt: Jeremy Lawrence; trans: Kathleen L. Komar, Peter Jelavich and Laurence Senelick; various composers and lyricists; (D) Charles Randolph-Wright and Carey Perloff; (S) Donald Eastman; (L) Mary Louise Geiger; (C) Gabriel Berry
Creditors, August Strindberg; trans: Paul Walsh; (D) Carey Perloff; (S) Donald Eastman; (L) Frances Aronson; (C) Candice Donnelly
Candide, adapt: Len Jenkin, from Voltaire; music and lyrics: David Lang; (D) David Esbjornson and Carey Perloff; (S) Hugh Landwehr; (L) Brian MacDevitt; (C) Teresa Snider-Stein; (CH) Lesley Farlow; (SD) John Kilgore

PRODUCTIONS 1992-1993

Goodnight Desdemona (Good Morning Juliet), Ann-Marie MacDonald; (D) David Esbjornson; (S) Donald Eastman; (L) Brian MacDevitt; (C) C.L. Hundley; (SD) John Kilgore
Scapin, book adapt: Shelley Berc and Andrei Belgrader, from Moliere; music and lyrics: Rusty Magee; (D) Andrei Belgrader; (S) Anita Stewart; (L) Stephen Strawbridge; (C) Candice Donnelly and Elizabeth Hope Clancy
Krapp's Last Tape, Samuel Beckett; (D) and (S) David Esbjornson; (L) Brian MacDevitt; (C) Jessica Grace; (SD) Dan Schreier

Classic Stage Company (CSC). Michael McCormick and Stanley Tucci in *Scapin*. Photo: T. Charles Erickson.

The Cleveland Play House. Howard Hesseman and Michele Tauber in *Man of the Moment*. Photo: Richard Termine.

The Cleveland Play House

JOSEPHINE R. ABADY
Artistic Director

DEAN R. GLADDEN
Managing Director

ROBERT A. BLATTNER
Board President

Box 1989
Cleveland, OH 44106
(216) 795-7010 (bus.)
(216) 795-7000 (b.o.)
(216) 795-7005 (fax)

FOUNDED 1915
Raymond O'Neill

SEASON
Sept.-June

FACILITIES
Kenyon C. Bolton Theatre
Seating Capacity: 612
Stage: proscenium

Francis E. Drury Theatre
Seating Capacity: 503
Stage: proscenium

Charles S. Brooks Theatre
Seating Capacity: 159
Stage: proscenium

FINANCES
July 1, 1992-June 30, 1993
Expenses: $6,700,000

CONTRACTS
AEA LORT (C) and TYA

The Cleveland Play House is America's oldest not-for-profit theatre, founded in 1915. We are an American theatre—our repertory reflects our view of contemporary American society through the exploration of new plays and new ways of interpreting American and world classics. Our first priority has always been the quality of the work on our stages, and more than half our resources are allocated to new-play development and production, including DiscoveReads, our annual new-play development series, and world and American premieres by such authors as Arthur Miller, Tennessee Williams, Bertolt Brecht, Alan Ayckbourn and Paul Zindel. Other programs include the MFA candidate's Lab Company, a children's theatre series and many special outreach initiatives. We provide the artists who work here with an environment that fosters creativity and experimentation, participation and commitment, and with an audience that is an active partner in creating theatre. For as we sit together in the dark—laughing, crying and experiencing live performance—we discover the best that we are as human beings.
—*Josephine R. Abady*

PRODUCTIONS 1991-1992

Sound design by Jeffrey Montgomerie.

The Night of the Iguana, Tennessee Williams; (D) Larry Arrick; (S) Ursula Belden; (L) Ann G. Wrightson; (C) Deborah Shaw
David's Mother, Bob Randall; (D) Josephine R. Abady; (S) James Morgan; (L) Marc B. Weiss; (C) C.L. Hundley
You Can't Take It With You, George S. Kaufman and Moss Hart; (D) Peter Mark Schifter; (S) David Potts; (L) Ann G. Wrightson; (C) Karen Krenz
Spunk, adapt: George C. Wolfe, from Zora Neale Hurston; music: Chic Street Man; (D) Claude Purdy; (S) David Potts; (L) Susan A. White; (C) Paul Tazewell
The Heidi Chronicles, Wendy Wasserstein; (D) Roger T. Danforth; (S) Vaughan Edwards; (L) Richard Devin; (C) Linda Fisher
A Quarrel of Sparrows, James Duff; (D) Kenneth Elliott; (S) David Potts; (L) Mary Jo Dondlinger; (C) John Glaser
Man of the Moment, Alan Ayckbourn; (D) Josephine R. Abady; (S) David Potts; (L) Richard Winkler; (C) Linda Fisher
Days of Wine and Roses, JP Miller; (D) Jack Hofsiss; (S) David Jenkins; (L) Peter Kaczorowski; (C) Julie Weiss

PRODUCTIONS 1992-1993

Sound design by Jeffrey Montgomerie.

Of Thee I Sing, book: George S. Kaufman and Morrie Ryskind; music: George Gershwin; lyrics: Ira Gershwin; (D) Peter Mark Schifter; (S) Lawrence Miller; (L) Richard Winkler; (C) David C. Paulin; (MD) Evans Haile; (CH) Ted Pappas
Fugue, Leonora Thuna; (D) Kenneth Frankel; (S) Marjorie Bradley Kellogg; (L) Ann G. Wrightson; (C) Jess Goldstein
The Philadelphia Story, Philip Barry; (D) Sheldon Epps; (S) James Leonard Joy; (L) Jeff Davis; (C) Judy Dearing
Jar the Floor, Cheryl L. West; (D) Tazewell Thompson; (S) and (L) Joseph P. Tilford; (C) Kay Kurta
The Misanthrope, Moliere; adapt: Neil Bartlett; (D) Roger T. Danforth; (S) Bob Phillips, Jr.; (L) Richard Winkler; (C) Mimi Maxmen
The Butcher's Daughter, Wendy Kesselman; (D) Leslie Swackhamer; (S) Tony Straiges; (L) Beverly Emmons; (C) Paul Tazewell
The House of Blue Leaves, John Guare; (D) Josephine R. Abady; (S) David Potts; (L) Dennis Parichy; (C) Linda Fisher
Heartbeats, conceived: Amanda McBroom and Bill Castellino; book, music and lyrics: Amanda McBroom; addtl music: Gerald Sternbach, Michael Brourman, Tom Snow and Craig Safan; (D) and (CH) Bill Castellino; (S) Linda Hacker; (L) Richard Winkler; (C) Charlotte M. Yetman; (MD) Ann-Carol Pence

Cleveland Public Theatre

JAMES A. LEVIN
Artistic Director

AMANDA SHAFFER
Producing Director

C. ELLEN CONNALLY
Board Chairperson

6415 Detroit Ave.
Cleveland, OH 44102
(216) 631-2727
(216) 523-1440 (fax)

FOUNDED 1983
James A. Levin

SEASON
Year-round

FACILITIES
Seating Capacity: 99-240
Stage: flexible

FINANCES
July 1, 1992-June 30, 1993
Expenses: $290,000

Cleveland Public Theatre's purpose is to serve the serious emerging theatre artist by providing both resources and a nurturing environment, allowing the artist to explore forms and styles, the dynamics of the human condition, and man's/woman's relationship to the earth, death, life and other beings. We encourage the taking of risks in both form and substance, believing that the arts should confront and examine the political and social milieu which shapes our lives. To this end, many of Cleveland Public Theatre's resources are directed not only at the artist but at members of the public who are not traditionally theatregoers. For example, we target inner-city youth for outreach and theatre training with the hope that if we can tap into the joy, passion and desperation of these lives, this will one day translate into a ripple of affirmation and possibility. We produce and present a wide range of performance genres: plays, dance, music, performance art and interdisciplinary work, and we are particularly committed to emerging artists in our region.

—James A. Levin

PRODUCTIONS 1991-1992

The Balcony, Jean Genet; adapt: James Slowiak and Lisa Wolford; (D) James Slowiak; (S) Douglas-Scott Goheen; (L) Andrew Kaletta; (C) Pamela Keech

Sonic Disturbance, conceived: Dennis Maxfield and Amy Sparks; (D) Dennis Maxfield and Amy Sparks; (L) Andrew Kaletta; (SD) Rich Masarik

Volare, Dario D'Ambrosi; (D) Dario D'Ambrosi; (S) and (C) Silvia Tramparullo and Carmela Spiteri; (L) Howard Thies

The Light Inside, Ann St. James; (D) Lee Worley; (S) Debbie Malcolm; (L) Leslie Moynihan; (C) Barbara J. Quill; (SD) Chris Shimp

Night, Night Max, Michael Salinger; (D) Michael Salinger; (S) and (C) The Nova Lizard Project; (L) Leslie Moynihan; (SD) Ron Slabe

10th Festival of New Plays: Various playwrights; various directors; (L) Andrew Kaletta

Kitchen Table U, conceived: Yvetta; book and lyrics: Yvetta, Linda Thomas-Jones, Andika and Kenyette Adrine-Robinson; music: Linda Thomas-Jones and Yvetta; (D) Yvetta; (S) David Ellison and John Rivera-Resto; (L) Dennis Dugan; (MD) Linda Thomas-Jones; (CH) Yvetta and Linda Thomas-Jones

Play, Samuel Beckett, **Quarks**, William Borden and **Maximum Tumescence: A Triptych of the Geometry of Love**, Edmund Santa Vicca; (D) Alan Trethewey; (S) and (C) Hazel Reid; (L) Andrew Kaletta

The Chapel of Perpetual Desire Presents A Liturgical Circus of Religious Fervor and Live Sex on Stage, conceived: Amanda Shaffer; book: Linda Eisenstein and Amanda Shaffer (with CPT ensemble); music and lyrics: Linda Eisenstein; (D) and (S) Amanda Shaffer; (L) Andrew Kaletta; (C) Elizabeth Gardner and Amanda Shaffer; (MD) and (SD) Karen E. Bull; (CH) Lisa Seppi

Map of My Mother, Mike Geither; (D) Rob Handel; (S) and (C) Mike Geither; (L) Andrew Kaletta

PRODUCTIONS 1992-1993

Path With No Moccasins, Shirley Cheechoo; (D) Richard Greenblatt; (S) James Plaxton; (L) Patsy Lang; (C) Blake Debassige; (SD) Evan Turner

A Girl's Guide to Chaos, Cynthia Hempel; (D) Amanda Shaffer; (S) Dennis Marold; (L) Debbie Malcolm; (C) Terri Gelzer

Social Work: An Election Year Fantasy, Joan Holden, Gregory R. Tate and Tanya Shaffer; (D) and (S) Daniel Chumley; (C) Lorenza Elena Marcais

The Christopher Columbus Follies, Cathy Cevoli, with the Underground Railway Theatre; (D) Downing Cless and Wes Sanders; (S) David Fichter; (L) Carl Wieting; (C) Carson M. Eddy

The Recital of the Bird, adapt: Massoud Saidpour, from Avecinna and **The Ancients**, James Slowiak; (D) Massoud Saidpour (*The Recital of the Bird*), James Slowiak (*The Ancients*; (S) and (C) Inda Blatch-Geib; (L) Max Barton, II

Power Pipes, Spiderwoman Theatre (Lisa Mayo, Gloria Miguel and Muriel Miguel); (S) Nancy Bardawil

11th Festival of New Plays: Various playwrights; various directors; (L) Andrew Kaletta

A Rat's Mass, Adrienne Kennedy and **The Life of a Worm**, kj Warren; (D) Caroline Jackson-Smith; (S) Blake Ketchum; (L) Dennis Dugan; (C) Hazel Reid; (SD) Jordan Davis

The Scarlet Letters, Frank Green; (D), (S), (L) and (C) Frank Green; (SD) Luigi Bob-Drake

The Prince of Madness, Dario D'Ambrosi; (D) Dario D'Ambrosi; (S) and (C) Carmela Spiteri; (L) Marcello Iazzetti

Mother's Work, James Slowiak; (D) James Slowiak; (S) Douglas-Scott Goheen; (L) Andrew Kaletta; (C) Inda Blatch-Geib

The Karmic Games, book and lyrics: Michael Sepesy; music: Karen E. Bull and Michael Sepesy; (D) Amanda Shaffer; (S) R.C. Naso and Jennifer Cuthbertson; (L) Jason Jaffery; (C) Terri Gelzer; (MD) and (SD) Karen E. Bull

Cleveland Public Theatre. Asha Padamadan in *Mother's Work*. Photo: Robert Schnellbacher.

Coconut Grove Playhouse

ARNOLD MITTELMAN
Producing Artistic Director

VICKI GRAYSON
General Manager

STEPHEN O'FARRELL
Board Chairman

3500 Main Highway
Miami, FL 33133
(305) 442-2662 (bus.)
(305) 442-4000 (b.o.)
(305) 444-6437 (fax)

FOUNDED 1977
Players Repertory Theater

SEASON
Nov.-June

FACILITIES
Arthur F. & Alice E. Adams Mainstage
Seating Capacity: 1,130
Stage: proscenium

Encore Room
Seating Capacity: 135
Stage: flexible

FINANCES
July 1, 1992-June 30 1993
Expenses: $3,850,000

CONTRACTS
AEA LORT (B) and (D)

The work of Coconut Grove Playhouse, Florida's largest regional theatre, complements Miami's role as a multicultural world capital. A priority is to create work, dramatic and musical, that is truly developing a new theatre literature by American or international artists whose roots and/or themes are Latin. The Playhouse presents residents and international tourists with innovative and original world, national and regional premieres, including the world premieres of *Tango Pasion*, Cy Coleman's *Let 'Em Rot!* and *The Big Love*, which transferred directly to Broadway, as did *Run for Your Wife*. Productions of *Matador* and the world premieres of *Mixed Blessings*, *Fame: the Musical* and *Miami Lights* moved to national and international stages. The Playhouse's

Coconut Grove Playhouse. Gustavo Marcelo Russo, Armando Orzuza, Pilar Alvarez and Luis Castro in *Tango Pasion*. Photo: Jo Winstead.

multifaceted educational/outreach programs make theatre accessible to the community, while its classes and in-school tours expose young people to relevant social issues they encounter as members of a culturally diverse community.
—Arnold Mittelman

PRODUCTIONS 1991-1992

Sound design by Steve Shapiro unless otherwise noted.

Blues in the Night, conceived: Sheldon Epps; various composers and lyricists; (D) Sheldon Epps; (S) and (L) Douglas D. Smith; (C) Ellis Tillman; (MD) Rahn Coleman; (CH) Patricia Wilcox; (SD) Philip G. Allen

Tales of Tinseltown, book and lyrics: Michael Colby; music: Paul Katz; (D) and (CH) Tony Stevens; (S) James Tilton; (L) John Hastings; (C) Lindsay W. Davis; (MD) David Krane; (SD) Philip G. Allen

Forever Plaid, book: Stuart Ross; various composers and lyricists; (D) and (CH) Stuart Ross; (S) Neil Peter Jampolis; (L) Jane Reisman; (C) Debra Stein; (MD) James Raitt; (SD) Philip G. Allen

I Hate Hamlet, Paul Rudnick; (D) Robert Kalfin; (S) Tony Straiges; (L) James Tilton; (C) Ellis Tillman

The Substance of Fire, Jon Robin Baitz; (D) Tony Giordano; (S) and (L) James Tilton; (C) Ellis Tillman

Too Short to be a Rockette, conceived: Gary Smith; book: Buz Kohan and Bruce Vilanch; music: Larry Grossman, et al; lyrics: Buz Kohan, et al; (D) Gary Smith; (S) Roy Christopher; (L) Ken Billington; (C) Ret Turner; (MD) Vincent Falcone; (CH) Walter Painter; (SD) Philip G. Allen

The Lady from Havana, Luis Santeiro; (D) Max Ferra; (S) Stephen Lambert; (L) Todd Wren; (C) Ellis Tillman

Family Secrets, Sherry Galser and Greg Howell; (D) Irene Pinn, after Art Wolff; (S) Stephen Lambert; (L) Todd Wren; (C) Ellis Tillman

Agape, conceived: Judith Delgado and Patricia Dolan Gross; music: Fred Desena; lyrics: Patricia Dolan Gross; (D) Patricia Dolan Gross; (S) Stephen Lambert; (C) Ellis Tillman; (MD) Fred Desena

PRODUCTIONS 1992-1993

Sound design by Steve Shapiro unless otherwise noted.

Give 'Em Hell, Harry!, Samuel Gallu; (D) Samuel Gallu; (S) Stephen Lambert; (L) Todd Wren

Tango Pasion, conceived: Mel Howard; various composers and lyricists; (D) Mel Howard; (S) and (C) John Falabella; (L) Richard Pilbrow and Dawn Chiang; (MD) Jose Libertella and Luis Stazo; (SD) Jan Nebozenko

Lips Together, Teeth Apart, Terrence McNally; (D) Tony Giordano; (S) and (L) James Tilton; (C) Ellis Tillman

Don't Dress for Dinner, adapt: Robin Hawdon, from Marc Camoletti; (D) Pamela Hunt; (S) and (L) James Tilton; (C) Ellis Tillman

Him, Her & You, conceived: Robert Shields; (D) Robert Shields; (S) James Tilton; (L) John McLain; (C) Carolyn Ford

Beau Jest, James Sherman; (D) Robert Kalfin; (S) and (L) James Tilton; (C) Ellis Tillman

Marriage Play, Edward Albee; (D) Arnold Mittelman; (S) and (L) James Tilton; (C) Ellis Tillman

Carreno, Pamela Ross; (D) Gene Frankel; (S) Stephen Lambert; (L) Todd Wren

Sweet Justice, Patricia Dolan Gross; (D) Patricia Dolan Gross; (S) Stephen Lambert; (C) Ellis Tillman

The Colony Studio Theatre

BARBARA BECKLEY
Producing Director

AMANDA DIAMOND
Managing Director

1944 Riverside Drive
Los Angeles, CA 90039
(213) 665-0280 (bus.)
(213) 665-3011 (b.o.)
(213) 667-3235 (fax)

FOUNDED 1975
Terrance Shank, Barbara Beckley, Michael Wadler

SEASON
Year-round

FACILITIES
Studio Theatre Playhouse
Seating Capacity: 99
Stage: thrust

FINANCES
Oct. 1, 1991-Sept. 30, 1992
Expenses: $275,680

CONTRACTS
AEA 99-seat theatre plan

At the Colony Studio Theatre, we strive with every production to create a direct emotional connection, a sense of warmth and intimacy between artists and audience. This intent informs everything we do, from the plays we select to the performing style we foster, and even extends to the way we train our house staff. As a result, we have a unique and personal relationship with our audience, which continues to grow year after year. (We are now over 90 percent subscribed and are looking for a larger space.) We produce familiar classics, previously produced plays that may have been overlooked, and new works. In selecting plays, we reject current trends towards political correctness, negativism, alienation and confrontation for its own sake. Our goal is to present a balance of dramas, comedies and musicals that entertain, uplift and enlighten, and have a particular resonance for today's audiences.
—Barbara Beckley

The Colony Studio Theatre. Lisa Beezley, Lisa Gates and Ceptembre Anthony in *The Farndale Avenue Housing Estate Townswomen's Guild Dramatic Society Murder Mystery*. Photo: Joe Lambie.

PRODUCTIONS 1991-1992

Sets by Susan Gratch and lighting by Ted C. Giammona unless otherwise noted.

The Farndale Avenue Housing Estate Townswomen's Guild Dramatic Society Murder Mystery, David McGillivray and Walter Zerlin, Jr.; (D) David McGillivray; (L) Debra Garcia Lockwood

To Grandmother's House We Go, Joanna M. Glass; (D) Scott Segall; (S) D. Silvio Volonte; (L) Jamie McAllister; (SD) Vince Acosta

True West, Sam Shepard; (D) David Rose; (S) D. Silvio Volonte; (L) Russell Boris; (SD) Vince Acosta

Oxford's Will, Jerry Fey; (D) Jules Aaron; (L) J. Kent Inasy and D. Silvio Volonte

The Lion in Winter, James Goldman; (D) Gordon D. Lee; (L) D. Silvio Volonte; (C) Don Woodruff; (SD) Vince Acosta

Candide, book adapt: Hugh Wheeler, from Voltaire; music: Leonard Bernstein; lyrics: Richard Wilbur; addtl lyrics: Stephen Sondheim and John LaTouche; (D) and (CH) Evan Weinstein; (L) Jamie McAllister; (MD) Steven Applegate

Waiting for the Parade, John Murrell; (D) Carol Newell; (L) Russell Boris; (C) Don Woodruff; (SD) Michael Wadler

PRODUCTIONS 1992-1993

Sets by Susan Gratch and lighting by Ted C. Giammona unless otherwise noted.

The Front Page, Ben Hecht and Charles MacArthur; (D) David Rose; (L) Guido Girardi; (SD) Michael Wadler

Tomfoolery, music and lyrics: Tom Lehrer; (D), (L) and (CH) Todd Nielsen

When the Bough Breaks, Robert Clyman; (D) Michael Haney; (S) D. Silvio Volonte; (L) Jamie McAllister; (SD) John Fisher

The Fantasticks, book adapt and lyrics: Tom Jones, from Edmond Rostand; music: Harvey Schmidt; (D), (C) and (CH) Don Woodruff; (L) Russell Boris; (MD) Tom Boyer

Rags, book: Joseph Stein; music: Charles Strouse; lyrics: Stephen Schwartz; (D) and (CH) Todd Nielsen; (L) Ted Ferreira; (MD) Steven Applegate; (SD) Todd Meier

I Can Fit My Fist in My Mouth, Carissa Channing; (D) David Rose; (L) Russell Boris; (SD) Annie Heller and Jeffrey Steefel

17 Days, Rick Garman; (D) Robert O'Reilly; (S) Richard D. Bluhm; (L) Ken Booth; (SD) Paul Anthony Navarro

Cornerstone Theater Company

BILL RAUCH
Artistic Director

ALISON CAREY
Founding Director

STEPHEN GUTWILLIG
Managing Director

JACK MONDERER
Board Chair

1653 18th St., #6
Santa Monica, CA 90404
(310) 449-1700
(310) 453-4347 (fax)

FOUNDED 1986
Alison Carey, Bill Rauch

SEASON
Year-round

FINANCES
July 1, 1991-June 30, 1992
Expenses: $347,363

Cornerstone Theater Company works alone as a professional ensemble and in collaboration with diverse communities across the United States. The consensus-run ensemble spent six years producing epic interactions between classic plays and specific rural communities: Moliere's disintegrating and combative families in the Kansas farmland, Shakespeare's civil strife in the segregated streets of Mississippi, Aeschylus' ancient rituals on the modern Native American reservation. In 1992, Cornerstone settled in Los Angeles to create shows with and for this city's underserved, multilingual residents, while continuing to pursue projects nationwide. Recent projects include an updated Sanskrit epic performed in English, Spanish, Mandarin and Korean with 30 residents of a downtown housing complex for seniors. The ensemble increasingly works with diverse professional guest artists and commissions new plays and adaptations. Cornerstone uses theatre to build bridges between disparate communities, uniting people through the creative process. We work to help build a new, inclusive American theatre.

—*Bill Rauch*

PRODUCTIONS 1991-1992

Music and lyrics by David Reiffel, direction by Bill Rauch and sets by Lynn Jeffries.

The Winter's Tale: An Interstate Adventure, book adapt: company, from William Shakespeare; (L) Mary-Ann Greanier; (C) Lynn Jeffries and Jeanne E. Amis; (MD) David Reiffel; (CH) Sabrina Peck; (SD) Bruce Odland

I Can't Pay the Rent, company-developed; (C) Lynn Jeffries

PRODUCTIONS 1992-1993

Direction by Bill Rauch and sets and costumes by Lynn Jeffries unless otherwise noted.

The Toy Truck, adapt: Peter Sagal and company, from King Sudraka; (L) Loren Brame; (SD) Nathan Wong

A Midsummer Night's Dream, adapt: company, from William Shakespeare; (C) Sal Taschetta and Lynn Jeffries

Rushing Waters, book and lyrics: Migdalia Cruz; music: Danny Vicente, Darren Brady and LaRue Marshall; (L) Geoff Korf; (MD) Danny Vicente and Darren Brady; (CH) Jan Kirsch

Cornerstone Theater Company. Donahue Tom, Jaqueline DeSantiago, Harris Craig, Jr. and Joanne Takahashi in *Rushing Waters*.

The Coterie

JEFF CHURCH
Artistic Director

JOETTE M. PELSTER
Executive Director

LYDIA BUTLER
Board President

2450 Grand Ave.
Kansas City, MO 64108
(816) 474-6785 (bus.)
(816) 474-6552 (b.o.)
(816) 474-6785 (fax)

FOUNDED 1979
Judith Yeckel, Vicky Lee

SEASON
Year-round

FACILITIES
Seating Capacity: 220-234
Stage: flexible

FINANCES
Jan. 1, 1992-Dec. 31, 1992
Expenses: $475,525

The Coterie is a professional theatre dedicated to presenting theatre for all ages that educates as well as entertains. By producing a wide range of material, be it classic or contemporary, original scripts or adaptations of classic works of literature, we strive to break through existing stereotypes of what children want or can comprehend—to present material which challenges traditional views of theatre for young audiences and which opens lines of communication among races, sexes and generations.

—*Jeff Church*

PRODUCTIONS 1992

Sets and costumes by Brad Shaw, lighting by Art Kent and sound design by Greg Mackender unless otherwise noted.

The Red Badge of Courage, adapt: Thomas W. Olson, from Stephen Crane; (D) Terry O'Reagan and Jeff Church; (C) Mary Traylor

Most Valuable Player, Mary Hall Surface and the California Theatre Center; (D) Chris Glaze; (S) Jeff Robinson

Mr. Raccoon & His Friends, adapt: Lisa Cordes, from Eugene McCarthy; (D) Jeff Church; (C) Gayla Voss

Neverland, adapt: Patricia Ludwick, from James M. Barrie; (D) Jeff Church; (C) Mary Traylor

The Red Sneaks, book, music and lyrics: Elizabeth Swados; (D) Lisa Cordes; (S) Laura Burkhart; (MD) Molly Jessup; (CH) Brad Shaw

The Meeting, Jeff Stetson; (D) Brad Shaw

Winnie the Pooh, adapt: Kristen Sergel, from A.A. Milne; (D) Linda Ade Brand; (S) Laura Burkhart

PRODUCTIONS 1993

Direction by Jeff Church, sets and costumes by Brad Shaw, lighting by Art Kent and sound design by Greg Mackender unless otherwise noted.

Oliver Twist, adapt: Terry O'Reagan, from Charles Dickens; (C) Patrick Shanahan

Wolf Child: The Correction of Joseph, Edward Mast; (S) Laura Burkhart; (C) Celena Mayo Fernandez

Blazing the Outback, Marlo Morgan; (S) and (C) Celena Mayo Fernandez

Bunnicula, adapt: James Sie, from James Howe; music and lyrics: Douglas Wood and James Sie; (D) Linda Ade Brand; (S) Celena Mayo Fernandez; (MD) Molly Jessup

Dinosaurus, Edward Mast and Lenore Bensinger; (S) Brad Shaw and Ron Megee; (C) Lynda K. Myers

Anne of Green Gables, adapt: Joanna Blythe, from L.M. Montgomery; (C) Gayla Voss

My Children! My Africa!, Athol Fugard; (C) Gregg Benkovich

Winnie the Pooh, adapt: Kristen Sergel, from A.A. Milne; (D) Brad Shaw

The Coterie. David Solovieff and Miles McBroome in *Oliver Twist*. Photo: Marianne Kilroy.

Court Theatre

NICHOLAS RUDALL
Executive Director

SANDRA KARUSCHAK
Managing Director

ROBERT McDERMOTT
Board Chair

5535 South Ellis Ave.
Chicago, IL 60637
(312) 702-7005 (bus.)
(312) 753-4472 (b.o.)
(312) 702-6417 (fax)

FOUNDED 1955
Nicholas Rudall

SEASON
Sept.-June

FACILITIES
Abelson Auditorium
Seating Capacity: 251
Stage: thrust

FINANCES
July 1, 1992-June 30, 1993
Expenses: $1,610,000

CONTRACTS
AEA CAT

Through fresh interpretations of the classics and contemporary masterworks, Court Theatre presents a repertory that reflects and challenges our culturally diverse patrons. Court has produced such works as the American premiere of Mustapha Matura's *Playboy of the West Indies*, Wole Soyinka's *The Lion and the Jewel* and the world premiere adaptations of *Creation* and *The Passion* from *The Mystery Cycle*. In the 1992-93 season, Court Theatre established the Associate Artist Program, the latest step in our long-range plan for restoring artistic collaboration to all phases of professional theatre. Associate artists serve as a "think tank" in developing repertory, and will collaborate as a nuclear company in the repertory's creation and production. Since 1981, Court has also been a leader in extensive education and outreach programs for students and adults. Each season our high school matinee program serves 3,500 students whose schools range from Chicago's inner city to suburban areas.

—*Nicholas Rudall*

PRODUCTIONS 1991-1992

Candide, book adapt: Hugh Wheeler, from Voltaire; music: Leonard Bernstein; lyrics: Richard Wilbur, addtl lyrics: Stephen Sondheim and John LaTouche; (D) Travis Stockley; (S) Katherine Ross; (L) John Culbert; (C) Frances Maggio, (MD) Barbara Schubert

Measure for Measure, William Shakespeare; (D) Nicholas Rudall; (S) and (C) Jeff Bauer; (L) Rita Pietraszek; (SD) David Zerlin

The Mystery Cycle: Creation, adapt: Bernard Sahlins, from the English Mystery plays; (D) Nicholas Rudall and Bernard Sahlins; (S) and (C) John Paoletti and Mary Griswold; (L) Michael S. Philippi; (SD) Robert Neuhaus

The Gigli Concert, Tom Murphy; (D) William Woodman; (S) Joseph Nieminski; (L) Robert Christen; (C) Nanette Acosta; (SD) David Zerlin

Comedians, Trevor Griffiths; addtl material: Aaron Freeman; (D) Barney Simon; (S) and (C) Jeff Bauer; (L) Rita Pietraszek

PRODUCTIONS 1992-1993

Othello, William Shakespeare; (D) Eric Simonson; (S) John Musial; (L) Peter Gottlieb; (C) Karin Simonson Kopischke; (SD) Brian Reed

Court Theatre. *The Mystery Cycle: Creation*. Photo: Matthew Gilson.

The House of Blue Leaves, John Guare; (D) Philip Killian; (S) Joseph Nieminski; (L) Rita Pietraszek; (C) Frances Maggio; (SD) David Zerlin

The Mystery Cycle: Creation and *The Passion*, adapt: Bernard Sahlins, from the English Mystery plays; (D) Nicholas Rudall and Bernard Sahlins; (S) and (C) Mary Griswold and Fortuna Taxi; (L) Michael S. Philippi; (SD) Robert Neuhaus

Electra, Sophocles; trans: Nicholas Rudall; (D) Mikhail Mokeiev; (S) John Culbert; (L) Rita Pietraszek; (C) Jeff Bauer; (SD) David Zerlin

Pantomine, Derek Walcott; (D) Jonathan Wilson; (S) and (L) Michael S. Philippi; (C) Jeff Bauer; (SD) Joe Cerqua

Crossroads Theatre Company

RICARDO KHAN
Artistic Director

KENNETH B. McCLAIN
Managing Director

FRANK A. BOLDEN
Board President

7 Livingston Ave.
New Brunswick, NJ 08901
(908) 249-5581 (bus.)
(908) 249-5560 (b.o.)
(908) 249-1861 (fax)

FOUNDED 1978
Ricardo Khan, L. Kenneth Richardson

SEASON
Sept.–May

FACILITIES
Seating Capacity: 264
Stage: thrust

FINANCES
July 1, 1992–June 30, 1993
Expenses: $2,600,000

CONTRACTS
AEA LORT (D)

We exist in a society that persists in perpetuating images on screen and stage that depict black people in socially limited, culturally deprived and spiritually debilitating ways. This fact has reinforced the sense of despair felt by so many black artists—those who can, through their art and the media, help correct these social misperceptions. Artists are among the most powerful of truth messengers and must, therefore, be encouraged to sing above the confusing sounds of despair and cause art to resound with a power that renews. This is why at Crossroads, we choose not to design seasons of plays but of people. Our associate artists program supports African-American writers, directors, actors and designers, asking them, "What have you always dreamed of working on, but for some reason never could?" By providing a "safe haven" for artists like Ruby Dee, Avery Brooks, Micki Grant, George C. Wolfe, Mbongeni Ngema, Sandra Reaves, Denise Nicholas and Leslie Lee, we have produced significant contributions to world theatre and spawned a new generation of black innovators.
—*Ricardo Khan*

PRODUCTIONS 1991-1992

Black Orpheus, OyamO; music: Ray Hollman; (D) Ricardo Khan; (S) Daniel Proett; (L) Bill Grant; (C) Toni-Leslie James; (CH) Dianne MacIntyre; (SD) Rob Gorton

Oak and Ivy, Kathleen McGhee-Anderson; (D) Shirley Jo Finney; (S) Peter Harrison; (L) Natasha Katz; (C) Myrna Colley-Lee

The Love Space Demands, Ntozake Shange; music: Billy "Spaceman" Patterson; (D) Talvin Wilks; (S) Richard Carroll; (L) Heather Carson; (C) Toni-Leslie James; (CH) Micki Davidson; (SD) Carmen Whip

The Talented Tenth, Richard Wesley; (D) Harold Scott; (S) John Ezell; (L) Jackie Manassee; (C) Susan Soetaert; (SD) Carmen Whip

The Genesis Festival:
The Disappearance, adapt: Ruby Dee, from Rosa Guy; (D) Kenneth Johnson
Mothers, Kathleen McGhee-Anderson; (D) Shirley Jo Finney
Koulaba, Joseph Walker; (D) Joseph Walker
Willie and Esther, James Graham Bronson; (D) Dwight Cook
Kate's Sister, Maisha Baton; (D) Dawn Renee Jones
A Family Affair, Andrea Loney; (D) Seret Scott
Dream, Anna Deavere Smith; (D) Ricardo Khan

PRODUCTIONS 1992-1993

Slow Dance on the Killing Ground, William Hanley; (D) Kenneth Johnson; (S) John Ezell; (L) Shirley Prendergast; (C) Mary Mease Warren; (SD) Dan Hochstine and Robert LaPierre

Crossroads Theatre Company. Khalil Kain and Ruby Dee in *The Disappearance*. Photo: Rich Pipeling.

Betsey Brown, book adapt: Ntozake Shange and Emily Mann, from Ntozake Shange; music: Baikida Carroll; lyrics: Ntozake Shange, Emily Mann and Baikida Carroll; (D) Ricardo Khan; (S) David Mitchell; (L) Jackie Manassee; (C) Toni-Leslie James; (MD) Tom Bridwell; (CH) George Faison; (SD) Rob Gorton

The Disappearance, adapt: Ruby Dee, from Rosa Guy; (D) Harold Scott; (S) John Ezell; (L) Jackie Manassee; (C) Theoni V. Aldredge; (SD) Rob Gorton

Mothers, Kathleen McGhee-Anderson; (D) Shirley Jo Finney; (S) Peter Harrison; (L) Victor En Yu Tan; (C) Myrna Colley-Lee; (SD) Janet Kalas

The Late Great Ladies of Blues & Jazz, adapt: Sandra Reaves, various composers and lyricists; (D) Ricardo Khan; (S) Daniel Proett; (L) Shirley Prendergast; (SD) Rob Gorton

The Genesis Festival:
Sunshine Playlot, Dominic Taylor; (D) Donald Douglass
Acted Within Proper Departmental Procedure, John Redwood; (D) Lillie-Marie Redwood
Talking Bones, Shay Youngblood; (D) Laurie Carlos
And the World Laughs, Karimah; (D) Ricardo Khan
Homer Gee and the Raphsodies, Ifa Bayeza; (D) Talvin Wilks

Cumberland County Playhouse

JIM CRABTREE
Producing Director

KATHY VANLANDINGHAM
Staff and Financial Manager

STEVEN C. DOUGLAS
Board Chairperson

Box 484
Crossville, TN 38557
(615) 484-4324 (bus.)
(615) 484-5000 (b.o.)

FOUNDED 1965
Margaret Keyes Harrison, Moses Dorton, Paul Crabtree

SEASON
Year-round

FACILITIES
Mainstage
Seating Capacity: 478
Stage: proscenium

Theater-in-the-Woods
Seating Capacity: 199
Stage: arena

Adventure Theater
Seating Capacity: 150-220
Stage: flexible

FINANCES
Jan. 1, 1992-Dec. 31, 1992
Expenses: $958,969

CONTRACTS
AEA Guest Artist

Our home is a town of 6,500 in a rural Appalachian county where we serve more than 90,000 people a year, drawn from the greater Knoxville-Nashville-Chattanooga region. We combine a resident company with guest artists drawn largely from the Southeast, and produce a broad repertoire of new works and revivals, musicals and opera. A major focus for us is new work rooted in rural America, Tennessee and Appalachia.
—*Jim Crabtree*

PRODUCTIONS 1992

Steel Magnolias, Robert Harling; (D) Mary Crabtree; (S) John Partyka; (L) and (SD) Stephen Shaw; (C) Renee Garrett

Tales of a Fourth Grade Nothing, adapt: Bruce Mason, from Judy Blume; (D) and (SD) Austin Tichenor; (S) Dan Backlund; (L) John Partyka; (C) Renee Garrett

Jesus Christ Superstar, music: Andrew Lloyd Webber; lyrics: Tim Rice; (D) Jim Crabtree; (S) Leonard Harman; (L) John Partyka; (C) Johann Stegmeir; (MD) Ann Crabtree; (CH) Pam Atha-Harrod; (SD) Matthew Parker

The 1940's Radio Hour, book: Walton Jones; various composers and lyricists; (D) and (CH) Abigail Crabtree; (S) Ron Keller; (L) Michael D. Klima; (C) Renee Garrett; (MD) Stephen Purdy; (SD) Victor Mecyssne

South Pacific, book adapt: Oscar Hammerstein, II and Joshua Logan, from James A. Michener; music: Richard Rodgers; lyrics: Oscar Hammerstein, II; (D) Mary Crabtree; (S) Leonard Harman; (L) Ken White; (MD) Ann Crabtree; (SD) Victor Mecyssne

Of Mice and Men, adapt: Carlisle Floyd, from John Steinbeck; music: Carlisle Floyd; (D) Jim Crabtree; (S) Leonard Harman; (L) Ken White; (C) Sarah Buchanan; (MD) Jonathan May

To Kill a Mockingbird, adapt: Christopher Sergel, from Harper Lee; (D) and (S) Jim Crabtree; (L) John Partyka; (C) Renee Garrett

Anne of Green Gables, book adapt: Donald Harron, from L.M. Montgomery; music: Norman Campbell; lyrics: Donald Harron and Norman Campbell; (D) and (CH) Abigail Crabtree; (S) and (L) Leonard Harman; (C) Mary Crabtree; (MD) JR McAlexander; (SD) Matthew Parker

Amahl and the Night Visitors, book, music and lyrics: Gian Carlo Menotti; (D) and (S) Jim Crabtree; (L) John Partyka; (C) Renee Garrett; (MD) Jonathan May; (CH) Stephanie Lynge; (SD) Matthew Parker

PRODUCTIONS 1993

You're a Good Man, Charlie Brown, book, music and lyrics: Clark Gesner; (D) Mark Cabus; (S) Jim Crabtree; (L) John Partyka; (C) Renee Garrett; (MD) Charles Irvin; (CH) Stephanie Lynge

I Remember Mama, adapt: John Van Druten, from Kathryn Forbes; (D) Jim Crabtree; (S) Leonard Harman; (L) Wally Eastland; (C) Renee Garrett

The Women of Troy, adapt: Don Taylor, from Euripides; (D) Abigail Crabtree; (S) Jim Crabtree; (L) Steve Woods; (C) Virginia Johnson

Big River, book adapt: William Hauptman, from Mark Twain; music and lyrics: Roger Miller; (D) Abigail Crabtree; (S) Leonard Harman; (L) Ted Doyle; (C) Virginia Johnson; (MD) JR McAlexander; (SD) Jim Crabtree and Heather Nichols

Pump Boys and Dinettes, John Foley, Mark Hardwick, Debra Monk, Cass Morgan, John Schimmel and Jim Wann; (D) and (S) Jim Crabtree; (L) John Partyka; (C) Renee Garrett; (MD) JR McAlexander; (SD) Howard Rose

The Foreigner, Larry Shue; (D) Abigail Crabtree; (S) and (L) John Partyka; (C) Renee Garrett

Oklahoma!, book adapt and lyrics: Oscar Hammerstein, II, from Lynn Riggs; music: Richard Rodgers; (D) Abigail Crabtree; (S) Joseph Varga; (L) John Horner; (C) Mary Crabtree; (MD) Ann Crabtree; (CH) Stephanie Lynge; (SD) Jim Crabtree and Heather Nichols

The Grapes of Wrath, adapt: Frank Galati, from John Steinbeck; (D) Jim Crabtree; (S) Leonard Harman; (L) Steve Woods; (C) Renee Garrett; (SD) Jim Crabtree and Heather Nichols

Christy, book adapt and lyrics: Sandy Kalan and Shirley Dolan,

Cumberland County Playhouse. Robert Marshall and Carol Ann Edwards in *Of Mice and Men*. Photo: Chase J. Glass.

from Catherine Marshall; music: Sandy Kalan and Ken McCaw; (D) Jim Crabtree; (S) Leonard Harman; (L) Ted Doyle; (C) Renee Garrett; (MD) Ann Crabtree; (CH) Michele Colvin; (SD) Howard Rose
The Boys Next Door, Tom Griffin; (D) Mary Crabtree
Cinderella, book adapt and lyrics: Oscar Hammerstein, II, from Charles Perrault; music: Richard Rodgers; (D) Abigail Crabtree; (L) Ted Doyle

Dallas Theater Center

RICHARD HAMBURGER
Artistic Director

ROBERT YESSELMAN
Managing Director

MRS. ROBERT TED ENLOE, III
Board Chairman

3636 Turtle Creek Blvd.
Dallas, TX 75219-5598
(214) 526-8210 (bus.)
(214) 526-8857 (b.o.)
(214) 521-7666 (fax)

FOUNDED 1959
Robert D. Stecker, Sr., Beatrice Handel, Paul Baker, Dallas Citizens

SEASON
Sept.-June

FACILITIES
Kalita Humphreys Theater
Seating Capacity: 466
Stage: thrust

Arts District Theater
Seating Capacity: 500
Stage: flexible

FINANCES
July 1, 1991-June 30, 1992
Expenses: $3,620,346

CONTRACTS
AEA LORT (C) and (D)

Located as it is in the very heart of our country, the Dallas Theater Center aims to create a national theatre center, galvanizing and uniting artists from the region and around the country. The Theater Center is committed to supporting the work of the most exciting, daring and uncompromising theatre artists, as well as to serving its richly diverse community through the plays it presents and the many special programs it offers—from the humanities series to Project Discovery, an outreach program serving thousands of students throughout the area. Utilizing our two exciting mainstage spaces and our many studio spaces, we present a wide array of work that attempts to push the boundaries of conventional theatrical form and language. Our primary focus is on the fresh reinterpretation of the classics and on the exploration of innovative new plays in all stages of development, as may be seen in our Big D Festival of the Unexpected.
—*Richard Hamburger*

PRODUCTIONS 1991-1992

Costumes by Donna M. Kress and sound design by Lamar Livingston unless otherwise noted.

A Midsummer Night's Dream, William Shakespeare; (D) David Petrarca; (S) Russell Metheny; (L) James F. Ingalls; (SD) Rob Milburn
The Substance of Fire, Jon Robin Baitz; (D) Richard Hamburger; (S) Anita Stewart; (L) Christopher Akerlind; (SD) David Budries
A Christmas Carol, book adapt: Adrian Hall, from Charles Dickens; music and lyrics: Richard Cumming; (D) Randy Moore; (S) E. David Cosier, Jr.; (L) Russell H. Champa; (CH) Claire Williamson
The Importance of Being Earnest, Oscar Wilde; (D) Malcolm Morrison; (S) John Iacovelli; (L) Russell H. Champa
I Hate Hamlet, Paul Rudnick; (D) Lou Salerni; (S) Jerry R. Williams; (L) David Martin Jacques
Miss Evers' Boys, David Feldshuh; (D) Claude Purdy; (S) James D. Sandefur; (L) Christina Giannelli; (SD) Dwight Andrews
Taking Steps, Alan Ayckbourn; (D) Lou Salerni; (S) Jerry R. Williams; (L) Russell H. Champa

PRODUCTIONS 1992-1993

Costumes by Donna M. Kress and sound design by Lamar Livingston unless otherwise noted.

Dallas Theater Center. Jennifer Griffin and Liz Mikel in *A Streetcar Named Desire*. Photo: Carl Davis.

A Streetcar Named Desire, Tennessee Williams; (D) Richard Hamburger; (S) Christopher Barreca; (L) Christopher Akerlind; (C) Martha Hally; (SD) Janet Kalas
A Christmas Carol, book adapt: Dennis Powers and Laird Williamson, from Charles Dickens; music: Lee Hoiby and Tim Weil; lyrics: Laird Williamson; (D) Lonny Price; (S) William Barclay; (L) Phil Monat; (MD) Tim Weil; (CH) Joey McKneely; (SD) David Natinsky
Another Time, Ronald Harwood; (D) Vivian Matalon; (S) and (L) Neil Peter Jampolis
The Misanthrope, Moliere; trans: Neil Bartlett; (D) Jackson Phippin; (S) Tony Straiges; (L) Christopher Akerlind; (C) Robert Wojewodski
Spunk, adapt: George C. Wolfe, from Zora Neale Hurston; music: Chic Street Man; (D) Reggie Montgomery; (S) Anita Stewart; (L) Donald Holder; (CH) Stephanie Berry
A Doll House, Henrik Ibsen; trans: Christopher Hampton; (D) Richard Hamburger; (S) Christopher Barreca; (L) Stephen Strawbridge; (C) Robert Wojewodski; (SD) Janet Kalas
Lady Day at Emerson's Bar and Grill, Lanie Robertson; (D) Victoria Bussert; (S) Russ Borski; (L) Mary Jo Dondlinger; (SD) Charles Kinnard

The Big D Festival of the Unexpected:
The America Play, Suzan-Lori Parks; (D) Liz Diamond; (S) Riccardo Hernandez; (L) Deborah Reitman; (C) Donna M. Kress; (SD) Guy Whitemore
Porcelain, Chay Yew; (D) Richard Hamburger; (S) Beje Fort; (L) Ed Schmitt; (C) Donna M. Kress
Simpatico, Roger Babb; music: 'Blue' Gene Tyranny; (D) Roger Babb; (S) Michael Fajans; (L) Pat Dignan; (C) Gabriel Berry, with Angela Wendt; (CH) Rocky Bornstein

48 DAVID GORDON/PICK UP COMPANY

David Gordon/Pick Up Company. Scott Cunningham, Jonathan Walker, Karen Evans-Kandel and Gayle Tufts in *The Mysteries and What's So Funny?* Photo: Jack Vartoogian.

David Gordon/Pick Up Company

DAVID GORDON
Director

JUNE POSTER
Managing Director

131 Varick St., Room 901
New York, NY 10013
(212) 627-1213
(212) 627-1005 (fax)

FOUNDED 1971
David Gordon

SEASON
Variable

FINANCES
July 1, 1992-June 30, 1993
Expenses: $533,000

The Pick Up Company provides a stable yet fluid structure through which I can create and present my work in live performance and media. The number of performers and type of venue vary according to the project. My work functions across forms. Language is used as dialogue, as commentary to suggest circumstance and/or relationship. Sometimes the words are our music. Most frequently the music is taped, layered and referential. The design elements, performance clothing, objects, visual devices are usually determined early enough in the rehearsal period to facilitate their integration into the action, to connect them with the movement. The movement is eclectic, sometimes gestural, sometimes balletic, sometimes eccentric, always connected to a base of pedestrian, behavioral activity. I find, in retrospect, that there are recurring themes in my work. Art, Life, Connection and Relationship, Communication, Death, and the determination not to repeat myself.
—*David Gordon*

PRODUCTIONS 1991-1993

The Mysteries and What's So Funny?, David Gordon; music: Philip Glass; (D) and (CH) David Gordon; (S) and (C) Red Grooms; (L) Dan Kotlowitz; (MD) Alan Johnson; (SD) David Meschter

Delaware Theatre Company

CLEVELAND MORRIS
Artistic Director

DAVID EDELMAN
Managing Director

PETER H. FLINT
Board Chairman

200 Water St.
Wilmington, DE 19801
(302) 594-1104 (bus.)
(302) 594-1100 (b.o.)
(302) 594-1107 (fax)

FOUNDED 1979
Cleveland Morris,
Peter DeLaurier

SEASON
Oct.-Apr.

FACILITIES
Seating Capacity: 389
Stage: proscenium

FINANCES
July 1, 1992-June 30, 1993
Expenses: $1,166,649

CONTRACTS
AEA letter of agreement

The Delaware Theatre Company is the state's only professional theatre. We seek to offer an encompassing, diverse examination of the art of theatre through our annual programs that mix well-known classics with unknown new plays, as well as lesser-known vintage plays with familiar contemporary works. In all cases, we seek plays of lasting social and literary value, worthy of thoughtful consideration by both artist and viewer, and produced in a style designed to strengthen the force of the playwright's language and vision. Our presentations are produced in a boldly modern facility that opened in November 1985, located on Wilmington's historic riverfront. The company offers a wide variety of ancillary and educational programs in an effort to assist the general public in finding the art of theatre an ongoing and joyful addition to their lives and community.
—*Cleveland Morris*

PRODUCTIONS 1991-1992

Lighting by Bruce K. Morriss and costumes by Marla Jurglanis unless otherwise noted.

Amadeus, Peter Shaffer; (D) Cleveland Morris; (S) Eric Schaeffer; (SD) Joseph K. Dombroski

Delaware Theatre Company. Gerald Richards, Maureen Silliman, Stanja Lowe and Timothy Wahrer in *The Cocktail Hour*. Photo: Richard C. Carter.

Cotton Patch Gospel, book: Tom Key and Russell Treyz, from Clarence Jordan; music and lyrics: Harry Chapin; (D) Danny Peak; (S) Rebecca G. Frederick
T Bone N Weasel, Jon Klein; (D) Cleveland Morris; (S) Karen TenEyck
Noel Coward at the Cafe de Paris, Will Stutts; music and lyrics: Noel Coward; (D) Adelle S. Rubin; (S) William Werner
The Price, Arthur Miller; (D) Alex Dmitriev; (S) Eric Schaeffer

PRODUCTIONS 1992-1993

Costumes by Marla Jurglanis unless otherwise noted.

Antigone, Jean Anouilh, after Sophocles; adapt: Lewis Galantiere; (D) Cleveland Morris; (S) Dan Boylen; (L) Curt Senie; (SD) Rich Leibfried
Mountain, Douglas Scott; (D) John Henry Davis; (S) Philipp Jung and Peter Harrison; (L) Dennis Parichy; (C) David C. Woolard; (SD) John Gromada
The Matchmaker, Thornton Wilder; (D) Cleveland Morris; (S) Lewis Folden; (L) Rebecca G. Frederick; (SD) Rich Leibfried
The Immigrant, Mark Harelik; (D) Howard J. Millman; (S) Lewis Folden; (L) Ken Lapham
The Cocktail Hour, A.R. Gurney, Jr.; (D) Allan Carlsen; (S) Eric Schaeffer; (L) Christopher Gorzelnik

Dell'Arte Players Company

MICHAEL FIELDS, DONALD FORREST, JOAN SCHIRLE
Co-Artistic Directors

BOBBI RICCA
Administrative Director

Box 816
Blue Lake, CA 95525
(707) 668-5663
(707) 668-5665 (fax)

FOUNDED 1971
Jael Weisman, Alain Schons, Joan Schirle, Carlo Mazzone-Clementi, Jane Hill, Michael Fields, Jon Paul Cook

SEASON
Year-round touring
Mad River Festival in July

FACILITIES
Dell'Arte Studio
Seating Capacity: 100
Stage: flexible

Dell'Arte Amphitheatre
Seating Capacity: 250
Stage: thrust

FINANCES
Oct. 1, 1991-Sept. 30, 1992
Expenses: $333,464

CONTRACTS
AEA letter of agreement

Dell'Arte Players Company is a rurally based touring theatre ensemble which performs nationally and internationally. The four core-company artists share 16 years of collaborative work on original theatre pieces. Our nonurban point of view and themes for many of our major works come from the California north coast where we live. The creative focus of our original work is on strong textual values expressed in a highly physical performance style; the integration of acting, text, music, movement and content is a primary goal of our ensemble process. Our unique style has brought invitations to perform with regional repertory theatres in large-scale works such as Peter Barnes's *Red Noses*. We also do extended teaching residencies and extensive outreach in our rural region. Our commitment to influencing theatre through traditional popular forms is also reflected in the training we offer at the Dell'Arte School of Physical Theatre. As recognition of our work grows, we move closer toward our vision of becoming an international center for the exploration and development of physical theatre traditions and their relationship to contemporary forms.
—*Michael Fields*

PRODUCTIONS 1991-1992

Direction by Jael Weisman and lighting by Michael Foster unless otherwise noted.

Redwood Curtain: The Scar Tissue Mystery Trilogy
Intrigue at Ah-Pah, Michael Fields, Donald Forrest, Joan Schirle, Jael Weisman, Steve Most and Mara Sabinson; music: Lisa Garcia and Joan Schirle; (S) Alain Schons; (C) Cindy Claymore; (MD) Gina Leishman
The Road Not Taken, Michael Fields, Donald Forrest, Joan Schirle and Jael Weisman; music: Tony Heimer; (S) Ivan Hess; (C) Nancy Betts; (MD) Gina Leishman
Fear of Falling, Michael Fields, Donald Forrest, Joan Schirle and Jael Weisman; music: Gina Leishman; (S) Alain Schons; (C) Mary Scott; (MD) Gina Leishman

Malpractice or Love's the Best Doctor, adapt: Michael Fields, Donald Forrest, Michele Linfante and Jael Weisman, from Moliere; (S) Andy Stacklin; (C) Mimi Mace
The Truly Remarkable Turkey Drive of 1912, Peter Buckley; (D) Michael Fields; (S) Raymond Gutierrez; (C) Mary Scott

PRODUCTIONS 1992-1993

Lighting by Michael Foster.

Korbel, Michael Fields, Donald Forrest, Joan Schirle and Jael Weisman; (D) Jael Weisman; (S) Raymond Gutierrez; (C) Jinkie Lee Boyce; (SD) Stephan Vernier
Punch!, Joan Schirle; (D) Michael Fields; (S) Raymond Gutierrez; (C) Mary Scott; (SD) Walter Whitney
Slapstick, Michael Fields, Donald Forrest, Joan Schirle and Jael Weisman; music: Gina Leishman; (D) Jael Weisman; (S) Alain Schons; (C) Nancy Jo Smith; (MD) Gina Leishman
Blowin Smoke, Jane Hill; (D) Joan Schirle; (S) Raymond Gutierrez; (C) Mary Scott; (SD) Patrick Gavin
The Wreck of the Good Ship "Humboldt", Peter Buckley; (D) Michael Fields; (S) Raymond Gutierrez; (C) Mary Scott; (SD) Stephan Vernier

Dell'Arte Players Company. Mikael Kingvall in *Punch!* Photo: Lezley Troxell.

Denver Center Theatre Company

DONOVAN MARLEY
Artistic Director

KEVIN K. MAIFELD
Executive Director

BARBARA E. SELLERS
Producing Director

DONALD R. SEAWELL
Board Chairman

1050 13th St.
Denver, CO 80204
(303) 893-4000 (bus.)
(303) 893-4100 (b.o.)
(303) 825-2117 (fax)

FOUNDED 1980
Donald R. Seawell

SEASON
Sept.-June

FACILITIES
The Stage
Seating Capacity: 550
Stage: thrust

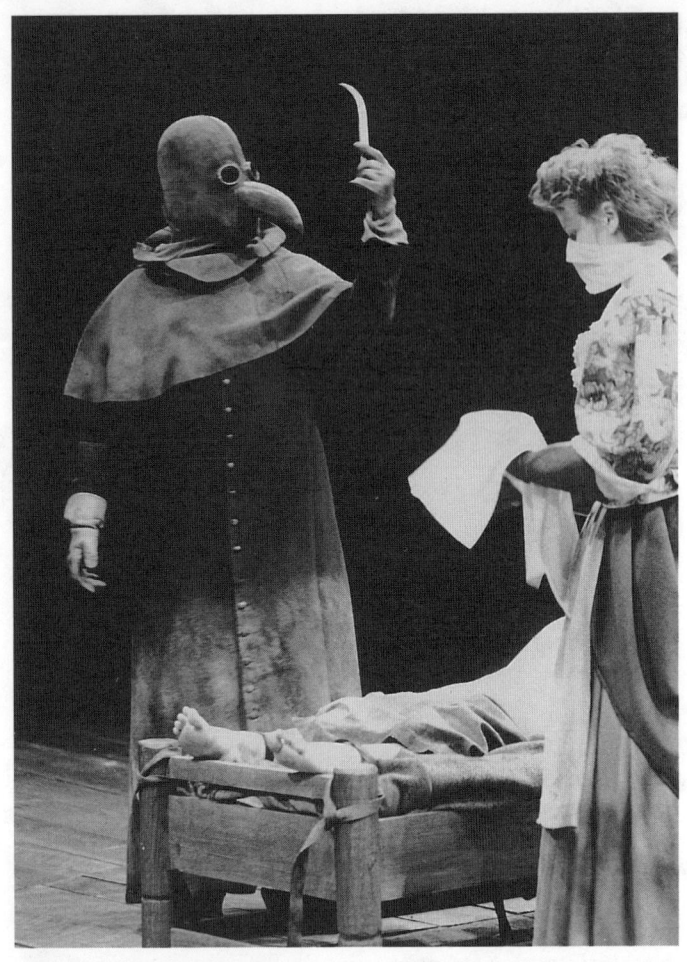

Denver Center Theatre Company. Sean Hennigan and Katherine Heasley in *The Living*. Photo: Terry Shapiro.

The Space
Seating Capacity: 450
Stage: arena

The Source
Seating Capacity: 154
Stage: thrust

The Ricketson
Seating Capacity: 195
Stage: proscenium

FINANCES
July 1, 1992-June 30, 1993
Expenses: $5,080,650

CONTRACTS
AEA LORT (C) and (D), and TYA

The Denver Center Theatre Company is a resident ensemble committed to the long-range development of a production style unique to this Rocky Mountain company. Central to this search is the operation of a theatre conservatory that clarifies and unifies the work of our professional artists through ongoing training. Our mature artists pursue company continuity through the selection and training of young artists to sustain the ideals, disciplines and traditions of the company. A vigorous play development program is designed to search for playwrights to give the ensemble a regional voice with global perspective. One-third to one-half of each season is comprised of world premieres. The remainder of a 12-production season examines world classics from a contemporary perspective, and explores both the major works of preeminent American playwrights and lost or obscure works that deserve to be reintroduced into the American repertoire.
—*Donovan Marley*

PRODUCTIONS 1991-1992

Lighting by Charles R. MacLeod and costumes by Andrew V. Yelusich unless otherwise noted.

The Rose Tattoo, Tennessee Williams; (D) Laird Williamson; (S) Andrew V. Yelusich; (SD) Joel Underwood

Other People's Money, Jerry Sterner; (D) Donovan Marley; (S) Bill Curley; (C) Barbara Bush; (SD) Jim Kaiser

Home, Samm-Art Williams; (D) Israel Hicks; (S) Richard L. Hay; (C) Patricia A. Whitelock; (SD) Joel Underwood

A Christmas Carol, book adapt: Dennis Powers and Laird Williamson, from Charles Dickens; music: Lee Hoiby and Tim Weil; lyrics: Laird Williamson; (D) Laird Williamson; (S) Robert Blackman; (CH) Ann McCauley

Julius Caesar, William Shakespeare; (D) Laird Williamson; (S) Andrew V. Yelusich; (L) Don Darnutzer; (SD) Joel Underwood

To Kill a Mockingbird, adapt: Christopher Sergel, from Harper Lee; (D) Randal Myler; (S) Vicki Smith; (C) Barbara Bush; (SD) Jim Kaiser

Tartuffe, Moliere; trans: Richard Wilbur; (D) Nagle Jackson; (S) Vicki Smith; (L) Don Darnutzer; (C) Michael Ganio; (SD) Joel Underwood

Arsenic and Old Lace, Joseph Kesselring; (D) Randal Myler; (S) Andrew V. Yelusich; (SD) Jim Kaiser

They Shoot Horses, Don't They?, book adapt and lyrics: Nagle Jackson, from Horace McCoy; music: Robert Sprayberry; (D) Alan Bailey; (S) Andrew V. Yelusich; (MD) Deborah R. Lapidus; (CH) Edie Cowan; (SD) Jim Kaiser

Uncertainty, Garrison Esst; (D) Anthony Powell; (S), (L) and (C) Pavel Dobrusky; (SD) Joel Underwood

Wolf-Man, Elizabeth Egloff; (D) Evan Yionoulis; (S), (L) and (C) Pavel Dobrusky; (SD) Joel Underwood

Evil Little Thoughts, Mark D. Kaufmann; (D) Israel Hicks; (S) Bill Curley; (L) Robert A. Keosheyan; (C) Nancy Bassett; (SD) Jim Kaiser

PRODUCTIONS 1992-1993

Lighting by Charles R. MacLeod and costumes by Andrew V. Yelusich unless otherwise noted.

The Grapes of Wrath, adapt: Frank Galati, from John Steinbeck; (D) Donovan Marley; (S) and (L) Pavel Dobrusky; (C) Jeannie Davidson; (SD) Jim Kaiser

Candida, George Bernard Shaw; (D) Anthony Powell; (S) Andrew V. Yelusich; (SD) Joel Underwood

A Christmas Carol, book adapt: Dennis Powers and Laird Williamson, from Charles Dickens; music: Lee Hoiby and Tim Weil; lyrics: Laird Williamson; (D) Laird Williamson; (S) Robert Blackman; (CH) Ann McCauley; (SD) Jim Kaiser

The Piano Lesson, August Wilson; (D) Israel Hicks; (S) Bill Curley; (C) Barbara Bush; (SD) Joel Underwood

A Quiet Little Wedding, adapt: Laird Williamson, from Eugene Labiche and Marc Michel; music: Larry Delinger; (D) Laird Williamson; (S) Richard Seger; (L) Don Darnutzer; (MD) Samuel Lancaster; (CH) Ann McCauley; (SD) Jim Kaiser

Hedda Gabler, Henrik Ibsen; trans: Csanad Z. Siklos; adapt: Douglas Hughes; (D) Nagle Jackson; (S) Vicki Smith; (SD) Joel Underwood

A Connecticut Yankee in King Arthur's Court, adapt: Randal Myler, from Mark Twain; (D) Randal Myler; (S) and (L) Pavel Dobrusky; (C) Barbara Bush; (SD) Jim Kaiser

The Man Who Wrote Peter Pan, John Fraser; (D) John Fraser; (S) Bill Curley

Bon Voyage, book: Jeffrey Hatcher; music and lyrics: Noel Coward; (D) Bruce K. Sevy; (S) Andrew V. Yelusich; (L) Don Darnutzer; (MD) Scott Warrender; (CH) Chad Henry; (SD) Jim Kaiser

The Living, Anthony Clarvoe; (D) Nagle Jackson; (S) Vicki Smith; (C) Lyndall L. Otto; (SD) Joel Underwood

Monte Carlo, Lydia Stryk; (D) Jennifer McCray Rincon; (S) Richard L. Hay; (L) Robert A. Keosheyan; (C) Patricia A. Whitelock; (SD) Joel Underwood

Detroit Repertory Theatre

BRUCE E. MILLAN
Artistic Director

FRED WILLIAMS
Board Chair

13103 Woodrow Wilson Ave.
Detroit, MI 48238
(313) 868-1347
(313) 868-1705 (fax)

FOUNDED 1957
Bruce E. Millan, Barbara
Busby, T. O. Andrus

SEASON
Nov.-June

FACILITIES
Seating Capacity: 196
Stage: proscenium

FINANCES
Jan. 1, 1992-Dec. 31, 1992
Expenses: $314,997

CONTRACTS
AEA SPT

The Detroit Repertory's purpose over the past 35 years has been to build a first-class professional theatre by assembling a resident company of theatre artists recruited from among local professionals in the field; to seed new plays and bring worthwhile forgotten plays back to life; to expand the creative possibilities of theatre by increasing the opportunities for participation of all artists regardless of their ethnic or racial origins or gender; to reach out to initiate the uninitiated; to build a theatre operation that is "close to the people" by acting as a catalyst for the revitalization of the neighborhood in which the theatre resides; and to attract audiences reflecting the cultural and ethnic diversity of southeastern Michigan.
—*Bruce E. Millan*

PRODUCTIONS 1991-1992

Lighting by Kenneth R. Hewitt, Jr., costumes by B.J. Essen and sound design by Burr Huntington unless otherwise noted.

Detroit Stories, Kim Carney, Janet Pound and Stephen Mack Jones; (D) Barbara Busby; (S) Marylynn Kacir
Miss Evers' Boys, David Feldshuh; (D) Yolanda Fleischer; (S) Bruce E. Millan
Other People's Money, Jerry Sterner; (D) Bruce E. Millan; (S) Richard J. Smith and Bruce E. Millan
Scully and Royce, Jeffrey Haddow; (D) Dolores Andrus; (S) Robert Katkowsky

PRODUCTIONS 1992-1993

Lighting by Kenneth R. Hewitt, Jr., costumes by B.J. Essen and sound design by Burr Huntington unless otherwise noted.

Homeward Bound, Elliott Hayes; (D) William Boswell; (S) Robert Katkowsky; (SD) John W. De Monaco
My Children! My Africa!, Athol Fugard; (D) Barbara Busby; (S) Marylynn Kacir
Unchanging Love, adapt: Romulus Linney, from Anton Chekhov; (D) Barbara Busby; (S) Robert Katkowsky
Three Card Monte and The Royal Flush, Daniel Du Plantis; (D) Bruce E. Millan; (S) John Stevens

Detroit Repertory Theatre. Roosevelt Johnson and Mack Palmer in *Detroit Stories*. Photo: Bruce E. Millan.

El Teatro Campesino

LUIS VALDEZ
Artistic Director

PHILLIP ESPARZA
Managing Director

Box 1240
San Juan Bautista, CA 95045
(408) 623-2444
(408) 623-4127 (fax)

FOUNDED 1965
Luis Valdez

SEASON
Variable

FACILITIES
ETC Playhouse
Seating Capacity: 150
Stage: flexible

Mission San Juan Bautista
Seating Capacity: 300
Stage: arena

FINANCES
Oct. 1, 1992-Sept. 30, 1993
Expenses: $950,000

CONTRACTS
AEA SPT and LORT (D)

El Teatro Campesino continues to explore the curative, affirmative power of live perfomance on actors and audiences alike, through its global vision of society. We remain acutely aware of the role of theatre as a creator of community, in the firm belief that the future belongs to those who can imagine it. We thus imagine an America born of the worldwide cultural fusion of our times, and see as our aesthetic and social purpose the creation of theatre that illuminates that inevitable future. To achieve this purpose, our evolving complex in San Juan Bautista continues to function as a research-and-development center, a place to explore the evolution of new works, new images and new ideas. Our aim is to maintain a dynamic crossroads for talent: a place where children can work with adults, teenagers with senior citizens, professionals with nonprofessionals, Latinos with Euro-Americans, Asian Americans, Afro-Americans and Native Americans. Once works are refined in San Juan Bautista, the more successful plays and productions are produced professionally in larger urban venues. Our productions of *Corridos!*, *La Pastorela*, *Simply Maria* and *I Don't Have to Show You No Stinking Badges* are examples of this process. Our theatre work is simple, direct, complex and profound, but it works. In the heart, *el corazon*, of a way of life.
—*Luis Valdez*

PRODUCTIONS 1991-1992

Sets by Joseph Cardinalli, lighting by Lisa Larice and costumes by Leticia Arellano unless otherwise noted.

Putting Flesh Back on the Bones, company-developed; (D) Maria Candelaria and Kinan Valdez; (L) Tomas Salas and Juan Candelaria; (SD) Anahuac Valdez
Praying For Laughter, Fran Hernandez, Suzi Sanford, Anahuac Valdez, Joseph Velasco and Kirk Ward; (D), (S) and (L) Joseph Velasco; (SD) Ned Herbert

Prospect, Octavio Solis; (D) Tony Curiel
La Pastorela, adapt: Luis Valdez, from Medieval Shepherd's play; (D) Rosa Maria Escalante; (S) Victoria Petrovich; (L) Rick Larsen; (MD) David Silva; (CH) Janet Johns
How Else Am I Supposed To Know I'm Still Alive, Evelina Fernandez and *Simply Maria*, Josefina Lopez; (D) Socorro Valdez; (SD) David Silva

PRODUCTIONS 1992-1993

Sets by Joseph Cardinalli, lighting by Lisa Larice and costumes by Leticia Arellano unless otherwise noted.

Emiliano, Peter Edwards and Ana Martinez Guerrera; (D) Tony Curiel; (S) Victoria Petrovich; (L) Brenda Berry; (MD) Joseph Julian Gonzalez; (CH) Janet Johns
El Fin del Mundo, Luis Valdez; (D) and (S) Luis Valdez; (L) Milt Commons; (SD) Mino Valdez
La Virgen del Tedeyac, adapt: Luis Valdez; (D) Rosa Maria Escalante; (S) Victoria Petrovich; (L) Rick Larsen; (MD) Joseph Julian Gonzalez; (CH) Janet Johns; (SD) Pancho Rodriguez
How Else Am I Supposed To Know I'm Still Alive, Evelina Fernandez and *Simply Maria*, Josefina Lopez; (D) Amy Gonzalez; (SD) David Silva
Prospect, Octavio Solis; (D) Octavio Solis; (L) Rick Larsen; (SD) Pancho Rodriguez

El Teatro Campesino. Paulina Macias Sahagun and Carlos Gonzalez in *La Pastorela*. Photo: Brad Shirakawa.

Emmy Gifford Children's Theater

JAMES LARSON
Artistic Director

MARK HOEGER
Executive Director

SUSIE BUFFETT
Board President

3504 Center St.
Omaha, NE 68105
(402) 345-4852 (bus.)
(402) 345-4849 (b.o.)
(402) 344-7255 (fax)

FOUNDED 1949
19 child advocacy agencies, Emmy Gifford

SEASON
Sept.-June

FACILITIES
Seating Capacity: 500
Stage: proscenium

FINANCES
June 1, 1992-May 31, 1993
Expenses: $1,150,000

CONTRACTS
AEA Guest Artist

At the Emmy Gifford Children's Theater we believe that children's theatre is an exciting and suitable performance mode for experimentation. Children have different psychological and aesthetic needs from those of adults, primarily because a child's cerebral design is synaptically more active. For children, fantasy and antirealism are the norm. Thus, artists in children's theatre have startling freedom in the theatrical choices they can make to break out of the straightjacket of stultifying, ossified realism—the traditional theoretical and formal style out of which most U.S. theatre artists have developed.
—*James Larson*

PRODUCTIONS 1991-1992

Costumes by Sherri Geerdes unless otherwise noted.

The Velveteen Rabbit, book adapt and lyrics: James Still, from Margery Williams; music: Marty Magnuson; (D) Roberta Larson; (S) Greg Hill; (L) Bill Van Deest
Hansel and Gretel, adapt: Max Bush, from The Brothers Grimm; (D) James Larson; (S) and (L) Film and Stage Services
Charlie and the Chocolate Factory, adapt: Richard R. George, from Roald Dahl; (D) Michael Wilhelm; (S) Heartland Scenic Studios; (L) Steven D. Wheeldon
Humpty Dumpty, adapt: Gail Erwin, from Mother Goose; (D) Mark Hoeger; (L) Steven D. Wheeldon; (C) Kenda Slavin
A Woman Called Truth, Sandra Fenichel Asher; (D) Laura Partridge-Nedds; (S) Tracy Thies; (L) Paul Smith
White as Snow, Red as Blood, adapt: V. Clasgow Kostc, from The Brothers Grimm; (D) James Larson; (S) Larry Kaushansky; (L) Bob Welk
Charlotte's Web, adapt: Joseph Robinette, from E.B. White; (D) Kevin Ehrhart; (S) David Tidwell; (L) Tracy Thies

PRODUCTIONS 1992-1993

Lighting by Sheila Malone and costumes by Sherri Geerdes unless otherwise noted.

Rumpelstiltskin, adapt: Brenda Joyce Dubay, from The Brothers Grimm; (D) Tim Carroll; (S) Sheila Malone
Tatterhood, adapt: Robert Bly, from the Norwegian folk tale; (D) Mark Hoeger; (S) Larry Kaushansky; (L) Bob Welk
Rocky and Bullwinkle, adapt: Bruce Hurlbut, from the TV series; (D) Stephanie Anderson; (S) Greg Hill
Dandelion, Judith Martin; (D) Roberta Larson; (S) Tracy Thies; (C) Robyn Munger
The Council, William S. Yellow Robe, Jr.; (D) William S. Yellow Robe, Jr.; (S) and (L) Bill Van Deest; (S) Steve Stacy
The Dancing Spider, adapt: Marilyn Osterman and Marilyn Kluge, from West African folk tales; music: Orville Johnson; (D) Laura Partridge-Nedds; (S) and (L) Bill Van Deest; (MD) Servalia Johnson; (CH) Trudy Monette
Little Lord Fauntleroy, book adapt, music and lyrics: Gail Erwin, from Francis Hodgson Burnett; (D) Stephanie Anderson; (S) James Othuse; (MD) Lynda Oswalt; (CH) M.L. Miller

Emmy Gifford Children's Theater. Kevin Barratt and Laura Marr in *Hansel and Gretel*. Photo: James Keller.

Are You My Mother?, adapt: Doug Marr, from P.D. Eastman; music: Roberta Larson and Carole Waterman; (D) Alexander Gelman; (S) Michael Alley; (L) Mike Reese

Hansel and Gretel, adapt: Max Bush, from The Brothers Grimm; (D) James Larson; (S) and (L) Film and Stage Services

The Empty Space Theatre

EDDIE LEVI LEE
Artistic Director

MELISSA HINES
Managing Director

MONTY G. DENNISON
Board Chairman

3509 Fremont Ave. N
Seattle, WA 98103-0301
(206) 547-7633 (bus.)
(206) 547-7500 (b.o.)
(206) 547-7635 (fax—call first)

FOUNDED 1970
M. Burke Walker, James Royce, Julian Schembri, Charles Younger

SEASON
Variable

FACILITIES
Fremont Palace
Seating Capacity: 150
Stage: proscenium

FINANCES
Oct. 1, 1991–Sept. 30, 1992
Expenses: $779,073

CONTRACTS
AEA letter of agreement

The Empty Space Theatre provides an opportunity for theatre artists, as well as artists in other disciplines, to collaborate on new works and new forms in a supportive atmosphere. The Space, one of the first theatres in the country to present the works of Mamet and Shepard, is drawn mostly to contemporary, cutting-edge works, and to artists who are initiative-driven and don't take themselves so damn seriously. Most of our plays are world or Northwest premieres, with an occasional offbeat look at a classic. This year, we plan to start a Northwest Playwrights' Lab and to revive our late-night experimental series. All of our programs are grounded in the belief that, in order for theatre to be a joyous experience, artists and audience must find communion through a series of shared experiences that are challenging, unique to live theatre and ultimately inspiring.
—*Eddie Levi Lee*

Note: During the 1991-92 and 1992-93 seasons, Kurt Beattie served as artistic director.

PRODUCTIONS 1991-1992

Kitty-Kitty and *Last Supper*, Edward Sampson and Matt Smith; (D) Rita Giomi (*Kitty-Kitty*), Rita Giomi and Mark Sheppard (*Last Supper*); (L) Karl Treibs

Arden of Faversham, Anonymous; (D) John Russell Brown; (S) and (L) Tim Saternow; (C) Frances Kenny; (SD) Steven M. Klein

Wolf at the Door, Erik Ehn; (D) Susan Fenichell; (S) Peggy McDonald; (L) Michael Wellborn; (C) Sarah Winberg; (SD) Steven M. Klein

Dr. Terror's 3-D House of Theatre, company-developed, and *Blood Orgy of the Bermuda Triangle Zombie Assassins*, Eddie Levi Lee and Larry Larson; music: Peter Silbert, David Pascal and John Engerman; (D) Empty Space Ensemble; (S) Charlene Hall; (L) Rick Paulsen; (C) Paul Chi-Ming Louey; (CH) Steve Tomkins; (SD) David Pascal

Dark Rapture, Eric Overmyer; (D) Kurt Beattie; (S) Peggy McDonald; (L) Michael Wellborn; (C) Paul Chi-Ming Louey; (SD) David Pascal

The Search for Signs of Intelligent Life in the Universe, Jane Wagner; (D) Stefan Rowny and Tom Spiller; (S) Kathryn Rathke; (L) Brian Duea; (C) Sherry Lyon; (SD) David Pascal

PRODUCTIONS 1992-1993

Some Things You Need to Know Before the World Ends (A Final Evening With the Illuminati), Eddie Levi Lee and Larry Larson; (D) V. Joy Lee; (S) Gary Smoot; (L) Roberta Russell; (C) Virgil C. Johnson; (SD) David Pascal

Mad Forest, Caryl Churchill; (D) Daniel Farmer; (S) Karen Gjelsteen; (L) Cynthia Bishop; (C) Paul Chi-Ming Louey; (SD) Steven M. Klein

Hell on Wheels, Mary Lathrop; (D) Rita Giomi; (S) Charlene Hall; (L) Roberta Russell; (C) Kathleen Maki; (SD) David Pascal

En Garde Arts

ANNE HAMBURGER
Producer

KAREN DALZELL
Associate Producer/Managing Director

JON DEMBROW
Board Chairperson

The Empty Space Theatre. Rene Laigo, Babo Harrison, Gregg Loughridge, Tom Spiller and Todd Jefferson Moore in *Arden of Faversham*. Photo: Chris Bennion.

EN GARDE ARTS

En Garde Arts. *Another Person is a Foreign Country*. Photo: William Rivelli.

225 Rector Place, Suite 3A
New York, NY 10280
(212) 941-9793 (bus.)
(212) 274-8123 (b.o.)
(212) 343-1137 (fax)

FOUNDED 1986
Anne Hamburger

SEASON
Variable

FINANCES
Sept. 1, 1992-Aug. 31, 1993
Expenses: $550,000

CONTRACTS
AEA Showcase Code Tier IV and letter of agreement

I formed En Garde Arts for the following reasons: to produce site-specific theatre; to cultivate the expression of new ideas through the ongoing development of this dynamic theatrical form; to bring together every stratum of society in celebration of shared cultural and human values; to create urban spectacles of living art and architecture in collaboration with talented artists; to provide these artists with all the support a human being can muster; to become an arts organization that truly belongs and responds to the city and its people; to reawaken people to the possibilities of the artform. Since these words first announced En Garde's mission, the company has produced eight seasons of highly visual, event-oriented theatre in strange and wonderful locations throughout New York City. These plays form a body of work that defines En Garde's concept of site-specific theatre. They are performances in unconventional and distinctive settings, inspired and informed by the history and current use of the sites which serve as our stage.

—Anne Hamburger

PRODUCTIONS 1991-1992

Occasional Grace, Michael Ahn, Neena Beber, Migdalia Cruz and Talvin Wilks; (D) Bill Rauch; (L) Brian Aldous; (C) Claudia Brown; (SD) Eric Liljestrand

Another Person is a Foreign Country, Charles L. Mee, Jr.; (D) Anne Bogart; (S) Kyle Chepulis; (L) Carol Mullins; (C) Claudia Brown; (SD) Eric Liljestrand

Vanquished by Voodoo, Laurie Carlos; (D) Laurie Carlos; (S) Kyle Chepulis; (L) Brian Aldous; (C) Natalie Walker; (SD) Tim Palmer

PRODUCTIONS 1992-1993

Lighting by Brian Aldous unless otherwise noted.

Strange Feet, Mac Wellman; (D) Jim Simpson; (S) Kyle Chepulis; (C) Mary Myers; (SD) Eric Liljestrand

Cacodemon King, adapt: Bernard Chatreux, from William Shakespeare; trans: Jeffrey Kime; (D) Didier Flamand; (S) Fred Codom; (C) Mary Myers; (SD) Sheafe Walker

Marathon Dancing, Laura Harrington; (D) Anne Bogart; (L) Jason Boyd; (SD) Carlos A. Murillo

Orestes, adapt: Charles L. Mee, Jr., from Euripides; (D) Tina Landau; (S) Kyle Chepulis; (C) James Schuette; (SD) John Gromada

Ensemble Theatre of Cincinnati

DAVID A. WHITE, III
Artistic Director

JOHN W. VISSMAN
Managing Director

GORDON C. GREENE
Board Chairman

1127 Vine St.
Cincinnati, OH 45210
(513) 421-3556 (bus.)
(513) 421-3555 (b.o.)
(513) 421-8002 (fax)

FOUNDED 1985
David A. White, III

SEASON
Sept.-July

FACILITIES
Seating Capacity: 190
Stage: thrust

FINANCES
July 1, 1992-June 30, 1993
Expenses: $648,459

CONTRACTS
AEA SPT

Ensemble Theatre of Cincinnati is a professional, nonprofit artistic team dedicated to the development and presentation of new works and artistic challenges. ETC creates these new works through a unique collaborative process utilizing locally based actors, directors and designers. Our new work outreach goes beyond our subscription season; ETC's annual Young Playwright Festival and Local Playwright Workshops enhance the artistic process that we as an ensemble are seeking to create within our community. By putting the word "regional" back into regional theatre, ETC has created an artistic home for its members, as well as providing our audiences with fresh, new voices in the American theatre.

—David A. White, III

PRODUCTIONS 1991-1992

Sets by Ron Shaw, lighting by Jeff Gress and costumes by Gretchen Sears unless otherwise noted.

Everything in the Garden, adapt: Edward Albee, from Giles Cooper; (D) Edward Albee; (S) Ruth Sawyer; (L) Ron Shaw; (C) Janet Beason

Ensemble Theatre of Cincinnati. Berni Weber and Claire Slemmer in *Lotus Hooks*. Photo: Sandy Underwood.

Jack and the Beanstalk, book adapt: David A. White, III; music and lyrics: David Kisor; (D) David A. White, III; (MD) David Kisor; (CH) Mark Diamond

The Chronicles of Plague, Aralee Strange; (D) David A. White, III; (L) Anne Barnes

The School for Scandal, Richard Brinsley Sheridan; (D) Drew Fracher; (S) Ruth Sawyer; (C) Jeff Gress

Lake Street Extension, Lee Blessing; (D) Jeanne Blake; (S) Michael Blankenship

That Serious He-Man Ball, Alonzo D. Lamont, Jr.; (D) Charles Holmond; (C) Janet Beason

Downwinder Dance, Gary Stewart; (D) Gary Stewart; (C) Lori Scheper

PRODUCTIONS 1992-1993

Lighting by Jeff Gress unless otherwise noted.

After the Fall, Arthur Miller; (D) Rebecca Miller; (S) Ron Shaw; (C) Rebecca Senske

Seascape, Edward Albee; (D) Edward Albee; (S) Kevin Murphy; (C) Rebecca Senske

Cinderella, book adapt: Eric Schmiedl, from Charles Perrault; music and lyrics: David Kisor; (D) David A. White, III; (S) Ruth Sawyer; (C) Gretchen Sears; (MD) David Kisor; (CH) Mark Diamond

Lotus Hooks, Kate Dahlgren; (D) David A. White, III; (S) and (L) Ron Shaw; (C) Susan Wenman

Freemen and Lunatics, Joseph McDonough; (D) Mark Mocahbee; (S) Kevin Murphy; (C) Susan Wenman

Zorro, adapt: David Richmond and Drew Fracher, from Johnston McCulley; (D) Drew Fracher; (S) Michael Blankenship; (L) Ron Shaw; (C) Gretchen Sears; (SD) John Henry Kreitler

First Stage Milwaukee

ROB GOODMAN
Producer/Artistic Director

JOHN HEDGES
Managing Director

MARINA S. KREJCI
Board President

929 North Water St.
Milwaukee, WI 53202
(414) 273-7121 (bus.)
(414) 273-7206 (b.o.)
(414) 273-5480 (fax)

FOUNDED 1987
Archie Sarazin

SEASON
Oct.-May

FACILITIES
Todd Wehr Theater
Seating Capacity: 500
Stage: thrust

FINANCES
July 1, 1992-June 30, 1993
Expenses: $950,000

CONTRACTS
AEA TYA

First Stage Milwaukee is a theatre whose audience is young people: children, adolescents, teenagers, young adults. As a theatre for young people we are dedicated to producing works, both new and classic, which explore the world through the eyes of youth. At any given age, our world is full of mystery, wonder, joy, tragedy, and all the complexities of human relationships and experiences. First Stage Milwaukee chooses material that explores and exposes these complexities, enabling young people to understand, experience or perhaps simply acknowledge them in ways that will impact their daily lives. To this end the company uses a broad range of children's and world literature, including scripted plays and new adaptations. We believe theatre is full of possibilities for today's young people as it takes them beyond the ordinary into worlds that engage the imagination, stimulate the mind and deeply touch the heart.
—*Rob Goodman*

PRODUCTIONS 1991-1992

Direction by Rob Goodman, sets by Rick Rasmussen and lighting by Robert Zenoni unless otherwise noted.

The Ugly Duckling, book adapt: Pamela Sterling, from Hans Christian Andersen; music and lyrics: Chris Limber; (S) Charles Erven; (C) Sraa Davidson; (MD) Chris Limber; (CH) Rick Ney

First Stage Milwaukee. Lee Palmer, Margaret Pierson-Bates and Monica C. Farrell in *A Woman Called Truth*.

The Best Christmas Pageant Ever, adapt: Barbara Robinson; (S) Tom Colwin; (C) Therese Donarski

Hans Brinker or the Silver Skates, adapt: Thomas W. Olson, from Mary Maples Dodge; (C) Rick Rasmussen

Animal Farm, book adapt: Peter Hall, from George Orwell; music: Richard Peaslee; lyrics: Adrian Mitchell; (D) Michael Moynihan; (C) Rick Rasmussen

One Thousand Cranes, book: Colin Thomas; music and lyrics: Michael Silversher; (C) Deborah Kossup-Kennedy; (SD) Michael Silversher

PRODUCTIONS 1992-1993

Direction by Rob Goodman, sets by Rick Rasmussen and lighting by Robert Zenoni unless otherwise noted.

Winnie the Pooh, book adapt: Kristen Sergel, from A.A. Milne; music and lyrics: John Tanner; (S) Charles Erven; (C) Ellen Kozak; (MD) John Tanner; (CH) Elaine Parsons

The Best Christmas Pageant Ever, adapt: Barbara Robinson; (D) William Theisen; (S) Tom Colwin; (C) Therese Donarski

A Woman Called Truth, Sandra Fenichel Asher; (D) Lee Palmer; (S) Charly Palmer; (C) Amy Horst

The Outsiders, adapt: Christopher Sergel, from S.E. Hinton; (D) Jon Kretzu; (C) Rick Rasmussen; (SD) John Tanner

Heidi, adapt: Thomas W. Olson, from Johanna Spyri; (C) Rick Rasmussen

Bridge to Terabithia, book adapt and lyrics: Katherine Paterson and Stephanie Tolan, from Katherine Paterson; music: Steve Liebman; (S) Danila Korogodsky; (L) Spencer Mosse; (C) Karin Simonson Kopischke; (MD) Lisa Smith; (CH) Ron Anderson; (SD) John Tanner

Florida Studio Theatre. Charles Tuthill and Eric Tazares in *The Sum of Us*. Photo: E. Reed.

Florida Studio Theatre

RICHARD HOPKINS
Artistic Director

JAYNE DOWD
General Manager

DENNIS McGILLICUDDY
Board President

1241 North Palm Ave.
Sarasota, FL 34236
(813) 366-9017 (bus.)
(813) 366-9796 (b.o.)
(813) 955-4137 (fax)

FOUNDED 1973
Jon Spelman

SEASON
Jan.-Sept.

FACILITIES
Seating Capacity: 165
Stage: flexible

FINANCES
Oct. 1, 1991-Sept. 30, 1992
Expenses: $803,807

CONTRACTS
AEA SPT

In the 1990s Florida Studio Theatre has firmly established itself as a resident contemporary theatre presenting alternative, thought-provoking work, and as a center for creating and presenting new works in its region. Primary programs include summer and winter mainstage seasons which total seven productions dedicated to contemporary writers and serve 7,000 subscribers annually; a New Play Development program which throughout the year produces three major festivals devoted to national, Florida and young playwrights; educational programs which include children's and adult workshops, camps and a statewide in-school Write A Play tour; and the Cabaret Theatre, which produces traditional and nontraditional productions in a dinner-and-drink setting. The driving mission of FST is to cause the creation of new plays and to educate and develop audiences for these new works.

—*Richard Hopkins*

PRODUCTIONS 1991-1992

Sets by Jeffrey W. Dean, lighting by Paul D. Romance and costumes by Barbara Pope unless otherwise noted.

Heartbeats, conceived: Amanda McBroom and Bill Castellino; book, music and lyrics: Amanda McBroom; addtl music: Gerald Sternbach, Michelle Brourman, Tom Snow and Craig Safan; (D) and (CH) Bill Castellino; (C) Cheryll DeRue; (MD) Gerald Sternbach
Prelude to a Kiss, Craig Lucas; (D) Scott Burkell
Execution of Justice, Emily Mann; (D) Richard Hopkins
Greetings, Tom Dudzick; (D) Bradford Wallace; (C) Cheryll DeRue
At Wit's End, Jack Fournier; (D) Steven Ramay
Good Evening, Peter Cook and Dudley Moore; (D) Richard Hopkins
Dear Liar, adapt: Jerome Kilty, from George Bernard Shaw and Mrs. Patrick Campbell; (D) David O'Hara; (C) Cheryll DeRue

PRODUCTIONS 1992-1993

Direction by Richard Hopkins, sets by Jeffrey W. Dean and lighting by Joseph Oshry unless otherwise noted.

Oil City Symphony, Mike Craver, Debra Monk, Mark Hardwick and Mary Murfitt; (D) Richard Hopkins and Mary Ehlinger
Talking With, Jane Martin
The Sum of Us, David Stevens; (D) John Ulmer; (C) Vicky Small
Dream Catchers, various playwrights; (C) Abby Littethun

Ford's Theatre

FRANKIE HEWITT
Producing Director

MICHAEL GENNARO
Managing Director

WILLIAM F. McSWEENY
Board Chairman

511 Tenth St. NW
Washington, DC 20004
(202) 638-2941 (bus.)
(202) 347-4833 (b.o.)
(202) 347-6269 (fax)

FOUNDED 1968
Frankie Hewitt

SEASON
Oct.-July

FACILITIES
Seating Capacity: 699
Stage: proscenium

FINANCES
Oct. 1, 1991-Sept. 30, 1992
Expenses: $5,654,026

CONTRACTS
AEA Special Production

For more than 25 years, Ford's has been diligent in its efforts to stage work that consistently appeals to a culturally diverse, family-oriented audience. Ford's has dedicated itself to providing the resources necessary to create opportunities for emerging composers and writers and to further diversify the ethnic and youth makeup of its audience. At the core of Ford's artistic mission is the development and production of new musicals—a uniquely American art form. Ford's Theatre has staged 55 musicals; *Don't Bother Me I Can't Cope*, *Your Arms Too Short to Box with God*, *Amen Corner*, *All Night Strut*, *Truly Blessed*, *Hot Mikado*, *Elmer Gantry*, *Conrack* and *Captains Courageous* are among those that premiered at Ford's Theatre. Many productions have subsequently received Broadway engagements and national tours. In addition, Ford's emphasis on the African-American experience has brought the black musical into the mainstream, adding significantly to the musical repertoire of American theatre.

—*Frankie Hewitt*

Ford's Theatre. Kel O'Neill and John Dossett in *Captains Courageous*. Photo: Joan Marcus.

Free Street Programs. *Teen Street*. Photo: Dan Rest.

PRODUCTIONS 1991-1992

Will Rogers' U.S.A., adapt: Paul Shyre; (D) Paul Shyre; (S), (L) and (C) Eldon Elder

A Christmas Carol, adapt: David H. Bell, from Charles Dickens; (D) David H. Bell; (S) Daniel Proett; (L) David Kissel; (C) D. Polly Kendrick

Zora Neale Hurston, Laurence Holder; (D) Wynn Handman; (L) Shirley Prendergast

Conrack, book adapt: Granville Burgess, from Pat Conroy; music: Lee Pockriss; lyrics: Anne Croswell; (D) Lonny Price; (S) Ann Sheffield; (L) Stuart Duke; (C) Charlotte M. Yetman; (MD) Tim Weil; (CH) Gregg Burge

PRODUCTIONS 1992-1993

Captains Courageous, book adapt and lyrics: Patrick Cook, from Rudyard Kipling and the film version; music: Frederick Freyer; (D) and (CH) Graciela Daniele; (S) Christopher Barreca; (L) Jules Fisher and Peggy Eisenhauer; (C) Ann Hould-Ward; (MD) James Kowal; (SD) Peter Fitzgerald

A Christmas Carol, adapt: David H. Bell, from Charles Dickens; (D) David H. Bell; (S) Daniel Proett; (L) David Kissel; (C) D. Polly Kendrick

Solemn Oaths and Looney Tunes, Mark Russell

The Good Times Are Killing Me, Lynda Barry; (D) Mark Brokaw; (S) Rusty Smith; (L) Donald Holder; (C) Ellen McCartney; (SD) Janet Kalas

Five Guys Named Moe, book: Clarke Peters; music and lyrics: Louis Jordan, et al.; (D) and (CH) Charles Augins; (S) Tim Goodchild; (L) Rick Belzer; (C) Gail Brassard; (MD) Hilton C. Felton, Jr.; (SD) Peter Fitzgerald

Free Street Programs

(formerly Free Street Theater)

DAVID SCHEIN
Artistic Director

JULIE GLAZER
Executive Director

CARROL RUSSELL SHERER
Board President

1419 West Blackhawk
Chicago, IL 60622
(312) 772-7248
(312) 465-7059 (fax)

FOUNDED 1969
Patrick Henry, Perry Baer

SEASON
Year-round touring

FINANCES
Apr. 1, 1992-Mar. 31, 1993
Expenses: $275,000

CONTRACTS
AEA letter of agreement

Free Street Theatre is an outreach organization dedicated to developing new audiences and participants for the performing arts. We pursue this goal by creating original performance material based on the experiences of the people we seek to engage. Frequently, performers are drawn from the community that has inspired the work—such as an inner-city neighborhood (*Project!*), or the community of the elderly (Free Street Too). Their experiences are interpreted through music, dance and theatre by Free Street's artistic staff. The resultant performance pieces are unique documentaries of aspects of the contemporary American condition which speak both to and for the community. Some of our companies operate on Actors' Equity contracts, others do not; but all maintain the highest standards. Although the surroundings and trappings may be low-rent, our endeavor is to make the experience high art.

—*David Schein*

PRODUCTIONS 1991-1993

All productions grow out of Free Street programs. Representative titles include ***Teen Street***, directed by Ron Bieganski, and ***Parenteen Theater***, directed by Maria McCray.

Fulton Theatre Company

(formerly Fulton Opera House)

KATHLEEN A. COLLINS
Artistic Director

LETTIE HERBERT
Managing Director

JOHN W. ESPENSHADE
Board President

Box 1865
Lancaster, PA 17603-1865
(717) 394-7133 (bus.)
(717) 397-7425 (b.o.)
(717) 397-3780 (fax)

FOUNDED 1963
Fulton Opera House Foundation

SEASON
Oct.-May

FACILITIES
Fulton Opera House
Seating Capacity: 909
Stage: proscenium

FINANCES
Oct. 1, 1991-Sept. 30, 1992
Expenses: $833,178

CONTRACTS
AEA letter of agreement

The Fulton Theatre Company, housed in the magnificent Fulton Opera House, produces contemporary American plays. By concentrating on works that explore powerful social issues, we are striving to create theatre that breathes new life into these venerable old bricks. Our educational outreach programs include classes for children and adults and a touring production that reaches more than 30,000 young people annually. We are gathering a company of artists committed to building a vital and challenging regional theatre here in the midst of this conservative, nonmetropolitan community.

—*Kathleen A. Collins*

Fulton Theatre Company. *The Gifts of the Magi*.

FULTON THEATRE COMPANY

PRODUCTIONS 1991-1992

Direction by Kathleen A. Collins, sets by Robert Klingelhoefer, lighting by Bill Simmons and costumes by Chib Gratz unless otherwise noted.

The Heidi Chronicles, Wendy Wasserstein; (SD) Pamela J. Nunnelley
The Gifts of the Magi, book adapt: Mark St. Germain, from O. Henry; music: Randy Courts; lyrics: Randy Courts and Mark St. Germain; (C) Marla Jurglanis; (MD) John O'Neill
Miss Evers' Boys, David Feldshuh; (D) Ron Nakahara
The Middle Ages, A.R. Gurney, Jr.; (D) Maureen Heffernan; (C) Beth Dunkelberger; (SD) Pamela J. Nunnelley

Theatre For Young Audiences:
Another Columbus, Barry Kornhauser

PRODUCTIONS 1992-1993

Direction by Kathleen A. Collins, sets by Robert Klingelhoefer, lighting by Bill Simmons and costumes by Chib Gratz unless otherwise noted.

Reckless, Craig Lucas
Great Expectations, adapt: Barbara Field, from Charles Dickens; (C) Beth Dunkelberger
The Lady in Red, Elizabeth Blake
I Hate Hamlet, Paul Rudnick

Theatre For Young Audiences:
Unexpected Universe, adapt: Barry Kornhauser, from children's poetry; music: Stephen Spiese; (D) Barry Kornhauser; (C) Beth Dunkelberger; (MD) Stephen Spiese

George Street Playhouse

GREGORY S. HURST
Producing Artistic Director

DIANE CLAUSSEN
Managing Director

AL D'AUGUSTA
Board President

9 Livingston Ave.
New Brunswick, NJ 08901
(908) 846-2895 (bus.)
(908) 246-7717 (b.o.)
(908) 247-9151 (fax)

FOUNDED 1974
John Herochik, Eric Krebs

SEASON
Sept.-Apr.

FACILITIES
George 367
Seating Capacity: 367
Stage: thrust

George 99
Seating Capacity: 99
Stage: flexible

State Theatre
Seating Capacity: 1,800
Stage: proscenium

FINANCES
July 1, 1992-June 30, 1993
Expenses: $2,385,679

CONTRACTS
AEA LORT (C)

For two decades we have made theatre an arena where uniqueness is celebrated, where audiences are inspired by the richness and diversity of the human experience. We are imagining regional theatre at its best: an art form that illuminates great moments in our lives. Our focus on developing new plays and musicals is balanced by innovative productions of classic and contemporary plays. Our investment in new plays by established and emerging playwrights who speak to the concerns and experience of all humankind earns for our stage the commitment of the finest actors. We actively remove physical, financial, cultural and generational barriers through innovative programs that open our door to all who wish to enter. Our Outreach Touring Company presents five issue-oriented plays annually to more than 100,000 students statewide, promoting theatre as a tool for self-awareness and understanding and as a vehicle for beauty and imagination.
—*Gregory S. Hurst*

PRODUCTIONS 1991-1992

Sets by Deborah Jasien, lighting by Donald Holder and costumes by Barbara Forbes unless otherwise noted.

George Street Playhouse. James Whitmore and Audra Lindley in *Foxfire*. Photo: Miguel Pagliere.

The Engagement, Richard Vetere; (D) Matthew Penn; (L) Paul Armstrong
Anna Christie, Eugene O'Neill; (D) Kevin Dowling; (S) Jane Musky; (SD) Randy Courts
I Ought To Be in Pictures, Neil Simon; (D) Gregory S. Hurst; (C) Sue Ellen Rohrer
Separation, Tom Kempinski; (D) Susan Kerner; (L) Michael Giannitti
Sarah and Abraham, Marsha Norman; (D) Jack Hofsiss; (S) David Jenkins; (L) Beverly Emmons; (C) Julie Weiss and Gary Lisz; (SD) David Yazbek
Other People's Money, Jerry Sterner; (D) Wendy Liscow; (S) Atkin Pace; (SD) David Budries
Zara Spook and Other Lures, Joan Ackermann; (D) Pamela Berlin; (S) Loren Sherman

PRODUCTIONS 1992-1993

Sets by Deborah Jasien, lighting by Donald Holder and costumes by Barbara Forbes unless otherwise noted.

Near the End of the Century, Tom Dulack; (D) Gregory S. Hurst

Idioglossia, Mark Handley; (D) and (SD) Tom O'Horgan; (S) Perry Arthur Kroeger; (L) Paul Armstrong
Three Men on a Horse, John Cecil Holm and George Abbott; (D) Gregory S. Hurst; (S) Atkin Pace; (SD) Jim Swonger
Spine, Bill C. Davis; (D) Bill C. Davis; (C) Sue Ellen Rohrer
Morning Dew with Trellis, Richard Browner; (D) Wendy Liscow; (S) Atkin Pace; (L) F. Mitchell Dana; (SD) Jim Swonger
The Fields of Ambrosia, book and lyrics: Joel Higgins; music: Martin Silvestri; (D) Gregory S. Hurst; (L) Howard Werner and Donald Holder; (C) Hillary Rosenfeld; (MD) Sariva Goetz; (CH) Lynn Taylor-Corbett; (SD) Fox and Perla, Ltd.
Foxfire, Hume Cronyn and Susan Cooper; (D) Matthew Penn; (C) Sue Ellen Rohrer; (SD) Jonathan Holtzman

Germinal Stage Denver

ED BAIERLEIN
Director/Manager

2450 West 44th Ave.
Denver, CO 80211
(303) 455-7108

FOUNDED 1974
Ed Baierlein, Ginger Valone,
Sallie Diamond, Jack McKnight

SEASON
Oct.-Aug.

FACILITIES
Seating Capacity: 100
Stage: thrust

FINANCES
Sept. 1, 1992-Aug. 31, 1993
Expenses: $93,000

Germinal Stage Denver is the hostile witness of regional theatres—an eight-table family restaurant, slaughtering our own pigs in the backyard, going easy on the gravy—sprouts available upon request. We're an actors' theatre, semi-rough, minimalist when we can afford it, still doggedly hopelessly vaguely postmodern, but backpedaling forward to ritual, advancing rearward to modern, or sidestepping to shamelessly theatrical in more lucid moments. We have declared the two-year battle against political correctness won and, licking our wounds, contemplate the Gauntlet of Accessibility. Goals for the next two years: 1) vigorous outreach to underserved local Boeotian community; 2) continual search for wealthy but empathetic private patron. Outlook: desolate to ghastly.

—*Ed Baierlein*

PRODUCTIONS 1991-1992

Direction, sets and lighting by Ed Baierlein and costumes by Sallie Diamond unless otherwise noted.

Getting Married, George Bernard Shaw; (C) Judy Graese
The Iceman Cometh, Eugene O'Neill
Woman in Mind, Alan Ayckbourn; (L) Stephen R. Kramer
The Three Sisters, Anton Chekhov; adapt: Ed Baierlein; (C) Ava T. Coleman
Mountain, Douglas Scott; (D), (S) and (L) Stephen R. Kramer

PRODUCTIONS 1992-1993

Direction, sets and lighting by Ed Baierlein and costumes by Sallie Diamond unless otherwise noted.

The Importance of Being Earnest, Oscar Wilde; (C) Judy Graese
Travesties, Tom Stoppard
Old Times, Harold Pinter; (S) and (L) Stephen R. Kramer
Goose and Tomtom, David Rabe; (S) Ed Baierlein and Angie Lee
Play Strindberg, Friedrich Durrenmatt; trans: James Kirkup

Germinal Stage Denver. Ed Baierlein, Ginger Valone and Sallie Diamond in *Old Times*. Photo: Strack Edwards.

GeVa Theatre

HOWARD J. MILLMAN
Producing Artistic Director

TIMOTHY J. SHIELDS
Managing Director

ANTHONY ZERBE
Associate Artistic Director

LINDA CORNELL WEINSTEIN
Board Chairman

75 Woodbury Blvd.
Rochester, NY 14607
(716) 232-1366 (bus.)
(716) 232-GEVA (b.o.)
(716) 232-4031 (fax)

FOUNDED 1972
William Selden, Cynthia Mason Selden

SEASON
Sept.-June

FACILITIES
Elaine P. Wilson Theatre
Seating Capacity: 552
Stage: thrust

FINANCES
July 1, 1992-June 30, 1993
Expenses: $3,398,690

CONTRACTS
AEA LORT (B)

GeVa Theatre enters its third decade with a renewed sense of ardor for producing theatre that has meaning and impact for the audiences that view it. GeVa presents a distinctive variety of theatre experience including the classics of the world and American stage, revivals, musicals, and contemporary dramas and comedies. Associate artistic director Anthony Zerbe has specific responsibilities for the production of new plays for the main stage and for the French Roast Festival, a staged reading series, and he works with playwrights in developing that work. We are committed to continuing to produce projects of dramatic scope and impact. We seek diversity in our audience, staff, board, volunteers, actors, directors and designers and want them to feel that GeVa is an artistic home for them. Each brings a differing need, but the feeling that these diverse groups can find their artistic home at GeVa is a forceful and guiding thought for us.

—*Howard J. Millman*

PRODUCTIONS 1991-1992

Pump Boys and Dinettes, John Foley, Mark Hardwick, Debra Monk, Cass Morgan, John Schimmel and Jim Wann; (D) Peter Glazier; (S) Chris Shriver; (L) Phil Monat; (C) Maria Marrero; (SD) James Wildman
Other People's Money, Jerry Sterner; (D) Howard J. Millman; (S) Bob Barnett; (L) F. Mitchell Dana; (C) Dana Harnish Tinsley; (SD) Dan Roach
Accomplice, Rupert Holmes; (D) Stephan Rothman; (S) David Jenkins; (L) Betsy Adams; (C) Dana Harnish Tinsley; (SD) Dan Roach
A Christmas Carol, adapt: Eberle Thomas, from Charles Dickens; (D) Barbara Redmond; (S) Bob Barnett; (L) Nic Minetor; (C) Pamela Scofield; (SD) Dan Roach
Anything Goes, book: Guy Bolton, P.G. Wodehouse, Howard Lindsay and Russel Crouse; music and lyrics: Cole Porter; (D) and (CH) Diana Baffa-Brill; (S) Keven Lock; (L) F. Mitchell Dana; (C) Mark Hughes; (MD) Mark R. Goodman; (SD) Adam Sperry
Nora, adapt: Ingmar Bergman, from Henrik Ibsen; trans: Frederick J. Marker and Lise-Lone Marker; (D) Margaret Booker; (S) Alexander Okun; (L) John Michael Deegan; (C) John Carver Sullivan; (SD) Adam Sperry
The Member of the Wedding, Carson McCullers; (D) Woodie King, Jr.; (S) Felix E. Cochren; (L) Shirley Prendergast; (C) Dana Harnish Tinsley; (SD) Adam Sperry

Reflections:
Sets by James Fenhagen, lighting by Kirk Bookman, costumes by Susan E. Mickey and sound design by James Wildman.

Peephole, Shem Bitterman; (D) Steve Zuckerman
Ellen Universe Joins the Band, David Rush; (D) Anthony Zerbe
Barbeque in 29 Palms, Wendy MacLeod; (D) Martin L. Platt

PRODUCTIONS 1992-1993

Lend Me a Tenor, Ken Ludwig; (D) Arthur Storch; (S) James Noone; (L) Phil Monat; (C) Pamela Scofield; (SD) James Wildman

GeVa Theatre. Deborah LaCoy and Eberle Thomas in *Accomplice*. Photo: Gelfand-Piper Photography.

Mount Allegro, adapt: Eberle Thomas and Barbara Redmond, from Jerre Mangione; (D) Eberle Thomas; (S) Bob Barnett; (L) Kirk Bookman; (C) Mimi Maxem; (SD) Kevin Dunayer
A Christmas Carol, adapt: Eberle Thomas, from Charles Dickens; (D) Eberle Thomas; (S) Bob Barnett; (L) Nic Minetor; (C) Pamela Scofield
Tintypes, book: Mary Kyte, Mel Marvin and Gary Pearle; music: John McKinney; lyrics: Mel Marvin; (D) Howard J. Millman; (S) Bob Barnett; (L) Kirk Bookman; (C) Dana Harnish Tinsley; (MD) Corrine Aquilina; (CH) Jim Hoskins; (SD) Kevin Dunayer
The Sum of Us, David Stevens; (D) Jamie Brown; (S) James Noone; (L) Phil Monat; (C) Randall E. Klein; (SD) James Wildman
Of Mice and Men, John Steinbeck; (D) Tony Curiel; (S) Victoria Petrovich; (L) Creon Thorne; (C) Dana Harnish Tinsley; (SD) Kevin Dunayer

Reflections:
Sets by Robert Thayer, lighting by Mary Louise Geiger, costumes by Susan E. Mickey and sound design by Kevin Dunayer.

A Penny for the Guy, Lanie Robertson; (D) Martin L. Platt
Criminal Hearts, Jane Martin; (D) Anthony Zerbe
What is Art?, Wm. S. Leavengood; (D) Sue Lawless

Goodman Theatre

ROBERT FALLS
Artistic Director

ROCHE SCHULFER
Executive Director

MICHAEL MAGGIO
Associate Artistic Director

FRANK GALATI
Associate Director

JAMES E. ANNABLE
Board Chairman

200 South Columbus Drive
Chicago, IL 60603
(312) 443-3811 (bus.)
(312) 443-3800 (b.o.)
(312) 263-6004 (fax)

FOUNDED 1925
Art Institute of Chicago

SEASON
Year-round

FACILITIES
Goodman Mainstage
Seating Capacity: 683
Stage: proscenium

Goodman Studio Theatre
Seating Capacity: 135
Stage: proscenium

FINANCES
July 1, 1992-June 30, 1993
Expenses: $7,467,500

CONTRACTS
AEA LORT (B+) and (D)

The Goodman is Chicago's largest and oldest nonprofit theatre, and we take advantage of its great resources to produce classic and contemporary works of size—large in both imagination and physical scale. Our goal is to infuse the classics with the energy usually reserved for new works, and to treat new plays with the care and reverence usually given to the classics. Every aspect of the Goodman should reflect the richness of our city's varied cultures, and our efforts to diversify our staff, to reach out to new audiences in our community and to broaden the range of what we program in our Mainstage and Studio theatres are steps toward that goal. Looking toward our future, we are expanding our efforts to develop younger audiences through our program of free student matinees and close collaboration with Chicago's public schools.

—*Robert Falls*

PRODUCTIONS 1991-1992

Miss Evers' Boys, David Feldshuh; (D) Kenneth Leon; (S) Michael Olich; (L) Robert Peterson; (C) Susan E. Mickey; (SD) Dwight Andrews
A Christmas Carol, adapt: Tom Creamer, from Charles Dickens; (D) Steve Scott; (S) Joseph Nieminski; (L) Robert Christen; (SD) Rob Milburn and David Naunton
Twelfth Night, William Shakespeare; (D) Neil Bartlett; (S) and (C) Richard Hudson; (L) Scott Zielinski; (SD) Rob Milburn
On the Open Road, Steve Tesich; (D) Robert Falls; (S) George Tsypin; (L) Michael S. Philippi; (C) Gabriel Berry; (SD) Rob Milburn
The Good Person of Setzuan, Bertolt Brecht; trans: Sheldon Patinkin; (D) Frank Galati; (S) Loy Arcenas; (L) James F. Ingalls; (C) Susan Hilferty; (SD) Rob Milburn
Riverview, John Logan; various composers and lyricists; (D) Robert Falls; (S) Thomas Lynch; (L) Michael S. Philippi; (C) Nan Cibula-Jenkins; (MD) Helen Gregory; (CH) Marcia Milgrom Dodge; (SD) Richard Woodbury

Goodman Theatre. Steve Pickering and Jordan Charney in *On the Open Road*. Photo: Liz Lauren.

Down the Shore, Tom Donaghy; (D) David Petrarca; (S) and (C) Linda Buchanan; (L) Robert Christen; (SD) Rob Milburn

Home and Away, Kevin Kling; (D) Steven Dietz; (L) Robert Christen

Spunk, adapt: George C. Wolfe, from Zora Neale Hurston; music: Chic Street Man; (D) and (CH) Donald Douglass; (S) Amy Smith; (L) Ken Bowen; (C) Birgit Rattenborg Wise; (SD) David Naunton

PRODUCTIONS 1992-1993

Spic-O-Rama, John Leguizamo; (D) Peter Askin; (L) Ken Bowen

The Skin of Our Teeth, Thornton Wilder; (D) David Petrarca; (S) Michael Yeargan; (L) Christopher Akerlind; (C) Catherine Zuber; (SD) Rob Milburn

A Christmas Carol, adapt: Tom Creamer, from Charles Dickens; (D) Steve Scott; (S) Joseph Nieminski; (L) Robert Christen; (SD) Rob Milburn and David Naunton

Two Trains Running, August Wilson; (D) Lloyd Richards; (S) Tony Fanning; (L) Geoff Korf; (C) Chrisi Karvonides-Dushenko; (SD) Rob Milburn

Marvin's Room, Scott McPherson; (D) David Petrarca; (S) Linda Buchanan; (L) Robert Christen; (C) Claudia Boddy; (SD) Rob Milburn

Black Snow, adapt: Keith Reddin, from Mikhail Bulgakov; (D) Michael Maggio; (S) Linda Buchanan; (L) James F. Ingalls; (C) Martin Pakledinaz; (SD) Rob Milburn

Cry, the Beloved Country, book adapt: Frank Galati, from Alan Paton; music: Kurt Weill; lyrics: Maxwell Anderson; (D) Frank Galati; (S) Loy Arcenas; (L) James F. Ingalls; (C) Susan Hilferty; (SD) Rob Milburn

Wings, book adapt and lyrics: Arthur Perlman, from Arthur Kopit; music: Jeffrey Lunden; (D) Michael Maggio; (S) Linda Buchanan; (L) Robert Christen; (C) Birgit Rattenborg Wise; (MD) Bradley Vieth; (SD) Richard Woodbury

Puddin 'n Pete, Cheryl L. West; (D) Gilbert McCauley; (S) Clay Snider; (L) Robert Shook; (C) Yslan Hicks; (SD) Richard Woodbury

The Baltimore Waltz, Paula Vogel; (D) Mary Zimmerman; (S) Scott Bradley; (L) Rita Pietraszek; (C) Allison Reeds; (SD) Michael Bodeen

Reno Once Removed, Reno; (D) Evan Yionoulis; (L) Dan Kotlowitz

Goodspeed Opera House

MICHAEL P. PRICE
Executive Director

SUE FROST
Associate Producer

ROBERT F. NEAL
Board President

Box A
East Haddam, CT 06423
(203) 873-8664 (bus.)
(203) 873-8668 (b.o.)
(203) 873-2329 (fax)

FOUNDED 1963
Goodspeed Opera House Foundation

SEASON
Apr.-Dec.

FACILITIES
Goodspeed Opera House
Seating Capacity: 398
Stage: proscenium

Goodspeed-at-Chester/The Norma Terris Theatre
Seating Capacity: 200
Stage: proscenium

FINANCES
Jan. 1, 1993-Dec. 31, 1993
Expenses $3,990,000

CONTRACTS
AEA LORT (B) and (D)

Celebrating its 30th anniversary in 1993, the Goodspeed Opera House is dedicated to the heritage, preservation and development of the musical theatre. Producing both classical and contemporary musicals, the Opera House has sent 13 productions to Broadway, including *Annie*, *Shenandoah* and *Man of La Mancha*. Goodspeed was awarded a special Tony award in 1980 for its significant contributions to this important artform. Goodspeed's second stage, Goodspeed-at-Chester/The Norma Terris Theatre, provides an intimate performing space exclusively for new works of musical theatre. Here, writers and creative staff have a rare opportunity to develop a "musical-in-progress" before an audience. Goodspeed operates the Library of the Musical Theatre, a resource center which houses performance and archival materials, and publishes *Show Music* magazine, a national publication on the musical theatre. Both are part of Goodspeed's continuing commitment to the musical theatre.
—*Michael P. Price*

Goodspeed Opera House. Sophie Hayden and Spiro Malas in *The Most Happy Fella*. Photo: Diane Sobolewski.

PRODUCTIONS 1991

The Most Happy Fella, book, music and lyrics: Frank Loesser; (D) Gerald Gutierrez; (S) John Lee Beatty; (L) Craig Miller; (C) Jess Goldstein; (MD) Tim Stella; (CH) Liza Gennaro

Arthur: The Musical, book adapt and lyrics: David Crane and Marta Kauffman, from the original screenplay; music: Michael Skloff; (D) Joseph Billone; (S) Linda Hacker; (L) John Hastings; (C) Beba Shamash; (MD) Tim Stella; (CH) Tony Stevens

Here's Love, book adapt, music and lyrics: Meredith Willson, from *Miracle on 34th Street*; (D) Larry Carpenter; (S) James Leonard Joy; (L) Craig Miller; (C) John Falabella; (MD) Mark Mitchell; (CH) Daniel Pelzig

Woody Guthrie's American Song, book: Peter Glazer; music and lyrics: Woody Guthrie; (D) Peter Glazer; (S) Philipp Jung; (L) David Noling; (C) Baker S. Smith; (MD) Malcolm Ruhl; (CH) Jennifer Martin

Conrack, book adapt: Granville Burgess, from Pat Conroy; music: Lee Pockriss; lyrics: Anne Croswell; (D) Lonny Price; (S) Ann Sheffield; (L) Stuart Duke; (C) Charlotte M. Yetman; (MD) Tim Weil; (CH) Gregg Burge

PRODUCTIONS 1992

It's a Bird, It's a Plane, It's Superman, book: David Newman and Robert Benton; music: Charles Strouse; lyrics: Lee Adams; (D) Stuart Ross; (S) Neil Peter Jampolis; (L) Kirk Bookman; (C) Lindsay W. Davis; (MD) Michael O'Flaherty; (CH) Michele Assaf

Paint Your Wagon, book and lyrics: Alan Jay Lerner; music: Frederick Loewe; (D) Andre Ernotte; (S) James Noone; (L) Phil Monat; (C) John Carver Sullivan; (MD) Michael O'Flaherty; (CH) Tony Stevens

Animal Crackers, book: George S. Kaufman and Morrie Ryskind; music and lyrics: Bert Kalmar and Harry Ruby; (D) Charles Repole; (S) John Falabella; (L) Craig Miller; (C) David Toser; (MD) Albin Konopka; (CH) Tony Stevens

Heartbeats, conceived: Amanda McBroom and Bill Castellino; book, music and lyrics: Amanda

McBroom; addtl music: Gerald Sternbach, Michael Brourman, Tom Snow and Craig Stefan; (D) and (CH) Bill Castellino; (S) Linda Hacker; (L) Craig Lathrop; (C) Charlotte M. Yetman; (MD) Ann-Carol Pence
Some Sweet Day, book: Don Jones and Mac Pirkle; music and lyrics: Si Kahn; (D) Mac Pirkle; (S) Brian J. Laczko; (L) Stuart Duke; (C) Charlotte M. Yetman; (MD) Stan Tucker
Good Sports, book: Susan Rice; music and lyrics: Carol Hall; (D) and (CH) J. Randall Hugill; (S) James Morgan; (L) Mary Jo Dondlinger; (C) Charlotte M. Yetman; (MD) Michael O'Flaherty

Great American History Theatre

**LYNN LOHR,
LANCE S. BELVILLE
Co-Artistic Directors**

**THOMAS H. BERGER
General Manager**

**DAVID BYRD
Board President**

30 East 10th St.
St. Paul, MN 55101
(612) 292-4323

FOUNDED 1978
Lynn Lohr, Lance S. Belville

SEASON
Oct.-June

**FACILITIES
Crawford Livingston Theatre
Seating Capacity: 597
Stage: thrust**

**FINANCES
July 1, 1992-June 30, 1993
Expenses: $525,500**

**CONTRACTS
AEA SPT**

The Great American History Theatre exists to develop world premieres that connect with audiences and speak to their lives. The theatre uses history, folklore, social issues, narratives and oral histories as the launching platforms for the imaginations of playwrights. The theatre focuses first on the untold stories of the Midwest but also offers its audiences a window to other people and other times and places: Brazil, Ireland, Sweden and the Southwest. The theatre seeks offbeat, surreal stagings and likes to transform airplane hangars or forts into theatres, or its own performing space into a speakeasy or an open-pit mine/union hall. Touring nationally with companies as large as 15, the theatre also is at home in rural communities, burrowing in with long-term research/writing/production workshops.
—*Lynn Lohr, Lance S. Belville*

PRODUCTIONS 1991-1992

Sets and lighting by Chris Johnson and costumes by Katherine Kohl unless otherwise noted.

Scum City, David Hawley; (D) Ron Peluso; (SD) Ryan Julien
Through the Wheat, adapt: Thomas W. Olson, from Thomas Boyd; (D) Stephen DiMenna; (C) Nayna Ramey; (SD) John Michener
A Country Christmas Carol, book adapt: Ed Graczyk, from Charles Dickens; music: David Tolley; lyrics: John Dempsey; (D) and (CH) Michael Ellison; (S) Robin W. McIntyre; (MD) Andrea Herschler
The Meeting, Jeff Stetson; (D) Chuck Smith; (S) and (L) Tim Oien; (C) Glenn Billings; (SD) Corbiere Boynes
The Life and Times of Deacon A.L. Wiley, Gregory Alan-Williams; (D) Alex Thomas; (S), (L) and (C) Gregory Alan-Williams
Irish Stew, Frank McCourt; (D) Lynn Lohr; (S) Thomas H. Berger; (C) Frank McCourt
Olle from Laughtersville, book: Lance S. Belville; music and lyrics: Olle Skratthult; (D) Lynn Lohr; (S) Nayna Ramey; (MD) Sally Reynolds; (CH) Michael Ellison
Small Town Triumphs, adapt: Lance S. Belville, Bart Sutter and Ross Sutter, from Bart Sutter; and *Cowboy Colors*, adapt: Lance S. Belville, Paul Zarzyski and Stephen DiMenna, from Paul Zarzyski; (D) Stephen DiMenna; (L) Nayna Ramey; (C) Mary Beth Gangler Ast; (MD) Ross Sutter (*Small Town Triumphs*) and Marya Hart (*Cowboy Colors*)

PRODUCTIONS 1992-1993

A Country Christmas Carol, book adapt: Ed Graczyk, from Charles Dickens; music: David Tolley; lyrics: John Dempsey; (D) and (CH) Michael Ellison; (S) Robin W. McIntyre; (L) Chris Johnson; (C) Katherine Kohl; (MD) Marya Hart
The Meeting, Jeff Stetson; (D) Chuck Smith; (S) and (L) Tim Oien; (C) Glenn Billings; (SD) Corbiere Boynes
The Life and Times of Deacon A.L. Wiley, Gregory Alan-Williams; (D) Alex Thomas; (S), (L) and (C) Gregory Alan-Williams
The Great Gatsby, book adapt: John Carlile, from F. Scott Fitzgerald; (D) Stephen DiMenna; (S) Thomas H. Berger; (L) Thomas H. Berger and Chris Johnson; (C) Matthew LeFebvre; (SD) Stephen DiMenna, Michael Ellison and Ryan Julien
Scott and Zelda: The Beautiful Fools, Lance S. Belville; (D) Stephen DiMenna; (S) Thomas H. Berger; (L) Thomas H. Berger and Chris Johnson; (C) Katherine Kohl; (SD) Stephen DiMenna and Ryan Julien
Days of Rondo, adapt: Gregory Alan-Williams, from Evelyn Fairbanks; (D) Gregory Alan-Williams; (S) and (L) Chris Johnson; (C) Diedre Whitlock; (SD) Ryan Julien

Great Lakes Theater Festival

**GERALD FREEDMAN
Artistic Director**

**ANNE B. DesROSIERS
Managing Director**

**MARY ANN JORGENSON,
WILLIAM E. MacDONALD, III
Board Co-Chairmen**

1501 Euclid Ave., Suite 423
Cleveland, OH 44115-2108
(216) 241-5490 (bus.)
(216) 241-6000 (b.o.)
(216) 241-6315 (fax)

Great American History Theatre. Delores Wade, Naina Taaj Ajmal Brown and Weymuth Bowen, Jr. in *Days of Rondo*. Photo: Gerald Gustafson.

Great Lakes Theater Festival. Robert Foxworth in *Cyrano de Bergerac*. Photo: Roger Mastroianni.

FOUNDED 1962
Community members

SEASON
Oct.-May

FACILITIES
Ohio Theatre
Seating Capacity: 643
Stage: proscenium

FINANCES
Feb. 1, 1992-May 31, 1993
Expenses: $3,234,441

CONTRACTS
AEA LORT (B)

Though the Great Lakes Theatre Festival continues to uphold the mandate for classical theatre that launched it, we have been challenging our perception of what that responsibility means. We are interested in the whole spectrum of American plays—not only the acknowledged great works, but the culturally significant plays and musicals that placed Broadway in the mainstream of American entertainment from the 1920s through the 1950s. And we are interested in pursuing the special resonance that comes from seeing world classics side by side with new plays. With regard to performance style, I am drawn to actors adept at both classic drama and musicals. I find a kinship between doing Shakespeare, for example, and musical theatre. The presentational styles—the soliloquies in one form, the songs in the other—each require a high-energy performance level that forms a visceral relationship with an audience and that is very much my signature.
—*Gerald Freedman*

PRODUCTIONS 1991-1992

Direction by Gerald Freedman unless otherwise noted.

Uncle Vanya, Anton Chekhov; trans: Michael Frayn; (S) John Ezell; (L) Thomas Skelton; (C) Lawrence Casey; (SD) Stan Kozak
Paul Robeson, Phillip Hayes Dean; (D) Harold Scott; (S) John Ezell and Gene Emerson Friedman; (L) Shirley Prendergast
A Christmas Carol, adapt: Gerald Freedman, from Charles Dickens; (S) John Ezell and Gene Emerson Friedman; (L) Mary Jo Dondlinger; (C) James Scott; (SD) Tom Mardikes and Stan Kozak
The Ohio State Murders, Adrienne Kennedy; (S) Gerald Freedman and John Ezell; (L) Cynthia Stillings; (C) Alfred Kohout; (SD) Stan Kozak
Mother Courage, Bertolt Brecht; trans: Eric Bentley; (L) Mary Jo Dondlinger; (C) Jeanne Button; (SD) Douglas Stein

PRODUCTIONS 1992-1993

Sets by John Ezell, costumes by James Scott and sound design by Stan Kozak unless otherwise noted.

Cyrano de Bergerac, Edmond Rostand; trans: Anthony Burgess; (D) Gerald Freedman; (L) Thomas Skelton
Rough Crossing, Tom Stoppard; (D) Victoria Bussert; (L) Mary Jo Dondlinger
A Christmas Carol, adapt: Gerald Freedman, from Charles Dickens; (D) Victoria Bussert; (S) John Ezell and Gene Emerson Friedman; (L) Mary Jo Dondlinger; (SD) Tom Mardikes and Stan Kozak
Sisters, Wives and Daughters, adapt: Claire Bloom, from William Shakespeare; (L) Cynthia Stillings
Othello, William Shakespeare; (D) Harold Scott; (L) Jackie Manassee; (C) Daniel L. Lawson

The Group: Seattle's MultiCultural Theatre

TIM BOND
Artistic Director

PAUL O'CONNELL
Producing Director

LAIRD HARRIS
Board President

305 Harrison
Seattle, WA 98109
(206) 441-9480 (bus.)
(206) 441-1299 (b.o.)
(206) 441-9839 (fax)

FOUNDED 1978
Gilbert Wong, Ruben Sierra, Scott Caldwell

SEASON
Sept.-June

FACILITIES
Carleton Playhouse
Seating Capacity: 192
Stage: thrust

FINANCES
July 1, 1992-June 30, 1993
Expenses: $1,004,577

CONTRACTS
AEA SPT and TYA

For more than 15 years, the Group has been at the forefront of the national movement to desegregate the American theatre. Our vision of a world without borders is reflected in the cultural diversity of our casting, play selection, staff, board of trustees and loyal audience. We are creating a multicultural, equal-opportunity theatre—a truly "American theatre" that is inclusive of and empowering to the disenfranchised peoples who compose our diverse world community and that seeks out unique voices representative of the myriad of cultural perspectives that enrich the American experience. Our company's heart and soul are deeply rooted in the idea of community. Each season we present mainstage premieres by both new and established playwrights and help to develop writers from diverse backgrounds in our MultiCultural Theatre Works series. Our educational programs, new-play labs and mainstage productions all are infused with the belief that passionate, vital and entertaining theatre can open up the minds and hearts of our society and ask important questions.
—*Tim Bond*

PRODUCTIONS 1991-1992

You Can't Take It With You, George S. Kaufman and Moss Hart; (D) Paul O'Connell; (S) Peggy McDonald; (L) Kyle Iddings; (C) Kathleen Maki; (SD) Steven M. Klein

The Group: Seattle's MultiCultural Theatre. Martha A. Del Rio, Monica J. Martinez and Mariana Vasquez in *Real Women Have Curves*. Photo: John Stamets.

Alfred Stieglitz Loves O'Keeffe, Lanie Robertson; (D) Rita Giomi; (S) and (C) Yuri Degtjar; (L) Collier Woods; (SD) David Pascal
Who Causes the Darkness, Marion Isaac McClinton; (D) Terry Bellamy; (S) Larry Rickel; (L) Darren McCroom; (C) Kathleen Maki; (SD) David Pascal
Real Women Have Curves, Josefina Lopez; (D) Susana Tubert; (S) Rex Carleton; (L) Jim Verdery; (C) Kathy Hunt
Meetings, Mustapha Matura; (D) Tim Bond; (S) Rex Carleton; (L) Darren McCroom; (C) Kathleen Maki
Voices of Christmas, Ruben Sierra and Colleen Carpenter-Simmons; (D) David Koch; (S) Aime Miller-Rickel; (L) Darren McCroom; (C) Marianne O'Brien

PRODUCTIONS 1992-1993

Lighting by Darren McCroom.

Dear Miss Elena Sergeyevna, Ludmilla Razymovskaya; trans: Zoltan Schmidt and Roger Downey; (D) Tim Bond; (S) Yuri Degtjar; (C) Kathleen Maki; (SD) Steven M. Klein
The Snowflake Avalanche, Y York; (D) Mark Lutwak; (S) Robert Dahlstrom; (C) Francis Kenney; (SD) Wayne Horvitz
Tod, the Boy, Tod, Talvin Wilks; (D) Tim Bond; (S) Carey Wong; (C) Michael Murphy; (SD) Jim Ragland
Kind Ness, Ping Chong; (D) Ping Chong
A...My Name is Still Alice, conceived: Joan Micklin Silver and Julianne Boyd; various composers and lyricists; (D) Jacqueline Moscou; (S) Robert Dahlstrom; (C) Michael Murphy; (MD) Richard Gray; (CH) Michele Blackmon
Voices of Christmas, Ruben Sierra and Colleen Carpenter-Simmons; (D) Michele Blackmon; (S) Yuriko Uematsu; (C) Wanda Walden

The Guthrie Theater

GARLAND WRIGHT
Artistic Director

EDWARD A. MARTENSON
Executive Director

MARGARET WURTELE
Board President

725 Vineland Place
Minneapolis, MN 55403
(612) 347-1100 (bus.)
(612) 377-2224 (b.o.)
(612) 347-1188 (fax)

FOUNDED 1963
Tyrone Guthrie, Peter Zeisler, Oliver Rea

SEASON
July-Mar.

FACILITIES
The Guthrie Theater
Seating Capacity: 1,315
Stage: thrust

The Guthrie Laboratory
Seating Capacity: 300
Stage: flexible

FINANCES
Apr. 1, 1992-Mar. 31, 1993
Expenses: $9,866,946

CONTRACTS
AEA LORT (A) and (D)

We at the Guthrie firmly commit our efforts to artistic excellence at every level, to the greatest plays of the world repertoire, to the actor as the central communicator of the ideas and poetry within those plays, and to the imagination and its transforming power.

—*Garland Wright*

PRODUCTIONS 1991-1992

Direction by Garland Wright and lighting by Marcus Dilliard unless otherwise noted.

Death of a Salesman, Arthur Miller; (D) Sheldon Epps; (S) James Leonard Joy; (L) Allen Lee Hughes; (C) Judy Dearing
The Man Who Came to Dinner, George S. Kaufman and Moss Hart; (D) Laird Williamson; (S) and (C) Andrew V. Yelusich
The Illusion, Pierre Corneille; trans: Ranjit Bolt; (S) and (C) Anita Stewart
Fantasio, Alfred de Musset; trans: Richard Howard; (S) Douglas Stein; (L) Allen Lee Hughes; (C) Susan Hilferty; (SD) Steve Bennett
The Tempest, William Shakespeare; (D) Jennifer Tipton; (S) and (C) John Conklin; (L) Scott Zielinski; (SD) Hans Peter Kuhn
A Christmas Carol, adapt: Barbara Field, from Charles Dickens; (D) Sari Ketter; (S) Jack Barkla; (C) Jack Edwards
The Persecution and Assassination of Jean-Paul Marat as Performed by the Inmates of the Asylum of Charenton Under the Direction of the Marquis de Sade, Peter Weiss; adapt: Adrian Mitchell; trans: Geoffrey Skelton; music: Richard Peaslee; (S) John Arnone; (C) David C. Woolard; (MD) Eric Kodner

PRODUCTIONS 1992-1993

Direction by Garland Wright, sets by Douglas Stein, lighting by Marcus Dilliard and costumes by Susan Hilferty unless otherwise noted.

Iphigenia at Aulis, Euripides; trans: W.S. Merwin and George E. Dimock, Jr.
Agamemnon, Aeschylus; trans: Robert Lowell
Electra, Sophocles; trans: Kenneth McLeish
The Winter's Tale, William Shakespeare; (D) Douglas Hughes; (S) Hugh Landwehr; (C) Catherine Zuber
The Seagull, Anton Chekhov; trans: Jean-Claude van Itallie; (L) James F. Ingalls
A Christmas Carol, adapt: Barbara Field, from Charles Dickens; (D) Sari Ketter; (S) Jack Barkla; (C) Jack Edwards
The Good Hope, Herman Heijermans; trans: Lilian Saunders and Caroline Heijermans-Houwink (D) Bartlett Sher; (SD) Peter Still

The Guthrie Theater. Isabell Monk in *Iphigenia at Aulis*. Photo: Michal Daniel.

Hangar Theatre. Tony Freeman, Jeff Gardner and Jane Wasser in *Man of La Mancha*. Photo: Jon Reis/PhotoLink.

Hangar Theatre

ROBERT MOSS
Artistic Director

LYNN FITZPATRICK
Managing Director

JULIA BONNEY
Board President

Box 205
Ithaca, NY 14851
(607) 273-8588 (bus.)
(607) 273-4497 (b.o.)
(607) 273-4516 (fax—call first)

FOUNDED 1975
Tom Niederkorn, Agda Osborn, Howard Dillingham, Nelson Delavan, Ruth Houghton, William Schmidt

SEASON
June-Aug.

FACILITIES
Seating Capacity: 381
Stage: thrust

FINANCES
Oct. 1, 1991-Sept. 30, 1992
Expenses: $420,999

CONTRACTS
AEA letter of agreement

The Hangar operates throughout the summer in what was once an airplane hangar. Its thrust stage creates an exciting dynamic between the performer and the audience in the 381-seat house. The repertoire tends to consist of contemporary plays that have achieved some recognition, plus an occasional Shaw or Moliere. A musical is also an annual event. The theatre is strongly artist-driven. The directors and designers all influence the selection of plays. What is unique and powerful at the Hangar is the collaborative process among the artists. The titles may be familiar, but the productions are not. There is also an extremely active auxiliary production unit called the Lab Company, which is comprised of 20 undergraduate actors and 5 graduate-level directors selected by the Drama League of New York. Lab Company members produce 15 plays of their own, mostly originals, which are free to the public and performed prior to and immediately following mainstage events. The Lab Company also produces five original plays for younger audiences.

—*Robert Moss*

PRODUCTIONS 1991-1992

Sets by David Birn, lighting by Kerro Knox 3, costumes by Tracy Christensen and sound design by Chuck Hatcher unless otherwise noted.

The Heidi Chronicles, Wendy Wasserstein; (D) Robert Moss; (C) Kristin Yungkurth
Man of La Mancha, book adapt: Dale Wasserman, from Miguel de Cervantes; music: Mitch Leigh; lyrics: Joe Darion; (D) and (CH) Andrew Grose; (C) Kristin Yungkurth; (MD) Frederick Willard
The Miracle Worker, William Gibson; (D) Erica Gould; (S) David Zinn
A Life in the Theatre, David Mamet; (D) Robert Moss; (L) Brian MacDevitt
M. Butterfly, David Henry Hwang; (D) Michael Mayer; (L) Brian MacDevitt; (SD) Christien Methot

PRODUCTIONS 1992-1993

Sound design by Chuck Hatcher.

Shirley Valentine, Willy Russell; (D) Robert Moss; (S) Andrew Hall; (L) Daniel C. Hall; (C) Kaye Voyce
Evita, music: Andrew Lloyd Webber; lyrics: Tim Rice; (D) and (CH) Joseph Patton; (L) Christien Methot; (C) Cynthia Ann Orr Brookhouse; (MD) Richard de Rosa
Candida, George Bernard Shaw; (D) Robert Moss; (S) Andrew Hall; (L) Brian MacDevitt; (C) Michael Krass
A View from the Bridge, Arthur Miller; (D) Michael Mayer; (S) David Birn; (L) Brian MacDevitt; (C) Michael Krass
Lips Together, Teeth Apart, Terrence McNally; (D) William Foeller; (S) Tony Cisek; (L) Matt Zelkowitz; (C) Kate Underhill
Love Letters, A.R. Gurney, Jr.; (D) Robert Moss and James Peck

Hartford Stage Company

MARK LAMOS
Artistic Director

Hartford Stage Company. *Falsettoland*. Photo: T. Charles Erickson.

HARTFORD STAGE COMPANY

STEPHEN J. ALBERT
Managing Director

ELLIOT F. GERSON
Board President

50 Church St.
Hartford, CT 06103
(203) 525-5601 (bus.)
(203) 527-5151 (b.o.)

FOUNDED 1964
Jacques Cartier

SEASON
Oct.-June

FACILITIES
John W. Huntington Theatre
Seating Capacity: 489
Stage: thrust

FINANCES
July 1, 1992-June 30, 1993
Expenses: $3,500,000

CONTRACTS
AEA LORT (B)

The work at Hartford Stage reflects the desire to explore every possible kind of theatrical style, whether through new plays, commissioned translations of old plays or adaptations of theatrical works. Our work is centered on the production of texts from the past—primarily works by Shakespeare, but also plays by Schnitzler, Shaw, Moliere and Ibsen. Occasionally plays from the recent past are also revived, and fully half of each season is devoted to world premieres or to second productions of new plays by U.S. writers.

—*Mark Lamos*

PRODUCTIONS 1991-1992

Sound design by David Budries.

March of the Falsettos, book, music and lyrics: William Finn; and *Falsettoland*, book: William Finn and James Lapine; music and lyrics: William Finn; (D) Graciela Daniele; (S) Ed Wittstein; (L) David F. Segal; (C) Judy Dearing; (MD) Henry Aronson
All's Well That Ends Well, William Shakespeare; (D) Mark Lamos; (S) Loy Arcenas; (L) Christopher Akerlind; (C) Catherine Zuber
Who's Afraid of Virginia Woolf?, Edward Albee; (D) Paul Weidner; (S) John Conklin; (L) Natasha Katz; (C) Jess Goldstein
Hidden Laughter, Simon Gray; (D) Mark Lamos; (S) Christopher Barreca; (L) Stephen Strawbridge; (C) Candice Donnelly
Heartbreak House, George Bernard Shaw; (D) Michael Langham; (S) Douglas Stein; (L) Pat Collins; (C) Ann Hould-Ward
Reckless, Craig Lucas; (D) Lisa Peterson; (S) Anita Stewart; (L) Peter Kaczorowski; (C) Melina Root

PRODUCTIONS 1992-1993

Sound design by David Budries.

Tartuffe, Moliere; trans: Richard Wilbur; (D) Mark Lamos; (S) Christine Jones; (L) Scott Zielinski; (C) Tom Broecker
Pill Hill, Samuel Kelley; (D) Marion Isaac McClinton; (S) James D. Sandefur; (L) Allen Lee Hughes; (C) Paul Tazewell
Martin Guerre, book adapt and lyrics: Laura Harrington, from the original screenplay; music: Roger Ames; (D) Mark Lamos; (S) Michael Yeargan; (L) Jennifer Tipton; (C) Jess Goldstein; (MD) Sue Anderson; (CH) Liza Gennaro
Marisol, Jose Rivera; (D) Michael Greif; (S) Debra Booth; (L) Kenneth Posner; (C) Gabriel Berry
The Cover of Life, R.T. Robinson; (D) Richard Corley; (S) Marjorie Bradley Kellogg; (L) Kirk Bookman; (C) Merrily Murray-Walsh
Herringbone, book: Tom Cone; music: Walter Edgar Kennon; lyrics: Ellen Fitzhugh; (D) Graciela Daniele; (S) Christopher Barreca; (L) Peggy Eisenhauer; (C) Ann Hould-Ward

Hippodrome State Theatre

MARY HAUSCH
Producing Director

MICHAEL CURRY
Business Manager

25 Southeast Second Place
Gainesville, FL 32601
(904) 373-5968 (bus.)
(904) 375-4477 (b.o.)
(904) 371-9130 (fax)

FOUNDED 1973
Mary Hausch, Marilyn Wall-Asse, Kerry McKenney, Bruce Cornwell, Gregory von Hausch, Orin Wechsberg

SEASON
Year-round

FACILITIES
Mainstage
Seating Capacity: 266
Stage: thrust

Second Stage
Seating Capacity: 86
Stage: flexible

FINANCES
June 1, 1991-May 31, 1992
Expenses: $1,430,661

CONTRACTS
AEA LORT (D)

The Hippodrome State Theatre has been nationally recognized for its imaginative theatre that spans contemporary, classic and international boundaries. The Hippodrome was founded as an artistic cooperative in 1973. The collective artistic input, along with intensely individual visions and stylistic variety, creates the theatre's unique premieres, translations, original adaptations of screenplays and classical works. Internationally recognized playwrights, including Tennessee Williams, Adrian Mitchell, Eric Bentley, Lee Breuer, Mario Vargas Llosa and Brian Thomson, have all collaborated with the theatre's company to produce world premieres on the Hippodrome stage. Other programs include the Teen Playwright Festival, the New Play Reading Series, an intern/conservatory program, an artistic residency program, and a Theatre for Young Audiences that has created 15 original plays and performed for more than two million children. The theatre's Improvisational Teen Theatre utilizes improvisational performances and discussion groups to address problems prevalent among teens, such as drug addiction, sexual abuse, suicide, pregnancy and AIDS.

—*Mary Hausch*

PRODUCTIONS 1991-1992

Direction and sets by Carlos Francisco Asse, lighting by Robert Robins and costumes by Marilyn Wall-Asse unless otherwise noted.

Lend Me a Tenor, Ken Ludwig
Accomplice, Rupert Holmes; (D) and (SD) Lauren Caldwell
Lettice and Lovage, Peter Shaffer; (D) Mary Hausch; (SD) Ken Melvin and Michael Hall
M. Butterfly, David Henry Hwang; (D) Mary Hausch; (SD) Rocky Draud
A Christmas Carol, book adapt and lyrics: Carlos Francisco Asse, from Charles Dickens; music: James Wren; (MD) James Wren; (CH) Richard Rose
West Side Story, book: Arthur Laurents; music: Leonard Bernstein; lyrics: Stephen Sondheim; (MD) Mark Janas; (CH) Jillian Johnson
Nunsense, book, music and lyrics: Dan Goggin; (MD) Kathy Tyrell

Hippodrome State Theatre. Mary Jo Catlett and Dylan Thue-Jones in *Marvin's Room*. Photo: Randy Batista/Media Image.

PRODUCTIONS 1992-1993

Direction and sets by Carlos Francisco Asse, lighting by Robert Robins and costumes by Marilyn Wall-Asse unless otherwise noted.

Prelude to a Kiss, Craig Lucas; (D) Mary Hausch; (SD) Rocky Draud

Lips Together, Teeth Apart, Terrence McNally; (D) and (SD) Lauren Caldwell

A Christmas Carol, book adapt and lyrics: Carlos Francisco Asse, from Charles Dickens; music: James Wren; (MD) James Wren; (CH) Richard Rose

From the Mississippi Delta, Dr. Endesha Ida Mae Holland; (D) Shirley Basfield Dunlap; (SD) Marion J. Caffey

Dancing at Lughnasa, Brian Friel; (SD) Carlos Francisco Asse

Marvin's Room, Scott McPherson; (D) Mary Hausch; (S) Dan Conway; (SD) Rocky Draud

Six Women with Brain Death or Expiring Minds Want to Know, book: Christy Brandt, Cheryl Benge, Rosanna E. Coppedge, Valerie Fagan, Ross Freese, Mark Houston, Sandee Johnson and Peggy Pharr; music: Mark Houston; (D) Lauren Caldwell; (MD) Mark Houston; (CH) Richard Rose

Honolulu Theatre for Youth

PAMELA STERLING
Artistic Director

JANE CAMPBELL
Managing Director

DAVID M. TAYLOR
Board President

2846 Ualena St.
Honolulu, HI 96819-1910
(808) 839-9885
(808) 839-7018 (fax)

FOUNDED 1955
Nancy Corbett

SEASON
July-May

FACILITIES

Castle High Theatre
Seating Capacity: 667
Stage: proscenium

Kaimuki High Theatre
Seating Capacity: 667
Stage: proscenium

McCoy Pavilion
Seating Capacity: 500
Stage: flexible

Richardson Theatre
Seating Capacity: 800
Stage: proscenium

Mamiya Theatre
Seating Capacity: 500
Stage: proscenium

FINANCES
June 1, 1992-May 31, 1993
Expenses: $1,200,000

Honolulu Theatre for Youth is dedicated to producing high-quality theatre for young audiences. It offers a broad spectrum of plays each season, from literary classics and childhood favorites to plays dealing with contemporary social issues and Pacific Rim cultures. HTY annually tours statewide with two major productions. Our education program provides materials, workshops and classes to teachers and students. Additionally, HTY actively encourages the development of new plays by commissioning works and sponsoring a young playwrights program through Very Special Arts Hawaii. HTY has provided international outreach programs and has toured to American Samoa, Micronesia and Australia. The ethnic mix of the HTY company is as diverse as the people of Hawaii: Nontraditional casting is the norm. The exploration of cultures, values and theatre forms is what HTY is all about.

—*Pamela Sterling*

PRODUCTIONS 1991-1992

Revenge of Space Pandas, David Mamet; (D) Daniel A. Kelin, II; (S) and (L) Jo Scheder; (C) Cindy Miles; (SD) Michael Mau

The Reluctant Dragon, adapt: Mary Hall Surface, from Kenneth Grahame; (D) Pamela Sterling; (S) Don Ranney; (L) Lloyd S. Riford, III; (C) Julie James

Theatrefest '91:
Direction by Daniel A. Kelin, II

Honolulu Theatre for Youth. *The Servant of Two Masters*. Photo: Lew Harrington.

The Martha War, Daniel London
The Broken Bough, Ramon Arjona, IV
Portraits in Shame, Alfred J.S. Silva

Spoon River Anthology, adapt: Charles Aidman, from Edgar Lee Masters; (D) Pamela Sterling; (S) Don Paine; (L) Sandy Sandelin; (C) Cindy Miles; (SD) Wendell Ing

The Council, William S. Yellow Robe, Jr.; (D) William S. Yellow Robe, Jr.; (S) Don Yanik; (C) Susan Jozefiak

The Dance and the Railroad, David Henry Hwang; (D) Ron Nakahara; (S) Don Yanik; (C) Susan Jozefiak

Tofa Samoa, Victoria Nalani Kneubuhl; (D) Pamela Sterling; (S) Bob Campbell; (C) Susan Jozefiak

Giant's Baby, Allen Ahlberg; (D) Kathleen A. Collins; (S) Joseph D. Dodd; (L) Gerald Kawaoka; (C) Hugh Hanson

Tall Tales and Small People, Kyle Kakuno, Roslyn Freitas and Pamela Sterling; (D) Pamela Sterling; (S) Gary Richardson; (C) Hugh Hanson

PRODUCTIONS 1992-1993

According to Coyote, John Kauffman; (D) Carlotta Kauffman; (S) Don Yanik; (L) Jeff Robbins; (SD) Michael Holten

The Secret Garden, adapt: Pamela Sterling, from Frances Hodgson Burnett; (D) Clayton Corzatte; (S) Bill Forrester; (L) Lloyd S. Riford, III; (C) Karen Ledger

Theatrefest 92:
Direction by Daniel A. Kelin, II

The Mouse Esquire, Justin Brossier
Impossible Dreams, Kimberly J. Rupp
Flower Therapy, Naomi Long

The Servant of Two Masters, Carlo Goldoni; trans: John Alan Wyatt; (D) Randall Duk Kim and Anne Occhiogrosso; (S) Bob Campbell; (L) Jo Scheder; (C) Ada Akaji; (SD) Roslyn Freitas

Just So Stories, adapt: Victoria Nalani Kneubuhl, from Rudyard Kipling; (D) Paul Cravath; (S) Meleanna Meyer; (C) Susan Jozefiak

Tales of the Grotesque, adapt: Eberle Thomas, from Edgar Allan Poe; (D) Daniel A. Kelin, II; (S) Wayne Kischer; (C) Susan Jozefiak; (SD) Michael K. Hase and Gary Richardson

Everyone Knows What a Dragon Looks Like, adapt: Daniel A. Kelin, II, from Jay Williams; (D) Pamela Sterling; (S) Joseph D. Dodd; (L) Don Ranney; (C) Hugh Hanson; (SD) Michael Mau

Crying to Laugh, Marcel Sabourin; trans: John Van Burek; (D) Pamela Sterling; (S) MJ Matsushita; (L) Darren Hochstedler; (C) Hugh Hanson; (SD) Gary Richardson

Popcorn and Peanut Butter, Michael K. Hase; music: Roslyn Freitas; (D) Karen Yamamoto Hackler; (S) Debra Drown; (C) Cynthia See

Horizon Theatre Company. *The Good Times are Killing Me.* Photo: Kathryn Kolb.

Horizon Theatre Company

LISA ADLER
Co-Artistic/Managing Director

JEFF ADLER
Co-Artistic/Technical Director

JESSICA R. LINDEN
Board President

Box 5376, Station E
Atlanta, GA 30307
(404) 523-1477 (bus.)
(404) 584-7450 (b.o.)

FOUNDED 1983
Lisa Adler, Jeff Adler

SEASON
Sept.-June

FACILITIES
Seating Capacity: 170
Stage: flexible

FINANCES
July 1, 1992-June 30, 1993
Expenses: $305,000

CONTRACTS
AEA SPT

Now in its 10th season, Horizon Theatre Company brings to Atlanta's audiences Atlanta, southeastern and world premieres of contemporary plays. We seek out the best of today's plays and playwrights, and new plays that have received acclaim across the country and abroad. We are also beginning to develop new work that speaks specifically to our audience, particularly plays that deal with urban southern themes and/or with the concerns of women. All of the plays we present address the social, political and personal issues of our times; they are thought-provoking, but also entertaining, accessible and often life-affirming. We have a small resident ensemble and are known for the high-quality ensemble acting that has become Horizon's trademark. In addition to our mainstage season, our programs include a Horizon Teen Acting Ensemble and Young Playwrights program.
—*Lisa Adler, Jeff Adler*

PRODUCTIONS 1991-1992

Sets by Jane Williams Flank, lighting by Kevin McDermott, costumes by Yvonne Lee and sound design by Thom Jenkins unless otherwise noted.

The Heidi Chronicles, Wendy Wasserstein; (D) Lisa Adler
Full Moon, Reynolds Price; (D) Jeff Adler; (SD) Lisa Adler
Our Country's Good, adapt: Timberlake Wertenbaker, from Thomas Keneally; (D) Rosemary Newcott; (C) Joanna Schmink
B-Movie, The Play, Tom Wood; (D) Jeff Adler and Teresa DeBerry; (C) Joanna Schmink; (SD) Bryan Mercer

PRODUCTIONS 1992-1993

Sets by Lynne Porter, costumes by Kevin McDermott and sound design by Thom Freeman unless otherwise noted.

Prelude to a Kiss, Craig Lucas; (D) Lisa Adler; (SD) Thom Jenkins
Marvin's Room, Scott McPherson; (D) Jeff Adler
The Film Society, Jon Robin Baitz; (D) Jeff Adler; (S) John Thigpen
The Good Times Are Killing Me, Lynda Barry; (D) Lisa Adler; (S) Tony Loadholt; (SD) Lionel Hamilton and Lynda Barry

Horse Cave Theatre

WARREN HAMMACK
Director

PAMELA WHITE
Associate Director

JANE BARTHELME
Board President

Box 215
Horse Cave, KY 42749
(502) 786-1200 (bus.)
(502) 786-2177,
(800) 342-2177 (b.o.)
(502) 786-5298 (fax)

FOUNDED 1977
Horse Cave citizens

SEASON
June-Dec.

FACILITIES
Seating Capacity: 346
Stage: thrust

FINANCES
Oct. 1, 1991-Sept. 30, 1992
Expenses: $397,802

CONTRACTS
AEA letter of agreement

Horse Cave Theatre is a resident professional theatre ensemble serving regional and national audiences. Under the same artistic direction since its inception, the theatre presents contemporary plays, new scripts and classics in rotating repertory, and seeks to encourage the development of theatre artists, with a particular commitment to Kentucky playwrights. Under the Kentucky Voices program, the theatre has presented nine works by seven Kentucky authors. Believing that the spark of a live performance is a powerful teaching tool, the theatre provides a wide range of educational programs, including a comprehensive outreach program wherein the plays of Shakespeare and classic American plays are presented at the theatre for students from across the region. Study guides, discussions and in-service training for teachers supplement the program. In May 1993, the theatre dedicated a newly renovated and expanded facility which enhances the theatre's technical capabilities and enables it to serve audiences year-round.
—*Warren Hammack*

PRODUCTIONS 1991-1992

Sets by Sam Hunt, lighting by Gregory Etter, costumes by Jennifer Noe and sound design by Wesley Jay Akers unless otherwise noted.

Horse Cave Theatre. Michael Hankins and Kirk Davis in *The Boys Next Door*. Photo: Warren Hammack.

Panic in Paris, Georges Feydeau; trans: Barnett Shaw; (D) Warren Hammack

The Boys Next Door, Tom Griffin; (D) and (S) Pamela White

His First, Best Country, Jim Wayne Miller; (D) Warren Hammack

The Tempest, William Shakespeare; (D) Liz Bussey; (C) Rebecca Shouse

Sleuth, Anthony Shaffer; (D) Liz Bussey; (S) Gregory Etter; (C) Rebecca Shouse

PRODUCTIONS 1992-1993

Direction by Warren Hammack, sets by Sam Hunt, lighting by James E. Boyter, Jr., costumes by Jennifer Noe and sound design by Howard Rose unless otherwise noted.

You Can't Take It With You, George S. Kaufman and Moss Hart; (D) Liz Bussey; (S) Eric Wegener

Marvin's Room, Scott McPherson; (D) and (S) Pamela White

The Crucible, Arthur Miller

Dancing at Lughnasa, Brian Friel; (D) Ryland Merkey

Julius Caesar, William Shakespeare

The Dickens Christmas Carol Show, adapt: Arthur Scholey, from Charles Dickens

Huntington Theatre Company

PETER ALTMAN
Producing Director

MICHAEL MASO
Managing Director

PETER VERMILYE
Board Chairman

264 Huntington Ave.
Boston, MA 02115-4606
(617) 266-7900 (bus.)
(617) 266-0800 (b.o.)
(617) 353-8300 (fax)

FOUNDED 1982
Boston University

SEASON
Sept.-June

FACILITIES
Boston University Theatre
Seating Capacity: 855
Stage: proscenium

Huntington Theatre Company. *Cymbeline*. Photo: Richard Feldman.

FINANCES
July 1, 1992-June 30, 1993
Expenses: $5,800,000

CONTRACTS
AEA LORT (B)

The Huntington Theatre Company is dedicated to producing annual seasons of classic and contemporary plays that are acted, directed and designed at a standard of excellence comparable to that of the nation's leading professional companies. In producing plays of any era or style, we enjoy and admire truthful situations, vivid characters, sound dramatic construction, eloquent language, imaginative staging with well-balanced casts and the finest possible level of craftsmanship. We continually seek to devote ourselves to the great masterpieces of dramatic literature and to produce them in their true spirit; we strive to respond to today's issues and emotions by presenting literate, trenchant contemporary plays new to Boston; and we aim to be enterprising and cosmopolitan in choosing worthy writing from the international theatrical heritage representing varied countries and periods. We believe that a flexible, allied family of professionals who share this vision will best extend, fulfill and serve our theatre's vision.
—*Peter Altman*

PRODUCTIONS 1991-1992

The Snow Ball, A.R. Gurney, Jr.; (D) Jack O'Brien; (S) Douglas W. Schmidt; (L) David F. Segal; (C) Steven Rubin; (SD) Jeff Ladman

Tartuffe, Moliere; trans: Richard Wilbur; (D) Jacques Cartier; (S) Hugh Landwehr; (L) Roger Meeker; (C) John Falabella

The Little Foxes, Lillian Hellman; (D) Kyle Donnelly; (S) Linda Buchanan; (L) Rita Pietraszek; (C) Lindsay W. Davis

Cymbeline, William Shakespeare; (D) Larry Carpenter; (S) John Falabella; (L) Marcia Madeira; (C) David Murin

The Way of the World, William Congreve; (D) Sharon Ott; (S) Kate Edmunds; (L) Stephen Strawbridge; (C) Erin Quigley; (SD) Stephen LeGrand

A Christmas Carol, adapt: Larry Carpenter, from Charles Dickens; (D) Larry Carpenter; (S) James Leonard Joy; (L) Craig Miller; (C) Mariann Verheyen; (SD) Ed McDermid

PRODUCTIONS 1992-1993

Pal Joey, book adapt: Richard Greenberg, from John O'Hara; music: Richard Rodgers; lyrics: Lorenz Hart; (D) David Warren; (S) John Arnone; (L) Peter Kaczorowski; (C) Toni-Leslie James; (MD) Ted Sperling; (CH) Thommie Walsh; (SD) Daryl Bornstein

Long Day's Journey into Night, Eugene O'Neill; (D) Edward Gilbert; (S) Karl Eigsti; (L) Nicholas Cernovitch; (C) Mariann Verheyen

My Mother Said I Never Should, Charlotte Keatley; (D) Charles Towers; (S) John Falabella; (L) Jackie Manassee; (C) Barbra Kravitz; (SD) Eileen Smithheimer

Undiscovered Country, adapt: Tom Stoppard, from Arthur Schnitzler; (D) Jacques Cartier; (S) Kate Edmunds; (L) Roger Meeker; (C) John Falabella

Arms and the Man, George Bernard Shaw; (D) Larry Carpenter; (S) James Leonard Joy; (L) Marcia Madeira; (C) David Murin

A Christmas Carol, adapt: Larry Carpenter, from Charles Dickens; (D) Larry Carpenter; (S) James Leonard Joy; (C) Mariann Verheyen; (SD) John Kilgore

Illinois Theatre Center

STEVE S. BILLIG
Artistic Director

ETEL BILLIG
Managing Director

DONNA JEMILO
Board Chairman

400A Lakewood Blvd.
Park Forest, IL 60466
(708) 481-3510
(708) 481-3693 (fax)

ILLINOIS THEATRE CENTER

FOUNDED 1976
Steve S. Billig, Etel Billig

SEASON
Year-round

FACILITIES
Illinois Theatre Center
Seating Capacity: 187
Stage: thrust

Park Forest Amphitheatre
Seating Capacity: 400
Stage: arena

FINANCES
Sept. 1, 1992-Aug. 31, 1993
Expenses: $265,000

CONTRACTS
AEA CAT

The Illinois Theatre Center was founded in 1976 in the belief that a vigorous artistic and cultural life should be part of all communities. It is through theatre that we hope to enrich the quality of life for all area residents. Through the world of theatre we want our audiences to appreciate man's infinite diversity of expression and the vast range of human invention. Along with our seven-play mainstage season, we have an active outreach program which provides special programming for the elderly, the handicapped and the economically disadvantaged. We also hold an annual free outdoor Classics Festival.

—*Steve S. Billig*

PRODUCTIONS 1991-1992

Direction by Steve S. Billig, sets by Wayne Adams, lighting and sound design by Jonathan Roark and costumes by Pat Decker unless otherwise noted.

After the Dancing in Jericho, P.J. Barry
Fences, August Wilson; (S) and (L) Archway Scenic
Fanny, book adapt and lyrics: S.N. Behrman and Joshua Logan, from Marcel Pagnol; music: Harold Rome; (S) Archway Scenic; (L) Wayne Adams; (C) Elea Crowther; (MD) Jonathan Roark; (CH) Ed Kross
The Cemetery Club, Ivan Menchell; (S) Jonathan Roark and Wayne Adams
The Rabbit Foot, Leslie Lee; (D) Etel Billig; (L) Archway Scenic; (C) Elea Crowther
I'm Not Rappaport, Herb Gardner; (D) Wayne Adams; (S) Jonathan Roark
Penny Serenade, Steve S. Billig; various composers and lyricists; (L) Wayne Adams; (C) Jewel-Ann Creations

PRODUCTIONS 1992-1993

Direction by Steve S. Billig, sets by Wayne Adams, lighting and sound design by Jonathan Roark and costumes by Pat Decker unless otherwise noted.

Homeward Bound, Elliott Hayes; (D) Steve S. Billig and Wayne Adams; (S) Jonathan Roark
Amigo's Blue Guitar, Joan MacLeod; (D) Wayne Adams; (S) Proctor
Olympus On My Mind, book and lyrics: Barry Harman; music: Grant Sturiale; (S) and (L) Archway Scenic; (C) Leigh Ann Ruyle; (MD) Jonathan Roark; (CH) Blair Bybee
The Piano Lesson, August Wilson; (S) Jonathan Roark
Our Country's Good, adapt: Timberlake Wertenbaker, from Thomas Keneally; (C) Jewel-Ann Creations
My Son the Lawyer is Drowning, Doug MacLeod; (D) Steve S. Billig and Wayne Adams; (S) Jonathan Roark
Romance/Romance, book adapt and lyrics: Barry Harman, from Arthur Schnitzler and Jules Renard; music: Keith Herrmann; (C) Stephen and Diane Moore; (MD) Jonathan Roark; (CH) Blair Bybee

Illusion Theater. Peter Macon and Melba Perry in Objects in the Mirror are Closer than They Appear. *Photo: Bill Carlson.*

Illinois Theatre Center. A.C. Smith, Al Boswell, Reri Barrett, Darryl Rocky Davis in The Piano Lesson. *Photo: Todd Panagopoulos.*

Illusion Theater

MICHAEL ROBINS
Executive Producing Director

BONNIE MORRIS
Producing Director

WILLIAM VENNE
Managing Director

SHELLY ENGELSMA
Board President

528 Hennepin Ave., Suite 704
Minneapolis, MN 55403
(612) 339-4944 (bus.)
(612) 338-8371 (b.o.)
(612) 337-8042 (fax)

FOUNDED 1974
Michael Robins, Carole Harris Lipschulz, Bonnie Morris

SEASON
Dec.-July

FACILITIES
Hennepin Center for the Arts
Seating Capacity: 220
Stage: modified thrust

FINANCES
Jan. 1, 1992-Dec. 31, 1992
Expenses: $946,253

CONTRACTS
AEA SPT

Illusion Theater's mission is to create theatre that illuminates the human condition by addressing the illusions, myths and realities of our times, and to use the power of theatre to be a catalyst for personal and social change. Illusion Theater is committed to developing new voices, expressing ideas that reflect a variety of cultural perspectives and contributing to positive social change. We have guided the creation of more than 100 new works in collaboration with playwrights, actors, directors, composers, designers and human-service professionals. Our nationally acclaimed sexual abuse prevention play, *Touch*, was created in 1978 and was the beginning of our Prevention Program. This educational awareness program is focused on promoting healthy sexuality and relationships through the prevention of sexual abuse, interpersonal violence, HIV/AIDS and sexual harassment.

—*Michael Robins, Bonnie Morris*

PRODUCTIONS 1992

Sets by James Salen and costumes by John Strauss unless otherwise noted.

Objects in the Mirror are Closer than They Appear, Mark Cryer and Lester Purry; (D) Lester Purry; (L) Darren McCroom; (SD) Brandon Smith

Kind Ness, Ping Chong; (D) and (S) Ping Chong; (L) Frederic Desbois; (C) Mel Carpenter; (SD) Brian Hallas

River's Edge, Susan Delattre, Diane Elliot, Margie Fargnoli, Rebecca Frost and Erika Thorne; (D) the playwrights; (L) James Salen; (C) Mary Claire Lowy O'Brien; (SD) Hamsa Hanzak

Covers, Carolyn Goezler, *Wishbone*, Judy McGuire, and *Confessions*, Ben Krielkamp; (D) the playwrights; (L) Robin Macgregor; (SD) Daron Walker

Do Not Pass Go, Kim Hines; (D) Michael Robins; (S) Steve Reiser; (L) Darren McCroom

Gold, Jawn Fleming and Louise Smith; (D) Jawn Fleming and Louise Smith; (S) Paul Krajniak; (L) David Vogel

Among Our Own, Eric Anderson; (D) Gary Gisselman; (S) Dean Holzman; (L) Barry Browning; (C) Lori Sullivan Worthman; (SD) Anita Ruth

If We Never Meet Again, Josette Antomarchi, Beth Gilleland, Mary McDevitt and Sue Scott; (D) the playwrights; (L) James Salen

December, Myron Johnson, Bonnie Morris and Michael Robins; music and lyrics: Michael Keck; (D) Myron Johnson, Bonnie Morris and Michael Robins; (L) Barry Browning; (C) Thea Ennen and Lyle Jackson; (MD) Michael Keck; (CH) Myron Johnson; (SD) Ezra Gold

PRODUCTIONS 1993

Sets by James Salen, lighting by Thomas Campbell, costumes by Thea Ennen and sound design by Brandon Smith unless otherwise noted.

From the Mississippi Delta, Dr. Endesha Ida Mae Holland; (D) Shirley Jo Finney; (L) Darren McCroom

Cut on the Bias and *Do Not Pass Go*, Kim Hines; (D) Michael Robins; (L) David Vogel

Oracle Mountain, Michael Smith; (D) Jim Stowell

Queer Thinking, Patrick Scully; (D) Patrick Scully

In the White Harvest: The Importance of Road Construction, Laura Littleford; (D) Laura Littleford

Christopher's Shirt, Eric Anderson; (D) Risa Brainin

Enlightenments on an Enchanted Island, Marion Isaac McClinton; (D) Marion Isaac McClinton

Whistling Girls & Crowing Hens, Beth Gilleland

The Independent Eye

CONRAD BISHOP
Producing Director

ELIZABETH FULLER
Associate Producing Director

ROBERT WEBBER
Board Chair

115 Arch St.
Philadelphia, PA 19106
(215) 925-2838

FOUNDED 1974
Conrad Bishop, Elizabeth Fuller

SEASON
Variable

FACILITIES
Old City Stage Works
Seating Capacity: 49
Stage: flexible

FINANCES
July 1, 1992-June 30, 1993
Expenses: $91,881

The Independent Eye is a progressive ensemble devoted to new plays and new visions of classics. We look for startling, deeply felt stories, leapfrogging through styles to find the right language for each. We often start a work without knowing whether it's to be funny, grisly, or both; for us, theatre is an art of juggling extremes to bring us into intense *presence*—to sit with the assembled tribe and feel the pain and promise of being human. Always, at the core: Is the story's heart true? Surprising? Our stake in telling it? Since 1974, the Eye has toured 34 states and produced resident seasons in Lancaster, Penn. before relocating to Old City Stage Works in Philadelphia, as a base for creating new work, touring and developing video, radio drama and co-productions. We've gone through continual changes in structure, strategy and where to hang our hats—all to keep the center true.

—Conrad Bishop

PRODUCTIONS 1991-1992

Plays by Conrad Bishop and Elizabeth Fuller, and direction, sets and lighting by Conrad Bishop unless otherwise noted.

Tapdancer; (S) John Whiting; (C) Sharon S.Q. Campbell

Rash Acts; (C) Nancy Whiting

Dividing Lines

The Man that Corrupted Hadleyburg, adapt: Conrad Bishop, from Mark Twain

PRODUCTIONS 1992-1993

Plays by Conrad Bishop and Elizabeth Fuller, and direction, sets and lighting by Conrad Bishop unless otherwise noted.

Loveplay; (S) Conrad Bishop and Elizabeth Fuller

Reality: Friend or Foe?

Rash Acts; (C) Nancy Whiting

Dividing Lines

Indiana Repertory Theatre

LIBBY APPEL
Artistic Director

JANET ALLEN
Associate Artistic Director

BRIAN PAYNE
Managing Director

DAVID H. KLEIMAN
Board President

140 West Washington St.
Indianapolis, IN 46204-3465
(317) 635-5277 (bus.)
(317) 635-5252 (b.o.)
(317) 236-0767 (fax)

FOUNDED 1972
Edward Stern, Gregory Poggi, Benjamin Mordecai

SEASON
Oct.-May

FACILITIES
Mainstage
Seating Capacity: 607
Stage: proscenium

Upperstage
Seating Capacity: 269
Stage: proscenium

Cabaret
Seating Capacity: 150
Stage: thrust

The Independent Eye. Elizabeth Fuller and Conrad Bishop in *Rash Acts*.

Indiana Repertory Theatre. *Hamlet*. Photo: Tod Martens.

FINANCES
July 1, 1992-June 30, 1993
Expenses: $3,357,700

CONTRACTS
AEA LORT (C) and (D), and TYA

As Indiana's only resident professional theatre, the IRT's mission embraces a broad spectrum of activities, addressing an audience extending from those in whom an appreciation of theatre must be awakened to those who seek the most innovative and provocative in the arts. In the Mainstage subscription series we dedicate our energies to bringing together artists of diverse backgrounds and points of view to create a season of classic and contemporary plays. We seek to rediscover the classics, eliciting fresh perspectives on them and exploring them for their relevance to our community. Similarly, we examine contemporary work for its pungent and challenging questions about our lives. IRT's combined educational outreach programs bring more than 40,000 students annually to the theatre: to matinees of our mainstage productions; to a special high school program, Classic Theatre for Youth; and to Junior Works, a project to which we have dedicated our Upperstage theatre, aiming to develop a young, multicultural company of professional actors to perform three plays annually for junior high school audiences. We are convinced that we can have a profound impact on the lives of these young audiences.

—*Libby Appel*

Note: During the 1991-92 season, Janet Allen served as interim artistic director.

PRODUCTIONS 1991-1992

Sound design by Milo Miller.

Major Barbara, George Bernard Shaw; (D) John David Lutz; (S) Craig Clipper; (L) Stuart Duke; (C) Catherine F. Norgren
Charley's Aunt, Brandon Thomas; (D) Gavin Cameron-Webb; (S) G.W. Mercier; (L) Rachel Budin; (C) Gail Brassard
The Road to Mecca, Athol Fugard; (D) Amy Saltz; (S) and (C) G.W. Mercier; (L) Robert Wierzel
Spunk, adapt: George C. Wolfe, from Zora Neale Hurston; music: Chic Street Man; (D) Thomas W. Jones, II; (S) Russell Metheny; (L) Michael Lincoln; (C) Goldie Dicks
The Cocktail Hour, A.R. Gurney, Jr.; (D) Nicholas Hormann; (S) and (C) Ann Sheffield; (L) Donald Holder
Twelfth Night, William Shakespeare; (D) Travis Preston; (S) Christopher Barreca; (L) Stephen Strawbridge; (C) Ann Sheffield
The Gifts of the Magi, book adapt and lyrics: Mark St. Germain, from O. Henry; music: Randy Courts; (D) Laurel Eldredge Goetzinger; (S) Jeffrey D. Schneider; (L) Joel Grynheim; (C) Deborah L. Shippee; (MD) Terry Woods; (CH) Michelle Jarvis
Huck Finn's Story, adapt: Aurand Harris, from Mark Twain; (D) Michael Lipton; (S) Chib Gratz; (L) Betsy Cooprider-Bernstein; (C) Deborah L. Shippee
The Secret History of the Future, James Still; (D) Janet Allen; (S) Mickey White; (L) DW Phineas Perkins; (C) Jennifer Q. Smith

PRODUCTIONS 1992-1993

Sound design by Milo Miller.

Yerma, Federico Garcia Lorca; trans: Christopher Martin; music: Gerardo Dirie; (D) Libby Appel; (S) William Bloodgood; (L) Robert Peterson; (C) Deborah M. Dryden; (CH) David Hochoy
The Miser, Moliere; trans: Douglas Hughes; (D) Richard Russell Ramos; (S) Peter Harrison; (L) Peter Maradudin; (C) David C. Paulin
Miss Evers' Boys, David Feldshuh; (D) Libby Appel; (S) Joel Fontaine; (L) Robert Peterson; (C) Arthur Ridley
And a Nightingale Sang, C.P. Taylor; (D) Philip Killian and Libby Appel; (S) Michael C. Smith; (L) Peter Maradudin; (C) Elizabeth Novak
Shirley Valentine, Willy Russell; (D) Seret Scott; (S) Russell Metheny; (L) Stuart Duke; (C) Azan Kung
Hamlet, William Shakespeare; (D) Libby Appel; (S) Michael C. Smith; (L) Robert Peterson; (C) Constanza Romero
Tales from the Arabian Nights, Michael Bigelow Dixon; music: Jan Cole; (D) and (CH) Peter Amster; (S) and (C) John Paoletti; (L) Betsy Cooprider-Bernstein
Rosa Parks and the Montgomery Bus Boycott, Sue Greenberg; (D) Donald Griffin; (S) Amy Smith; (L) Kathy Perkins; (C) Wendy Meaden
The Red Badge of Courage, adapt: Thomas W. Olson, from Stephen Crane; (D) Loretta Yoder; (S) Wes Peters; (L) Betsy Cooprider-Bernstein; (C) Jeanette DeJong

INTAR Hispanic American Arts Center

MAX FERRA
Artistic Director

EVA BRUNE
Managing Director

STANLEY T. STAIRS
Board Chairman

Box 788
New York, NY 10108
(212) 695-6134
(212) 268-0102 (fax)

FOUNDED 1966
Max Ferra, Frank Robles, Elsa Ortiz Robles, Gladys Ortiz, Benjamin Lopez, Antonio Gonzalez-Jaen, Oscar Garcia

SEASON
July-June

FACILITIES
INTAR on Theatre Row
Seating Capacity: 99
Stage: proscenium

INTAR Two
Seating Capacity: 75
Stage: proscenium

Playhouse 91
Seating Capacity: 299
Stage: proscenium

FINANCES
July 1, 1992-June 30, 1993
Expenses: $1,093,748

CONTRACTS
AEA letter of agreement

INTAR Hispanic American Arts Center includes a theatre and a multicultural visual-arts gallery. Our theatre program is developmental in nature. In addition to our mainstage season, we present theatrical works-in-progress and a series of readings of new plays. INTAR's aim is to see Hispanic voices take their place in the forefront of our nation's arts expression. We continue to respond to the ever-changing nature of this rich and vital American voice through commissioning, presenting, touring and interdisciplinary collaborations. Our mission today remains as focused as it was 28 years ago: to identify, develop and present the work of Hispanic-American theatre artists and multicultural visual artists, as well as to introduce outstanding works by internationally respected Latin artists to American audiences.

—*Max Ferra*

PRODUCTIONS 1991-1992

Our Lady of the Tortilla, Luis Santeiro; (D) Max Ferra; (S) Charles McCarry; (L) Michael Chybowski; (C) Claudia Stephens; (SD) Gary Harris

The Lady from Havana, Luis Santeiro; (D) Max Ferra; (S) and (C) Campbell Baird; (L) Debra Dumas; (SD) Fox and Perla, Ltd.

Any Place But Here, Caridad Svich; (D) George Ferencz; (S) Bill Stabile; (L) Ernie Barbarash; (C) Sally Lesser; (SD) Alina Avila

PRODUCTIONS 1992-1993

Daedalus in the Belly of the Beast, Marco Antonio de la Parra; trans: Joanne Pottlitzer; adapt: Alfredo Castro and Francesca Lombardo; (D) Alfredo Castro; (S) and (L) Curtis Dretsch; (C) David Kutos; (SD) David Kutos and Curtis Dretsch

Words Divine, Ramon del Valle-Inclan; trans and adapt: Lorenzo Mans; (D) Max Ferra; (S) and (C) Rimer Cardillo; (L) Mark McCullough; (SD) Fox and Perla, Ltd.

Nostalgia Tropical, conceived: Max Ferra; various composers and lyricists; (D) Max Ferra; (S) Riccardo Hernandez; (L) Jennifer Tipton; (C) Randy Barcelo; (MD) Meme Solis; (CH) Victor Cuellar; (SD) Fox and Perla, Ltd.

INTAR Hispanic American Arts Center. Christopher Coucill and Ofelia Medina in *Words Divine*. Photo: Paula Court.

Intiman Theatre Company. Reiko Aylesworth and Ronald Hippe in *Peter Pan*. Photo: Chris Bennion.

Intiman Theatre Company

WARNER SHOOK
Artistic Director

IDA S. COLE
Board President

Box 19760, Seattle, WA 98109
(206) 626-0775 (bus.)
(206) 626-0782 (b.o.)
(206) 626-0778 (fax)

FOUNDED 1972
Margaret Booker

SEASON
May-Dec.

FACILITIES
Intiman Playhouse
Seating Capacity: 424
Stage: thrust

FINANCES
Jan. 1, 1992-Dec. 31, 1992
Expenses: $2,400,000

CONTRACTS
AEA LORT (C)

What I aspire to in my work is to find the very essence of the human condition in a play, crystallize that essence and present it to an audience in theatrical terms. If I've done my job correctly, all participants are enlightened, informed, uplifted and entertained. Like my predecessor, I am committed to presenting plays of stature (works whose themes endure and continue to speak to us)—a healthy mixture of established classics, challenging contemporary works and world-premiere plays. Encouraging the art of our time is necessary to guarantee the cultural health of our future. Hopefully, at Intiman, our world-premiere plays will become the established classics of tomorrow. As artists, we are the overseers of our cultural heritage. We present the stories that examine who we are: how we behave and think, how we change and grow. We are at the very heartbeat of our civilization.

—*Warner Shook*

Note: During the 1992 season, Elizabeth Huddle served as artistic director.

PRODUCTIONS 1992

Sets and costumes by David Zinn unless otherwise noted.

Macbeth, William Shakespeare; (D) Susan Fenichell; (L) Mary Louise Geiger; (SD) Steven M. Klein

Catherine: Concerning the Fateful Origins of Her Grandeur, with Diverse Musical Interludes, Three Elephants and No Ballet, book and lyrics: Louisa Rose; music: Jim Ragland; (D) Elizabeth Huddle; (S) Craig Labenz; (L) Meg Fox; (C) Todd Roehrman; (MD) and (SD): Jim Ragland; (CH) Robert Davidson

Antigone, Jean Anouilh; trans: Barbara Bray; (D) Daniel Renner; (L) Meg Fox; (SD) Robert Davidson
How the Other Half Loves, Alan Ayckbourn; (D) M. Burke Walker; (S) Craig Labenz; (L) Rick Paulsen; (C) Frances Kenny; (SD) Steven M. Klein
Warrior, Shirley Gee; (D) Susan Fenichell; (L) Michael Wellborn; (C) Todd Roehrman; (SD) David Pascal
Peter Pan, James M. Barrie; (D) Edward Payson Call; (S) Karen Gjelsteen; (L) Don Darnutzer; (SD) Larry Delinger and Chris Walker

PRODUCTIONS 1993

Sets by Michael Olich unless otherwise noted.

Faith Healer, Brian Friel; (D) Warner Shook; (L) Peter Maradudin; (C) Frances Kenny; (SD) Jim Ragland
The Importance of Being Earnest, Oscar Wilde; (D) Victor Pappas; (L) Greg Sullivan; (C) David Zinn; (SD) David Pascal
From the Mississippi Delta, Dr. Endesha Ida Mae Holland; (D) Jacqueline Moscou; (L) Allen Lee Hughes; (C) Constanza Romero; (SD) David Pascal
"Master Harold"...and the boys, Athol Fugard; (D) Edward Payson Call
Intimate Exchanges, Alan Ayckbourn; (D) Elizabeth Huddle; (L) Rick Paulsen
Peter Pan, James M. Barrie; (D) Edward Payson Call; (S) Karen Gjelsteen; (L) Don Darnutzer; (C) David Zinn; (SD) Larry Delinger and Chris Walker

Irondale Ensemble Project. *Antigone*. Photo: Gerry Goodstein.

Irondale Ensemble Project

JIM NIESEN
Artistic Director

TERRY GREISS
Executive Director

BARBARA HAUBEN ROSS
Board Chairperson

Box 1314, Old Chelsea Station
New York, NY 10011
(212) 633-1292
(212) 633-2078 (fax)

FOUNDED 1983
Jim Niesen, Terry Greiss, Barbara MacKenzie-Wood

SEASON
Variable

FACILITIES
Hudson Guild
Seating Capacity: 99
Stage: proscenium

House of Candles
Seating Capacity: 70
Stage: flexible

FINANCES
July 1, 1992-June 30, 1993
Expenses: $397,000

CONTRACTS
AEA letter of agreement

Irondale is a research theatre company with roots in improvisation, extensive movement work and collaborative writing techniques. Typically the theatre uses a variety of performance styles to explore classic texts and re-form them into new pieces located in the context of contemporary times. Since 1983 Irondale has created more than 20 original works for the theatre, staged the American premiere of Brecht's *Conversations in Exile*, and established an extensive outreach program in the New York City jails, high school special education programs and alternative high schools. The company tours nationally and internationally and, since 1990, has collaborated with Walter Thompson and the Walter Thompson Orchestra. The Irondale AIDS Improv Team works throughout the school year to inform New York City students about safe sex practices and the facts of HIV infection. Irondale's educational techniques are made accessible nationally through the CINE award-winning *Game Video*.
—*Jim Niesen*

PRODUCTIONS 1991-1992

Sets by Kennon Rothchild, lighting by Hilarie Blumenthal and costumes by Elena Pellicciaro.

AIDS Show, company-developed; (D) Molly Hickok
Antigone, Sophocles; adapt: company; music: Walter Thompson; (D) Jim Niesen; (MD) Steve Osgood; (CH) Annie-B Parson
The Hostage, Brendan Behan; (D) Barbara MacKenzie-Wood

PRODUCTIONS 1992-1993

Sets by Kennon Rothchild, lighting by Hilarie Blumenthal and costumes by Elena Pellicciaro.

AIDS Show, company-developed; (D) Nicole Potter
Antigone, Sophocles; adapt: company; music: Walter Thompson; (D) Jim Niesen; (MD) Walter Thompson; (CH) Annie-B Parson
Past Times, company-developed; (D) Nicole Potter
Saint Joan of the Stockyards, Bertolt Brecht; trans: Ralph Manheim; music: Walter Thompson; (D) Jim Niesen; (MD) Walter Thompson; (CH) Carrie Owerko

Jean Cocteau Repertory

ROBERT HUPP
Artistic Director

SCOTT SHATTUCK
Producing Director

ROBERT W. BEREND, ALAN I. GOLDMAN
Board Co-Chairs

Bouwerie Lane Theatre
330 Bowery
New York, NY 10012
(212) 677-0060
(212) 777-6151 (fax)

FOUNDED 1971
Eve Adamson

SEASON
Aug.-June

FACILITIES
Bouwerie Lane Theatre
Seating Capacity: 140
Stage: proscenium

FINANCES
July 1, 1992-June 30, 1993
Expenses: $425,000

The Cocteau is a resident company of artists performing in rotating repertory those works of world theatre which by their very nature demand to live on a stage. The company is committed to Jean Cocteau's "poetry of the theatre" in which all elements of production—performance, design, music—fuse into a whole that illuminates the heart of the play and elevates it into a "dramatic poem." Whether approaching a classic or a contemporary work of provocative content and structure, the Cocteau strives to create that unique production style appropriate to each play which will engage the audience intellectually and emotionally. Meeting this artistic challenge in rotating repertory requires a disciplined and flexible resident acting company, as well as bold and imaginative designers and directors. Towards that end, the Cocteau has developed and continued to nurture a growing community of repertory-oriented theatre artists.
—*Robert Hupp*

Jean Cocteau Repertory. Mark Waterman, Robert Ierardi, Craig Smith and Grant Neale in *Galileo*. Photo: Gerry Goodstein.

PRODUCTIONS 1991-1992

Costumes by Jonathan Bixby unless otherwise noted.

The Skin of Our Teeth, Thornton Wilder; (D) Robert Hupp; (S) and (L) Giles Hogya; (SD) Ellen Mandel
Geneva, George Bernard Shaw; (D) Casey Kizziah; (S) Robert Joel Schwartz; (L) Brian Aldous; (SD) Ellen Mandel
Galileo, Bertolt Brecht; trans: Charles Laughton; (D) and (L) Eve Adamson; (S) John Brown; (SD) Haze Greenfield
Mary Stuart, Friedrich Schiller; trans: Robert David MacDonald; (D) Casey Kizziah; (S) George Xenos; (L) Brian Aldous; (C) Gregory Gale
Endgame, Samuel Beckett; (D) and (L) Eve Adamson; (S) John Brown
The Vanek Plays, Vaclav Havel; trans: Jan Novak and Vera Blackwell; (D) David Fishelson; (S) Patrick Heydenburg; (L) Brian Aldous

PRODUCTIONS 1992-1993

Under Milk Wood, Dylan Thomas; (D) Robert Hupp; (S) and (L) Giles Hogya; (C) Andrea Gibbs; (SD) Ellen Mandel
An Old Actress in the Role of Dostoevsky's Wife, Edvard Radzinsky; trans: Alma H. Law; (D) Eve Adamson; (S) and (L) Giles Hogya; (C) Susan Soetaert; (SD) Joseph Ciolino
The Caretaker, Harold Pinter; (D) and (L) Eve Adamson; (S) John Brown; (C) Ofra Confino
The Idiot, adapt: David Fishelson, from Fyodor Dostoevski; (D) David Fishelson; (S) Robert Joel Schwartz; (L) Brian Aldous; (C) Susan Soetaert; (SD) Ellen Mandel
Much Ado About Nothing, William Shakespeare; (D) Robert Hupp; (S) George Xenos; (L) Brian Aldous; (C) Susan Soetaert; (SD) Ellen Mandel
The Cenci, Percy Bysshe Shelley; (D) and (L) Eve Adamson; (S) John Brown; (C) Steven F. Graver; (SD) Dennis Green

Jewish Repertory Theatre

RAN AVNI
Artistic Director

STEPHEN LEVY
General Manager

EVELYN CLYMAN
Board President

92nd Street Y
1395 Lexington Ave.
New York, NY 10128
(212) 415-5550 (bus.)
(212) 831-2000 (b.o.)
(212) 415-5575 (fax)

FOUNDED 1974
Ran Avni

SEASON
Oct.-June

FACILITIES
Playhouse 91
Seating Capacity: 299
Stage: proscenium

FINANCES
July 1, 1992-June 30, 1993
Expenses: $500,000

The Jewish Repertory Theatre is now in its 20th season. JRT has revived such treasured classics as *Awake and Sing!*, *Green Fields* and *Incident at Vichy*; has rediscovered forgotten American works such as *Me and Molly*, *Unlikely Heroes*, *Success Story* and *Cantorial*; has shed new light on the plays of Chekhov, Pinter, Sartre and des Ghelderode; has produced a series of new musicals including *Vagabond Stars*, *Up from Paradise*, *Kuni-Lemi* (which won four Outer Critics Circle Awards, including Best Off Broadway Musical), *Pearls*, *The Special*, *The Shop on Main Street*, *Chu Chem* and *Theda Bara and the Frontier Rabbi*. The JRT Writers' Lab, led by associate director Edward M. Cohen, does readings, workshops and miniproductions aimed at developing the works of young writers. This program has resulted in JRT productions of *Taking Steam*, *Benya the King*, *36*, *Crossing Delancy*, *Bitter Friends* and other plays which are now being produced throughout the country.
—*Ran Avni*

PRODUCTIONS 1991-1992

Shmulnik's Waltz, Allan Knee; (D) Gordon Hunt; (S) Ray Recht; (L) Betsy Finston; (C) David Loveless
A Life in the Theatre, David Mamet; (D) Kevin Dowling; (S) Rob Odorisio; (L) Brian Nason; (C) Teresa Brooks
The Sunset Gang, book and lyrics, Warren Adler; music: L. Russel Brown; (D) Edward M. Cohen; (S) Ray Recht; (L) Spencer Moss; (C) Edi Giguere; (MD) Andrew Howard; (CH) Ricarda O'Conner
The Last Laugh, adapt: Michael Hardstark, from Anton Chekhov; (D) Lou Jacob; (S) Rob Odorisio; (L) Teresa Snider-Stein; (C) Brian Nason

PRODUCTIONS 1992-1993

God of Vengeance, Sholem Asch; adapt: Stephen Fife; (D) Ran Avni; (S) Rob Odorisio; (L) Betsy Finston; (C) Gail Cooper-Hecht

Jewish Repertory Theatre. Roslyn Kind and Robert Ari in *Show Me Where the Good Times Are*. Photo: Carol Rosegg/Martha Swope Associates.

Theda Bara and the Frontier Rabbi, book: Jeff Hochhauser; music: Bob Johnston; lyrics: Jeff Hochhauser and Bob Johnston; (D) and (CH) Lynn Taylor-Corbett; (S) Michael C. Smith; (L) Tom Sturge; (C) Tom Reiter; (MD) Michael Rafter; (SD) Scott Stauffer

The King of Carpets, Joel Hammer; (D) Edward M. Cohen; (S) Ray Recht; (L) Brian Nason; (C) Brenda Rousseau; (SD) Michael Grumer

Show Me Where the Good Times Are, book adapt: Leonora Thuna, from Moliere; music: Kenneth Jacobson; lyrics: Rhoda Roberts; (D) Warren Enters; (S) Michael Bottari and Ronald Case; (L) Michael J. Baldassari; (C) Hal George; (MD) Darren R. Cohen; (CH) Dennis Grimaldi; (SD) Scott Stauffer

Jomandi Productions, Inc.

THOMAS W. JONES, II
Co-Artistic Director

MARSHA A. JACKSON
Co-Artistic Director/
Managing Director

BOB HOLMES
Board Chairperson

1444 Mayson St. NE
Atlanta, GA 30324
(404) 876-6346 (bus.)
(404) 873-1099 (b.o.)
(404) 872-5764 (fax)

FOUNDED 1978
Thomas W. Jones, II,
Marsha A. Jackson

SEASON
Oct.-June

FACILITIES
14th St. Playhouse
Seating Capacity: 378
Stage: proscenium

Center Stage
Seating Capacity: 900
Stage: arena

FINANCES
July 1, 1992-June 30, 1993
Expenses: $816,412

CONTRACTS
AEA SPT

At Jomandi's philosophical and aesthetic center is the assertion of the African-American presence in a global community. That presence, while informed by tradition, concurrently acknowledges the present and future possibilities. From this center evolves the design of our programs. Jomandi's upcoming season continues the development of an aesthetic within an ever-changing universe. The company's artistic voice is an articulation of the newest works from established and emerging playwrights. The commitment to tour productions nationally and internationally this year, while maintaining a schedule of productions in Atlanta, underscores the company's mission to fulfill the cultural needs of the widest possible community. As architects of the future, Jomandi will continue to redefine the means by which African-American artists examine the values of a new world culture. In this way, the company contributes to a future that encourages cultural pluralism and, specifically, an appreciation of the African-American presence, while capitalizing on the economic and development potentials of theatre in a world marketplace.

—*Marsha A. Jackson,
Thomas W. Jones, II*

PRODUCTIONS 1991-1992

Direction by Andrea Frye, lighting by Paul Evans, III and sound design by Craig Cousins unless otherwise noted.

The Colored Museum, George C. Wolfe; (S) Art Johnson; (L) Rae Williams; (C) Goldie Dicks

Still Life, book: Thomas W. Jones, II; various composers and lyricists; (D) Thomas W. Jones, II; (S) Tony Loadholt; (C) Andre Peck; (MD) Jerome Roberson; (CH) Andre Peck, Ron Frazier and Jackie Crenshaw

Spunk, adapt: George C. Wolfe, from Zora Neale Hurston; music: Chic Street Man; (S) Art Johnson; (C) Sharlene Ross

The Meeting, Jeff Stetson; (D) Chuck Smith; (S) and (L) Tim Oien; (C) Glenn Billings; (SD) Corbiere Boynes

Today, Valetta Anderson; (S) Art Johnson and Debi Barber; (C) Edouard

Sisters, Marsha A. Jackson; (D) Thomas W. Jones, II; (S) John Harris and Debi Barber; (L) John Harris; (C) Debi Barber

The Wizard of Hip, Thomas W. Jones, II; (D) Kenneth Leon; (S) Tony Loadholt; (C) Goldie Dicks

Do Lord Remember Me, James de Jongh; (S) and (L) John Harris; (S) Andrea Frye and Craig Cousins

PRODUCTIONS 1992-1993

Jar the Floor, Cheryl L. West; (D) Andrea Frye; (S) Annie Blackburn; (L) Christian Epps; (C) Sharlene Ross

The Fisherman, Dianne Houston; (D) and (SD) Thomas W. Jones, II; (S) Art Johnson; (L) Randall Cox; (C) Sharlene Ross

She'll Find Her Way Home, Valetta Anderson; (D) and (SD) Andrea Frye; (S) Art Johnson and Debi Barber; (L) Paul Evans, III; (C) Sharlene Ross

The Meeting, Jeff Stetson; (D) Chuck Smith; (S) and (L) Tim Oien; (C) Glenn Billings; (SD) Corbiere Boynes

The Wizard of Hip, Thomas W. Jones, II; (D) Kenneth Leon; (S) Tony Loadholt; (L) Paul Evans, III; (C) Goldie Dicks

Bessie's Blues, book: Thomas W. Jones, II; music: Thomas W. Jones, II and Keith Rawls; various lyricists; (D) Thomas W. Jones, II; (S) Art Johnson; (L) Christian Epps; (C) Goldie Dicks; (MD) Keith Rawls; (CH) Patdro Harris

Jomandi Productions, Inc. Bernardine Mitchell in *Bessie's Blues*. Photo: Shiela Turner.

La Jolla Playhouse

DES McANUFF
Artistic Director

TERRENCE DWYER
Managing Director

ROBERT BLACKER
Associate Artistic Director

WILLARD P. VANDERLAAN
Board President

Box 12039
La Jolla, CA 92039
(619) 550-1070 (bus.)
(619) 550-1010 (b.o.)
(619) 550-1075 (fax)

FOUNDED 1947
Gregory Peck, Dorothy McGuire, Mel Ferrer

SEASON
May-Nov.

FACILITIES
Mandell Weiss Theatre
Seating Capacity: 492
Stage: proscenium

Mandell Weiss Forum
Seating Capacity: 384
Stage: thrust

FINANCES
Nov. 1, 1991-Oct. 31, 1992
Expenses: $5,824,719

CONTRACTS
AEA LORT (B) and (C) contracts

The La Jolla Playhouse provides a home in which theatre artists can gather, share ideas and extend themselves. At the heart of each project we produce is a director, playwright or performer who can impact the development of our art form and help define the course of American theatre. We encourage a variety of genres and styles, believing that the vitality of the American theatre is bound to our rich and diverse theatrical and cultural heritage. We produce new work and classics side by side because we believe that they inform each other—that working on classics expands contemporary artists' ideas about theatre, and that new works keep classics honest by reminding us that they must be pertinent. This juxtaposition allows artists and audiences alike to examine contemporary issues in a historical context.

—*Des McAnuff*

PRODUCTIONS 1992

Sets by Robert Brill, lighting by John Martin and costumes by Janice Benning unless otherwise noted.

The Glass Menagerie, Tennessee Williams; (D) Douglas Hughes; (S) Andrei Both; (L) Peter Maradudin; (C) David C. Woolard; (SD) Michael Roth

Le Petomane, adapt: Paul Magid, from Howard Patterson (co-produced by The Flying Karamazov Brothers); (D) Robert Woodruff; (S) Douglas Stein; (C) Susan Hilferty and Candice Cain; (SD) James LeBrecht

The Who's Tommy, book adapt and lyrics: Pete Townshend and Des McAnuff; music: The Who; (D) Des McAnuff; (S) John Arnone; (L) Frances Aronson; (C) David C. Woolard; (MD) Joseph Church; (CH) Wayne Cilento; (SD) Steve Kennedy

What the Butler Saw, Joe Orton; (D) Michael Greif; (S) John Arnone; (L) David Thayer; (SD) Jeff Ladman

Playland, Athol Fugard; (D) Athol Fugard; (S) and (C) Susan Hilferty; (L) Dennis Parichy; (SD) David Budries

Marisol, Jose Rivera; (D) Tina Landau; (SD) John Gromada

The Swan, Elizabeth Egloff; (D) Lisa Peterson; (SD) John Gromada

Much Ado About Nothing, William Shakespeare; (D) Des McAnuff; (L) Chris Parry; (C) David C. Woolard; (SD) Michael Roth

PRODUCTIONS 1993

Children of Paradise: Shooting a Dream, adapt: Steven Epp, Felicity Jones, Dominique Serrand and Paul Walsh, from Marcel Carne and Jacques Prevert (co-produced by Theatre de la Jeune Lune); (D) Dominique Serrand; (S) Vincent Gracieux; (L) Frederic Desbois; (C) Trina Mrnak

Arms and the Man, George Bernard Shaw; (D) Lisa Peterson; (S) Robert Brill; (L) Chris Kortum; (C) Christina Haatainen; (SD) Michael Roth

The Hairy Ape, Eugene O'Neill; (D) Matthew Wilder; (S) Robert Brill; (L) David Thayer; (C) Cynthia Bolin; (SD) Michael Roth

Luck, Pluck & Virtue, adapt: James Lapine, from Nathanael West; (D) James Lapine; (S) Adrianne Lobel; (L) Chris Parry; (C) Martin Pakledinaz

The Mission, Richard Montoya, Ric Salinas and Herbert Siquenza (co-produced by Culture Clash); (D) Tony Curiel; (S) Victoria Petrovich; (L) Jose Lopez

Sweet & Hot, conceived: Julianne Boyd; music: Harold Arlen; various lyricists; (D) Julianne Boyd; (S) Ken Foy; (L) Howell Binkley; (C) David C. Woolard; (MD) Danny Holgate; (CH) Hope Clarke

La Jolla Playhouse. Michael Cerveris and Nino Pamaran in *The Who's Tommy*. Photo: Ken Howard.

La MaMa Experimental Theater Club

ELLEN STEWART
Founder/Artistic Director

MERYL VLADIMER
Associate Director

FRANK CARUCCI
Board President

74A East 4th St.
New York, NY 10003
(212) 254-6468 (bus.)
(212) 475-7710 (b.o.)
(212) 254-7597 (fax)

FOUNDED 1961
Ellen Stewart

SEASON
Oct.-June

FACILITIES
Annex Theater
Seating Capacity: 299
Stage: flexible

1st Floor Theater
Seating Capacity: 99
Stage: flexible

The "Club" (Cabaret)
Seating Capacity: 125
Stage: thrust

The Galleria
Seating Capacity: 60
Stage: flexible

FINANCES
July 1, 1992-June 30, 1993
Expenses: $945,000

CONTRACTS
AEA Off Broadway and Showcase Code

La MaMa E.T.C. has been consistently changing the face of theatre since 1961. Here, artists from more than 70 nations have found a supportive environment which nurtures and applauds creative risk-taking, and an audience interested not in an individual production but in the development of an artist's work over time. Still located on New York's Lower East Side, where it has become a vital and stabilizing component of its neighborhood, La MaMa has grown from its early basement theatre with nine tables and chairs into a multipurpose complex housing two theatres, a cabaret, seven floors of free rehearsal space, nonprofit office spaces, an art gallery, and an archive documenting the history of Off-Off-Broadway theatre. La MaMa produces 60 to 70 productions yearly, and has been honored with over 60 Obie awards and dozens of Drama Desk, Bessie, Audelco and Villager awards. Through our diverse productions we are able to reach out to audiences who tend to be isolated geographically and culturally from the theatre experience. La MaMa's artists are traveling the globe, serving as ambassadors of experimental culture in all corners of the world, testifying to the importance of this unique laboratory of cultural exploration.

—Ellen Stewart

PRODUCTIONS 1991-92

Lighting by Howard Thies unless otherwise noted.

Futz, Rochelle Owens; (D), (S) and (SD) Tom O'Horgan; (C) Ellen Stewart
Volare, Dario Di Ambrosi; (D) and (S) Dario Di Ambrosi
Motel Blue 19, Edgar Oliver; (D) Jason Bauer; (S) Helen Oliver
Punch Me in the Stomach, Deb Filler and Alison Summers; (D) Alison Summers
Basement, Denise Stoklos; (D), (L), (C) and (SD) Denise Stoklos; (S) Denise Stoklos and Isla Jay
Nosferatu, Ping Chong; (D) Ping Chong; (S) Miguel Lopez-Castillo; (C) Carol Ann Pelletier; (SD) Brian Hallas
Explosions, Virlana Tkacz and Wanda Phipps; (D) Virlana Tkacz; (S) and (L) Watoku Ueno; (C) Carol Ann Pelletier
Shatterhand Massecree, John Jesurun; (D) and (S) John Jesurun; (L) Jeff Nash
Haunted House, book, music and lyrics: John Moran; (D), (S) and (MD) John Moran
Hibiscus Story, conceived: Michael Walter Harris; book: Ann Harris, Daniel Barry, Frederic Harris and Rebecca Stone; music and lyrics: Mary Lou Harris; (D) Jacque Lynn Colton; (S) Donald Brooks; (C) Rich Kiamco and Angel Jack; (MD) Kevin D. Mayes; (CH) Michelle Azar and cast; (SD) David Pascal
Egypt, adapt: David Herskovits and Douglas Langworthy, from William Shakespeare (co-produced by Target Margin Theater); (D) David Herskovits; (S) Marsha Ginsberg; (L) Lenore Doxsee; (C) David Zinn; (SD) John Collins
Lesbians Who Kill, Peggy Shaw and Lois Weaver (co-produced by Split Britches); (C) Susan Young
Iphigenia in Tauris, Richard Lattimore; adapt: Yannis Houvardas, from Euripides; (D) Yannis Houvardas; (S) and (C) Dionyssis Fotopoulos
God's Country, Steven Dietz (co-produced by The Barrow Group); (D) Leonard Foglia; (S) Michael McGarty; (L) Russell H. Champa; (C) Nina Canter
Photo Op, book and lyrics: James Sienna; music: Conrad Cummings (co-produced by Ridge Theater); (D) Bob McGrath; (S) Lauri Olinder; (C) Elizabeth Evers; (SD) Tim Schellenbaum
Kanashibetsu, Soh Kuramoto (co-produced by Furand Group of Japan); (D) Soh Kuramoto; (L) Yoshiaki Yamada; (C) Hisako Hiraki; (SD) Kayoko Yamamoto
Haarlem Nocturne, book: Murray Horwitz and Andre DeShields; music and lyrics: Marc Shaiman; (D) and (CH) Andre DeShields; (S) Mark Tambella; (C) Chico Kassinoir; (MD) Billy Swindler
Iron Lung, John Jesurun; (D) and (SD) John Jesurun; (S) Jun Maeda; (L) Jeff Nash
Kafka, Father & Son, Mark Rozovsky; trans: Elena Prischepenko; (D), (S) and (C) Leo Shapiro; (L) Blu; (SD) Kyle Chepulis
Akin, John Kelly; music: Richard Peaslee; (D) and (CH) John Kelly; (S) Huck Snyder; (L) Howell Binkley; (C) Donna Zakowska; (MD) Robert Pace; (SD) Tim Schellenbaum
A City Called Forest, Kurt Fulton, Melanie Monios and Richard Schachter; (D) Kurt Fulton, Melanie Monios and Richard Schachter
Der Golem, lyrics: Moni Ovadia; music: Alessandro Nidi; (D) Moni Ovadia; (S) and (C) Pierluigi Bottazzi; (L) Gigi Saccomandi; (CH) Elisabeth Boeke
Flight of Chung Sop Lee, Kim Fui-Kyung; (D) Lee Yun-Taek; (S) Shin Sun-Hi; (C) Choi Hyung-O; (C) Choi Bo-Kyoung and You Soon-Bok
Fallen Angel, book, music and lyrics: William Boesky; (D) Rob Greenberg; (S) David Bim; (L) Christopher Akerlind; (C) Wendy Rolf; (MD) Steve Postel; (SD) Dave Ferdinand

PRODUCTIONS 1992-1993

Lighting by Howard Thies unless otherwise noted.

Hippolytos, adapt: Vasilios Calitsis, from Euripides; trans: Robert Bagg; (D) Vasilios Calitsis; (S) George Tsurdinis; (C) Prema Karanth; (SD) Tim Schellenbaum
Yunus, book adapt: Ellen Stewart, from Talat Halman and Huseyn Kat; trans: Erol Keskin; music: Ellen Stewart, Genji Ito and Yukio Tsuji; lyrics: Ellen Stewart and Talat Halman; (D) and (S) Ellen Stewart; (C) Selcuk Gurisik; (SD) Tim Schellenbaum
Baby, Fourteen Clowns and Xylophone, Susan Sherman; (D) John Morace; (S) Loyan Beausoleil; (L) Diana Arecco; (C) Sally Young and Hefi Bohem; (SD) John Delaney
Deungsinbul; (D) Hyunyup Lee and Kyoon Kim; (S) and (C) Ja Kyoung Kim; (L) Mikiko Takanashi; (SD) Jun Maeda
Tales From Hollywood, Christopher Hampton; (D) Seth Barrish; (S) Markas Henry; (L) Eileen H. Dougherty; (C) Nina Canter; (SD) One Dream
Deshima, Ping Chong; (D) Ping Chong; (S) Ping Chong and Watoku Ueno; (L) Thomas C. Hase; (C) Carol Ann Pelletier; (SD) Robert Bosh and Brian Hallas
Underground, Theodora Skipitares; (D) Theodora Skipitares; (S) Holly Laws; (L) Liz Lee
Big Butt Girls/Hard Headed Women, Rhodessa Jones; (D) Idris Ackamoor

La MaMa Experimental Theater Club. Denise Stoklos in *500 Years—A Fax from Denise Stoklos to Christopher Columbus*. Photo: Bel Pedrosa.

Faust/Gastronome, adapt: Richard Schechner, from Goethe, et al; music: Ralph Denzer and Michelle Kinney; (D) Richard Schechner; (S) Chris Muller; (L) Lenore Doxsee; (C) Constance Hoffman
Ghost—Live From Gallillee, book and lyrics: Edgar Nkosi White; music: Genji Ito; (D) and (S) George Ferencz; (C) Sally Lesser; (MD) Genji Ito; (SD) Tim Schellenbaum
500 Years–A Fax from Denise Stoklos to Christopher Columbus, Denise Stoklos; (D) Denise Stoklos; (L) Denise Stoklos and Annette Ter Meulen; (C) Veronica Franca
Point of Debarkation, John Jesurun; (D) and (SD) John Jesurun; (S) John Jesurun and Jun Maeda; (L) Jeff Nash
Angel From Montgomery, book, music and lyrics: William Boesky; (D) Richard Caliban
Every Day Newt Burman, book, music and lyrics: John Moran; (D) Bob McGrath; (S) Lauri Olinder; (C) Elizabeth Evers; (SD) Tim Schellenbaum
Blind Sight, trans and adapt: Virlana Tkacz, Wanda Phipps and Watoku Ueno; (D) Virlana Tkacz; (S) and (L) Watoku Ueno; (C) Carol Ann Pelletier
The Prince of Madness, Dario Di Ambrosi; (D) Dario Di Ambrosi
The White Whore and The Bit Player, book: Tom Eyen; music: Henry Krieger; lyrics: Ellen Stewart; (D) Eric Concklin; (S) and (L) David Adams; (C) Susan Young; (MD) Henry Krieger; (SD) Tim Schellenbaum
Cheek to Cheek, book and lyrics: The Harris Sisters; music: The Harris Sisters, Ann Harris, Peter Kwaloff and Bob Cutarella; (D) Brad Friedman; (S) Daniel Kuchar; (C) Nicole Katz; (MD) Steve Weisberg
Extended Forecast, Franz Xaver Kroetz; adapt: Erica Bilder and Estelle Parsons; (D) Erica Bilder; (S) and (L) Watoku Ueno; (C) Theodora Skipitares
Mosquito Succulence, Edgar Oliver; (D) Jason Bauer; (S) Helen Oliver; (C) Leslie Lowe
Stump the Host, David Sedaris; (D) Warren David Keith; (S) Hugh Hamrick
WOMBmanWARs, Judith Alexa Jackson; (D) Paul McIsaac
The Wrong Mistake, book and lyrics: Jim Neu; music: Harry Mann and Neal Kirkwood; (D) Jim Neu and SK Dunn; (S) David Nunemaker; (MD) Harry Mann and Neal Kirkwood; (CH) Harry Mann

L. A. Theatre Works

SUSAN ALBERT LOEWENBERG
Executive Director

GALE COHEN
Managing Director

DOUGLAS JEFFE
Board President

681 Venice Blvd.
Venice, CA 90291
(310) 827-0808 (bus.)
(213) 660-8587 (b.o.)
(213) 827-4949 (fax)

FOUNDED 1974
Susan Albert Loewenberg, Robert Greenwald, Jeremy Blahnik

SEASON
Oct.-July

FACILITIES
Guest Quarters Suite Hotel (Santa Monica/Chicago/Waltham)
Seating Capacity: 400
Stage: ballroom

FINANCES
Oct, 1, 1992-Sept. 30, 1993
Expenses: $322,300

CONTRACTS
AEA LORT (D) and 99-seat theatre plan

As producing director of L.A. Theatre Works, my task has been to guide the evolution of the company—from an informally organized group of theatre artists exploring ways to make theatre in unorthodox settings such as prisons and community workshops to a formal producing organization that develops and presents the work of playwrights from the U.S. and abroad. Our new L.A. Theatre Works Radio Company, an ensemble of distinguished, classically trained actors who share our ideas about theatre, enlarges our artistic scope through innovative productions of both classic and contemporary plays for radio. Our commitment is to new work, new forms and the explication of a particular vision. As a post-Brechtian theatre that truly mirrors the "unease" of modern culture, we want our audience to experience the exhilaration of change, as opposed to the emotional release that comes from artifice. We support and nurture our theatrical vision through our Radio Theatre Series for New Plays and through collaborations involving conceptual directors, playwrights and designers.
—*Susan Albert Loewenberg*

L.A. Theatre Works. JoBeth Williams recording *The Crimson Thread*. Photo: Ed Goldstein.

PRODUCTIONS 1991-1992

Direction by Robert Robinson and sound design by Steve Barker unless otherwise noted.

Serious Money, Caryl Churchill; (SD) Gerald Sternbach
Bad Axe, P.J. Barry
Gulf War and *Black*, Joyce Carol Oates; (D) Peggy Shannon
A Telegram from Heaven, adapt: Dennis Bailey and Dinah Manoff, from Arnold Manoff; (D) Dinah Manoff
Absent Forever, John Hopkins; (D) Peggy Shannon
Pericles, Prince of Tyre, adapt: Peggy Shannon, from William Shakespeare; (D) Peggy Shannon
At Long Last Leo, Mark Stein; (D) Steven D. Albrezzi
Say Zebra, Sherry Coman
Mastergate, Larry Gelbart; (D) Dudley Knight; (SD) Ron Streicher
Exchange, Yuri Trifonov; trans: Martin Jenkins; adapt: Michael Frayn; (D) Martin Jenkins; (SD) Ron Streicher
Buk: The Life and Times of Charles Bukowski, Paul Pedito; (D) Frank Condon; (SD) Ron Streicher
New York Profiles, Kirsten Dahl; (SD) Ron Streicher
My Visits with MGM, Edit Villarreal; (D) Peggy Shannon; (SD) Ron Streicher

PRODUCTIONS 1992-1993

Direction by Robert Robinson and sound design by Ray Guarna unless otherwise noted.

Mayhem: The Invasion, Tim Robbins; (D) Tim Robbins
Bang the Drum Slowly, adapt: Eric Simonson, from Mark Harris; (D) Eric Simonson
Tears of Rage, Doris Baizley; (D) Valerie Landsburg
The Crimson Thread, Mary Hanes
Golf with Alan Shepard, Carter W. Lewis
Fuente Ovejuna, Lope de Vega; adapt and trans: Adrian Mitchell
Make and Break, Martin Jarvis
Incunabula, Incunabulorum, Anna Nicholas
Of One Blood, Andrew White; (D) Andrew White
To Distraction, Cecilia Fannon; (D) JoBeth Williams
The Swan, Elizabeth Egloff
Park Your Car in Harvard Yard, Israel Horovitz; (D) Mark Ward

Lincoln Center Theater. Madeline Kahn, Jane Alexander and Christine Estabrook in *The Sisters Rosensweig*. Photo: Martha Swope.

Lincoln Center Theater

ANDRE BISHOP
Artistic Director

BERNARD GERSTEN
Executive Producer

LINDA LEROY JANKLOW
Board Chairman

150 West 65th St.
New York, NY 10023
(212) 362-7600 (bus.)
(212) 239-6200 (b.o.)
(212) 873-0761 (fax)

FOUNDED 1985
Lincoln Center for the Performing Arts, Inc.

SEASON
Year-round

FACILITIES
Vivian Beaumont Theater
Seating Capacity: 1,100
Stage: thrust

Mitzi E. Newhouse Theater
Seating Capacity: 299
Stage: thrust

FINANCES
July 1, 1992-June 30, 1993
Expenses: $19,517,000

CONTRACTS
AEA LORT (A) and (C)

PRODUCTIONS 1991-1992

Two Shakespearean Actors, Richard Nelson; (D) Jack O'Brien; (S) David Jenkins; (L) Jules Fisher; (C) Jane Greenwood; (SD) Jeff Ladman

The Most Happy Fella, book, music and lyrics: Frank Loesser; (D) Gerald Gutierrez; (S) John Lee Beatty; (L) Craig Miller; (C) Jess Goldstein; (MD) Tim Stella; (CH) Liza Gennaro; (SD) Scott Lehrer

The Substance of Fire, Jon Robin Baitz; (D) Daniel Sullivan; (S) John Lee Beatty; (L) Arden Fingerhut; (C) Jess Goldstein; (SD) Scott Lehrer

Four Baboons Adoring the Sun, John Guare; music: Stephen Edwards; (D) Peter Hall; (S) Tony Walton; (L) Richard Pilbrow; (C) Willa Kim; (MD) Michael Barrett; (SD) Paul Arditti

PRODUCTIONS 1992-1993

The Sisters Rosensweig, Wendy Wasserstein; (D) Daniel Sullivan; (S) John Lee Beatty; (L) Pat Collins; (C) Jane Greenwood; (SD) Guy Sherman/Aural Fixation

My Favorite Year, book adapt: Joseph Dougherty, from the original screenplay; music: Stephen Flaherty; lyrics: Lynn Ahrens; (D) Ron Lagomarsino; (S) Thomas Lynch; (L) Jules Fisher; (C) Patricia Zipprodt; (MD) Ted Sperling; (CH) Thommie Walsh; (SD) Scott Lehrer

Playboy of the West Indies, adapt: Mustapha Matura, from John Millington Synge; (D) Gerald Gutierrez; (S) John Lee Beatty; (L) James F. Ingalls; (C) Paul Tazewell; (SD) Serge Ossorguine

Live Oak Theatre

DON TONER
Producing Artistic Director

ANNA MORMAN WELCH
Administrative Director

GREG MARCHBANKS
Board President

311 Nueces
Austin, TX 78701
(512) 472-5143
(512) 472-7199 (fax)

FOUNDED 1982
Mac Williams, Jeanette Brown

SEASON
Year-round

FACILITIES
Seating Capacity: 215
Stage: proscenium

FINANCES
Oct. 1, 1991-Sept. 30, 1992
Expenses: $507,811

CONTRACTS
AEA SPT

We believe that theatre provides communal nourishment of mind and spirit for better understanding of our world and fuller enjoyment of our lives. We are committed to providing the live-theatre experience to the broadest possible audience through professional productions of the best classic and contemporary plays, with a special commitment to development and production of new works. The signing of a contract with Actors' Equity in 1989 reflects our desire to create a theatre where the creative life of the actor is supported and given opportunity to grow. Recognizing an additional responsibility to nurture emerging playwrights and to further the development and presentation of their work, we present at least one premiere production as part of our regular season. Live Oak Theatre has instituted a New Plays Award program which attracts more than 400 new scripts annually from across the country.

—*Don Toner*

PRODUCTIONS 1991-1992

The Best Little Whorehouse in Texas, book: Larry L. King and Peter Masterson; music and lyrics: Carol Hall; (D), (S) and (C) Bil Pfuderer; (L) Robert Whyburn; (MD) Noel Alford; (CH) Randall Soileau

A Texas Romance, Ellsworth Schave; (D) Don Toner; (S) and (C) Devon Painter; (L) Robert Whyburn

A Midsummer Night's Dream, William Shakespeare; (D) Bill Watson; (S) and (L) Richard Isackes; (C) Gaye Bowen

An O. Henry Christmas, adapt: Ellsworth Schave and Don Toner, from O. Henry; (D) Steve Shearer; (S) Gary van der Wege; (L) Don Toner; (C) Nina Proctor; (SD) Lou Rigler

Live Oak Theatre. *Dancing at Lughnasa*. Photo: Kirk R. Tuck.

The House of Blue Leaves, John Guare; (D), (S) and (C) Joe York; (L) Robert Whyburn; (SD) Lou Rigler

Prelude to a Kiss, Craig Lucas; (D) Michael Hankin; (S) and (L) Tim Poertner; (C) Stephanie Moore; (SD) Lou Rigler

Bosque County, Texas, Steven Fromholz and Don Toner; (D) Don Toner; (S) Bil Pfuderer; (L) Ken Hudson; (C) Sung Shin

Nunsense, book, music and lyrics: Dan Goggin; (D) and (CH) Acia Gray; (L) Ken Hudson; (MD) Bradley Vieth

PRODUCTIONS 1992-1993

Fiddler on the Roof, book adapt: Joseph Stein, from Sholom Aleichem; music: Jerry Bock; lyrics: Sheldon Harnick; (D) Don Toner; (S) Gary van der Wege; (L) Ken Hudson; (C) Irlyn Toner; (MD) Jerry Peperone; (CH) Randall Soileau

The Crucible, Arthur Miller; (D) Peter Sheridan; (S) Gary van der Wege; (L) Rossa Sheridan; (C) Jill Parker-Jones

A Child's Christmas in Wales, adapt: Jerry Brooks and Adrian Mitchell, from Dylan Thomas; (D) and (S) Don Toner; (L) Rory McClure; (C) April Blackburn; (SD) Lou Rigler

Lend Me a Tenor, Ken Ludwig; (D) Bill Watson; (S) Tim Poertner; (L) Don Toner; (C) Ken Johnson

Dancing at Lughnasa, Brian Friel; (D) and (S) Don Toner; (L) Rory McClure; (C) April Blackburn

The Golden Shadows Old West Museum, Larry L. King; (D) Don Toner; (S) Ken Johnson; (L) Rory McClure; (C) Jill Parker-Jones

Nine, adapt: Mario Fratti, from Federico Fellini, et al; book: Arthur Kopit; music and lyrics: Maury Yeston; (D) Rod Caspers; (S) Don Toner and Joe York; (L) Rory McClure; (C) Ken Johnson; (MD) Allen Robertson; (CH) Kelly James Patterson

Living Stage Theatre Company

ROBERT A. ALEXANDER
Director

VANESSA EATON
Managing Director

DAVID E. SHIFFRIN
Board Chairman

6th and Maine Ave. SW
Washington, DC 20024
(202) 554-9066
(202) 488-4056 (fax)
(202) 484-0247 TTY

FOUNDED 1966
Robert A. Alexander

SEASON
Sept.-June

FACILITIES
Seating Capacity: 124
Stage: flexible

FINANCES
July 1, 1992-June 30, 1993
Expenses: $686,500

CONTRACTS
AEA LORT (D)

The fundamental belief of Living Stage is that everyone is an artist. Living Stage enhances this artistry through improvised productions, combined with workshops, designed to actively engage the audience in the creative process. Living Stage inspires creativity and promotes a positive view of the self and the world. Living Stage's work focuses on children and special-needs audiences. In addition to performances and workshops, we offer training in the creative process for adults who work with children. Attendees include educators, artists, social activists and community organization workers. The training is offered through residencies—locally, nationally and internationally. We are most interested now in finding ways to show how the power of the artistic imagination can create positive change in our society. The future will include more work with adults to ensure that our philosophies and techniques will be utilized on a greater scale, along with public forums that provide an opportunity to explore solutions to societal problems such as racism, sexism, violence, drug abuse and poverty.

—*Robert A. Alexander*

PRODUCTIONS 1991-1992

Ongoing improvisational performance/workshop sessions directed by Robert A. Alexander.

Lynched Hopes and Unsung Songs, Traci Halima Williams; (D) Robert A. Alexander

PRODUCTIONS 1992-1993

Ongoing improvisational performance/workshop sessions directed by Robert A. Alexander.

Daddy, Daddy Go Away! I Don't Like the Games You Play, Traci Halima Williams; (D) Robert A. Alexander

Long Wharf Theatre

ARVIN BROWN
Artistic Director

M. EDGAR ROSENBLUM
Executive Director

JOHN TILLINGER
Literary Consultant

GORDON EDELSTEIN
Artistic Associate

Living Stage Theatre Company. Oran Sandel and students in an improvisational performance/workshop. Photo: Kelly Jerome.

JANICE MUIRHEAD
Artistic Administrator

FRED E. WALKER
Board Chairman

222 Sargent Drive
New Haven, CT 06511
(203) 787-4284 (bus.)
(203) 787-4282 (b.o.)
(203) 776-2287 (fax)

FOUNDED 1965
Harlan Kleiman, Jon Jory

SEASON
Sept.-June

FACILITIES
Newton Schenck Stage
Seating Capacity: 487
Stage: thrust

Stage II
Seating Capacity: 199
Stage: flexible

FINANCES
July 1, 1991-June 30, 1992
Expenses: $4,265,000

CONTRACTS
AEA LORT (B) and (C)

Long Wharf Theatre is committed to plays that deal with character, incorporating those ethical, social, political, moral and aesthetic principles that help to define the human condition. We present classics and neglected works in a way that will open up our vision of the past, present and future; provide a forum for contemporary theatre voices by introducing new works of established and emerging playwrights; and foster creativity by supporting research and development of new plays and ideas. Long Wharf Theatre is dedicated

Long Wharf Theatre. Frank Langella in *Booth is Back*. Photo: T. Charles Erickson.

to cultivating audiences that reflect the State of Connecticut and the diversity of our cities and our rural and suburban areas; serving as a forum for the examination of historical and current issues through humanities programs; and nurturing tomorrow's audiences through an arts-in-education initiative which enriches and enlightens the children of our community. We accomplish these goals within a supportive working environment for our staff and theatre artists.

—*Arvin Brown*

PRODUCTIONS 1991-1992

Booth is Back, Austin Pendleton; (D) Arvin Brown; (S) John Lee Beatty; (L) Dennis Parichy; (C) Jess Goldstein

Adventures in the Skin Trade, book adapt: John Tillinger and James Hammerstein, from Dylan Thomas; music: Thomas Fay; lyrics: James Hammerstein; (D) John Tillinger; (S) John Lee Beatty; (L) Tharon Musser; (C) Jane Greenwood; (MD) Thomas Fay; (CH) Danny Herman

The Philanthropist, Christopher Hampton; (D) Gordon Edelstein; (S) Hugh Landwehr; (L) Peter Kaczorowski; (C) Candice Donnelly

An Enemy of the People, Henrik Ibsen; adapt: Arthur Miller; (D) John Tillinger; (S) Donald Eastman; (L) Arden Fingerhut; (C) Robert Wojewodski

A Touch of the Poet, Eugene O'Neill; (D) Arvin Brown; (S) Michael Yeargan; (L) Christopher Akerlind; (C) David Murin

PRODUCTIONS 1992-1993

A Month in the Country, Ivan Turgenev; adapt: Isaiah Berlin; (D) Arvin Brown; (S) Loren Sherman; (L) Mark Stanley; (C) Jess Goldstein

Once Removed, Eduardo Machado; (D) John Tillinger; (S) John Lee Beatty; (L) Pat Collins; (C) Jane Greenwood; (SD) Donna Riley

The Day the Bronx Died, Michael Henry Brown; (D) Gordon Edelstein; (S) Hugh Landwehr; (L) Donald Holder; (C) Candice Donnelly; (SD) John Gromada

The Misanthrope, Moliere; trans: Richard Wilbur; (D) Edward Gilbert; (S) and (C) Mark Negin; (L) Nicholas Cernovitch

Absurd Person Singular, Alan Ayckbourn; (D) Arvin Brown; (S) Michael Yeargan; (L) Arden Fingerhut; (C) David Murin

Mabou Mines

LEE BREUER, RUTH MALECZECH, FREDERICK NEUMANN, TERRY O'REILLY
Artistic Directorate

JOHN McGRATH
Associate Director

DAVID PREMINGER
Board Chairman

150 First Ave.
New York, NY 10009
(212) 473-0559
(212) 473-2410 (fax)

FOUNDED 1970
David Warrilow, Ruth Maleczech, Philip Glass, Lee Breuer, JoAnne Akalaitis

SEASON
Year-round

FINANCES
July 1, 1992-June 30, 1993
Expenses: $312,050

CONTRACTS
AEA Guest Artist

Mabou Mines is an artistic collective based in New York City. The company has produced 42 works for theatre, film, video and radio during its 23-year history and has performed all over the U.S., and in Europe, Japan, South America, Israel and Australia. Combining the visual, aural, musical and sculptural arts with dramatic texts, and synthesizing film, video and live performances through the art of the actor, Mabou Mines has produced experimental theatre pieces that integrate aesthetic content with political substance. We have sought to make art that redefines the culture, punctures what is, pushes the limits of what's thinkable—to raise difficult issues in paradoxical ways and to challenge audiences with new ways of looking at our world. In this, our 23rd year, we have instituted the Resident Artists Program of Mabou Mines/Suite to encourage other artists to develop experimental works on the edge of an ever more conservative society. We feel strongly the need to continue working, to gather strength from the world community of artists and to share our vision with a hungry audience.

—*Ruth Maleczech for the members of Mabou Mines*

Mabou Mines. Terry O'Reilly and Black-Eyed Susan in *The Bribe*. Photo: Dona Ann McAdams.

Madison Repertory Theatre

D. SCOTT GLASSER
Artistic Director

VICKI STEWART
Managing Director

ROBERT J. KAY
Board President

122 State St., Suite 201
Madison, WI 53703-2500
(608) 256-0029 (bus.)
(608) 266-9055 (b.o.)
(608) 256-7433

FOUNDED 1969
Katherine Waack, Vicki Stewart

SEASON
July-May

FACILITIES
Isthmus Playhouse of Madison Civic Center
Seating Capacity: 335
Stage: thrust

FINANCES
July 1, 1992-June 30, 1993
Expenses: $677,000

CONTRACTS
AEA SPT

As it celebrates its 25th season, Madison Repertory Theatre—Wisconsin's only year-round Equity theatre outside Milwaukee—continues to welcome a diverse audience to plays that reflect a wide range of human experience. The repertoire includes contemporary plays and musicals as well as revivals of distinguished 20th-century works and classics. Regardless of genre, style or period, the goal of each production is to present the work with freshness and originality, to seek the most talented artists and to collaborate with them to achieve strong ensemble acting and outstanding production values—in other words, to create a memorable experience. Priorities for the future are: cultural diversity in our company and in our audience, the development and presentation of new plays that have particular resonance for audiences in this region, and expansion of the theatre's reputation for hiring the finest actors for individual productions and inviting them into a hospitable and creative atmosphere.
—*D. Scott Glasser*

Note: During the 1991-92 and 1992-93 seasons, Joseph Hanreddy served as artistic director.

PRODUCTIONS 1991-1992

Sets by Frank Schneeberger and lighting by Thomas C. Hase unless otherwise noted.

Nunsense, book, music and lyrics: Dan Goggin; (D) and (CH) John Staniunas; (L) David Gipson; (C) Kahlei A. Slick and Mary Waldhart; (MD) Jack Forbes Wilson
Eleemosynary, Lee Blessing; (D) Kristine Thatcher; (C) Mary Waldhart
Waiting for Godot, Samuel Beckett; (D) Joseph Hanreddy; (C) Mary Waldhart
Arms and the Man, George Bernard Shaw; (D) Joseph Hanreddy; (C) Mary Waldhart and Anna Stevens; (SD) Tom Hamer
The Crucible, Arthur Miller; (D) Joseph Hanreddy; (C) Mary Waldhart and Anna Stevens; (SD) Tom Hamer
Other People's Money, Jerry Sterner; (D) Joseph Hanreddy; (C) Dawna Gregory and Mary Waldhart; (SD) David Budries

PRODUCTIONS 1992-1993

Sets by Frank Schneeberger, lighting by Thomas C. Hase, costumes by Mary Waldhart and sound design by Tom Hamer unless otherwise noted.

Baby, book: Sybille Pearson; music: David Shire; lyrics: Richard Maltby, Jr.; (D) and (CH) John Staniunas; (L) Kenneth Kloth
A Streetcar Named Desire, Tennessee Williams; (D) D. Scott Glasser; (SD) Michael Croswell
American Buffalo, David Mamet; (D) Joseph Hanreddy
I Hate Hamlet, Paul Rudnick; (D) J.R. Sullivan; (C) Jon R. Accardo
The Recruiting Officer, George Farquhar; (D) Joseph Hanreddy; (S) Joseph Varga; (SD) Michael Croswell
Our Country's Good, adapt: Timberlake Wertenbaker, from Thomas Keneally; (D) Joseph Hanreddy; (SD) Michael Croswell

Madison Repertory Theatre. Brenda Bedard and Angela Yannon in *A Streetcar Named Desire*. Photo: Zane Williams.

Mad River Theater Works

JEFF HOOPER
Producing Director

SUSAN BANKS
Producing Associate

JOYCE WOODRUFF
Board Chair

PRODUCTIONS 1991-1992

In the Jungle of Cities, Bertolt Brecht; trans: Gerhard Nellhaus; book adapt: Anne Bogart; music: Judson Wright; lyrics: Anne Bogart and Judson Wright (co-produced by New York Shakespeare Festival and VIA Theater); (D) Anne Bogart; (S) Donald Eastman; (L) Heather Carson; (C) Gabriel Berry; (MD) Judson Wright; (SD) Jacob Burckhardt and L.B. Dallas
CEO, Stig Larsson; trans: Joe Martin (co-produced by Classic Stage Company); (D) Frederick Neumann; (S) Kevin J. Roach, concept: Frederick Neumann; (L) Mahlon Kruse; (C) Anna Gorman; (SD) Panaiotis

PRODUCTIONS 1992-1993

The Warrior Ant, Part 7C, The Ma Ha Bhar Ant A, Lee Breuer; music: I Ketut Partha, I Wayan Mardika Bhuwana, Christopher Romero and Tom Burkhardt; (D) Lee Breuer; (S) and (L) Richard Nonas; (SD) Christopher Romero
The Bribe, Terry O'Reilly; music: John Zorn; (D) Ruth Maleczech; (S) and (L) Richard Nonas; (C) Ann-Marie Wright and Toby Niesen; (SD) John Collins and Nathan Guisinger

83

Mad River Theater Works

Box 248
West Liberty, OH 43357
(513) 465-6751 (bus.)
(513) 465-1580 (b.o.)

FOUNDED 1978
Jeff Hooper

SEASON
Year-round touring

FACILITIES
Tent Theater
Seating Capacity: 325
Stage: flexible

FINANCES
Sept. 1, 1992-Aug. 31, 1993
Expenses: $354,080

CONTRACTS
AEA Guest Artist

Mad River Theater Works is a rural professional repertory theatre based in west central Ohio. Our purpose is to create original plays drawn from the history and culture of rural America and perform those plays primarily for audiences from farms and small towns. We use theatre and music to explore the stories of people who have confronted change in the past in order to inform and illuminate the choices that we face in the future. In particular, we focus on issues of community breakdown, racism and tolerance, the importance of individual cultures and the changing role of women. Our programming consists of a summer home season in our tent theatre in rural Ohio, six months of educational touring and outreach, and three months of touring full-length plays from our repertoire throughout the United States.
—*Jeff Hooper*

PRODUCTIONS 1991-1992

Direction by Jeff Hooper and costumes by Laurie Collins unless otherwise noted.

Riverboatin', Jeff Hooper; music: Bob Lucas; (MD) Bob Lucas
A Christmas Carol, book adapt: Jeff Hooper, from Charles Dickens; music and lyrics: Bob Lucas and Rick Good; (MD) Bob Lucas
The Return of Kate Shelley, Jeff Hooper
Cry of the Americas, Jeff Hooper and Lance Henson; (D) Darla Cash
Freedom Bound, book: Jeff Hooper; music and lyrics: Bob Lucas; (MD) Vickie Hilliard
Coyote Road, book: Jeff Hooper and Lance Henson; music: Andy Teirstein; lyrics: Jeff Hooper, Lance Henson and Andy Teirstein; (S) and (L) Martin Bluestein; (MD) Lee Tomboulian

PRODUCTIONS 1992-1993

Direction by Susan Banks and costumes by Laurie Collins unless otherwise noted.

Starting Out Small, Jeff Hooper
Mystic Voices, Harrison Lowe; (D) Jeff Hooper
Whick Wack, Jeff Hooper
Freedom Bound, book: Jeff Hooper; music and lyrics: Bob Lucas; (D) Jeff Hooper; (MD) J.D. Nelson (resident), Andy Cohen and Bob Thompson (tour)
Back Way Back, Jeff Hooper; (S) Jeff Hooper
Black Hats, book: Jeff Hooper; music and lyrics: Bob Lucas; (S) Steve Brownless; (MD) Lee Tomboulian
Shooting Star, book: Jeff Hooper; music: Bob Lucas and Willy Schwarz; lyrics: Bob Lucas; (D) Jeff Hooper; (MD) William Barrett

Mad River Theater Works. Pam Clouse and Harrison Lowe in *Mystic Voices*. Photo: Mike Hall/Studio Expressions.

Magic Theatre

MAME HUNT
Artistic Director

ALBERT HASSON
Managing Director

MAUREEN SULLIVAN
Board President

Bldg. D, Fort Mason Center
San Francisco, CA 94123
(415) 441-8001 (bus.)
(415) 441-8822 (b.o.)
(4150 771-5505 (fax)

FOUNDED 1967
John Lion

SEASON
Oct.-July

FACILITIES
North Side
Seating Capacity: 160
Stage: thrust

South Side
Seating Capacity: 170
Stage: proscenium

FINANCES
Sept. 1, 1991-Aug. 31, 1992
Expenses: $1,260,700

CONTRACTS
AEA BAT

For over 25 years, the Magic has been a theatre dedicated to the primary creative voice in the theatre: the playwright. The Magic exists to offer contemporary playwrights an artistic home that is nurturing, challenging, truthful and passionate. In addition to producing six new plays a year, including several world premieres, the Magic engages in many collaborations with local and national artists and companies. We provide an artistic home for several Associate Artists who are supported with commissions, residencies, readings and workshops. Since our home in San Francisco embraces a phenomenal diversity of cultures and means of artistic expression, our mission is to strive to reflect the diversity of those voices. We develop and produce the work of artists who share our obsessions, and our obsessions are with a world that often contradicts expectations, is culturally diverse, political in its sensibilities and on the cutting edge of the integration of form and content.
—*Mame Hunt*

Note: During the 1991-92 season, Harvey Seifter served as general director. During the 1992-93 season, Larry Eilenberg served as artistic director.

PRODUCTIONS 1991-1992

Sets by Pamela Peniston, lighting by Jeff Rowlings, costumes by Laura Hazlett and sound design by Kim Foscato unless otherwise noted.

Love Diatribe, Harry Kondoleon; (D) Albert Takazauckas; (S) Don Weinger; (L) Kurt Landisman; (C) Kate Irvine; (SD) Barney Jones
Hunger, Peter Mattei; (D) Mary Forcade; (S) Amy Trachtenberg; (L) Jim Cave

Magic Theatre. Ellen Idelson and Michael Chinyamurindi in *The Brief But Exemplary Life of the Living Goddess*. Photo: David Allen.

Fat Men in Skirts, Nicky Silver; (D) R.A. White; (S) Jeff Rowlings; (L) Dirk Epperson; (C) Allison Connor; (SD) Andy Murdock
Greek, Steven Berkoff; (D) Paul Hellyer; (S) Karl Rawicz; (C) Susan Doepner; (SD) J.A. Deane
Oscar and Bertha, Maria Irene Fornes; (D) Maria Irene Fornes; (S) and (C) Sandra Woodall; (L) Jennifer Norris
Angel of Death, Charlie Schulman; (D) David Dower; (SD) Bob Davis
Reasons to Live, Han Ong; (D) Brian Kulick
XXX Love Act, Cintra Wilson; (D) Richard Corley
Cross-Dressing in the Depression, Erin Cressida Wilson; (D) Harvey Seifter; (S) Jeffrey Struckman; (L) Kurt Landisman; (C) Beaver Bauer; (SD) Barney Jones

PRODUCTIONS 1992-1993

Sets and lighting by Jeff Rowlings and costumes by Marianne Flippin unless otherwise noted.

The Baltimore Waltz, Paula Vogel; (D) Phyllis S.K. Look; (S) Shevra Tait; (C) Fumiko Bielefeldt; (SD) Kim Foscato
The Brief But Exemplary Life of the Living Goddess, Neena Beber; (D) Marcus Stern; (S) Jeff Hunt; (L) Alex Nichols; (C) Allison Connor; (SD) J.A. Deane
Unquestioned Integrity: The Hill/Thomas Hearings, adapt: Mame Hunt, from U.S. Senate transcripts; (D) Ellen Sebastian; (C) Kim Porter; (SD) Greg Robinson
Trouble, Steve Friedman; (D) Barbara Damashek; (S) Marsha Ginsberg; (L) Jim Cave; (SD) J. Raoul Brody
Why We Have a Body, Claire Chafee; (D) Jayne Wenger; (L) Jim Cave; (SD) Bob Davis
Watch Your Back, Gary Leon Hill; (D) David Ford; (S) Marsha Ginsberg; (L) Jim Cave; (SD) Bob Davis
The Substance of Fire, Jon Robin Baitz; (D) John C. Fletcher; (S) Shevra Tait; (C) Max Szadek; (SD) J.A. Deane

Manhattan Theatre Club

LYNNE MEADOW
Artistic Director

BARRY GROVE
Managing Director

MICHAEL H. COLES
Board Chairman

453 West 16th St., 2nd Floor
New York, NY 10011
(212) 645-5590 (bus.)
(212) 581-1212 (b.o.)
(212) 691-9106 (fax)

FOUNDED 1970
Peregrine Whittlesey, A. Joseph Tandet, George Tabori, Gerard L. Spencer, Margaret Kennedy, A. E. Jeffcoat, Barbara Hirschl, William Gibson, Gene Frankel, Philip Barber

SEASON
Variable

FACILITIES
City Center Stage I
Seating Capacity: 299
Stage: proscenium

City Center Stage II
Seating Capacity: 150
Stage: flexible

FINANCES
July 1, 1992-June 30, 1993
Expenses: $6,400,000

CONTRACTS
AEA Off Broadway

Manhattan Theatre Club has a long tradition of developing and presenting important new works by American and international writers. We also produce earlier works we believe have not been fully interpreted or appreciated in the past, as well as New York premieres of plays that originated in American regional theatres. Many of the plays presented at MTC have gone on to be produced on Broadway, in London, in regional theatres nationwide and as major motion pictures. The flexibility of our two spaces enables us to offer greater visibility in a Stage I production, with production standards of the highest possible quality, as well as a more developmental environment in Stage II for new works by emerging and established playwrights, composers and lyricists. MTC's Writers in Performance series has, for nearly 22 years, presented an international array of writers of all genres whose works demonstrate the diversity and power of contemporary literature. Our subscription audience numbers close to 17,000. MTC is accessible to the broadest community through group discounts, free-ticket distribution, sign-interpreted performances, and an educational outreach program that combines in-class curriculum with exposure to live theatre for students at the intermediate and high school level.

—*Lynne Meadow*

PRODUCTIONS 1991-1992

A Piece of My Heart, Shirley Lauro; (D) Allen R. Belknap; (S) James Fenhagen; (L) Richard Winkler; (C) Mimi Maxmen; (SD) John Kilgore
Boesman and Lena, Athol Fugard; (D) Athol Fugard; (S) and (C) Susan Hilferty; (L) Dennis Parichy
A Small Family Business, Alan Ayckbourn; (D) Lynne Meadow; (S) John Lee Beatty; (L) Peter Kaczorowski; (C) Ann Roth; (SD) Tom Sorce
The Extra Man, Richard Greenberg; (D) Michael Engler; (S) Loy Arcenas; (L) Donald Holder; (C) Jess Goldstein; (SD) Scott Lehrer
Beggars in the House of Plenty, John Patrick Shanley; (D) John Patrick Shanley; (S) Santo Loquasto; (L) Natasha Katz; (C) Lindsay W. Davis; (SD) Bruce Ellman
Sight Unseen, Donald Margulies; (D) Michael Bloom; (S) James Youmans; (L) Donald Holder; (C) Jess Goldstein; (SD) Michael Roth
Groundhog, book, music and lyrics: Elizabeth Swados; (D) Elizabeth Swados; (S) and (C) G.W. Mercier; (L) Natasha Katz; (SD) Ed Fitzgerald

Manhattan Theatre Club. Frances Conroy and John Heard in *The Last Yankee*. Photo: Gerry Goodstein.

85

The Innocents' Crusade, Keith Reddin; (D) Mark Brokaw; (S) Bill Clarke; (L) Michael R. Moody; (C) Ellen McCartney; (SD) Janet Kalas

PRODUCTIONS 1992-1993

Mad Forest, Caryl Churchill (co-produced by New York Theatre Workshop); (D) Mark Wing-Davey; (S) and (C) Marina Draghici; (L) Christopher Akerlind; (SD) Mark Bennett

The Years, Cindy Lou Johnson; (D) Jack Hofsiss; (S) Loren Sherman; (L) Peter Kaczorowski; (C) Lindsay W. Davis; (SD) John Kilgore

Putting It Together, conceived: Stephen Sondheim and Julia McKenzie; music and lyrics: Stephen Sondheim; (D) Julia McKenzie; (S) Robin Wagner; (L) Tharon Musser; (C) Theoni V. Aldredge; (MD) Scott Frankel; (CH) Bob Avian; (SD) Scott Lehrer

A Perfect Ganesh, Terrence McNally; (D) John Tillinger; (S) Ming Cho Lee; (L) Stephen Strawbridge; (C) Santo Loquasto; (SD) Scott Lehrer

Joined at the Head, Catherine Butterfield; (D) Pamela Berlin; (S) James Noone; (L) Natasha Katz; (C) Alvin Perry; (SD) John Kilgore

The Last Yankee, Arthur Miller; (D) John Tillinger; (S) John Lee Beatty; (L) Dennis Parichy; (C) Jane Greenwood; (SD) Scott Lehrer

Jenny Keeps Talking, Richard Greenberg; (D) Risa Bramon Garcia; (S) Shelley Barclay; (L) Brian Nason; (C) Rita Ryack; (SD) Bruce Ellman

Pretty Fire, Charlayne Woodard; (D) Pamela Berlin; (S) Shelley Barclay; (L) Brian Nason; (C) Rita Ryack; (SD) Bruce Ellman

Playland, Athol Fugard; (D) Athol Fugard; (S) and (C) Susan Hilferty; (L) Dennis Parichy; (SD) David Budries

Marin Theatre Company

LEE SANKOWICH
Artistic Director

REGINA LICKTEIG
Managing Director

W. PHILIP WOODARD
Board President

397 Miller Ave.
Mill Valley, CA 94941
(415) 388-5200 (bus.)
(415) 388-5208 (b.o.)
(415) 388-0768 (fax)

FOUNDED 1966
Sali Lieberman

SEASON
Sept.-May

FACILITIES
Mainstage
Seating Capacity: 250
Stage: proscenium

Sali Lieberman Studio Theatre
Seating Capacity: 125
Stage: thrust

FINANCES
July 1, 1992-June 30, 1993
Expenses: $1,023,977

CONTRACTS
AEA BAT

Marin Theatre Company. Nancy Palmer Jones, Carla Befera, Marcia Pizzo, Anni Long and Cynthia Bassham in *The Women*. Photo: Joseph Greco.

The Marin Theatre Company focuses its energies on using the theatre to its full potential as a medium unique in its immediacy, affinity for illusion and distinctive ability to engage, stimulate, move, enlighten and entertain. While we present plays from varied periods and cultures, our emphasis is on developing and premiering new works, introducing contemporary plays lacking previous local exposure and performing American classics. We dedicate ourselves to supporting and compensating artists; to seeking, producing and casting plays that reflect a wide diversity of ethnic, social and cultural backgrounds; and to serving as a training ground for future actors, directors, designers, writers and technicians. Through the Marin Theatre Company School for Theatre Arts, our youth programs offer the opportunity for future artists and audiences to learn, perform and grow; and the school's home, the Sali Lieberman Studio Theatre, will also be used to encourage the development of new talent and original works. The Marin Theatre Company seeks to be a creative, fertile environment with a national reputation for excellence.

—*Lee Sankowich*

PRODUCTIONS 1991-1992

Let Me Sing and I'm Happy, music and lyrics: Irving Berlin, Ira Gershwin, George Gershwin, Oscar Hammerstein, II and Jerome Kern; (D) Alan Johnson; (S) Scott Barringer and Norman E. Barringer; (L) Ellen Shireman; (C) Bill Belew; (MD) Paul Horner; (CH) Donna McKechnie and Alan Johnson

Cobb, Lee Blessing; (D) Lee Sankowich; (S) Steve Coleman; (L) Thomas E. Hansen; (C) Karin Simonson Kopischke; (SD) Adam Liberman

Born Yesterday, Garson Kanin; (D) Richard Seyd; (S) Jeff Hunt; (L) Kurt Landisman; (C) Gail Russell; (SD) John Flanders

A Dream of Wealth, Arthur Giron; (D) Lee Sankowich; (S) Steve Coleman; (L) Novella T. Smith; (C) Laura Hazlett

Arms and the Man, George Bernard Shaw; (D) Barbara Damashek; (S) Alla Chertok-Tripolsky; (L) John Flanders; (C) Gail Russell; (SD) Michael Allen

PRODUCTIONS 1992-1993

The Women, Clare Boothe Luce; (D) Lee Sankowich; (S) Steve Coleman; (L) Kurt Landisman; (C) Laura Hazlett; (SD) Steven Dietz

Lady Day at Emerson's Bar and Grill, Lanie Robertson; (D) Danny Duncan; (S) Joel Eis; (L) Maurice Vercoutere; (C) Jheri; (SD) Darren J. Taylor

A Shayna Maidel, Barbara Lebow; (D) Lee Sankowich; (S) Karl Rawicz; (L) Ellen Shireman; (C) Gail Russell; (SD) Michael Allen

The Price, Arthur Miller; (D) Richard Rossi; (S) Shevra Tait; (L) Thomas E. Hansen; (C) Anna Oliver; (SD) Steven Dietz

Lend Me a Tenor, Ken Ludwig; (D) Albert Takazauckas; (S) Barbara Mesney; (L) Kurt Landisman; (C) Jeffrey Larsen; (SD) William Tracy

Mark Taper Forum

GORDON DAVIDSON
Artistic Director

CHARLES DILLINGHAM
Managing Director

KAREN S. WOOD
General Manager

STEPHEN F. HINCHLIFFE, JR.
Board President

135 North Grand Ave.
Los Angeles, CA 90012
(213) 972-7353 (bus.)
(213) 972-7392 (b.o.)
(213) 972-0746 (fax)

FOUNDED 1967
Gordon Davidson

SEASON
Year-round

FACILITIES
Mark Taper Forum
Seating Capacity: 760
Stage: thrust

Taper, Too
Seating Capacity: 99
Stage: flexible

FINANCES
July 1, 1992-June 30, 1993
Expenses: $10,530,000

CONTRACTS
AEA LORT (A) and (B)

Over the past 26 years the Mark Taper Forum has pursued a distinct and vigorous mission: to create, nurture and maintain a theatre that is socially and culturally aware; that continually examines and challenges the assumptions of our culture, community and society; and that expands the aesthetic boundaries of theatre as an art form. The Taper is committed to nurturing new voices and new forms for the American theatre; to enlightening, amazing, challenging and entertaining our audience by reflecting on our stages the rich multicultural heritage found in Los Angeles; and to encouraging tomorrow's audience through programming that addresses the concerns and challenges the imagination of young people. The future of the Mark Taper Forum lies in the pursuit of artistic excellence, aesthetic daring and community service. The challenge of these goals will continue to provide impetus to our broad-based programming as we begin our second quarter-century.
—*Gordon Davidson*

PRODUCTIONS 1991-1992

Spunk, adapt: George C. Wolfe, from Zora Neale Hurston; music: Chic Street Man; (D) George C. Wolfe; (S) Loy Arcenas; (L) Donald Holder; (C) Toni-Leslie James; (CH) Hope Clarke

Henceforward, Alan Ayckbourn; (D) Tom Moore; (S) Ralph Funicello; (L) Peter Maradudin; (C) Robert Blackman; (SD) Jon Gottlieb

The Kentucky Cycle, Robert Schenkkan; (D) Warner Shook; (S) Michael Olich; (L) Peter Maradudin; (C) Frances Kenny

Richard II, William Shakespeare; (D) Robert Egan; (S) Yael Pardess; (L) R. Stephen Hoyes; (C) Robert Blackman; (SD) Nathan Birnbaum

Unfinished Stories, Sybille Pearson; (D) Gordon Davidson; (S) Peter Wexler; (L) Martin Aronstein; (C) Csilla Marki; (SD) Jon Gottlieb

Fire in the Rain/Singer in the Storm, Holly Near; (D) Timothy Near; (S) Kate Edmunds; (L) Peter Maradudin; (C) Marianna Elliott; (SD) Jon Gottlieb

PRODUCTIONS 1992-1993

Angels in America, Tony Kushner; (D) Oskar Eustis, with Anthony Taccone; (S) John Conklin; (L) Pat Collins; (C) Gabriel Berry; (SD) Jon Gottlieb

The Substance of Fire, Jon Robin Baitz; (D) Daniel Sullivan; (S) John Lee Beatty; (L) Arden Fingerhut; (C) Jess Goldstein; (SD) Scott Lehrer

Scenes From an Execution, Howard Barker; (D) Robert Allan Ackerman; (S) Yael Pardess, concept: Richard Macdonald; (L) Arden Fingerhut; (C) Dona Granata; (SD) Jon Gottlieb

Twilight: Los Angeles, 1992, Anna Deavere Smith; (D) Emily Mann; (S) Robert Brill; (L) Allen Lee Hughes; (C) Candice Donnelly; (SD) Jon Gottlieb

Lips Together, Teeth Apart, Terrence McNally; (D) John Tillinger; (S) John Lee Beatty; (L) Ken Billington; (C) Jane Greenwood; (SD) Jon Gottlieb

Mark Taper Forum. Anna Deavere Smith in *Twilight: Los Angeles, 1992*. Photo: Jay Thompson.

McCarter Theatre Center for the Performing Arts

EMILY MANN
Artistic Director

JEFFREY WOODWARD
Managing Director

LIZ FILLO
Board President

91 University Place
Princeton, NJ 08540
(609) 683-9100 (bus.)
(609) 683-8000 (b.o.)
(609) 497-0369 (fax)

FOUNDED 1972
Daniel Seltzer

SEASON
Sept.-May

FACILITIES
McCarter Theatre
Seating Capacity: 1,078
Stage: proscenium

FINANCES
July 1, 1992-June 30, 1993
Expenses: $4,962,488

CONTRACTS
AEA LORT (B+)

McCarter's vision is to create a theatre of testimony—a theatre engaged in a dialogue with the world around it, one that pays tribute to the enduring power of the human spirit and the scope of the imagination. Each season, McCarter Theatre Center produces a drama series augmented by performances of music and dance and special events featuring artists of national and international repute. The creation of theatre remains at the heart of McCarter's mission, and the theatre's goals are threefold: to evolve into a world-class theatre; to present a diverse season of classic and contemporary plays; and to reinvigorate our audiences by welcoming and encouraging participation by all members of our community. Integral to our mission is the

McCarter Theatre Center for the Performing Arts. Kim Cattrall and Peter Francis James in *Miss Julie*. Photo: T. Charles Erickson.

sponsorship of work that is multi-ethnic and multicultural, and service to the community through broad-based outreach programming, including school assemblies and workshops, student matinees, study guides and audio-described performances.

—Emily Mann

PRODUCTIONS 1991-1992

Indians, Arthur Kopit; (D) George Faison; (S) Eduardo Sicangco; (L) Timothy Hunter; (C) Randy Barcelo

A Christmas Carol, adapt: David Thompson, from Charles Dickens; (D) Scott Ellis; (S) Michael Anania; (L) Peter Kaczorowski; (C) Lindsay W. Davis; (SD) Abe Jacob

The Three Sisters, Anton Chekhov; trans: Lanford Wilson; (D) Emily Mann; (S) Michael Yeargan; (L) Pat Collins; (C) Jennifer von Mayrhauser

Marriage Play, Edward Albee; (D) Edward Albee; (S) and (C) Derek McLane; (L) Howell Binkley

The Triumph of Love, Pierre Carlet de Marivaux; trans: Stephen Wadsworth, with Nadia Benabid; adapt: Stephen Wadsworth; (D) Stephen Wadsworth; (S) Thomas Lynch; (L) Christopher Akerlind; (C) Martin Pakledinaz

PRODUCTIONS 1992-1993

Cat on a Hot Tin Roof, Tennessee Williams; (D) Emily Mann; (S) Derek McLane; (L) Peter Kaczorowski; (C) Jennifer von Mayrhauser; (SD) Mark Bennett

Between East and West, Richard Nelson; (D) Jack Hofsiss; (S) David Jenkins; (L) Beverly Emmons; (C) Gary Lisz

A Christmas Carol, adapt: David Thompson, from Charles Dickens; (D) Scott Ellis; (S) Michael Anania; (L) Peter Kaczorowski; (C) Lindsay W. Davis; (SD) Abe Jacob

Miss Julie, August Strindberg; trans: Michael Tremonte; adapt: Emily Mann; (D) Emily Mann; (S) Thomas Lynch; (L) Pat Collins; (C) Jennifer von Mayrhauser

Sweet & Hot, conceived: Julianne Boyd; music: Harold Arlen; various lyricists; (D) Julianne Boyd; (S) Ken Foy; (L) Howell Binkley; (C) David C. Woolard; (MD) Danny Holgate; (CH) Hope Clarke; (SD) Stephen G. Smith

Much Ado About Nothing, William Shakespeare; (D) Michael Kahn; (S) Derek McLane; (L) Howell Binkley; (C) Martin Pakledinaz; (SD) Gil Thompson

Merrimack Repertory Theatre

DAVID G. KENT
Artistic Director

KEITH STEVENS
General Manager

NANCY L. DONAHUE
Board Chair

Box 228
Lowell, MA 01853
(508) 454-6324 (bus.)
(508) 454-3926 (b.o.)
(508) 441-0222 (fax)

FOUNDED 1979
Mark Kaufman, John Briggs

SEASON
Sept.-May

FACILITIES
Liberty Hall
Seating Capacity: 386
Stage: 3/4 thrust

FINANCES
July 1, 1992-June 30, 1993
Expenses: $949,000

CONTRACTS
AEA LORT (D)

With new artistic leadership and the establishment of a resident company of actors and directors, MRT has expanded its artistic and stylistic reach. MRT's community of artists is committed to a stage language that is rich and exotic, to a stage poetry that is lyrical and musical, and to the plurality of views and attitudes found in our own multicultural region. MRT's artistic vision is rooted in a belief that the theatre is a mysterious and wonderful journey where there are no borders, only new frontiers. In pursuit of this vision MRT continues its evolution, serving the area with a new performance series, a new play series and comprehensive educational, training and outreach programs. In the spring of 1993, MRT originated the world premiere of *The Survivor: A Cambodian Odyssey*, the first in the Lowell Trilogy of stories from within the theatre's own community. From freshly conceived approaches to Shakespeare and Chekhov to the diverse passions of O'Neill and Beckett, MRT recognizes that theatrical truth can help us experience meaning, and see ourselves and our desires in a creative, moral and original way.

—David G. Kent

Merrimack Repertory Theatre. Dawn Akemi Saito, Francois Chau, Ernest Abuba and Eva Lee in *The Survivor: A Cambodian Odyssey*. Photo: Kevin Harkins.

PRODUCTIONS 1991-1992

A Moon for the Misbegotten, Eugene O'Neill; (D) Jonathan Epstein; (S) Alison Ford; (L) James Fulton; (C) Jane Alois Stein

Round and Round the Garden, Alan Ayckbourn; (D) Robert Walsh; (S) Alison Ford; (L) Dave Brown; (C) Kevin Pothier; (SD) Pip Biancamano, III

A Christmas Carol, adapt: Richard McElvain, from Charles Dickens; (D) Richard McElvain; (S) Charles Morgan; (L) Steven Rosen; (C) Lisa Cody

A Pack of Lies, Hugh Whitemore; (D) Steve McConnell; (S) Alison Ford; (L) James F. Franklin; (C) Gail Buckley

Uncle Vanya, Anton Chekhov; trans: Vlada Chernomordik; adapt: David Mamet; (D) David G. Kent; (S) and (C) Gary English; (L) Kendall Smith

Living in Exile, Jon Lipsky; (D) Jon Lipsky; (S) Gary English; (L) Dave Brown; (C) Jane Alois Stein

Shirley Valentine, Willy Russell; (D) Richard Rose; (S) Charles Morgan; (L) Dave Brown; (C) Jane Alois Stein

PRODUCTIONS 1992-1993

Rumors, Neil Simon; (D) David Michael Fox; (S) Maureen Fish and Margo Zdravkovic; (L) Dave Brown; (C) Jane Alois Stein

Our Town, Thornton Wilder; (D) David G. Kent; (S) and (L) Clifton Taylor; (C) Amanda Aldridge; (SD) Todd Shilhanek

A Christmas Carol, adapt: Richard McElvain, from Charles Dickens; (D) Richard McElvain; (S) Charles Morgan; (L) Steven Rosen; (C) Lisa Cody

Twelfth Night, William Shakespeare; (D) Steve McConnell; (S) Maureen Fish and Margo Zdravkovic; (L) James F. Franklin; (C) Jane Alois Stein; (SD) Todd Shilhanek

Talley's Folly, Lanford Wilson; (D) Grey Johnson; (S) Charles Morgan; (L) Dave Brown; (C) Lisa Cody; (SD) Todd Shilhanek

The Survivor: A Cambodian Odyssey, adapt: Jon Lipsky, from Haing S. Ngor and Roger Warner; (D) David G. Kent; (S) and (C) Gary English; (L) Kendall Smith; (SD) Todd Shilhanek

Amadeus, Peter Shaffer; (D) Ted Kazanoff; (S) Leslie Taylor; (L) John Ambrosone; (C) Jane Alois Stein; (SD) Todd Shilhanek

Mill Mountain Theatre

JERE LEE HODGIN
Executive/Artistic Director

MICHAEL WARNER
Board President

1 Market Square SE
Roanoke, VA 24011-1437
(703) 342-5730 (bus.)
(703) 342-5740 (b.o.)
(703) 224-1238 (fax)

FOUNDED 1964
Don Carter, Marta Byer

SEASON
Year-round

FACILITIES
Mainstage
Seating Capacity: 411
Stage: proscenium

Theatre B
Seating Capacity: 125
Stage: flexible

FINANCES
Oct. 1, 1992-Sept. 30, 1993
Expenses: $1,111,904

CONTRACTS
AEA Guest Artist

Mill Mountain Theatre is in its 30th-anniversary season. It has grown from a seasonal stock company to a year-round regional theatre with diverse programming. Perhaps what characterizes it most is a dedication to going beyond simply being "live theatre." We strive to be a theatre that is *alive* and *vital*. This means serving not only our audience but theatre artists and our profession as well. That commitment has encouraged challenge and risk-taking at all levels of our programming—our education, outreach and enrichment programs; our Festival of New Works; and our selection of material for both main and alternate stages. We are dedicated to theatre which makes a difference and theatre which changes the lives of those making and witnessing it.

—*Jere Lee Hodgin*

Mill Mountain Theatre. Herbert Mark Parker and Lynne-Marie Brown in *The Piano Lesson*.

PRODUCTIONS 1991-1992

Direction by Ernest Zulia, sets and lighting by John Sailer and costumes by Anne M. Toewe unless otherwise noted.

Woody Guthrie's American Song, book: Peter Glazer; music and lyrics: Woody Guthrie; (D) Jere Lee Hodgin; (MD) David Caldwell; (CH) Colleen Kelly

Children of Eden, book: John Caird; music and lyrics: Stephen Schwartz; (C) Johann Stegmeir; (MD) David Caldwell; (CH) Lesley Farlow; (SD) Reid Henion

And We Were Left Darkling, Lynn Elliott; (D) Mary Best-Bova; (SD) Tina Decker

White Money, Julie Jensen

The Piano Lesson, August Wilson; (D) Jere Lee Hodgin

Lend Me a Tenor, Ken Ludwig; (D) Jere Lee Hodgin; (C) Robert Croghan

110 in the Shade, book: N. Richard Nash; music: Harvey Schmidt; lyrics: Tom Jones; (MD) David Caldwell; (CH) Colleen Kelly

All I Really Need To Know I Learned In Kindergarten, book adapt: Ernest Zulia, from Robert Fulghum; music: David Caldwell; lyrics: Robert Fulghum; (MD) David Caldwell

PRODUCTIONS 1992-1993

Direction by Ernest Zulia, sets and lighting by John Sailer and costumes by Anne M. Toewe unless otherwise noted.

Pump Boys and Dinettes, book, music and lyrics: John Foley, Mark Hardwick, Debra Monk, Cass Morgan, John Schimmel and Jim Wann; (MD) David Caldwell; (CH) Wendy Overly; (SD) Jeff Busche

A Wonderful Life, book adapt and lyrics: Sheldon Harnick, from the original screenplay; music: Joe Raposo; (D) Jere Lee Hodgin; (C) Janis Martin; (MD) David Caldwell; (CH) Richard Stafford

In the Presence, Sallie Bingham; (D) Mary Best-Bova

Partial Objects, Sherry Kramer

Hamlet, William Shakespeare; (D) Jere Lee Hodgin; (S) and (C) Robert Croghan

The Velveteen Rabbit, book adapt, music and lyrics: Barnes Boffey and Paul Pilcher, from Margery Williams; (D) Biff Baron; (MD) Larry Bixler; (CH) Candace Oerltling

The Search for Signs of Intelligent Life in the Universe, Jane Wagner

42nd Street, book adapt: Michael Stewart and Mark Bramble, from the original screenplay; music: Harry Warren; lyrics: Al Dubin; (C) Robert Croghan; (MD) David Caldwell; (CH) Gail Benedict

Foxfire, Hume Cronyn and Susan Cooper; (D) Jere Lee Hodgin

Milwaukee Chamber Theatre

MONTGOMERY DAVIS
Artistic Director

CARLA SLAWSON
General Manager

ARTHUR LASKIN
Board President

158 North Broadway
Milwaukee, WI 53202
(414) 276-8842 (bus.)
(414) 291-7800 (b.o.)
(414) 277-4477 (fax)

FOUNDED 1975
Montgomery Davis, Ruth Schudson

SEASON
Oct.-June

FACILITIES
Mainstage
Seating Capacity: 310
Stage: proscenium

Studio Theatre
Seating Capacity: 95
Stage: flexible

FINANCES
July 1, 1992-June 30, 1993
Expenses: $342,086

CONTRACTS
AEA SPT

The Chamber Theatre has been committed for over a decade to performing works of a literate and/or classical nature, including those presented in our annual Shaw Festival. The performances emphasize the actor's art and mainly involve artists living and working in Wisconsin. Our permanent move to a new theatre with two audience-engaging spaces gives us the capability to develop new and more experimental works. We also aim to produce one work a year that is accessible and available to student audiences.
—Montgomery Davis

PRODUCTIONS 1991-1992

Direction by Montgomery Davis, sets by Pat Doty, lighting by Andrew Meyers, costumes by Debra Krajec and sound design by Laura Gordon unless otherwise noted.

Shirley Valentine, Willy Russell; (S) Ken Johnson; (L) Dan Brovarney; (C) Dawn B. Worth; (SD) William Jay Venzke
A Few Good Men, Aaron Sorkin; (S) Skelly Warren; (L) Robert Zenoni; (C) Robert Liebhauser; (SD) William Jay Venzke
84 Charing Cross Road, adapt: Janes Roose-Evans, from Helene Hanff; (L) Chester Loeffler-Bell; (C) Karalee Dawn; (SD) Montgomery Davis

Shaw Festival:
Misalliance, George Bernard Shaw; (D) D. Scott Glasser
The Lady's Not For Burning, Christopher Fry
Far Fetched Fables, George Bernard Shaw

PRODUCTIONS 1992-1993

Vincent, adapt: Leonard Nimoy, from Phillip Stephens; (D) Montgomery Davis; (S) Sandra J. Strann; (L) Leroy Stoner; (C) Karalee Dawn; (SD) Laura Gordon
Lettice and Lovage, Peter Shaffer; (D) Ken Cazan; (S) Skelly Warren; (L) Dan Brovarney; (C) Debra Krajec and Robert Liebhauser; (SD) Jonathan Smoots
My Children! My Africa!, Athol Fugard; (D) D. Scott Glasser; (S) Rick Rasmussen; (L) Andrew Meyers; (C) William F. Wedepohl; (SD) Jonathan Smoots

Shaw Festival:
Timon of Athens, William Shakespeare; (D) Montgomery Davis; (S) John Story; (L) Andrew Meyers; (C) Debra Krajec; (SD) David Cecsarini
The Millionairess, George Bernard Shaw; (D) Denise Coffey; (S) Joan Devlin; (L) Andrew Meyers; (C) Debra Krajec; (SD) David Cecsarini

Milwaukee Chamber Theatre. James Tasse and Jonathan Smoots in *Timon of Athens*.

Milwaukee Repertory Theater

JOSEPH HANREDDY
Artistic Director

SARA O'CONNOR
Managing Director

VINCENT L. MARTIN
Board President

108 East Wells St.
Milwaukee, WI 53202
(414) 224-1761 (bus.)
(414) 224-9490 (b.o.)
(414) 224-9097 (fax)

FOUNDED 1954
Mary John

SEASON
Sept.-May

FACILITIES
Powerhouse Theater
Seating Capacity: 720
Stage: thrust

Stiemke Theater
Seating Capacity: 198
Stage: flexible

Stackner Cabaret
Seating Capacity: 116
Stage: proscenium

Pabst Theater
Seating Capacity: 1,393
Stage: proscenium

FINANCES
July 1, 1992-June 30, 1993
Expenses: $4,033,000

CONTRACTS
AEA LORT (A), (C) and (D)

Our work at the Milwaukee Rep is based on the belief that a sustained commitment to the growth and development of a diverse ensemble of artists provides us with the potential to achieve theatrical work that is richer, more personal and more meaningful than that which would result from any other way of organizing theatre. In order to increase our awareness of the world and keep our artistic vision ever expanding, we foster exchanges and collaborations with international companies; invite forward-thinking, innovative theatre artists to work with us; and maintain an in-house laboratory that develops new works and explores fresh approaches to established texts. To strengthen our relationship to our community we commission work specific to our region and maintain a community service program that uses the theatre as an educational tool in the development of imagination, skills and self-esteem in populations for whom the life-enhancing experience of theatre is presently inaccessible.
—Joseph Hanreddy

Note: During the 1991-92 and 1992-93 seasons, John Dillon served as artistic director.

PRODUCTIONS 1991-1992

Sets by John Story, lighting by Chester Loeffler-Bell and costumes by Dawna Gregory unless otherwise noted.

Our Town, Thornton Wilder; (D) John Dillon; (S) Steven Rubin; (L) William H. Grant, III; (C) Michael Krass
The House of Bernarda Alba, Federico Garcia Lorca; trans: Michael Dewell and Carmen Zapata; (D) Rene Buch; (S) Pavel Dobrusky; (L) Jason Sturm; (C) Sam Fleming

Milwaukee Repertory Theater. *Moot.* Photo: Jay Westhauser.

Missouri Repertory Theatre

GEORGE KEATHLEY
Artistic Director

JAMES D. COSTIN
Executive Director

MARK S. GILMAN
Board President

4949 Cherry St.
Kansas City, MO 64110
(816) 235-2727 (bus.)
(816) 235-2700 (b.o.)
(816) 235-5367 (fax)

FOUNDED 1964
Patricia McIlrath, James D. Costin

SEASON
Sept.-May

FACILITIES
Helen F. Spencer Theater
Seating Capacity: 730
Stage: flexible

Unicorn Theater
Seating Capacity: 170
Stage: thrust

FINANCES
July 1, 1992-June 30, 1993
Expenses: $3,717,903

CONTRACTS
AEA LORT (B)

The Gin Game, D.L. Coburn; (D) Libby Appel; (S) Michael C. Smith; (L) Peter Maradudin; (C) Constanza Romero

All the Tricks but One, Gilles Segal; trans: Sara O'Connor; (D) Kenneth Albers; (S) Victor A. Becker; (L) Robert Jared; (C) Sam Fleming

Death of a Salesman, Arthur Miller; (D) John Dillon; (S) Laura Maurer; (L) Robert Peterson; (C) Sam Fleming

Moot, John Leicht; (D) John Dillon; (C) Charles Berliner; (SD) John Tanner

A Christmas Carol, adapt: Amlin Gray, from Charles Dickens; (D) Kenneth Albers; (S) Stuart Wurtzel; (L) Dan Kotlowitz; (C) Carol Oditz

Other People's Money, Jerry Sterner; (D) Joseph Hanreddy; (S) Kenneth Kloth; (L) Thomas C. Hase; (SD) David Budries

Meetings, Mustapha Matura; (D) Tim Bond; (S) Rick A. Rasmussen; (L) Kenneth Kloth; (C) Ellen Kozak

An Evening of Mamet, Gray and Linney, David Mamet, Amlin Gray and Romulus Linney; (D) Norma Saldivar; (S) Pat Doty; (L) Linda Essig; (C) Cecelia Mason

Imago: The Theatre Mask Ensemble, conceived: Carol Uselman and Jerry Mouawad; music: Daniel Brandt, Fred Chalenor and Courtney Von Drehle

2 X 5 X 4, conceived: Seth Glassman; music: John Kander; lyrics: Fred Ebb; (D) Pamela Hunt; (L) Rick Rasmussen; (C) Rey Dobeck

Greater Tuna, Jaston Williams, Joe Sears and Ed Howard; (D) Kenneth Albers

Appalachian Voices, Edward Morgan; music: Steve Hickman, Edward Morgan and Jon Newlin; (D) Edward Morgan

Lady Day at Emerson's Bar and Grill, Lanie Robertson; (D) William Partlan; (S) Steve Krahnke, after Jack Barkla

Mother Jones: The Most Dangerous Woman in America, book: Ronnie Gilbert; music and lyrics: Si Kahn; (D) Norma Saldivar; (S) Kate Henderson

PRODUCTIONS 1992-1993

Sets by John Story, lighting by Jeff Stroman and costumes by Wayne White unless otherwise noted.

M. Butterfly, David Henry Hwang; (D) Kenneth Albers; (S) Victor A. Becker; (L) Dan Kotlowitz; (C) Sam Fleming

The Greater Good, adapt: Amlin Gray, from Arthur Schnitzler; (D) John Dillon; (S) Kate Edmunds; (L) Derek Duarte; (C) Constanza Romero

The Foreigner, Larry Shue; (D) George Keathley; (S) Vicki Smith; (L) Linda Essig; (C) Dawna Gregory

Ambrosio, adapt: Romulus Linney, from Matthew G. Lewis; (D) John Dillon; (S) E. David Cosier, Jr.; (L) William H. Grant, III; (C) Judy Dearing

A Raisin in the Sun, Lorraine Hansberry; (D) Kenneth Leon; (S) Dex Edwards; (L) Ann G. Wrightson; (C) Sam Fleming

The Tempest, William Shakespeare; (D) John Dillon; (S) and (L) Kevin Rigdon; (C) Sam Fleming; (SD) John Tanner

A Christmas Carol, adapt: Amlin Gray, from Charles Dickens; (D) Kenneth Albers; (S) Stuart Wurtzel; (L) Robert Jared; (C) Carol Oditz

My Visits with MGM, Edit Villarreal; (D) Norma Saldivar; (S) Pat Doty; (L) Linda Essig; (C) Cecelia Mason

Rajeckas & Intraub, conceived: Paul Rajeckas and Neil Intraub; (L) Vaughn Patterson

How I Got That Story, Amlin Gray; (D) Joseph Hanreddy; (L) Kenneth Kloth; (C) Karin Simonson Kopischke

Betrayal, Harold Pinter; (D) Norma Saldivar; (S) Victor A. Becker; (L) Kenneth Kloth; (C) Sam Fleming

Hula Hoop Sha-Boop, Larry Deckel, John Leicht and John Tanner; various composers and lyricists; (D) Larry Deckel; (L) Jeff Stroman; (C) Dawna Gregory; (CH) Darci Brown Wutz

Rodgers and..., conceived: Jack Forbes Wilson and Kaye Stiefel; music: Richard Rodgers; various lyricists; (D) Peter Amster; (S) Kate Henderson

Duke's Place, conceived: Mercedes Ellington; music: Duke Ellington; various lyricists; (D) and (CH) Mercedes Ellington; (S) John Devlin; (MD) Diana B.

An Irish Reunion, Edward Morgan; various composers and lyricists; (D) Edward Morgan

The Tall and the Short of It, Will Clinger and Jim FitzGerald; various composers and lyricists

---

Theatre can be a mirror for the soul. It provides a context for understanding ourselves and our world which can lead to moments of enlightenment and connection to others. The job of Missouri Repertory Theatre is to capture on stage universal, timeless aspects of human behavior. Classics and plays about to become classics are the continuum of history, providing a background for each of us and our lives. For this reason new plays continue to be a high priority for us. Playwright's Stage (formerly Second Stage) provides a program of readings and productions that are thought-provoking, compelling and entertaining. Theatre at Missouri Rep is a collaboration that creates a unique world onstage, visually, aurally and, ultimately, emotionally.

—*George Keathley*

Missouri Repertory Theatre. Benjamin Evett, Jayne Houdyshell and John Plumpis in *Broadway Bound*. Photo: Frank Siraguso.

PRODUCTIONS 1991-1992

Sets by John Ezell, lighting by Robert Murphy, costumes by Vincent Scassellati and sound design by Tom Mardikes unless otherwise noted.

King Lear, William Shakespeare; (L) Curt Ostermann
I'm Not Rappaport, Herb Gardner; (D) Mary G. Guaraldi; (S) Gene Emerson Friedman; (C) Martha Hally
A Christmas Carol, adapt: Barbara Field, from Charles Dickens; (D) Ross Freese; (L) Joseph Appelt; (C) Baker S. Smith
The Lady from Maxim's, Georges Feydeau; trans: John Mortimer; (D) Gerald Freedman; (C) James Scott; (SD) Stan Kozak
Lady Day at Emerson's Bar and Grill, Lanie Robertson; (D) George Keathley; (L) Jackie Manassee
A View from the Bridge, Arthur Miller; (D) Edward Stern; (S) John Jensen; (C) Dorothy L. Marshall
The Cocktail Hour, A.R. Gurney, Jr.; (D) Mary G. Guaraldi; (S) Joseph Nieminski

Playwright's Stage:
Villains, B. Burgess Clark; (D) Mary G. Guaraldi; (S) Robert Murphy; (C) Gregg Benkovich

PRODUCTIONS 1992-1993

Direction by George Keathley, sets by John Ezell, lighting by Robert Murphy, costumes by Vincent Scassellati and sound design by Tom Mardikes unless otherwise noted.

Romeo and Juliet, William Shakespeare; (L) Curt Ostermann
Broadway Bound, Neil Simon; (S) Joseph Nieminski; (L) Kathy Perkins; (C) Baker S. Smith
A Christmas Carol, adapt: Barbara Field, from Charles Dickens; (D) Ross Freese; (L) Joseph Appelt; (C) Baker S. Smith
Ma Rainey's Black Bottom, August Wilson; (D) Claude Purdy; (S) James D. Sandefur; (L) Phil Monat; (C) Paul Tazewell
Rough Crossing, adapt: Tom Stoppard, from Ferenc Molnar; (D) Ross Freese and George Keathley; (C) James Scott
Death of a Salesman, Arthur Miller; (S) Gene Emerson Friedman; (L) Jeff Davis; (C) Baker S. Smith
The Fantasticks, book adapt and lyrics: Tom Jones, from Edmond Rostand; music: Harvey Schmidt; (D) Mary G. Guaraldi; (S) Robert Murphy; (C) Vikki Marshall; (MD) Molly Jessup
A Midsummer Night's Dream, William Shakespeare

Playwright's Stage:
Purple Hearts, B. Burgess Clark; (D) B. Burgess Clark; (S) Robert Murphy; (C) Gregg Benkovich; (SD) Rod Attebury
Hollywood Canteen, Ron Wilson; (D) Mary G. Guaraldi; (S) Ann Keehbaugh; (L) Jarrett Bertoncin; (C) Becky Larson; (SD) Rod Attebury

Mixed Blood Theatre Company

JACK REULER
Managing/Artistic Director

JIM McCARTHY
Board President

1501 South Fourth St.
Minneapolis, MN 55454
(612) 338-0937 (bus.)
(612) 338-6131 (b.o.)

FOUNDED 1976
Jack Reuler

SEASON
Sept.-May

FACILITIES
Seating Capacity: 200
Stage: flexible

FINANCES
July 1, 1992-June 30, 1993
Expenses: $966,000

CONTRACTS
AEA Twin Cities Area

It is my contention that Mixed Blood Theatre Company foreshadows the American regional theatre of the future: a well-paid, well-trained, multiracial staff of artists and administrators presenting flexible seasons that integrate original works with the tried-and-true in rotating rep, with no subscription yet with accessible admission rates. I would like our new-play programming to remain strong, multifaceted and *production-oriented*. I am very proud that we are able to pay our actors salaries commensurate with their worth; that our touring programs promote cultural pluralism through more than 300 performances each year in 15 states; and that our training program is unique in America. Above all, our artistic quality and production values are at a zenith. For me theatre is a vehicle for artistry, entertainment and education, and for effecting world change.
—*Jack Reuler*

PRODUCTIONS 1991-1992

Sets by Robert Fuecker, lighting by Charles D. Craun, costumes by Chris Cook and sound design by Herbie Woodruff unless otherwise noted.

The Grapes of Wrath, adapt: Frank Galati, from John Steinbeck; (D) Jeff Perry; (L) Barry Browning

Mixed Blood Theatre Company. Morgan Duncan and Isabell Monk in *Cincinnati Man*. Photo: Mike Paul/Act II Photography.

Cincinnati Man, Syl Jones; (D) Don Cheadle
Black Belts, Jevetta Steele and Jack Reuler; (D) Jack Reuler

PRODUCTIONS 1992-1993

Sets by Nayna Ramey, lighting by Scott Peters, costumes by Chris Cook and sound design by Herbie Woodruff unless otherwise noted.

The King of the Kosher Grocers, Joe Minjares; (D) Marion Isaac McClinton
Road to Nirvana, Arthur Kopit; (D) Mike Kissin
The Boys Next Door, Tom Griffin; (D) John Clark Donahue; (S) Kevin Egelund; (C) Anne Ruben; (SD) Lawrence Fried
A...My Name is Still Alice, conceived: Julianne Boyd and Joan Micklin Silver; various composers and lyricists; (D) Sari Ketter and Risa Brainin; (L) Michael Klaers; (MD) Sanford Moore; (CH) Marvette Knight; (SD) Scott W. Edwards

Music-Theatre Group

LYN AUSTIN
Producing Director

DIANE WONDISFORD
General Director

ROSITA SARNOFF
Board Chair

29 Bethune St.
New York, NY 10014
(212) 924-3108
(212) 255-1981 (fax)

FOUNDED 1971
Lyn Austin

SEASON
Variable

FINANCES
July 1, 1992-June 30, 1993
Expenses: $500,000

CONTRACTS
AEA LORT (B) and Off Broadway

Music-Theatre Group is a leading force in commissioning, developing and presenting new, innovative major music-theatre in New York, the Berkshires, across the country and abroad. Our work explores new creative territory, weaving together music, theatre, dance and the visual arts. The *New York Times* writes that "MTG is producing one of the most innovative and original bodies of work in the American theatre." Among the many distinguished works in MTG's canon are Julie Taymor/Elliot Goldenthal's *Juan Darien*, Martha Clarke's *The Garden of Earthly Delights* and *Vienna: Lusthaus*, Stanley Silverman and Richard Foreman's *Love and Science* and *Africanus Instructus*, and our innovative version of Virgil Thomson and Gertrude Stein's *The Mother of Us All*. MTG sends its work out *to* diverse audiences, rather than assuming that they will come to a single performance space distant from their home base. We constantly explore and identify unique performance spaces where there is a compelling meeting ground between our artists and those they want to reach.
—*Lyn Austin*

PRODUCTIONS 1991-1992

Costumes by Donna Zakowska unless otherwise noted.

Diary of an African American, book, music and lyrics: Hannibal Peterson; (D) Oz Scott; (L) Peter West; (C) Judy Dearing; (MD) Rahn Burton; (SD) One Dream
Life in the Lost Track, book, music and lyrics: Edward Flower; (L) Bill Beautyman
Akin, book: John Kelly; music: Richard Peaslee; lyrics: Mark Campbell; (D) and (CH) John Kelly; (S) Huck Snyder; (L) Howell Binkley; (MD) Roberto Pace; (SD) Tim Schellenbaum
Cooking the World, book and lyrics: Robert Berky; music: William Harper; (D) Paul Walker; (S) Donna Zakowska; (L) Paul Bartlett; (SD) Bob Bielecki

PRODUCTIONS 1992-1993

Costumes by Donna Zakowska unless otherwise noted.

Palm Court, music: Stanley Silverman; various lyricists; (D) Diane Wondisford; (S) Carl Sprague; (L) Bill Beautyman
The Mother of Us All, music: Virgil Thomson; lyrics: Gertrude Stein; (D) Stanley Silverman; (S) Carl Sprague; (L) Bill Beautyman; (MD) Richard Cordova
Cooking the World, book and lyrics: Robert Berky; music: William Harper; (D) Paul Walker; (S) Donna Zakowska; (L) Paul Bartlett; (SD) Bob Bielecki
Ring Around the Rosie..., conceived: David Parsons; music: Richard Peaslee; lyrics: Mark Campbell; (D) and (CH) David Parsons; (L) Howell Binkley
Hey Love, conceived: Richard Maltby, Jr.; music: Mary Rodgers; various lyricists; (D) Richard Maltby, Jr.; (L) and (SD) Mat Berman; (C) David C. Woolard; (MD) Patrick S. Brady

Music-Theatre Group. Hannibal Peterson in *Diary of an African American*. Photo: Tom Brazil.

National Jewish Theater

JEFF GINSBERG,
SUSAN PADVEEN
Co-Artistic Directors

FRAN BRUMLIK
Producing Director

CHARLOTTE NEWBERGER
Board Chair

5050 West Church St.
Skokie, IL 60077
(708) 675-2200 (bus.)
(708) 675-5070 (b.o.)
(708) 675-2914 (fax)

FOUNDED 1986
Jewish Community Centers of Chicago

SEASON
Oct.-July

FACILITIES
Zollie and Elaine Frank Theater
Seating Capacity: 250
Stage: flexible

FINANCES
July 1, 1992-June 30, 1993
Expenses: $452,900

CONTRACTS
AEA CAT

The National Jewish Theater is dedicated to the exploration of the contemporary Jewish experience through a wide variety of theatrical styles and stories—as always, redefining and rejuvenating the role that theatre plays in the lives of our diverse community. Our mandate is to produce theatre that will energize its audiences, and help them to understand who they are and how they can exist and thrive in an ethnically diverse society without losing their roots and their identity. As artists, we can explore our existence within the context of being Jewish today. We challenge ourselves to confront the hard issues of the Jewish-American experience and hope that our productions inspire fervent debate. Change is inevitable. The NJT must be a place where world events can be watched and analyzed, where existing dramatic material of the Jewish-American experience can be presented, and where we can support new work that in style

National Jewish Theater. Tim Ferrin and Brian Kolb in *In My Father's Court*. Photo: Lisa Ebright.

and content speaks to who we are and who we want to be.
—*Jeff Ginsberg, Susan Padveen*

Note: During the 1991-92 season, Arnold Aprill served as artistic director.

PRODUCTIONS 1991-1992

Sets by Richard and Jacqueline Penrod, costumes by Frances Maggio and sound design by Wm. T. Griffeth unless otherwise noted.

The Heidi Chronicles, Wendy Wasserstein; (D) Sheldon Patinkin; (S) Mary Griswold; (L) Rita Pietraszek; (SD) Dabney Forest
In My Mother's House, adapt: Arnold Aprill, from Kim Chernin; (D) Estelle Spector; (L) Todd Hensley; (SD) Robert Neuhaus
Sins of the Father, Chaim Potok; (D) David Cromer; (S) Jane Gault; (L) Geoffrey Bushor
In My Father's Court, adapt: Arnold Aprill and Jacqueline Penrod, from Isaac Bashevis Singer; (D) Arnold Aprill; (L) Chris Phillips

PRODUCTIONS 1992-1993

Sets by Richard and Jacqueline Penrod and costumes by Jessica Hahn.

The Songs of War, Murray Schisgal; (D) Susan Padveen; (L) Mary M. Badger; (SD) Dabney Forest
The Wizards of Quiz, Steve Feffer; (D) Jeff Ginsberg; (L) Chris Phillips; (SD) Robert Neuhaus
The Price, Arthur Miller; (D) B.J. Jones; (L) Robert Shook; (SD) Sonia Kholomanian
Puttin' on the Ritz, music and lyrics: Irving Berlin; (D) Sheldon Patinkin; (L) Rita Pietraszek; (MD) Kingsley Day; (CH) James Corti

Nebraska Theatre Caravan

CHARLES JONES
Founding Director

CAROLYN RUTHERFORD
Managing Director

L.B. THOMAS
Board President

6915 Cass St.
Omaha, NE 68132
(402) 553-4890 (bus.)
(402) 553-0800 (b.o.)
(402) 553-6288 (fax)

FOUNDED 1976
Charles Jones, Omaha Community Playhouse

SEASON
Sept.-May

FACILITIES
Omaha Community Playhouse
Seating Capacity: 600
Stage: proscenium

Fonda-McGuire Theatre
Seating Capacity: 250
Stage: flexible

FINANCES
July 1, 1992-June 30, 1993
Expenses: $1,053,085

CONTRACTS
AEA Guest Artist

The Nebraska Theatre Caravan is the professional touring wing of the Omaha Community Playhouse, the largest community theatre in the nation and the only community theatre to sponsor a national professional touring company. The original mission of the Caravan is to provide high-quality entertainment and educational opportunities to communities where distance, financial limitations or lack of appropriate resources have hindered or prevented such activities. However, we are finding that the company is now providing performances and workshops to cities of all sizes across the U.S. and Canada, as well as in our home state. The 15-member resident company now works together eight months each year. Our dream is to have year-round employment for the professional company that not only performs in our home theatre's Fonda-McGuire Series, but also tours nationally and internationally.
—*Charles Jones*

PRODUCTIONS 1991-1992

Direction by Carl Beck, sets by Steven D. Wheeldon and costumes by Kathleen Gossman unless otherwise noted.

The Mystery of Edwin Drood, book adapt, music and lyrics: Rupert Holmes, from Charles Dickens; (C) Amy Schmidt; (MD) Jonathan Cole; (CH) Kathy Wheeldon

Nebraska Theatre Caravan. Kathryn Hammond, Matthew Kamprath, Camille Carrell, Cork Ramer and Joe Arnold in *The Mystery of Edwin Drood*. Photo: Stuart Allen Scott.

Great Expectations, adapt: Barbara Field, from Charles Dickens; (D) Susan Baer Beck
Ichabod!, book adapt and lyrics: Charles Jones, from Washington Irving; music: Jonathan Cole; (D) Eleanor Brodie Jones; (MD) Jonathan Cole; (CH) Joanne Cady
A Christmas Carol, adapt: Charles Jones, from Charles Dickens; (S) and (L) James Othuse; (C) Tom Crisp

PRODUCTIONS 1992-1993

Direction by Susan Baer Beck, sets and lighting by Steven D. Wheeldon and sound design by Barry Anderson unless otherwise noted.

Carnival, book: Michael Stewart; music and lyrics: Bob Merrill; (D) Carolyn Rutherford; (C) Wendy Stark; (MD) Ron Guthrie; (CH) Kathy Wheeldon
The Martian Chronicles, Ray Bradbury; (L) Laurel Shoemaker; (C) Denise Ervin
Junglebook, adapt: Edward Mast, from Rudyard Kipling; (L) Laurel Shoemaker; (C) John Gergel
A Christmas Carol, adapt: Charles Jones, from Charles Dickens; (D) Carl Beck; (S) and (L) James Othuse; (C) Tom Crisp

New American Theater

J.R. SULLIVAN
Producing Director

JOHN C. PICK
Board President

118 North Main St.
Rockford, IL 61101
(815) 963-9454 (bus.)
(815) 964-8023 (b.o.)
(815) 963-7215 (fax)

FOUNDED 1972
J.R. Sullivan

SEASON
Year-round

FACILITIES
David W. Knapp Theater
Seating Capacity: 282
Stage: thrust

AMCORE Cellar Theater
Seating Capacity: 100
Stage: flexible

FINANCES
July 1, 1992-June 30, 1993
Expenses: $1,129,498

CONTRACTS
AEA SPT

New American Theater's mission is to produce a wide range of works from the American and world repertory, with a focus on contemporary and new work. It is also the theatre's mission to build an ensemble of artists in residence who will, in addition to their mainstage work, work with the community in outreach programs that will further establish the art of theatre as vital to the area. With the production of plays from the world and modern American repertory, the theatre seeks to reaffirm the values inherent in these works. With the development of new plays in its Amcore space, and later on the main stage, it seeks to generate new and lasting work for the American stage and to develop new audiences, especially among populations traditionally underserved by the arts in our country. New American Theatre seeks to be a theatre of surprising diversity and consistent quality for all.

—*J.R. Sullivan*

PRODUCTIONS 1991-1992

Direction by J.R. Sullivan, lighting by Peter Gottlieb and costumes by Jon R. Accardo unless otherwise noted.

Sunday in the Park with George, book: James Lapine; music and lyrics: Stephen Sondheim; (S) Bruce Bergner; (MD) Andrew Levine; (CH) Cathy Susan Pyles
A Walk in the Woods, Lee Blessing; (D) Allan Carlsen; (S) and (C) Cathy Susan Pyles; (L) Todd Hensley
A Christmas Carol, adapt: Amlin Gray, from Charles Dickens; (S) James Wolk; (SD) Rob Milburn
Other People's Money, Jerry Sterner; (S) William D. Carey; (SD) Rob Milburn and Michael Bodeen
The Mousetrap, Agatha Christie; (D) Allan Carlsen; (S) Jon R. Accardo and Mark Lohman; (L) Thomas Hase
Shirley Valentine, Willy Russell; (S) Michael S. Philippi

The Mystery of Irma Vep, Charles Ludlam; (S) Jon R. Accardo and William D. Carey; (L) Thomas Hase

PRODUCTIONS 1992-1993

Direction by J.R. Sullivan, lighting by Peter Gottlieb and costumes by Jon R. Accardo unless otherwise noted.

The Nerd, Larry Shue; (D) Allan Carlsen; (S) Stephen Packard; (L) Susan McElhaney
You Can't Take It With You, George S. Kaufman and Moss Hart; (S) and (C) Jon R. Accardo and Jon Paoletti; (L) Geoffrey Bushor; (SD) Michael Bodeen
A Christmas Carol, adapt: J.R. Sullivan, from Charles Dickens; (S) Michael S. Philippi; (SD) Rob Milburn
Love Letters, A.R. Gurney, Jr.; (D) Bern Sundstedt; (S) Jon R. Accardo
The Piano Lesson, August Wilson; (D) Donald Douglass; (S) James Wolk; (L) Thomas C. Hase; (C) Nick Harris
The Passion of Dracula, adapt: Bob Hall and David Richmond, from Bram Stoker; (S) Michael S. Philippi; (SD) Michael Bodeen
Private Lives, Noel Coward; (S) Jon R. Accardo
Steel Magnolias, Robert Harling; (D) Stephen F. Vrtol, III; (S) Phillip Jay Hickox; (L) Todd Hensley

New American Theater. Gail Dartez, Pat Bauerlein, Colleen Burns and Julia Thudium in *Steel Magnolias*. Photo: John McGinty.

New Dramatists

ELANA GREENFIELD
Co-Director/Artistic Programs

PAUL SLEE
Co-Director/Development

JANA JEVNIKAR
Co-Director/Administration and Finance

ISOBEL ROBINS KONECKY
Board President

424 West 44th St.
New York, NY 10036
(212) 757-6960
(212) 265-4738 (fax)

FOUNDED 1949
John Wharton, Richard Rodgers, Michaela O'Hara, Howard Lindsay, Moss Hart, Oscar Hammerstein, II, John Golden

SEASON
Sept.-May

FACILITIES
Mainstage
Seating Capacity: 90
Stage: flexible

Lindsay/Crouse Studio
Seating Capacity: 60
Stage: flexible

FINANCES
July 1, 1992-June 30, 1993
Expenses: $510,000

CONTRACTS
AEA letter of agreement

New Dramatists provides the time, space and tools for playwrights to develop their vision and their work. The organization, now entering its fifth decade, is firmly established as the country's oldest workshop for playwrights. The eclectic group of playwrights who make up New Dramatists at any given time are chosen by a panel of their peers for a seven-year term. With the advice and supervision of the artistic staff, member playwrights define the process of development for themselves. To this end, in addition to the program of readings and workshops, the writers have a variety of services available including a resident director and dramaturg, writer studios and exchanges with theatres in other countries. We are Dedicated to the Playwright.

—Elana Greenfield

PRODUCTIONS 1991-1992

Running for Blood No. 3, Migdalia Cruz; (D) Marjorie Van Halteren
The Happy Prince, book and lyrics: Laura Harrington; music: Christopher Drobny; (D) Alma Becker
The America Play, Suzan-Lori Parks; (D) Liz Diamond
Braille Garden, Darrah Cloud
Babes in Toyland, Laura Harrington
Disappeared, Phyllis Nagy; (D) Beth Schachter
Awake, Phyllis Nagy; (D) Beth Schachter
The Universal Wolf, Joan Schenkar; (D) Liz Diamond
Frozen in Time, Migdalia Cruz, Erik Ehn, Jeffrey M. Jones, Sherry Kramer, Eduardo Machado, Wendy MacLeod, Pedro Pietri, Joan Schenkar, Ana Maria Simo and Joe Sutton; (D) Eduardo Machado, Beth Schacter and Fritz Ertl
The Reincarnation of Jamie Brown, Lynne Alvarez; (D) John Pynchon Holms
Black Forest, Anthony Giardina; (D) Doug Wagner
When Night is Near, Willy Holtzman; (D) John Pynchon Holms
Anatomy of Suicide, Kate Moira Ryan; (D) Suzanne Bennett
Windshook, Mary Gallagher; (D) Phil Soltanoff
Across a Crowded Room, Eduardo Machado; (D) Anne Bogart
Girl Bar, Phyllis Nagy; (D) Anne Bogart
Chaos, book and lyrics: Matthew Maguire; music: Michael Gordon; (D) Anne Bogart, (MD) Charles Berigan
To My Chagrin, Ben Seigler
Alabama Rain, Heather McCutchen; (D) Anne Bogart
Fur, Migdalia Cruz; (D) Stephen Pickover
Once Removed, Eduardo Machado; (D) Mark Brokaw
The Devils, Elizabeth Egloff
Voir Dire, Joe Sutton; (D) Evan Yionoulis
The River Book, Erik Ehn; (D) Brian Mertes
Lake Street Extension, Lee Blessing; (D) Jeanne Blake
Nacre, Erik Ehn; (D) Fritz Ertl
The Year of My Mothers Birth, Erik Ehn; (D) Fritz Ertl
Real Life, Susan Yankowitz; (D) Melia Bensussen
Dream House, Darrah Cloud
The Opium Wars, book and lyrics: Ana Maria Simo; music: Zeena Parkins; (D) Linda Chapman
Sanctuary, Laura Cunningham, Mary Gallagher, Romulus Linney, Lisa Loomer, Wendy MacLeod, Peter Mattei, OyamO, Kate Moira Ryan, Joan Schenkar, Ana Maria Simo and Donald Wollner; (D) Marya Cohn, Elana Greenfield, Michael Mayer, Lisa Peterson and Ana Maria Simo
Things That Break, Sherry Kramer; (D) Jesse Allen
Weldon Rising, Phyllis Nagy; (D) Lisa Peterson
Mormons in Malibu, Wendy Hammond; (D) Julian Webber
What a Man Weighs, Sherry Kramer; (D) Liz Diamond
A Permanent Signal, Sherry Kramer
The Quilting Circle, Heather Schuster; (D) Heather Schuster
Sight Retrieved, Kate Moira Ryan; (D) Lisa Peterson
The Closer, Willy Holtzman; (D) John Pynchon Holms
Sin, Wendy MacLeod
Hanna, Frank Gagliano; (D) Sara Romersberger
My Chekov Light, Frank Gagliano
The Day God Died, Bonnie Bluh; (D) Craig Lowy
Succulence, Phil Wilmott; (D) Lisa Peterson
Lady Chieftains, Willy Holtzman; (D) Calvin Skaggs
Planet of the Mutagens, Mary Gail; (D) Lisa Peterson
Stealing the Scene, Phil Wilmott; (D) Lisa Peterson

PRODUCTIONS 1992-1993

Y York: No Props, Y York; (D) Mark Lutwak
Clearance Sale at the Five and Dime, David Hanson; (D) Elaine Smith
The Will, Paolo De Paola; (D) Ernie Barbarash
Sabina, Willy Holtzman
Greater Good, adapt: Amlin Gray, from Arthur Schnitzler; (D) Lawrence J. Jost
Early Dismissal, Willy Holtzman; (D) John Pynchon Holms
George and Elba, Ed Einhorn; (D) Ernie Barbarash
Pacific Ocean, Roger Arturo Durling; (D) Mark Brokaw
The Saga of the Famous Mrs. Grimes, Gary Carsel; (D) Sharon Mazer
Hadley's Mistake, Kate Moira Ryan; (D) Robert Woodruff
Voir Dire, Joe Sutton; (D) Clinton Turner Davis
The Sirens, Darrah Cloud; (D) Seret Scott
Rushing Waters, Migdalia Cruz; (D) Liz Diamond
Mother Clap's Molly House, John C. Russell; (D) Michael Mayer
Borders of Loyalty, Michael Henry Brown; (D) Marion Isaac McClinton
Hunters of the Soul, Marion Isaac McClinton; (D) Seret Scott
The Day the Bronx Died, Michael Henry Brown; (D) Gordon Edelstein
Stupid Kids, John C. Russell; (D) Michael Mayer
Delire D'Interpretations, Fiona Templeton; (D) Lisa Peterson
Honor Song For Crazy Horse, Darrah Cloud; (D) Lisa Peterson
The Benefits of Doubt, Joe Sutton; (D) David Chambers
Cruising Close to Crazy, Laura Cunningham; (D) Jim Simpson
The Cemetery Man, Jennifer Fox; (D) Lisa Peterson
A Gun, A Book, A Photograph, A Name, John C. Russell; (D) Janie Geiser
Mormons in Malibu, Wendy Hammond; (D) Julian Webber
Sabina, Willy Holtzman; (D) John Pynchon Holms
Thin Air, Beth Kracklauer; (D) Tracy Brigden
Anarchy in the OK, Erik Ehn; (D) Erik Ehn
Better Him Than Me, Heather McCutchen; (D) Alice Jankell
Freefall, Charles Smith; (D) Jim Simpson
Romance Concerto, Daniel Therriault; (D) Sergio Castilla
In the Land of Giants, Roger Arturo Durling; (D) Travis Preston
Enlightenments, Marion Isaac McClinton; (D) Jim Simpson
Shoeman, Marion Isaac McClinton; (D) Marion Isaac McClinton
The Devils, Elizabeth Egloff; (D) Robert Woodruff
Benny Kozo, Jim Simpson
Sacred Rhythms, Eduardo Machado
Thin Air, Lynne Alvarez
Sabina, Willy Holtzman
Julie Johnson, Wendy Hammond
The Accident, Carol Mack
Cigarettes and Moby Dick, Migdalia Cruz
Death Catches the Hunter, Biyi Bandele Thomas
Enlightenments, Marion Isaac McClinton
Resurrections in the Season of the Longest Drought, Biyi Bandele Thomas
Bathtub, Wendy MacLeod
Machines Cry Wolf, Wendy MacLeod
Dante and Virgil Go Dancing, John C. Russell
Eddie, Lynne Alvarez
Windshook, Mary Gallagher

New Federal Theatre

WOODIE KING, JR.
Producer

LINDA HERRING
Managing Director

LEON GILDIN
Board Chairman

466 Grand St.
New York, NY 10002
(212) 598-0400

FOUNDED 1970
Woodie King, Jr.

SEASON
Sept.-June

FINANCES
July 1, 1991-June 30, 1992
Expenses: $256,136

CONTRACTS
AEA letter of agreement

New Federal Theatre. Grenoldo Frazier, Denise Burse-Mickelbury and Guy Davis in *Robert Johnson: Trick the Devil*. Photo: Martha Holmes.

Growing out of the New York State Council on the Arts Ghetto Arts Program, the New Federal Theatre was officially founded by Woodie King, Jr. at Henry Street Settlement. Now in its 23rd season, the New Federal Theatre has carved a much admired special niche for itself in the New York and national theatre worlds. Specializing in minority drama, it has brought the joy of the living stage to the many minority audience members who live in the surrounding Lower East Side community and the greater metropolitan area. It has brought minority playwrights, actors and directors to national attention, and has sponsored a variety of ethnic theatre groups and events.
—*Woodie King, Jr.*

PRODUCTIONS 1991-1992

Zion, book: Beverly Trader; music and lyrics: Uzee Brown; (D) and (CH) Thomas W. Jones, II; (S) and (L) Richard Harmon; (C) Gregory Glenn; (MD) Uzee Brown; (SD) Carmen Griffin

Chain and *Late Bus to Mecca*, Pearl Cleage; (D) Imani; (S) George Xenos; (L) Melody Beal; (C) Ornyece; (SD) Bill Toles

Testimony, Safiya Henderson-Holmes; (D) and (C) Raina Von Waldenburg; (S) Nathan Jones; (L) Mary Liquori

PRODUCTIONS 1992-1993

Christchild, J.E. Franklin; (D) Irving Vincent; (S) Felix E. Cochren; (L) Jeff Guzik; (C) Judy Dearing; (SD) Bill Toles

Robert Johnson: Trick the Devil, book: Bill Harris; music and lyrics: Guy Davis and Robert Johson; (D) Woodie King, Jr.; (S) Richard Harmon; (L) Antoinette Tynes; (C) Judy Dearing; (MD) Guy Davis and Grenoldo Frazier

New Jersey Shakespeare Festival

BONNIE J. MONTE
Artistic Director

MICHAEL STOTTS
Managing Director

A. GARY SHILLING
Board Chairman

c/o Drew University
36 Madison Ave.
Madison, NJ 07940
(201) 408-3278 (bus.)
(201) 408-5600 (b.o.)
(201) 408-3361 (fax)

FOUNDED 1963
Paul Barry

SEASON
June-Sept.

FACILITIES
Bowne Theatre
Seating Capacity: 244
Stage: thrust

Other Stage
Seating Capacity: 108
Stage: flexible

FINANCES
Jan. 1, 1992-Dec. 31, 1992
Expenses: $726,480

CONTRACTS
AEA SPT and letter of agreement

The New Jersey Shakespeare Festival's mission is twofold. Dedicated to producing the plays of Shakespeare and other classic masterworks, NJSF is committed to the notion that through its longevity classical theatre can shed light on current concerns and issues, holding a mirror up to our lives and helping us understand personal dilemmas and those common to the human race. Classic works can also help us understand those who look and live differently, serving as a force for social and political change. Classics can accomplish these things as effectively as our contemporary plays because they have a history and a perspective. They show us where we've come from, what mankind is, what it will always be, and how we have changed and evolved. At their best, classics can show us where to go. We are interested in this kind of work because it illuminates, not just because it exists. A second and equal focus of our mission is to nurture new talent *and* new audiences for the American stage; to strengthen and expand the venues for young professionals; and to do our part, especially through working with young people, to revitalize the tradition of theatre-going in this country.
—*Bonnie J. Monte*

PRODUCTIONS 1992

Sound design by Donna Riley unless otherwise noted.

Macbeth, William Shakespeare; (D) Bonnie J. Monte; (S) Chris Muller; (L) Steven Rosen; (C) Constance Hoffman

The Importance of Being Earnest, Oscar Wilde; (D) Dylan Baker; (S) Michael V. Sims; (L) Scott Zielinski; (C) Cynthia Dumont

Henry IV, Part 1, William Shakespeare; (D) Peggy Shannon; (S) James Youmans; (L) Michael R. Moody; (C) Victoria Petrovich

The Taming of the Shrew, book adapt and lyrics: Mark Milbauer and David Becker, from William Shakespeare; music: David Becker; (D) Mark Milbauer and David Becker; (S) Jerry Hubert; (L) Andrew Hancock; (C) Ronna Rothenberger; (CH) and (SD) David Becker

The Seagull, Anton Chekhov; trans: Jean-Claude van Itallie; (D) Bonnie J. Monte; (S) Rob Odorisio; (L) Bruce Auerbach; (C) Hwa K.C. Park

Much Ado About Nothing, William Shakespeare; (D) Jimmy Bohr; (S) Rob Odorisio; (L) Michael Giannitti; (C) B. Christine McDowell

New Jersey Shakespeare Festival. Tom Brennan and Carrie Nye in *The Seagull*. Photo: Gerry Goodstein.

PRODUCTIONS 1993

Sound design by Donna Riley unless otherwise noted.

The Taming of the Shrew, William Shakespeare; (D) Dylan Baker; (S) Michael V. Sims; (L) Scott Zielinski; (C) Susan Branch

Arms and the Man, George Bernard Shaw; (D) Bonnie J. Monte; (S) Rob Odorisio; (L) Steven Rosen; (C) Maggie Morgan

Othello, William Shakespeare; (D) Robert Walsh; (S) Shelley Barclay; (L) Bruce Auerbach

Measure for Measure, adapt: Mark Milbauer, from William Shakespeare; (D) Mark Milbauer

Ghosts, Henrik Ibsen; trans: Michael Meyer; (D) Ellis Rabb; (S) and (L) James Tilton

The Comedy of Errors, William Shakespeare; (D) Bonnie J. Monte; (S) Michael Ganio; (L) Michael Giannitti; (C) Tom Broecker

New Mexico Repertory Theatre

DREW MARTORELLA
Producing Director

BOB MacDONALD
Managing Director

JOEL FAYE BENNET
Board President

Box 9279
Santa Fe, NM 87504-9279
(505) 983-2382 (bus.)
(505) 984-2226 (b.o.)
(505) 984-1296 (fax)

Box 789
Albuquerque, NM 87103-0789
(505) 243-4577 (bus.)
(505) 764-1700 (b.o.)

FOUNDED 1983
Andrew Shea, Steven Schwartz-Hartley, Clayton Karkosh

SEASON
Year-round

FACILITIES
KiMo Theatre
Seating Capacity: 755
Stage: proscenium

Santa Fe Armory for the Arts
Seating Capacity: 340
Stage: thrust

FINANCES
July 1, 1992-June 30, 1993
Expenses: $1,142,000

CONTRACTS
AEA LORT (D)

Founded in 1983, the Rep is New Mexico's only fully professional theatre and member of the League of Resident Theatres. The Rep regularly produces both in the state's largest city, Albuquerque, and in the state capital, Santa Fe. The Rep serves 50,000 audience members each year. The purpose of the New Mexico Repertory Theatre is to create and present entertaining, provocative and innovative works of theatrical art; to serve as a major theatrical resource for the Southwest; to educate present and future audiences in a greater appreciation of theatre; and to illumine the human condition.

—*Drew Martorella*

Note: During the 1991-92 season, Rosario Provenza served as interim artistic director. During the 1992-93 season, Martin L. Platt served as artistic director.

PRODUCTIONS 1991-1992

Brilliant Traces, Cindy Lou Johnson; (D) Roberta Levitow; (S) Rosario Provenza; (L) Paulie Jenkins; (C) Tina Cantu Navarro; (SD) Mitchell Greenhill

Burn This, Lanford Wilson; (D) Susan Fenichell; (S) A. Clark Duncan; (L) Mary Louise Geiger; (C) Teresa Snider-Stein

The Mystery of Irma Vep, Charles Ludlam; (D) Jules Aaron; (S) Rosario Provenza; (L) Michael Gilliam; (C) Ann Bruice

Blood Knot, Athol Fugard; (D) Gordon Gray; (S) and (C) Scott Bradley; (L) Mary Louise Geiger

Our Lady of the Tortilla, Luis Santeiro; (D) Jose Guadalupe Saucedo; (S) Rosario Provenza; (L) Jose Lopez; (C) Tina Cantu Navarro; (SD) Chris Koff

PRODUCTIONS 1992-1993

Pump Boys and Dinettes, John Foley, Mark Hardwick, Debra Monk, Cass Morgan, John Schimmel and Jim Wann; (D) Maggie Lamee; (S) Rosario Provenza; (L) Mary Louise Geiger; (C) Susan E. Mickey; (SD) Daryl Bornstein

The Glass Menagerie, Tennessee Williams; (D) Martin L. Platt; (S) and (C) David Crank; (L) Kirk Bookman

Love Letters, A.R. Gurney, Jr.; (D) Ted Weiant; (L) Lynn Janick; (SD) Stacie Johnson

Arms and the Man, George Bernard Shaw; (D) Richard Russell Ramos; (S) Russell Parkman; (L) Robert Wierzel; (C) Alan Armstrong

Woman in Mind, Alan Ayckbourn; (D) Martin L. Platt; (S) Russell Parkman; (L) Robert Wierzel; (C) Holly Poe Durbin; (SD) Stacie Johnson

New Mexico Repertory Theatre. Raye Lankford and Guy Paul in *Arms and the Man*. Photo: Martin Perea.

New Repertory Theatre

LARRY LANE
Artistic Director

STEPHEN C. COPPICK
Managing Director

BONNIE CLENDENNING
Board Chair

Box 418
Newton Highlands, MA 02161
(617) 332-1646
(617) 527-5217 (fax)

FOUNDED 1984
Larry Lane, Kathryn Lubar, Nora Singer, Richard Fairbanks, Donna Glick

SEASON
Sept.-May

FACILITIES
Seating Capacity: 150
Stage: thrust

FINANCES
Aug. 1, 1991-July 31, 1992
Expenses: $463,628

CONTRACTS
AEA SPT

Our audiences come to the theatre to be moved and exposed. They want to share in the mysterious contact between actor and actor, actor and audience. In our small, 150-seat thrust-stage theatre, such contact is very direct. Detail is magnified. Actors can work small and still cast a spell. For this reason, we work to produce with meticulous care and concern for detail. Our interest in contact extends also to our connection with the community through many post-show discussions, classes, forums and workshops that explore the plays we produce—their themes, their relevance and the feelings they engender. In a culture in which any sense of "community" seems increasingly absent, we believe that theatre should be a gathering point, a place where artists and audiences explore what is difficult, consoling and challenging.

—*Larry Lane*

New Repertory Theatre. Peter Husovsky and Peter Bubrisky in *The Lisbon Traviata*. Photo: Eric Levenson.

PRODUCTIONS 1991-1992

Sets and lighting by Eric Levenson unless otherwise noted.

The Circle, Somerset Maugham; (D) Robert Walsh; (C) Frances Nelson McSherry
True West, Sam Shepard; (D) Clinton Turner Davis; (L) Steven Rosen; (C) Jennifer Tingle; (SD) Billie Cox
Lady Day at Emerson's Bar and Grill, Lanie Robertson; (D) Joe Brancato; (S) and (L) Richard Fairbanks; (C) Charlotte Asbury
A Shayna Maidel, Barbara Lebow; (D) Alan Brody; (C) Frances Nelson McSherry; (SD) Billie Cox
The Cocktail Hour, A.R. Gurney, Jr.; (D) Larry Lane; (S) Jennifer Lansdale; (L) L. Stacy Eddy; (C) Gail Buckley

PRODUCTIONS 1992-1993

Sets and lighting by Eric Levenson and sound design by Billie Cox unless otherwise noted.

And a Nightingale Sang, C.P. Taylor; (D) Larry Lane; (S) Jennifer Lansdale; (L) Linda O'Brien; (C) Donna May
The Lisbon Traviata, Terrence McNally; (D) Ingrid Sonnichsen; (L) Steven Rosen; (C) Carson M. Eddy
Arms and the Man, George Bernard Shaw; (D) Munson Hicks; (S) Steven Capone; (L) L. Stacy Eddy; (C) Gail Buckley
My Children! My Africa!, Athol Fugard; (D) Joanna Zazofsky; (C) Charlotte Asbury
The Company of Angels, Alan Brody; (D) Larry Lane; (S) Steven Capone; (C) Donna May

New Stage Theatre

JANICE ENGELHARDT
Managing Director

CAROL DAILY
Board President

Box 4792
Jackson, MS 39296-4792
(601) 948-3533 (bus.)
(601) 948-3531 (b.o.)
(601) 948-3538 (fax)

FOUNDED 1966
Jane Reid-Petty

SEASON
Year-round

FACILITIES
Meyer Crystal Auditorium
Seating Capacity: 364
Stage: proscenium

Jimmy Hewes Room
Seating Capacity: 100
Stage: flexible

FINANCES
July 1, 1992-June 30, 1993
Expenses: $665,000

CONTRACTS
AEA letter of agreement

We create an environment where the artist can do his or her best work. Everybody at New Stage talks about plays, and exploration is not limited to rehearsal and production meetings. Mississippi audiences are bred on the rich literary heritage of the state, and our emphasis on new playwrights evolves from this heritage. Our special programming of the Eudora Welty New Plays Series, for example, encourages writers both locally and nationally. Our statewide touring program spotlights scenes from Shakespeare and Mississippi fiction writers. Minority involvement is a priority, and our commitment to this principle is reflected in the composition of our intern company and our acting company.
—*Jane Reid-Petty*

Note: During the 1991-92 season, Jane Reid-Petty served as artistic director.

PRODUCTIONS 1991-1992

Direction by Jane Reid-Petty, sets and costumes by Janet Gray, and lighting by David Castaneda unless otherwise noted.

Nunsense, book, music and lyrics: Dan Goggin; (L) Charles Morrison; (MD) Randy Redd; (CH) Felton Smith
The Lion in Winter, James Goldman; (D) Ivan Rider
A Christmas Carol, adapt: John Jakes, from Charles Dickens; (D) Kevin Kinley; (S) John Ovington; (L) Joseph B. Musumeci, Jr.; (SD) Kevin Kinley and John Dunn
The Cocktail Hour, A.R. Gurney, Jr.; (D) Ivan Rider; (L) Joseph Oshry
Charlotte's Web, adapt: Joseph Robinette, from E.B. White; (D) Francine Thomas; (S) Marvin L. White and Jimmy Robertson; (L) Nick Wurzel and Andre Golden
Eden, book: Frank Wood, Jr.; music: David Womack; lyrics: Frank Wood, Jr. and David Womack; (MD) Randy Redd; (CH) Lori Leshner
Abundance, Beth Henley; (SD) Mark Johnson

PRODUCTIONS 1992-1993

Direction by Ivan Rider and sets and lighting by Janet Gray unless otherwise noted.

Dirty Work at the Crossroads, Bill Johnson; (L) Nick Wurzel
Romance/Romance, book and lyrics: Barry Harman; music: Keith Herrmann; (D) and (CH) Karen Azenberg; (L) Joseph Oshry
Edna Earle, adapt: Jane Reid-Petty, with Eudora Welty; (L) Derek Donovan
A Christmas Carol, adapt: Ivan Rider, from Charles Dickens; (S) Sandy McNeal and Jimmy Robertson; (L) Kenneth J. Lewis
The Glass Menagerie, Tennessee Williams; (D) Jane Reid-Petty; (L) Derek Donovan; (C) Diane Donovan; (SD) Mark Johnson
Lettice and Lovage, Peter Shaffer; (D) Stephen Hollis; (L) John Wilson; (SD) Jeremy Donovan
The Lion, the Witch and the Wardrobe, adapt: Joseph Robinette, from C.S. Lewis; (D) Francine Thomas; (S) Derek Donovan; (L) John Wilson; (SD) Jeremy Donovan
I Hate Hamlet, Paul Rudnick; (D) Ivan Rider; (L) Derek Donovan; (SD) Jeremy Donovan

New Stage Theatre. Francine Thomas in *The Glass Menagerie*.

New York Shakespeare Festival

GEORGE C. WOLFE
Producer

JASON STEVEN COHEN
Managing Director

**H. SCOTT HIGGINS,
ROBERT W. PITTMAN**
Board Co-Chairmen

Joseph Papp Public Theater
425 Lafayette St.
New York, NY 10003
(212) 589-7100 (bus.)
(212) 598-7150 (b.o.)
(212) 589-7199 (fax)

FOUNDED 1954
Joseph Papp

SEASON
Year-round

FACILITIES
Newman Theater
Seating Capacity: 299
Stage: proscenium

Anspacher Theater
Seating Capacity: 275
Stage: 3/4 arena

Martinson Hall
Seating Capacity: 169
Stage: proscenium

LuEsther Hall
Seating Capacity: 159
Stage: flexible

Susan Stein Shiva Theater
Seating Capacity: 104
Stage: flexible

Delacorte Theater, Central Park
Seating Capacity: 1,932
Stage: thrust

FINANCES
Sept. 1, 1992-Aug. 31, 1993
Expenses: $9,472,000

CONTRACTS
AEA LORT (B) and Off Broadway (A) and (C) contracts

Since 1954, when Joseph Papp founded the New York Shakespeare Festival, it has been operated in the belief that a theatre with the highest professional standards can attract, and should be made available to, a broadly-based public. From this guiding philosophy a contemporary theatre of extraordinary range and quality has emerged, rooted in the classics but with new American plays as its primary focus. Each summer since 1956, NYSF has presented free outdoor productions of the classics throughout New York City, and since 1962, at the Delacorte Theater in Central Park. At the Joseph Papp Public Theater, a repertoire of new American plays and several generations of American actors, directors and designers have grown and matured. In 1988, the Festival embarked on a marathon of Shakespeare's entire 36-play canon with the foremost American actors. Since my appointment as producer in 1993, NYSF has renewed its commitment to discovering and nurturing new voices and sustaining mature artists who reflect the full range of contemporary America's diverse landscape, thereby attracting the broad-based publics (both new and loyal) whose many stories they reflect.

—*George C. Wolfe*

PRODUCTIONS 1991-1992

In the Jungle of Cities, Bertolt Brecht; trans: Gerhard Nellhaus; book adapt: Anne Bogart; music: Judson Wright; lyrics: Anne Bogart and Judson Wright (co-produced by Mabou Mines and VIA Theater); (D) Anne Bogart; (S) Donald Eastman; (L) Heather Carson; (C) Gabriel Berry; (MD) Judson Wright; (SD) Jacob Burckhardt and L.B. Dallas

Pericles, William Shakespeare; (D) Michael Greif, (S) John Arnone; (L) Frances Aronson; (C) Gabriel Berry; (SD) Mark Bennett

Moving Beyond the Madness–A Festival of New Voices:
curator: George C. Wolfe; various playwrights; various directors; (L) Dan Kotlowitz

The Home Show Pieces, David Greenspan; (D) David Greenspan; (S) William Kennon; (L) David Bergstein; (C) Elsa Ward

'Tis Pity She's a Whore, John Ford; (D) JoAnne Akalaitis; (S) John Conklin; (L) Mimi Jordan Sherin; (C) Gabriel Berry; (SD) John Gromada

Blood Wedding, Federico Garcia Lorca; trans: Langston Hughes; adapt: Melia Bensussen; (D) Melia Bensussen; (S) Derek McLane; (L) Peter Kaczorowski; (C) Franne Lee

Fires in the Mirror, Anna Deavere Smith; (D) Christopher Ashley; (S) James Youmans; (L) Debra J. Kletter; (C) Candice Donnelly

As You Like It, William Shakespeare; (D) Adrian Hall; (S) Eugene Lee; (L) Natasha Katz; (C) Melina Root

The Comedy of Errors, William Shakespeare; (D) CaCa Rossett; (S) and (C) Jose De Ancieta Costa; (L) Peter Kaczorowski

PRODUCTIONS 1992-1993

You Could Be Home By Now, Ann Magnuson (co-produced by Women's Project & Productions); (D) David Schweizer; (S) Bill Clarke; (L) Heather Carson; (C) Pilar Limosner; (SD) Eric Liljestrand

Texts for Nothing, Samuel Beckett; (D) Joseph Chaikin; (S) Christine Jones; (L) Beverly Emmons; (C) Mary Brecht; (SD) Gene Ricciardi

Woyzeck, Georg Buchner; trans: Henry J. Schmidt; (D) JoAnne Akalaitis; (S) Marina Draghici; (L) Mimi Jordan Sherin; (C) Gabriel Berry; (SD) John Gromada

Mo' Madness–A Festival of New Voices:
curator: George C. Wolfe; various playwrights; various directors; (L) Dan Kotlowitz; (SD) Gene Ricciardi

On the Open Road, Steve Tesich; (D) Robert Falls; (S) Donald Eastman; (L) Kenneth Posner; (C) Gabriel Berry; (SD) John Gromada

Wings, book adapt and lyrics: Arthur Perlman, from Arthur Kopit; music: Jeffrey Lunden; (D) Michael Maggio; (S) Linda Buchanan; (L) Robert Christen; (C) Birgit Rattenborg Wise; (MD) Bradley Vieth; (SD) Richard Woodbury

Memory Tricks, Marga Gomez; (D) Roberta Levitow; (S), (L) and (C) Linda Buchanan; (SD) Jeff Bova

Deep in a Dream of You, David Cale; (D) David Petrarca; (S), (L) and (C) Linda Buchanan; (SD) Rob Millburn

Marisol, Jose Rivera (co-produced by Hartford Stage Company); (D) Michael Greif; (S) Debra Booth; (L) Kenneth Posner; (C) Angela Wendt and Gabriel Berry; (SD) David Budries

Measure for Measure, William Shakespeare; (D) Michael Rudman; (S) John Lee Beatty; (L) Peter Kaczorowski; (C) Toni-Leslie James; (SD) Tom Morse

All's Well That Ends Well, William Shakespeare; (D) Richard Jones; (S) and (C) Stewart Laing; (L) Mimi Jordan Sherin; (SD) Tom Morse

New York Shakespeare Festival. *All's Well That Ends Well*. Photo: Martha Swope.

New York State Theatre Institute

PATRICIA Di BENEDETTO SNYDER
Producing Director

ED. LANGE
Associate Artistic Director

SHARON ROBINSON
President, Citizens for NYSTI

Box 28
Troy, NY 12181-0028
(518) 274-3200 (bus.)
(518) 274-3256 (b.o.)
(518) 274-3815 (fax)

FOUNDED 1976
Patricia Di Benedetto Snyder, Empire State Youth Theatre Institute (State University of New York), Governor Nelson A. Rockefeller Empire State Plaza Performing Arts Center Corporation

SEASON
Sept.-June

FACILITIES
Schacht Fine Arts Center
Seating Capacity: 900
Stage: proscenium

FINANCES
Apr. 1, 1993-Mar. 30, 1994
Expenses: $1,050,000

CONTRACTS
AEA TYA

Known until 1990 as the Empire State Institute for the Performing Arts (ESIPA), the newly named New York State Theatre Institute has undergone numerous changes which have left the central mission of its 17-year history unaltered. With the enthusiastic support of the public, the Institute has left the parentage of the State University and has been reconstituted by the New York State Legislature as a public benefit corporation. We have moved from Albany's art center known as "the Egg" and at present perform temporarily at Russell Sage College. Our commitment to tomorrow manifests itself in our efforts to produce high-quality, challenging theatre for young people and their families; to develop new works that speak clearly to a diverse, changing world and offer a broader cultural perspective; and to provide young people with provocative arts-in-education programs that open doors as they open eyes to new ways of seeing, learning and understanding.
—*Patricia Di Benedetto Snyder*

PRODUCTIONS 1991-1992

Direction by Ed. Lange, sets by Victor A. Becker, lighting by Betsy Adams, costumes by Brent Griffin, and sound design by Matt Elie unless otherwise noted.

Pinocchio, adapt: Sandra Deer, from Carlo Collodi; (L) Lenore Doxsee; (SD) Dan Toma
Beauty and the Beast, adapt: Ray Bono, from Mme. Le Prince de Beaumont; (C) Karen Kammer
Yours, Anne, book, adapt and lyrics: Enid Futterman, from Anne Frank; music: Michael Cohen; (D) Terence Lamude; (S) Bill Stabile; (L) John McLain; (C) Karen Kammer; (MD) Mark Brockley
Sherlock's Last Case, Charles Marowitz; (S) Richard Finkelstein
The Wizard of Oz, book adapt: John Kane, from L. Frank Baum; music: Harold Arlen; lyrics: E.Y. Harburg; (D) Patricia Di Benedetto Snyder; (S) Richard Finkelstein; (L) John McLain; (MD) Caryl Gershman; (CH) Adrienne Posner; (SD) Omni Tech

PRODUCTIONS 1992-1993

Direction by Ed. Lange, sets and lighting by Victor A. Becker, costumes by Brent Griffin, and sound design by Matt Elie unless otherwise noted.

Sleeping Beauty, adapt: Richard Shaw and the company, from Charles Perrault; (D) Joseph Balfior and Adrienne Posner; (S) Marsha Lovis Eck; (L) Lloyd S. Riford, III; (C) Patrizia von Brandenstein
To Kill a Mockingbird, adapt: Christopher Sergel, from Harper Lee; (C) Karen Kammer
Slow Dance on the Killing Ground, William Hanley; (L) Victor En Yu Tan; (SD) Dan Toma
The Secret Garden, adapt: Thomas W. Olson, from Frances Hodgson Burnett; (D) Terence Lamude; (L) Ann G. Wrightson

New York Theatre Workshop. John Curless, J. Smith-Cameron and Robert Stanton in *Owners*. Photo: Martha Swope.

New York State Theatre Institute. Harlin C. Kearsley and Joel Aroeste in *Slow Dance on the Killing Ground*. Photo: Tim Raab/Northern Photo.

New York Theatre Workshop

JAMES C. NICOLA
Artistic Director

NANCY KASSAK DIEKMANN
Managing Director

STEPHEN GRAHAM
Board Chair

220 West 42nd St., 18th Floor
New York, NY 10036
(212) 302-7737 (bus.)
(212) 302-NYTW (b.o.)
(212) 391-9875 (fax)

FOUNDED 1979
Stephen Graham

SEASON
Oct.-June

FACILITIES
Perry Street Theatre (1991-92)
Seating Capacity: 99
Stage: flexible

New York Theatre Workshop (1992-93)
Seating Capacity: 150
Stage: proscenium

FINANCES
July 1, 1992-June 30, 1993
Expenses: $924,000

CONTRACTS
AEA letter of agreement

NEW YORK THEATRE WORKSHOP

New York Theatre Workshop maintains its commitment to producing works of artistic merit that provide society with a perspective on our history and on the events and institutions that shape our lives. Each season we present four-to-six fully mounted productions of literate, unconventional plays. These new works are primarily developed from continuing relationships with writers and directors. We seek out artists who can combine an interest in the exploration of theatrical forms with intelligent and substantial content, and who can maintain the highest standards of quality. In addition to a New Works Series, we present New Directors/New Directions, which provides opportunities for both the most promising directors of the next generation and established theatre artists; and O Solo Mio, an annual festival of solo performance art. Our Mondays at Three program, and summer residencies at the Hotchkiss School and Dartmouth College, provide forums for presentation of and comment on work in progress, and for discussion of current social and artistic issues, thereby creating a sense of community amongst artists and staff.

—James C. Nicola

PRODUCTIONS 1991-1992

Sound design by Mark Bennett unless otherwise noted.

Mad Forest, Caryl Churchill; (D) Mark Wing-Davey; (S) and (C) Marina Draghici; (L) Christopher Akerlind

Time Flies When You're Alive, Paul Linke; (D) Mark W. Travis; (L) Pat Dignan

Lypsinka! A Day in the Life, John Epperson; (D) Michael Leeds; (S) James Schuette; (L) Mark McCullough; (C) Anthony Wong; (SD) Mark Bennett and James van Bergen

Punch Me in the Stomach, Deb Filler and Alison Summers; (D) Alison Summers; (S) George Xenos; (L) Pat Dignan

PRODUCTIONS 1992-1993

C. Colombo Inc. Export/Import, Genoa, Leo Bassi; (D) Christopher Grabowski; (S), (L) and (C) Anita Stewart; (SD) Mark Bennett

Owners and *Traps*, Caryl Churchill; (D) Mark Wing-Davey *(Owners)*; Lisa Peterson *(Traps)*; (S) Derek McLane; (L) Christopher Akerlind; (C) Gabriel Berry; (SD) John Gromada

The Opium War, book and lyrics: Ana Maria Simo; music: Zeena Parkins; (D) Linda Chapman; (L) Heather Carson

O Solo Mio Festival: various playwrights, various directors

Just Add Water Festival: various playwrights, various directors

Brave Smiles...Another Lesbian Tragedy, Maureen Angelos, Babs Davey, Dominique Dibbell, Peg Healey and Lisa Kron (co-produced by the Five Lesbian Brothers); (D) Kate Stafford; (S) Jamie Leo; (L) Diana Arecco; (C) Susan Young; (SD) Peg Healey

Novel Stages

DAVID BASSUK
Artistic Director

DAVID URRUTIA
Executive Director

BRIAN JOYCE
Managing Director

STEVEN TUTTLEMAN
Board Chairman

7001 Mc Callum St.
Philadelphia, PA 19119-3038
(215) 843-6152 (bus.)
(215) 963-0345 (b.o.)
(215) 843-4410 (fax)

FOUNDED 1989
David Bassuk, Donna Browne, Elizabeth Cuthrell, Brian Joyce, Barbara Pitts, Christopher Stewart, Clista Townsend, David Urrutia

SEASON
Sept.-May

FACILITIES
Stage III
Seating Capacity: 120
Stage: proscenium

FINANCES
July 1, 1992-June 30, 1993
Expenses: $251,000

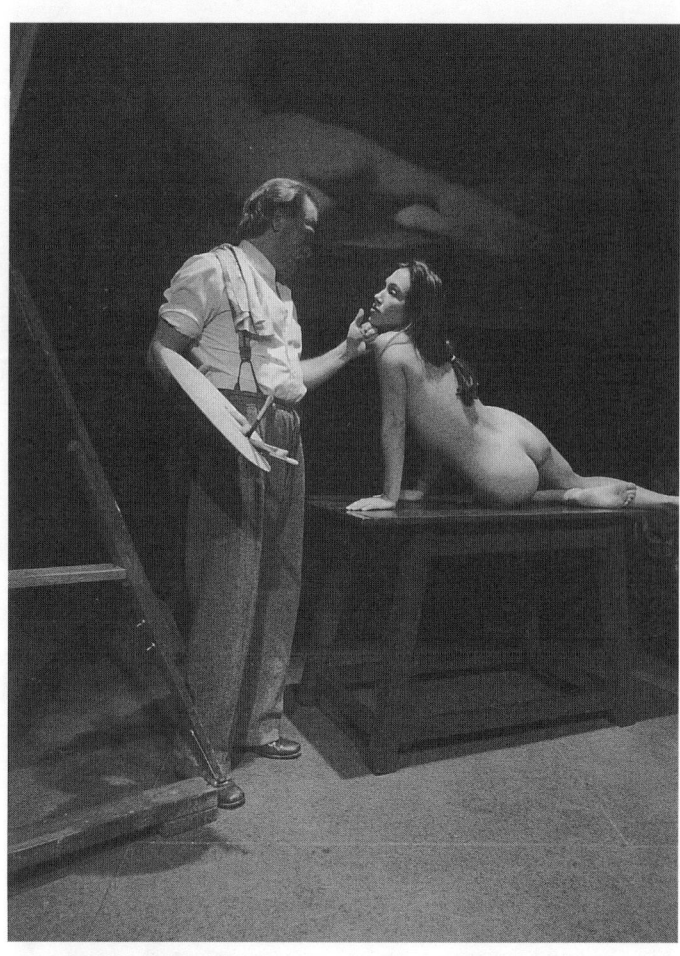

CONTRACTS
AEA SPT

Novel Stages integrates a passion for the mind with a sensual aesthetic. The company is dedicated to developing and producing innovative contemporary plays, presenting classics of world theatre and developing a company of actors and writers. Novel Stages generates theatre which engages audiences. The connection is made through important texts, diverse voices and a definition of theatre as an artform. In four years, Novel Stages has produced 18 productions, 9 of which were world premieres. The company's new work has often been adapted from nondramatic literary sources, and often from very challenging texts by such revered authors as Emile Zola, William Faulkner and Italo Calvino, and by contemporary writers such as Nadine Gordimer, Luisa Valenzuela, Paul Theroux, Lorrie Moore and Chaim Potok. Many aspects of the company's daring aesthetic have been born out of unusual collaborations with visual artists and composers. The company has often collaborated with other cultural and social organizations in Philadelphia in the creation of new work and new approaches to play development. We continue to be challenged by what is novel—ideas and impulses that renew.

—David Bassuk

Novel Stages. H. Michael Walls and Irene Bedard in *Marks in the Water*. Photo: Charles Stewart/Stewart Visual.

PRODUCTIONS 1991-1992

Direction and sound design by David Bassuk, sets and lighting by Brian Joyce and costumes by Patricia Heitman unless otherwise noted.

Marks in the Water, Clista Townsend; (S) John Schmidt; (L) Russell Wadbrook

The Green Bird, Carlo Gozzi; trans: Albert Bermel; music: Adam Grant; (D) Jim Calder; (CH) Siegfrido Agular

Romeo and Juliet, William Shakespeare; (C) Clista Townsend

The Sound and the Fury, adapt: Clista Townsend and Brian Joyce, from William Faulkner; (S) David Bassuk

PRODUCTIONS 1992-1993

Direction by David Bassuk, sets and lighting by Brian Joyce, costumes by Clista Townsend and sound design by Kevin Francis unless otherwise noted.

Metamorphosis, adapt: Steven Berkoff, from Franz Kafka; (D) Brian Joyce; (L) Jim Cackovich

Alice in Concert, book adapt, music and lyrics: Elizabeth Swados, from Lewis Carroll; (D) and (CH) Bill Castellino; (S) Philadelphia Anti-Grafitti Network; (L) Russell Wadbrook; (C) Mary La Boissere; (MD) Christopher Sapienza

The Cherry Orchard, Anton Chekhov; trans: David Bassuk; (C) Kelly Reeves

The Baltimore Waltz, Paula Vogel; music: Kevin Francis

Oakland Ensemble Theatre

SHARON WALTON
Producing Director

Oakland Ensemble Theatre. Zorana Edun in *The Magical Adventures of Pretty Pearl*. Photo: Harry Wade.

EMILY DUNCAN
Board President

1428 Alice St., Suite 306
Oakland, CA 94612
(510) 763-7774 (bus.)
(510) 238-7222 (b.o.)
(510) 763-7536 (fax)

FOUNDED 1974
Ron Stacker Thompson

SEASON
Nov.-May

FACILITIES
The Alice Arts Center
Seating Capacity: 399
Stage: thrust

FINANCES
July 1, 1992-June 30, 1993
Expenses: $632,000

CONTRACTS
AEA BAT

In the past 20 years, OET has grown and evolved from a community theatre to the only professional resident theatre in Oakland, with a commitment to producing theatre from an African-American perspective. In fulfilling this purpose, we reaffirm our commitment to the African-American community by presenting works which explore issues from our unique position as probably the most American of all hyphenated Americans. And we strengthen our bonds to audiences of the ethnically diverse population of the Bay Area by demonstrating that our celebration of the African-American experience does not negate or denigrate the voices of other cultures, but simply brings to the fore this perspective, among many. I am proud of the viewpoint that OET presents; for it is not a foreign viewpoint, but one that has been formulated by the contributions of a specific culture to the greater culture that is America.

—*Sharon Walton*

PRODUCTIONS 1991-1992

That Serious He-Man Ball, Alonzo D. Lamont, Jr.; (D) John Doyle; (S) Pamela Peniston; (L) Stephanie Johnson; (C) Suzanne Jackson

Frederick Douglass Now, adapt: Roger Guenveur Smith, from Frederick Douglass; (D) Roger Guenveur Smith

The Magical Adventures of Pretty Pearl, adapt: Kim Hines, from Virginia Hamilton; (D) Gilbert McCauley; (S) Joel Eis; (L) Stephanie Johnson; (C) Suzanne Jackson

PRODUCTIONS 1992-1993

The Colored Museum, George C. Wolfe; (D) Sharon Walton; (S) and (C) Suzanne Jackson; (L) Stephanie Johnson

Dark Cowgirls & Prairie Queens, Linda Parris-Bailey; (D) Tom Bullard

I Witness, Mary Miller; (D) Sharon Walton; (S) Pamela Peniston; (L) Criswell Murray; (C) Callie Floor

Odyssey Theatre Ensemble

RON SOSSI
Artistic Director

DAVID A. MILLS
Business Manager

MAURICE C. LEVIN
Board President

2055 South Sepulveda Blvd.
West Los Angeles, CA 90025
(310) 477-2055
(310) 444-0455 (fax)

FOUNDED 1969
Ron Sossi

SEASON
Variable

FACILITIES
Odyssey 1
Seating Capacity: 99
Stage: thrust

Odyssey 2
Seating Capacity: 99
Stage: thrust

Odyssey 3
Seating Capacity: 99
Stage: thrust

FINANCES
July 1, 1992-June 30, 1993
Expenses: $660,000

CONTRACTS
AEA 99-seat Theatre Plan

The Odyssey Theatre Ensemble's prime *raison d'etre* is the production of exploration-oriented projects drawn from contemporary, classical and original sources, with a strong leaning toward international and multicultural work. Almost every Odyssey production is, in some important sense, an adventure in form—an attempt to push outward the boundaries of theatrical possibility. Year by year, more Odyssey-evolved work moves out into the larger theatre world. OTE's long-running world premiere production of Steven Berkoff's *Kvetch* opened Off Broadway; *The Chicago Conspiracy Trial* by Ron Sossi and Frank Condon received an ACE award for its production on HBO and was a recent hit of the Chicago theatre scene; Odyssey's *Tracers* has enjoyed long runs throughout the U.S. and Europe; and OTE-developed *McCarthy* moved on to the Milwaukee Repertory Theater. Its innovation-oriented nine-play and lab seasons, its resident Hispanic Unit (LAAFO) and its ever-burgeoning literary program rank the Odyssey as one of the West Coast's leading experimental and process-oriented theatres.

—*Ron Sossi*

Odyssey Theatre Ensemble. *The Bacchae*. Photo: Jan Deen.

PRODUCTIONS 1992

Virtus, Gregg Loughridge; (D) Gregg Loughridge; (S) Michael Olich; (L) Meg Fox and Sindy Slater; (C) Frances Kenny

Only Kidding!, Jim Geoghan; (D) Larry Arrick; (S) Karen Schulz; (L) Joe Damiano; (C) Jeffrey L. Ullman; (SD) Paul Garrity

A Map of the World, David Hare; (D) Allan Miller; (S) Paul William Hawker; (L) Gary Floyd; (C) Pauline Cronin; (SD) John Bryant

God's Country, Steven Dietz; (D) Frank Condon; (S) Don Llewellyn; (L) Doc Ballard and Lynne Peryon; (C) Diane E. Shapiro; (SD) Michael Mortilla

Ivona, Princess of Burgundia, Witold Gombrowicz; various translators; (D) Stefan Kruck; (S) Robert W. Zentiss; (L) Doc Ballard; (C) Denise Blasor and Angela Calin; (SD) Michael Young-Evans

El Grande de Coca-Cola, Ron House, John Neville-Andrews, Alan Shearman, Diz White and Sally Willis; (D) Ron House and Diz White; (S) and (C) Diz White; (L) Lynne Peryon

The Importance of Being Irish, Shay Duffin; (D) Richard Cary

PRODUCTIONS 1993

Lighting by Doc Ballard unless otherwise noted.

The Bacchae, Euripides; various translators; (D) Ron Sossi; (S) Don Llewellyn; (C) Kathi O'Donohue; (C) Neal San Teguns

Puntila and Matti, Bertolt Brecht; trans: Ralph Manheim; (D) Tony Abatemarco; (S) Jeffrey D. Schneider; (L) Sean David Forrester; (C) Kit McCall

Incommunicado, Tom Dulack; (D) Tom Dulack; (S) Jerry Rojo; (C) Sigrid Insull; (SD) Andrea Centazzo

Love Suicide at Schofield Barracks, Romulus Linney; (D) Harris Yulin; (S) Brian Alan Reed; (L) David Flad; (C) Linda Kenmore and Lindsay Stewart

Imperceptible Mutabilities in the Third Kingdom, Suzan-Lori Parks; (D) Peter Brosius; (S) Neil Patel; (C) Suzanne Jackson; (SD) Karl Lundeberg

The Art of Success, Nick Dear; (D) Al Rossi; (S) Merry-Beth Noble; (L) Dietrich F. Juengling; (C) Eddie Bledsoe; (SD) Andrea Centazzo

Frauleins in Underwear, conceived: Ron Sossi; various composers and lyricists; trans: Carl R. Mueller, with Friedrich and Melodie Hollaender and Michael Feingold; (D) Ron Sossi; (S) Cara Hoepner; (C) Sigrid Insull; (MD) Sandy Rohr and Jason Michael Alexander; (CH) Maureen Robinson

Blue Corridor, book, music and lyrics: Mimi Seton; (D) Mark Bringelson; (S) Jason Loewith; (C) Eddie Bledsoe; (MD) Gary Simmons; (CH) Zonnie Bauer

Old Globe Theatre

JACK O'BRIEN
Artistic Director

CRAIG NOEL
Executive Director

TOM HALL
Managing Director

BOBBIE QUICK
Board President

Box 2171
San Diego, CA 92112-2171
(619) 231-1941 (bus.)
(619) 239-2255 (b.o.)
(619) 231-5879 (bus. fax)
(619) 231-1037 (b.o. fax)

FOUNDED 1937
Community members

SEASON
Jan.-Nov.

FACILITIES
Seating Capacity: 581
Stage: flexible

Lowell Davies Festival Theatre
Seating Capacity: 612
Stage: thrust

Cassius Carter Centre Stage
Seating Capacity: 225
Stage: arena

FINANCES
Nov. 1, 1991-Oct. 31, 1992
Expenses: $9,354,244

CONTRACTS
AEA LORT (B), (B+) and (C)

I believe the network of regional theatres is in transition, moving toward its inevitable emergence as the American National Theatre. The Old Globe Theatre, a bastion of craft, skill and technique, has kept the classical tradition flourishing in Southern California for 58 years. From the vantage point of this tradition, we offer remarkable venues to writers and artists who formerly flocked to New York for exposure and artistic freedom. Across this country, over the last decade or so, our ability to articulate the classics has shrunk in direct proportion to the influence of film and television, but the Globe still offers an opportunity to actors, directors and designers to

Old Globe Theatre. Alaina Reed Hall, Mary Gordon Murray and Randy Graff in *A...My Name is Still Alice*. Photo: Ken Howard.

stretch their talents and add to their skills in a healthy, competitive market alongside the literature that has sustained theatre for hundreds of years. Currently, the influx of major American writers premiering their newest works at this theatre shows the healthy relationship between the classics and new American plays. By juxtaposing the contemporary and the classical we offer audiences the most vigorous, comprehensive theatre experience possible.

—*Jack O'Brien*

PRODUCTIONS 1992

Direction by Jack O'Brien, sets by Ralph Funicello, costumes by Robert Wojewodski and sound design by Jeff Ladman unless otherwise noted.

The Old Boy, A.R. Gurney, Jr.; (D) Paul Benedict; (S) and (L) Kent Dorsey; (C) Christine Dougherty

The School for Husbands and *The Flying Doctor*, Moliere; adapt: Richard Wilbur (*The School for Husbands*), Albert Bermel (*The Flying Doctor*); (D) Edward Payson Call; (S) Robert Dahlstrom; (L) David F. Segal; (C) Michael Krass

Shirley Valentine, Willy Russell; (D) Craig Noel; (S) Nick Reid; (L) Barth Ballard

Bargains, Jack Heifner; (L) Ashley York Kennedy

Mr. Rickey Calls A Meeting, Ed Schmidt; (D) Sheldon Epps; (L) Barth Ballard; (C) Christina Haataainen

A...My Name is Still Alice, conceived: Joan Micklin Silver and Julianne Boyd; various composers and lyricists; (D) Joan Micklin Silver and Julianne Boyd; (S) Cliff Faulkner; (L) David F. Segal; (C) David C. Woolard; (MD) Henry Aronson; (CH) Liza Gennaro; (SD) Jeff Ladman and Tony Tait

Two Gentlemen of Verona, William Shakespeare; (D) Laird Williamson; (S) Richard Seger; (L) Peter Maradudin; (C) Andrew V. Yelusich

Breaking Up, Michael Cristofer; (D) Stuart Ross; (S) Richard Seger; (L) Ashley York Kennedy; (C) Michael Krass

Interior Decoration, William Hamilton; (L) David F. Segal; (C) Michael Krass

Lost Highway, conceived: Randal Myler and Mark Harelik; music and lyrics: Hank Williams; (D) Randal Myler; (S) Richard L. Hay; (L) Peter Maradudin; (C) Andrew V. Yelusich; (MD) Mark Harelik and Dan Wheetman; (SD) Tony Tait

From the Mississippi Delta, Dr. Endesha Ida Mae Holland; (D) Seret Scott; (L) Ashley York Kennedy

The Winter's Tale, William Shakespeare; (L) David F. Segal

Forever Plaid, book: Stuart Ross; various composers and lyricists; (D) and (CH) Stuart Ross; (S) Neil Peter Jampolis; (L) Jane Reisman; (C) Debra Stein; (MD) James Raitt; (SD) Tony Tait

Pastorela '92: A Shepherds' Play, adapt: Raul Moncada; various composers and lyricists; (D) William A. Virchis; (S) John Iacovelli; (C) Dione Lebhar; (MD) Carlos A. Mendoza and Michael Gonzales: (CH) Carlos A. Mendoza

PRODUCTIONS 1993

Direction by Jack O'Brien, costumes by Andrew V. Yelusich and sound design by Jeff Ladman unless otherwise noted.

Light Sensitive, Jim Geoghan; (D) Andrew J. Traister; (S) Nick Reid; (L) Barth Ballard; (C) Clare Henkel

Redwood Curtain, Lanford Wilson; (D) Marshall W. Mason; (S) John Lee Beatty; (L) Dennis Parichy; (C) Laura Crow; (SD) Chuck London and Stewart Werner

Ghosts, Henrik Ibsen; trans: Nicholas Rudall; (S) Ralph Funicello; (L) Ashley York Kennedy; (C) Dona Granata

Falsettos, book: William Finn and James Lapine; music and lyrics: William Finn; (D) James Lapine; (S) Douglas Stein; (L) Frances Aronson; (C) Ann Hould-Ward; (MD) Ben Whiteley; (SD) Peter Fitzgerald

Out of Purgatory, Carol Galligan; (D) Benny Sato Ambush; (S) Ralph Funicello and Jane LaMotte; (L) Ashley York Kennedy

Morning's at Seven, Paul Osborn; (D) Craig Noel; (S) Richard Seger; (L) Barth Ballard

All's Well That Ends Well, William Shakespeare; (D) Sheldon Epps; (S) Richard Hoover; (L) Robert Peterson; (C) Dona Granata

Damn Yankees, book adapt: George Abbott and Douglass Wallop, from Douglass Wallop; music and lyrics: Richard Adler and Jerry Ross; (S) Douglas W. Schmidt; (L) David F. Segal; (C) David C. Woolard; (MD) James Raitt; (CH) Rob Marshall

The King of the Kosher Grocers, Joe Minjares; (D) Craig Noel; (S) Joel Fontaine; (L) Robert Peterson; (C) Dona Granata

Ballad of the Blacksmith, Mercedes Rein and Jorge Curi; trans: Raul Moncada; (D) Rene Buch; (S) Robert Weber Federico; (L) Robert Peterson

King Lear, William Shakespeare; (S) Ralph Funicello; (L) David F. Segal; (C) Robert Morgan

Burning Hope, Douglas Michilinda; (D) Andrew J. Traister; (S) Kent Dorsey; (L) Ashley York Kennedy

Olney Theatre

BILL GRAHAM, JR.,
JIM PETOSA
Producing Directors

WILLIAM H. GRAHAM
Board President

Box 550, Route 108
Olney, MD 20830
(301) 924-4485 (bus.)
(301) 924-3400 (b.o.)
(301) 924-2654 (fax)

FOUNDED 1942
C.Y. Stephens

SEASON
May-Dec., Mar.

FACILITIES
Seating Capacity: 552
Stage: proscenium

FINANCES
Jan. 1, 1993-Dec. 31, 1993
Expenses: $1,900,000

CONTRACTS
AEA COST Mini contract

Olney Theatre has long enjoyed a reputation for excellence as an adventurous summer theatre. We are now entering a new phase of

Olney Theatre. Alan Wade and Valerie Leonard in *Voice of the Prairie*. Photo: Stan Barouh.

our history, which includes four sections of the corporation. The theatre's primary program, the Olney Theatre's Summer Season, provides a balanced selection of new plays, area premieres, new musicals and significant revivals. The theatre is proud of its creation of strong ensembles and a nurturing environment for writers, directors, actors and designers. Olney Theatre's Winter Season, a new concept for us at the theatre, is conceived as a laboratory and showcase that will provide full productions of new works. National Players, a development program now beginning its 45th annual national tour, continues its mission of providing classical and significant 20th-century dramas to young audiences who have limited access to live theatre. The Acorn Family Theatre Project presents and produces plays that are designed for very young audiences and their parents.

—*Bill Graham, Jr., Jim Petosa*

PRODUCTIONS 1992

Sets by James Kronzer, lighting by Daniel MacLean Wagner, costumes by Rosemary Pardee and sound design by Gary Daum unless otherwise noted.

Prelude to a Kiss, Craig Lucas; (D) Jim Petosa
Illegal Motion, Bernie Deleo; (D) James Waring; (S) and (L) Carl F. Gudenius
I Hate Hamlet, Paul Rudnick; (D) Bill Graham, Jr.
The Miracle Worker, William Gibson; (D) Jim Petosa; (S) Thomas F. Donahue; (C) Gail Stewart Beach; (SD) Lee Eskey
Wuthering Heights, book adapt, music and lyrics: Edward Trach, from Emily Bronte; (D) John Going; (S) James Wolk; (L) Martha Mountain; (C) Pamela Scofield; (MD) John Aschenbrenner; (CH) Carole Graham Lehan; (SD) Ron Ursano
The Grapes of Wrath, adapt: Frank Galati, from John Steinbeck; (D) Jim Petosa and Bill Graham, Jr.
As You Like It, William Shakespeare; (D) Jim Petosa and Bill Graham, Jr.; (C) Helen Q. Huang

PRODUCTIONS 1993

Sets by James Kronzer, lighting by Daniel MacLean Wagner, costumes by Rosemary Pardee and sound design by Lee Eskey unless otherwise noted.

The Voice of the Prairie, John Olive; (D) Jim Petosa
The Tavern, adapt: George M. Cohan, from Cora Dick Gantt; (D) Bill Graham, Jr.; (S) Thomas F. Donahue
Lend Me a Tenor, Ken Ludwig; (D) John Going; (L) Martha Mountain; (SD) Neil McFadden
Shadowlands, William Nicholson; (D) Jim Petosa; (S) Russell Metheny; (SD) David Kriebs
Show Me Where the Good Times Are, book adapt: Leonora Thuna, from Moliere; music: Kenneth Jacobson; lyrics: Rhoda Roberts; (D) Bill Graham, Jr.; (MD) Rob Bowman; (CH) Carole Graham Lehan; (SD) Timothy Thompson
Romeo and Juliet, William Shakespeare; (D) Jim Petosa and Halo Wines; (C) Jane Schloss Phelan
1984, adapt: Robert Owens, Wilton E. Hall, Jr. and William A. Miles, Jr., from George Orwell; (D) Jim Petosa and Halo Wines; (C) Helen Q. Huang

Omaha Magic Theatre

JO ANN SCHMIDMAN
Producing Artistic Director

2309 Hanscom Blvd.
Omaha, NE 68105
(402) 346-1227

FOUNDED 1968
Jo Ann Schmidman

SEASON
Year-round

FACILITIES
Magic Theatre-Farnam
Seating Capacity: 93
Stage: flexible

Magic Theatre-16th St.
Seating Capacity: 100
Stage: flexible

FINANCES
June 1, 1991-May 31, 1992
Expenses: $436,714

A cutting-edge, multidisciplinary performance ensemble of artists collaborates out of Omaha, Neb. It is our object to make fresh, committed performance that integrates text, music, sound, environmental installation, projections, performers and directorial concept, and finds innovative ways to engage audiences. Our theatre is run by women artists; we publish and tour our original works nationally. Our primary mission is to provide fine art services for artists and audiences. Through a mix of new and traditional theatricality, we seek to impact, impassion and provide an active forum for audiences in this otherwise passive world. Our new, additional facility allows us four times the space to realize artistic visions. We're the proud publishers of *Right Brain Vacation Photos: New Plays and Production Photographs from the Omaha Magic Theatre 1972-1992*, an extraordinarily beautiful, large-format photographic journey through the plays and playwrights we've produced.

—*Jo Ann Schmidman*

PRODUCTIONS 1991-1992

Direction and choreography by Jo Ann Schmidman and sets by Sora Kimberlain unless otherwise noted.

Deadweight, Susan Harris Smith; (D), (S) and (L) Hollie McClay and William York Hyde; (C) Hollie McClay; (SD) Kietryn Zychal
Sound Fields, Megan Terry, Jo Ann Schmidman and Sora Kimberlain; (S) Sora Kimberlain and Jo Ann Schmidman; (L) Jo Ann Schmidman; (C) Sora Kimberlain and Megan Terry; (SD) Beth Kattelman, Jon Lindley and Megan Terry
Body Leaks, book and lyrics: Megan Terry, Jo Ann Schmidman and Sora Kimberlain; music: Marianne de Pury, Luigi Waites and Megan Terry; (L) Jo Ann Schmidman; (C) Kenda Slavin and Robert N. Gilmer; (SD) Luigi Waites and Megan Terry
Pro Game, book and lyrics: Megan Terry; music: Jon Lindley; (D) Jo Ann Schmidman, with Hollie McClay; (L) Jo Ann Schmidman, with Jon Lindley; (C) Hollie McClay and Jo Ann Schmidman; (SD) Jon Lindley
India Plays, Megan Terry; (L) Jo Ann Schmidman, with Jon Lindley; (C) Hollie McClay and Jo Ann Schmidman; (SD) Jon Lindley

PRODUCTIONS 1992-1993

Direction, choreography and lighting by Jo Ann Schmidman, and sets by Sora Kimberlain unless otherwise noted.

Pro Game, book and lyrics: Megan Terry; music: Jon Lindley; (D) Jo Ann Schmidman, with Hollie McClay; (L) Jo Ann Schmidman, with Jon Lindley; (C) Hollie McClay, with Jo Ann Schmidman; (SD) Jon Lindley
India Plays, Megan Terry; (L) Jo Ann Schmidman, with Jon Lindley; (C) Hollie McClay, with Jo Ann Schmidman; (SD) Jon Lindley
The Plucky and Spunky Show, Susan Nussbaum and Mike Ervin; (D) Doug Marr; (S) Jo Ann Schmidman and Sora Kimberlain; (C) Marsha Johnson; (SD) Jo Ann Schmidman

Omaha Magic Theatre. Sora Kimberlain, Hollie McClay, Jon Lindley and Jo Ann Schmidman in *Sound Fields*. Photo: Megan Terry.

Body Leaks, book and lyrics: Megan Terry, Jo Ann Schmidman and Sora Kimberlain; music: Marianne de Pury, Luigi Waites and Megan Terry; (C) Kenda Slavin and Robert N. Gilmer; (SD) Luigi Waites and Megan Terry

Floating Milkpods, David Brink; (D) David Brink; (C) Diane Degan and Faboo Tchoupitoulous; (SD) Eric Freiberg

Soap Scum, David Brink; (D) David Brink; (C) Faboo Tchoupitoulous

Do You See What I'm Saying, Megan Terry; (D) Brian Bengtson; (S) Sora Kimberlain, Bill Farmer, Russ Bloomquist and Jo Ann Schmidman; (C) Rose Marie Whiteley

Barriers—Soft and Hard, Jo Ann Schmidman and Sora Kimberlain; (S) Sora Kimberlain and Jo Ann Schmidman; (C) Rose Marie Whiteley

Belches on Couches, Megan Terry, Jo Ann Schmidman and Sora Kimberlain; (C) Kenda Slavin; (SD) Megan Terry and Jo Ann Schmidman

O'Neill Theater Center

GEORGE C. WHITE
President

LLOYD RICHARDS
Artistic Director, National Playwrights Conference

PAULETTE HAUPT
Artistic Director, Music Theater Conference

STEPHEN WOOD
Board Chairman

305 Great Neck Rd.
Waterford, CT 06385
(203) 443-5378
(203) 443-9653 (fax)

NYC Office:
234 West 44th St., Suite 901
New York, NY 10036
(212) 382-2790
(212) 921-5538 (fax)

FOUNDED 1964
George C. White

SEASON
July-Aug.

FACILITIES
Margo & Rufus Rose Barn
Seating Capacity: 200
Stage: flexible

Instant Theater
Seating Capacity: 200
Stage: arena

Amphitheater
Seating Capacity: 300
Stage: thrust

FINANCES
Sept. 1, 1991-Aug. 31, 1992
Expenses: $2,015,561

CONTRACTS
AEA LORT (D)

The O'Neill Theater Center is an alliance of programs which foster the development of new plays, music-theatre, puppetry and theatre criticism. The center also has extensive international exchange programs for playwrights, critics and students. In addition, it houses an accredited theatre training program for students, a museum and a library, and provides extensive outreach and education programs for the community. Named for Eugene O'Neill, America's only Nobel Prize-winning playright, who spent his formative years in the area, the center honors his memory by: initiating and harboring projects of value to the theatre; challenging existing theatrical "truths"; creating an environment for examination, experimentation and deliberation; providing a venue for national and international theatrical interaction, discussion and exchange; and protecting and preserving our native theatrical heritage.

—*George C. White*

PRODUCTIONS 1992

The Spinning Top, Ilya Chlakishvili; trans: Michael Yurieff; (D) Alexander Velikovsky

I Have Often Dreamed of Arriving Alone in a Strange Country..., Patricia Cobey; (D) Amy Saltz

Hero At Last, Frederick G. Dillen; (D) Jay Broad

Charlie's Wedding Day, Patricia Goldstone; (D) William Partlan

O'Neill Theater Center. National Playwrights Conference. Photo: A. Vincent Scarano.

Scotland Road, Jeffrey Hatcher; (D) William Partlan

Eulogy, Ted Hoover; (D) Margaret Booker

Empathy, Inc., Jerry Isaacs; (D) Oz Scott

A Thimble of Smoke, Elroyce Jones; (D) Jay Broad

Straight Man, Ian Kerner; (D) Jay Broad

Tough Call, Ronald Kidd; (D) William Partlan

Arthur and Leila, Cherylene Lee; (D) Margaret Booker

Voodoo Nickel, Patti Patton; (D) Oz Scott

Blackwater, J. Dakota Powell; (D) Amy Saltz

Different, Susan Arnout Smith; (D) Jay Broad

Avenue X, book, music and lyrics: John Jiler and Ray Leslee; (D) Mark Brokaw; (MD) Chapman Roberts

Christina Alberta's Father, book adapt, music and lyrics by Polly Pen, from H.G. Wells; (D) Andre Ernotte; (MD) Kristen Blodgette

The Wild Swans, book and lyrics: Adele Ahronheim; music: Ben Schaechter; (D) Worth Gardner; (MD) Rob Bowman

PRODUCTIONS 1993

The Book of Lamb, Kirk Aanes; (D) William Partlan

You Send Me, Rick Cleveland; (D) Jay Broad

The Interrogation, Evert Eden; (D) Amy Saltz

Killing Jazz, Frederic Glover; (D) Oz Scott

Mysterious Connections, Peter Hardy; (D) Oz Scott

17 Black, Wm. S. Leavengood; (D) Jay Broad

The Valley of the Human Spirit, Lesli-Jo Morizono; (D) William Partlan

Locked Doors and Lightning Bugs, Jett Parsley; (D) Oz Scott

White Oak, Hunt Scarritt; (D) Oz Scott

Entries, Bernardo Solano; (D) Amy Saltz

A Name for the Moon, Thomas W. Stephens; (D) William Partlan

The Cradle of Maybe, Gay Walch; (D) Jay Broad
Marina, Youri Volkov; (D) Youri Volkov
The Gig, book adapt, music and lyrics: Douglas J. Cohen, from Frank D. Gilroy; (D) Victoria Bussert; (MD) James Laev
Time and Again, book, music and lyrics: Jack Viertel and Walter Edgar Kennon, from Jack Finney; (D) John Znidarsic; (MD) Michael Kosarin and David La Marshe

Ontological-Hysteric Theater

RICHARD FOREMAN
Artistic Director

SUSAN LATHAM
Administrative Director

**PAUL SCHIFF BERMAN,
SOPHIE HAVILAND**
Theater Administrators

c/o Performing Artservices
260 West Broadway
New York, NY 10013-2259
(212) 941-8911 (bus.)
(212) 533-4650 (b.o.)
(212) 334-5149 (fax)

FOUNDED 1968
Richard Foreman

SEASON
Year-round

FACILITIES
Ontological at Saint Mark's Theater
Seating Capacity: 80
Stage: flexible

FINANCES
July 1, 1992-June 30, 1993
Expenses: $125,520

Since 1968 I have evolved my own idiosyncratic theatre language, which is nevertheless applicable to many different moods, subjects and settings. I attempt to stretch the employment of that language further each year, which in itself seems self-evident. But, more important, I try to build into my plays secret reflections upon the inevitable failure involved in pursuing such a goal.
—Richard Foreman

PRODUCTIONS 1991-1992

The Mind King, Richard Foreman; (D), (S), (L), (C) and (SD) Richard Foreman

PRODUCTIONS 1992-1993

Samuel's Major Problems, Richard Foreman; (D), (S), (L), (C) and (SD) Richard Foreman

Ontological-Hysteric Theater. Thomas Jay Ryan, Steven Rattazzi and Jill Dreskin in *Samuel's Major Problems*. Photo: Paula Court.

The Open Eye: New Stagings. Ricky Genaro and Stephanie Marshall in *The Odyssey*. Photo: Scott Humbert.

The Open Eye: New Stagings

AMIE BROCKWAY
Artistic Director

ADRIENNE J. BROCKWAY
Production/Business Manager

DAN BERKOWITZ
Board Chairman

270 West 89th St.
New York, NY 10024
(212) 769-4141 (bus.)
(212) 769-4143 (b.o.)
(212) 595-0336 (fax)

FOUNDED 1972
Jean Erdman, Joseph Campbell

SEASON
Oct.-June

FACILITIES
Seating Capacity: 115
Stage: proscenium

FINANCES
July 1, 1992-June 30, 1993
Expenses: $265,000

CONTRACTS
AEA TYA and letter of agreement

The Open Eye: New Stagings draws on the creative power of the theatre arts—music, dance, drama and comedy—to mount innovative productions, many based on ancient myths and folklore, that appeal to people of all cultures and ages. Our commitment to the city's youth, and those from surrounding suburban and rural regions, is seen in productions and arts-in-education programs that help foster a strong sense of community and emphasize the power of diverse cultures. Through timely original works and classics, or plays by important writers from the more recent past, we seek to bring people together, communicate our shared heritage and provide a fresh perspective on universal human experience.
—Amie Brockway

PRODUCTIONS 1991-1992

Sets, lighting and costumes by Adrienne J. Brockway unless otherwise noted.

Eagle or Sun, Sabina Berman; trans: Isabel Saez; adapt: Amie Brockway; (D) Amie Brockway

The Death and Life of Sherlock Holmes, Susan Zeder; (D) Russell Treyz; (L) Spencer Moss; (C) Marianne Powell-Pa

A Woman Called Truth, Sandra Fenichel Asher; (D) Ernest Johns

Eye on Directors Festival: various playwrights, various directors

PRODUCTIONS 1992-1993

Sets, lighting and costumes by Adrienne J. Brockway unless otherwise noted.

The Odyssey, adapt: Amie Brockway, from Homer; (D) Amie Brockway

The Wise Men of Chelm, book and lyrics: Sandra Fenichel Asher; music: Richard Henson and Kyle Williams; (D) Amie Brockway; (CH) Adina Kaufman Popkin

Freedom is My Middle Name, Lee Hunkins; (D) Ernest Johns

Eye on Directors Festival: various playwrights, various directors

---

Oregon Shakespeare Festival

HENRY WORONICZ
Artistic Director

WILLIAM W. PATTON
Executive Director

JOHN HASSEN
Board President

Box 158
Ashland, OR 97520
(503) 482-2111 (bus.)
(503) 482-4331 (b.o.)
(503) 482-0446 (fax)

Box 9008
Portland, OR 97207
(503) 248-6309 (bus.)
(503) 274-6588 (b.o.)
(503) 796-6509 (fax)

FOUNDED 1935
Angus Bowmer

SEASON
Nov.-Apr. (Portland)
Feb.-Oct. (Ashland)

FACILITIES
Angus Bowmer Theatre
Seating Capacity: 600
Stage: modified thrust

Black Swan
Seating Capacity: 140
Stage: flexible

Elizabethan Theatre
Seating Capacity: 1200
Stage: outdoor

Intermediate Theatre, Portland
Seating Capacity: 885
Stage: proscenium

FINANCES
Nov. 1, 1991-Oct. 31, 1992
Expenses: $11,644,555

CONTRACTS
AEA special LORT (B)

The Oregon Shakespeare Festival's mission is to bring to life the essential event of theatre: the creation of a passionate communion between artists and audience. The Festival exists to expand and enhance that communion, to illuminate and broaden the boundaries of shared human experience, and to explore and embrace that which is unique to the theatre. Using Shakespeare's plays as our standard and inspiration, we are committed to producing theatre of the highest artistic quality while maintaining and developing a skilled and flexible professional company; to performing in repertory a broad range of plays chosen to celebrate and investigate the breadth of vision and depth of insight that we find in Shakespeare; to seeking and nurturing a diverse, active audience drawn from a wide geographical area, as an essential creative partner. These commitments grow from our fidelity to our individual imaginations, to each other as company members and to our audience. In all these relationships, we seek a dynamic interaction fueled by curiosity and challenge, tempered by awareness and understanding, and shaped by simplicity, patience and compassion.

—Henry Woronicz

PRODUCTIONS 1991-1992

Fences, August Wilson; (D) Benny Sato Ambush; (S) Edward Burbridge; (L) Stephanie Johnson; (C) Myrna Colley-Lee; (SD) David Maltby

Seasons Greetings, Alan Ayckbourn; (D) Philip Killian; (S) Michael C. Smith; (L) James Sale; (C) David Kay Mickelsen; (SD) John J. Gibson

The Guardsman, Ferenc Molnar; trans: James Keller; (D) Dennis Bigelow; (S) William Bloodgood; (L) Robert Peterson; (C) Deborah M. Dryden; (SD) David de Berry

Betrayal, Harold Pinter; (D) Dennis Bigelow; (S) Michael C. Smith; (L) Ann G. Wrightson; (C) Debra Bruneaux

King Lear, William Shakespeare; (D) Richard Seyd; (S) Cliff Faulkner; (L) Peter Maradudin; (C) Shigeru Yaji

All's Well That Ends Well, William Shakespeare; (D) Henry Woronicz; (S) Richard L. Hay; (L) Robert Peterson; (C) David Kay Mickelsen

Toys in the Attic, Lillian Hellman; (D) Cynthia White; (S) Michael Ganio; (L) Robert Peterson; (C) Claudia Everett

The Playboy of the Western World, John Millington Synge; (D) Fontaine Syer; (S) William Bloodgood; (L) James Sale; (C) Candice Cain

Restoration, Edward Bond; (D) Penny Metropulos; (S) Vicki Smith; (L) James Sale; (C) Frances Kenny

The Firebugs, Max Frisch; trans: Michael Bullock; (D) Barbara Damashek; (S) Robert Brill; (L) Michael Holcombe; (C) Sarah Nash Gates

La Bete, David Hirson; (D) Henry Woronicz; (S) William Bloodgood; (L) James Sale; (C) Deborah M. Dryden

Othello, William Shakespeare; (D) Jerry Turner; (S) William Bloodgood; (L) Robert Peterson; (C) Jeannie Davidson

Oregon Shakespeare Festival. Ray Porter in *La Bête*. Photo: Christopher Briscoe.

Henry VI, Part 3, William Shakespeare; (D) Pat Patton; (S) Richard L. Hay; (L) Robert Peterson; (C) Barbara Bush
As You Like It, William Shakespeare; (D) James Edmondson; (S) Michael C. Smith; (L) Robert Peterson; (C) Deborah M. Dryden
The Ladies of the Camellias, Lillian Garrett-Groag; (D) Kenneth Albers; (S) William Bloodgood; (L) James Sale; (C) Michael Olich
Heathen Valley, Romulus Linney; (D) Kirk Boyd; (S) William Bloodgood; (L) James Sale; (C) Elizabeth Novak

PRODUCTIONS 1992-1993

The Glass Menagerie, Tennessee Williams; (D) Henry Woronicz; (S) Richard L. Hay; (L) Robert Jared; (C) Debra Bruneaux
The Ladies of the Camellias, Lillian Garrett-Groag; (D) Kenneth Albers; (S) William Bloodgood; (L) James Sale; (C) Michael Olich
Twelfth Night, William Shakespeare; (D) Pat Patton; (S) William Bloodgood; (L) Robert Peterson; (C) David Kay Mickelsen
Lips Together, Teeth Apart, Terrence McNally; (D) Penny Metropulos; (S) Robert Brill; (L) Derek Duarte; (C) Sarah Nash Gates
Spunk, adapt: George C. Wolfe, from Zora Neale Hurston; music: Chic Street Man; (D) Debra Wicks; (S) Michael C. Smith; (L) Collier Woods; (C) Claudia Everett
Richard III, William Shakespeare; (D) James Edmondson; (S) William Bloodgood; (L) James Sale; (C) Deborah M. Dryden
A Flea in Her Ear, Georges Feydeau; trans: John Mortimer; (D) Kenneth Albers; (S) Richard L. Hay; (L) Robert Peterson; (C) Charles Berliner
Joe Turner's Come and Gone, August Wilson; (D) Clinton Turner Davis; (S) Mike Fish; (L) James Sale; (C) Candice Cain
Cymbeline, adapt: Henry Woronicz and the ensemble, from William Shakespeare; (D) Henry Woronicz and the ensemble; (S) William Bloodgood; (L) Robert Peterson; (C) Carole Wheeldon
Light in the Village, John Clifford; (D) Kirk Boyd; (S) Richard L. Hay; (L) Rachel Budin; (C) Wanda Walden

Lips Together, Teeth Apart, Terrence McNally; (D) Penny Metropulos; (S) Robert Brill; (L) Derek Duarte; (C) Sarah Nash Gates
The Baltimore Waltz, Paula Vogel; (D) Barbara Damashek; (S) William Bloodgood; (L) Robert Peterson; (C) Susan Tsu
Mad Forest, Caryl Churchill; (D) Fontaine Syer; (S) Curt Enderle; (L) Michael Holcombe; (C) Deborah M. Dryden
The Illusion, Pierre Corneille; trans: Tony Kushner; (D) Pat Patton; (S) Richard L. Hay; (L) Michael Holcombe; (C) Claudia Everett
Antony and Cleopatra, William Shakespeare; (D) Charles Towers; (S) William Bloodgood; (L) James Sale; (C) Candice Cain
The White Devil, John Webster; (D) Jerry Turner; (S) Richard L. Hay; (L) James Sale; (C) Elizabeth Novak
A Midsummer Night's Dream, William Shakespeare; (D) Cynthia White; (S) Michael Ganio; (L) James Sale; (C) John Carver Sullivan

Organic Theater Company

JEFF NEAL, STEVE PICKERING, PETER RYBOLT, SARAH TUCKER (Chair)
Artistic Committee

JEFF NEAL
General Manager

KATHLEEN B. GILLIG
Board President

3319 North Clark St.
Chicago, IL 60657
(312) 327-2427 (bus.)
(312) 327-5588 (b.o.)
(312) 327-8947 (fax)

FOUNDED 1969
Carolyn Purdy-Gordon,
Stuart Gordon

SEASON
Sept.-June

FACILITIES
Mainstage
Seating Capacity: 400
Stage: modified thrust

Greenhouse Lab
Seating Capacity: 90
Stage: proscenium

Greenhouse South Hall
Seating Capacity: 40-60
Stage: flexible

FINANCES
July 1, 1992-June 30, 1993
Expenses: $400,000

CONTRACTS
AEA CAT

The Organic Theater Company is committed to the creation of new plays and adaptations. In keeping with the history of the Organic, we continue to explore popular culture—adventure, horror, science fiction—modern mythology, if you will. We look for writers with a spirit of adventure, who create imaginative worlds and populate them with unique citizens, who have a gloriously rich or inventive use of language, and who understand the kinetic energy of theatrical performance. Our contract with our audience is to take them on a journey of discovery, and theirs with us is to invest their imagination, so that together we can stimulate our minds, engage our hearts and feed our souls.

—*Jeff Neal, Steve Pickering, Peter Rybolt, Sarah Tucker*

Note: During the 1991-92 season, Richard Fire served as artistic director.

PRODUCTIONS 1991-1992

Victims, Antony Van Zyl; (D) Michael E. Myers; (S), (L) and (C) Margaret L. Nelson; (SD) Galen G. Ramsey
Nixon: Live! The Future is Now, Frank Melcori; (D) Richard Fire; (S) Eric Wegener; (L) Andrew Meyers
A Few Simple Truths, conceived: Richard Fire; book: Anne McGravie, et al; music and lyrics: Howard Berkman, Andy Haben, Nate Herman, Juan Lopez,

Organic Theater Company. Alison Halstead and Scott Denny in *52*. Photo: Leigh Loranger.

Robert McNaughton and Tom Yore; (D) Michael J. Gellman; (S) and (L) Robert G. Smith; (C) Vicki Justice; (MD) Chris Farrell and Nate Herman

Couch Piece, Ann Boyd and Julia Neary; (D) Ann Boyd and Julia Neary; (S) Maurice Chasse; (L) Paul Foster; (SD) Michael Bodeen

Coming Back, Jeffrey Lieber; (D) Bruce Orendorf; (S) Maurice Chasse; (L) Paul Foster; (SD) Ned Mochel and David Naunton

PRODUCTIONS 1992-1993

Lighting by Paul Foster unless otherwise noted.

S2, Edward Mast; (D) Sarah Tucker; (S) Steve Pickering; (L) Margaret L. Nelson; (C) Edward Ranson; (SD) Jim Marcus

In the Flesh, adapt: Steve Pickering and Charley Sherman, from Clive Barker; (D) Charley Sherman; (S) Steve Pickering and Greg Ballmann; (C) Stephanie Ferrell; (SD) Michael Bodeen

The Pornographic Man, Jim Marcus; (D) Meghan Strell; (S) Cheryl Anne Levin; (C) Ebenezer Inawat

A Child Is Born, Stan Nevin; (D) Jeff Neal; (S) Peter Rybolt; (L) Christine Jones; (C) Renee Starr Liepins; (SD) Paul Foster

Gulliver's Last Travels, adapt: Lawrence Bommer, from Jonathan Swift; (D) Steve Scott; (S) Cheryl Anne Levin; (L) Margaret L. Nelson; (C) Erica Hoelscher; (SD) Liane LeMaster

Role Play, Eric Berg; (D) Paul Frellick; (S) Robert G. Smith; (C) Renee Starr Liepins; (SD) David Zerlin

In the Flesh, adapt: Steve Pickering and Charley Sherman, from Clive Barker; (D) Charley Sherman; (S) Steve Pickering, Greg Ballmann and Cheryl Anne Levin; (C) Stephanie Ferrell; (SD) Michael Bodeen

Pan Asian Repertory Theatre

TISA CHANG
Artistic/Producing Director

RUSSELL MURPHY
Business Manager

JEFF CHIN
Board Chairman

47 Great Jones St.
New York, NY 10012
(212) 505-5655 (bus.)
(212) 245-2660 (b.o.)
(212) 505-6014 (fax)

FOUNDED 1977
Tisa Chang

SEASON
Oct.-May

FACILITIES
Playhouse 46
Seating Capacity: 151
Stage: arena

FINANCES
Sept. 1, 1992-Aug. 31, 1993
Expenses: $500,000

CONTRACTS
AEA letter of agreement and LORT (D)

Pan Asian Rep, celebrating its 17th year, is the premiere New York theatre of Asian-American actors and directors, producing the works of Asian-American playwrights, Asian masterworks translated into English and innovative adaptations of Western classics. A resident ensemble was established in 1987 to ensure artistic continuity, and creative challenges are provided through commissions, collaborations with guest artists, intercultural projects and such explorations into the music-theatre form as *Cambodia Agonistes* and the *Three Kingdoms* project. The next stage of our evolution will emphasize global artistic outreach as well as educational and community service in cities where we tour annually. The individual artistic voice of the theatre's founder has grown into the collective chorus of Senior Artists, sophisticated staff, younger and newer audiences, and national programs which transcend geographic and ethnic boundaries.
—*Tisa Chang*

PRODUCTIONS 1991-1992

Sound design by Ty Sanders unless otherwise noted.

The Dressing Room, Kunio Shimizu; trans: John K. Gillespie; adapt: Chiori Miyagawa; (D) Kati Kuroda; (S) Atsushi Moriyasu; (L) Tina Charney; (C) Eiko Yamaguchi

Letters to a Student Revolutionary, Elizabeth Wong; (D) Ernest Abuba; (S) Kyung Won Chang; (L) Anne Somogye; (C) Maggie Raywood

Fairy Bones, Laurence Yep; (D) Tina Chen; (S) Atsushi Moriyasu; (L) Deborah Constantine; (C) Juliet Ouyoung; (SD) James van Bergen

PRODUCTIONS 1992-1993

Sets by Robert Klingelhoefer, costumes by Juliet Ouyoung and sound design by James van Bergen unless otherwise noted.

Cambodia Agonistes, book and lyrics: Ernest Abuba; music: Louis Stewart; (D) Tisa Chang; (L) Deborah Constantine; (MD) Jack Jarrett; (CH) H.T. Chen and Sam-Oeun Tes

Letters to a Student Revolutionary, Elizabeth Wong; (D) Ernest Abuba; (S) Kyung Won Chang; (L) Anne Somogye; (C) Maggie Raywood; (SD) Ty Sanders

A Doll House, Henrik Ibsen; adapt: John Briggs; (D) John Briggs; (L) Bill Simmons

Pan Asian Repertory Theatre. Daniel Dae Kim and Karen Lee in *A Doll House*. Photo: Corky Lee.

PCPA Theaterfest

JACK SHOUSE
Managing Artistic Director

JUDY FROST
Business Manager

MICHAEL BRADY
Board Chair

Box 1700
Santa Maria, CA 93456
(805) 928-7731 (bus.)
(800) PCPA-123 (b.o.)
(805) 928-7506 (fax)

PCPA Theaterfest

FOUNDED 1964
Donovan Marley

SEASON
Year-round

FACILITIES
Marian Theatre
Seating Capacity: 508
Stage: thrust

Festival Theatre
Seating Capacity: 772
Stage: thrust

Severson Theatre
Seating Capacity: 200
Stage: flexible

FINANCES
Oct. 1, 1991-Sept. 30, 1992
Expenses: $2,757,321

CONTRACTS
AEA U/RTA

We, as theatre artists, performers and craftsmen, share our product with our audience in an attempt to entertain and create a heightened awareness of the human condition, and to promote a better understanding of what our roles are as individuals and contributors to society. This collaboration is the essence of the theatre. It is the artist who initiates the creative process and the audience who responds, thus maintaining a cycle of realization and growth for both. At PCPA Theaterfest we create an environment for those artists dedicated to taking that creative initiative. We strive to protect and nurture a theatrical process we feel is vital to our development as individuals and our growth as a civilization. As a performing company and conservatory, we commit ourselves to serving the community and our professional staff and students by producing an even wider variety of theatrical works of excellence, while preserving our tradition of offering the classics of world theatre, new plays, contemporary plays, and the new and classic in American musical theatre.

—*Jack Shouse*

PRODUCTIONS 1991-1992

Sets by Everett Chase, lighting by Michael A. Peterson, costumes by Judith A. Ryerson and sound design by Jeff Mockus unless otherwise noted.

The Wizard of Oz, book adapt: John Kane, from L. Frank Baum; music: Harold Arlen; lyrics: E.Y. Harburg; (D) Jack Shouse; (S) Norm Spencer; (MD) Jeremy Mann; (CH) Carolyn Shouse

Dandelion Wine, Ray Bradbury; (D) Jonathan Gillard Daly; (S) Lisa Moran; (L) David Lee Cuthbert; (C) Leo Cortez

Jesus Christ Superstar, music: Andrew Lloyd Webber; lyrics: Tim Rice; (D) and (CH) Brad Carroll; (C) Norm Spencer; (MD) Jeremy Mann

Joseph and His Amazing Technicolor Dreamcoat, music: Andrew Lloyd Webber; lyrics: Tim Rice; (D) and (CH) Brad Carroll; (MD) Jeremy Mann

Noises Off, Michael Frayn; (D) Paul Barnes; (S) Norm Spencer; (L) David Lee Cuthbert; (C) Abby Hogan

Big River, book adapt: William Hauptman, from Mark Twain; music and lyrics: Roger Miller; (D) Paul Barnes; (S) Lisa Moran; (L) David Lee Cuthbert; (MD) Jeremy Mann; (CH) Karen Barbour

Lend Me a Tenor, Ken Ludwig; (D) Frederick Barbour; (C) Marcia Rodriguez; (SD) Eric O. Cronwall

PRODUCTIONS 1992-1993

Direction by Brad Carroll, sets by Norm Spencer, lighting by Michael A. Peterson, costumes by Judith A. Ryerson and sound design by Jeff Mockus unless otherwise noted.

Cinderella, book adapt and lyrics: Oscar Hammerstein, II, from Charles Perrault; music: Richard Rodgers; (MD) Brad Carroll; (CH) Karen Barbour

Cyrano de Bergerac, Edmond Rostand; adapt: Anthony Burgess; (D) Roger DeLaurier; (L) David Lee Cuthbert

Into the Woods, book: James Lapine; music and lyrics: Stephen Sondheim; (C) Marcia Rodriguez; (MD) Michael Gribbin

Oklahoma!, book adapt and lyrics: Oscar Hammerstein, II, from Lynn Riggs; music: Richard Rodgers; (L) David Lee Cuthbert; (CH) Karen Barbour

Ain't Misbehavin', conceived: Murray Horwitz and Richard Maltby, Jr.; music and lyrics: Fats Waller, et al; (D) and (CH) Andrea Frye; (S) Ryk Souza; (C) Marcia Rodriguez

West Side Story, book: Arthur Laurents; music: Leonard Bernstein; lyrics: Stephen Sondheim; (D) Paul Barnes; (S) Jack Shouse; (C) Marcia Rodriguez; (MD) Brad Carroll; (CH) Michael Bernard

The Immigrant, Mark Harelik; (D) Frederick Barbour; (L) David Lee Cuthbert

Great Expectations, adapt: Gale Fury Childs, from Charles Dickens; (D) Roger DeLaurier; (C) Katrina Souza

Joseph and His Amazing Technicolor Dreamcoat, music: Andrew Lloyd Webber; lyrics: Tim Rice; (S) Tim Hogan; (MD) Brad Carroll

The Little Foxes, Lillian Hellman; (D) Paul Barnes; (S) Jack Shouse; (L) David Lee Cuthbert

Love Letters, A.R. Gurney, Jr.; (D) Roger DeLaurier; (S) Tim Hogan; (C) Katrina Souza

PCPA Theaterfest. *Jesus Christ Superstar*. Photo: Tom Smith/Images.

Pennsylvania Stage Company

CHARLES RICHTER
Artistic Director

ELLEN BAKER BALTZ
Managing Director

PATRICIA CARLIS
Board President

837 Linden St.
Allentown, PA 18101
(215) 434-6110 (bus.)
(215) 433-3394 (b.o.)
(215) 433-6086 (fax)

FOUNDED 1977
Anna Rodale

SEASON
Sept.-June

FACILITIES
J. I. Rodale Theatre
Seating Capacity: 274
Stage: proscenium

FINANCES
July 1, 1992-June 30, 1993
Expenses: $1,369,506

CONTRACTS
AEA LORT (D)

Pennsylvania Stage Company is the major professional theatre in the Lehigh Valley region of Pennsylvania. The company presents high-quality productions of plays and musicals that deal with important concerns with honesty and artistry. Our seven-play mainstage season is supplemented by an extensive outreach program that presents touring productions in schools and community agencies, a program to develop new plays by Pennsylvania writers, and a community theatre school that serves both children and adults. We strive to produce work that speaks to a diverse population in a way that will foster a healthy intellectual and emotional life in a community in the midst of social and economic change. To this end we are attempting to build a company of professional theatre artists who believe in the value of the communal cultural experience possible only on the living stage.

—*Charles Richter*

Pennsylvania Stage Company. Colleen Gallagher and Mathew Arkin in *Little Footsteps*. Photo: Hub Willson.

Note: During the 1991-92 season, Peter Wrenn-Meleck served as producing artistic director.

PRODUCTIONS 1991-1992

Sets by Sarah Baptist unless otherwise noted.

The Immigrant, Mark Harelik; (D) Charles Richter; (S) and (L) Paul Wonsek; (C) Patricia Adshead; (SD) Dru P. Allard
Ain't Misbehavin', conceived: Murray Horwitz and Richard Maltby, Jr.; music and lyrics: Fats Waller, et al; (D) Mercedes Ellington; (L) Kenneth Posner; (C) George Bergeron
Ho Ho Ho the Christmas Show, Bruce W. Coyle and Fred Greene; (D) Fred Greene; (S) William Kreider; (L) John Rankin; (C) Gail Cooper-Hecht
Smiling Through, Ivan Menchell; (D) Howard Rossen; (L) Tom Sturge; (C) Jose M. Rivera
The Cocktail Hour, A.R. Gurney, Jr.; (D) Scott Edmiston; (S) and (L) Curtis Dretsch; (C) Charlotte M. Yetman
Theme and Variations, Samuil Alyoshin; trans: Michael Glenny; (D) Peter Wrenn-Meleck; (S) Paul Wonsek; (L) Joseph Arnold; (C) Audrey Stables
Candida, George Bernard Shaw; (D) Scott Edmiston; (L) John Rankin; (C) Barbra Kravitz
Lend Me a Tenor, Ken Ludwig; (D) Dennis Delaney; (S) and (L) Bennet Averyt; (C) Margaret Shyne Benson

PRODUCTIONS 1992-1993

Sets by Sarah Baptist unless otherwise noted.

Smoke on the Mountain, Constance Ray; (D) John Foley; (L) Joseph Arnold; (C) Patricia Adshead
Fences, August Wilson; (D) Charles Dumas; (S) David Gallo; (L) Joseph Arnold; (C) Myrna Colley-Lee; (SD) Geoff Zink
The Gift of the Magi, book adapt, music and lyrics: Peter Ekstrom, from O. Henry; (D) Dennis Delaney; (L) John Hessler; (C) Audrey Stables
Mountain, Douglas Scott; (D) Thomas Gruenewald; (S) and (L) Curtis Dretsch; (C) Audrey Stables; (SD) Geoff Zink
Little Footsteps, Ted Tally; (D) Jay E. Raphael; (S) and (L) Fred Kolo; (C) Elizabeth Covey; (SD) Geoff Zink
Bus Stop, William Inge; (D) Pam Pepper; (S) and (L) Bennet Averyt; (C) Myrna Colley-Lee; (SD) Geoff Zink
Shirley Valentine, Willy Russell; (D) Kim Rubenstein; (S) and (C) David Gallo; (L) Donald Holder
Beau Jest, James Sherman; (D) Charles Richter; (L) Curtis Dretsch; (C) Audrey Stables

Penumbra Theatre Company

LOU BELLAMY
Artistic Director

MAURINE D. KNIGHTON
Managing Director

DAVID TAYLOR
Board Chairman

270 North Kent St.
St. Paul, MN 55102
(612) 224-4601 (bus.)
(612) 224-3180 (b.o.)
(612) 224-7074 (fax)

FOUNDED 1976
Lou Bellamy

SEASON
Aug.-June

FACILITIES
Seating Capacity: 260
Stage: thrust

FINANCES
July 1, 1992-June 30, 1993
Expenses: $1,140,000

CONTRACTS
AEA SPT

The Penumbra Theatre Company's mission is to create productions that are artistically excellent, thought-provoking, relevant and entertaining. Penumbra's goals are: to increase public awareness of the significant contributions that African Americans have made in creating a diversified American theatrical tradition; to encourage a culturally diverse and all-inclusive America by using theatre to teach, criticize, comment and model; to use theatre to create an American mythology that includes African Americans and other people of color in every thread of the fabric of our society; to redefine and expand the consciousness of our audiences and our theatrical communities to include a sympathetic and realistic portrayal of people of color; to encourage the staging of plays that address the African-American experience; and to continue to maintain and stabilize a black performing arts community. Mainstage productions, tours, lectures and conferences contribute to these ends.

—Lou Bellamy

PRODUCTIONS 1991-1992

Direction by Marion Isaac McClinton, sets by Paul Brown, lighting by Mike Wangen, costumes by Anne Ruben and sound design by Terry Tilley unless otherwise noted.

Penumbra Theatre Company. Tom Carey, Abdul Salaam El Raz-Zac in *King of Coons*. Photo: R. Dushaine.

Pecong, Steve Carter; (D) Edmund Cambridge; (S) Michael Burden; (C) Anthony Gorzycki; (SD) Martin B. Gwinup
Generations of the Dead in the Abyss of Coney Island Madness, Michael Henry Brown; (CH) Bruce Thompson
Black Nativity, Langston Hughes; (D) Lewis Whitlock, III; (S) Gregory O. Ray
Shine!, Syl Jones; (S) W.J.E. Hammer
The Mojo and the Sayso, Aishah Rahman; (D) Laurie Carlos; (S) Seitu Ken Jones
The Mighty Gents, Richard Wesley; (D) Lou Bellamy
Dutchman, Amiri Baraka (LeRoi Jones)

PRODUCTIONS 1992-1993

Lighting by Mike Wangen and costumes by Anne Ruben unless otherwise noted.

The Last Minstrel Show, book, music and lyrics: John Davidson; (D) Richard D. Thompson; (S) Jerry Berebitsky; (C) Charles Autry; (CH) Garry Lewis and Marvette Knight
Shakin' the Mess Outta Misery, Shay Youngblood; (D) Robbie McCauley; (S) Lori Sullivan-Wothman; (SD) Terry Tilley
Black Nativity, Langston Hughes; (D) Lewis Whitlock, III; (S) Gregory O. Ray
King of Coons, Michael Henry Brown; (D) Lou Bellamy; (S) Paul Brown; (SD) Terry Tilley
Willie and Esther, James Graham Bronson; (D) Jennifer Nelson; (S) Paul Brown; (SD) Martin Ruben
The Piano Lesson, August Wilson; (D) Marion Isaac McClinton; (S) W.J.E. Hammer; (SD) Terry Tilley

The People's Light and Theatre Company

DANNY S. FRUCHTER
Producing Director

GREGORY T. ROWE
Managing Director

WILLIAM F. DRAKE
Board President

39 Conestoga Road
Malvern, PA 19355-1798
(215) 647-1900 (bus.)
(215) 644-3500 (b.o.)
(215) 640-9521 (fax)

FOUNDED 1974
Ken Marini, Richard L. Keeler, Danny S. Fruchter, Margaret E. Fruchter

SEASON
Variable

FACILITIES
Main Stage
Seating Capacity: 325-400
Stage: flexible

Steinbright Stage
Seating Capacity: 160-220
Stage: flexible

FINANCES
Feb. 1, 1992-Jan. 31, 1993
Expenses: $2,133,506

CONTRACTS
AEA LORT (D)

At People's Light we present work unique to our resident ensemble through a multiyear phased development process. Phased development relies on actors, directors, designers and writers to conceive, train, rehearse, reconsider and revise over sufficient time to bring our best ideas to the stage, rather than our first ideas. We commit ourselves and most of our resources to our company of artists and to the community in which we live, including the 50,000 young people we serve in Project Discovery, our educational program. Beginning in 1993, we expanded our reach to the full diversity of our community with a Free Summer Theatre Festival. Concentration on large-scale work and extraordinary dedication to outreach and diversity describe our artistic commitment. We are committed to serving our art so completely that we feel we can do it properly only by dedicating a serious chunk of our lives to it—it takes years of working together to make social art. And that vision is defining our immediate future.
—*Danny S. Fruchter*

PRODUCTIONS 1992

Talley's Folly, Lanford Wilson; (D) Aaron Posner; (S) Phillip A. Graneto; (L) Curt Seine; (C) Michele Osherow; (SD) Bob Perdick

The People's Light and Theatre Company. Lou Ferguson in *My Children! My Africa!* Photo: Mark Garvin.

My Children! My Africa!, Athol Fugard; (D) David Ingram; (S) James F. Pyne, Jr.; (L) Deborah Peretz; (C) Shirley Horwith; (SD) Charles T. Brastow
On the Way Home, Stephen Wade; (D) Milton Kramer

Short Stuff Festival:
Sets and lighting by James F. Pyne, Jr., costumes by Shirley Horwith and Marla Jurglanis and sound design by Charles T. Brastow.

Roman Fever, adapt: Hugh Leonard, from Edith Wharton; (D) Tom Teti
The Man with the Flower in His Mouth, Luigi Pirandello; trans: William Murray; (D) Louis Lippa
The Happy Journey, Thornton Wilder; (D) Danny S. Fruchter
Dutchman, Amiri Baraka (LeRoi Jones); (D) Stephen Novelli
The Woodman and the Goblins, Don Nigro; (D) Alda Cortese
Chicks, Grace McKeaney; (D) Stephen Novelli
Molly and James, Sheila Walsh; (D) Carla Belver
Bus Riley's Back in Town, William Inge; (D) David Ingram
The American Century, Murphy Guyer; (D) Bob McCracken
The Eye of the Beholder, Kent Broadhurst; (D) Tom Teti, Stephen Novelli and Peter DeLaurier
Postcards, Carol Mack; (D) Bob McCracken
Our Lady of the Alley, Louis Lippa; (D) Ken Marini
La Putana: A Romance, Louis Lippa; (D) Louis Lippa
The Sicilian Wife, Louis Lippa; (D) Paul Meshejian
Immigrants, Louis Lippa; (D) Ken Marini

The Realists, Murphy Guyer; (D) Bob McCracken

The Playboy of the Western World, John Millington Synge; (D) Abigail Adams; (S) and (L) James F. Pyne, Jr.; (C) Marla Jurglanis
The Wizard of Hip, Thomas W. Jones, II; (D) Kenneth Leon; (S) James F. Pyne, Jr.; (L) Jeff Guzik
A Christmas Carol, adapt: Peter DeLaurier, from Charles Dickens; (D) Peter DeLaurier; (S) James F. Pyne, Jr.; (L) Deborah Peretz; (C) Andrea Barrier and Deborah Rooney; (SD) Alan Gardener

PRODUCTIONS 1993

Sets and lighting by James F. Pyne, Jr. and sound design by Charles Brastow unless otherwise noted.

Faith Healer, Brian Friel; (D) Abigail Adams; (S) and (L) William McNeil Marshall; (C) Marla Jurglanis
A Raisin in the Sun, Lorraine Hansberry; (D) Ceal Phelan; (C) M. Michael Montgomery
John Brown's Body, Stephen Vincent Benet; (D) Danny S. Fruchter and Bob Devin Jones
The Importance of Being Earnest, Oscar Wilde; (D) Michael McCallion; (L) Deborah D. Peretz; (C) Shirley Horwith and Marla Jurglanis
Our Town, Thornton Wilder; (D) Danny S. Fruchter; (C) Shirley Horwith
Glengarry Glen Ross, David Mamet; (D) Stephen Novelli; (C) Shirley Horwith and Marla Jurglanis
Peter Pan, James M. Barrie; adapt: Abigail Adams

Perseverance Theatre

MOLLY D. SMITH
Artistic Director

LYNETTE TURNER
Producing Director

TOM LINKLATER
Board President

914 Third St.
Douglas, AK 99824
(907) 364-2421
(907) 364-2603 (fax)

FOUNDED 1979
Molly D. Smith

SEASON
Year-round

FACILITIES
Mainstage
Seating Capacity: 150
Stage: flexible

Phoenix Stage
Seating Capacity: 60
Stage: flexible

Voices Stage
Seating Capacity: 175
Stage: flexible

FINANCES
July 1, 1992-June 30, 1993
Expenses: $981,650

Perseverance Theatre is located in Juneau, the capital of Alaska, a community of 28,000 that is inaccessible by road. Alaska's rich cultural heritage and its environmental and social background contribute profoundly to the artistic direction and scope of Perseverance Theatre. The complex personality of the state encompasses many kinds of people: winners and losers, people out to get rich quick, Aleuts, Tlingits, Filipinos, Eskimos, whites, oil tycoons and environmentalists looking for the "last frontier." Our major artistic goal is to wrestle with this spirit, this uniquely Alaskan experience and, using a company of multitalented artists with differing performance traditions from around the state, develop a voice for it. We produce a full season of classical and contemporary theatre on our main stage (including at least one new play by an Alaskan playwright) as well as productions on our Phoenix and Voices stages. We also tour the state and offer extensive training programs.
—*Molly D. Smith*

PRODUCTIONS 1991-1992

Direction by Molly D. Smith unless otherwise noted.

Hedda Gabler, Henrik Ibsen; trans: Gerry Bamman and Irene B. Berman; (S), (L) and (C) Pavel Dobrusky; (SD) Tim Wilson
Amigo's Blue Guitar, Joan MacLeod; (D) Laura Stribling; (S) Dan DeRoux; (L) P. Dudley Riggs; (C) Aaron J. Elmore; (SD) Diane Martin
The Caucasian Chalk Circle, Bertolt Brecht; trans: Eric Bentley; (L) Arthur Rotch; (C) Marta Ann Lastufka; (MD) Bruce J. Hanson and Peter Salett; (CH) Lynette Turner
The Mystery of Irma Vep, Charles Ludlam; (D) Rita Giomi; (S) Bill Hudson; (L) John E. Miller; (C) Barbara Casement and Aaron J. Elmore; (SD) Kathryn Kurtz and Arthur Rotch
The Collected Works of Billy the Kid, Michael Ondaatje; (S) Arthur Rotch; (L) Allen Lee Hughes; (C) Vikki Benner
In Two Worlds, Earl Atchak; (D) Kate Bowns and Jamison McLean; (S) and (C) Bill and Clarissa Hudson; (L) Arthur Rotch
Fishmas, Merry Ellefson; (D) Laura Stribling; (S), (L), (C) and (SD) Vikki Benner
The Rez Sisters, Tomson Highway; (D) Tim Wilson; (S) Vikki Benner; (L) Debra Stovern; (C) Vikki Benner and Dana Schnick
The Lady Lou Revue, book and lyrics: Gordon Duffy; music: Alan Chapman; (D) Laura Stribling; (S) Arthur Rotch; (L) John E. Miller; (C) Barbara Casement; (MD) Bruce J. Hanson; (CH) Katie Jenson

PRODUCTIONS 1992-1993

Genesis, adapt: Darrah Cloud, from the Bible (D) Molly D. Smith; (S), (L) and (C) Pavel Dobrusky
American Buffalo, David Mamet; (D) Rita Giomi; (S) and (L) Arthur Rotch; (C) Aaron J. Elmore; (SD) Lee Harris
Waiting for the Parade, John Murrell; (D) Laura Stribling; (S) Sheila Wyne; (L) Debra Stovern; (C) Barbara Casement; (SD) Bruce J. Hanson
The Grapes of Wrath, adapt: Frank Galati, from John Steinbeck; (D) Tim Dang and Luan Schooler; (S) Arthur Rotch; (L) Vikki Benner; (C) Katie Jenson; (SD) Tim Wilson
Don Juan, adapt: Per-Olav Sorensen, from various sources; (D), (S), (L) and (C) Per-Olav Sorensen and Pavel Dobrusky; (SD) Arthur Rotch
The Plucky and Spunky Show, Susan Nussbaum and Mike Ervin; (D) Mel Sandvik; (S) Brett Wolfe; (C) Deborah Smith; (SD) Mel Sandvik and Lori Roland
The Meeting, Jeff Stetson; (D) Lynette Turner; (S) Tobin Clark; (L) P. Dudley Riggs; (C) Betsy Kunibe; (SD) Glenda Carino
The Lady Lou Revue, book and lyrics: Gordon Duffy; music Alan Chapman; (D) Laura Stribling; (S) Arthur Rotch; (L) Tobin Clark; (C) Barbara Casement; (MD) Bruce J. Hanson; (CH) Katie Jenson

Perseverance Theatre. John Walcutt and Patrick Moore in *The Collected Works of Billy the Kid*. Photo: Suzanne Drapeaux.

Philadelphia Drama Guild

MARY B. ROBINSON
Artistic Director

ALAN LEVEY
Managing Director

CARL A. POSSE
Board Chairman

Robert Morris Bldg.
100 North 17th St.
Philadelphia, PA 19103
(215) 563-7530 (bus.)
(215) 898-6791 (b.o.)
(215) 563-0954 (fax)

FOUNDED 1956
Sidney S. Bloom and community members

SEASON
Oct.-May

FACILITIES
Zellerbach Theater at the Annenberg Center
Seating Capacity: 900
Stage: thrust

FINANCES
June 1, 1992-May 31, 1993
Expenses: $2,500,000

CONTRACTS
AEA LORT (B+)

The Philadelphia Drama Guild is committed to fresh explorations of the greatest plays of world literature; to the commissioning, development and production of new plays; and to a wide range of voices from many different cultures. The work onstage is initiated whenever possible by a core group of theatre artists, and developed over a period of time before it is produced. Education and outreach programs include extensive work with schools, the hearing-impaired and adult literacy students, and there is a strong commitment at every level to developing a more ethnically diverse audience. The Drama Guild is a theatre that strives to connect: to bridge the gaps of time, culture, geography, gender, age and race, and to celebrate the common humanity beneath our surface diversity through the communal event of live theatre.
—*Mary B. Robinson*

115

PHILADELPHIA DRAMA GUILD

Philadelphia Drama Guild. Orlagh Cassidy and Tandy Cronyn in *The Misanthrope*. Photo: Kenneth Kauffman.

PRODUCTIONS 1991-1992

Direction by Mary B. Robinson, sets by Allen Moyer and sound design by Robert D. Biasetti unless otherwise noted.

Macbeth, William Shakespeare; (L) Dennis Parichy; (C) James Scott
Dog Lady and *The Cuban Swimmer*, Milcha Sanchez-Scott; (L) Arden Fingerhut; (C) Tina Cantu Navarro
Joe Turner's Come and Gone, August Wilson; (D) Walter Dallas; (S) Charles McClennahan; (L) Shirley Prendergast; (C) Judy Dearing
Redwood Curtain, Lanford Wilson; (D) Marshall W. Mason; (S) John Lee Beatty; (L) Dennis Parichy; (C) Laura Crow; (SD) Chuck London and Stewart Werner
A Moon for the Misbegotten, Eugene O'Neill; (L) Arden Fingerhut; (C) Michael Krass

PRODUCTIONS 1992-1993

Sets by Allen Moyer and sound design by Connie Lockwood unless otherwise noted.

The Misanthrope, Moliere; trans: Tony Harrison; (D) Mary B. Robinson; (L) Arden Fingerhut; (C) Michael Krass
Death and the Maiden, Ariel Dorfman; (D) Mark Brokaw; (S) Scott Bradley; (L) Mary Louise Geiger; (C) Jess Goldstein
Spunk, adapt: George C. Wolfe, from Zora Neale Hurston; music: Chic Street Man; (D) Walter Dallas; (S) Felix E. Cochren; (L) Shirley Prendergast; (C) Veronica Worts; (MD) Barry Sames; (CH) Lisa D. White
Strictly Dishonorable, Preston Sturges; (D) Melia Bensussen; (L) Brian MacDevitt; (C) Michael Krass
Nora, adapt: Ingmar Bergman, from Henrik Ibsen; trans: Frederick J. Marker and Lise-Lone Marker; (D) Mary B. Robinson; (L) Arden Fingerhut and Brian MacDevitt; (C) Michael Krass; (SD) John Gromada

Philadelphia Festival Theatre for New Plays

CAROL ROCAMORA
Artistic/Producing Director

EMILY GOTTSCHALK
Managing Director

JONATHAN KLEIN
Board Chairman

1515 Locust St., 7th Fl.
Philadelphia, PA 19102
(215) 735-1500 (bus.)
(215) 898-6791 (b.o.)
(215) 735-7753 (fax)

FOUNDED 1981
Carol Rocamora

SEASON
Oct.-June

FACILITIES
Harold Prince Theatre
Seating Capacity: 211
Stage: flexible

FINANCES
July 1, 1992-June 30, 1993
Expenses: $800,000

CONTRACTS
AEA LORT (D)

The Philadelphia Festival Theatre for New Plays is an independent, nonprofit professional theatre dedicated to the production of new plays by contemporary playwrights for the purpose of enriching the cultural life of the region and contributing to the development of dramatic literature. Founded in 1981, the theatre has produced 76 world premieres, more than three-quarters of which have gone on to future life in production or publication across the country and abroad. The major programs offered by Festival Theatre include its mainstage season, playwrights' residencies, Previewers Reading Series, Curtain Call discussions, the Dennis McIntyre Playwriting Award and educational outreach. In addition, Festival Theatre commissions and develops new translations, adaptations and foreign premieres, as well as new American work.

—*Carol Rocamora*

PRODUCTIONS 1991-1992

Lighting by Curt Senie, costumes by Vickie Esposito and sound design by Connie Lockwood unless otherwise noted.

Bobby, Can You Hear Me?, Judy GeBauer; (D) Carol Rocamora; (S) Phillip A. Graneto; (C) Janus Stefanowicz
The Champagne Charlie Stakes, Bruce Graham; (D) James J. Christy; (S) James Wolk
The Play of Lights, Chaim Potok; (D) Carol Rocamora; (S) Allen Moyer; (L) Karen TenEyck
A Small Delegation, Janet Neipris; (D) Susan H. Schulman; (S) Ming Cho Lee

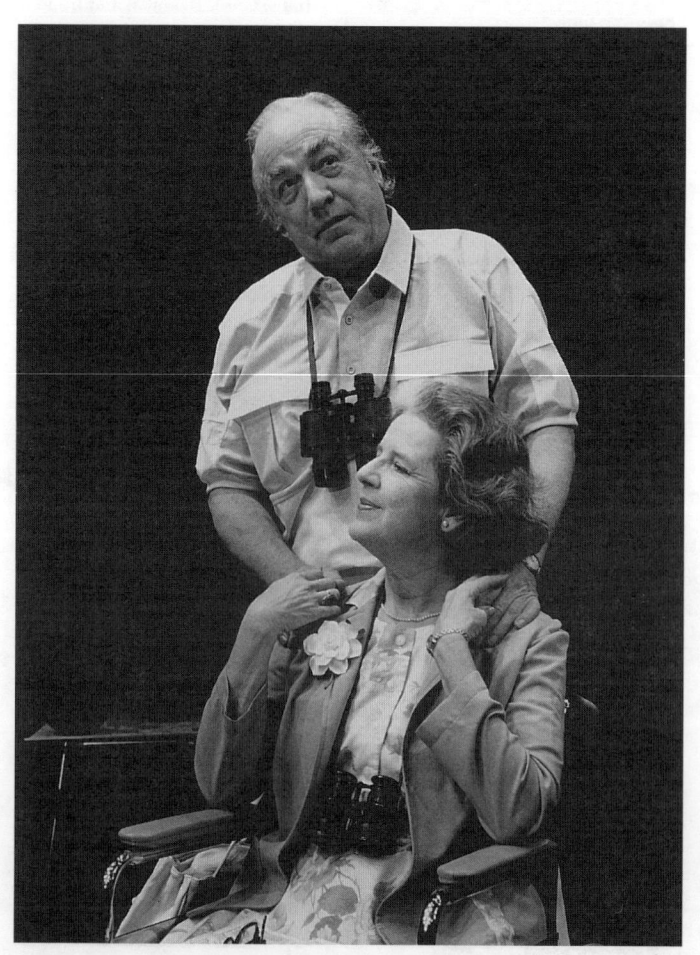

Philadelphia Festival Theatre for New Plays. John MacKay and Marcia Mahon in *The Champagne Charlie Stakes*. Photo: Stan Sadowski.

The Philadelphia Theatre Company. A. Benard Cummings, Kevin Davis, Lex Monson, Rony Clanton and Sharon Washington in *Miss Evers' Boys*. Photo: Mark Garvin.

PRODUCTIONS 1992-1993

Direction by Carol Rocamora, lighting by Jerold R. Forsyth, costumes by Vickie Esposito and sound design by Connie Lockwood unless otherwise noted.

The Seagull, Anton Chekhov; trans and adapt: Carol Rocamora; (S) James Wolk
A Very Nice Neighborhood, Bruce Graham; (D) James J. Christy; (S) James Wolk
The Big Numbers, Craig Wright; (S) David P. Gordon
Effie's Burning, Valerie Windsor; (S) Karen TenEyck

The Philadelphia Theatre Company

SARA GARONZIK
Producing Artistic Director

ADA COPPOCK
General Manager

MONIKA KRUG
Board President

21 South 5th St.
The Bourse Bldg.
Philadelphia, PA 19106
(215) 592-8333 (bus.)
(215) 735-0631 (b.o.)
(215) 592-6456 (fax)

FOUNDED 1974
Robert Hedley, Jean Harrison

SEASON
Oct.-May

FACILITIES
Plays and Players Theater
Seating Capacity: 324
Stage: proscenium

FINANCES
Sept. 1, 1992-Aug. 31, 1993
Expenses: $800,000

CONTRACTS
AEA LORT (D)

The Philadelphia Theatre Company retains a strong commitment to celebrating the genius and diversity of the American playwright, producing the emerging as well as the established contemporary American voice. Our STAGES new-play program, founded in 1986, augments this mission by offering readings, commissions and a mentor program to noteworthy writers. Of the 38 scripts developed in STAGES, 16 have gone on to production or publication. PTC is an urban theatre with a strong humanitarian conscience. More and more, we are concerned with forging strong links to our community. Panels and symposiums that place our work in context and create an ongoing dialogue with the audience are an essential part of our programming. Most important, however, is our wish to remain a nurturing home to major artists by offering them an enlightened and supportive environment that allows them to accomplish their best work.

—*Sara Garonzik*

PRODUCTIONS 1991-1992

National Anthems, Dennis McIntyre; (D) Lynn M. Thomson; (S) Paul Wonsek; (L) Stuart Duke; (C) David Murin; (SD) Jeff Chestek
Miss Evers' Boys, David Feldshuh; (D) Christopher Ashley; (S) and (L) Paul Wonsek; (C) Jess Goldstein
Lady-Like, Laura Shamas; (D) Jules Aaron; (S) John Iacovelli; (L) Kevin Rigdon; (C) Ann Bruice
Nagasaki Dust, W. Colin McKay; (D) Jules Aaron; (S) Loren Sherman; (L) Dennis Parichy; (C) Walker Hicklin; (SD) Jeff Chestek
Stages New Play Festival 1992: various playwrights; (D) Lynn M. Thomson

PRODUCTIONS 1992-1993

Prelude to a Kiss, Craig Lucas; (D) Lynn M. Thomson; (S) Karen TenEyck; (L) William H. Grant, III; (C) M. Michael Montgomery
Mountain, Douglas Scott; (D) John Henry Davis; (S) Philipp Jung and Peter Harrison; (L) Dennis Parichy; (C) David C. Woolard; (SD) John Gromada
Tiny Tim Is Dead, Barbara Lebow; (D) Frank Wittow; (S) William Barclay; (L) Stuart Duke; (C) Janus Stefanowicz; (SD) John Gromada
Lips Together, Teeth Apart, Terrence McNally; (D) Christopher Ashley; (S) and (L) Paul Wonsek; (C) Judy Dearing; (SD) Connie Lockwood
Stages New Play Festival 1993: various playwrights, various directors

The Phoenix Theatre Company

BRAM LEWIS
Artistic Director

JOEL B. WARREN
Managing Director

PAUL DEF. HICKS
Board Chairman

Box 236
Purchase, NY 10577
(914) 251-6288 (bus.)
(914) 251-6200 (b.o.)
(914) 251-6289 (fax)

FOUNDED 1988
Bram Lewis

SEASON
June-Aug.

FACILITIES
PEPSICO Theatre
Seating Capacity: 500
Stage: proscenium

FINANCES
Oct. 1, 1991-Sept. 30, 1992
Expenses: $480,000

CONTRACTS
AEA SPT

The Phoenix Theatre Company is an ensemble company. Our task is to provide our community with the most excellent theatre our professional talent, organization and material resources can produce.

The Phoenix Theatre Company. *Morning's at Seven*.

We perform a challenging repertory to highlight the diversity and creativity of our work as an *ensemble*, and to remind our public and ourselves of the theatre's most potent (and human) ingredient: transformation. Further, we believe we are partners with our community and that as such we should take an active role in education, facilitating language arts and skills in schools, colleges and community centers.

—Bram Lewis

PRODUCTIONS 1992

Sets and lighting by James Tilton, costumes by David Charles and sound design by Guy Sherman / Aural Fixation unless otherwise noted.

Morning's at Seven, Paul Osborn; (D) Ellis Rabb
The Old Boy, A.R. Gurney, Jr.; (D) Stephen Collins
Twelfth Night, William Shakespeare; (D) Bram Lewis; (C) Jan Finnell

PRODUCTIONS 1993

Sets and lighting by James Tilton, costumes by James Scott and sound design by Guy Sherman /Aural Fixation unless otherwise noted.

End of Summer, S.N. Behrman; (D) Kent Paul; (S) Tim Saternow
Sullivan and Gilbert, Ken Ludwig; music: Arthur Sullivan; lyrics: W.S. Gilbert; (D) Marcia Milgrom Dodge
Long Day's Journey into Night, Eugene O'Neill; (D) Bram Lewis

Ping Chong and Company

PING CHONG
Artistic Director

BRUCE ALLARDICE
Managing Director

Ping Chong and Company. Dawn Saito in *Deshima*. Photo: Carol Rosegg/Martha Swope Associates.

ERICA BILDER
Board President

47 Great Jones St.
New York, NY 10012
(212) 529-1557
(212) 529-1703 (fax)

FOUNDED 1975
Ping Chong

SEASON
Year-round

FINANCES
July 1, 1992-June 30, 1993
Expenses: $275,000

I continue to be fascinated by the intersections that form our world, particularly the often violent meetings of race, culture, history, art and technology in the modern era. The clash of these forces has an almost geological aspect, one that constantly unearths fresh areas for artistic investigation. My collaborators and I have explored these new lands in a proliferation of styles and forms, respecting no orthodoxy and serving no master. It is our privilege as artists to create performances from this material as part of an ongoing dialogue with the 20th century.

—Ping Chong

PRODUCTIONS 1991-1992

Plays by Ping Chong and company, direction and choreography by Ping Chong, lighting by Howard Thies, costumes by Carol Ann Pelletier and sound design by Brian Hallas unless otherwise noted.

Elephant Memories, (S) Ping Chong and Matthew Yokobosky; (L) Thomas C. Hase; (C) Matthew Yokobosky
Nosferatu, (S) Ping Chong and Miguel Lopez-Castillo
Kind Ness, (S) Ping Chong
American Gothic, (S) Ping Chong and Bonnie Brinkley; (L) Ping Chong and Kathryn Eader; (C) Stephen Stratton

PRODUCTIONS 1992-1993

Plays by Ping Chong and company, direction and choreography by Ping Chong, lighting by Thomas C. Hase, costumes by Carol Ann Pelletier and sound design by Brian Hallas unless otherwise noted.

Undesirable Elements, (S) Ping Chong
Deshima, (S) Ping Chong and Watoku Ueno
Kind Ness, (S) and (L) Ping Chong

Pioneer Theatre Company

CHARLES MOREY
Artistic Director

CHRISTOPHER LINO
Managing Director

EDWARD BATES
Board Chairman

Pioneer Memorial Theatre
University of Utah
Salt Lake City, UT 84112
(801) 581-6356 (bus.)
(801) 581-6961 (b.o.)
(801) 581-5472 (fax)

FOUNDED 1962
C. Lowell Lees, University of Utah, local citizens

SEASON
Sept.-May

FACILITIES
Lees Main Stage
Seating Capacity: 1,000
Stage: proscenium

FINANCES
July 1, 1992-June 30, 1993
Expenses: $2,200,000

CONTRACTS
AEA LORT (B) and U/RTA

The Pioneer Theatre Company is the resident professional theatre of the University of Utah. PTC has the largest subscription audience of any arts organization in Utah and draws theatregoers from four western states. The company's mission is twofold: first, to provide the community with an ongoing resident theatre of the highest professional standards; and, second, to serve as an educational and cultural resource to the university community and a training ground for aspiring professionals. Central to this dual purpose is the assumption that the educational mission cannot be fulfilled without first satisfying the primary concern for artistic excellence. As befits PTC's position as the largest professional theatre in the region and a division of a major research university, the company produces a broad and eclectic repertoire focused upon the classics of world literature, augmented by contemporary work of distinction.

—Charles Morey

Pioneer Theatre Company. *The Grapes of Wrath*. Photo: Robert Clayton.

PRODUCTIONS 1991-1992

Direction by Charles Morey, sets by George Maxwell and lighting by Peter Willardson unless otherwise noted.

The Grapes of Wrath, adapt: Frank Galati, from John Steinbeck; (L) Karl Hass; (C) Elizabeth Novak

Henry V, William Shakespeare; (S) Gary English; (C) Carol Wells-Day

The 1940's Radio Hour, book: Walton Jones; various composers and lyricists; (D) Richard Russell Ramos; (S) Peter Harrison; (C) Linda Sarver; (MD) James Prigmore

The Mystery of Irma Vep, Charles Ludlam; (D) John Laywood; (L) Angelo O'Dierno; (C) David C. Paulin

Uncle Vanya, Anton Chekhov; trans: Constance Garnett; (S) Ariel Ballif; (C) K.L. Alberts

Lettice and Lovage, Peter Shaffer; (D) Libby Appel; (S) Peter Harrison; (C) Carol Wells-Day

My Fair Lady, book adapt and lyrics: Alan Jay Lerner, from George Bernard Shaw; music: Frederick Lowe; (L) Richard Winkler; (C) David C. Paulin; (MD) James Prigmore; (CH) Jayne Luke

PRODUCTIONS 1992-1993

Direction by Charles Morey, sets by George Maxwell and lighting by Peter Willardson unless otherwise noted.

A Day in Hollywood/A Night in the Ukraine, book and lyrics: Dick Vosburgh; music: Frank Lazarus; (D) and (CH) Pamela Hunt; (L) Robert Jared; (C) Carol Wells-Day; (MD) James Prigmore

Much Ado About Nothing, William Shakespeare; (D) Richard Russell Ramos; (S) Larry Kanshansky; (C) Linda Sarver

Private Lives, Noel Coward; (L) Ann G. Wrightson; (C) K.L. Alberts

Fences, August Wilson; (D) Kenneth Washington; (S) Peter Harrison; (C) Carol Wells-Day

O, Pioneers!, adapt: Darrah Cloud, from Willa Cather; (S) Ariel Ballif; (C) K.L. Alberts

Lend Me a Tenor, Ken Ludwig; (S) Rob Odorisio; (L) Mary Louise Geiger; (C) Bill Brewer

Evita, music: Andrew Lloyd Webber; lyrics: Tim Rice; (D) John Going; (C) David C. Paulin; (MD) James Prigmore; (CH) Jayne Luke

Pittsburgh Public Theater

EDWARD GILBERT
Artistic Director

DANIEL B. FALLON
Managing Director

RICHARD H. DANIEL
Board Chairman

Allegheny Square
Pittsburgh, PA 15212-5349
(412) 323-8200 (bus.)
(412) 321-9800 (b.o.)
(412) 323-8550 (fax)

FOUNDED 1975
Joan Apt, Margaret Rieck, Ben Shaktman

SEASON
Sept.-June

FACILITIES
Theodore L. Hazlett, Jr. Theater
Seating Capacity: 452
Stage: flexible

FINANCES
Sept. 1, 1992-Aug. 31, 1993
Expenses: $3,842,705

CONTRACTS
AEA LORT (B)

Pittsburgh Public Theater seeks to present the finest plays of the American and world repertoire to the widest possible audience in a city noted for its cultural diversity. We aim to bring together gifted theatre artists and to provide a setting in which they can reach for excellence. We believe that the art of theatre, practiced with distinction, sheds light on the human condition, and holds out the promise that members of the human family can learn to treat one another with greater wisdom and compassion than they have in the past. Currently, the board and staff of the Public are heavily engaged in planning for the construction of a new theatre complex in Pittsburgh's downtown Cultural District. We are working hard to expand and improve all aspects of our operation in preparation for our move to a new home.
—*Edward Gilbert*

Note: During the 1991-92 season, William T. Gardner served as producing director.

PRODUCTIONS 1991-1992

Costumes by Laura Crow and sound design by James Capenos unless otherwise noted.

Hamlet, William Shakespeare; (D) Ron Daniels; (S) and (C) Antony McDonald; (L) Frances Aronson; (SD) Maribeth Back

I Do! I Do!, book and lyrics: Tom Jones; music: Harvey Schmidt; (D) Maureen Heffernan; (S) Ray Recht; (L) Phil Monat; (C) Michael J. Cesario; (MD) Nathan Hurwitz; (CH) David Wanstreet

The Three Sisters, Anton Chekhov; adapt: Corinne Jacker; (D) William T. Gardner; (S) Charles McCarry; (L) Brian McDevitt

The Cocktail Hour, A.R. Gurney, Jr.; (D) Peter Bennett; (S) Gary English; (L) Andrew David Ostrowski

A Moon for the Misbegotten, Eugene O'Neill; (D) Lee Sankowich; (S) Anne Mundell; (L) Phil Monat; (C) Barbara Anderson

The Sum of Us, David Stevens; (D) Marshall W. Mason; (S) John Lee Beatty; (L) Mal Sturchio

PRODUCTIONS 1992-1993

Sound design by James Capenos unless otherwise noted.

Ma Rainey's Black Bottom, August Wilson; (D) Claude Purdy; (S) Vicki Smith; (L) Phil Monat; (C) Paul Tazewell

Inspecting Carol, Daniel Sullivan and the Seattle Repertory Resident Acting Company; (D) David Saint; (S) Loren Sherman; (L) Donald Holder; (C) Michael J. Cesario

Pittsburgh Public Theater. *Mad Forest*. Photo: Gerry Goodstein.

Mad Forest, Caryl Churchill; (D) Mark Wing-Davey; (S) and (C) Marina Draghici; (L) Peter Maradudin; (SD) Mark Bennett and James van Bergen

The Old Lady's Guide to Survival, Mayo Simon; (D) Alan Mandell; (S) Ray Recht; (L) Dennis Parichy; (C) Marianna Elliott

Cobb, Lee Blessing; (D) Lee Sankowich; (S) Anne Mundell; (L) Phil Monat; (C) Barbara Anderson

The School for Wives, Moliere; trans: Richard Wilbur; (D) Edward Gilbert; (S) Mark Negin; (L) Nicholas Cernovitch; (C) Mark Negin

Playhouse on the Square

JACKIE NICHOLS
Executive Producer

ELIZABETH HOWARD
Administrative Director

RANDALL REAGAN
Board President

51 South Cooper St.
Memphis, TN 38104
(901) 725-0776 (bus.)
(901) 726-4656 (b.o.)
(901) 272-7530 (fax)

FOUNDED 1968
Jackie Nichols

SEASON
Year-round

FACILITIES
Playhouse on the Square
Seating Capacity: 260
Stage: proscenium

Circuit Playhouse
Seating Capacity: 140
Stage: proscenium

FINANCES
July 1, 1991-June 30, 1992
Expenses: $788,747

Playhouse on the Square, the only professional company in the Memphis/Mid-South area, serves a broad constituency in a diverse ethnic and cultural community approaching one million people. We produce a varied season and are committed to providing long-term employment to a core acting company and artistic staff. The resident-company concept therefore requires us to seek out versatile individuals to support the seasons selected, individuals who are committed to ensemble growth. This philosophy provides artists the opportunity to work on and expand their skills in productions for which they may not normally be considered. The manageable size of our organization and our dedication to our principles help us maintain our goals in a society that embraces specialization and discourages personal long-term commitment. We also have well-established and highly effective theatre-for-youth and outreach programs dedicated to the audience of the future.
—*Jackie Nichols*

PRODUCTIONS 1991-1992

Direction by Ken Zimmerman, sets by Chuck Britt, lighting by Dean Davis and costumes by Alex Allesandri Bruce unless otherwise noted.

Oklahoma!, book adapt and lyrics: Oscar Hammerstein, II, from Lynn Riggs; music: Richard Rodgers; (S) Craig Spain; (L) John Rankin; (MD) Tom Johnson; (CH) Judith Wombwell

Uncle Vanya, Anton Chekhov; trans: John Murrell; (D) Kate Davis; (S) Henry Swanson

Peter Pan, book: James M. Barrie; music: Mark Charlap; lyrics: Carolyn Leigh; (S) Joe Ragey; (MD) Tom Johnson; (CH) Cynthia Oliver

The Heidi Chronicles, Wendy Wasserstein; (D) Jerry Chipman; (S) Scott Blake; (SD) Dean Davis

Death of a Salesman, Arthur Miller; (S) Mike Nichols; (SD) Ross Rice

Oil City Symphony, Mike Craver, Mark Hardwick, Debra Monk and Mary Murfitt

Fences, August Wilson; (D) Bob Devin Jones; (SD) Dean Davis

The Cocktail Hour, A.R. Gurney, Jr.; (D) Gene Crain; (S) Greg D. Boyd; (L) Chuck Britt

Godspell, book: John Michael Tebelak; music and lyrics: Stephen Schwartz; (D) Cecelia Pickle; (L) Duane Pagano; (C) Jeff A.R. Jones; (MD) Tom Johnson; (CH) Barbara Powell and Linda Savage

More Fun Than Bowling, Steven Dietz; (S) Tina M. Newhauser; (L) Duane Pagano; (C) Jeff A.R. Jones

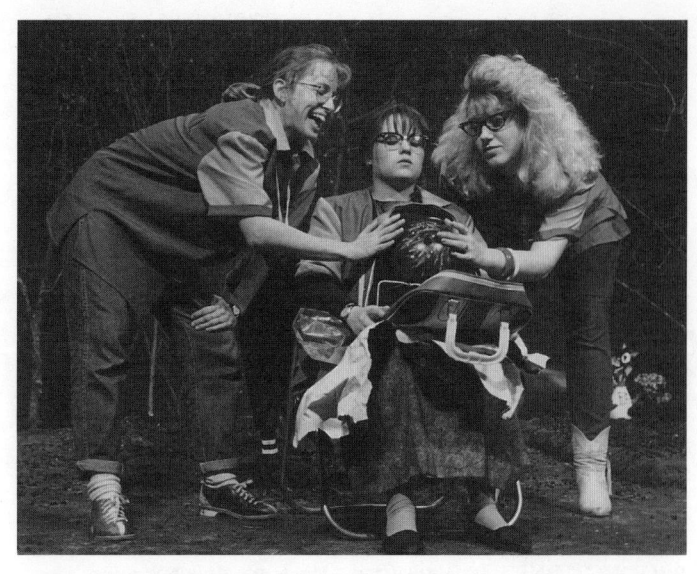

The Lion, the Witch and the Wardrobe, book adapt: Jules Tasca, from C.S. Lewis; music: Thomas Tierney; lyrics: Ted Drachman; (D) Michael Donahue; (S) Jackie Nichols; (L) John Rankin; (C) Jeff A.R. Jones; (MD) Tom Johnson

Independence, Lee Blessing; (D) Dave Landis; (S) Tina M. Newhauser; (L) Duane Pagano; (C) Jeff A.R. Jones; (SD) Gary Larkin

The Gamblers, Valerie Smith; (D) Cecelia Pickle; (S) Chuck Britt and Jackie Nichols; (L) Duane Pagano; (C) Jeff A.R. Jones; (SD) Pam Rickman

Nothing Sacred, George F. Walker; (D) Michael Donahue; (S) Steve Jones; (L) Duane Pagano; (C) Jeff A.R. Jones; (SD) Melissa Marquis

Closer Than Ever, conceived: Steven Scott Smith; music: David Shire; lyrics: Richard Maltby, Jr.; (D) Bennett Wood; (S) Jackie Nichols; (L) Tina M. Newhauser; (C) Jeff A.R. Jones; (MD) Tom Johnson; (CH) Vera Stephenson

PRODUCTIONS 1992-1993

Direction by Ken Zimmerman, sets by Chuck Britt, lighting by Dean Davis and costumes by Alex Allesandri Bruce unless otherwise noted.

Carousel, book and lyrics: Oscar Hammerstein, II; music: Richard Rodgers; (S) Chuck Britt and Jackie Nichols; (MD) Tom Johnson; (CH) Judith Wombwell; (SD) Dean Davis

Our Country's Good, adapt: Timberlake Wertenbaker, from Thomas Keneally; (D) Ken McCulough; (S) Pamela Goss; (SD) Melissa Marquis

Peter Pan, book: James M. Barrie; music: Mark Charlap; lyrics: Carolyn Leigh; (S) Joe Ragey; (MD) Tom Johnson; (CH) Kim Sanders

M. Butterfly, David Henry Hwang; (D) Tom Prewitt; (S) Brantley Ellzey; (SD) Dean Davis

Inherit the Wind, Jerome Lawrence and Robert E. Lee; (S) Kathy Haaga

Little Shop of Horrors, book adapt and lyrics: Howard Ashman, from Charles Griffith; music: Alan Menken; (D) Cecelia Pickle; (MD) Tom Johnson

Dearly Departed, David Bottrell and Jessie Jones

Goodnight Desdemona (Good Morning Juliet), Ann-Marie MacDonald; (D) Terry Scott; (S) Tina M. Newhauser; (C) Jeff A.R. Jones; (SD) Mark Pergolizzi

The Lion, the Witch and the Wardrobe, book adapt: Jules Tasca, from C.S. Lewis; music: Thomas Tierney; lyrics: Ted Drachman; (D) Michael Donahue; (S) Jackie Nichols; (L) John Rankin; (C) Jeff A.R. Jones; (MD) Tom Johnson

Shadowlands, William Nicholson; (D) Gene Crain; (S) Jackie Nichols; (L) John Rankin; (C) Jeff A.R. Jones

Prelude to a Kiss, Craig Lucas; (D) Anthony Isbell; (S) Jackie Nichols; (L) Chuck Britt; (C) Jeff A.R. Jones; (SD) Ted Sherman

Playhouse on the Square. Tracey Zerwig, Rebecca Kolber and Alison Franck in *More Fun than Bowling*. Photo: Sam Leakley.

Assassins, book: John Weidman; music and lyrics: Stephen Sondheim; (D) Barry Fuller; (S) Stephen Pair; (L) Stephen Forsyth; (C) Jeff A.R. Jones; (SD) Charles Grace
The Adventures of Tom Sawyer, adapt: Timothy Mason, from Mark Twain; (D) Michael Donahue; (L) Chuck Britt; (C) Jeff A.R. Jones
Reckless, Craig Lucas; (D) Anthony Isbell; (S) Ted Thomas; (L) Shelly Callahan; (C) Jeff A.R. Jones
Six Women with Brain Death or Expiring Minds Want to Know, book: Cheryl Benge, Christy Brandt, Rosanna E. Coppedge, Valerie Fagan, Ross Freese, Mark Houston, Sandee Johnson and Peggy Pharr Wilson; lyrics: Mark Houston; (D) Ken McCulough; (S) Shelly Callahan; (L) Chuck Britt; (C) Ramona Ward
Cementville, Jane Martin; (D) Cecelia Pickle; (S) Chuck Britt; (C) Jeff A.R. Jones; (SD) Darron L. West

PlayMakers Repertory Company

MILLY S. BARRANGER
Producing Director

DAVID HAMMOND
Associate Producing Director

PlayMakers Repertory Company. Stephen Shelley, Neil Maffin, Ed Wagenseller and Brent Langdon in *Hamlet*. Photo: Biar Orrell.

MARY ROBIN WELLS
Administrative Director

CB# 3235 Graham Memorial Bldg. 052A
Chapel Hill, NC 27599-3235
(919) 962-1122 (bus.)
(919) 962-PLAY (b.o.)
(919) 962-4069 (fax)

FOUNDED 1976
Arthur L. Housman

SEASON
Sept.-May

FACILITIES
Paul Green Theatre
Seating Capacity: 499
Stage: thrust

PlayMakers Theatre
Seating Capacity: 285
Stage: proscenium

FINANCES
July 1, 1992-June 30, 1993
Expenses: $1,137,950

CONTRACTS
AEA LORT (D)

PlayMakers Repertory Company was founded as a professional producing organization and theatrical training conservatory in association with the department of dramatic art at the University of North Carolina at Chapel Hill. Within two decades the company has presented 93 productions, including 7 premieres. PlayMakers has a dual commitment to artistic excellence and to the training of young professionals who work with the company for three years prior to entering the profession. We are committed to producing a season of classic and contemporary works, using guest artists and a resident ensemble of actors, directors, designers and craftspeople who collaborate to produce a primarily classical repertoire. In doing so, we aim to enrich the imaginative and spiritual lives of North Carolina audiences. At all times, PlayMakers' dual role as a professional theatre and a training center demonstrates a unique collaboration between an educational institution and the profession.
—*Milly S. Barranger*

PRODUCTIONS 1991-1992

Sets by Bill Clarke, lighting by Marcus Dilliard and sound design by Pamela Emerson unless otherwise noted.

Hard Times, adapt: Stephen Jeffreys, from Charles Dickens; (D) David Hammond; (L) Robert Wierzel; (C) McKay Coble
A Shayna Maidel, Barbara Lebow; (D) Ray Dooley; (L) Mary Louise Geiger; (C) Bobbi Owen
The Nutcracker: A Play, adapt: David Hammond, from E.T.A. Hoffman; (D) David Hammond; (C) McKay Coble
Who's Afraid of Virginia Woolf?, Edward Albee; (D) William Woodman; (S) and (C) Russell Parkman
Eleemosynary, Lee Blessing; (D) Kathryn Long; (S) Anita Stewart; (C) Sharon S.Q. Campbell
Twelfth Night, William Shakespeare; (D) Martin L. Platt; (S) Russell Parkman; (L) Robert Wierzel; (C) Bill Clarke

PRODUCTIONS 1992-1993

Sets by Bill Clarke, lighting by Marcus Dilliard and sound design by Pamela Emerson unless otherwise noted.

The Little Foxes, Lillian Hellman; (D) Stephen Stout; (S) Russell Parkman; (L) Ashley York Kennedy; (C) McKay Coble
Prelude to a Kiss, Craig Lucas; (D) Ray Dooley; (S) and (C) Russell Parkman; (L) Mary Louise Geiger
The Nutcracker: A Play, adapt: David Hammond, from E.T.A. Hoffman; (D) Dede Corvinus; (C) McKay Coble
Tartuffe, Moliere; trans: Sara O'Connor; (D) David Hammond; (L) Mary Louise Geiger; (C) Bill Clarke
Some Americans Abroad, Richard Nelson; (D) Evan Yionoulis; (S) and (C) McKay Coble
Hamlet, William Shakespeare; (D) David Hammond; (L) Robert Wierzel; (C) Bill Clarke

The Playwrights' Center

DAVID MOORE, JR.
Executive Director

LORI-ANNE WILLIAMS
Managing Director

PERRY KETCHUM
Board President

2301 Franklin Ave. E
Minneapolis, MN 55406
(612) 332-7481
(612) 332-6037 (fax)

FOUNDED 1971
Erik Brogger, Thomas G. Dunn, Barbara Field, Jon Jackoway

SEASON
Year-round

FACILITIES
Playwrights' Center
Seating Capacity: 175
Stage: flexible

Rarig Center (Playlabs)
Seating Capacity: 300
Stage: thrust

FINANCES
July 1, 1992-June 30, 1993
Expenses: $508,501

CONTRACTS
AEA letter of agreement

The Playwrights' Center fuels the contemporary theatre by providing services that support the development and public appreciation of playwrights and playwriting. The center is committed to artistic excellence; diversity of aesthetic, culture, age and gender; playwright leadership in governance; advocacy of playwrights' work; and freedom of expression. Since 1971 the center has assisted more than 600 playwrights across the country through playwright-driven initia-

121

The Playwrights' Center. Workshop of *The Dead Book*. Photo: Dee Henry Williams.

tives. Core programs include script workshops and public readings employing seasoned actors and artists; PlayLabs, a developmental workshop and conference held each August; 18 annual playwriting awards totaling over $100,000, including national McKnight and Jerome Fellowships; Many Voices, a pilot program of residencies and training for writers of color; developmental exchanges and residencies linking artists and producers in major theatre communities; a national, tiered playwright membership program offering information and career services; and a range of educational and touring initiatives reaching school and community audiences of more than 30,000 a year.
—David Moore, Jr.

PRODUCTIONS 1992

Hope for Breakfast, Marisha Chamberlain; (D) Lou Salerni
Buffalo Hair, Carlyle Brown; (D) Lou Bellamy
Last Total Eclipse, Patty Lynch; (D) Kent Stephens
The Dead Book, Bill Corbett; (D) Wendy Knox
A Family Man, Tom Szentgyorgyi; (D) Kent Stephens
The Scrub, Chris Cinque; (D) Melia Bensussen

PRODUCTIONS 1993

Bitter Homes and Gardens, Luis Alfaro; (D) Roxanne Rogers
What to Say, Peter Fagal; (D) Douglas Hughes
Alchemy of Desire/Deadman's Blues, Caridad Svich; (D) Lisa Peterson
The Job, Shem Bitterman; (D) Leslie Swackhamer
Helen of Athens, Buffy Sedlachek; (D) Cynthia White

Playwrights Horizons

DON SCARDINO
Artistic Director

JUDITH O. RUBIN
Board Chairman

LYNN LANDIS
General Manager

416 West 42nd St.
New York, NY 10036
(212) 564-1235 (bus.)
(212) 279-4200 (b.o.)
(212) 594-0296 (fax)

FOUNDED 1971
Robert Moss

SEASON
Variable

FACILITIES
Mainstage
Seating Capacity: 145
Stage: proscenium

Studio Theatre
Seating Capacity: 72
Stage: flexible

FINANCES
Sept. 1, 1992-Aug. 31, 1993
Expenses: $4,464,000

CONTRACTS
AEA Off Broadway

Playwrights Horizons is dedicated to the support and development of contemporary American playwrights, composers and lyricists and to the production of their work.
—Don Scardino

PRODUCTIONS 1991-1992

Marvin's Room, Scott McPherson; (D) David Petrarca; (S) Linda Buchanan; (L) Robert Christen; (C) Claudia Boddy
Break, *Agnes*, *Eulogy for Mister Hamm* and *Lucky Nurse*, book, music and lyrics: Michael John LaChiusa; (D) Kirsten Sanderson; (S) Derek McLane; (L) Debra J. Kletter; (C) David Sawaryn; (MD) Joshua Rosenblum
The End of the Day, Jon Robin Baitz; (D) Mark Lamos (S) John Arnone; (L) Pat Collins; (C) Jess Goldstein; (SD) David Budries
Man, Woman, Dinosaur, Regina M. Porter; (D) Melia Bensussen; (S) Allen Moyer; (L) Brian MacDevitt; (C) Karen Perry; (SD) Bruce Ellman
Little Egypt, Lynn Siefert; (D) Roberta Levitow; (S) James Noone; (L) Robert Wierzel; (C) Mary Myers; (SD) John Gromada
Flaubert's Latest, Peter Parnell; (D) David Saint; (S) James Noone; (L) Kenneth Posner; (C) Jane Greenwood; (SD) John Gromada

PRODUCTIONS 1992-1993

On the Bum, Neal Bell; (D) Don Scardino; (S) Allen Moyer; (L) Kenneth Posner; (C) Sharon Lynch; (SD) John Gromada
Man in His Underwear, Jay Tarses; (D) Kevin Dowling; (S) Rob Odorisio; (L) Michael Lincoln; (C) Therese A. Bruck; (SD) Jeremy Grody
The Heliotrope Bouquet by Scott Joplin & Louis Chauvin, Eric Overmyer; (D) Joe Morton; (S) Richard Hoover; (L) Phil Monat; (C) Judy Dearing; (SD) Bruce Odland
Sophistry, Jonathan Marc Sherman; (D) Nicholas Martin; (S) Allen Moyer; (L) Kenneth Posner; (C) Michael Krass; (SD) Jeremy Grody
Later Life, A.R. Gurney, Jr.; (D) Don Scardino; (S) Ben Edwards; (L) Brian MacDevitt; (C) Jennifer von Mayrhauser; (SD) Guy Sherman/Aural Fixation
Avenue X, book, music and lyrics: John Jiler and Ray Leslee; (D) Mark Brokaw; (S) Loy Arcenas; (L) Donald Holder; (C) Ellen McCartney; (MD) Chapman Roberts; (SD) Janet Kalas

The Pollard Theatre

CHARLES C. SUGGS, II
Producing Director

MARILYN BRANCH
President, Guthrie Arts and Humanities Council

Playwrights Horizons. Nancy Marchand and Roger Rees in *The End of the Day*. Photo: T. Charles Erickson.

The Pollard Theatre. Robert Matson and Brenda S. Williams in *Cabaret*. Photo: Charles C. Suggs, II.

Box 38
Guthrie, OK 73044
(405) 282-2802 (bus.)
(405) 282-2800 (b.o.)

FOUNDED 1987
Charles C. Suggs, II

SEASON
Year-round

FACILITIES
The Pollard Theatre
Seating Capacity: 250
Stage: proscenium

Stage II
Seating Capacity: 90
Stage: proscenium

FINANCES
July 1, 1992-June 30, 1993
Expenses: $349,100

Humanity is shaped by many powerful forces, not the least of which is Society, the ever-present pressure to reduce life to order. Society searches the chaos of life for its rational aspects, bringing the weapons of logic and reason to bear upon them, creating the faith of law and order. Some of life remains chaotic, however, because by its very nature it is irrational and unreasonable. Love and hate, joy and despair, beauty and fear simply cannot be reduced to logic. Theatre is humankind's refuge from that chaos with which reason is unable to deal. Its processes allow us to confront this chaos without the fear or risk inherent in life itself. The Pollard is a space in which theatre artists of significant vision and skill, working across disciplinary boundaries while developing continuing relationships with each other, produce plays that grapple with that chaos.

—*Charles C. Suggs, II*

PRODUCTIONS 1992

Direction, sets and lighting by Charles C. Suggs, II and costumes by Michael James unless otherwise noted.

The Imaginary Invalid, Moliere; trans: Miles Malleson; (D) Steven Vincent; (S) Michael James; (L) Jim Evans; (SD) Michael James
Greater Tuna, Jaston Williams, Joe Sears and Ed Howard; (D) Brenda S. Williams
A...My Name is Alice, conceived: Joan Micklin Silver and Julianne Boyd; various composers and lyricists; (D) and (CH) Rebecca Skupin; (MD) Rebecca Skupin and David Hargis
Arsenic and Old Lace, Joseph Kesselring; (D) Sandy Williams; (S) Michael James
"Master Harold"...and the boys, Athol Fugard; (D) Steven Vincent
Lettice and Lovage, Peter Shaffer
The Best Little Whorehouse in Texas, book: Larry L. King and Peter Masterson; music and lyrics: Carol Hall; (S) Fred Christoffel; (MD) Bernard Jones; (CH) Rebecca Skupin
M. Butterfly, David Henry Hwang; (SD) Lucia Hwong
The Mystery of Irma Vep, Charles Ludlam; (D) Brenda S. Williams; (S) Michael Sullivan
A Territorial Christmas Carol, adapt: Stephen P. Scott, from Charles Dickens; (D) Sandy Williams; (S) Gary Varner; (SD) Charles C. Suggs, II

PRODUCTIONS 1993

Direction, sets and lighting by Charles C. Suggs, II and costumes by Michael James unless otherwise noted.

The Life of Galileo, Bertolt Brecht; trans Charles Laughton; (D) Steven Vincent
Love Letters, A.R. Gurney, Jr.
Cabaret, book adapt: Joe Masteroff, from Christopher Isherwood; music: John Kander; lyrics: Fred Ebb; (S) Michael Sullivan; (MD) Edie Hamilton; (CH) Rebecca Skupin
The Immigrant, Mark Harelik; (D) Robert Matson; (L) Jim Evans
The Search for Signs of Intelligent Life in the Universe, Jane Wagner
Prelude to a Kiss, Craig Lucas; (D) Rebecca Wooldridge; (S) and (L) Michael Sullivan
The Passion of Dracula, adapt: Bob Hall and David Richmond, from Bram Stoker; (D) Robert Thompson
Dancing at Lughnasa, Brian Friel
Shadowlands, William Nicholson
A Territorial Christmas Carol, adapt: Stephen P. Scott, from Charles Dickens; (D) Rebecca Skupin; (S) Gary Varner; (SD) Charles C. Suggs, II

Pope Theatre Company

(formerly Theatre Club of the Palm Beaches)

LOUIS TYRRELL
Producing Director

NANCY BARNETT
Company Manager

LAURIE GILDAN
Board President

262 South Ocean Blvd.
Manalapan, FL 33462
(407) 585-3404 (bus.)
(407) 585-3433 (b.o.)
(407) 588-4708 (fax)

FOUNDED 1987
Louis Tyrrell

SEASON
Nov.-Aug.

FACILITIES
Lois Pope Theatre
Seating Capacity: 250
Stage: thrust

FINANCES
Oct. 1, 1992-Sept. 30, 1993
Expenses: $1,800,000

CONTRACTS
AEA letter of agreement

Pope Theatre Company (formerly known as Theatre Club of the Palm Beaches) continues to challenge an ever-expanding audience with some of the best new works in contemporary theatre. Whether thought-provoking, issue-driven or innovative in style, the company's productions reflect a collective dedication to making theatre an integral part of our community life. While committed to the support and development of a Florida community of theatre artists, our artistic collaboration extends across the country. Our company has experienced strong, continued growth with a move to our own theatre facility in the 1991-92 season, and our subscriber base has expanded to better than 6,000 during our first six seasons. Our primary mission includes the establishment of a new generation of audiences and artists through our Learning Stage educational program, which reaches more than

Pope Theatre Company. Warren Kelley and John Felix in *Some Things You Need to Know Before the World Ends*. Photo: Debra Hesser.

50,000 students annually with company-created works focusing on relevant issues. In addition, the New Voices series assists playwrights by providing public readings of developing works, and a new play-commissioning program supports the work of some of America's finest dramatists.

—*Louis Tyrrell*

PRODUCTIONS 1991-1992

Direction by J. Barry Lewis and costumes by Carol Provonsha unless otherwise noted.

A Smaller Place, Mitch Giannunzio; (D) Vincent Dowling; (S) Suzanne Clement Jones; (L) Victor A. Becker; (C) Mark Pirolo

Cat's-Paw, William Mastrosimone; (D) John Briggs; (S) Stephen Placido, Jr.; (L) Pamela A. Mara; (C) Christine E. Field; (SD) Kristen R. Kuipers

Some Things You Need to Know Before the World Ends (A Final Evening with the Illuminati), Larry Larson and Eddie Levi Lee; (S) Rex Fluty; (L) Richard Crowell; (C) Mark Pirolo; (SD) R. Mesmer

The Gravity of Honey, Bruce E. Rodgers; (D) Tony Giordano; (S) Hugh Landwehr; (L) Clifton Taylor; (SD) Craig Ames

Lost Electra, Bruce E. Rodgers; (S) Victor A. Becker; (L) Pamela A. Mara; (C) Suzette Bridges

Moon Over the Brewery, Bruce Graham; (S) Stephen Placido, Jr.; (L) Pamela A. Mara

Mama Drama, Leslie Ayvazian, Donna Daley, Christine Farrell, Rita Nachtmann and Ann Sachs; (D) Ann Sachs; (S) Eugene Lee; (L) Richard Crowell

The Belle of Amherst, William Luce; (D) Peter Bennett; (S) Allen D. Cornell; (L) Suzanne Clement Jones

PRODUCTIONS 1992-1993

Direction by J. Barry Lewis, costumes by Suzette Bridges and sound design by Jon M. Loflin unless otherwise noted.

Shmulnik's Waltz, Allan Knee; (S) Allen D. Cornell; (L) Pamela A. Mara

Early One Evening at the Rainbow Bar and Grill, Bruce Graham; (D) Louis Tyrrell; (S) Victor A. Becker; (L) Suzanne Clement Jones; (C) Carol Provonsha

The Sum of Us, David Stevens; (S) Stephen Placido, Jr.; (L) Richard Crowell; (C) Carol Provonsha

No Way to Treat a Lady, book adapt, music and lyrics: Douglas J. Cohen, from William Goldman; (S) David Trimble; (L) Suzanne Clement Jones; (MD) Michael Lavine; (CH) Michael DiFonzo

Moonshadow, Richard Hellesen; (D) Lynnette Barkley; (S) and (L) Victor A. Becker; (C) Marty Grusby

Ripe Conditions, Claudia Allen; (S) David Trimble; (L) Howard Werner

Always...Patsy Cline, book: Ted Swindley; various composers and lyricists; (D) Ted Swindley; (S) Allen D. Cornell; (L) Albert C. Mathers; (MD) Craig Ames

Portland Repertory Theater

GEOFFREY SHERMAN
Artistic Director

NANCY WELCH ALLEN
Executive Director

KAREN WHITMAN
Board Chair

Two World Trade Center
25 Southwest Salmon St.
Portland, OR 97204-3233
(503) 224-4491

FOUNDED 1980
Mark Allen, Nancy D. Welch

SEASON
Sept.-June

FACILITIES
World Trade Center
Seating Capacity: 230
Stage: proscenium

PCPA (Portland Center for the Performing Arts)
Seating Capacity: 150
Stage: proscenium

FINANCES
July 1, 1992-June 30, 1993
Expenses: $1,150,000

CONTRACTS
AEA letter of agreement

The Portland Repertory Theater is the oldest professional theatre company in the city. We are committed to the presentation of the finest and most innovative of both American and international drama and are presently engaged in a thorough examination of our artistic policy in order to expand the nature and quantity of our work. To achieve this goal we intend to increase the level of compensation for all artists involved with the theatre; to establish a second performance space of considerable flexibility to facilitate the production of new work by both emerging and established playwrights; to vigorously encourage new actors, directors

Portland Repertory Theater. Diana Van Fossen, Mark Allen, Tobias Andersen and Euan McLeod in *Shadowlands*. Photo: Owen Carey.

and designers; and to promote exchanges of work with other companies—locally, nationally and internationally. In reflecting the complexity of our existence, theatre can be a wondrous celebration of humanity. From the first words produced by the playwright to each and every performance, we believe there should be evolution—continual flux and movement brought about by the presence of an ever-changing group of people we call our audience.

—*Geoffrey Sherman*

PRODUCTIONS 1991-1992

Direction by Geoffrey Sherman, sets by Jim Weisman, lighting by Gary E. Cotter and costumes by Terri Lewis unless otherwise noted.

Speed-the-Plow, David Mamet; (D) John Daines
The Explorators Club, W.F. Schmidt
The Price, Arthur Miller; (D) Pat Patton; (S) Susan Taylor
Lettice and Lovage, Peter Shaffer; (S) Gary E. Cotter
Unchanging Love, adapt: Romulus Linney, from Anton Chekhov; (D) Allen Nause
Lend Me a Tenor, Ken Ludwig

PRODUCTIONS 1992-1993

Direction by Geoffrey Sherman, sets and lighting by Jim Weisman, costumes by Terri Lewis and sound design by Drew Flint unless otherwise noted.

The Substance of Fire, Jon Robin Baitz
Shadowlands, William Nicholson; (S) and (L) Paul Wonsek
Hay Fever, Noel Coward; (D) Jon Dretzu; (S) Susan Taylor
Henceforward, Alan Ayckbourn; (D) Jeff Steitzer; (L) Drew Flint
No Way to Treat a Lady, book adapt, music and lyrics: Douglas J. Cohen, from William Goldman; (S) Peter Rossing; (L) Drew Flint; (MD) Karl Mansfield; (CH) Jeanette Harris
The Piano Lesson, August Wilson; (D) Debra Wicks; (S) and (L) Paul Wonsek
A Christmas Carol, adapt: Geoffrey Sherman, from Charles Dickens; (L) Drew Flint
Paul Robeson, Phillip Hayes Dean; (D) Phillip Hayes Dean; (S) Polly Allen Robbins; (L) Jeff Forbes

Portland Stage Company

GREG LEAMING
Artistic Director

WILLIAM CHANCE
Managing Director

PEGGY SIEGLE
Board President

Box 1458
Portland, ME 04104
(207) 774-1043 (bus.)
(207) 774-0465 (b.o.)
(207) 774-0576 (fax)

FOUNDED 1974
Ted Davis

SEASON
Oct.-May

FACILITIES
Portland Performing Arts Center
Seating Capacity: 290
Stage: proscenium

FINANCES
June 1, 1992-May 31, 1993
Expenses: $1,004,672

CONTRACTS
AEA LORT (D)

Portland Stage Company is dedicated to the cultivation of wonder in the theatrical arts through a process of engagement, entertainment and education. Our community is both the immediate geographical community of Portland, Maine and the larger, more elusive national theatre community. We address the most important concerns and beliefs of the community, and do so with the highest level of artistry and theatrical imagination. We provide a home for artists by surrounding them with a supportive atmosphere in which experimentation and invigorating exploration are not only made possible but strongly encouraged. We work to meet the needs of our community by engaging it in a lively discussion of immediate concerns. Our productions engage the audience with humor, with inventive forms, with clear and intelligent discussion. Our educational programs pinpoint and meet the needs of both teachers and students. Our outreach and humanities programs provide a forum for further investigation of ideas and concerns. Our goal is to inject the much needed element of surprise into the culture of Portland, of Maine and of our national theatre community.

—*Greg Leaming*

Note: During the 1991-92 season, Richard Hamburger served as artistic director.

Portland Stage Company. Mark Arnold and John Greisemer in *The Mandrake*. Photo: David A. Rodgers.

PRODUCTIONS 1991-1992

Lighting by Christopher Akerlind unless otherwise noted.

Goblin Market, book adapt and lyrics: Polly Pen and Peggy Harmon, from Christina Rossetti; music: Polly Pen; (D) Evan Yionoulis; (S) G.W. Mercier; (L) Scott Zielinski; (C) Teresa Snider-Stein; (MD) Dan Sticco
My Children! My Africa!, Athol Fugard; (D) John Pynchon Holms; (S) Debra Booth; (L) Steven L. Shelley; (C) Susan Brown
The Mandrake, Niccolo Machiavelli; trans and adapt: Wallace Shawn; (D) Richard Hamburger; (S) Anita Stewart; (C) Martha Hally
Fool for Love, Sam Shepard; (D) Rob Greenberg; (S) Russell Parkman; (C) Anita Stewart
The Substance of Fire, Jon Robin Baitz; (D) Richard Hamburger; (S) Anita Stewart; (C) Donna M. Kress; (SD) David Budries

A Little Festival of the Unexpected:
various playwrights, various directors

PRODUCTIONS 1992-1993

On the Verge, Eric Overmyer; (D) Greg Leaming; (S) Rob Odorisio; (L) Mimi Jordan Sherin; (C) Candice Cain; (SD) Rob Gorton
Holiday Memories, adapt: Russell Vandenbroucke, from Truman Capote; (D) Tom Prewitt; (S) and (C) Anita Stewart; (L) Christopher Akerlind; (SD) Erich Stratmann
Hedda Gabler, Henrik Ibsen; trans: Gerry Bamman and Irene B. Berman; (D) Roberta

126 PORTLAND STAGE COMPANY

Levitow; (S) Rosario Provenza; (L) Robert Wierzel; (C) Tom Broecker; (SD) Mitchell Greenhill

The Baltimore Waltz, Paula Vogel; (D) Greg Leaming; (S) Debra Booth; (L) Dan Kotlowitz; (C) Susan Picinich; (SD) James van Bergen

The Mystery of Irma Vep, Charles Ludlam; (D) Davis Hall; (S) Rob Odorisio; (L) Scott Zielinski; (C) Tom Broecker

Borders of Loyalty, Michael Henry Brown; (D) Marion Isaac McClinton; (S) James Noone; (L) Kenneth Posner; (C) Elsa Ward

A Little Festival of the Unexpected:
various playwrights, various directors

The Purple Rose Theatre Company. Elizabeth Keiser, Wayne David Parker and Marilyn Mays in *Necessities*. Photo: T. Newell Kring.

The Purple Rose Theatre Company

T. NEWELL KRING
Artistic Director

ALAN RIBANT
Managing Director

JEFF DANIELS
Executive Director/Board President

137 Park St.
Chelsea, MI 48118
(313) 475-5817 (bus.)
(313) 475-7902 (b.o.)

FOUNDED 1991
Jeff Daniels, Bartley H. Bauer, Doug Beaumont, T. Newell Kring

SEASON
Year-round

FACILITIES
Garage Theatre
Seating Capacity: 119
Stage: thrust

FINANCES
Sept. 1, 1992-Aug. 31, 1993
Expenses: $465,000

CONTRACTS
AEA SPT

Located in the small village of Chelsea, an hour's drive from both Detroit and Lansing, the Purple Rose Theatre Company is an experiment in what might be termed "second-wave" regional theatre—that is, the effort to extend the range of regional theatre beyond the city limits of urban America and into a rural setting. That an audience exists for such efforts is irrefutable: In the first two and a half years of operation, more than 42,000 patrons have visited our 119-seat thrust-stage theatre to see nine productions, seven of which have been unpublished original works. Therefore, as we look to the future, the Purple Rose Theatre Company will continue to serve two primary goals: to provide the region with its own resident professional theatre, and to seek out and enourage those plays and playwrights that speak to the distinct sensibilities of a mid-American audience.
—*T. Newell Kring*

PRODUCTIONS 1991-1992

Kuru, Josh C. Manheimer; (D) T. Newell Kring; (S) Bartley H. Bauer; (L) Dana White; (C) Joanne Johnson; (SD) Bill Lelbach
Ties That Bind, Kitty S. Dubin; (D) Julie Nessen; (S) and (C) Gaetane Bertol; (L) Victor En Yu Tan
More Fun Than Bowling, Steven Dietz; (D) John Seibert; (S) Bartley H. Bauer; (L) Peter Beudert; (C) Nancy Davis; (SD) David J. Kron
The Tropical Pickle, Jeff Daniels; (D) T. Newell Kring; (S) and (C) Greg Gillette; (L) Dana White

PRODUCTIONS 1992-1993

Possessed—The Dracula Musical, book adapt: Robert Marasco and Jason Darrow, from Bram Stoker; music: Carter Cathcart; lyrics: Jason Darrow; (D) Jim Posante; (S) T. Newell Kring; (L) Dana White; (C) Edith Leavis Bookstein; (MD) Steve DeDocs and James Christian Nissen
Necessities, Velina Hasu Houston; (D) Mary Bremer; (S) Bartley H. Bauer; (L) Victor En Yu Tan; (C) Nancy Davis
National Anthems, Dennis McIntyre; (D) T. Newell Kring; (S) Gary Decker; (L) Peter Beudert; (C) Jeanette DeJong
Nooner, Kim Carney; (D) Guy Sanville; (S) Bartley H. Bauer; (L) Daniel C. Walker; (C) Edith Leavis Bookstein

Remains Theatre

NEEL KELLER
Artistic Director

R.P. SEKON
Producing Director

GEORGIA FOGELSON
Board President

1800 North Clybourn Ave.
Chicago, IL 60614
(312) 335-9595 (bus.)
(312) 335-9800 (b.o.)
(312) 335-0620 (fax)

FOUNDED 1979
Jim Roach, Earl Pastko, David Alan Novak, D.W. Moffett, Lindsay McGee

SEASON
Variable

FACILITIES
Seating Capacity: 250
Stage: thrust

FINANCES
July 1, 1992-June 30, 1993
Expenses: $1,153,631

CONTRACTS
AEA CAT

Remains was founded by a group of die-hard Chicagoans and we remain a very Chicago place. We don't rehearse during Bulls or Bears games, we eat way too much pizza, and we draw on the city's raw energy to create our work. As we approach our 15th year, we are producing work that responds to life in Chicago, we are working with more diverse artists and attracting more diverse audiences. We are trying to spark conversa-

Remains Theatre. Gerry Becker and Christopher Donahue in *Laughter in the Dark*. Photo: Liz Lauren.

tions, question assumptions and bridge gaps. We hope to build a theatre that reflects our city. Next time you're in Chicago drop by for a drink at the bar, a game on the TV and a show in our space.
—Neel Keller

Note: During the 1991-92 and 1992-93 seasons, Larry Sloan served as artistic director.

PRODUCTIONS 1991-1992

The Chicago Conspiracy Trial, adapt: Ron Sossi and Frank Condon, from trial transcripts; (D) Frank Condon; (S) and (L) Kevin Snow; (C) Sraa Davidson; (SD) Michael Bodeen
The Actor Retires, Bruce Norris; (D) Mary Zimmerman
Mishuganismo, Susan Nussbaum; (D) Mike Nussbaum; (S) and (C) Sraa Davidson; (L) Richard Lundy; (SD) Christian Petersen
Laughter in the Dark, adapt: Mary Zimmerman, from Vladimir Nabokov; (D) Mary Zimmerman; (S) John Musial; (L) Kenneth Moore; (C) Sarah J. Holden; (SD) Michael Bodeen
I Want Someone to Eat Cheese With, Jeff Garlin; (D) Mick Napier; (C) Edith Head

PRODUCTIONS 1992-1993

Sound design by Christian Petersen unless otherwise noted.

Once In Doubt, Raymond J. Barry; (D) Raymond J. Barry; (S) and (L) Kevin Snow; (C) Laura Cunningham
Of Thee I Sing, book: George S. Kaufman and Morrie Ryskind; lyrics: Ira Gershwin; music: George Gershwin; (D) Larry Sloan; (S) Stephanie R. Gerckens; (L) Rita Pietraszek; (C) Frances Maggio; (MD) Jeff Lewis; (CH) Timothy O'Slynne
Rehearsal for the Apocalypse, Del Close and David Pasquesi; (D) Del Close and David Pasquesi
Snakebit, David Marshall Grant; (D) Campbell Scott; (S) Jeff Bauer; (L) Kevin Snow; (C) Laura Cunningham
The Day Room, Don DeLillo; (D) Neel Keller; (S) and (L) Michael S. Philippi; (C) Frances Maggio; (SD) Richard Woodbury

Repertorio Español

RENE BUCH
Artistic Director

GILBERTO ZALDIVAR
Producer

138 East 27th St.
New York, NY 10016
(212) 889-2850
(212) 686-3732 (fax)

FOUNDED 1968
Gilberto Zaldivar, Rene Buch

SEASON
Year-round

FACILITIES
Gramercy Arts Theatre
Seating Capacity: 140
Stage: proscenium

FINANCES
Sept. 1, 1992-Aug. 31, 1993
Expenses: $1,500,000

The Repertorio Español has three components, all acclaimed for their artistic achievements and their service to the Hispanic community in the U.S. The dramatic ensemble is a true repertory company presenting more than 12 productions a year, from the classics of Spain's Golden Age to the great 20th-century plays of Latin America and Spain, and new plays by emerging Hispanic-American playwrights. The musical company, since 1981, has introduced zarzuelas and Spanish operettas, as well as anthologies of music from Mexico, Puerto Rico, Spain and Cuba. Dance is represented by Pilar Rioja, the Spanish dancer, who has been an invited artist since 1973. The company gives year-round performances at the historic Gramercy Arts Theatre and performs on tour throughout the U.S. Its services for students are acclaimed as some of the most effective by the New York City Cultural Affairs commissioner. Recent highlights include the inauguration of an infrared simulcast system offering audiences English translations, and a series of productions directed by three of Latin America's most respected and innovative directors.
—Rene Buch

PRODUCTIONS 1991-1992

Direction by Rene Buch and sets, lighting and costumes by Robert Weber Federico unless otherwise noted.

La Candida Erendira, adapt: Jorge Ali Triana and Carlos Jose Reyes, from Gabriel Garcia Marquez; trans: Rene Buch and Felipe Gorostiza; (D) Jorge Ali Triana; (S) Lilliana Villegas; (C) Rosario Lozano; (SD) German Arrieta
El Carbon que ha Sido Brasa, J. Sanchez del Rio
Esperando la Carroza, Jacobo Langsner; (D) Braulio Villar
Botanica, Dolores Prida; (D) Manuel Martin, Jr.; (S) Randy Barcelo
El Alcalde de Zalamea, Pedro Calderon de la Barca; trans: Adrian Mitchell
La Casa de Bernarda Alba, Federico Garcia Lorca

Repertorio Español. Alexia Murray, Ofelia Gonzalez and Juan Carlos Mallo in *La Candida Erendira*. Photo: Gerry Goodstein.

La Nonna, Roberto Cossa; trans: Raul Moncada; (D) Braulio Villar
Cafe con Leche, Gloria Gonzalez
Luisa Fernanda, book and lyrics: Federico Moreno Toroba and Guillermo Fernandez Shaw; music: Federico Moreno Torroba; (MD) Pablo Zinger; (CH) Adolfo Vazquez
Los Jibaros Progresistas, book: Ramon Mendez Quinones; music and lyrics: Manuel B. Gonzales; (MD) Pablo Zinger
Mexico Romantico, various composers and lyricists; (MD) Pablo Zinger; (CH) Adolfo Vazquez
Puerto Rico: Encanto y Cancion, various composers and lyricists; (MD) Pablo Zinger; (CH) Adolfo Vazquez
Habana: Antologia Musical, various composers and lyricists; (MD) Pablo Zinger; (CH) Adolfo Vazquez
Nova Velha Estoria, adapt: Antunes Filho, from Charles Perrault; (D) Antunes Filho; (S) and (C) J.C. Serroni; (L) Davi de Brito; (SD) Raul Teixeira
Pension para Senoritas, Soraya Maria; (D) and (C) Soraya Maria

PRODUCTIONS 1992-1993

Direction by Rene Buch and sets, lighting and costumes by Robert Weber Federico unless otherwise noted.

Bodas de Sangre, Federico Garcia Lorca; trans: Felipe Gorostiza; (SD) Nicolas Uribe
La Candida Erendira, adapt: Jorge Ali Triana and Carlos Jose Reyes, from Gabriel Garcia Marquez; trans: Rene Buch and Felipe Gorostiza; (D) Jorge Ali Triana, (S), (L) and (C) Lilliana Villegas; (SD) German Arrieta
El Carbon que ha Sido Brasa, J. Sanchez del Rio
Botanica, Dolores Prida; (D) Manuel Martin, Jr.; (S) and (C) Randy Barcelo
Esperando la Carroza, Jacobo Langsner; (D) Braulio Villar
La Casa de Bernarda Alba, Federico Garcia Lorca
La Nonna, Roberto Cossa; trans: Raul Moncada; (D) Braulio Villar
Cafe con Leche, Gloria Gonzalez
El Eclipse, Carlos Olmos; (SD) Nicolas Uribe
Los Jibaros Progresistas, book: Ramon Mendez Quinones; music and lyrics: Manuel B. Gonzales; (MD) Pablo Zinger
Mexico Romantico, various composers and lyricists; (MD) Pablo Zinger; (CH) Adolfo Vazquez
Puerto Rico: Encanto y Cancion, various composers and lyricists; (MD) Pablo Zinger; (CH) Adolfo Vazquez
Noche Antillana, various composers and lyricists; (MD) Pablo Zinger; (CH) Adolfo Vazquez
Yo Me Bajo en la Prozima. Y Usted?, Adolfo Marsillach; adapt: Braulio Villar; (D) Braulio Villar

The Repertory Theatre of St. Louis

STEVEN WOOLF
Artistic Director

MARK D. BERNSTEIN
Managing Director

RICHARD A. LIDDY
Board President

Box 191730
St. Louis, MO 63119
(314) 968-7340 (bus.)
(314) 968-4925 (b.o.)
(314) 968-9638 (fax)

FOUNDED 1966
Webster College

SEASON
Sept.-Apr.

FACILITIES
Mainstage
Seating Capacity: 733
Stage: thrust

Studio
Seating Capacity: 125
Stage: flexible

Lab Space
Seating Capacity: 75
Stage: flexible

FINANCES
June 1, 1992-May 31, 1993
Expenses: $4,175,000

CONTRACTS
AEA LORT (C) and (D), and TYA

A partnership with community, audiences, artists, technicians and administrators that started 27 years ago and keeps strengthening and evolving makes the Repertory Theatre of St. Louis an integral part of the artistic life of this region. An eclectic mix of styles creates a widely varied season: mainstage selections offer work from many sources, giving a wide view of theatre literature to our largest audience; our Studio Theatre explores the new, the old seen in new ways, poetry, music and sometimes season-long themes; the Imaginary Theatre Company, our touring component, plays throughout Missouri and surrounding states, using literature and specially comissioned scripts as its basis for introducing theatre to younger audiences; the Lab series focuses on playwrights, giving them a full rehearsal period and a professional cast and director to work on a new script. Through these activities and others, the Rep seeks to develop audiences who become strong advocates for live performance.

—*Steven Woolf*

PRODUCTIONS 1991-1992

Cyrano, Edmond Rostand; trans: Brian Hooker; (D) Martin L. Platt; (S) David Crank; (L) Peter E. Sargent; (C) Alan Armstrong
Other People's Money, Jerry Sterner; (D) Steven Woolf; (S) Carolyn L. Ross; (L) Max De Volder; (C) Holly Poe Durbin;
The 1940's Radio Hour, book: Walton Jones; various composers and lyricists; (D) John Going; (S) John Roslevich, Jr.; (L) Peter E. Sargent; (C) Dorothy L. Marshall; (MD) Byron Grant; (CH) Rob Marshall
Miss Evers' Boys, David Feldshuh; (D) Libby Appel; (S) Joel Fontaine; (L) Robert Peterson; (C) Arthur Ridley
A View from the Bridge, Arthur Miller; (D) Edward Stern; (S) John Jensen; (L) Robert Murphy; (C) Dorothy L. Marshall; (SD) Tom Mardikes
Almost September, conceived: David Schechter; book and lyrics: David Schechter and Steven Lutvak; music: Steven Lutvak; (D) David Schechter; (S) John Ezell; (L) Max De Volder; (C) John Carver Sullivan
Okiboji, Conrad Bishop and Elizabeth Fuller; (D) Susan Gregg; (S) and (C) Arthur Ridley; (L) Mark P. Wilson
The Swan, Elizabeth Egloff; (D) Susan Gregg; (S) and (L) Dale F. Jordan; (C) John Carver Sullivan
March of the Falsettos, book, music and lyrics: William Finn; and *Falsettoland*, book: William Finn and James Lapine; music and lyrics: William Finn; (D) and (CH) Pamela Hunt; (S) Daniel Robinson; (L) Peter E. Sargent; (C) J. Bruce Summers; (MD) Larry Pressgrove
Rikki Tikki Tavi, adapt: Lynne Alvarez, from Rudyard Kipling; (D) Jeffrey Matthews; (S) Nicholas Kryah; (C) J. Bruce Summers
The Nutcracker and the Mouse King, adapt: Jahnna Beecham and Malcolm Hillgartner, from E.T.A. Hoffman; (D) Tom Martin; (S) Derek Stenborg; (C) Holly Poe Durbin

The Repertory Theatre of St. Louis. Doan Jaroenngarm, Song Liling, Fan Yi-Song and Sawako Tamishige in *M. Butterfly*. Photo: Judy Andrews.

A Thousand Cranes, Kathryn Schultz Miller; (D) Jeffrey Matthews; (S) Nicholas Kryah; (C) Holly Poe Durbin

The Travelling Jekyll and Hyde Show, adapt: Russell Davis, from Robert Louis Stevenson; (D) Jeffrey Matthews; (S) Nicholas Kryah; (C) Carole Tucker

Savages, book: John B. Justice; music and lyrics: Tommy Thompson; (D) Susan Gregg

PRODUCTIONS 1992-1993

M. Butterfly, David Henry Hwang; (D) Edward Stern; (S) and (C) Marie Anne Chiment; (L) Peter E. Sargent

Dracula, adapt: Charles Morey, from Bram Stoker; (D) Charles Morey; (S) Peter Harrison; (L) Max De Volder; (C) John Carver Sullivan

A Funny Thing Happened on the Way to the Forum, book: Burt Shevelove and Larry Gelbart; music and lyrics: Stephen Sondheim; (D) and (CH) Pamela Hunt; (S) John Roslevich, Jr.; (L) Peter E. Sargent; (C) Dorothy L. Marshall

Six Degrees of Separation, John Guare; (D) Steven Woolf; (S) Carolyn L. Ross; (L) Max De Volder; (C) Dorothy L. Marshall

Woman in Mind, Alan Ayckbourn; (D) Susan Gregg; (S) John Ezell; (L) Dale F. Jordan; (C) Alan Armstrong

Pygmalion, George Bernard Shaw; (D) John Going; (S) Joel Fontaine; (L) Allen Lee Hughes; (C) Jeffrey Struckman

Show and Tell, Anthony Clarvoe; (D) Susan Gregg; (S) and (L) Max De Volder; (C) J. Bruce Summers; (SD) Stephen Burns Kessler

The Mystery of Irma Vep, Charles Ludlam; (D) Tom Martin; (S) William F. Schmiel; (L) Glenn Dunn; (C) J. Bruce Summers

Sight Unseen, Donald Margulies; (D) Steven Woolf; (S) and (C) Michael Ganio; (L) John Wylie

Rats!! The Pied Piper of Hamlin, adapt: Lynne Alvarez; (D) Jeffrey Matthews; (S) Nicholas Kryah; (C) J. Bruce Summers

The Voyage of the Red Hat, adapt: Constance Congdon, from a Celtic folktale; (D) Tom Martin; (S) and (C) Devon Painter

Fire or Ice, Jahnna Beecham and Malcolm Hillgartner; (D) Jahnna Beecham and Malcolm Hillgartner; (S) Bruce Bergner; (C) Louis Bird

Young Rube, book adapt: John Pielmeier, from George W. George; music and lyrics: Matthew Selman; (D) Susan Gregg; (MD) Larry Pressgrove

Riverside Theatre

ALLEN D. CORNELL
Artistic Director

LYNN T. POTTER
Executive Director

JUDITH BALPH
Board President

Box 3788
Vero Beach, FL 32964
(407) 231-5860 (bus.)
(407) 231-6990 (b.o.)
(407) 234-5298 (fax)

FOUNDED 1985
Vero Beach Community Theatre Trust

SEASON
Oct.-May

FACILITIES
Seating Capacity: 633
Stage: proscenium

FINANCES
June 1, 1992-May 31, 1993
Expenses: $1,200,000

CONTRACTS
AEA letter of agreement

Our theatre exists because its community has been involved since day one of its existence. We are a reflection of this unique Floridian place, this time, this society. Our artists are very much like the professional guides who venture forth on the river here to expose the uninitiated to the profundity of ultramarine shadows along mangrove-lined shores. They are the navigators who bridge the inlet between the art of nature and the nature of art. Our place is called the Treasure Coast. Gold escudos are found on these shores. We believe theatre, too, is like a prodigious strongbox and that we as artists hold the key to the bounty within. The programs we produce are an eclectic mixture of the past and present. They are designed to reaffirm the commitment of the initiated and enlist the uninitiated. We are fortunate to live and work in an extraordinarily beautiful place. Our theatre is a celebration of this good fortune.

—*Allen D. Cornell*

PRODUCTIONS 1991-1992

Sets and lighting by Allen D. Cornell unless otherwise noted.

Harvey, Mary Chase; (D) Peter Bennett; (C) Chris Carpenter

The Boys Next Door, Tom Griffin; (D) Mary G. Guaraldi; (C) Chris Carpenter and Michele Siler; (SD) Pamela Emerson

Rodgers & Hart, book: Richard Lewine and John Fearnley; music: Richard Rodgers; lyrics: Lorenz Hart; (D) and (CH) Steven Smeltzer; (C) Chris Carpenter; (MD) Brian Spitler

South Pacific, book adapt: Oscar Hammerstein, II and Joshua Logan, from James A. Michener; music: Richard Rodgers; lyrics: Oscar Hammerstein, II; (D) and (CH) Katrina Ploof; (C) Steven Crouse; (MD) Brian Spitler

Cotton Patch Gospel, book adapt: Tom Key and Russell Treyz, from Clarence Jordan; music and lyrics: Harry Chapin; (D) Cathey Crowell Sawyer; (C) Jennie L. Davis; (MD) Roland Kausen; (SD) Michael Hamlin

The Belle of Amherst, William Luce; (D) Allen D. Cornell

Riverside Theatre. Jeff Herbst and Gordon Reinhart in *Billy Bishop Goes to War*. Photo: Egan Rasmusson.

PRODUCTIONS 1992-1993

Oil City Symphony, Mike Craver, Mark Hardwick, Debra Monk and Mary Murfitt; (D) Mike Craver and Mark Hardwick; (C) Gordon DeVinney, Mike Craver and Mark Hardwick; (SD) Michael Gerbhardt

Oliver, book adapt, music and lyrics: Lionel Bart, from Charles Dickens; (D) and (CH) Katrina Ploof; (C) Suzette Bridges; (MD) Brian Spitler; (SD) Michael Gerbhardt

Lend Me a Tenor, Ken Ludwig; (D) Peter Bennett; (S) Gary English; (C) Suzette Bridges; (SD) Gary Barie

Camelot, book adapt and lyrics: Alan Jay Lerner, from T.H. White; music: Frederick Loewe; (D) Allen D. Cornell; (C) Suzette Bridges; (MD) Brian Spitler; (CH) Katrina Ploof; (SD) Gary Barie

Billy Bishop Goes to War, John Gray and Eric Peterson; (D) Mary G. Guaraldi; (S) and (L) Robert Murphy; (C) Susie Brooks; (SD) Gary Barie

Stardust, book: Albert Harris; lyrics: Mitchell Parish; music: various composers; (D) and (CH) Donald Brenner; (C) Michelle Meade; (MD) Brian Spitler; (SD) Tom Davis

THE ROAD COMPANY

The Road Company. Catina Lowery and Paula Larke in *Bite the String Snake*. Photo: Paul Gobble.

The Road Company

**ROBERT H. LEONARD,
CHRISTINE MURDOCK,
EUGENE WOLF**
Co-Artistic Directors

JAN HEARNE
General Manager

CHARLES MONTFORD
Board President

Box 5278 EKS
Johnson City, TN 37603
(615) 926-7726

FOUNDED 1975
Robert H. Leonard

SEASON
Sept.-June

FACILITIES
Beeson Hall
Seating Capacity: 150
Stage: flexible

FINANCES
July 1, 1992-June 30, 1993
Expenses: $130,000

We believe theatre is a community event. The Road Company is a working environment for artists who want to apply their skills to the investigation and expression of our community in upper east Tennessee. The ensemble works on the premise that theatre is a compact between the artists and the audience—artistically and organizationally. The successful theatre event happens when the audience joins the imagination of the production during performance. This belief assumes the enjoyment of theatre is active not passive. It also assumes a long-term relationship between the ensemble and the community. These concepts do not define or restrict subject matter, form or style. These are matters of constant investigation. What subjects are actually of concern? To whom? What style or form is effective within the framework of content and audience aesthetic? These issues and the artistic growth of the ensemble constitute the basis of our dramaturgy. We tour our own works to communities all over Tennessee and the nation.
—*Robert H. Leonard, Christine Murdock, Eugene Wolf*

Note: During the 1991-92 and 1992-93 seasons, Robert H. Leonard served as artistic director.

PRODUCTIONS 1991-1992

A Holiday Evening With Friends, company-developed and directed; (SD) Phil Leonard
Ghosts, Henrik Ibsen; trans: Nicholas Rudall; (D) Shawn Gulyas; (S) Andrew Myers; (L) Harold J. Hunter; (C) Tonja Peterson; (SD) Phil Leonard
Bite the String Snake, conceived: Barbara Carlisle, company-developed; music: Paula Larke, Michael Urich, Ed Snodderly and Mapopa Mtonga; (D) Robert H. Leonard; (S) Randy Ward; (L) Beate M. Czogalla; (C) Charlotte Aiken; (CH) Ann Kilkelly; (SD) David Wedin
Echoes & Postcards, company-developed and designed; (D) Robert H. Leonard

PRODUCTIONS 1992-1993

Echoes & Postcards, company-developed and designed; (D) Robert H. Leonard
The Fever, Wallace Shawn; (D) Robert H. Leonard
The Bear Facts, Jo Carson; (D) and (L) Robert H. Leonard; (C) Linda Benemann
Bite the String Snake, conceived: Barbara Carlisle, company-developed; music: Paula Larke, Michael Urich, Ed Snodderly and Mapopa Mtonga; (D) Robert H. Leonard; (S) Randy Ward; (L) Beate M. Czogalla; (C) Charlotte Aiken; (CH) Ann Kilkelly; (SD) David Wedin

Roadside Theater

DUDLEY COCKE
Director

DONNA PORTERFIELD
Administrative Director

DEE DAVIS
Board Chair

306 Madison St.
Whitesburg, KY 41858
(606) 633-0108
(606) 633-1009 (fax)

FOUNDED 1974
Appalshop, Inc.

SEASON
Year-round

FACILITIES
Appalshop Theater
Seating Capacity: 175
Stage: thrust

FINANCES
Oct. 1, 1991-Sept. 30, 1992
Expenses: $418,000

Roadside is an ensemble of actors, musicians, designers, writers, directors and managers, most of whom grew up in the Appalachian mountains. Appalachia is the subject of the theatre's original plays, and the company has developed its theatrical style from its local heritage of storytelling, mountain music and oral history. In making indigenous theatre and creating a body of native dramatic literature, Roadside sees itself as continuing its region's cultural

Roadside Theater. Kim Cole, Tommy Bledsoe and Rema Keen in *Pretty Polly*. Photo: Jeff Whetstone.

tradition. Roadside's hometown has 1,200 people; coal mining is the main occupation. The theatre tours nationally year-round, often performing for rural and working-class audiences, and conducting residencies that examine and celebrate local life. Roadside is an integral part of the multimedia organization Appalshop, which also produces work about Appalachia through the media of film, television, radio, photography, music and sound recording, and visual art.

—*Dudley Cocke*

PRODUCTIONS 1991-1992

Mountain Tales and Music, company-developed and directed; various composers and lyricists; (L) and (SD) Ben Mays; (MD) Tommy Bledsoe

Red Fox and Second Hangin', Don Baker and Ron Short; (D) Don Baker and Dudley Cocke; (L) Don Baker

South of the Mountain, book, music and lyrics: Ron Short; (D) Dudley Cocke and Ron Short; (L) and (MD) Ron Short; (SD) Ben Mays

Pretty Polly, Don Baker and Ron Short; (D) Dudley Cocke and Ron Short; (L) Ben Mays

Leaving Egypt, Ron Short; (D) Dudley Cocke; (L) Ron Short

Junebug Jack, company-developed; music and lyrics: Michael Keck and Ron Short; (D) Dudley Cocke and Steven Kent; (MD) Michael Keck and Ron Short; (L) and (SD) Ben Mays

PRODUCTIONS 1992-1993

Mountain Tales and Music, company-developed and directed; various composers and lyricists; (L) and (SD) Ben Mays; (MD) Tommy Bledsoe

South of the Mountain, book, music and lyrics: Ron Short; (D) Dudley Cocke and Ron Short; (L) and (MD) Ron Short; (SD) Ben Mays

Pretty Polly, Don Baker and Ron Short; (D) Dudley Cocke and Ron Short; (L) Ben Mays

Leaving Egypt, Ron Short; (D) Dudley Cocke; (L) Ron Short

Junebug Jack, company-developed; music and lyrics: Michael Keck and Ron Short; (D) Dudley Cocke and Steven Kent; (MD) Michael Keck and Ron Short; (L) and (SD) Ben Mays

Roundabout Theatre Company

TODD HAIMES
Artistic Director

ELLEN RICHARD
General Manager

CHRISTIAN C. YEGEN, JR.
Board Chairman

1530 Broadway
New York, NY 10036
(212) 719-9393 (bus.)
(212) 869-8400 (b.o.)
(212) 869-8817 (fax)

FOUNDED 1965
Gene Feist, Elizabeth Owens

SEASON
Oct.-Sept.

FACILITIES
Criterion Center Theatre
Seating Capacity: 499
Stage: thrust

Susan Bloch Theatre
Seating Capacity: 152
Stage: arena

FINANCES
Sept. 1, 1992-Aug. 31, 1993
Expenses: $5,175,000

CONTRACTS
AEA LORT (B)

Now celebrating its 27th year and its second season in its new home at the Criterion Center theatre in the heart of Broadway, Roundabout Theatre Company remains dedicated to producing the highest quality revivals of classic theatre. Our mission is to explore established works in an effort to introduce and reintroduce these masterpieces from our theatrical heritage to a present-day audience; to establish and cultivate relationships with the great artists of our time; to nurture the talents of the next generation of great artists; and to develop a theatre-going audience for the future. Roundabout continues its commitment to assuring that classic theatre is accessible to and appreciated by a diverse audience through its innovative audience development program and its arts education program. Through these efforts, Roundabout ensures that classic theatre remains a vital part of New York's cultural life.

—*Todd Haimes*

PRODUCTIONS 1991-1992

Sound design by Douglas J. Cuomo unless otherwise noted.

The Homecoming, Harold Pinter; (D) Gordon Edelstein; (S) John Arnone; (L) Peter Kaczorowski; (C) William Ivey Long; (SD) Philip Campanella

The Visit, Friedrich Durrenmatt; trans: Maurice Valency; (D) Edwin Sherin; (S) Thomas Lynch; (L) Roger Morgan; (C) Frank Krenz

Hamlet, William Shakespeare; (D) Paul Weidner; (S) Christopher Barreca; (L) Natasha Katz; (C) Martin Pakledinaz

The Price, Arthur Miller; (D) John Tillinger; (S) John Lee Beatty; (L) Dennis Parichy; (C) Jane Greenwood

The Real Inspector Hound and *The Fifteen Minute Hamlet*, Tom Stoppard; (D) Gloria Muzio; (S) John Lee Beatty; (L) Pat Collins; (C) Jess Goldstein

Roundabout Theatre Company. Natasha Richardson and Liam Neeson in *Anna Christie*. Photo: Carol Rosegg/Martha Swope Associates.

PRODUCTIONS 1992-1993

Lighting by Peter Kaczorowski and sound design by Douglas J. Cuomo unless otherwise noted.

The Show-off, George Kelly; (D) Brian Murray; (S) Ben Edwards; (C) David Charles

Anna Christie, Eugene O'Neill; (D) David Leveaux; (S) John Lee Beatty; (L) Marc B. Weiss; (C) Martin Pakledinaz

Candida, George Bernard Shaw; (D) Gloria Muzio; (S) David Jenkins; (C) Jess Goldstein

She Loves Me, book adapt: Joe Masteroff, from Miklos Laszlo; music: Jerry Bock; lyrics: Sheldon Harnick; (D) Scott Ellis; (S) Tony Walton; (C) David Charles and Jane Greenwood; (MD) David Loud; (CH) Rob Marshall; (SD) Tony Meola

Black Comedy and *White Liars*, Peter Shaffer; (D) Gerald Gutierrez; (S) John Lee Beatty; (L) Craig Miller; (C) Jess Goldstein

Round House Theatre. Sarah Marshall and Marty Lodge in *Elektra*. Photo: Geri Olson.

Round House Theatre

JERRY WHIDDON
Producing Artistic Director

KATHA KISSMAN
Managing Director

JEFFREY B. DAVIS
Board President

12210 Bushey Drive
Silver Spring, MD 20902
(301) 217-6770 (bus.)
(301) 217-3300 (b.o.)
(301) 217-6819 (fax)

FOUNDED 1978
June Allen, Montgomery County Department of Recreation

SEASON
Sept.-June

FACILITIES
Seating Capacity: 218
Stage: thrust

FINANCES
July 1, 1991-June 30, 1992
Expenses: $992,913

CONTRACTS
AEA SPT

In an increasingly urbanized world, we constantly yearn for ways to nurture a sense of community, for when we feel truly part of the "tribe," we are more confident that issues will be addressed and solutions found, and then celebrations can be truly joyous. Theatre can be a powerful agent of community bonding when audiences are willing to share the adventure of new voices and new ways of looking at ourselves. Theatre imbues us with purpose. We welcome the commitment to making our art accessible through classes, through performances in schools and through our mainstage productions. It is through all these programs that we at the Round House reacquaint ourselves with the actor's impulse. Why theatre is "needed" becomes simply and wonderfully obvious. That joy comes full circle in the darkened room where a member of the tribe tells a story.

—*Jerry Whiddon*

PRODUCTIONS 1991-1992

Sets by Joseph B. Musumeci, Jr., costumes by Rosemary Pardee and sound design by Neil McFadden unless otherwise noted.

Willie and Esther, James Graham Bronson; (D) Jennifer Nelson; (L) Prince No-Ra
Apocalyptic Butterflies, Wendy MacLeod; (D) Gillian Drake; (S) James Kronzer; (L) Joseph B. Musumeci, Jr.
Elektra, Sophocles; trans and adapt: Ezra Pound and Rudd Fleming; (D) Tom Prewitt; (L) Neil McFadden; (SD) Dan Schrader
Tintypes, Mary Kyte, Mel Marvin and Gary Pearle; various composers and lyricists; (D) Mary Hall Surface; (S) Thomas F. Donahue; (L) Christopher Townsend; (MD) George Fulginiti-Shakar; (CH) Karma Camp; (SD) Dan Schrader
A Day in the Death of Joe Egg, Peter Nichols; (D) Laurence Maslon; (L) Dan Schrader

PRODUCTIONS 1992-1993

Sets by Joseph B. Musumeci, Jr., costumes by Rosemary Pardee and sound design by Neil McFadden unless otherwise noted.

Pentecost, Stewart Parker; (D) Kevin Kinley; (L) Joseph B. Musumeci, Jr.; (SD) Dan Schrader
Sand Mountain, Romulus Linney; (D) Edward Morgan; (S) Elizabeth Jenkins; (L) Neil McFadden
Antigone, Jean Anouilh; trans: Lewis Galantiere; adapt: Laurence Maslon; (D) Laurence Maslon; (L) Dan Schrader
Daytrips, Jo Carson; (D) Gillian Drake; (S) Elizabeth Jenkins; (L) Dan Schrader and Joseph B. Musumeci, Jr.
The Art of Waiting, Rob Shinn; (D) Tom Prewitt; (S) Elizabeth Jenkins; (L) Dan Schrader and Joseph B. Musumeci, Jr.
Criminals in Love, George F. Walker; (D) Jeff Davis; (S) James Kronzer; (L) Neil McFadden; (SD) Dan Schrader

Sacramento Theatre Company

MARK CUDDY
Artistic Director

DAVID M. HAGAR
Managing Director

BARRY KOHN
Board President

1419 H St.
Sacramento, CA 95814
(916) 446-7501 (bus.)
(916) 443-6722 (b.o.)
(916) 446-4066 (fax)

FOUNDED 1942
Eleanor McClatchy

SEASON
Sept.-May

FACILITIES
Mainstage
Seating Capacity: 301
Stage: proscenium

Stage Two
Seating Capacity: 86
Stage: flexible

FINANCES
July 1, 1992-June 30, 1993
Expenses: $1,251,637

CONTRACTS
AEA LORT (D) and letter of agreement

Sacramento Theatre Company is the only professional resident

Sacramento Theatre Company. Elisabeth Nunziato and Joe Kane in *Speed-the-Plow*. Photo: Rudy Meyers.

theatre company in California's capital. This brings with it several responsibilities including: responding to the city's sociopolitical makeup, taking subscribers on journeys through their hearts and minds, and making contributions to the American theatre both artistically and administratively. We are building a trust with our audience that secures our future and allows them the ownership that they deserve. Our task is to select plays of dramatic stature and present them vividly, clearly and boldly, making demands of ourselves and our audience. We strive to create a cathartic experience which will enhance a sense of community within the theatre. The theatre can be a focal point for the exchange of ideas and emotions among members of a shared community. Above all, we want the Sacramento Theatre Company to be a sane place to work and an adventurous place to visit.

—*Mark Cuddy*

PRODUCTIONS 1991-1992

Direction by Mark Cuddy, lighting by Kathryn Burleson and sound design by David de Berry unless otherwise noted.

All My Sons, Arthur Miller; (S) Nicholas Dorr; (C) Patricia Polen
A Raisin in the Sun, Lorraine Hansberry; (D) Tim Ocel; (S) Eric Sinkkonen; (L) Maurice Vercoutere; (C) Phyllis Kress
How to Succeed in Business Without Really Trying, book: Abe Burrows, Jack Weinstock and Willie Gilbert; music and lyrics: Frank Loesser; (S) Barbara Mesney; (C) Carolyn Lancet; (MD) Charles Lucas; (CH) Sheri-Kurk Stockdale
Fifth of July, Lanford Wilson; (D) Tim Ocel; (S) Jeffrey Struckman; (C) B. Modern; (SD) Clay Wilcox
Latins Anonymous, Luisa Leschin, Armando Molina, Rick Najera and Diane Rodriguez; (D) Rick Najera; (S) Jeff Hunt; (L) Maurice Vercoutere; (C) Loren Tripp; (SD) Steve Wisely
At the Still Point, Jordon Roberts; (S) Nicholas Dorr; (L) Maurice Vercoutere; (C) Skipper Skeoch; (SD) Steve Wisely

PRODUCTIONS 1992-1993

Direction by Tim Ocel and lighting by Kathryn Burleson unless otherwise noted.

The Immigrant, Mark Harelik; (D) Mark Cuddy; (S) Mark Hopkins; (C) Carolyn Lancet
The Heidi Chronicles, Wendy Wasserstein; (D) Dennis Bigelow; (S) Jeffrey Struckman; (L) Maurice Vercoutere; (C) Debra Bruneaux; (SD) David de Berry
A Christmas Carol, adapt: Richard Hellesen, from Charles Dickens; (S) Ralph Fetterly; (C) Skipper Skeoch; (SD) David de Berry
Twelfth Night, William Shakespeare; (D) Mark Cuddy; (S) Eric Sinkkonen; (C) B. Modern; (SD) David de Berry
Electra, Sophocles; adapt: E.F. Watling; (S) Nicholas Dorr; (C) B. Modern
Speed-the-Plow, David Mamet; (D) Roberta Levitow; (S) Rosario Provenza; (C) Patricia Polen
The Glass Menagerie, Tennessee Williams; (S) Eric Sinkkonen; (L) Maurice Vercoutere; (C) Skipper Skeoch; (SD) Allen Branson and Rick Gott
Pain of the Macho, Rick Najera; (D) Rick Najera; (S) Matthew Berry; (L) Mark Hopkins; (C) Skipper Skeoch; (SD) Garrett Langston-Perkins

The Salt Lake Acting Company

EDWARD J. GRYSKA
Producing Artistic Director

VICTOR RICKMAN
Board President

168 West 500 N
Salt Lake City, UT 84103
(801) 363-0526 (bus.)
(801) 363-SLAC (b.o.)
(801) 363-8681 (fax)

FOUNDED 1970
Edward J. Gryska

SEASON
Year-round

FACILITIES
Seating Capacity: 150-220
Stage: thrust

FINANCES
Sept. 1, 1992-Aug. 31, 1993
Expenses: $535,130

The Salt Lake Acting Company presents a unique and innovative repertoire of plays, including world and regional premieres and award-winning contemporary plays. Since its inception, the company has supported new works and new playwrights, particularly Utah writers, and is proud to have delivered new works and new writers to the forefront of an international theatre community. The company is committed to producing theatre of the highest artistic integrity. It serves the needs of a responsive audience and continues to make a significant contribution to the world of professional theatre.

—*Edward J. Gryska*

PRODUCTIONS 1991-1992

Sets by Cory Dangerfield and lighting by Catherine L. Owens unless otherwise noted.

Nine, adapt: Mario Fratti, from Federico Fellini, et al; book: Arthur Kopit; music and lyrics: Maury Yeston; (D) Edward J. Gryska; (C) Steve Rasmussen and Carolyn Wood; (MD) Ron Van Woerden
K-Mille, Aden Ross; (D) Kenneth Washington; (L) Megan McCormick; (C) Keven Myhre; (SD) Vince Frates
The Lisbon Traviata, Terrence McNally; (D) Edward J. Gryska; (S) and (C) Keven Myhre; (L) Kiyono Oshiro; (SD) Reiner Peery
Abundance, Beth Henley; (D) James Morrison; (C) Steve Rasmussen; (SD) Michael Roth and Reiner Peery
Nunsense, book, music and lyrics: Dan Goggin; (D) Rafael Colon Castanera; (S) Marnie Sears; (C) Steve Rasmussen; (MD) Michael Johnson

PRODUCTIONS 1992-1993

Lighting by Catherine L. Owens unless otherwise noted.

God's Country, Steven Dietz; (D) Rick VanNoy; (S) and (C) Keven Myhre; (L) Nicholas Cavallaro; (SD) Richard Jewkes

The Salt Lake Acting Company. Toni Byrd and Laurie Johnson in *The Kathy & Mo Show: Parallel Lives*. Photo: Jess Allen.

133

Salt Lake Salt Lake, book, music and lyrics: Edward J. Gryska, Richard Jewkes and Ron Van Woerden; (D) Edward J. Gryska; (S) Cory Dangerfield; (C) Steve Rasmussen; (MD) Ron Van Woerden

The Kathy & Mo Show: Parallel Lives, Kathy Najimy and Mo Gaffney; (D) Ellen Graham; (S) John Wayne Cook; (C) Steve Rasmussen; (SD) Cris Paulsen

FF: The Brontes, Aden Ross; (D) Charles Lynn Frost; (S) Brian Jones; (C) Catherine Zublin; (SD) Richard Jewkes

Love Letters, A.R. Gurney, Jr.; (D) Edward J. Gryska; (S) Cory Dangerfield

Greater Tuna, Jaston Williams, Joe Sears and Ed Howard; (D) James Morrison; (S) Marnie Sears; (L) Gary Justesen; (C) Keven Myhre; (SD) Cris Paulsen

Oil City Symphony, Mike Craver, Mark Hardwick, Debra Monk and Mary Murfitt; (D) and (S) Richard Jewkes; (L) Wilton Koernig; (C) Christine Murdoch

San Diego Repertory Theatre

DOUGLAS JACOBS
Artistic Director

SAM WOODHOUSE
Producing Director

JEFFREY M. SHOHET
Board President

79 Horton Plaza
San Diego, CA 92101
(619) 231-3586 (bus.)
(619) 235-8025 (b.o.)
(619) 235-0939 (fax)

FOUNDED 1976
Sam Woodhouse, Douglas Jacobs

SEASON
Oct.-June

FACILITIES
Lyceum Stage
Seating Capacity: 570
Stage: modified thrust

Lyceum Space
Seating Capacity: 250
Stage: flexible

FINANCES
Jan. 1, 1992-Dec. 31, 1993
Expenses: $1,730,000

CONTRACTS
AEA letter of agreement

Based on the conviction that theatre continually reinvents itself through an ongoing blending of all the arts, the San Diego Repertory Theatre operates its two theatres as a multidisciplinary, multicultural arts complex. We produce our own season for nine months of the year; during the other three months we book, present or rent our theatre to other artists. Our eclectic programming is based on the belief that the arts should reflect the diversity of the world around and within us, and that the theatre is a uniquely appropriate place to explore the boundaries and borders of life and art. Our seasons emphasize contemporary plays, seldom-seen classics and revivals of well-known classics. We are committed to ensemble development, nontraditional casting and lifelong training for professionals; and to explorations of music, dance, visual arts and poetry, in order to expand and deepen the range of theatrical expression.

—Douglas Jacobs

PRODUCTIONS 1991-1992

I Ain't Yo' Uncle, book adapt and lyrics: Robert Alexander, from Harriet Beecher Stowe and George Aiken (co-produced by the San Francisco Mime Troupe); music: Elliot Kavee, Dred Scott, Dan Hart and Stephen C. Foster; (D) Daniel Chumley; (S) Alan Curreri; (L) Gregory R. Tate; (C) Kiko Shimosato; (MD) Elliot Kavee

A Tale of Two Cities, adapt: Everett Quinton, from Charles Dickens; (D) Sam Woodhouse; (S) and (C) Jack Taggart; (L) Diane Boomer; (SD) Lawrence Czoka

A Christmas Carol, adapt: Douglas Jacobs, from Charles Dickens; (D) Scott Feldsher; (S) Robert Brill; (L) Ashley York Kennedy; (C) Emmelle Holmes; (SD) Michael Roth

Abingdon Square (La Plaza Chica), Maria Irene Fornes; (D) Maria Irene Fornes; (S) Robert Brill; (L) Anne Militello; (C) Jack Taggart

Ruby's Bucket of Blood, book: Julie Hebert; music and lyrics: Mark Bingham; (D) Sam Woodhouse; (S) Jane LaMotte and Robert Brill; (L) Ashley York Kennedy and Diane Boomer; (C) Mary Larson; (SD) Mark Bingham and Jim Brooks; (MD) Mark Bingham

Mirandolina, Carlo Goldoni; adapt: Melissa Cooper; (D) Douglas Jacobs; (S) John Redman; (L) Diane Boomer; (C) Ingrid Helton; (SD) Michael Roth

The Women, Clare Boothe Luce; (D) Anne Bogart; (S) Victoria Petrovich; (L) Brenda Berry; (C) Catherine Meacham Hunt

PRODUCTIONS 1992-1993

Spunk, adapt: George C. Wolfe, from Zora Neale Hurston; music: Chic Street Man; (D) Thomas W. Jones, II; (S) Victoria Petrovich; (L) Ashley York Kennedy; (C) Mary Larson; (MD) Kevin Moore; (SD) Jeff Ladman

The Queen's Garden and *Obake!*, Brenda Wong Aoki; (D) Jael Weisman; (S) Steven La Ponsie; (L) Jose Lopez; (C) Dori Quan

A Christmas Carol—The Gospel According to Dickens, book adapt: Douglas Jacobs, from Charles Dickens; music and lyrics: Osayande Baruti; (D) Sam Woodhouse and Osayande Baruti; (S) Victoria Petrovich; (L) Brenda Berry; (C) Kay Peebles; (MD) Ricky Womack; (CH) Osayande Baruti; (SD) Mitch Grant

The Latins Anonymous Lifetime Achievement Awards, Cris Franco, Luisa Leschin, Armando Molina, Diane Rodriguez; (D) Jose Luis Valenzuela; (S) Steven La Ponsie and Gronk; (L) Jose Lopez; (C) Patssi Valdez; (SD) Mark Friedman

The Dybbuk, adapt: Golda Weman, from S. Ansky; (D) Todd Salovey; (S) Neil Patel; (L) Brenda Berry; (C) Mary Larson

Always...Patsy Cline, book: Ted Swindley; various composers and lyricists; (D) Ted Swindley; (L) Raymond Thompson, with KEONI; (C) Sherry Wilson; (MD) Vicki Eckard; (SD) Mitch Grant

Death and the Maiden (La Muerte y La Doncella), Ariel Dorfman; (D) Douglas Jacobs; (S) Jane LaMotte; (L) John Martin; (C) Judy Watson; (SD) Michael Roth

San Diego Repertory Theatre. Marco Rodriguez and Rose Portillo in *Death and the Maiden/La Muerte y la Doncella*. Photo: Ken Jacques.

San Jose Repertory Theatre. *Rumors*. Photo: Nicholas Crepea.

San Jose Repertory Theatre

TIMOTHY NEAR
Artistic Director

ALEXANDRA U. BOISVERT
Managing Director

STEVEN P. MOULDS
Board President

Box 2399
San Jose, CA 95109-2399
(408) 291-2266 (bus.)
(408) 291-2255 (b.o.)
(408) 995-0737 (fax)

FOUNDED 1980
James P. Reber

SEASON
Oct.-Aug.

FACILITIES
The Montgomery Theater
Seating Capacity: 535
Stage: proscenium

Mayer Theatre
Seating Capacity: 505
Stage: proscenium

FINANCES
July 1, 1991-June 30, 1992
Expenses: $2,200,000

CONTRACTS
AEA LORT (C) and TYA

San Jose Repertory Theatre performs in the Montgomery Theater in downtown San Jose, the 11th largest city in the nation and one that has become the cultural center of Silicon Valley. The theatre gives focus to this culturally diverse and widespread community by producing seasons of visually exciting, challenging and evocative plays selected from both classical and contemporary periods. In addition to striving to reflect and enhance its own community through mainstage productions and the Red Ladder Theatre Company (the Rep's outreach project for youth-at-risk), the Rep works to contribute on a national level to the essential growth of live theatre in the United States, developing new plays and encouraging artists to take an innovative approach to existing work. The Rep provides a creative, nurturing environment that offers unique theatre experiences for artists and audiences alike.
—Timothy Near

PRODUCTIONS 1991-1992

Sound design by Brian Studler unless otherwise noted.

The Little Foxes, Lillian Hellman; (D) Timothy Near; (S) David J. Hoffman; (L) Ashley York Kennedy; (C) Jeffrey Struckman
The 1940's Radio Hour, Walton Jones; various composers and lyricists; (D) Timothy Near; (S) and (C) Jeffrey Struckman; (L) Peter Maradudin
My Visits with MGM, Edit Villarreal; (D) Peggy Shannon; (S) and (L) Martyn Bookwalter; (C) Victoria Petrovich
Hay Fever, Noel Coward; (D) John McCluggage; (S) Rick Goodwin; (L) Derek Duarte; (C) Christine Dougherty
The Master Builder, Henrik Ibsen; trans: Jerry Turner; (D) Libby Appel; (S) Kent Dorsey; (L) Peter Maradudin; (C) Deborah M. Dryden; (SD) Benton Delinger
Cole, book: Alan Strachman and Benny Green; music and lyrics: Cole Porter; (D) and (CH) Bick Goss; (S) Kent Dorsey; (L) Derek Duarte; (C) Christine Dougherty; (MD) Carl Danielson; (SD) Michael Ferguson
Remember or Repeat, John McCluggage; (D) John McCluggage

PRODUCTIONS 1992-1993

Lighting by Derek Duarte unless otherwise noted.

Woody Guthrie's American Song, book: Peter Glazer; music and lyrics: Woody Guthrie; (D) Peter Glazer; (S) Philipp Jung; (C) Susan Snowden; (SD) Stephen LeGrand
Harvey, Mary Chase; (D) John McCluggage; (S) Kate Edmunds; (L) Jerald Enos; (C) Jeffrey Struckman; (SD) Paul Preston Overton
The Baby Dance, Jane Anderson; (D) Timothy Near; (S) and (C) Jeffrey Struckman; (SD) Paul Preston Overton
The Innocents, adapt: William Archibald, from Henry James; (D) John McCluggage; (S) Kent Dorsey; (C) Pamela Lampkin; (SD) Paul Preston Overton
Rumors, Neil Simon; (D) Peggy Shannon; (S) Joel Fontaine; (SD) Sergio Avila

Seattle Children's Theatre

LINDA HARTZELL
Artistic Director

THOMAS PECHAR
Managing Director

CRAIG E. SCHUMAN
Board President

Box 9640
Seattle, WA 98109-0640
(206) 443-0807 (bus.)
(206) 441-3322 (b.o.)
(206) 443-0442 (fax)

FOUNDED 1975
Seattle City Parks Department, Jenifer McClauchlan Carlson, Molly Welch Reed

SEASON
Sept.-June

FACILITIES
The Charlotte Martin Theatre
Seating Capacity: 485
Stage: proscenium

PONCHO Theatre (1991-1993)
Seating Capacity: 280
Stage: proscenium

FINANCES
July 1, 1992-June 30, 1993
Expenses: $2,300,000

CONTRACTS
AEA TYA

Seattle Children's Theatre. Barry Johnson in *The Velveteen Rabbit*. Photo: Chris Bennion.

Seattle Children's Theatre has a national reputation for producing innovative, thought-provoking professional theatre for young audiences and their families. We have commissioned more than 55 new works for young audiences since our founding in 1975, and our scripts have been produced by theatres across the country. In 1993-94, SCT celebrates its inaugural season in the newly built Charlotte Martin Theatre. Combining functional design with whimsical detail, the building houses state-of-the-art facilities in a structure that reflects our commitment to children and high-quality theatre. To enhance the educational experience of the mainstage season, SCT offers a wide variety of programs, including classroom workshops, study guides and postplay discussions. In addition, SCT brings mainstage and educational plays to schools through its regional touring program, and provides year-round classes in acting and theatre skills for grades K-12, taught by professional artists. Audiences of all ages deserve thoughtful, well-crafted professional theatre. Creative discovery inspired by a sophisticated, entertaining theatre experience is my vision of Seattle Children's Theatre.
—*Linda Hartzell*

PRODUCTIONS 1991-1992

The Firebird, R.N. Sandberg; trans: Natalia Sirikh; (D) Susan Glass Burdick; (S) Robert A. Gardiner and Jane E. Price; (L) Rogue Conn; (C) Fagilla Selskaya; (SD) Steven M. Klein

Nancy and Plum, adapt: Chad Henry, from Betty MacDonald; (D) Linda Hartzell; (S) Bill Forrester; (L) Patty Mathieu; (C) Catherine Meacham Hunt; (SD) Michael Holten

Charlotte's Web, adapt: Joseph Robinette, from E.B. White; (D) Rita Giomi; (S) Edie Whitsett; (L) Jennifer Lupton; (C) Paul Chi-Ming Louey; (SD) David Pascal

Roll of Thunder, Hear My Cry, adapt: Ed Shockley, from Mildred D. Tayler; (D) Tim Bond; (S) Jennifer Lupton; (L) Collier Woods; (C) Melanie Burgess; (SD) Steven M. Klein

Make Me Pele for a Day, Ted Sod; (D) Linda Hartzell; (S) Jane E. Price and Robert A. Gardiner; (L) Darren McCroom; (C) Mark Mitchell; (SD) Robert A. Langley

PRODUCTIONS 1992-1993

Invisible Friends, Alan Ayckbourn; (D) Rita Giomi; (S) Don Yanik; (L) Rogue Conn; (C) Paul Chi-Ming Louey; (SD) Robert A. Langley

Doctor Dolittle in the Moon, book adapt, music and lyrics: Chad Henry, from Hugh Lofting; (D) Linda Hartzell; (S) Shelley Henze Schermer; (L) Brenda Berry; (C) Catherine Meacham Hunt; (MD) Daryl Spadaccini; (CH) Marianne Claire Roberts; (SD) Michael Holten

The Invisible Man, adapt: Len Jenkin, from H.G. Wells; (D) Linda Hartzell; (S) Robert A. Gardiner and Jane E. Price; (L) Rogue Conn; (C) Paul Chi-Ming Louey; (SD) Steven M. Klein

The Velveteen Rabbit, adapt: B. Burgess Clark, from Margery Williams; (D) Pamela Sterling; (S) Edie Whitsett; (L) Michael Wellborn; (C) Catherine Meacham Hunt; (SD) David Pascal

Dragonwings, Laurence Yep; (D) Phyllis S.K. Look; (S) Joseph D. Dodd; (L) David K.H. Elliott; (C) Lydia Tanji; (SD) Scott Koue

Ramona Quimby, adapt: Len Jenkin, from Beverly Cleary; (D) Stephen Terrell; (S) Jennifer Lupton; (L) Patty Mathieu; (C) Melanie Burgess; (SD) Steven M. Klein

Seattle Repertory Theatre

DANIEL SULLIVAN
Artistic Director

DOUGLAS HUGHES
Associate Artistic Director

BENJAMIN MOORE
Managing Director

STANLEY D. SAVAGE
Board Chairman

155 Mercer St.
Seattle, WA 98109
(206) 443-2210 (bus.)
(206) 443-2222 (b.o.)
(206) 443-2379 (fax)

FOUNDED 1963
Bagley Wright

SEASON
Oct.-May

FACILITIES
Bagley Wright Theatre (Mainstage)
Seating Capacity: 856
Stage: proscenium

PONCHO Forum (Stage 2)
Seating Capacity: 133
Stage: flexible

FINANCES
July 1, 1991-June 30, 1992
Expenses: $5,554,912

CONTRACTS
AEA LORT (B+) and (D)

The Seattle Repertory Theatre continues to support a resident acting company, offering long-term employment to members who are cast across a season of six Mainstage and three Stage 2 productions. Both the Mainstage and Stage 2 offer work ranging from the classics to world premieres. Each year we seek to collaborate with other nonprofit theatres to present a special production on the Mainstage, thus providing extra time for the resident company to prepare subsequent productions. A strong commitment to new work is reflected in workshop productions of four new scripts every spring. Building the resources of a resident acting company and developing new plays remain parallel artistic priorities. Outreach programs include workshops and performances in the schools and a tour of a Mainstage production to venues across the country.
—*Daniel Sullivan*

Seattle Repertory Theatre. Mario Arrambide, Jonathan Adams, John Aylward and Mark Nelson in *Julius Caesar*. Photo: Chris Bennion.

PRODUCTIONS 1991-1992

Sound design by Steven M. Klein unless otherwise noted.

Twelfth Night, William Shakespeare; (D) Douglas Hughes; (S) Hugh Landwehr; (L) Peter Maradudin; (C) Catherine Zuber

M. Butterfly, David Henry Hwang; (D) David Saint; (S) David Gallo; (L) Kenneth Posner; (C) Michael Olich

Redwood Curtain, Lanford Wilson; (D) Marshall W. Mason; (S) John Lee Beatty; (L) Dennis Parichy; (C) Laura Crow; (SD) Chuck London and Stewart Werner

When We Are Married, J.B. Priestley; (D) Nagle Jackson; (S) Marjorie Bradley Kellogg; (L) Kirk Bookman; (C) Michael Olich

Hedda Gabler, Henrik Ibsen; trans: Csanad Z. Siklos; adapt: Douglas Hughes; (D) Douglas Hughes; (S) Anita Stewart; (L) Nancy Schertler; (C) Michael Olich

The Good Times Are Killing Me, Lynda Barry; (D) Mark Brokaw; (S) Rusty Smith; (L) Donald Holder; (C) Ellen McCartney; (SD) Janet Kalas

The Lisbon Traviata, Terrence McNally; (D) Mark Brokaw; (S) Bill Clarke; (L) Tim Saternow; (C) Rose Pederson

Inspecting Carol, Daniel Sullivan and the Resident Acting Company; (D) Daniel Sullivan; (S) Andrew Wood Boughton; (L) Rick Paulsen; (C) Robert Wojewodski; (SD) Michael Holten

Marvin's Room, Scott McPherson; (D) Robin Lynn Smith; (S) Scott Weldin; (L) Rick Paulsen; (C) Rose Pederson; (SD) David Hunter Koch

PRODUCTIONS 1992-1993

Sound design by Steven M. Klein unless otherwise noted.

Julius Caesar, William Shakespeare; (D) Douglas Hughes; (S) Andrei Both; (L) Peter Maradudin; (C) Caryn Neman; (SD) SADHAPPY and Jim Ragland
Inspecting Carol, Daniel Sullivan and the Resident Acting Company; (D) Daniel Sullivan; (S) Andrew Wood Boughton; (L) Rick Paulsen; (C) Robert Wojewodski; (SD) Michael Holten
Lips Together, Teeth Apart, Terrence McNally; (D) David Saint; (S) James Noone; (L) Kenneth Posner; (C) David Murin
The Flying Karamazov Brothers in The Brothers Karamazov, Paul Magid; (D) Daniel Sullivan; (S) Andrew Wood Boughton; (L) Allen Lee Hughes; (C) Caryn Neman
Heartbreak House, George Bernard Shaw; (D) Adrian Hall; (S) Eugene Lee; (L) Natasha Katz; (C) Catherine Zuber
The Piano Lesson, August Wilson; (D) Lloyd Richards; (S) E. David Cosier, Jr.; (L) Ashley York Kennedy; (C) Constanza Romero; (SD) G. Thomas Clark
The Substance of Fire, Jon Robin Baitz; (D) Michael Bloom; (S) Bill Clarke; (L) Brian Gale; (C) Rose Pederson
Spunk, adapt: George C. Wolfe, from Zora Neale Hurston; music: Chic Street Man; (D) Jacqueline Moscou; (S) and (C) Michael Olich; (L) Meg Fox; (SD) David Pascal
Eye of God, Tim Blake Nelson; (D) Douglas Hughes; (S) Andrew Wood Boughton; (L) Greg Sullivan; (C) Rose Pederson; (SD) Michael Roth

Second Stage Theatre. Mary Beth Hurt, Brian Kerwin, Jennifer Tilly, Jeffrey DeMunn and Daniel Gerroll in *One Shoe Off*. Photo: Susan Cook.

Second Stage Theatre

CAROLE ROTHMAN
Artistic Director

SUZANNE SCHWARTZ DAVIDSON
Producing Director

CAROL FISHMAN
Producing Director

ANTHONY C.M. KISER
Board Chairman

Box 1807, Ansonia Station
New York, NY 10023
(212) 787-8302 (bus.)
(212) 873-6103 (b.o.)
(212) 877-9886 (fax)

FOUNDED 1979
Robyn Goodman, Carole Rothman

SEASON
Oct.-Aug.

FACILITIES
McGinn/Cazale Theatre
Seating Capacity: 108
Stage: proscenium

FINANCES
July 1, 1991-June 30, 1992
Expenses: $1,229,434

CONTRACTS
AEA letter of agreement

Second Stage Theatre was founded in July 1979 to produce American plays that we felt deserved a second chance. These included plays that were ahead of their time, not accessible to a wide audience or obscured by inferior productions. This "second staging" not only rescued some great works from obscurity, but launched the careers of many actors, directors and playwrights. As relationships developed, artists wanted to bring their original concepts to the theatre. So in 1982 we expanded our misson to include presenting new plays by our developing corps of writers. These plays include *Painting Churches* and *Coastal Disturbances* by Tina Howe, and *Spoils of War* by Michael Weller. Throughout our 12 seasons Second Stage has been honored with 18 Obie awards, 2 Clarence Derwent Awards, 4 Theatre World Awards, 4 Outer Critics Circle Awards and 4 Tony nominations.

—*Carole Rothman*

PRODUCTIONS 1991-1992

Dearly Departed, David Bottrell and Jessie Jones; (D) Gloria Muzio; (S) Allen Moyer; (L) Donald Holder; (C) Ellen McCartney; (SD) Mark Bennett
Before It Hits Home, Cheryl L. West; (D) Tazewell Thompson; (S) Loy Arcenas; (L) Nancy Schertler; (C) Paul Tazewell; (SD) Susan R. White
Red Diaper Baby, Josh Kornbluth; (D) Joshua Mostel; (S) Randy Benjamin; (L) Pat Dignan; (C) Susan Lyall; (SD) Guy Sherman/Aural Fixation
Spike Heels, Theresa Rebeck; (D) Michael Greif; (S) James Youmans; (L) Kenneth Posner; (C) Candice Donnelly; (SD) Mark Bennett

PRODUCTIONS 1992-1993

A...My Name is Still Alice, conceived: Joan Micklin Silver and Julianne Boyd; various composers and lyricists; (D) Joan Micklin Silver and Julianne Boyd; (S) Andrew Jackness; (L) David F. Segal; (C) David C. Woolard; (MD) Ian Herman; (CH) Hope Clarke
One Shoe Off, Tina Howe; (D) Carole Rothman; (S) Heidi Landesman; (L) Richard Nelson; (C) Susan Hilferty; (SD) Mark Bennett
Time on Fire, Evan Handler; (D) Marcia Jean Kurtz; (S) Rob Odorisio; (L) Kenneth Posner; (SD) Guy Sherman/Aural Fixation
Loose Knit, Theresa Rebeck; (D) Beth Schachter; (S) Santo Loquasto; (L) Frances Aronson; (C) Elsa Ward; (SD) Mark Bennett

7 Stages

DEL HAMILTON
Artistic Director

LISA MOUNT
Managing Director

ALEX P. ORFINGER
Board Chairman

1105 Euclid Ave. NE
Atlanta, GA 30307
(404) 522-0911 (bus.)
(404) 523-7647 (b.o.)
(404) 522-0913 (fax)

FOUNDED 1979
Faye Allen, Del Hamilton

SEASON
Sept.-June

FACILITIES
Mainstage Theater
Seating Capacity: 250
Stage: flexible

Back Door Theater
Seating Capacity: 100
Stage: flexible

FINANCES
Jan. 1, 1992-Dec. 31, 1992
Expenses: $328,000

CONTRACTS
AEA SPT

7 Stages engages artists and audiences by focusing on social, spiritual and political values in contemporary culture. Much of the work we do centers on issues of concern to our artists and audiences, and we try to examine both the specific circumstances and the larger meaning inherent in the conflicts we face. Primary emphasis

7 Stages. Saul Williams, Carolyn Cook and LeRoy Mitchell, Jr. in *My Children! My Africa!*. Photo: Jonathan Burnette.

is given to the support and development of new plays, new playwrights and new methods of collaboration. Our developmental process is based on meeting needs articulated by the artists we work with, especially those from the Southeast. We are committed to bringing international plays and performing artists to our community to share their wisdom, to bring different cultures into intimate contact and to promote artistic exchanges. We also maintain a Peforming Arts Center which is a home for arts groups based in Atlanta and a way to foster the development of new theatre companies.

—Del Hamilton

PRODUCTIONS 1991-1992

Carmen Kittel, George Seidel; trans: Frank Heibert; (D) Lore Stefanek; (S), (L) and (C) Martin Kraemer; (SD) Tom Spock
Tiny Tim is Dead, Barbara Lebow (co-produced by Academy Theatre); (D) Frank Wittow; (S) Elliott Berman; (L) Jessica Coale
Almost Asleep, Julie Hebert; (D) and (C) Celeste Miller; (S) and (L) Eric Jennings; (SD) Klimchak
Waiting for Godot, Samuel Beckett; (D) Joseph Chaikin; (S) Linda Burgess; (L) Eric Jennings; (C) Kappitola Williams

PRODUCTIONS 1992-1993

Vivisections From the Blown Mind, Alonzo D. Lamont, Jr.; (D) Clinton Turner Davis; (S) Michael Franklin White; (L) Jeff Guzik; (C) Patsy Mills and Joanna Schmink; (SD) Thom Freeman and Celeste A-Re
My Children! My Africa!, Athol Fugard; (D) Del Hamilton; (L) Jessica Coale; (C) Joanna Schmink; (SD) Allen Green
Night Sky, Susan Yankowitz; (D) Del Hamilton; (S) and (L) Jeff Guzik; (SD) Allen Green
Angel Works (The Sandbox, Edward Albee; *The War in Heaven*, Sam Shepard and Joseph Chaikin; *Angel Fragments*, Sam Shepard, Joseph Chaikin and the ensemble); (D) Joseph Chaikin; (S) Linda Burgess; (L) Eric Jennings; (C) Joanna Schmink; (SD) Klimchak and Chip Epsten

U.S./Netherlands Touring and Exchange Project:
various playwrights, various directors

Shakespeare & Company

TINA PACKER
Artistic Director

DENNIS KRAUSNICK
Managing Director

NEIL COLVIN
Board Chairman

The Mount
Box 865
Lenox, MA 01240
(413) 637-1197 (bus.)
(413) 637-3353 (b.o.)
(413) 637-4274 (fax)

FOUNDED 1978
Tina Packer, Kristin Linklater, B.H. Barry, John Broome, Dennis Krausnick

SEASON
Mar.-Nov.

FACILITIES
Mainstage Theatre
Seating Capacity: 500
Stage: thrust

Stables Theatre
Seating Capacity: 108
Stage: flexible

Wharton Theatre
Seating Capacity: 72-94
Stage: arena

Oxford Court Theatre
Seating Capacity: 200
Stage: thrust

FINANCES
Oct. 1, 1991-Sept. 30, 1992
Expenses: $1,536,500

CONTRACTS
AEA letter of agreement

Shakespeare & Company is committed to creating a classical theatre which performs as the Elizabethans did—with the same passion for exploring universal truths, the same exploration of violence, physical grace in dance, and lust for language. This commitment is founded on the company's central aesthetic: the power of the spoken word. Shakespeare & Company has developed a distinctive philosophy of training which merges a classical approach to language with emotional truth in acting in order to free human expression from habitual limitations, restoring thought and language to their sensory, organic, atavistic roots, allowing potent communication between actor and audience. The company has three program areas: performance, professional actor and teacher training, and educational programming. The work on language is being used in other fields—business management, labor organization, and psychiatric and social well-being—but its research and development belong properly to theatre, where the unspoken can be spoken and the unconscious is made conscious.

—Tina Packer

PRODUCTIONS 1992

Direction by Tina Packer, sets and lighting by Steve Ball and costumes by John Pennoyer unless otherwise noted.

Inner House, adapt: Dennis Krausnick, from Edith Wharton; (D) Dennis Krausnick; (C) Arthur Oliver
Shirley Valentine, Willy Russell; (D) Patrick Swanson; (C) Andrea Zax
A Life in the Theatre, David Mamet; (D) Tina Packer and Dennis Krausnick; (C) Arthur Oliver
Custer Rides, James Daniels; (D) Patricia Daniels; (S) S. Mark Hoffman; (C) Joanna Medioli
Duet for One, Tom Kempinski; (C) Andrea Zax
Women of Will, adapt: Tina Packer, from William Shakespeare; (D) Gary Mitchell
The Mission of Jane/A Love Story, adapt: Gary Mitchell and Dennis Krausnick, from Edith Wharton; (D) Gary Mitchell and Dennis Krausnick; (C) Arthur Oliver
Julius Caesar, William Shakespeare
Maisie, adapt: Dennis Krausnick, from Henry James; (D) Dennis Krausnick; (C) Deborah A. Brothers

Shakespeare & Company. Jonathan Epstein and Tina Packer in *Women of Will*. Photo: Richard Bomberg.

The Taming of the Shrew, William Shakespeare; (D) John Hadden; (S) and (L) Hiroshi Iwasaki; (SD) Donald DiNicola
The Tale of a Tiger, Dario Fo; trans: Ron Jenkins; (D) Christopher Ashley; (C) Arthur Oliver
Manners and More, adapt: Dennis Krausnick and Karen MacDonald, from Edith Wharton; (D) Dennis Krausnick and Karen MacDonald
Much Ado About Nothing, William Shakespeare; (D) Gary Mitchell
Richard II, William Shakespeare
Troilus and Cressida, William Shakespeare; (D) Dennis Krausnick; (C) Andrea Zax
Two Gentlemen of Verona, William Shakespeare; (D) Tim Sankiavicus; (C) Andrea Zax

PRODUCTIONS 1993

Direction by Tina Packer, sets and lighting by Steve Ball and costumes by John Pennoyer unless otherwise noted.

Julius Caesar, William Shakespeare
Berkeley Square, adapt: John L. Balderston, from Henry James; (D) Dennis Krausnick and Tina Packer; (C) Arthur Oliver
Duet for One, Tom Kempinski; (C) Andrea Zax
Virginia, Edna O'Brien; (D) Normi Noel; (C) Arthur Oliver
A Memory of Splendor, adapt: Dennis Krausnick, from Henry James and Edith Wharton; (D) Dennis Krausnick
Mothers and Daughters, adapt: Sharon Werner and Dennis Krausnick, from Edith Wharton; (D) Allyn Burrows
The Landscape Painter, adapt: Stanley Richardson, from Henry James; (D) Dennis Krausnick; (C) Ed Baker
A Midsummer Night's Dream, William Shakespeare; (S) Terry Beckett; (L) Lenore Doxsee
Twelfth Night, William Shakespeare; (D) Jonathan Croy; (C) Arthur Oliver
On the Open Road, Steve Tesich; (D) Gary Mitchell
The Henry VI Chronicles, adapt: Jonathan Croy, from William Shakespeare; (D) Jonathan Croy
The Spirit Warrior's Dream, Ricardo Pitts-Wiley; (D) Ricardo Pitts-Wiley; (L) Bob Lott; (C) Andrea Zax
The Custom of the Country, adapt: Jane Stanton Hitchcock, from Edith Wharton; (D) Dennis Krausnick
The Scarlet Letter, adapt: Dennis Krausnick, from Nathaniel Hawthorne
Kerfol: A Ghost Story, adapt: Gary Mitchell, from Edith Wharton; (D) Dennis Krausnick

Shakespeare Repertory

BARBARA GAINES
Artistic Director

CRISS HENDERSON
Producing Director

PETER GOODHART
Board Chairman

820 Orleans Ave., Suite 340
Chicago, IL 60610
(312) 642-8394 (bus.)
(312) 642-2273 (b.o.)
(312) 642-8817 (fax)

FOUNDED 1987
Kathleen Buckley, Barbara Gaines, Susan Geffen, Camilla Hawk, Liz Jacobs, Tom Joyce

SEASON
Aug.-Apr.

FACILITIES
Ruth Page Theater
Seating Capacity: 310
Stage: thrust

FINANCES
July 1, 1992-June 30, 1993
Expenses: $750,000

CONTRACTS
AEA CAT and TYA

When Shakespeare put pen to paper he unleashed an avalanche of human behavior. Shakespeare Repertory's vision focuses on the humanity of his characters and on how they relate to each other and to us. One element that distinguishes the Rep's work is its reliance on the First Folio as its script and blueprint. The Folio scripts help the actor connect emotional behavior to the technical demands of the verse. Another important connection to be made is obviously between the audience and the actors. We want that connection to be immediate and exciting. The fact that we perform on a deep thrust stage gives the audience a feeling of participation rather than observation, and takes away any sense of distance. The students and teachers of Chicago are our partners in *Team Shakespeare*. More than 16,000 students annually participate in our education outreach program, which actively supports the work of teachers and the curriculum of Chicago's schools.
—*Barbara Gaines*

PRODUCTIONS 1991-1992

Pericles, William Shakespeare; (D) Barbara Gaines; (S) Michael Merritt; (L) Robert Shook; (C) Nan Zabriskie; (SD) Robert Neuhaus
Macbeth, William Shakespeare; (D) Roman Polak; (S) Michael Merritt; (L) Robert Shook; (C) Nan Cibula-Jenkins; (SD) Robert Neuhaus and Lloyd Broadnax King

Shakespeare Repertory. Greg Vinkler and Richard Kneeland in *King Lear*. Photo: Roger Lewin/Jennifer Girard Studio.

Shakespeare's Greatest Hits, adapt: Barbara Gaines, from William Shakespeare; (D) Barbara Gaines
Will Power on Tour, adapt: Kathleen Buckley, from William Shakespeare; (D) Kathleen Buckley

PRODUCTIONS 1992-1993

King Lear, William Shakespeare; (D) Barbara Gaines; (S) Michael S. Philippi; (L) Rita Pietraszek; (C) Nan Zabriskie; (SD) Robert Neuhaus and Lloyd Broadnax King
Romeo and Juliet and Julius Caesar...Nice Play, Shakespeare, adapt: Kevin Gudahl and Greg Vinkler, from William Shakespeare; (D) Kevin Gudahl and Greg Vinkler; (S) Kurt Sharp; (L) Deborah Acker; (C) Nanette Acosta; (SD) Michael Bodeen
Will Power on Tour, adapt: Kathleen Buckley, from William Shakespeare; (D) Kristine Thatcher

Shakespeare Santa Cruz

DANNY SCHEIE
Artistic Director

MARILYN GROSS
Board President

Performing Arts Complex
University of California
Santa Cruz, CA 95064
(408) 459-2121 (bus.)
(408) 459-4168 (b.o.)
(408) 459-3552 (fax)

FOUNDED 1982
Audrey Stanley, Karen Sinsheimer

SEASON
July-Sept.

FACILITIES
Sinsheimer-Stanley
Festival Glen
Seating Capacity: 650
Stage: flexible

Performing Arts Theater
Seating Capacity: 537
Stage: thrust

FINANCES
Jan. 1, 1992-Dec. 31, 1992
Expenses: $807,830

CONTRACTS AEA Guest Artist

Shakespeare Santa Cruz productions aggressively eschew Museum Shakespeare. The clash of a 400-year-old play with the present is primary; reconstruction of a time-gone-by-in-merrie-olde-England is of negligible interest. Ours is not a festival to visit for Disneyland scenery, morris-dancing-on-the-green, mince pasties, or actors who sound as if they were carefully bred on Planet Shakespeare. We have found that Elizabethan costumes and standard stage or British accents tend to obscure the meaning of character for the modern American audience. Our artistic mission is quite simple: Shakespeare must not bore. This is not achieved through Reverence of Beauty and Culture, but by pulling out the creative stops and doing anything that clarifies the story and the characters of Shakespeare's plays. Shakespeare Santa Cruz is a company that collides Shakespeare with *now*.

—*Danny Scheie*

Note: During the 1991-92 season, Michael Edwards served as artistic director.

PRODUCTIONS 1991

A Midsummer Night's Dream, William Shakespeare; (D) Danny Scheie; (S) Michael Edwards; (L) Maurice Vercoutere; (C) B. Modern; (SD) David Holmes
Our Town, Thornton Wilder; (D) Mark Rucker; (S) David Hoffmann; (L) Evan Parker; (C) Anna Oliver; (SD) Carmen Borgia
Measure for Measure, William Shakespeare; (D) Michael Edwards; (S) David Hoffmann; (L) Evan Parker; (C) Jeffrey Struckman; (SD) Carmen Borgia
Waiting for Godot, Samuel Beckett; (D) Audrey Stanley; (S) Michael Edwards; (L) Maurice Vercoutere; (C) David Draper; (SD) David Holmes

PRODUCTIONS 1992

Lighting by Mark Hager and Evan Parker.

The Taming of the Shrew, William Shakespeare; (D) Danny Scheie; (S) Skip Epperson; (C) B. Modern
A Doll House, Henrik Ibsen; adapt: Karin Magaldi-Unger; (D) Michael Edwards; (S) Joe Ragey; (C) Beaver Bauer; (SD) Wade Peterson
Macbeth, William Shakespeare; (D) Mark Rucker; (S) Skip Epperson; (C) Katherine Roth; (SD) Wade Peterson

The Shakespeare Tavern. Tony Wright and Mark Douglas-Jones in Romeo and Juliet. *Photo: Michael Holland.*

Shakespeare Santa Cruz. Jason Nunes, Francisco Reinoso, Tom Graves, Darius Stone and Kalli Jonsson in A Midsummer Night's Dream. *Photo: Ann Parker.*

The Shakespeare Tavern

JEFFREY WATKINS
Producing Artistic Director

TONY WRIGHT
Managing Director

GRETCHEN SCHULZ
Board Chairperson

Box 5436
Atlanta, GA 30307
(404) 874-9219 (bus.)
(404) 874-5299 (b.o.)
(404) 378-8767 (fax)

FOUNDED 1979
Elisabeth Lewis Corley, Jane Tuttle

SEASON
Aug.-June

FACILITIES
Seating Capacity: 210
Stage: flexible

FINANCES
May 1, 1992-Apr. 30, 1993
Expenses: $254,095

CONTRACTS
AEA SPT

The Shakespeare Tavern is in quest of pure theatre—a theatre whose reason for being is the communion of actor, audience and playwright. The Shakespeare Tavern is a place to eat, drink and nourish the soul, a place where actors and audiences alike can directly experience the works of Shakespeare and other great playwrights. It is a place where people do not just watch the trial of Saint Joan or the last moments of Romeo as he shares a final embrace with his wife. It is a place to share Joan's thoughts, to feel her heartbeat...to breathe with Romeo as his arms enfold his everlasting love. It is a magic place.

—*Jeffrey Watkins*

PRODUCTIONS 1991-1992

Direction, sets and lighting by Jeffrey Watkins and costumes by Carol Haynes unless otherwise noted.

The Merry Wives of Windsor, William Shakespeare; (C) Peter Vassil
The Lion in Winter, James Goldman
Romeo and Juliet, William Shakespeare

PRODUCTIONS 1992-1993

Direction, sets and lighting by Jeffrey Watkins and costumes by Carol Haynes unless otherwise noted.

As You Like It, William Shakespeare; (D) Tony Wright
Henry IV, Part 1, William Shakespeare
The Rover, Aphra Behn; (D) Tony Wright
Julius Caesar, William Shakespeare

The Shakespeare Theatre

MICHAEL KAHN
Artistic Director

JESSICA L. ANDREWS
Managing Director

LAWRENCE A. HOUGH
Board Chairman

301 East Capitol St. SE
Washington, DC 20003
(202) 547-3230 (bus.)
(202) 393-2700 (b.o.)
(202) 547-0226 (fax)

FOUNDED 1969
O.B. Hardison, Richmond Crinkley, Folger Shakespeare Library

SEASON
Year-round

FACILITIES
The Lansburgh
Seating Capacity: 447
Stage: modified proscenium

Carter Barron Amphitheater
Seating Capacity: 4,000
Stage: modified proscenium

FINANCES
July 1, 1992-June 30, 1993
Expenses: $5,500,000

CONTRACTS
AEA LORT (C) and (D)

The central issue of the Shakespeare Theatre is the development of an American classical style for the 1990s and beyond. Our true challenge is to connect the technical demands made on the classical actor (vocal range, articulation of the text, etc.) and the necessary emotional life (including the larger-than-real-life feelings that Shakespearean characters experience in connecting themselves to the cosmos) to the full use of the actor's intellectual powers and a highly physical acting style. Our other concerns include the need to merge multigenerational artists in all areas of the theatre in a true collaboration; to continue our policy of multicultural casting and staffing in artistic and administrative leadership positions; to expand our educational and outreach programs, including two weeks of free Shakespeare at Carter Barron Amphitheater; to address major social issues as the plays illuminate them; and to connect productively with the complex community in which we work and live.
—*Michael Kahn*

PRODUCTIONS 1991-1992

Direction by Michael Kahn unless otherwise noted.

Coriolanus, William Shakespeare; (D) William Gaskill; (S) and (C) Peter Hartwell; (L) Frances Aronson; (SD) Deniz Ulben
Saint Joan, George Bernard Shaw; (D) Sarah Pia Anderson; (S) Donald Eastman; (L) Nancy Schertler; (C) Barbra Kravitz; (SD) Dan Schreier
Much Ado About Nothing, William Shakespeare; (S) Derek McLane; (L) Howell Binkley; (C) Martin Pakledinaz; (SD) Gil Thompson
Measure for Measure, William Shakespeare; (S) Derek McLane; (L) Howell Binkley; (C) Lewis Brown; (SD) Adam Wernick
As You Like It, William Shakespeare; (S) Andrew Jackness; (L) Nancy Schertler; (C) Candice Donnelly; (SD) David Bishop

PRODUCTIONS 1992-1993

Direction by Michael Kahn, sets by Derek McLane and lighting by Howell Binkley unless otherwise noted.

Troilus and Cressida, William Shakespeare; (D) Bill Alexander; (S) and (C) Kit Surrey; (L) Nancy Schertler; (SD) Adam Wernick
Hamlet, William Shakespeare; (C) Catherine Zuber; (SD) Adam Wernick
The Comedy of Errors, William Shakespeare; (D) John Retallack; (S) Russell Metheny; (L) Daniel MacLean Wagner; (C) Candice Donnelly; (SD) George Fulginiti-Shakar
Mother Courage and Her Children, book adapt: Hanif Kareishi, from Bertolt Brecht; music: Louis Rosen; lyrics: Sue Davies; (C) Catherine Zuber; (MD) Jon Kalbfleisch; (CH) Karma Camp; (SD) John Burke
Much Ado About Nothing, William Shakespeare; (C) Martin Pakledinaz; (SD) Gil Thompson

Society Hill Playhouse

DEEN KOGAN
Managing Director

507 South 8th St.
Philadelphia, PA 19147
(215) 923-0211 (bus.)
(215) 923-0210 (b.o.)
(215) 923-1789 (fax)

FOUNDED 1959
Deen Kogan, Jay Kogan

SEASON
Year-round

The Shakespeare Theatre. Pat Carroll and Floyd King in *Mother Courage and Her Children*. Photo: Joan Marcus.

Society Hill Playhouse. Gloria Salmansohn and Walter Vail in *Beau Jest*. Photo: Paul Sirochman.

FACILITIES
Mainstage
Seating Capacity: 223
Stage: proscenium

Second Space
Seating Capacity: 99
Stage: flexible

FINANCES
July 1, 1992-June 30, 1993
Expenses: $318,134

CONTRACTS
AEA SPT and Guest Artist

The primary goal of Society Hill Playhouse was and is to present great contemporary plays to Philadelphians who might not otherwise see them. For years we produced the Philadelphia premieres of such playwrights as Brecht, Genet, Sartre, Frisch and Beckett. England's Arden, Wesker and Pinter first played here. American playwrights like Arthur Kopit, LeRoi Jones, Mark Medoff and James Sherman were first seen in Philadelphia at this theatre. During the years, many experiments pursued by other theatres of the world were also pursued by us in Philadelphia: public script-in-hand readings, playwrights' workshops, one-act play marathons, street theatre, youth theatre. As an arts institution functioning as much more than just a presenter of plays, our interaction with Philadelphians, not just as spectators but in every aspect of making theatre, produced an expanding commitment and role in the community, affecting many people. Our continued dedication to our original goals still leads us into new paths of community involvement.
—*Jay Kogan*

Note: During the 1991-92 and 1992-93 seasons, Jay Kogan served as artistic director.

PRODUCTIONS 1991-1992

Grease, book, music and lyrics: Jim Jacobs and Warren Casey; (D) and (CH) Jack Bloeser; (S) Michael Kleintop; (L) Stephen Keever; (C) Patrice Faulcon; (MD) Joe Goodrich
The Day Mary Shelley Met Charlotte Bronte, Eduardo Manet; trans: Vivian Cox; (D) Jay Kogan; (S) Barry Marron; (L) Stephen Keever; (C) Patrice Faulcon; (SD) Leonora Schildkraut
Nunsense, book, music and lyrics: Dan Goggin; (D) Dan Goggin; (S) Barry Marron; (L) Neil Tomlinson; (MD) Douglass Lutz; (CH) Felton Smith
Dancing to the River, Clay Goss; (D) Susan Turlish; (S) Fred Wright; (L) Neil Tomlinson; (C) Patrice Faulcon; (SD) Ray Buffington

PRODUCTIONS 1992-1993

Nunsense, book, music and lyrics: Dan Goggin; (D) Dan Goggin; (S) Barry Marron; (L) Neil Tomlinson; (MD) Douglass Lutz; (CH) Felton Smith
Beau Jest, James Sherman; (D) Deen Kogan; (S) Bruce Goodrich; (L) Stephen Keever; (C) S.D. Falk; (SD) Jeff Rubin
Miracle at Graceland, book: Dorothy Velasco; music: Malcolm Lowe; lyrics: James Giancarlo, Dorothy Velasco and Malcolm Lowe; (D) Domenick Scuder; (S) Bruce Goodrich; (L) Wes Hacking; (C) Danielle Corrado; (MD) Jack Carr; (CH) Wayne St. David
A Safe Place, Susan Turlish; (D) Susan Turlish; (S) Ray Buffington; (L) Neil Tomlinson

Source Theatre Company

PAT MURPHY SHEEHY
Producing Artistic Director

CAROL CRUSE
General Manager

RICHARD APPERSON
Board Chairman

1835 14th St. NW
Washington, DC 20009
(202) 232-8011 (bus.)
(202) 462-1073 (b.o.)
(202) 462-0676 (fax)

FOUNDED 1977
Bart Whiteman

SEASON
Year-round

FACILITIES
Seating Capacity: 101
Stage: thrust

FINANCES
Sept. 1, 1992-Aug. 31, 1993
Expenses: $419,000

CONTRACTS
AEA SPT

Source Theatre Company, celebrating its 17th season, is committed to producing innovative contemporary works, new plays and reinterpretations of the classics. Nurtured by a core of resident professionals, Source provides a home for the emerging Washington-area theatre artist. Source's artists have gained national prominence as playwrights, artistic directors and actors, and have founded innumerable smaller Washington-area theatres. The company's artistic vision is realized through a season of plays and outreach projects and a developmental new-play program, the heart of which is Source's annual Washington Theatre Festival, winner of the 1993 Helen Hayes Washington Post Award. During this new-play festival, one of the largest in the country and now in its 14th summer, Source produces workshop productions and readings of more than 50 scripts, submitted by both local and national playwrights, in venues throughout D.C. The theatre explores issues of importance to its diverse community while challenging its audience with provocative work.
—*Pat Murphy Sheehy*

PRODUCTIONS 1991-1992

Lighting by William A. Price, III unless otherwise noted.

more intimacies, Michael Kearns; (D) Kelly Hill; (SD) Darien Martus
The Art of Success, Nick Dear; (D) Joe Banno; (S) Michael Stepowany; (C) Mirielle Lellouche Key; (SD) Robin Heath and Joe Banno
Lloyd's Prayer, Kevin Kling; (D) Pat Murphy Sheehy; (S) Michael Stepowany; (C) Christina Rosendaul; (SD) David Crandall
The Talented Tenth, Richard Wesley; (D) Jennifer Nelson; (S) Michael Stepowany; (L) Prince No-Ra; (C) Jennifer Nelson; (SD) Mark Anduss
The Pearl, Judlyne A. Lilly; (D) Lisa Rose Middleton
Those Sweet Caresses, Lucy Tom Lehrer; (D) Elizabeth Robelen; (S) Michael Stepowany; (L) David Kriebs; (C) Mirielle Lellouche Key; (SD) Mark Anduss

White Money, Julie Jensen; (D) Randye Hoeflich; (S) Michael Stepowany; (L) Ayun Fedorcha; (C) Theresa Chevine; (SD) Neil McFadden
Red She Said, Eliot Byerrum; (D) Deborah Grossman
Psycho Beach Party, Charles Busch; (D) Jerry Manning; (S) Tony Cisek; (L) Christopher V. Lewton; (C) Hugh Hansen and Susan Anderson; (SD) Susan R. White and Eric Annis

PRODUCTIONS 1992-1993

Sets and lighting by William A. Price, III, costumes by Mirielle Lellouche Key and sound design by Mark Anduss unless otherwise noted.

Rock, Michael Kearns; (D) Kelly Hill
Executive Leverage, book: Joe Palka; music and lyrics: Rory Chalcroft; (D) Joe Banno; (S) Tim Goecke; (MD) Rory Chalcroft; (CH) Nick Bowling
Attack of the Capitol Hill Nazis, Patrick Kennedy; (D) Eric Winick

Shakin' the Mess Outta Misery, Shay Youngblood; (D) Jennifer Nelson; (S) Tim Goecke; (L) Nancy Ann Arnold
La Bete, David Hirson; (D) Randye Hoeflich; (S) James Kronzer; (C) Gweneth West; (SD) Neil McFadden
Murder as a Fine Art, Otho Eskin; (D) Stephen Jarrett

Coming of Age Festival:
Year of Pilgrimage, Doug Grissom; (D) Lisa Rose Middleton and Elizabeth Robelen
Dancing With Ourselves, Allyson Currin; (D) Rick Fiori
One Tit, a Dyke & Gin, Pennell Somsen; (D) Allyson Currin
Crushed Tomatoes, Donna DiNovelli; (D) Elizabeth Robelen; (C) Shirley Dubois
California Cowboy, Ernest Joselovitz; (D) Randye Hoeflich; (C) Shirley Dubois

Red Scare on Sunset, Charles Busch; (D) Joe Banno; (S) Michael Stepowany; (SD) Robin Heath

Source Theatre Company. Nancy Grosshans, Susan Ross and Christopher Wilson in *Those Sweet Caresses*. Photo: Jim Ronan.

South Coast Repertory

DAVID EMMES
Producing Artistic Director

MARTIN BENSON
Artistic Director

PAUL HAMMOND
Associate Producer

PAULA TOMEI
General Manager

THOMAS C. SUTTON
Board President

Box 2197
655 Town Center Drive
Costa Mesa, CA 92628-2197
(714) 957-2602 (bus.)
(714) 957-4033 (b.o.)
(714) 545-0391 (fax)

FOUNDED 1964
David Emmes, Martin Benson

SEASON
Sept.-June

FACILITIES
Mainstage
Seating Capacity: 507
Stage: modified thrust

Second Stage
Seating Capacity: 161
Stage: thrust

FINANCES
Sept. 1, 1992-Aug. 31, 1993
Expenses: $5,800,000

CONTRACTS
AEA LORT (B) and (D), and TYA

South Coast Repertory commits itself to exploring the most important human and social issues of our time and to testing the bounds of theatre's possibilities. While valuing all elements of theatrical production, we give primacy to the text and its creators. Through premiere productions and an array of developmental programs, we serve, nurture and establish long-term relationships with America's most promising playwrights. Around our core company of actors we have built a large and dynamic ensemble of artists, constantly infusing their work with the fresh perspective of artists new to our collaboration. We devote our financial resources to making theatre a viable and rewarding profession for all our artists. While striving to advance the art of theatre, we also serve our community with a variety of educational, multicultural and outreach programs designed to support our artistic mission.
—*David Emmes, Martin Benson*

PRODUCTIONS 1991-1992

Direction by Martin Benson, sets by Cliff Faulkner, lighting by Paulie Jenkins, costumes by Shigeru Yaji, and sound design by Michael Roth unless otherwise noted.

Heartbreak House, George Bernard Shaw; (D) John Iacovelli
The Extra Man, Richard Greenberg; (D) Michael Engler; (S) Philipp Jung; (L) Peter Maradudin; (C) Candice Donnelly
Twelfth Night, William Shakespeare; (D) David Chambers; (S) Ralph Funicello; (L) Tom Ruzika
The Philadelphia Story, Philip Barry; (D) Libby Appel; (L) Peter Maradudin; (C) Ann Bruice
Boundary Waters, Barbara Field; (S) Michael Devine; (L) Tom Ruzika; (C) Walker Hicklin
Woman in Mind, Alan Ayckbourn; (D) David Emmes; (C) Ann Bruice
A Christmas Carol, adapt: Jerry Patch, from Charles Dickens; (D) John-David Keller; (L) Tom and Donna Ruzika; (C) Dwight Richard Odle
Sight Unseen, Donald Margulies; (D) Michael Bloom; (L) Tom Ruzika; (C) Ann Bruice
The Caretaker, Harold Pinter; (D) Paul Marcus
Noah Johnson Had a Whore, Jon Bastian
Billy Bishop Goes to War, John Gray and Eric Peterson; (D) Ben Halley, Jr.; (S) and (C) E. Scott Shaffer; (L) Peter Maradudin
Hospitality Suite, Roger Rueff; (D) Steven D. Albrezzi; (S) and (C) Dwight Richard Odle; (L) Doc Ballard

PRODUCTIONS 1992-1993

Direction by Martin Benson, sets by Cliff Faulkner and lighting by Paulie Jenkins unless otherwise noted.

The Man Who Came to Dinner, George S. Kaufman and Moss Hart; (D) William Ludel; (L) Tom Ruzika; (C) Shigeru Yaji

144 SOUTH COAST REPERTORY

South Coast Repertory. Stephen Rowe, Randy Oglesby and Elizabeth Norment in *Sight Unseen*. Photo: Henry DiRocco.

Our Country's Good, adapt: Timberlake Wertenbaker, from Thomas Keneally; (S) Gerard Howland; (C) Walker Hicklin; (SD) Nathan Birnbaum

The Miser, Moliere; trans: David Chambers; (D) David Chambers; (S) Ralph Funicello; (L) Shigeru Yaji; (C) Chris Parry

Great Day in the Morning, Thomas Babe; (D) David Emmes; (S) Gerard Howland; (L) Walker Hicklin; (L) Peter Maradudin; (SD) Michael Roth

Hay Fever, Noel Coward; (D) William Ludel; (L) Peter Maradudin; (C) Ann Bruice

Shadowlands, William Nicholson; (S) John Iacovelli; (C) Ann Bruice; (SD) Michael Roth

A Christmas Carol, adapt: Jerry Patch, from Charles Dickens; (D) John-David Keller; (S) Tom and Donna Ruzika; (C) Dwight Richard Odle

Let's Play Two, Anthony Clarvoe; (D) Michael Bloom; (S) John Iacovelli; (L) Brian Gale; (C) Dwight Richard Odle; (SD) Nathan Birnbaum

Odd Jobs, Frank Moher; (D) David Emmes; (L) Tom Ruzika; (C) Ann Bruice; (SD) David Edwards

Intimate Exchanges, Alan Ayckbourn; (D) Mark Rucker; (L) Tom Ruzika; (C) Rhonda Earick

Waiting for Godot, Samuel Beckett; (S) Michael Devine; (L) Tom Ruzika; (C) Dwight Richard Odle

So Many Words, Roger Rueff; (D) Mark Rucker; (S) Dwight Richard Odle; (C) Todd Roehrman

Stage One: The Louisville Children's Theatre

MOSES GOLDBERG
Producing Director

G. JANE JARRETT
Managing Director

SAM C. CORBETT
Board President

425 West Market St.
Louisville, KY 40202
(502) 589-5946 (bus.)
(502) 584-7777,
(800) 283-7777 (b.o.)
(502) 589-5779 (fax)

FOUNDED 1946
Sara Spencer, Ming Dick

SEASON
Oct.-May

FACILITIES
Kentucky Center for the Arts
Bomhard Theater
Seating Capacity: 622
Stage: thrust

Louisville Gardens Theatre
Seating Capacity: 300
Stage: arena

FINANCES
June 1, 1991-May 31, 1992
Expenses: $1,286,745

CONTRACTS
AEA TYA

Stage One: The Louisville Children's Theatre provides theatre experiences for young people and families. Choosing plays for specific age groups, we attempt to develop the aesthetic sensitivity of our audience members, step by step, until they emerge from our program as committed adult theatregoers. We play to both school groups and weekend family audiences. Stage One is also committed to developing professionalism in theatre for young audiences, including upgrading artist compensation to the level of adult theatres our size. We perform an eclectic repertoire, including traditional children's plays, company-created pieces, commissioned plays, plays translated from other cultures and carefully selected works from the adult repertoire. Stage One operates in the belief that the classics (both ancient and modern) of folk and children's literature concern archetypal human relationships and are worthy of serious artistic exploration.

—*Moses Goldberg*

PRODUCTIONS 1991-1992

Direction by Moses Goldberg, lighting by Chuck Schmidt and costumes by Jan Finnell unless otherwise noted.

The Emperor's Nightingale, adapt: Laura Amy Schlitz, from Hans Christian Andersen; (S) Mike Grube

Stage One: The Louisville Children's Theatre. Jeremy Tow and Yetunde Adeyinka-De'Leon in *Scars and Stripes*. Photo: Richard Bram/N.Q.P.

Tales of a Fourth Grade Nothing, adapt: Bruce Mason, from Judy Blume; (D) Tom Schreier; (S) Mike Grube
Kringle's Window, Mark Medoff; (S) Jim Billings
Jack and the Beanstalk, book: Moses Goldberg; music and lyrics: Lisa Palas; (D) Tom Schreier; (S) James Smith; (C) Rebecca Shouse; (CH) Debra Macut
A Tale of Two Cities, book adapt, music and lyrics: Wendy Kesselman, from Charles Dickens; (S) James Ream; (MD) Scott Kasbaum
Rumpelstiltskin, book: Moses Goldberg; music and lyrics: Lisa Palas; (D) J. Daniel Herring; (S) Ken Terrill
Jemima Boone: Daughter of Kentucky, Moses Goldberg; (D) Curt L. Tofteland; (S) Ken Terrill

PRODUCTIONS 1992-1993

Direction by Moses Goldberg and lighting by Chuck Schmidt unless otherwise noted.

Foreigners: A Play of Cristoforo Colombo, Laura Amy Schlitz; (S) Gary Eckhart; (C) Jeff Kinard
The Tortoise and the Hare, Alan Broadhurst; (D) Tom Schreier; (S) Gary Eckhart; (C) Jeff Kinard
Kringle's Window, Mark Medoff; (D) Tom Schreier; (S) Jim Billings; (C) Jan Finnell
The Brave Little Tailor, Robert Miller; (S) Kelly Wiegant; (C) Donna Lawrence
Anne of Green Gables, adapt: R.N. Sandberg, from L.M. Montgomery; (D) Sherrie Shultz; (S) Mike Grube; (C) Martin Thaler; (SD) Chuck Schmidt
Winnie the Pooh, A.A. Milne; (D) David Lively; (S) Kelly Wiegant; (C) Donna Lawrence
The Analysis of Mineral #4, Moses Goldberg; (S) Ken Terrill; (C) Alice A. Jenkins
Aladdin, adapt: Moses Goldberg, from *The 1,001 Nights*; (D) J. Daniel Herring; (S) Ken Terrill; (C) Connie Furr
Scars and Stripes, Thomas Cadwaleder Jones; (D) Thomas Cadwaleder Jones; (S) Chuck Schmidt; (C) Christephor Gilbert

Stage West

JERRY RUSSELL
Artistic/Managing Director

JAMES COVAULT
Associate Director

JEFF DAVIS
Board President

Box 2587
Fort Worth, TX 76113
(817) 924-9454 (bus.)
(817) 784-9378 (b.o.)
(817) 924-9454 (fax)

FOUNDED 1979
Jerry Russell

SEASON
Year-round

FACILITIES
Seating Capacity: 200
Stage: thrust

FINANCES
Oct. 1, 1991-Sept. 30, 1992
Expenses: $402,380

CONTRACTS
AEA SPT

When Stage West was founded in a downtown storefront in 1979, our primary intent was to affect our audience emotionally and intellectually; to present theatre that was intimate and honest and would, hopefully, so involve our audience that the outside world would vanish. Often we've been successful. Our second strongest purpose was to provide employment for area artists and a safe environment for their work—a no-strings, no-bullshit place. In this we have succeeded totally. Last, we hoped to educate and broaden our audience through widely varied programming which would include classic, contemporary and original works. Again we have met that goal. Now we have broadened our scope to include multiracial programming, color-blind casting and an in-school performance company. And, finally, we are moving into our own home, a 200-seat thrust-stage theatre in a former movie house which we've bought and renovated. The future is bright and ever challenging.

—*Jerry Russell*

Stage West. Bill Garber, Rene Augesen and David Poynter in *Prelude to a Kiss*. Photo: Buddy Myers.

PRODUCTIONS 1991-1992

Direction and sound design by Jerry Russell, sets by Nelson Robinson, lighting by Michael O'Brien and costumes by James Covault unless otherwise noted.

I'm Not Rappaport, Herb Gardner; (D) Nick Sandys
Lend Me a Tenor, Ken Ludwig; (D) James Covault; (C) Margaret Mitchell
The Diviners, James Leonard, Jr.
Prelude to a Kiss, Craig Lucas; (D) James Covault
Tintypes, Mary Kyte, Mel Marvin and Gary Pearle; various composers and lyricists; (C) Margaret Mitchell; (MD) Leonard McCormick; (CH) Suzi McLaughlin
Ripe Conditions, Claudia Allen; (D) Buckley Sachs
The Promise, Jose Rivera
Banjo Dancing, Stephen Wade; (D) Milton Kramer; (S) and (SD) Samuel J. Hatcher; (C) Stephen Wade

PRODUCTIONS 1992-1993

Direction and sound design by Jerry Russell, sets and costumes by James Covault and lighting by Michael O'Brien unless otherwise noted.

Fences, August Wilson; (S) Samuel J. Hatcher
Taking Steps, Alan Ayckbourn; (D) James Covault
Tales of the Lost Formicans, Constance Congdon
Heartbreak House, George Bernard Shaw; (D) James Covault; (C) Jane Goodman
The Mystery of Irma Vep, Charles Ludlam; (S) Samuel J. Hatcher; (C) Jane Goodman
Alfred Stieglitz Loves O'Keeffe, Lanie Robertson; (D) James Covault; (S) Tamlyn Wright; (C) Jane Goodman
Breaking the Code, Hugh Whitemore; (D) Nick Sandys; (S) Tamlyn Wright; (C) Jane Goodman
Lost in Yonkers, Neil Simon

StageWest

ERIC HILL
Artistic Director

KATE MAGUIRE
Managing Director

MARIE STEBBINS
Board President

One Columbus Center
Springfield, MA 01103
(413) 781-4470 (bus.)
(413) 781-2340 (b.o.)
(413) 781-3741 (fax)

FOUNDED 1967
Stephen E. Hays

SEASON
Oct.-May

FACILITIES
S. Prestly Blake Theatre
Seating Capacity: 447
Stage: thrust

Winifred Arms Studio Theatre
Seating Capacity: 99
Stage: flexible

FINANCES
July 1, 1992-June 30, 1993
Expenses: $1,415,309

CONTRACTS
AEA LORT (C) and (D)

StageWest's artistic identity is reflected in its commitment to a company of artists whose ongoing collaboration in a varied and expanded repertoire forms the central condition of our work. The goals of the theatre are to develop and cultivate the artists; to present a full range of theatrical works to the broadest possible audience; to promote opportunities for creative individuals of all cultural backgrounds to exercise their artistic and technical skills; to train and develop young talent; and to continue to collaborate with other theatre companies. Ongoing classes for students and special projects in research and development continue through the season. An intern acting company works alongside the Equity company all season, and daily acting classes are offered to every company member throughout the season.

—*Eric Hill*

PRODUCTIONS 1991-1992

Direction by Eric Hill, sets by Keith Henery, lighting and sound design by David A. Strang and costumes by Polly Byers unless otherwise noted.

Hamlet, William Shakespeare; adapt: Eric Hill; (C) Eric Hill and Ellen Lauren
Taking Steps, Alan Ayckbourn; (D) Nick Faust; (L) Jeff Hill
My Children! My Africa!, Athol Fugard; (D) David Eppel; (S) Sarah Sullivan
Sea Marks, Gardner McKay; (D) Charles Towers; (S) Peter Kallok
The Cocktail Hour, A.R. Gurney, Jr.; (L) Jeff Hill
The Trojan Women, Euripides; adapt: Eric Hill; (S) Christopher L. Brown and Keith Henery

PRODUCTIONS 1992-1993

Direction by Eric Hill, lighting and sound design by David A. Strang and costumes by Polly Byers unless otherwise noted.

Lend Me a Tenor, Ken Ludwig; (D) Kent Thompson; (S) Jim Maronek; (L) Rachel Budin; (C) Gail Brassard; (SD) Rick Menke
Holiday Memories, adapt: Russell Vandenbroucke, from Truman Capote; (S) Todd Rosenthal
Other People's Money, Jerry Sterner; (S) Peter Kallok; (L) Jeff Hill
Cat on a Hot Tin Roof, Tennessee Williams; (D) Bruce Bouchard; (S) Keith Henery
Shirley Valentine, Willy Russell; (D) Pamela Berlin; (S) and (C) G.W. Mercier; (L) Jackie Manassee; (SD) David Wiggall
Love Letters, A.R. Gurney, Jr.; (D) Tom Blair
What You Will, adapt: Eric Hill, from William Shakespeare; (S) S. Michael Getz; (L) Jeff Hill; (SD) Lisa DeGrace

Stamford Theatre Works. Matthew Mabe, Wiley Moore and John Braden in *Cobb*. Photo: Jayson Byrd.

StageWest. Kelly Maurer and Susan Hightower in *Hamlet*.

Stamford Theatre Works

STEVE KARP
Artistic Director

PAUL HIGGINS
General Manager

NAN MILLER
Board President

95 Atlantic St.
Stamford, CT 06901
(203) 359-4414
(203) 356-1846 (fax)

FOUNDED 1988
Steve Karp

SEASON
Sept.-May

FACILITIES
Sacred Heart Academy-
Circle for the Arts
Seating Capacity: 150
Stage: flexible

FINANCES
July 1, 1992-June 30, 1993
Expenses: $225,000

CONTRACTS
AEA SPT

As if to prove the proposition that a community's cultural maturity lies in its ability to produce its own art, STW's boldly original, uniquely courageous and solidly professional theatre productions have firmly established it as one of the most exciting professional theatres in our region. Reflecting the cultural diversity of its southern Connecticut and Westchester County audience, STW productions have ranged from nostalgic classic comedies to plays with strong social relevance. With last season's popular American premiere of *Jigsaws* moving to New York, preceded there by our celebrated production of *Remembrance*, which was nominated "Best Off-Broadway Play" and is currently being produced throughout the world, STW is proving that the theatre hits of tomorrow are being created right here at STW today! Our enduring commitment is to build a theatre of energy, vitality and sustained professional quality—a theatre in which our imaginations and creative talents are constrained only by the limits of our financial resources.
—*Steve Karp*

PRODUCTIONS 1991-1992

Sets by Jerry Rojo and lighting and sound design by Rob Birarelli unless otherwise noted.

Listen to the Lions, John Ford Noonan; (D) Terence Lamude; (S) Duke Durfee; (L) Stuart Duke; (C) Barbara Forbes; (SD) Tom Gould
The Deal, Matthew Witten; (D) Steve Karp; (C) Linda Melloy
Elaine's Daughter, Mayo Simon; (D) Steve Karp; (C) Chris Lawton
Two, Ron Elisha; (D) Susie Fuller; (C) Chris Lawton; (SD) Christopher A. Granger

PRODUCTIONS 1992-1993

Lighting by Rob Birarelli, costumes by Chris Lawton and sound design by Christopher A. Granger unless otherwise noted.

Cobb, Lee Blessing; (D) Steve Karp; (S) Jerry Rojo
Jigsaws, Jennifer Rogers; (D) Susie Fuller; (S) David Goetsch
Murdering Green Meadows, Douglas Post; (D) Steve Karp; (S) David Goetsch
Breakfast with Les and Bess, Lee Kalcheim; (D) Susie Fuller; (S) Jerry Rojo

Steppenwolf Theatre Company

RANDALL ARNEY
Artistic Director

STEPHEN EICH
Managing Director

WILLIAM L. ATWELL
Board President

1650 North Halsted St.
Chicago, IL 60614
(312) 335-1888 (bus.)
(312) 335-1650 (b.o.)
(312) 335-0808 (fax)

FOUNDED 1976
Terry Kinney, Jeff Perry, Gary Sinise

SEASON
Year-round

FACILITIES
Mainstage
Seating Capacity: 500
Stage: proscenium

Studio
Seating Capacity: 100-300
Stage: flexible

FINANCES
Sept. 1, 1992-Aug. 31, 1993
Expenses: $4,000,000

CONTRACTS
AEA CAT

Seppenwolf Theatre Company is comprised of actors, directors, designers, administrative and production staffs, and a board of directors who work closely together towards a cooperative and common artistic vision. With a 30-member ensemble of actor-directors and a wide-ranging repertoire, Steppenwolf aims to provide exceptional theatre through a collective approach conducive to artistic growth and thus challenging to audience and actor alike. Each artist's commitment to the ensemble approach testifies to its worth. Seven of the nine original members remain with the group after 18 years. The company achieves a rare combination: Talented individuals put the group effort first and thereby simultaneously develop their own individual potential. Steppenwolf is committed to maintaining a permanent resident company in Chicago and to promoting the goals of the ensemble by the presentation of its works to new audiences. With the completion of its new permanent home in the spring of 1991, the opening of its second stage in the fall of 1993, and the addition of seven new ensemble members, these future commitments are ensured.
—*Randall Arney*

PRODUCTIONS 1991-1992

Lighting by Kevin Rigdon, costumes by Erin Quigley and sound design by Richard Woodbury unless otherwise noted.

Your Home in the West, Rod Wooden; (D) Tom Irwin; (S) Kevin Rigdon
A Summer Remembered, Charles Nolte; (D) Stephen Eich; (S) Michael Merritt; (C) Nan Cibula-Jenkins
A Slip of the Tongue, Dusty Hughes; (D) Simon Stokes; (S) Thomas Lynch; (C) Kaye Nottbusch

The Song of Jacob Zulu, Tug Yourgrau (D) Eric Simonson; (S) Kevin Rigdon; (L) Robert Christen; (SD) Rob Milburn
My Thing of Love, Alexandra Gersten; (D) Terry Kinney; (S) Michael Merritt; (SD) Rob Milburn

PRODUCTIONS 1992-1993

Sound design by Richard Woodbury unless otherwise noted.

Awake and Sing!, Clifford Odets; (D) Sheldon Patinkin; (S) Michael Merritt and Kurt Sharp; (L) Robert Shook; (C) Frances Maggio; (SD) Rob Milburn
Inspecting Carol, Daniel Sullivan and the Seattle Repertory Resident Acting Company; (D) Eric Simonson; (S) Peter Hartwell; (L) Kevin Rigdon; (C) Karin Simonson Kopischke
Road to Nirvana, Arthur Kopit; (D) Gary Sinise; (S) John Arnone; (L) James F. Ingalls; (C) Erin Quigley
Ghost in the Machine, David Gilman; (D) Jim True; (S) Kevin Rigdon; (L) Christine A. Solger; (C) Allison Reeds; (SD) Eric Huffman
Death and the Maiden, Ariel Dorfman; (D) Randall Arney; (S) Kevin Rigdon; (L) Howard Werner; (C) Nan Cibula-Jenkins

Steppenwolf Theatre Company. John Malkovich and Lizzy McInnerny in *A Slip of the Tongue*. Photo: Michael Brosilow.

St. Louis Black Repertory Company. Joseph Edwards and Ronald J. Himes in *The Meeting*. Photo: Bob Williams.

St. Louis Black Repertory Company

RONALD J. HIMES
Producing Director

DONNA M. ADAMS
General Manager

ARTHUR D. JORDAN
Board Chairman

634 North Grand Blvd.,
Suite 10-F
St. Louis, MO 63103
(314) 534-3807 (bus.)
(314) 534-3810 (b.o.)
(314) 533-3345 (fax)

FOUNDED 1976
Ronald J. Himes

SEASON
Jan.-July

FACILITIES
Grandel Square Theatre
Seating Capacity: 450
Stage: thrust

FINANCES
July 1, 1992-June 30, 1993
Expenses: $712,808

CONTRACTS
AEA SPT

St. Louis Black Repertory Company was founded to heighten the social, cultural and educational awareness of the community—and to create an ongoing arts program for that community. As the company has expanded so have our programs: We now produce six mainstage shows; we have an extensive educational component that includes four to six touring shows, workshops and residencies, and a professional intern program. We have also presented dance, music and film series. Our main stage has a strong commitment to producing the works of black American and Third World writers in an environment that supports not only the development of the work, but also the actors, directors and designers involved. Thus the majority of our productions are area and regional premieres, aimed at artistic rather than commercial success.

—*Ronald J. Himes*

PRODUCTIONS 1991-1992

Costumes by Antonitta Barnes and sound design by Bernard Hall unless otherwise noted.

A Soldier's Play, Charles Fuller; (D) Edward G. Smith; (S) James Burwinkel; (L) Kathy Perkins
The Trials of Brother Jero, Wole Soyinka; (D) Ronald J. Himes; (S) and (L) Chris Abernathy
Zora Neale Hurston, Laurence Holder; (D) Wynn Handman; (S) Terry Chandler; (L) Antoinette Tynes
Stories About the Old Days, Bill Harris; (D) Ronald J. Himes; (S) John Carver Sullivan; (L) Michael Williams
The Me Nobody Knows, book adapt: Robert Livingston and Herb Shapiro, from Stephen Joseph and Herb Shapiro; music: Gary William Friedman; lyrics: Will Holt; (D) Amy Loui; (S) Chris Abernathy; (L) Glenn Dunn; (CH) Danny Clark
Shakin' the Mess Outta Misery, Shay Youngblood; (D) Lorna Littleway; (S) Frank Bradley; (L) Kathy Perkins; (C) Laurie Trevethan

PRODUCTIONS 1992-1993

Sound design by David Medley unless otherwise noted.

The Piano Lesson, August Wilson; (D) Edward G. Smith; (S) Frank Bradley; (L) Kathy Perkins; (C) Antonitta Barnes
Zora Neale Hurston, Laurence Holder; (D) Wynn Handman; (S) James Burwinkel; (L) Antoinette Tynes
The Meeting, Jeff Stetson; (D) Stephen McKinley Henderson; (S) James Burwinkel; (L) Michael Williams; (C) Barbara Vaughan
Black Eagles, Leslie Lee; (D) Ronald J. Himes; (S) Charles McClennahan; (L) Kathy Perkins; (C) Barbara Vaughan
Jar the Floor, Cheryl L. West; (D) Ronald J. Himes; (S) Russell Metheny; (L) Christian Epps; (C) Laurie Trevethan
Purlie, book adapt: Ossie Davis, Philip Rose and Peter Udell, from Ossie Davis; music: Gary Geld; lyrics: Peter Udell; (D) Wayne Salomon; (S) John Roslevich, Jr.; (L) Glenn Dunn; (C) Devon Painter; (MD) Dello Thedford; (CH) Danny Clark

Studio Arena Theatre

GAVIN CAMERON-WEBB
Artistic Director

RAYMOND BONNARD
Producing Director

HENRY P. SEMMELHACK
Board President

710 Main St.
Buffalo, NY 14202-1990
(716) 856-8025 (bus.)
(716) 856-5650 (b.o.)
(716) 856-3415 (fax)

FOUNDED 1965
Neal DuBrock

SEASON
Sept.-June

FACILITIES
Mainstage
Seating Capacity: 637
Stage: thrust

Pfeifer Theatre
Seating Capacity: 350
Stage: thrust

FINANCES
July 1, 1992-June 30, 1993
Expenses: $3,204,080

CONTRACTS
AEA LORT (B)

Studio Arena's programming is designed to restore the theatre to a

Studio Arena Theatre. Pamela Gray, Terrell Anthony and Michael Schacht in *Catch Me If You Can*. Photo: Rand Schuster.

central place in the community. The focus of the work is on the actor. The actor is the starting point for an exploration of what happens between her/him and the audience to create a performance. Consequently, the work selected for production tends to be theatrical in nature, and it is produced in a way that prizes both the imagination of the artist and the audience. We wish to foster long-term relationships with artists, and we are committed to developing the regional talent. In addition to production, we support a wide range of activities in the schools and community which are central to the theatre's mission. As we are resident in a border city, we are actively developing international ties both in Canada and further abroad.

—*Gavin Cameron-Webb*

PRODUCTIONS 1991-1992

Sound design by Rick Menke unless otherwise noted.

Sweet 'N' Hot in Harlem, conceived: Robert Elliot Cohen; music: Harold Arlen; various lyricists; (D) Robert Elliot Cohen; (S) John Bonard Wilson; (L) Peter Kaczorowski; (C) Judy Dearing; (MD) M. Michael Fauss; (CH) Evelyn Thomas
Other People's Money, Jerry Sterner; (D) Kathryn Long; (S) Steven Perry; (L) Nancy Schertler; (C) Lauren K. Lambie
A Christmas Carol, adapt: Amlin Gray, from Charles Dickens; (D) David Frank; (S) and (L) Paul Wonsek; (C) Mary Ann Powell
Catch Me If You Can, Jack Weinstock and Willie Gilbert; (D) Frederick King Keller; (S) Gary Eckhart; (L) Paul Wonsek; (C) Lauren K. Lambie
Fences, August Wilson; (D) Edward G. Smith; (S) Felix E. Cochren; (L) Dennis Parichy; (C) Donna Massimo
The Immigrant, Mark Harelik; (D) Howard J. Millman; (S) Kevin Rupnik; (L) Phil Monat; (C) Maria Marrero
Love Letters, A.R. Gurney, Jr.; (D) Warren Enters; (S) Gerard P. Vogt; (L) Dennis Parichy

PRODUCTIONS 1992-1993

Sound design by Rick Menke unless otherwise noted.

Lend Me a Tenor, Ken Ludwig; (D) Kent Thompson; (S) Jim Maronek; (L) Rachel Budin; (C) Gail Brassard
Lost Electra, Bruce E. Rodgers; (D) Gavin Cameron-Webb; (S) and (C) G.W. Mercier; (L) Richard Devin
A Christmas Carol, adapt: Amlin Gray, from Charles Dickens; (D) Gavin Cameron-Webb, after David Frank; (S) and (L) Paul Wonsek; (C) Mary Ann Powell
The Dining Room, A.R. Gurney, Jr.; (D) Nagle Jackson; (S) Bill Clarke; (L) Q. Brian Sickels; (C) Donna Massimo
The Business of Murder, Richard Harris; (D) Frederick King Keller; (S) and (L) Paul Wonsek; (C) Charlotte M. Yetman
Miss Evers' Boys, David Feldshuh; (D) Edward G. Smith; (S) Harry A. Feiner; (L) William H. Grant, III; (C) Lauren K. Lambie
The Voyage of Mary C, Laurence Carr; (D) Gavin Cameron-Webb; (S) Robert Cothran; (L) Harry A. Feiner; (C) Lauren K. Lambie; (SD) Lia Vollack
A...My Name is Still Alice, conceived: Joan Micklin Silver and Julianne Boyd; various composers and lyricists; (D) and (CH) Darwin Knight; (S) Peter Harrison; (L) Victor En Yu Tan; (C) Lauren K. Lambie; (MD) Randall Kramer

The Studio Theatre

JOY ZINOMAN
Artistic/Managing Director

KEITH ALAN BAKER
Associate Managing Director/ Artistic Director, Secondstage

NANCY LINN PATTON
Board Chairperson

1333 P St. NW
Washington, DC 20005
(202) 232-7267 (bus.)
(202) 332-3300 (b.o.)
(202) 588-5262 (fax)

FOUNDED 1978
Joy Zinoman

SEASON
Year-round

FACILITIES
Mainstage
Seating Capacity: 200
Stage: thrust

Secondstage
Seating Capacity: 50
Stage: flexible

FINANCES
Sept. 1, 1991-Aug. 31, 1992
Expenses: $1,233,144

CONTRACTS
AEA SPT

The Studio Theatre, now in its 16th season, is a vital and vibrant artistic force, recognized as a major cultural institution in the nation's capital. Since its founding, the Studio has produced more than 80 productions, gaining a national reputation for intelligent and challenging work. The Studio Theatre offers a wide range of works emphasizing what is best in contemporary theatre today—area premieres of bold American and European works, innovative revivals of classic works, and arresting solo performance art. The developmental Secondstage nurtures emerging directors, designers and actors. The Acting Conservatory is the region's largest and most comprehensive training program. The Studio marked its 15th anniversary with the purchase of its permanent artistic home, realizing Phase 1 of the multiyear, three-phase *Campaign to Secure the Future*. As the downtown anchor of the developing "Uptown Arts District," the Studio is committed to the cultural revival of the historic 14th Street arts and entertainment area, and the revitalization of this dynamic urban community.

—*Joy Zinoman*

The Studio Theatre. Doug Brown, Any Waddell and Kenneth C. Jackson, Jr. in *Spunk*. Photo: Stan Barouh.

PRODUCTIONS 1991-1992

Sets by Russell Metheny, lighting by Daniel MacLean Wagner and sound design by Gil Thompson unless otherwise noted.

When I Was A Girl, I Used to Scream and Shout, Sharman Macdonald; (D) Joy Zinoman; (C) Ric Thomas Rice
The Women, Clare Boothe Luce; (D) John Going; (C) Don Newcomb

The American Plan, Richard Greenberg; (D) Rob Barron; (S) James Kronzer; (C) Helen Q. Huang
The Wizard of Hip, Thomas W. Jones, II; (D) Kenneth Leon; (S) Joy Zinoman and James Kronzer; (L) Jeff Guzik
Falsettoland, book: William Finn and James Lapine; music and lyrics: William Finn; (D) Joy Zinoman; (C) Ric Thomas Rice; (MD) Rob Bowman
Nobody Here But Us Chickens, Peter Barnes; (D) Maynard Marshall; (S) and (L) David R. Zemmels; (C) Cindy King
Alfred and Victoria: A Life, Donald Freed; (D) Keith Alan Baker; (S), (L) and (SD) G. Andrew Duthie; (C) T. Kay Hutchinson
Sincerity Forever, Mac Wellman; (D) Serge Seiden; (S) James Kronzer; (L) Bill Price; (C) Marie Schneggenburger; (SD) G. Andrew Duthie

PRODUCTIONS 1992-1993

Costumes by Helen Q. Huang and sound design by Gil Thompson unless otherwise noted.

The Bright and Bold Design, Peter Whelan; (D) Joy Zinoman; (S) Russell Metheny; (L) Donald Holder
The Lisbon Traviata, Terrence McNally; (D) John Going; (S) James Kronzer; (L) Daniel MacLean Wagner; (C) Ric Thomas Rice
Rosencrantz and Guildenstern Are Dead, Tom Stoppard; (D) Evan Yionoulis; (S) Russell Metheny; (L) Donald Holder
Imagine Drowning, Terry Johnson; (D) Joy Zinoman; (S) James Kronzer; (L) Daniel MacLean Wagner; (SD) Gil Thompson and Ron Ursano
Spunk, adapt: George C. Wolfe, from Zora Neale Hurston; music: Chic Street Man; (D) Ronald J. Himes; (S) Dan Conway; (L) William H. Grant, III; (C) Reggie Ray; (CH) Mike Malone
2-2-Tango, Daniel MacIvor; (D) Keith Alan Baker; (S) Giorgos Tsappas; (L) Marianne Meadows; (SD) H. Lee Gable
Hot Fudge, Caryl Churchill; (D) Serge Seiden; (S) Christopher L. Brown; (L) Cheryl Zook; (C) Jenni Blong; (SD) Kelly L. King

Syracuse Stage

TAZEWELL THOMPSON
Artistic Director

JAMES A. CLARK
Producing Director

ROBERT J. BENNETT
Board Chair

820 East Genesee St.
Syracuse, NY 13210-1508
(315) 443-4008 (bus.)
(315) 443-3275 (b.o.)
(315) 443-9846 (fax)

FOUNDED 1974
Arthur Storch

SEASON
Sept.-June

FACILITIES
John D. Archbold Theatre
Seating Capacity: 510
Stage: proscenium

Daniel C. Sutton Pavilion
Seating Capacity: 100
Stage: flexible

FINANCES
July 1, 1992-June 30, 1993
Expenses: $2,400,000

CONTRACTS
AEA LORT (C)

As the new artistic director of Syracuse Stage, I intend to produce populist theatre that mines the rich trove of American and international classics, and emphasizes the aggressive development of new plays in a cutting-edge, provocative and compelling manner. Entering its third decade, the Stage will hold as its guiding principle the choice of a repertoire whose primary aim is the pursuit of artistic excellence; whose scope encompasses the world's rich cultural diversity; whose theatrical realization will be visionary, innovative and bold; and whose literary content is intellectually challenging, emotionally uplifting, and sometimes iconoclastic and even shocking. Crucial to my mission is providing a supportive atmosphere where artists—actors, writers, designers, directors—are encouraged to explore the distant reaches of their imaginations, breaking through the mind's envelope to achieve the highest artistic merit. I am committed to the active participation of an ever-widening diverse core-audience base and the development of younger audiences through an educational outreach program in collaboration with public and private schools.
—*Tazewell Thompson*

Note: During the 1991-92 season, Arthur Storch served as producing artistic director.

PRODUCTIONS 1991-1992

Lighting by Phil Monat, costumes by Maria Marrero and sound design by James Wildman unless otherwise noted.

Pump Boys and Dinettes, John Foley, Mark Hardwick, Debra Monk, Cass Morgan, John Schimmel and Jim Wann; (D) Peter Glazer; (S) Chris Shriver; (MD) John DiPinto
The Country Wife, William Wycherley; (D) Julianne Boyd; (S) James Youmans; (L) Michael Newton Brown; (C) David C. Woolard
Tea, Velina Hasu Houston; (D) Julianne Boyd; (S) Craig Lathrop; (L) Victor En Yu Tan; (C) C.L. Hundley; (SD) Bruce Ellman
Androcles and the Lion, George Bernard Shaw; (D) Arthur Storch; (S) Victor A. Becker; (C) Pamela Scofield
The Sum of Us, David Stevens; (D) Jamie Brown; (S) James Noone; (L) Sandra Schilling; (C) Randall E. Klein
The Immigrant, Mark Harelik; (D) Howard J. Millman; (S) Kevin Rupnik; (SD) Jeffrey Karoff
Love Letters, A.R. Gurney, Jr.; (D) Arthur Storch; (L) Sandra Schilling

PRODUCTIONS 1992-1993

Sound design by James Wildman unless otherwise noted.

Lend Me a Tenor, Ken Ludwig; (D) Arthur Storch; (S) James Noone; (L) Phil Monat; (C) Pamela Scofield
A Christmas Carol, adapt: Gerardine Clark, from Charles Dickens; (D) William S. Morris; (S) Bob Barnett; (L) Victor En Yu Tan; (C) Maria Marrero
Hysterics, Le Clanche Du Rand; (D) Will Osborne; (S) Kerry Sanders; (L) Sandra Schilling; (C) Randall E. Klein
"Master Harold"...and the boys, Athol Fugard; (D) Jamie Brown; (S) James Noone; (L) Phil Monat; (C) Barbara Jenks; (SD) Brett Rominger
Awake and Sing!, Clifford Odets; (D) Arthur Storch; (S) R. Michael Miller; (L) Marc B. Weiss; (C) Pamela Scofield
Jar the Floor, Cheryl L. West; (D) Tazewell Thompson; (S) and (L) Joseph P. Tilford; (C) Kay Kurta; (SD) Susan R. White

Syracuse Stage. Benjamin White, Daryl Edwards and Allen Gilmore in *"Master Harold"...and the boys*. Photo: Doug Wanders.

Tacoma Actors Guild. Benny S. Cannon, Gregg Loughridge, Kevin C. Loomis in Virtus. *Photo: Fred Andrews.*

Tacoma Actors Guild

BRUCE K. SEVY
Artistic Director

KATE HAAS
Managing Director

PATRICIA SHUMAN
Board President

901 Broadway
Jones Building, 6th Floor
Tacoma, WA 98402-4404
(206) 272-3107 (bus.)
(206) 272-2145 (b.o.)
(206) 272-3358 (fax)

FOUNDED 1978
Rick Tutor, William Becvar

SEASON
Nov.-June

FACILITIES
Theatre on the Square
Seating Capacity: 304
Stage: modified proscenium/flexible

FINANCES
July 1, 1992-June 30, 1993
Expenses: $967,726

CONTRACTS
AEA letter of agreement

Tacoma Actors Guild continually strives to achieve the highest standards of excellence in the theatre it presents. TAG seeks to engage the community it serves in a dynamic partnership by constantly exploring challenging and entertaining works selected from the entire breadth of dramatic literature. Additionally, TAG sees the development of new works which contribute to the growth and development of American theatre as part of its greater artistic misson. In our efforts to become a true regional theatre center, we are committed to developing programs which will broaden our audience and reflect the diversity of the region. We will continue to expand programs like our student performance series and summer conservatory, and to develop other programs which provide theatre-related forums for community outreach. Our move to a brand-new facility in the fall of 1993 affords us greater opportunities for audience development and artistic growth.
—*Bruce K. Sevy*

PRODUCTIONS 1991-1992

Direction by Bruce K. Sevy, sets by Carey Wong, lighting by Michael Wellborn, costumes by Ron Erickson and sound design by Tom Utterback unless otherwise noted.

Lend Me a Tenor, Ken Ludwig; (L) Robert A. Jones
Straight Arrows, Colleen Dodson; (D) John Monteith and Beth Henley; (C) Colleen Dodson
A Christmas Carol, adapt: Chad Henry, from Charles Dickens
A...My Name is Still Alice, conceived: Joan Micklin Silver and Julianne Boyd; various composers and lyricists; (D) Christine Sumption; (S) Peggy McDonald; (L) Patty Mathieu; (C) Josie Gardner; (MD) Teresa Metzger; (CH) Jayne Muirhead
Orphans, Lyle Kessler; (D) William Becvar; (S) Jeff Frkonja; (L) Robert A. Jones
Rumors, Neil Simon; (D) Christine Sumption; (S) Bill Forrester; (L) Robert A. Jones; (C) Jeanne Arnold
Guys and Dolls, book adapt: Jo Swerling and Abe Burrows, from Damon Runyon; music and lyrics: Frank Loesser; (S) Bill Forrester; (MD) Richard Gray; (CH) Stephen Terrell

PRODUCTIONS 1992-1993

Lighting by Robert A. Jones, costumes by Ron Erickson and sound design by Tom Utterback unless otherwise noted.

I Hate Hamlet, Paul Rudnick; (D) Bruce K. Sevy; (S) Carey Wong; (L) Michael Wellborn
Beehive, conceived: Larry Gallagher; various composers and lyricists; (D) and (CH) Stephen Terrell; (S) Jennifer Lupton; (MD) Richard Gray
Virtus, Gregg Loughridge; (D) Gregg Loughridge; (S) Michael Olich; (C) Frances Kenny
The Voice of the Prairie, John Olive; (D) Steven E. Alter; (S) Bill Forrester; (SD) David Hunter Koch and Tom Utterback
Love Letters, A.R. Gurney, Jr.; (D) Bruce K. Sevy
Pump Boys and Dinettes, John Foley, Mark Hardwick, Debra Monk, Cass Morgan, John Schimmel and Jim Wann; (D) and (CH) Steve Tomkins; (S) Bill Forrester; (L) Michael Wellborn; (C) Karen Ledger; (MD) Richard Gray

Tennessee Repertory Theatre

MAC PIRKLE
Artistic Director

BRIAN J. LACZKO
Managing Director

JACK O. BOVENDER, JR.
Board President

427 Chestnut St.
Nashville, TN 37203
(615) 244-4878 (bus.)
(615) 741-7777 (b.o.)
(615) 244-1232 (fax)

FOUNDED 1985
Mac Pirkle, Martha Rivers Ingram

SEASON
Sept.-May

FACILITIES
James K. Polk Theatre
Seating Capacity: 1,010
Stage: modified thrust

FINANCES
July 1, 1991-June 30, 1992
Expenses: $1,599,981

CONTRACTS
AEA LORT (C)

Tennessee Repertory Theatre is in Nashville, a strong center of life and commerce in the South, and a prominent center for music and entertainment. Nashville is home to

Tennessee Repertory Theatre. James Judy and Betsy True in A Wonderful Life. *Photo: Rhea Rippey.*

151

some of the most talented songwriters, performers and publishers of music in the world. Our theatre is born out of the same basic human need as their music—the need to express the stories of our lives. The Rep is a place of stories. These stories are expressed sometimes with song but always with music. Many of them have been told for centuries, in different languages and in different countries, and many have been told only once. Tennessee Rep was founded with the simple mission of establishing high-quality professional theatre in Nashville. We accomplished this the same way any other theatre does—through hard work, good friends and creative problem-solving. Give us a call, come for a visit, and you might stay for a while.

—*Mac Pirkle*

PRODUCTIONS 1991-1992

Direction by Don Jones and sound design by Eric Swartz unless otherwise noted.

Grease, book, music and lyrics: Jim Jacobs and Warren Casey; (S) Craig Spain; (L) Jonathan R. Hutchins; (C) Jennifer S. Orth; (MD) Jeff Lisenby; (CH) Janet Younts

Ain't Got Long to Stay Here, Barry Scott; (D) Mac Pirkle; (S) Sandy Bates and Brian J. Laczko; (L) Brian J. Laczko; (C) Carmen Cavello

A Christmas Carol, adapt: Don Jones, from Charles Dickens; (S) Bennet Averyt; (L) Jonathan R. Hutchins; (C) Cindy Russell

Big River, book adapt: William Hauptman, from Mark Twain; music and lyrics: Roger Miller; (D) John Briggs; (S) and (L) Bennet Averyt; (C) Martha Harris Cooper; (MD) Stan Tucker; (CH) Janet Younts

Baby, book: Sybille Pearson; music: David Shire; lyrics: Richard Maltby, Jr.; (S) Craig Spain; (L) Jonathan R. Hutchins; (C) Johann Stegmeir; (MD) Stan Tucker; (CH) Rowena Soriano

PRODUCTIONS 1992-1993

Sound design by Eric Swartz unless otherwise noted.

The All Night Strut, Fran Charnas; various composers and lyricists; (D) and (CH) Eric Riley; (S) Sandy Bates; (L) Jeffrey A. Hall; (C) Jennifer S. Orth; (MD) Stan Tucker

Twelfth Night, William Shakespeare; (D) Barry Edelstein; (S) Norelle Sissons; (L) Steve Loftin; (C) Angela Wendt

A Wonderful Life, book adapt and lyrics: Sheldon Harnick, from the original screenplay; music: Joe Raposo; (D) Mac Pirkle; (S) Robert Cothran; (L) Jonathan R. Hutchins; (C) Bill Black; (MD) Stan Tucker; (CH) Edie Cowan

Phantom, book adapt: Arthur Kopit, from Gaston Leroux; music and lyrics: Maury Yeston; (D) John Briggs; (S) David Mitchell; (L) Brian J. Laczko; (C) Howard Tsvi Kaplan; (MD) Stan Tucker; (CH) Janet Younts

Cat on a Hot Tin Roof, Tennessee Williams; (D) Don Jones; (S) Craig Spain; (L) Scott Leathers; (C) David Kay Mickelsen; (SD) Tim Hubler and Eric Swartz

Thalia Spanish Theatre

SILVIA BRITO
Artistic/Executive Director

KATHRYN A. GIAIMO
Administrative Director

ANNA HARRSCH
Board Chairperson

Box 4368
Sunnyside, NY 11104
(718) 729-3880
(718) 729-3388 (fax)

FOUNDED 1977
Silvia Brito

SEASON
Year-round

FACILITIES
Seating Capacity: 74
Stage: proscenium

FINANCES
July 1, 1992-June 30, 1993
Expenses: $352,600

Thalia Spanish Theatre's mission is to produce and present high-quality, professional theatrical productions in order to promote and preserve Spanish and Latin American culture and heritage throughout the greater New York community. Thalia's specialty is *zarzuela* (Spanish operetta), the only lyrical heritage of the Spanish stage. Thalia is the only theatre in New York presenting traditional *zarzuela* with period costumes and sets. We've performed every year at the Festival of the Zarzuela in El Paso, Texas (the only one of its kind outside Spain) since it began in 1986. We've produced the American premieres of plays by celebrated Spanish playwrights Antonio Gala and Jaime Salom, and our Folklore Shows of music and dance from Spain and Latin America attract a wide audience. We've won 63 awards for artistic excellence, including 45 from ACE (Association of Critics of Entertainment) and the 1989 Encore Award of the Arts and Business Council.

—*Silvia Brito*

PRODUCTIONS 1991-1992

Direction by Silvia Brito, sets by Antonio Perez Melero, lighting and sound design by Jorge Prieto and costumes by Marta Gomez unless otherwise noted.

Los Claveles, book and lyrics: Sevilla and Carreno; music: Jose Serrano; (S) Sergio Vidal; (MD) Leopoldo Escalante

Tango & Folklore Argentino 1991, various composers and lyricists; (D) and (CH) Pedro Escudero; (S) Sergio Vidal

Celos Del Aire, Jose Lopez Rubio

Andrea Del Conte and the American Spanish Dance Theater, various composers and lyricists; (D) and (CH) Andrea Del Conte; (C) Chana Alvarez

Cena Para Dos, Santiago Moncada

Tango & Folklore Argentino 1992, various composers and lyricists; (D) and (CH) Pedro Escudero; (L) and (SD) Guillermo Escudero

PRODUCTIONS 1992-1993

Direction by Silvia Brito, sets lighting and sound design by Guillermo Escudero and costumes by Marta Gomez unless otherwise noted.

Las Leandras, book and lyrics: Gonzalez del Castillo and Munoz Roman; music: Francisco Alonso; (MD) Shellie K. Johnson; (CH) Laura and Pedro Escudero

Tango & Folklore Argentino 1992, various composers and lyricists; (D) and (CH) Pedro Escudero

Cena Para Dos, Santiago Moncada

Andrea Del Conte and the American Spanish Dance Theater, various composers and lyricists; (D) and (CH) Andrea Del Conte; (C) Chana Alvarez

Tango & Folklore Argentino 1993, various composers and lyricists; (D) and (CH) Pedro Escudero

Thalia Spanish Theatre. Georgia Galvez in *Las Leandras*. Photo: Rafael Llerena.

Theater at Lime Kiln. John Wayne Shafer, Bryan Thompson, Tommy Conway, Ben Jones and Patrick McCloskey in *Munci Meg*. Photo: W. Patrick Hinely Work/Play.

Theater at Lime Kiln

BARRY MINES
Artistic Director

KENNETH E. SHECK
Managing Director

ROBERT MARTIS
Board Chairman

Box 663
Lexington, VA 24450
(703) 463-7088 (bus.)
(703) 463-3074 (b.o.)
(703) 463-1082 (fax)

FOUNDED 1984
Don Baker, Tommy Spencer

SEASON
June-Aug.

FACILITIES
The Kiln
Seating Capacity: 299
Stage: proscenium

The Bowl
Seating Capacity: 350
Stage: proscenium

The Tent
Seating Capacity: 400
Stage: proscenium

FINANCES
Mar. 1, 1992-Feb. 28, 1993
Expenses: $570,349

CONTRACTS
AEA SPT

I believe the artistic backbone of Lime Kiln to be the creation and presentation of work that reflects the indigenous stories and music of our region. Accordingly, we extend an invitation to the members of the population we serve to knowledgeably evaluate our work from *their* perspective of this place. To present theatre that grows from this particular region is, by necessity, to incorporate within the fiber of the product a voice which exhibits the heritage, culture and history of the region. Lime Kiln is more than a unique *physical* place to see a production; its work *identifies* and *celebrates* our community's unique qualities and provides a way to express and a means to personify the identity indigenous to this region. In this way Lime Kiln educates its public by becoming a more thorough arts organization and a more responsible community member.
—Barry Mines

Note: During the 1991-92 and part of the 1992-93 seasons, Don Baker served as artistic director.

PRODUCTIONS 1992

Direction by Don Baker, lighting by Michael Gorman and sound design by Mike Anady unless otherwise noted.

Apple Dreams, Tom Ziegler; (S) Tom Ziegler; (C) Marshal McAden
Stonewall Country, book: Don Baker; music: Robin and Linda Williams; lyrics: Robin and Linda Williams and Don Baker; (D) and (CH) Marshal McAden; (MD) Clay Buckner
Tale of Cymbeline, William Shakespeare; adapt: Don Baker; (C) Thomas Preziosi
Roadside, book adapt, music and lyrics: Marshal McAden, from Lynn Riggs; (S) Bart McGeehon; (C) Thomas Preziosi

PRODUCTIONS 1993

Direction by William Rough, lighting by Michael Gorman and sound design by Mike Anady unless otherwise noted.

Scalding Steam & Lonesome Rails, Don Baker, Marshal McAden and Barry Mines; music: Marshal McAden; (MD) Marshal McAden
Munci Meg, Don Baker, Jack Merrick, Robin Mullins, Barry Mines, Cherie Sheppard and Tommy Conway; music and lyrics: Robin Mullins and Jack Herrick; (MD) Marshal McAden
3 Drops of Blood, book: Don Baker; music and lyrics: Robin Mullins; (MD) Marshal McAden
Stonewall Country, book: Don Baker; music: Robin and Linda Williams; Robin and Linda Williams and Don Baker; (D) Barry Mines
Apple Dreams, Tom Ziegler; (D) Ted Story; (S) Tom Ziegler; (C) Anne Chamberlain
Oedipus, Sophocles; adapt: Bill Goulet; (D) Marshal McAden; (L) Geoff Will; (C) Anne Chamberlain

The Theater at Monmouth

RICHARD SEWELL
Artistic Director

M. GEORGE CARLSON
Managing Director

RALPH CONANT
Board President

Box 385
Monmouth, ME 04259-0385
(207) 933-2952 (bus.)
(207) 933-9999 (b.o.)

FOUNDED 1970
Richard Sewell, Robert Joyce

SEASON
June-Sept.

FACILITIES
Cumston Hall
Seating Capacity: 275
Stage: thrust

FINANCES
Oct. 1, 1991-Sept. 30, 1992
Expenses: $200,000

CONTRACTS
AEA SPT

The Theater at Monmouth's rolling repertory season is mounted in a jewel box of a historic opera house, Cumston Hall. Using the plays of Shakespeare as our criterion and centerpiece, we draw from the whole range of classical—and some modern—literature. Our quest is always for actors comfortable with a wide scope of style and type, and scripts that respect the excitement and power of language.
—Richard Sewell

PRODUCTIONS 1991-1992

The Comedy of Errors, William Shakespeare; (D) and (C) Richard Sewell; (S) Jim Thurston and Richard Sewell; (L) Randy Emory
The Liar, Pierre Corneille; trans and adapt: Ranjit Bolt; (D) Christopher Rock; (S) Jim Thurston and Christopher Rock; (L) John Ervin; (C) Elisabeth Tobey
King Lear, William Shakespeare; (D) and (S) Christopher Rock; (L) Randy Emory; (C) Elisabeth Tobey

Our Country's Good, adapt: Timberlake Wertenbaker, from Thomas Keneally; (D) and (S) Christopher Rock; (L) John Ervin; (C) Elisabeth Tobey
Beauty and the Beast, adapt: Richard Sewell, from Mme. Le Prince de Beaumont; (D), (S), (L) and (C) Richard Sewell
Musicians of Bremen, adapt: Richard Sewell, from The Brothers Grimm; (D), (S), (L) and (C) Richard Sewell

PRODUCTIONS 1992-1993

Direction and sets by Christopher Rock and costumes by Elisabeth Tobey unless otherwise noted.

Waiting for Godot, Samuel Beckett; (L) and (C) Christopher Rock
Saint Joan, George Bernard Shaw; (L) Christopher Rock and Eva Mosely
A Midsummer Night's Dream, William Shakespeare; (D) and (S) Richard Sewell; (L) William P. Esty
Macbeth, William Shakespeare; (L) Christopher Rock and Eva Mosely

The Playboy of the Western World, John Millington Synge; (D) and (S) Richard Sewell; (L) William P. Esty
One Inch Fellow, Charles and Lola Wilcox; (L) and (C) Christopher Rock

---

Theatre de la Jeune Lune

BARBRA BERLOVITZ DESBOIS, VINCENT GRACIEUX, ROBERT ROSEN, DOMINIQUE SERRAND
Artistic Directors

SONJA HARRIDAY
Business Director

SUSAN ZEMKE
Board President

105 First St. N.
Minneapolis, MN 55401
(612) 332-3968 (bus.)
(612) 333-6200 (b.o.)
(612) 332-0048 (fax)

FOUNDED 1978
Dominique Serrand, Vincent Gracieux, Barbra Berlovitz Desbois

SEASON
Sept.-June

FACILITIES
Seating Capacity: 450
Stage: flexible

FINANCES
Aug. 1, 1992-July 31, 1993
Expenses: $820,000

Theatre de la Jeune Lune is a theatre of actors. What is important to us is what the actor puts on the stage when the curtain goes up—what happens in front of the audience. With that end result in mind, we enter into each production. There isn't a play we won't do. We could be interested in a classic, a modern work or an original new play. What we do with it is a different matter. We strive to make the play "ours," to bring across, as our audience would agree, our style. Our heart, passions and emotions open the paths to ideas. We create exactly what we want to, within our obvious financial restrictions. Every production is different and each play must be attacked from a new angle with our experience of the past. Pushing ourselves into new areas every year, we want to continue bringing exciting, eventful and important theatre to our community.

—*Dominique Serrand*

PRODUCTIONS 1991-1992

Crusoe, Friday, and the Island of Hope, Steven Epp, Felicity Jones and Dominique Serrand; (D) Dominique Serrand; (S) Vincent Gracieux; (L) Robert Rosen; (C) Barbra Berlovitz Desbois
The Nightingale, book adapt and lyrics: Tom Poole, from Hans Christian Andersen; music: Chan Poling; (D) Felicity Jones; (S) Steven Epp and Vincent Gracieux; (L) Robert Rosen; (C) Dominique Serrand; (MD) Michael Koerner
The Ballroom, Theatre de la June Leune; (D) Dominique Serrand; (S) Vincent Gracieux; (L) Frederic Desbois; (C) Anne Ruben; (SD) Herbie Woodruff

Theatre de la Jeune Lune. Dominique Serrand and Vincent Gracieux in *Scapin*. Photo: Donna Kelly.

The Theater at Monmouth. Kim Gordon, James Finnegan and Chloe Leamon in *Our Country's Good*. Photo: Christopher Rock.

Theater Emory

VINCENT MURPHY
Artistic Producing Director

PAT MILLER
Managing Director

ROBERT STRICKLAND
Board Chair, Emory University

Emory University
Atlanta, GA 30322
(404) 727-0524 (bus.)
(404) 727-6187 (b.o.)
(404) 727-6253 (fax)

FOUNDED 1982
James W. Flannery

SEASON
Aug.-April

FACILITIES
Mary Gray Munroe Theater
Seating Capacity: 121-150
Stage: flexible

The Studio, Annex B
Seating Capacity: 40-60
Stage: flexible

FINANCES
Sept. 1, 1992-Aug. 31, 1993
Expenses: $441,325

CONTRACTS
AEA SPT

Theater Emory is the producing organization of Emory University, presenting professional and student productions to engage theatregoers in ideas and images developed from new works and classics. The theatre functions in the best tradition of a research university—posing questions, challenging assumptions and examining values in search of a lasting truth. A theatre company cannot find itself by following some preexisting model. Theatres define themselves through a body of work, created by artists who treat themselves as researchers. The collaborators ask important questions, pursuing and staying open to all inherent possibilities. We have become such a product-oriented society, focused on the final results, that we are losing the idea of exploration, of experience. At Theater Emory, we produce theatre that evokes and opens ideas as well as conclusions and definitions. We look for profound ways to ask ourselves questions. We are here to suggest to society where it might go.
—*Vincent Murphy*

PRODUCTIONS 1991-1992

Caligula, Albert Camus; trans: Justin O'Brien; (D) Vincent Murphy; (S) Liz Elliott; (L) Dave Garrett and Judy Zanotti; (C) Andrew McIlroy; (SD) Scott Shankman
The Van Gogh Gallery, conceived: Vincent Murphy, written: Steve Murray; (D) Vincent Murphy, Norman Armour and Andrew McIlroy; (S) Leslie Taylor; (L) Judy Zanotti; (C) Judy Winograd
The Good Person of Setzuan, Bertolt Brecht; trans: Ralph Manheim; lyrics: David DeBerry; (D) Tim Ocel; (S) William Moore; (L) Judy Zanotti; (C) Leslie Taylor
Enough, Samuel Beckett; (D) Vincent Murphy; (S) and (C) Leslie Taylor; (L) Judy Zanotti

Every Other Monday:
various playwrights, various directors

PRODUCTIONS 1992-1993

The Oriki of a Grasshopper, Femi Osofisan; and *The Engagement*, Anton Chekhov; adapt: Femi Osofisan; (D), (S) and (C) Femi Osofisan
Enough, Samuel Beckett; (D) Vincent Murphy; (S) and (C) Leslie Taylor; (L) Judy Zanotti
The Little Prince, adapt: Kenny Raskin, from Antoine de Saint Exupery; (D) Kenny Raskin; (S) Rochelle Barker; (L) Judy Zanotti; (C) Stephanie Kaskel; (SD) Dennis West and Judy Zanotti

PRODUCTIONS 1992-1993

Children of Paradise: Shooting a Dream, adapt: Steven Epp, Felicity Jones, Dominique Serrand and Paul Walsh, from Marcel Carne and Jacques Prevert; (D) Dominique Serrand; (S) Vincent Gracieux; (L) Frederic Desbois; (C) Trina Mrnak
Scapin, Moliere; trans: Robert Rosen; (D) Robert Rosen; (S) Steven Epp and Vincent Gracieux; (L) Frederic Desbois; (C) Joel Sass

Hello and Goodbye, Athol Fugard; (D) Vincent Murphy; (S) Leslie Taylor; (L) and (SD) Judy Zanotti; (C) Judy Winograd
Statements After an Arrest Under the Immorality Act, Athol Fugard; (D) Brenda Bynum; (S) Leslie Taylor; (L) and (SD) Judy Zanotti; (C) Judy Winograd
The Trap, Frank Manley; (D) Vincent Murphy; (S) William Moore; (L) and (SD) Judy Zanotti; (C) Leslie Taylor
A Family Affair, Alexander Ostrovsky; adapt: Nick Dear; (D) Eugene Lazarev; (S) and (C) Leslie Taylor; (L) and (SD) Judy Zanotti
Your Children: The Testimony of Charles Manson, adapt: Dave Garrett; (D) Dave Garrett; (L) Katrina Walker
The Lear Project, adapt from William Shakespeare; (D) Janice Akers and Tim McDonough; (S) Leslie Taylor; (L) Whitney Banks and Fredrick Holloman

Theater Emory. Andrew McIlroy and Norman Armour in *Caligula*. Photo: Nancy Scherm.

Theatre for a New Audience

JEFFREY HOROWITZ
Artistic/Producing Director

PETER M. KINDLON
General Manager

THEODORE C. ROGERS
Board Chair

154 Christopher St., Suite 3D
New York, NY 10014-2839
(212) 229-2819 (bus.)
(212) 279-4200 (b.o.)
(212) 229-2911 (fax)

FOUNDED 1979
Jeffrey Horowitz

SEASON
Jan.-May

FACILITIES
St. Clement's Church
Seating Capacity: 175
Stage: proscenium

FINANCES
Sept. 1, 1992-Aug. 31, 1993
Expenses: $925,000

CONTRACTS
AEA letter of agreement

Theatre for a New Audience

Theatre for a New Audience. Christina Haag, Enid Graham and Melissa Bowen in *Love's Labour's Lost*. Photo: Gerry Goodstein.

Theatre for a New Audience produces Shakespeare and other classics and contemporary plays of poetic imagination, and builds audiences drawn from all ages and from diverse ethnic and economic backgrounds. The next stage of our development is to build a group of associate artists to promote artistic development and the continuity of shared values over time. An important goal of the associate artist program is to nurture artists through ongoing training and development, and to provide opportunities for artistic experimentation. Education is a fundamental part of our mission. We educate both through the plays we produce and through our arts education programs, which serve young people in our community's schools. Participants in these programs include underserved, at-risk and special-education students.
—*Jeffrey Horowitz*

PRODUCTIONS 1991-1992

The Comedy of Errors, William Shakespeare; (D) William Gaskill; (S) Power Boothe; (L) Frances Aronson; (C) Gabriel Berry

The New Americans, book, music and lyrics: Elizabeth Swados; (S) and (C) Skip Mercier; (L) Mary Louise Geiger

PRODUCTIONS 1992-1993

Henry V, William Shakespeare; (D) Barry Kyle; (S) Marina Draghici and Jay Durrwachter; (L) Steve Woods; (C) Marina Draghici and Hwa K.C. Park

Love's Labour's Lost, William Shakespeare; (D) Michael Langham; (S) Douglas Stein; (L) Matthew Frey; (C) Ann Hould-Ward; (SD) James van Bergen

Theater for the New City

CRYSTAL FIELD
Artistic Director

GEORGE BARTENIEFF
Executive Director

SEYMOUR HACKER
Board Chairman

155 First Ave.
New York, NY 10003
(212) 475-3302 (bus.)
(212) 254-1109 (b.o.)

FOUNDED 1971
Larry Kornfield, Crystal Field, George Bartenieff, Theo Barnes

SEASON
Year-round

FACILITIES
Johnson Theater
Seating Capacity: 99-240
Stage: flexible

Theater II
Seating Capacity: 99
Stage: proscenium

Theater III
Seating Capacity: 74
Stage: flexible

FINANCES
July 1, 1991-June 30, 1992
Expenses: $516,396

CONTRACTS
AEA letter of agreement

Theater for the New City, now in its 24th season, is a center dedicated to the discovery of relevant new writing and the nurturing of new playwrights. TNC has presented 600 new American plays to more than 750,000 audience members, including the premieres of works by playwrights like Sam Shepard, Maria Irene Fornes, Harvey Fierstein and Romulus Linney, and has also presented many of America's most important theatre companies and artists. TNC's commitment to new artists, lesser-known writers and young performers is evidenced by our Emerging Playwrights Program, our Street Theatre Performers Workshop and our extensive new play commissioning program. Each year, TNC provides 30,000 free admissions to members of 90 community, senior citizen and youth groups, and creates a free street-theatre traveling festival bringing outdoor performances to New York City's five boroughs. In 1986, after performing in rented spaces, TNC purchased a new home that is being converted into a community-based cultural and performance art center.
—*Crystal Field, George Bartenieff*

PRODUCTIONS 1991-1992

War and Peace, Crystal Field and Christopher Cherney; (D) Crystal Field; (S) Anthony Angel; (C) Lolly Alejandro, S. Degiez, Marc Borders and Allan Charlet

Accident, 9th Street Theater; (D) Joanne Schultz; (S) Donna Evans

Easy Living, Sam Harps; (D) and (S) Leon Pinkney; (C) Raymond Pizzaro

Downtown Psychobroads, Larry Myers; (D) Brad Friedman; (S) Barbara Hurley; (C) Loren Bevans

Squaring the Circle, Guy Gsell; (D) Thomas Gilpin; (S) Myrna Duarte

Long Journey Home, Laura Simms; (D), (S) and (C) Laura Simms

Walk Around the Block, Gail Conrad, (D) Gail Conrad; (S) Matthew Taneri; (C) Fifi Khabie

Powwow, Thunderbird Dancers; (D) Louis Mofsie; (L) Tommy Barker; (C) Frances Grumbly

Kill, Bina Sharif; (D) Bina Sharif; (S) Paula Sjoblomv; (C) Frances Grumbly

Library Love, Walter Corwin and A. Abrams; (S) James Jennings; (C) Anthony Angel

Hello, Mrs. President, Phoebe Legere; (S) and (C) Phoebe Legere

Dreamers of the Absolute, Phil Motherwell; (D) Lindsey Smith; (S) Tim Burns

Huipil II, Vira and Hortensia Colorado; (D) Ben Geboe; (S) Tom Moore; (C) Soni Moreno Primeau

Watermotions, Brian Keith Jackson; (D), (S) and (C) Brian Keith Jackson

Jamboree, David Sedaris; (D) Arnold Aprill; (S) Hugh Hamrick; (C) Jeffrey Wallach

Bunny & Doris, Sebastian Stuart; (D) Sebastian Stuart; (S) Jamie Leo; (C) Zsamira

Times Square Angel, Charles Busch; (D) Kenneth Elliott; (S) B.T. Whitehill; (C) John Glaser

The Flood, Rosalyn Drexler; (D) Rosalyn Drexler; (S) Tom Moore; (C) Lolly Alejandro

Weather Report, Margo Lee Sherman; (D) Margaret Harrington; (S) and (C) Katy Orrick

Felicia, Patricia Cobey; (D) Robert Bresnick; (S) Karen Fsakos; (C) Maureen Schell

Dust, Gary Goldberg; (D), (S) and (C) Gary Goldberg

Rivalry of Dolls, James Purdy; (D) John Eucker; (S) Myrna Duarte; (C) Delia Doherty

The Three Little Sisters, Robert Dahdah; (D) (S) and (C) Robert Dahdah

Eco-Festival:
various playwrights, various directors

Micropolis, Theodora Skipitares; (D) and (C) Theodora Skipitares; (L) Zdenek Kriz

Anna, Viveca Lindfors; (D) (S) and (C) Viveca Lindfors

Higher Powers, Stephen Fife; (D) Seth Gordon; (S) and (C) Michael Mariano

Angelina's Pizzeria, Eddie Di Donna; (D) Mark Marcante; (S) Anthony Angel; (C) Lolly Alejandro

Bombing the Cradle, David Willinger; (D) Monica Benitz; (S) M. Karimi-Hakak; (C) M. Dewayne Benitz

PRODUCTIONS 1992-1993

Christopher Columbus! Or, Business as Usual, Crystal Field and Christopher Cherney; (D) Crystal Field; (S) Anthony Angel; (C) Dawn Dewitt and G. Beck
Afterthoughts, Brian Keith Jackson; (D) D.J. Mendel; (S) and (C) David Paul
The Rain Always Falls, Gary Lasdun; (D) and (C) Rich Crooks; (S) Daniel Nichols
Color Blind, Terry Lee King; (D), (S), (L) and (C) Terry Lee King
The Return of the Raven and Other Stories, The Wise Guise; (S) and (C) Myrna Duarte
A Curious Tale, Margo Lee Sherman; (D) Kate Mennone; (S) Kate Brown; (C) Mary Myers
Blue Sky is a Curse, The Talking Band; (S) Tony Carruthers; (C) David Zinn
Who Collects the Pain?, Sean O'Connor, Manucher Harsini and Michael McGarty; (C) Lolly Alejandro
Monk 'n Bud, Laurence Holder; (D) Jasper McGruder; (S) Henrietta Lienke; (C) Rome Neal
Pineapple Face, Rosalyn Drexler; (D) John Vaccaro; (S) Noel MacFetrich; (C) Jerry Harding
Times Square Angel, Charles Busch; (D) Kenneth Elliott; (S) B.T. Whitehill; (C) E.K. Carr
Medea, Exavier Muhammad; (D) Exavier Muhammad; (S) and (C) Fran Sperling
Onafhankelijk Toneel, Dutch Theater Exchange Program
It Is It Is Not, Manuel Pareiras; (D) Maria Irene Fornes; (S) and (C) Carol Bailey
Blue Heaven, Karen Malpede; (D) Leo Shapiro and Karen Malpede; (S) Leo Shapiro; (C) Karen Young
The L-Word, Ed DuRante (co-produced by Talking Drum Theatre) (D) Kira Arne
40 Deuce, Alan Bowne; (D) Tom O'Horgan; (S) Perry Arthur Kroeger; (C) Todd Tomarrow
Rash Acts, Conrad Bishop and Elizabeth Fuller; (D) Conrad Bishop
My Ancestors' House, Bina Sharif; (D) Francisco Rivela; (S) and (C) Jose-Antonio Rouco
Nativity, Bread & Puppet Theater; (D) Peter Shumann
Toy Theater Festival, 9th Street Theater
Rising Sun, Falling Star, Yolanda Rodrieguez; (D) Bob Landau; (S) and (C) Charles McClennahan;
Neuro Sisters, Cora Hook and Lizzie Olesker; (D) Lizzie Olesker; (S) Christine Sinnott; (C) Carol Brys
The Bundle Man, Ilsa Gilbert; (D) Tom O'Horgan; (S) and (C) Perry Arthur Kroeger
Take to the Bed, Joan Rater; (D) Amy Rosenfeld; (S) Andras Kanegson; (C) Todd Thomas
Spain, Romulus Linney; (D) Romulus Linney; (L) Jeffrey Koger; (C) Teresa Snider-Stein
Thunder: Perfect Mind, Laura Simms and Julia Haines; (D), (S), (L) and (C) Julia Haines

Eco-Festival:
various playwrights, various directors

The Houseguests, Harry Kondoleon; (D) Tom Gladwell; (S) Chris Field; (C) David Zinn
Truus Bronkhorst, Dutch Theater Exchange Program
The Hunchback of Harlem, Winston Lovett; (D) Rome Neal; (S) Billy Graham
Smalltown Gals, Larry Myers; (D) Roger Mrazek; (S) Michelle Sibilia; (C) Myrna Duarte
1,000 Hours of Love, Bina Sharif; (D) Bina Sharif and Dawn Spring; (C) Gaetano Fazia
Stuffed Puppet, Dutch Theater Exchange Program
Warhol In Hell, Richie Heisler; (D) Zoe MacKay; (S) and (C) Julie Polk
The Upward Path to Ignorance, Walter Corwin; (S) and (C) Jerry Hsieh
Annual Pow Wow & Dance Concert (co-produced by Thunderbird Dancers); (D) Louis Mofsie
Get Hur, Ray Dobbins (co-produced by Bloolips) (D) Bette Bourne; (L) David Adams
Rubber Heat, Eddie Di Donna; (D) Mark Marcante; (S) Anthony Angel; (C) Mark Marcante
Venetian Fever, Yuri Belov; (D) Yuri Belov; (S) and (C) Nikita Polyansky
New Jersey/New York, Richard Hoehler; (D) and (S) Richard Hoehler; (C) Michelle Reish
La Roca, Sean Brown; (D), (S) (L) and (C) Robert Dahdah
Life's Too Short to Cry, Michael Vazquez; (D) Michael Vazquez; (S) Mark Marcante; (C) Lolly Alejandro
The Master and Margarita, adapt: Jean-Claude van Itallie, from Mikhail Bulgakov; (D) David Willinger; (S) Mark Symczak; (C) Tanya Serdiuk
The Crib, Gary Goldberg; (D), (S), (L) and (C) Gary Goldberg
After the Heart Is Broken, H.M. Koutoukas; (D) and (S) H.M. Koutoukas; (C) Carol Tauser
Stuart Sherman's 18th Spectacle, Stuart Sherman
The Bribe, Terry O'Reilly (co-produced by Theater for the New City); music: John Zorn; (D) Ruth Maleczech; (S) and (L) Richard Nonas; (C) Ann-Marie Wright and Toby Niesen; (SD) John Collins and Nathan Guisinger
Songs Lucifer Sang..., H.M. Koutoukas; (D) and (S) H.M. Koutoukas; (C) Carol Tauser

Theater for the New City. T. Cat Ford, Fred Burrell and Peter Ashton Wise in *Spain*. Photo: Jonathan Slaff.

Theatre IV

BRUCE MILLER
Artistic Director

PHILIP WHITEWAY
Managing Director

HERBERT CLAIBORNE, III,
THOMAS TULLIDGE, JR.
Board Co-Chairmen

7 West Marshall St.
Richmond, VA 23220
(804) 783-1688 (bus.)
(804) 344-8040 (b.o.)
(804) 775-2325 (fax)

FOUNDED 1975
Bruce Miller, Philip Whiteway

SEASON
Year-round

FACILITIES
Empire Theatre
Seating Capacity: 604
Stage: proscenium

Little Theatre
Seating Capacity: 84
Stage: proscenium

FINANCES
July 1, 1991-June 30, 1992
Expenses: $1,533,354

CONTRACTS
AEA SPT

Theatre IV. Bridget Gethins, Brian Ballantine, Nancy McMahon, Jacqueline Jones and Peter Berinato in *The Reluctant Dragon*. Photo: Eric Dobbs.

Theatre IV presents an eclectic mix of plays and musicals for adults, and an ambitious roster of original plays for children, teens and their families. As our company has grown, we have added more mainstream plays to our season (*The Rainmaker, Hamlet*), while continuing to produce contemporary plays which challenge our central Virginia audience (*The Normal Heart, Frankie and Johnny in the Clair de Lune, Stand-Up Tragedy*). Most of our budget is devoted to youth productions which tour extensively; we present more than 1,500 performances a year from San Juan to Chicago. Our original plays *Hugs and Kisses, Runners, Walking the Line* and *Dancing in the Dark* deal honestly and effectively with the issues of child sexual abuse, runaways, teenage suicide, substance abuse and adolescent pregnancy/sexual responsibility. Our home theatres—the grand Empire Theatre and the intimate Little Theatre—first opened in 1911 and are the oldest extant theatres in our state.

—*Bruce Miller*

PRODUCTIONS 1991-1992

Direction by John Glenn, sets by Terrie Powers and costumes by Thomas W. Hammond unless otherwise noted.

Four Part Harmony, book: Marcus J. Fisk; music and lyrics: Douglas E. Minerd; (S) Bill Jenkins; (L) James C. Ryan; (MD) Ron Barnett

Three Little Pigs, book and lyrics: Douglas Jones; music: Ron Barnett; (D) Robin Arthur; (L) Bruce Rennie

Babes in Toyland; book and new lyrics: Bruce Miller; original lyrics: Glen McDonough; music: Victor Herbert; (D) Bruce Miller; (L) James C. Ryan; (MD) Paul Deiss

Jack and the Beanstalk; book and lyrics: Douglas Jones; music: Ron Barnett; (L) Bruce Rennie

The Wind in the Willows, lyrics: Roger McGough and William Perry, from Kenneth Grahame; music: William Perry; (S) Brad Boynton; (L) Bruce Rennie; (MD) Jeri Cutler-Volz

A Shayna Maidel, Barbara Lebow; (D) Denise Simone; (S) Brad Boynton; (L) David Miller; (C) Nancy Allen; (SD) Richard Allison

Frankie and Johnny in the Clair de Lune, Terrence McNally; (D) Bruce Miller; (S) David Majewski; (L) Alasdair Denvil; (C) Alyne S. Burgess

Wait Until Dark, Frederick Knott; (D) John Moon; (S) James C. Ryan; (L) Bill Jenkins; (C) Colleen McDuffee

The Rainmaker, N. Richard Nash; (S) Eddie Pierce; (L) Rich Mason; (C) Elizabeth Weiss Hopper

PRODUCTIONS 1992-1993

Sets by Brad Boynton, lighting by James C. Ryan and costumes by Thomas W. Hammond unless otherwise noted.

Hamlet, William Shakespeare; (D) Gary C. Hopper; (C) Elizabeth Weiss Hopper

Shirley Valentine, Willy Russell; (D) and (S) John Moon; (C) Colleen McDuffee

Crimes of the Heart, Beth Henley; (D) Bruce Miller; (C) Sherry Harper

Closer Than Ever, conceived: Steven Scott Smith; lyrics: Richard Maltby, Jr.; music: David Shire; (D) Billy Dye; (S) Amy Bale; (L) Lynne M. Hartman

Winnie the Pooh, book adapt: Kristen Sergel, from A.A. Milne; music: Allen Jay Friedman; lyrics: A.A. Milne and Kristin Sergel; (D) John Glenn; (S) Terrie Powers; (L) Bruce Rennie

Snowflake, Gale LaJoye; (D), (S), (L) and (C) Gale LaJoye

The Reluctant Dragon, adapt: Mary Hall Surface, from Kenneth Grahame; (D) Staci Trowbridge; (L) Lynne M. Hartman

Cinderella, book adapt and lyrics: Oscar Hammerstein, II, from Charles Perrault; music: Richard Rodgers; (D) Joseph Pabst; (S) James C. Ryan; (L) Bruce Rennie; (MD) Paul Diess; (CH) Janet Clarkson

Theatre in the Square

MICHAEL HORNE
Producing Artistic Director

PALMER D. WELLS
Managing Director

CHERRY SPENCER-STARK
Board Chair

11 Whitlock Ave.
Marietta, GA 30064
(404) 425-5873 (bus.)
(404) 422-8369 (b.o.)
(404) 424-2637 (fax)

FOUNDED 1982
Michael Horne, Palmer D. Wells

SEASON
Sept.-June

FACILITIES
Main Stage
Seating Capacity: 226
Stage: proscenium

Theatre in the Square. William Hardy in *Death of a Salesman*. Photo: Kathryn Kolb.

Alley Stage
Seating Capacity: 60
Stage: flexible

FINANCES
July 1, 1992-June 30, 1993
Expenses: $750,000

CONTRACTS
AEA SPT

As the only year-round professional theatre in Georgia outside the Atlanta city limits, we face certain pressures, a few advantages and some vital responsibilities. We expose many people to their first and only live theatre. Among their numbers are young people, some of whom will decide to choose careers in the arts or at least include the arts as part of their adult lives. So, aside from fulfilling our own artistic sensibilities, we strive to educate and stimulate audiences. Our mission is to: program shows which appeal to our instincts because of strong writing, subject matter, suitability to our space and/or audience or the opportunity to showcase regional talent; build a loyal audience which will hunger for diverse work; acquire the resources to grow and diversify; and nurture talent and develop materials indigenous to the Southeast. We pride ourselves on varied work—from classics to new works—and run the gamut of comedies, dramas and musicals. We enjoy the challenge of making our small size work for us rather than limit us, often exchanging epic proportions for epic emotions.
—*Michael Horne*

PRODUCTIONS 1991-1992

Lighting by Liz Lee and sound design by Richard Robison unless otherwise noted.

Anastasia, Marcelle Maurette; trans: Guy Bolton; (D) Michael Horne; (S) Jeroy Hannah; (C) Michael Reynolds
Miracle Man, Joseph McDonough; (D) Jill Jane Clements; (S) Rochelle Barker; (C) Sylvia Hillyard
The 1940's Radio Hour, book: Walton Jones; various composers and lyricists; (D) Doug Kaye; (S) Duncan McKelvey; (C) David Mattox; (MD) Michael Monroe; (CH) Dee Wagner
Lend Me a Tenor, Ken Ludwig; (D) Frank Miller; (S) John Thigpen; (C) Stanley Poole
A Walk in the Woods, Lee Blessing; (D) Josephine Ayers; (S) John Thigpen; (C) Freddie Clements
Smoke on the Mountain, Constance Ray; (D) and (S) Dex Edwards; (L) Tim Robinson; (C) Ray Dudley

PRODUCTIONS 1992-1993

Lighting by Liz Lee and sound design by Richard Robison unless otherwise noted.

M. Butterfly, David Henry Hwang; (D) John Briggs; (S) Dex Edwards; (C) Stanley Poole
Taking Steps, Alan Ayckbourn; (D) Frank Miller; (S) Tim Habeger; (L) Ken Yunker; (C) Lynette Cram
The 1940's Radio Hour, book: Walton Jones; various composers and lyricists; (D) Marian Bolton; (S) Duncan McKelvey; (L) Ken Yunker; (C) Ray Dudley; (MD) Michael Monroe; (CH) Dee Wagner
Lettice and Lovage, Peter Shaffer; (D) Michael Horne; (S) Leslie Taylor; (C) Carol Haynes
Death of a Salesman, Arthur Miller; (D) John Stephens; (S) Rochelle Barker; (C) Greg Ansley; (SD) Bryan Mercer
Lips Together, Teeth Apart, Terrence McNally; (D) Michael Horne; (S) Rochelle Barker; (C) Michael Reynolds; (SD) Erica French

TheatreVirginia

GEORGE BLACK
Producing Artistic Director

HOWARD BUSBEE
Board President

2800 Grove Ave.
Richmond, VA 23221
(804) 367-0840 (bus.)
(8040 367-0831 (b.o.)
(804) 367-6849 (fax)

FOUNDED 1954
Virginia Museum of Fine Arts

SEASON
Oct.-May

FACILITIES
Mainstage
Seating Capacity: 494
Stage: proscenium

Second Stage
Seating Capacity: 239
Stage: proscenium

TheatreVirginia. Michael Oberlander in *The Immigrant*.

FINANCES
July 1, 1992-June 30, 1993
Expenses: $1,687,000

CONTRACTS
AEA LORT (C1) and (D)

At TheatreVirginia we aim to enhance the future by reaching out to new audiences while keeping in touch with our traditional artistry. Our programming aims at the widest acceptance through such outreach and education programs as Shakespeare in the Schools, New Voices and Visiting Professionals, as well as through internships and apprenticeships, and improved access for the physically challenged. Ultimately, we want to make productions that entertain by engaging our audiences in both expected and unexpected ways. We are devoted to "live theatre," by which we mean theatre that is vital and energetic. Whether doing new plays or familiar titles, TheatreVirginia tries to find what is fresh and interesting in each script as we bring it to the stage. Towards that goal, we eagerly seek plays, production ideas and designs— conventional or unconventional, new or old—through which our artists can create vigorous theatrical experiences.
—*George Black*

Note: During the 1991-92 and 1992-93 seasons, William Gregg served as artistic director.

PRODUCTIONS 1991-1992

Direction by William Gregg and sets by Keven Lock unless otherwise noted.

Other People's Money, Jerry Sterner; (L) F. Mitchell Dana; (C) Howard Tsvi Kaplan
Anything Goes, book: Guy Bolton, P.G. Wodehouse, Howard Lindsay and Russel Crouse; music and lyrics: Cole Porter; (D) and (CH) Diana Baffa-Brill; (L) F. Mitchell Dana; (C) Mark Hughes
West Memphis Mojo, Martin Jones; (L) Tina Gallegos; (C) Keven Lock
Scaramouche, Rafael Sabatini; adapt: Laurence Maslon; (D) B.H. Barry; (S) and (L) Marc B. Weiss; (C) Jane Greenwood
The Mystery of Irma Vep, Charles Ludlam; (L) Christopher T. Lau; (C) Mark Hughes (SD) Richard Allison

PRODUCTIONS 1992-1993

Direction by William Gregg and sets by Keven Lock unless otherwise noted.

Harvey, Mary Chase; (L) Terry Cermak; (C) Sue Griffin
A Little Night Music, book adapt: Hugh Wheeler, from Ingmar Bergman; music and lyrics: Stephen Sondheim; (D) David Schechter; (L) F. Mitchell Dana; (C) Mark Hughes; (MD) Andrew Howard; (CH) Liza Gennaro
As You Like It, William Shakespeare; (L) Tina Gallegos; (C) Keven Lock
The Immigrant, Mark Harelik (co-produced by Delaware Theater Company); (D) Howard J. Millman; (S) Lewis Folden, after Kevin Rupnik; (L) Ken Lapham, after Phil Monat; (C) Marla Jurglanis, after Maria Marrero
Lettice and Lovage, Peter Shaffer; (L) John Carter Hailey; (C) David Crank

TheatreWorks

ROBERT KELLEY
Artistic Director

RANDY ADAMS
Managing Director

PERRY IRVINE
Board Chairperson

470 San Antonio Road
Palo Alto, CA 94306
(415) 812-7550 (bus.)
(415) 329-2623, 903-6000 (b.o.)
(415) 812-7562 (fax)

FOUNDED 1970
Robert Kelley

SEASON
Year-round

FACILITIES
Mountain View Center for the Performing Arts
Seating Capacity: 625
Stage: proscenium

Lucie Stern Theatre
Seating Capacity: 425
Stage: proscenium

Cubberley Stage II
Seating Capacity: 110
Stage: flexible

FINANCES
June 1, 1992-May 31, 1993
Expenses: $1,750,000

CONTRACTS
AEA Guest Artist

TheatreWorks explores and celebrates the human spirit through contemporary plays, musicals of literary merit, new works in development and innovative reinterpretations of the classics, offering audiences in the San Francisco Bay Area a regional theatre of exceptional diversity. We are a theatre for all races and ages, a longtime leader in nontraditional casting and programming. Our mainstage season is selected to expand the social and artistic horizons of a large audience. STAGE II offers world and regional premieres in intimate spaces, and our recently launched Playwrights Forum develops and reads several new plays and musicals annually, many by our regional writers. As we celebrate our 24th season, we have focused our financial and artistic efforts on the growth and support of a multi-racial company, creating a community that will be a model of diversity and commitment for the larger community we serve.
—Robert Kelley

PRODUCTIONS 1991-1992

Direction by Robert Kelley, sets by Joe Ragey, lighting by John G. Rathman and sound design by Aodh Og O Tuama unless otherwise noted.

The Good Doctor, adapt: Neil Simon, from Anton Chekhov; (S) Bruce McLeod; (C) Fumiko Bielefeldt
Miami Lights, book adapt and lyrics: Jacques Levy, from John Millington Synge; music: Stanley Walden; (D) Randal K. West; (S) John Bonard Wilson; (C) Cassandra Carpenter; (MD) Lita B. Libaek; (CH) Susan V. Cashion
O, Pioneers!, book adapt and lyrics: Darrah Cloud, from Willa Cather; music: Kim D. Sherman; (C) Susan Archibald Grote; (MD) Tom Lindblade; (CH) Barbara Valente
Hi-Hat Hattie!, Larry Parr; various composers and lyricists; (D) Richard Hopkins; (S) Paul G. Vallerga; (L) Bruce McLeod; (C) Richard W. Battle; (MD) Rob Robinson
Les Liaisons Dangereuses, adapt: Christopher Hampton, from Choderlos de Laclos; (D) Rush Rehm; (S) John Bonard Wilson; (L) Barbara DuBois; (C) Pamela Lampkin
Peter Pan, book: James M. Barrie; lyrics: Carolyn Leigh; music: Mark Charlap; (L) Bruce McLeod; (C) Jill C. Bowers; (MD) Lita B. Libaek; (CH) Diane Silven
A Rosen by Any Other Name, adapt: Israel Horovitz, from Morley Torgov; (D) Ginger Drake; (S) Gary C. Mitchell; (L) Michael F. Ramsaur; (C) Allison Connor
Interpreters, Ronald Harwood; (D) Leslie Martinson; (L) M. Elizabeth Nelson; (C) Kristin Lewis
Sweeney Todd, book adapt: Hugh Wheeler, from Christopher Bond; music and lyrics: Stephen Sondheim; (S) Bruce McLeod; (C) Jill C. Bowers; (MD) Lita B. Libaek; (CH) Barbara Valente
Talk-Story, Jeannie Barroga; (D) Marc Hayashi; (S) Paul G. Vallerga; (L) Pamela Gray Bones; (C) Sherrol A. Simard; (SD) Shari Bethel
Shakin' the Mess Outta Misery, Shay Youngblood; (D) Anthony J. Haney; (S) Thomas J. Zofrea; (L) Stephanie A. Johnson; (C) Richard W. Battle
New Business, Tom Williams; (D) Amy Gonzalez; (L) Jim Cave; (C) T.J. Wilcock

PRODUCTIONS 1992-1993

Direction by Robert Kelley, sets by Joe Ragey, lighting by Maurice Vercoutere and sound design by Aodh Og O Tuama unless otherwise noted.

Prelude to a Kiss, Craig Lucas; (D) Tom Lindblade; (C) Allison Connor
The Human Comedy, book adapt and lyrics: William Dumaresq, from William Saroyan; (S) Gary C. Mitchell; (C) T.J. Wilcock; (MD) Lita B. Libaek; (CH) Yoko Young; (SD) Shari Bethel and Aodh Og O Tuama
M. Butterfly, David Henry Hwang; (S) Jeffrey Struckman; (C) Pamela Lampkin; (SD) Shari Bethel and Aodh Og O Tuama
God's Hands, book, music and lyrics: Douglas J. Cohen; (D) and (CH) Barbara Valente; (L) Pamela Gray Bones; (C) Loren Tripp; (MD) Lita B. Libaek; (SD) Shari Bethel
Jar the Floor, Cheryl L. West; (D) Harry J. Elam; (L) Stephanie Johnson; (C) Jill C. Bowers
Into the Woods, book: James Lapine; music and lyrics: Stephen Sondheim; (D) and (CH) Barbara Valente; (S) Michael Puff; (L) John G. Rathman; (C) Jill C. Bowers; (MD) Lita B. Libaek
A Normal Life, adapt: Erik Brogger, from Delmore Schwartz; (S) Joel Fontaine; (L) Michael F. Ramsaur; (C) Fumiko Bielefeldt; (SD) Shari Bethel
Theme and Variations, Samuil Alyoshin; trans: Michael Glenny; (D) Jeff Bengford; (S) Paul G. Vallerga; (L) Ed Hunter; (C) Sherrol A. Simard
Once on This Island, book adapt and lyrics: Lynn Ahrens, from Rosa Guy; music: Stephen Flaherty; (D) Anthony J. Haney; (S) John Bonard Wilson; (L) Kurt Landisman; (C) Suzanne Jackson; (MD) Lita B. Libaek; (CH) Danny Duncan
Mrs. Klein, Nicholas Wright; (D) Amy Glazer; (S) Bruce McLeod; (L) Jim Cave; (C) Kristin Lewis; (SD) Rich McCracken
The Royal Hunt of the Sun, Peter Shaffer; (L) John G. Rathman; (C) Fumiko Bielefeldt
Our Lady of the Tortilla, Luis Santeiro; (D) Amy Gonzalez; (S) Paul G. Vallerga; (L) Steven B. Mannshardt; (C) Karen Lim; (SD) Jeff Hanson

TheatreWorks. JoAnne Nagler, Willie Jackson, Woof Kurtzman, Kevin Blackton and Jack Davis in *New Business*. Photo: WPG Enterprises.

Theatreworks/USA

JAY HARNICK
Artistic Director

CHARLES HULL
Managing Director

ROBERT WOOD
Board Chairman

890 Broadway, 7th Floor
New York, NY 10003
(212) 677-5959 (bus.)
(212) 420-8202 (b.o.)
(212) 353-1632 (fax)

FOUNDED 1961
Jay Harnick, Robert K. Adams

SEASON
Sept.-June

FACILITIES
Promenade Theatre
Seating Capacity: 400
Stage: thrust

Town Hall
Seating Capacity: 1,500
Stage: proscenium

FINANCES
July 1, 1991-June 30, 1992
Expenses: $4,376,000

CONTRACTS
AEA TYA

After 32 seasons of creating theatre for young and family audiences, Theatreworks/USA continues to be inspired by the belief that young people deserve theatre endowed with the richness of content demanded by the most discerning adult audience. To that end, we have commissioned an ever-expanding collection of original works from established playwrights, composers and lyricists. Our creative roster includes Ossie Davis, Charles Strouse, Alice Childress, Joe Raposo, Thomas Babe, Mary Rodgers, Saul Levitt, John Forster, Leslie Lee, Lynn Ahrens, Stephen Flaherty, Jonathan Bolt, Marta Kauffman, David Crane, Michael Skloff, John Allen and Douglas J. Cohen. We are also dedicated to the development of fresh voices for the American theatre and encourage emerging playwrights to develop projects about issues that concern them and affect the young audiences they seek to address. We currently give more than a thousand performances annually in a touring radius encompassing 49 of the 50 states.
—*Jay Harnick*

PRODUCTIONS 1991-1992

Sets by Vaughn Patterson and music direction by Christopher McGovern unless otherwise noted.

Class Clown, book: Thomas Edward West; lyrics: Alison Hubbard; music: Kim Oler; (D) Steve Kaplan; (C) Sharon Lynch; (CH) Edie Cowan

Columbus, book: Jonathan Bolt; music: Douglas J. Cohen; lyrics: Thomas Toce; (D) Samuel D. Cohen, after David Holdgrive; (C) Julie Doyle; (MD) Douglas J. Cohen

Harold and the Purple Crayon, book adapt: Jane Merlin Shepard, from Crockett Johnson; music: Jon Ehrlich; lyrics: Robin Pogrebin and Jon Ehrlich; (D) Tony Phelan; (S) Rick Dennis; (C) Michael Krass; (MD) Jon Ehrlich; (CH) Elizabeth Keen

Heidi, book adapt: Sarah Schlesinger and David Evans, from Johanna Spyri; music: David Evans; lyrics: Sarah Schlesinger; (D) Michael Leeds; (S) Brian P. Kelly; (C) Julie Doyle; (MD) Bob Goldstone

Jekyll & Hyde, book adapt and lyrics: David Crane and Marta Kauffman, from Robert Louis Stevenson; music: Michael Skloff; (D) Mark Cole, after Jay Harnick; (C) Ann-Marie Wright; (CH) Christopher Scott

Freedom Train, book: Marvin Gordon; various composers and lyricists; (D) Michael-David Gordon; (S) Hal Tine; (C) Linda Geley; (CH) Gloria Jones Schultz

Rapunzel, book adapt and lyrics: David Crane and Marta Kauffman, from The Brothers Grimm; music: Michael Skloff; (D) John E. Brady, after Paul Lazarus; (S) Mavis Smith; (C) Joel Vig

The Velveteen Rabbit, book adapt and lyrics: James Still, from Margery Williams; music: Jimmy Roberts; (D) James Still, after Stuart Ross; (S) Dick Block; (C) Linda Geley, after Debra Stein; (MD) Jimmy Roberts; (CH) Janet Bogardus

PRODUCTIONS 1992-1993

Sets by Vaughn Patterson and costumes by Linda Geley unless otherwise noted.

Columbus, book: Jonathan Bolt; music: Douglas J. Cohen; lyrics: Thomas Toce; (D) Jonathan Bolt, after David Holdgrive; (C) Julie Doyle; (MD) Douglas J. Cohen

Freaky Friday, book adapt and lyrics: John Forster, from Mary Rodgers; music: Mary Rodgers; (D) Christopher Ashley; (C) Don Newcomb; (MD) John Boswell; (CH) Christopher Scott

Freedom Train, book: Marvin Gordon; various composers and lyricists; (D) Michael-David Gordon; (S) Hal Tine; (MD) Ron Drotos; (CH) Gloria Jones Schultz

From Sea to Shining Sea, book and lyrics: Arthur Perlman; music: Jeffrey Lunden; (D) Ted Pappas; (S) James Noone; (MD) Christopher McGovern

Heidi, book adapt: Sarah Schlesinger and David Evans, from Johanna Spyri; music: David Evans; lyrics: Sarah Schlesinger; (D) Michael Leeds; (S) Brian P. Kelly; (C) Julie Doyle; (MD) Christopher McGovern

Play to Win, book: James de Jongh and Carles Cleveland; music: Jimi Foster; lyrics: Jimi Foster, James de Jongh and Carles Cleveland; (D) Regge Life, after Bruce Butler; (D) Tom Barnes; (MD) Elliot Weiss; (CH) Jan Johnson

The Secret Garden, book adapt: Linda B. Kline and Robert Jess Roth, from Frances Hodgson Burnett; music: Kim Oler; lyrics: Alison Hubbard; (D) Marcus Olson, after Robert Jess Roth; (C) Deborah Rooney; (MD) Ron Drotos

Tom Sawyer, book adapt: Thomas Edward West, from Mark Twain; music: Michael Kessler; lyrics: Alison Hubbard and Greer Woodward; (D) John Henry Davis; (S) Peter Harrison; (C) Martha Hally; (MD) Robert Elhai; (CH) Elizabeth Keen

The Velveteen Rabbit, book adapt and lyrics: James Still, from Margery Williams; music: Jimmy Roberts; (D) James Still; (S) Dick Block; (C) Linda Geley, after Debra Stein; (MD) Jimmy Roberts; (CH) Janet Bogardus

Hansel and Gretel, book adapt: Michael Slade, from The Brothers Grimm; music: David Evans, after Engelbert Humperdinck; lyrics: Jane Smulyan; (D) Michael Mayer; (S) David Gallo; (C) Jana Rosenblatt and Danielle Hollywood; (MD) David Evans

Theatreworks/USA. Aaron Harnick, Robert Osborne, Anne O'Sullivan and Laura Stanczyk in *Tom Sawyer*. Photo: Gerry Goodstein.

Theatre X

JOHN SCHNEIDER
Artistic Director

PAMELA PERCY
Managing Director

LEONARD SOBCZAK
Board President

Box 92206
Milwaukee, WI 53202
(414) 278-0555
(414) 278-8233 (fax)

FOUNDED 1969
Conrad Bishop, Linda Bishop, Ron Gural

SEASON
Sept.-June

FACILITIES
Broadway Theatre Center
Seating Capacity: 99
Stage: flexible

FINANCES
Sept. 1, 1992-Aug. 31, 1993
Expenses: $225,000

Theatre X. *Pleasant Dreams.* Photo: Fred Graber.

The "X" in Theatre X, as conceived in 1969, represents the algebraic symbol for "the unknown factor." The motion-picture rating system, implemented years later, has complicated the associations of this symbol. The enigmatic implications of the "X" appropriately describe an aesthetic sensibility which seeks to represent an ever-changing present, to create a truly contemporary and illuminating theatre art. Theatre X's work is characterized by a combination of pseudo-naturalism and an equally self-conscious theatricality involving artifices derived from theatre history, mass culture and the ongoing fruits of interdisciplinary collaborations. It strives to say what is not said in a culture where content decays as words and images multiply. Theatre X's artistic mission, above all else, is to encourage and provoke the process of thinking for its audiences as well as for itself.

—*John Schneider*

PRODUCTIONS 1991-1992

Pilgrims of the Night, Len Jenkin; (D) John Schneider; (S) Jim Matson; (L) John Starmer; (C) Carri Skoczek; (SD) John Dereszynski

A Christmas Memory, adapt: Wesley Savick, from Truman Capote; and ***The Fifteen Minute Christmas Carol***, adapt: Mark Anderson, Flora Cokor and John Starmer, from Charles Dickens; (D) Wesley Savick *(Memory)*, Mark Anderson *(Carol)*; (S) Andrew Meyers; (L) John Starmer

Rhinoceros, Eugene Ionesco; adapt: Wesley Savick; (D) Wesley Savick; (S) R.H. Graham; (L) Andrew Meyers; (C) Carri Skoczek; (SD) Michael Vitali and John Dereszynski

Toute Une Nuit, Mark Anderson; (D) Mark Anderson; (S) and (L) Mark Anderson and John Starmer

American Nervousness, (co-produced by the Drawing Legion)

Liberace, The Magic of Believing, Pamela Woodruff and Wesley Savick; music: Michael Vitali; (D) Wesley Savick; (S) Ed Paschke; (L) Robert Zenoni; (C) Ellen Kozak; (MD) Randy Swiggum

PRODUCTIONS 1992-1993

Costumes by Carri Skoczek unless otherwise noted.

The Strength and Indifference of the Snow, company-developed, from George F. Kennan; (S) and (C) the company; (L) John Starmer; (SD) John Dereszynski

Pleasant Dreams, John Schneider; (D) John Schneider; (S) Jim Matson; (L) R.H. Graham; (SD) John Dereszynski

A Christmas Memory, adapt: Wesley Savick, from Truman Capote; (D) Wesley Savick; (S) and (L) John Starmer

The Long Christmas Dinner, Thornton Wilder; (D) Wesley Savick; (S) Carri Skoczek; (L) John Starmer

Quorum, Mark Anderson; (D) Mark Anderson; (S) John Starmer; (L) R.H. Graham

When You're Smiling, adapt: John Schneider, from August Strindberg; (D) John Schneider; (S) and (L) R.H. Graham; (SD) John Dereszynski

A Murder of Crows, Mac Wellman; (D) John Schneider; (S) and (L) R.H. Graham; (SD) John Dereszynski

Theatrical Outfit

PHILLIP DePOY
Producing Artistic Director

JUDY E. JOY
General Manager

DAVID H. COFRIN
Board President

Box 7098
Atlanta, GA 30357
(404) 872-0665
(404) 872-1164 (fax)

FOUNDED 1976
David Head, Sharon Levy

SEASON
Year-round

FACILITIES
Mainstage
Seating Capacity: 200
Stage: flexible

Downstairs
Seating Capacity: 100
Stage: flexible

FINANCES
July 1, 1992-June 30, 1993
Expenses: $317,332

CONTRACTS
AEA SPT

Theatrical Outfit, Atlanta's only new music theatre, produces work that is life-affirmingly optimistic, often funny, and has a wide array of spiritual values. We often speak directly to the audience, breaking the "fourth wall" between performer and audience, in productions that enlighten as well as engage. We are committed to a multiplicity of cultural influences in

Theatrical Outfit. Nina Jones, Tim Habeger and Heather Heath in *No Exit*. Photo: David Zeiger.

creating work that reacts intimately with audiences. Some of our work is original, some is collaboratively developed, and some is the result of new adaptation of classic theatre. All our works have music at the center. We hope to reimagine theatre, and recombine forms toward a total theatre: a form in which all other forms coincide, collaborate and coalesce—finally hammered into a unity, and founded in music. If the creation of the Universe was an act of celestial music, the creation of our little universe (a black box full of actors) can be the result of no less an effort.
—*Phillip DePoy*

PRODUCTIONS 1991-1992

Lighting by Hal McCoy unless otherwise noted.

Angels, book, music and lyrics: Phillip DePoy; (D) Carol Mitchell-Leon; (S) Scott Preston; (C) Steve Joslin; (MD) Phillip DePoy
Appalachian Christmas, book: Eddie Levi Lee and Phillip DePoy; various composers and lyricists; (D) and (MD) Phillip DePoy; (S) Bruce Starr
Ulysses, book adapt and lyrics: Tamara Hill and Scott DePoy, from Homer; (D) Brenda Porter and Jonathan Dew; (S) Young Goldstien Architects; (C) Steve Joslin
Lamb on Fire, Phillip DePoy; (D) Phillip DePoy; (S) Robert Teverino; (C) Cindy Hill and Robert Teverino
Rev. Tartuffe: A Divine Musical, book adapt: Andrew Ordover, from Moliere; various composers and lyricists; (D) Del Hamilton; (S) Robert Teverino; (C) Joseph D. Morgan; (MD) Phillip DePoy

PRODUCTIONS 1992-1993

Lighting by Hal McCoy and costumes by Lynette Cram unless otherwise noted.

The Playboy of the Western World, John Millington Synge; music and lyrics: Phillip DePoy; (D) John Stephens; (S) Dean Ota and Joe Rabun; (MD) Phillip DePoy; (CH) Erica Yoder
Appalachian Christmas, book: Eddie Levi Lee and Phillip DePoy; various composers and lyricists; (D) and (MD) Phillip DePoy; (S) Bruce Starr
No Exit, Jean-Paul Sartre; trans: Chris Kayser; (D) Didier Rousselet; (S) Jeroy Hannah
The Ladder, R.L. Beverly; (D) Charles Reed; (S) Robert Teverino
The Merchant of Venus, book adapt: Andrew Ordover, from William Shakespeare; music and lyrics: Phillip DePoy; (D) and (MD) Phillip DePoy; (S) Rochelle Barker; (L) Hal McCoy, Brett Crawford and Robert Teverino

Touchstone Theatre

BRIDGET GEORGE
Producing Director

RICHARD E. THULIN
Board President

321 East 4th St.
Bethlehem, PA 18015
(215) 867-1689
(215) 867-0561 (fax)

FOUNDED 1981
William George, Bridget George

SEASON
Sept.-July

FACILITIES
Seating Capacity: 75
Stage: flexible

FINANCES
Sept. 1, 1992-Aug. 31, 1993
Expenses: $399,100

Touchstone is a theatre home where our resident acting ensemble and visiting artists can generate and develop innovative work in an ongoing dialogue with diverse audiences, and foster intercultural and international collaborations. Our focus is on the process of the actor as creator and on work rich in metaphor, image, poetry, and an intimate and multilayered connection with the audience. We take our role in the community very seriously. The ensemble immerses itself in the tide of Bethlehem's diverse cultural spirit (48 different nationalities represented)—its day-to-day fears, joys, aspirations—and responds with a theatre of inner discovery, hope and revelation. Our work in the community includes long-term educational projects as well as collaborations with other community organizations in the creation of new work. Selected ensemble creations, premiered at Touchstone, join our touring repertory and have reached audiences throughout the East Coast and abroad.
—*Bridget George*

PRODUCTIONS 1991-1992

We All Fall Down, Eric Beatty and Susan Chase; (D) and (L) Daniel Stein; (S) and (C) Paule Sandoval Stein; (SD) Tim Frey
The Vulture Speaks, William Pope. L (co-produced by the Luftkugel Association); (D) Jim Calder; (S) and (C) Joan Harmon; (L) and (SD) Tim Frey
Make We Merry, Bridget George; (D) Barbara Pearson; (S) and (L) Ken Moses; (C) Mildred Greene
The Wizard of Hip, Thomas W. Jones, II; (D) Kenneth Leon; (S) Tony Loadholt; (L) Jeff Guzik
Whosis, John Farrell and Carol Llewellyn (co-produced by Figures of Speech Theatre); (D) the company; (S) John Farrell, Carol Llewellyn and Karen E. Nelson; (L) Stoney Cook; (SD) J.H. Phillips and Heath Allen
School Alley, Gary Webster; (D) Augustine Ripa; (S) and (L) Vicki Neal; (C) D. Polly Kendrick; (SD) Tim Frey

PRODUCTIONS 1992-1993

Daedalus in the Belly of the Beast, Marco Antonio de la Parra; trans: Joanne Pottlitzer; adapt: Alfredo Castro and Francesca Lombardo; (D) Alfredo Castro; (S) and (L) Curtis Dretsch; (C) David Kutos; (SD) Miguel Miranda
Zora Neale Hurston, Laurence Holder; (D) Wynn Handman; (S) Terry Chandler; (L) Antoinette Tynes

Touchstone Theatre. Daedalus in the Belly of the Beast. *Photo: B. Stanley.*

Holiday Memories, adapt: Russell Vandenbroucke, from Truman Capote; (D) Gerard Stropnicky; (S) and (L) Vicki Neal; (C) D. Polly Kendrick; (SD) Malcolm Ruhl
Antigone, company-developed, from Sophocles; (D) Jim Niesen; (S) Kennon Rothchild; (L) Hilarie Blumenthal; (C) Elena Pellicciaro; (SD) Walter Thompson
Candide, company-developed; adapt: William Pope. L and Sara Capwell, from Voltaire; (D) Jim Calder; (S) Rosemary Geseck and the company; (L) Rob Nowicki; (C) Jessica Szabo and Barbara Seyda; (SD) John Calder
The Pill Hill Stories, Jay O'Callahan; (D) Richard McElvain

Trinity Repertory Company

RICHARD JENKINS
Artistic Director

DENNIS E. CONWAY
General Manager

SARAH T. DOWLING
Board Chairman

201 Washington St.
Providence, RI 02903
(401) 521-1100 (bus.)
(401) 351-4242 (b.o.)
(401) 521-0447 (fax)

Trinity Repertory Company

FOUNDED 1963
Adrian Hall

SEASON
Year-round

FACILITIES
Upstairs Theatre
Seating Capacity: 550
Stage: thrust

Downstairs Theatre
Seating Capacity: 297
Stage: flexible

FINANCES
July 1, 1992-June 30, 1993
Expenses: $3,300,000

CONTRACTS
AEA LORT (B) and (C)

Now celebrating the start of its 30th season, Trinity Repertory Company continues to earn recognition for its dedication to its company of artists, its vigorous ensemble style of production, its long commitment to the development of original works and adaptations, and its daring and innovative approach to traditional materials. From its beginnings, Trinity Rep has supported two goals: to provide a permanent home for its resident artists and to engage its audience as participants, rather than spectators, in the theatre experience. Our annual audience of 175,000 includes nearly 9,000 subscribers, and more than 18,000 high school students who participate in our extraordinarily successful Project Discovery, a program to make theatre a part of students' regular curriculums.
—*Richard Jenkins*

PRODUCTIONS 1991-1992

Sets by Robert D. Soule, lighting by Michael Giannitti, costumes by William Lane and sound design by Anthony PM Ricci unless otherwise noted.

It's Only A Play, Terrence McNally; (D) David Wheeler; (L) John F. Custer
A Christmas Carol, adapt: Adrian Hall and Richard Cumming, from Charles Dickens; (D) Peter Gerety; (S) David A. Rotondo; (SD) Chris Turner
The Glass Menagerie, Tennessee Williams; (D) Richard Jenkins; (S) Eugene Lee; (L) Natasha Katz
Fences, August Wilson; (D) Clinton Turner Davis
Prelude to a Kiss, Craig Lucas; (D) Adrian Hall; (S) Eugene Lee; (L) Natasha Katz
Macbeth, William Shakespeare; (D) Richard Jenkins; (S) Eugene Lee; (SD) Chris Turner and Rachel Maloney
The Heidi Chronicles, Wendy Wasserstein; (D) Leonard Foglia; (S) Michael McGarty
Burn This, Lanford Wilson; (D) David Wheeler; (S) David A. Rotondo
One for the Money, Janice Duclos; (D) Janice Duclos; (L) Jeff Clark
Lend Me a Tenor, Ken Ludwig; (D) Tony Giordano; (L) Jeff Clark

PRODUCTIONS 1992-1993

Direction by Richard Jenkins, sets and lighting by Eugene Lee and costumes by William Lane unless otherwise noted.

The Seagull, Anton Chekhov; trans: Tori Haring-Smith
Lips Together, Teeth Apart, Terrence McNally; (D) Leonard Foglia; (S) Michael McGarty; (L) Russell H. Champa; (SD) Anthony PM Ricci
A Christmas Carol, adapt: Adrian Hall and Richard Cumming, from Charles Dickens; (D) Neal Baron; (S) David A. Rotondo; (L) Michael Giannitti; (SD) Chris Turner
Northeast Local, Tom Donaghy; (D) David Petrarca; (S) Linda Buchanan; (L) James F. Ingalls; (SD) Rob Milburn
The Hope Zone, Kevin Heelan
Come Back, Little Sheba, William Inge; (D) Ralph Waite; (S) Robert D. Soule; (L) Jeff Clark; (SD) Anthony PM Ricci
Twelfth Night, William Shakespeare; (SD) Chris Turner and Rachel Maloney
The Good Times Are Killing Me, Lynda Barry; (D) Clinton Turner Davis; (S) Robert D. Soule; (L) Jeff Clark

Trinity Repertory Company. Olympia Dukakis and Anne Scurria in The Hope Zone. *Photo: Mark Morelli.*

Unicorn Theatre

CYNTHIA LEVIN
Producing Artistic Director

DON SCHREINER
Business Manager

FRED FOWLER
Board President

3820 Main St.
Kansas City, MO 64111
(816) 531-3033 (bus.)
(816) 531-7529 (b.o.)
(816) 531-0421 (fax)

FOUNDED 1973
Liz Gordon, Ronald Dennis, James Cairns

SEASON
Sept.-June

FACILITIES
Seating Capacity: 200
Stage: thrust

FINANCES
July 1, 1992-June 30, 1993
Expenses: $281,000

CONTRACTS
AEA SPT

Unicorn Theatre is dedicated to exploring the issues that confront and affect our lives. Racism, terrorism, sexual persecution, mental illness and the AIDS crisis are topics on which the Unicorn has focused in recent productions, reinforcing our commitment to the idea that theatre is a provocative tool used to inspire emotional response, intellectual discussion and controversy. It is the power to incite that keeps us moving forward, testing our artistic boundaries and functioning outside the commercial mainstream. By producing lesser-known plays and playwrights, and premiering at least one previously unproduced play each season, we hope to nurture emerging voices in the American theatre. The strong sense of collaboration felt by the local actors, designers and directors who work here is reflected in the productions themselves. Our audiences' overwhelming response to the plays we produce confirms the need for this type of theatre in Kansas City.
—*Cynthia Levin*

PRODUCTIONS 1991-1992

Direction by Cynthia Levin, sets by Atif Rome and lighting by Art Kent unless otherwise noted.

Closer Than Ever, conceived: Steven Scott Smith; music: David Shire; lyrics: Richard Maltby, Jr.; (S) and (L) Gary Mosby; (C) Mary Traylor; (MD) Kent Barnhart; (CH) Jeanne Beechwood
The Lisbon Traviata, Terrence McNally; (D) Jeff Church; (L) Greg Westfall; (C) Rebecca S. Larson; (SD) Cynthia Levin
Vital Signs, Jane Martin; (D) Cynthia Levin, Ray Smith and Lisa Cordes; (S) Gary Mosby; (C) Cheryl Benge; (SD) Stephana Mackender
Eastern Standard, Richard Greenberg; (C) Mary Traylor and Gregg Benkovich; (SD) Roger Stoddard

Unicorn Theatre. Don Richard and Terry O'Reagan in *The Lisbon Traviata*.

The Ivory Alphabet, B. Burgess Clark (co-produced by Missouri Repertory Theatre); (D) Mary G. Guaraldi; (S) Gary Mosby; (L) Amy Harrod; (C) Gregg Benkovich; (SD) Tom Mardikes
Two Rooms, Lee Blessing; (C) Cheryl Benge; (SD) Roger Stoddard
Theatre Grottesco, John Flax and Elizabeth Wiseman; (D) John Flax; (S) and (L) David Salowich; (C) the company
Falsettoland, book: William Finn and James Lapine; music and lyrics: William Finn; (C) Gregg Benkovich; (MD) Kent Barnhart

PRODUCTIONS 1992-1993

Direction by Cynthia Levin, sets by Atif Rome and lighting by Art Kent unless otherwise noted.

Changin' Lanes, book, music and lyrics: Mark Houston; (D) Francis Cullinan; (S) Keith Brumley; (C) Buzz Smith; (SD) Cynthia Levin
The Swan, Elizabeth Egloff; (C) Mary Traylor; (SD) Roger Stoddard
Five in the Killing Zone, Lavonne Mueller; (D) Meredith Alexander; (S) and (L) Michael Amico; (C) Rebecca S. Larson; (SD) Cynthia Levin
Daytrips, Jo Carson; (C) Rebecca S. Larson; (SD) Roger Stoddard
Lips Together, Teeth Apart, Terrence McNally; (L) Chester E. White; (C) Gregg Benkovich; (SD) Roger Stoddard
The Heidi Chronicles, Wendy Wasserstein; (D) Carol Blitgen; (C) Linda Flake; (SD) Cynthia Levin

Utah Shakespearean Festival

FRED C. ADAMS
Executive Producer

CAMERON HARVEY
Producing Artistic Director

R. SCOTT PHILLIPS
Managing Director

VERL R. TOPHMAN
Board President

351 West Center St.
Cedar City, UT 84720
(801) 586-7880 (bus.)
(801) 586-7878 (b.o.)
(801) 865-8003 (fax)

FOUNDED 1961
Fred C. Adams, Douglas N. Cook

SEASON
June-Sept.

FACILITIES
Adams Memorial Theatre
Seating Capacity: 817
Stage: thrust

Randall L. Jones Theatre
Seating Capacity: 767
Stage: thrust

University Mainstage
Seating Capacity: 988
Stage: proscenium

FINANCES
Oct. 1, 1991-Sept. 30, 1992
Expenses: $2,345,000

CONTRACTS
AEA U/RTA

For years I dreamed, and schemed, to bring a modern revival of classical theatre to this often-neglected end of my state. Shakespeare was, from the beginning, to be my medium; to bring to each and every school child, farmer's wife and Native American on the reservation an opportunity to experience the universality and dimension of this master playwright was my mission. It was also my hope to create a training system in the classics; just as a pianist practices scales, an actor has to work in repertory with Shakespeare, Chekhov, Ibsen and Moliere. Today's theatre must also be as flexible and imaginatively creative as the Old Globe was to a Shakespeare or a Jonson, where the promising young undiscovered playwrights of America can be challenged, free from the restraints of "economic necessities" or "marketability." In our 33-year history, the Festival has merely scratched the surface of its potential.

—*Fred C. Adams*

PRODUCTIONS 1991-1992

Blithe Spirit, Noel Coward; (D) Philip Killian; (S) Richard Isackes; (L) Robert A. Shakespeare; (C) James Berton Harris; (SD) James Capenos
Cyrano de Bergerac, Edmond Rostand; trans: Brian Hooker; (D) John Neville-Andrews; (S) Richard Isackes; (L) Robert A. Shakespeare; (C) Linda Melloy; (SD) James Capenos
Julius Caesar, William Shakespeare; (D) Howard Jensen; (S) Richard Isackes; (L) Robert A. Shakespeare; (C) James Berton Harris; (SD) James Capenos
King Lear, William Shakespeare; (D) Kathleen F. Conlin; (S) Carolyn L. Ross; (L) Linda Essig; (C) Colleen Muscha; (SD) Pamela Emerson
The Merchant of Venice, William Shakespeare; (D) Eli Simon; (S) Carolyn L. Ross; (L) Linda Essig; (C) Chris Flaharty; (SD) Pamela Emerson
The Merry Wives of Windsor, William Shakespeare; (D) James J. Christy; (S) Carolyn L. Ross; (L) Linda Essig; (C) Bill Black; (SD) Pamela Emerson

PRODUCTIONS 1992-1993

Tartuffe, Moliere; trans: Richard Wilbur; (D) Paul Barnes; (S) Thomas C. Umfrid; (L) Linda Essig; (C) James Berton Harris; (SD) James Capenos
Our Town, Thornton Wilder; (D) William Leach; (S) Thomas C. Umfrid; (L) Linda Essig; (C) Rosemary Ingham; (SD) James Capenos
The Royal Family, George S. Kaufman and Edna Ferber; (D) Howard J. Millman; (S) Thomas C. Umfrid; (L) Linda Essig; (C) James Berton Harris; (SD) James Capenos
Timon of Athens, William Shakespeare; (D) Robert Cohen; (S) Anne Gibson; (L) Geoff Korf; (C) Janet Swenson; (SD) Steven M. Klein

Utah Shakespearean Festival. Michele Farr and Richard Kinter in *Tartuffe*. Photo: John Running.

166 UTAH SHAKESPEAREAN FESTIVAL

Victory Gardens Theater. Jeff Still and Martha Lavey in *Earth and Sky*. Photo: Suzanne Plunkett.

Richard II, William Shakespeare; (D) Kathleen F. Conlin; (S) Anne Gibson; (L) Geoff Korf; (C) Janice Stauffer; (SD) Steven M. Klein

A Midsummer Night's Dream, William Shakespeare; (D) James J. Christy; (S) Anne Gibson; (L) Geoff Korf; (C) Bill Black; (SD) Steven M. Klein

Victory Gardens Theater

DENNIS ZACEK
Artistic Director

JOHN P. WALKER
Managing Director

MARCELLE McVAY
Development Director

NANCY BRESEKE
Board President

2257 North Lincoln Ave.
Chicago, IL 60614
(312) 549-5788 (bus.)
(312) 871-3000 (b.o.)
(312) 549-2779 (fax)

FOUNDED 1974
David Rasche, June Pyskacek, Cecil O'Neal, Mac McGinnes, Roberta Maguire, Stuart Gordon, Cordis Fejer, Warren Casey

SEASON
Aug.-June

FACILITIES
Mainstage
Seating Capacity: 195
Stage: thrust

Studio
Seating Capacity: 60
Stage: proscenium

FINANCES
July 1, 1992-June 30, 1993
Expenses: $1,010,585

CONTRACTS
AEA CAT

Victory Gardens Theater is a not-for-profit professional developmental theatre unique in the city for its commitment to the Chicago artist, with a special emphasis on the playwright. The theatre features a number of basic programs, all geared toward playwright development. The mainstage series consists of five diverse multiethnic productions, many of which are world premieres. The studio series presents productions focusing on new work suited to a smaller space. The free Readers Theater series presents works-in-progress on a bimonthly basis. Residencies and workshops for Chicago playwrights occur throughout the year. The training center offers classes in all aspects of theatre and provides an opportunity for about a thousand students a year. The touring program usually features an abbreviated version of one of the mainstage shows, which is seen by more than 10,000 high school students a year. A number of areas interact to produce the same result—developmental theatre.
—*Dennis Zacek*

PRODUCTIONS 1991-1992

Sound design by Galen G. Ramsey unless otherwise noted.

Hauptmann, John Logan; (D) Terry McCabe; (S) James Dardenne; (L) Todd Hensley; (C) Claudia Boddy

Spiele '36 or the Fourth Medal, Steve Carter; (D) Sandy Shinner; (S) James Wolk; (L) Michael Rourke; (C) Margaret Morettini

The Death of Zukasky, Richard Strand; (D) Curt Columbus; (S) Chuck Drury; (L) Chris Phillips; (C) Frances Maggio

Working Magic, Margaret Hunt; (D) Sandy Shinner; (S) Jeff Bauer; (L) Ellen Jones; (C) Frances Maggio

The Show Host, Rodolfo Santana; trans: Juan Pazos; (D) Edward F. Torres; (S) Robert Martin; (L) Dana Low and John Imburgia; (C) Sraa Davidson; (SD) Jeff Webb

This Old Man Came Rolling Home, James Sherman; (D) Dennis Zacek; (S) James Dardenne; (L) Robert Shook; (C) Claudia Boddy

Smile Orange, Trevor Rhone; (D) Jaye Stewart; (S) Linda Lane; (L) David Gipson; (C) Jaye Stewart; (SD) Joe Plummer

PRODUCTIONS 1992-1993

Sound design by Galen G. Ramsey unless otherwise noted.

Earth and Sky, Douglas Post; (D) Curt Columbus; (S) James Dardenne; (L) Michael Rourke; (C) John Hancock Brooks, Jr.

Hospitality Suite, Roger Rueff; (D) John Swanbeck; (S) William Bartelt; (L) Chris Phillips; (C) Claudia Boddy

Spinning Into Blue, Sally Nemeth; (D) Sandy Shinner; (S) Jeff Bauer; (L) Kathy Perkins; (C) Margaret Morettini

Freefall, Charles Smith; (D) Dennis Zacek; (S) James Dardenne; (L) Todd Hensley; (C) Claudia Boddy

Kimchee and Chitlins, Elizabeth Wong; (D) Amy Ludwig; (S) Robert Martin; (L) David Gipson; (C) Robert Cornelius; (SD) Willy Steele

Ripe Conditions, Claudia Allen; (D) Sandy Shinner; (S) Patrick Kerwin; (L) Robert Shook; (C) Frances Maggio

Vineyard Theatre

DOUGLAS AIBEL
Artistic Director

BARBARA ZINN KRIEGER
Executive Director

JON NAKAGAWA
Managing Director

108 East 15th St.
New York, NY 10003-9689
(212) 353-3366 (bus.)
(212) 353-3874 (b.o.)
(212) 353-3803 (fax)

FOUNDED 1981
Barbara Zinn Krieger

SEASON
Variable

FACILITIES
Vineyard Theatre at 26th St.
Seating Capacity: 71
Stage: thrust

Dimson Theatre
Seating Capacity: 120
Stage: flexible

FINANCES
Sept. 1, 1991-Aug. 31, 1992
Expenses: $426,585

CONTRACTS
AEA letter of agreement

The Vineyard Theatre, a multiart chamber theatre now entering its second decade, produces new plays and musicals, music-theatre collaborations and revivals of works that have previously failed in the commercial arena. While the range of our programming is eclectic, we've been consistently drawn to writers with a distinctively poetic style and an affinity for adventurous theatrical forms. We hope to produce work that provides our audience with an experience that is at once emotional and visceral, and that gives our artists a true opportunity to collaborate and experiment with their material. Because the company sponsors several music programs, including early music and jazz, we've also attempted to explore different ways in which music can enhance and enrich a dramatic text. The opening of our new theatre at Union Square has been the realization of a dream for us, and we look forward to many new creative opportunities there.

—*Douglas Aibel*

PRODUCTIONS 1991-1992

Lighting by Phil Monat unless otherwise noted.

The Don Juan & the Non Don Juan, book: James Milton; music: Neil Radisch; lyrics: James Milton and David Goldstein; (D) Evan Yionoulis; (S) William Barclay; (L) A.C. Hickox; (C) Teresa Snider-Stein; (MD) Dale Rieling

Lady Bracknell's Confinement, Paul Doust, and ***The Party***, adapt: Ellen McLaughlin, from Virgina Woolf; (D) Maria Aitken, (*Lady Bracknell's Confinement*), David Esbjornson (*The Party*); (S) G.W. Mercier; (C) Muriel Stockdale (*Lady Bracknell's Confinement*); (SD) Bruce Ellman

One of the All-Time Greats, Charles Grodin; (D) Tony Roberts; (S) Allen Moyer; (C) Muriel Stockdale; (SD) Bruce Ellman

Juno, book adapt: Joseph Stein, from Sean O'Casey; music and lyrics: Marc Blitzstein; (D) Lonny Price; (S) William Barclay; (C) Gail Brassard; (MD) Grant Sturiale; (CH) Joey McKneely

PRODUCTIONS 1992-1993

Costumes by Gail Brassard unless otherwise noted.

Juno, book adapt: Joseph Stein, from Sean O'Casey; music and lyrics: Marc Blitzstein; (D) Lonny Price; (S) William Barclay; (L) Phil Monat; (MD) Grant Sturiale; (CH) Joey McKneely; (SD) Bruce Ellman

Pterodactyls, Nicky Silver; (D) David Warren; (S) James Youmans; (L) Donald Holder; (C) Teresa Snider-Stein; (SD) Brian Hallas

The Chocolate Ambassador, book and lyrics: Chip Lopez and Camille Saviola; music: Charles Greenberg; (D) Andre Ernotte; (S) Allen Moyer; (L) Brian Aldous; (MD) Richard Cordova; (CH) Lynn Taylor-Corbett; (SD) Brian Hallas

Christina Alberta's Father, book adapt, music and lyrics: Polly Pen, from H.G. Wells; (D) Andre Ernotte; (S) William Barclay; (L) Phil Monat; (MD) Madelyn Rubinstein; (CH) Lynn Taylor-Corbett

Virginia Stage Company. Kyme and Allen Hidalgo in *Ain't Misbehavin'*. Photo: Mark Edward Atkinson.

Vineyard Theatre. Anita Gillette and Dick Latessa in *Juno*. Photo: Carol Rosegg/Martha Swope Associates.

Virginia Stage Company

CHARLIE HENSLEY
Artistic Director

DOUG PERRY
Managing Director

SIDNEY N. ASKEW, JR.
Board President

Box 3770
Norfolk, VA 23514
(804) 627-6988 (bus.)
(804) 627-1234 (b.o.)
(804) 628-5958 (fax)

FOUNDED 1979
Community members

SEASON
Oct.-Mar.

FACILITIES
Wells Theatre
Seating Capacity: 677
Stage: proscenium

Second Stage
Seating Capacity: 100
Stage: flexible

FINANCES
July 1, 1992-June 30, 1993
Expenses: $1,282,484

CONTRACTS
AEA LORT (C)

Virginia Stage Company is committed to the presentation of plays representing a wide range of theatrical styles and periods. Utilizing resident artists and maintaining an ongoing relationship with actors, designers and craftsmen, VSC is dedicated to the development of theatrical artistry which will nourish artists' work both here and elsewhere. As the area's only professional theatre, VSC continues to educate, inspire and entertain its culturally diverse audience through play and production discussions, student performances and school touring, as well as mainstage productions. In its 15th season Virginia Stage will revive new play development on its second stage, which will create and develop works by regional playwrights that explore issues indigenous to the region.

—*Charlie Hensley*

Note: During parts of the 1991-1992 and 1992-93 seasons, Tom Gardner served as artistic director.

PRODUCTIONS 1991-1992

Costumes by Lisa A. Vollrath and sound design by Pamela J. Nunnelley unless otherwise noted.

Who's Afraid of Virginia Woolf?, Edward Albee; (D) Charles Towers; (S) E. David Cosier, Jr.; (L) Nancy Schertler

Ain't Misbehavin', conceived: Murray Horwitz and Richard Maltby, Jr.; music and lyrics: Fats Waller, et al; (D) and (CH) Marcia Milgrom Dodge; (S) James Noone; (L) Kenneth Posner; (MD) Reginald Royal

Arms and the Man, George Bernard Shaw; (D) Christopher Hanna; (S) Bill Clarke; (L) Mary Louise Geiger; (C) Candice Cain

Broadway Bound, Neil Simon; (D) Tom Gardner; (S) John Falabella; (L) Terry Cermak

PRODUCTIONS 1992-1993

Costumes by Lisa A. Vollrath and sound design by Pamela J. Nunnelley unless otherwise noted.

The Lion in Winter, James Goldman; (D) Tom Gardner; (S) Donald Eastman; (L) James F. Ingalls

From the Mississippi Delta, Dr. Endesha Ida Mae Holland; (D) Seret Scott; (S) Debra Booth; (L) Pat Dignan

The Immigrant, Mark Harelik; (D) Tom Gardner; (S) Donald Eastman; (L) Brian MacDevitt; (C) Dona Granata

Pump Boys and Dinettes, John Foley, Mark Hardwick, Debra Monk, Cass Morgan, John Schimmel and Jim Wann; (D) Jason Edwards; (S) Mark Cheney; (L) Kenton Yeager; (C) Guinevere W. Lee

The Walnut Street Theatre Company

BERNARD HAVARD
Executive Director

KEN WESLER
Managing Director

JOHN D. GRAHAM
Board President

825 Walnut St.
Philadelphia, PA 19107
(215) 574-3550 (bus.)
(215) 574-3550, ext. 4 (b.o.)
(215) 574-3598 (fax)

FOUNDED 1983
Bernard Havard

SEASON
Sept.-June

FACILITIES
Mainstage
Seating Capacity: 1,052
Stage: proscenium

Studio 3
Seating Capacity: 77
Stage: flexible

Studio 5
Seating Capacity: 99
Stage: flexible

FINANCES
June 1, 1992-May 31, 1993
Expenses: $4,971,937

CONTRACTS
AEA LORT (A) and (D)

I have a twofold purpose in the direction of this theatre: to cultivate the finest talent in all facets of the artform, and to present to the community all this artform has to offer—inspiration, provocation and gratification. I strive to create a fertile environment for theatre professionals and students to explore the vibrant tradition of the theatre, to challenge it and to enrich it. I have an ongoing commitment to develop new works in general and new musicals specifically. In the past two seasons, the Walnut has fostered the birth of two new musicals: *Another Kind of Hero* and *Twist*. In addition, the studio theatre series has proved a fertile environment for the nurturing of new works, as well as lesser-known pieces. The Walnut Street Theatre, built in 1809, is the oldest theatre in America. That brings with it both a responsibility and the privilege of carrying that tradition forward with as much vitality as possible.

—Bernard Havard

PRODUCTIONS 1991-1992

Shirley Valentine, Willy Russell; (D) Jeff Lee; (S) and (L) James Tilton

Jesus Christ Superstar, music: Andrew Lloyd Webber; lyrics: Tim Rice; (D) and (CH) Charles Abbott; (S) and (L) Paul Wonsek; (C) Barbara Forbes; (MD) Joseph Baker

The Lion in Winter, James Goldman; (D) Malcolm Black; (S) David Jenkins; (L) Thomas Skelton; (C) Ann Roth; (SD) Bill Conti

Rumors, Neil Simon; (D) William Roudebush; (S) Tony Straiges; (L) Paul Wonsek; (C) Robert Bevenger, Jr.

Another Kind of Hero, book and lyrics: Lezley Steele; music: E.A. Alexander; (D) Charles Abbott; (S) and (L) Paul Wonsek; (C) Gail Cooper-Hecht; (MD) Patrick S. Brady; (CH) Marcia Milgrom Dodge; (SD) Scott Smith

Joanna's Husband, David's Wife, Elizabeth Forsythe Hailey; (D) Paul Linke; (S) Judi Guralnick and Joe Celli; (L) Paul Richardson; (C) Katryn Richardson; (SD) Tristan Wilson

Walt Whitman, Will Stutts; (D) Greg Giovanni; (S) and (L) Stephen Keever; (C) Sandra-Christine

Down The Road, Lee Blessing; (D) Alexa Kelly; (S) Peter C. Harvey; (L) John Stephen Hoey; (C) Christine Hanak; (SD) Connie Lockwood

When I Was a Girl I Used to Scream and Shout, Sharman Macdonald; (D) Celine Havard; (S) Paul Trapani; (L) Paul Richardson; (C) Christine Hanak; (SD) Connie Lockwood

PRODUCTIONS 1992-1993

Lend Me a Tenor, Ken Ludwig; (D) William Roudebush; (S) and (L) Kenneth N. Kurtz; (C) Cathie McClellan; (SD) Connie Lockwood

Into the Woods, book: James Lapine; music and lyrics: Stephen Sondheim; (D) and (CH) Charles Abbott; (S) and (L) Paul Wonsek; (C) Lee J. Austin; (MD) Patrick S. Brady; (SD) Scott Smith

The Old Devils, adapt: Robin Hawdon, from Kingsley Amis; (D) Toby Robertson; (S) Franco Colavecchia; (L) Marcia Madeira; (C) Cathie McClellan

Henceforward, Alan Ayckbourn; (D) Charlie Hensley; (S) Rob Odorisio; (L) David Traylor; (C) Cathie McClellan; (SD) Doug Coates

Groucho: A Life in Revue, book: Arthur Marx and Robert Fisher; various composers and lyricists; (D) Frank Ferrante; (S) Michael Boyer; (L) Kim Hanson; (C) Jose M. Rivera; (MD) Phyllis Gessler

The Sum of Us, David Stevens; (D) Sally Mercer; (S) Peter C. Harvey; (L) Wes Hacking; (C) Jeanne Adams; (SD) Ken Moreland

Mrs. Klein, Nicholas Wright; (D) Granville Burgess; (S) Kathleen J. Padova; (L) Tom Turner; (C) Tracy E. D'Altilia; (SD) Ken Moreland

Cries in the Night, Michael Elkin; (D) Alexa Kelly; (S) and (L) Mark R. Bloom; (C) Jennifer Deal; (SD) Ken Moreland

Brilliant Traces, Cindy Lou Johnson; (D) Celine Havard; (S) Peter C. Harvey; (L) Wes Hacking; (C) Kevin E. Ross; (SD) Ken Moreland

Will Stutts' Tallulah!, Will Stutts; (D) Greg Giovanni; (C) Sarah Iams

The Walnut Street Theatre Company. Kathleen Welch Markel, Susan Clark and George Peppard in *The Lion in Winter*. Photo: Martha Swope.

West Coast Ensemble. Gammy L. Singer and Clyde Talley, II in *Playboy of the West Indies*. Photo: Bob Bayles.

West Coast Ensemble

LES HANSON
Artistic Director

ROCCO VIENHAGE
Theater Administrator

STEVE RADOSH
Board President

Box 38728
Los Angeles, CA 90038
(213) 871-8673 (bus.)
(213) 871-1052 (b.o.)
(213) 462-6741 (fax)

FOUNDED 1982
Les Hanson, John Lehne

SEASON
Year-round

FACILITIES
Theater A
Seating Capacity: 55
Stage: proscenium

Theater B
Seating Capacity: 72
Stage: flexible

FINANCES
Jan. 1, 1992-Dec. 31, 1992
Expenses: $232,868

CONTRACTS
AEA 99-seat theatre plan

The mission of West Coast Ensemble is to produce classical theatre, American plays, and new plays and musicals that promote growth for the audience and the company ensemble. West Coast Ensemble presents seasons of great diversity that serve both the community and the artists involved. The community is provided with a variety of works from many cultures that stimulate, challenge and entertain. The theatre exists for the company as well, providing an exciting and nurturing atmosphere by giving time and space for theatre artists' individual growth and development. Because of a strong belief that a busy performance schedule and continued professional training are inseparable, West Coast Ensemble offers a full schedule of classes and workshops to actors, directors and playwrights. Three annual festivals are specifically designed to encourage emerging playwrights—the Celebration of One-Acts, the Full-Length Play Competition and Musical Stairs.
—*Les Hanson*

PRODUCTIONS 1992

Gorey Stories, adapt: Stephen Currens, from Edward Gorey; music: David Aldrich; (D) Tony Tanner; (S) Ramsey Avery; (L) Jerry Abbitt; (C) Susan Watanabe; (MD) Darren Server; (CH) Martin Silvestri
Old Times, Harold Pinter; (D) Dan Kern; (S) and (L) Jim Barbaley; (C) Barbara Nova
Playboy of the West Indies, adapt: Mustapha Matura, from John Millington Synge; (D) Les Hanson; (S) Stuart R. Baur; (L) Patrick Pankhurst; (C) Aldora B. Mitchell; (SD) Matthew Beville
The Shakespeare Circle, book adapt and lyrics: Tony Tanner, from William Shakespeare; (D) Tony Tanner; (S) Ramsey Avery and Stella Rose; (L) Jerry Abbitt; (C) Angela Calin; (MD) Darren Server; (CH) Valerie Zisser Gould

Celebration of One Acts:
Sets by Richard Hench and lighting by Diane Shaver.

Anthesis, Shellen Lubin; (D) Richard J. Large
Basketball Jones, William Babula; (D) Gammy L. Singer
Fast!, A.E.O. Goldman; (D) Pamela Putch
Before Eva, William Scheer; (D) Claudia Jaffee
Blind Date, Tannis Galik; (D) Ann Farthing
Dessert at Waffle House, Breakfast Anytime, Christopher Kyle; (D) Steven Avalos

Light Up the Sky, Moss Hart; (D) Chris Hart; (S) and (L) Jim Barbaley; (C) Jeanne Reith
8 Miles from New York, Charles Avakian Freericks; (D) Avner Garbi; (S) Jim Barbaley; (L) Jerry Abbitt
Steal Away, Ramona King; (D) Gammy L. Singer; (S) Tom Brown; (L) Ves Weaver; (C) Naila Sanders; (SD) Matthew Beville

PRODUCTIONS 1993

The Much Ado Musical, book adapt and lyrics: Tony Tanner, from William Shakespeare; music: Darren Server; (D) and (CH) Tony Tanner; (S) Ramsey Avery; (L) Jerry Abbitt; (C) Angela Calin; (MD) Darren Server
August Snow, Reynolds Price; (D) Richard J. Large; (S) Alex Kolmanovsky; (L) Jerry Abbitt; (C) Barbara Nova
Equus, Peter Shaffer; (D) Jules Aaron
Charley's Aunt, Brandon Thomas
La Malasangre, Griselda Gambara
Bitter Cane, Genny Lim
Suddenly Last Summer, Tennessee Williams
The Human Comedy, book adapt and lyrics: William Dumaresq, from William Saroyan; music: Galt MacDermot

White River Theatre Festival

STEPHEN LEGAWIEC
Artistic Director

STEVEN LEON
Managing Director

ALEX HUPPE
Board President

Box 336
White River Junction, VT 05001
(802) 295-6221 (bus.)
(802) 296-2505 (b.o.)
(802) 295-6101 (fax)

FOUNDED 1988
Stephen Legawiec, Steven Leon

SEASON
June-Dec.

FACILITIES
Briggs Opera House
Seating Capacity: 245
Stage: thrust

FINANCES
May 1, 1992-Apr. 30, 1993
Expenses: $252,922

CONTRACTS
AEA SPT

White River Theatre Festival presents a variety of dramatic genres from contemporary and classic literature, creating theatre pieces which not only entertain but challenge its audience. White River Theatre Festival contributes to the body of world theatre by developing new plays, by offering fresh interpretations of classics and by exploring new theatrical conventions. A permanent component of White River Theatre Festival is the Invisible Theatre Project, an ongoing exploration of theatre as a spiritual, nonintellectual medium.
—*Stephen Legawiec*

PRODUCTIONS 1992

Direction and sets by Stephen Legawiec, lighting by Steven Leon and costumes by Angela Brande unless otherwise noted.

Arsenic and Old Lace, Joseph Kesselring; (D) Steven Leon; (C) Adrienne Cedeno

White River Theatre Festival. Allison Metcalf and Gary Tucker in *A Midsummer Night's Dream*.

The Puppetmaster of Lodz, Gilles Segal; trans: Sara O'Connor; (D) Jayme Koszyn; (S) Jan Chambers; (C) Rachel Kurland
Hard Times, adapt: Stephen Jeffreys, from Charles Dickens; (C) Adrienne Cedeno
Evita, book and lyrics: Tim Rice; music: Andrew Lloyd Webber; (D) Mara Sabinson; (S) Robert M. Raiselis; (MD) Harry Richardson; (CH) Theresa Borden
Clarence Darrow, David Rintels; (D) Michael Friedman; (S) Robert M. Raiselis
Twelfth Night, William Shakespeare; (C) Stephen Legawiec
Amadeus, Peter Shaffer; (D) Steven Leon; (S) Victor A. Becker
The Minotaur, company-developed; (L) and (C) Stephen Legawiec

PRODUCTIONS 1993

Direction and sets by Stephen Legawiec, lighting by Steven Leon and costumes by Angela Brande unless otherwise noted.

Candide, book adapt: Hugh Wheeler, from Voltaire; music: Leonard Bernstein; lyrics: Richard Wilbur; addtl lyrics: Stephen Sondheim and John LaTouche; (D) Kevin Cotter; (S) Daniele Perna; (MD) Fred Frabotta
A Midsummer Night's Dream, William Shakespeare; (C) Stephen Legawiec
Come Up and See Me Sometime, Stephen Legawiec; (D) Rob Barron
Our Country's Good, adapt: Timberlake Wertenbaker, from Thomas Keneally; (D) Michael Friedman; (S) Robert M. Raiselis; (C) Sarah Stone
The Minotaur and *The Medicine Show*, company-developed
Lend Me a Tenor, Ken Ludwig; (D) Robert M. Raiselis
The Caucasian Chalk Circle, Bertolt Brecht; trans: Ralph Manheim
The Snow Queen, adapt: Stephen Legawiec, from Hans Christian Andersen
Sleuth, Anthony Shaffer; (S) Robert M. Raiselis; (L) Steven Leon and Thomas Fusco; (C) Adrienne Cedeno
A Christmas Carol, adapt: Charles Jones, from Charles Dickens; (S) Robert M. Raiselis

Williamstown Theatre Festival

PETER HUNT
Artistic/Executive Director

WILLIAM STEWART
Managing Director

WILLIAM H. EVERETT
Board President

Box 517
Williamstown, MA 01267
(413) 458-3200 (bus.)
(413) 597-3400 (b.o.)
(413) 458-3147 (fax)

FOUNDED 1955
Nikos Psacharopoulos, Trustees of the Williamstown Theatre Festival

SEASON
June-Aug.

FACILITIES
Adams Memorial Theatre
Seating Capacity: 521
Stage: proscenium

The Other Stage
Seating Capacity: 96
Stage: thrust

FINANCES
Dec. 1, 1991-Nov. 30, 1992
Expenses: $1,669,179

CONTRACTS
AEA CORST (X) and letter of agreement

Williamstown Theatre Festival is devoted to the growth of the individual artist. Through productions of classics and epic works on its main stage, new works focusing on the playwright at its Other Stage and adaptations of world literature in its Free Theatre, WTF offers its extended family of actors, directors, designers and writers an array of theatrical challenges rarely available elsewhere. As an educational institution concerned with the future of the theatre, WTF champions intensive programs for interns and apprentices. These involve training and opportunities for constant interaction between talented students and gifted professionals, and the results are both revitalizing and inspirational. WTF dedicates itself to being a haven—a place where artists have done, and will continue to do, their best work.
—*Peter Hunt*

PRODUCTIONS 1992

Lighting by Betsy Finston and costumes by Kimberly Schnormeier unless otherwise noted.

The Threepenny Opera, book and lyrics: Bertolt Brecht; trans and adapt: Marc Blitzstein; music: Kurt Weill; (D) Peter Hunt; (S) John Conklin; (L) Peter Hunt; (C) Merrily Murray-Walsh; (MD) Christopher Drobny; (CH) Ann Reinking
The Guardsman, Ferenc Molnar; trans: Frank Marcus; (D) Michael Bloom; (S) Peter Harrison; (L) Rui Rita; (C) Connie Singer
The Visit, Friedrich Durrenmatt; trans: Maurice Valency; (D) Peter Hunt; (S) Hugh Landwehr; (L) Arden Fingerhut; (C) Jeanne Button; (SD) Darron L. West
2, Romulus Linney; (D) Tom Bullard; (S) E. David Cosier, Jr.; (L) Jeffrey Koger; (C) Teresa Snider-Stein; (SD) Darron L. West
The Sweet By 'n' By, Frank Higgins; (D) David Dorwart; (S) Maureen Fish and Margo Zdravkovic; (L) Rui Rita; (C) Jess Goldstein

Williamstown Theatre Festival. *The Threepenny Opera*. Photo: Richard Feldman.

The Will and Bart Show, Jim Lehrer; (D) Tina Ball; (S) Jana Bialon
Black, Joyce Carol Oates; (D) Gordon Hunt; (S) Tom Baker
Hotel Oubliette, Jane Anderson; (D) Jenny Sullivan; (S) Emily J. Beck; (SD) Martin Desjardins
Alone Together: Betty Buckley in Concert, (D) Syd Sidner; (S) Sherri Adler; (L) David Reynolds; (C) Richard Shawn Dudley; (MD) Ken Werner
A Midsummer Night's Dream, William Shakespeare; (D) Neel Keller; (S) Steven Thompson; (L) Benjamin Pearcy; (C) Ken Mooney

PRODUCTIONS 1993

Lighting by Rui Rita and sound design by Rob Smith unless otherwise noted.

The Madwoman of Chaillot, Jean Giraudoux; adapt: Maurice Valency; (D) Tom Moore; (S) Christine Jones; (C) Carrie Robbins
Nora, Henrik Ibsen; trans: Frederick J. Marker and Lise-Lone Marker; adapt: Ingmar Bergman; (D) Michael Bloom; (S) Peter Harrison; (C) Paul Tazewell
Counsellor-at-Law, Elmer Rice; (D) Peter Hunt; (S) Peter Harrison; (C) Claudia Stephens
An Inspector Calls, J.B. Priestley; (D) John Badham; (S) Hugh Landwehr; (C) Therese A. Bruck
Fourplay, Alan Ayckbourn, Ferenc Molnar, Ring Lardner and George S. Kaufman, and Serafin and Joaquin Quintero; (D) David Saint; (S) David Mitchell; (L) Ken Billington; (C) Jane Greenwood
Therese Raquin, adapt: Neal Bell, from Emile Zola; (D) Michael Greif; (S) Betsy McDonald; (L) Betsy Finston; (C) Deanna Berg
If We Are Women, Joanna M. Glass; (D) Austin Pendleton; (S) C. David Russell; (L) Betsy Finston; (C) Maureen Schell; (SD) Matthew Bennett
The Waiting Room, Lisa Loomer; (D) David Schweizer; (S) Douglas Huszti; (L) Betsy Finston; (C) Jeanette DeJong; (SD) Mitchell Greenhill and Matthew Bennett
Dirt, Bruce Gooch; (D) Jenny Sullivan; (S) Paul Melia; (L) Betsy Finston; (C) Deanna Berg
As You Like It, William Shakespeare; (D) Alice Jankell; (S) and (C) Anduin R. Havens; (L) Benjamin Pearcy

The Wilma Theater

BLANKA ZIZKA, JIRI ZIZKA
Artistic/Producing Directors

LORI OTT
Interim Managing Director

MAN SHAW
Board Chairman

2030 Sansom St.
Philadelphia, PA 19103-4417
(215) 963-0249 (bus.)
(215) 963-0345 (b.o.)
(215) 963-0377 (fax)

FOUNDED 1973
Liz Stout, Linda Griffith

SEASON
Sept.-June

FACILITIES
Seating Capacity: 106
Stage: proscenium

FINANCES
Aug. 1, 1992-July 31, 1993
Expenses: $1,399,819

CONTRACTS
AEA letter of agreement

The Wilma Theater presents theatre as an artform that engages both audience and artists in an adventure of aesthetic and philosophical reflection on the complexities of contemporary life. We believe that a fine performance of a great play is one of the most rewarding experiences our culture provides. The Wilma relies on the selection of powerful, compelling scripts, to which mixed media add another dimension, allowing each production to evolve beyond the confines of verbal communication into the world of metaphor and poetic vision. Our productions are a synthesis of many artistic disciplines—visual arts, music, choreography, writing, acting; our challenge lies in finding new connections among these disciplines to illuminate the dramatic essence of the script. Our staging utilizes a succession of impermanent images, cinematic and three-dimensional, to heighten the inner emotional realities of the characters and create a unique scenic rhythm that captures our age of constant speed, surprise and visual stimulation.

—*Blanka Zizka, Jiri Zizka*

PRODUCTIONS 1991-1992

A Tale of Two Cities, adapt: Everett Quinton, from Charles Dickens; (D) John Going; (S) James Wolk; (L) Jerold R. Forsyth; (C) Hiroshi Iwasaki; (SD) Adam Wernick
Achilles: A Kabuki Play, adapt: Karen Sunde, from Homer (co-produced by The People's Light and Theatre Company)
When She Danced, Martin Sherman; (D) Blanka Zizka; (S) and (C) Anne C. Patterson; lyrics: Jerold R. Forsyth; (SD) Arthur Stidfole and Joyce Lieberman
The Virgin Molly, Quincy Long; (D) Jiri Zizka; (S) James Wolk; (L) Jerold R. Forsyth; (C) Maxine Hartswick; (SD) Adam Wernick

PRODUCTIONS 1992-1993

Lighting by Jerold R. Forsyth unless otherwise noted.

Halcyon Days, Steven Dietz; (D) Jiri Zizka; (S) Karen TenEyck; (C) Maxine Hartswick; (SD) Adam Wernick
Lady Day at Emerson's Bar and Grill, Lanie Robertson; (D) Blanka Zizka; (S) Andrei W. Efremoff; (C) Maxine Hartswick

The Wilma Theater. Carol Mayo Jenkins and Philip Lynch in *When She Danced*. Photo: Joseph Nettis.

Oedipus The King, Sophocles; trans: Stephen Berg and Diskin Clay; (D) Blanka Zizka; (S) Andrei W. Efremoff; (C) Anne C. Patterson
Etta Jenks, Marlane Meyer; (D) Jiri Zizka; (S) Jerry Rojo; (C) Sarah Iams; (SD) Jonathan Sher

Wisdom Bridge Theatre

JEFFREY ORTMANN
Producing Director

JOHN CONLON, JACK JOHNSON
Board Co-Chairmen

1559 West Howard St.
Chicago, IL 60626
(312) 743-0486 (bus.)
(312) 743-6000 (b.o.)
(312) 743-1614 (fax)

FOUNDED 1974
David Beaird

SEASON
Sept.-July

FACILITIES
Seating Capacity: 196
Stage: proscenium

172 WISDOM BRIDGE THEATRE

Wisdom Bridge Theatre. Ahmed Elkassabany and Robert Scogin in *M. Butterfly*.

FINANCES
Aug. 1, 1992-July 31, 1993
Expenses: $750,000

CONTRACTS
AEA CAT

Wisdom Bridge Theatre is located in a second-story loft space in a dynamic and culturally diverse neighborhood on the northernmost edge of Chicago. The theatre's guiding tenet is that "the bridge to wisdom lies in the continual asking of questions." The theatre focuses on plays which ask large questions about society, art and the political system, producing both new works and innovative interpretations of classics. WBT also embraces the power of theatre as a tool for increasing global understanding, and has toured productions to Austria, England, Scotland and Israel. In addition to WBT's main emphasis on producing plays on Howard Street, the theatre also plays a significant role in the community in which it is located. WBT has a nationally recognized outreach program that works with local primary and secondary schools, senior centers, social service agencies, restaurants, the neighborhood (economic) development corporation and community groups.

—*Jeffrey Ortmann*

PRODUCTIONS 1991-1992

Falsettoland, book: William Finn and James Lapine; music and lyrics: William Finn; (D) Jeffrey Ortmann; (S) Kevin Rigdon; (L) Michael Rourke; (C) Claudia Boddy; (MD) Tim Schirmer; (CH) James Corti
My Children! My Africa!, Athol Fugard; (D) Terry McCabe; (S) Chip Yates; (L) Michael Rourke; (C) Sraa Davidson
The Richest Dead Man Alive, Theatre Grottesco; (L) Ian Rosenkranz
M. Butterfly, David Henry Hwang; (D) Jeffrey Ortmann; (S) John Murbach; (L) Barbara Reeder and Michael Rourke; (C) Nanalee Raphael-Schirmer

PRODUCTIONS 1992-1993

Direction by Terry McCabe unless otherwise noted.

The Picture of Dorian Gray, adapt: Paul Edwards, from Oscar Wilde; (S) Jeff Bauer; (L) Barbara Reeder and Michael Rourke; (C) Claudia Boddy; (SD) Paul Edwards
Triple Exposure, Jim Geoghan; (S) Jacqueline Penrod and Richard Penrod; (L) Michael Rourke; (C) Claudia Boddy
Life During Wartime, Keith Reddin; (D) Michael Maggio; (S) Rob Hamilton; (L) Chris Phillips; (C) Lynn Sandberg; (SD) Michael Bodeen and Joe Cerqua
Showbiz, John Logan; (S) Jeff Bauer; (L) Kevin Rigdon; (C) Christine Birt

Women's Project & Productions

JULIA MILES
Artistic Director

MARY ANN HANSEN
Managing Director

PAT SCHOENFELD
Board Chairperson

7 West 63rd St.
New York, NY 10023
(212) 873-3040 (bus.)
(212) 873-3767 (b.o.)
(212) 873-3788 (fax)

FOUNDED 1978
Julia Miles

SEASON
Oct.-June

FACILITIES
Seating Capacity: flexible
Stage: proscenium

FINANCES
July 1, 1992-June 30, 1993
Expenses: $580,000

CONTRACTS
AEA letter of agreement

I founded the Women's Project with one goal—to bring women to the forefront of the American theatre. Through a variety of innovative programs, including high-quality professional productions, Next Stage work-in-progress productions, rehearsed readings, the Directors' Forum, Departures, Southern Exposure and an active advocacy program, the Women's Project creates a supportive environment in which women can experiment, exchange ideas and see their work expertly brought to the stage. Our educational outreach program, "Ten Centuries of Women Playwrights," examines the fascinating lives and work of women playrights from the 10th century to the present. The Women's Project currently has 389 artistic members, and has produced 67 new plays, edited 5 play anthologies and helped to develop literally hundreds of new plays by women. The WPP works with women theatre artists of all cultures whose unique perspectives and authentic voices encourage us to examine our society deeply and insightfully.

—*Julia Miles*

Women's Project & Productions. Mia Katigbak, Mary Mara and Carls Corfman in *Dream of a Common Language*. Photo: Martha Holmes.

PRODUCTIONS 1991-1992

Approximating Mother, Kathleen Tolan; (D) Gloria Muzio; (S) David Jenkins; (L) Jackie Manassee; (C) Elsa Ward; (SD) Mark Bennett

Chain and *Late Bus to Mecca*, Pearl Cleage; (D) Imani; (S) George Xenos; (L) Melody Beal; (C) Ornyece; (SD) Bill Toles

Dream of a Common Language, Heather McDonald; (D) Liz Diamond; (S) Anita Stewart; (L) Michael Chybowski; (C) Sally Lesser; (SD) Dan Schreier

PRODUCTIONS 1992-1993

You Could Be Home By Now, Ann Magnuson (co-produced by the New York Shakespeare Festival); (D) David Schweizer; (S) Bill Clarke; (L) Heather Carson; (C) Pilar Limosner; (SD) Eric Liljestrand

Frida, book: Hilary Blecher; music: Robert Xavier Rodriguez; lyrics: Migdalia Cruz; (D) Hilary Blecher; (S) Andrew Jackness; (L) Robert Wierzel; (C) Ann Roth and Robert de Mora; (MD) Robert Kapilow; (CH) Hope Clarke; (SD) Theatre Sound

Skirting the Issues, various composers and lyricists; (D) Sue Lawless; (MD) Sande Campbell

The Brooklyn Trojan Women, Carole Braverman; (D) Margot Breier; (S) Ted Glass; (L) Heather Rogan; (C) Leslie Yarmo; (SD) Bart Fasbender

Amphibians, Molly Haskell; (D) Joan Vail Thorne

Woolly Mammoth Theatre Company

HOWARD SHALWITZ
Artistic Director

NANCY TURNER HENSLEY
Producing Associate

MOLLY WHITE
Associate Director

SUNNY JUNG SCULLY
Board President

1401 Church St. NW
Washington, DC 20005
(202) 234-6130 (bus.)
(202) 393-3939 (b.o.)
(202) 667-0904 (fax)

FOUNDED 1980
Howard Shalwitz, Roger Brady

SEASON
Oct.-July

FACILITIES
Seating Capacity: 132
Stage: thrust

FINANCES
Sept. 1, 1992-Aug. 31, 1993
Expenses: $565,483

CONTRACTS
AEA SPT

Woolly Mammoth is committed to producing innovative new plays with provocative points of view, unusual techniques and styles, and exceptional verbal and theatrical energy. Roughly half our plays are world premieres, and the rest regional or American premieres. We work closely with playwrights on script development, and nurture a 12-member acting company which includes some of Washington's most noted performers. Woolly Mammoth produces a four-play subscription series, plus an "Odd Evenings" series of solo and small ensemble works. In 1994 we are mounting a festival of solo performers from around the country called "Single Exposures." Woolly Mammoth has developed an innovative program called "Outside Woolly," which uses the arts to build bridges among the diverse populations of our neighborhood. The program includes commissioned murals, theatre workshops to serve the clients of area service organizations, and a major outdoor production slated for the summer of 1995.
—*Howard Shalwitz*

PRODUCTIONS 1991-1992

Sets by Lewis Folden unless otherwise noted.

Mud People, Keith Huff; (D) Grover Gardner; (L) Christopher Townsend; (C) Rosemary Ingham; (SD) Dan Schrader

African Tourist, Drury Pifer; (D) Howard Shalwitz; (S) Tom Meyer; (L) Christopher Townsend; (C) Rosemary Pardee and Lynn Steinmetz; (SD) Ron Ursano

Woolly Mammoth Theatre Company. Jason Kravits in *Free Will & Wanton Lust*. Photo: Stan Barouh.

Life During Wartime, Keith Reddin; (D) Lee Mikeska Gardner; (L) Daniel MacLean Wagner; (C) Howard Vincent Kurtz; (SD) Ron Ursano

Kvetch, Steven Berkoff; (D) Howard Shalwitz; (L) Lewis Folden; (C) Jane Schloss Phelan; (SD) Dan Schrader

PRODUCTIONS 1992-1993

Sets by James Kronzer unless otherwise noted.

Billy Nobody, Stanley Rutherford; (D) Howard Shalwitz; (S) Lou Stancari; (L) Kim Peter Kovac; (C) Howard Vincent Kurtz; (SD) Dan Schrader

Free Will & Wanton Lust, Nicky Silver; (D) Nicky Silver; (L) David R. Zemmels; (C) Rosemary Ingham; (SD) Hugh Caldwell

The Mask, Namu Lwanga; (D), (C) and (SD) Namu Lwanga; (L) Stephanie Johnson

The Cockburn Rituals, John Strand; (D) Jennifer Mendenhall; (L) Christopher Townsend; (C) Susan Anderson; (SD) Neil McFadden

Strindberg In Hollywood, Drury Pifer; (D) Howard Shalwitz; (S) Lewis Folden; (L) Martha Mountain; (C) Howard Vincent Kurtz; (SD) Neil McFadden

The Wooster Group

ELIZABETH LeCOMPTE, WILLEM DAFOE, SPALDING GRAY, JIM CLAYBURGH, PEYTON SMITH, KATE VALK, RON VAWTER
Artistic Directors

CYNTHIA HEDSTROM
Producing Director

Box 654, Canal St. Station
New York, NY 10013
(212) 966-9796 (bus.)
(212) 966-3651 (b.o.)

FOUNDED 1975

SEASON
Variable

FACILITIES
The Performing Garage
Seating Capacity: 200
Stage: flexible

FINANCES
July 1, 1991-June 30, 1992
Expenses: $742,167

The Wooster Group has worked together for more than 15 years producing original theatre and media pieces. Wooster Group productions are composed by the Group and directed by Elizabeth LeCompte. The Group's theatre works join an ongoing repertoire and are periodically revived in conjunction with new work. All the work is created and produced at the group's permanent theatre space, the Performing Garage, a space that is collectively owned and operated by the group. The company's season is flexible, and the group regularly tours throughout Europe and the United States.

—The Wooster Group

PRODUCTIONS 1991-1992

Brace Up!, Anton Chekhov; trans: Paul Schmidt; adapt: the company; (D) Elizabeth LeCompte; (S) Jim Clayburgh; (L) Jennifer Tipton; (C) Elizabeth Jenyon

PRODUCTIONS 1992-1993

Fish Story—Part 1, adapt: the company, from Eugene O'Neill; (D) Elizabeth LeCompte; (S) Jim Clayburgh; (L) Clay Shirky; (SD) James Johnson

Fish Story—Part 2, company-developed; (D) Elizabeth LeCompte; (S) Jim Clayburgh; (L) Clay Shirky; (C) Ellen McCartney, with the company; (SD) James Johnson

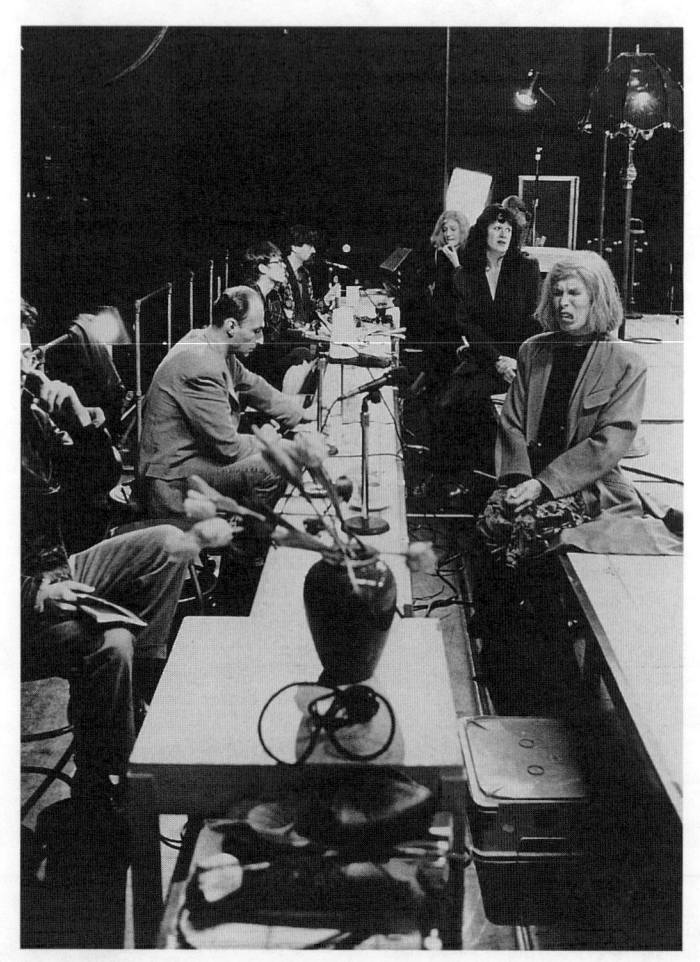

Worcester Foothills Theatre Company. Sean Cutler and Eda Roth in *Brighton Beach Memoirs*. Photo: Patrick O'Connor.

Worcester Foothills Theatre Company

MARC P. SMITH
Executive Producer/Artistic Director

TAMARA A. BETHEL
Board President

074 Worcester Center
100 Front St.
Worcester, MA 01608
(508) 754-3314 (bus.)
(508) 754-4018 (b.o.)

FOUNDED 1974
Marc P. Smith

SEASON
Oct.-May

FACILITIES
Foothills Theatre
Seating Capacity: 349
Stage: proscenium

FINANCES
June 1, 1992-May 31, 1993
Expenses: $953,500

CONTRACTS
AEA letter of agreement

I think of artistic success when I see people from all parts of our diverse community gather together in our theatre. To me, they are doing something much more than "seeing" a play. They are *considering* all the elements that go into any production: the ideas, the plot, the characters, the sets, costumes, lights, props, sound, etc. More and more of our audience members have become "repeat business," and they are becoming educated in the complexities of this very human endeavor we call theatre. As this happens, they realize their own importance as an audience that participates in creating a dynamic dialogue between a community and its artists. Of course, people then talk to others about what they've experienced. How many more people are then affected by what happens in our theatre? This multiplication will only happen over a period of time if people care. And that brings us round robin. I think of artistic success as presenting a program of what a community truly cares about.

—*Marc P. Smith*

PRODUCTIONS 1991-1992

Sets by Don Ricklin, lighting by L. Stacy Eddy, costumes by Kent Street and sound design by J. Patrick McGrail unless otherwise noted.

Brighton Beach Memoirs, Neil Simon; (D) Thomas Oullette; (L) Penny L. Remsen
Sea Marks, Gardner McKay; (D) Roger Hendricks Simon; (L) Spencer Mosse
Bell, Book, and Candle, John Van Druten; (D) Jack Magune; (S) Richard Russell; (L) Steven Rosen
Steel Magnolias, Robert Harling; (D) James B. Nicola
The Great American Backstage Musical, book: Billy Solly and Donald Ward; music and lyrics: Billy Solly; (D) and (CH) Michael Oster; (MD) Jonathan Goldberg

The Wooster Group. *Brace Up!* Photo: Bob Van Dantzig.

The Brewster Papers, Marc P. Smith; (D) Marc P. Smith; (S) Bill Savoy; (L) Jim Albergini
A Funny Thing Happened on the Way to the Forum, book: Burt Shevelove and Larry Gelbart; music and lyrics: Stephen Sondheim; (D) and (CH) Jim L'Ecuyer; (S) Richard Russell; (MD) Arthur Finstein

PRODUCTIONS 1992-1993

Lighting by L. Stacy Eddy, costumes by Andrew J. Poleszak and sound design by Michael Versteegt unless otherwise noted.

I Hate Hamlet, Paul Rudnick; (D) Robert Walsh; (S) Richard Russell
Shirley Valentine, Willy Russell; (D) Richard Rose; (S) Charles Morgan; (L) Ellen Gould; (C) Jane Alois Stein
Arsenic and Old Lace, Joseph Kesselring; (D) Ingrid Sonnichsen; (S) Don Ricklin
Side by Side by Sondheim, book: Ned Sherrin; music: Stephen Sondheim, Leonard Bernstein, Mary Rodgers, Richard Rodgers and Jule Styne; lyrics: Stephen Sondheim; (D) and (CH) Michael Oster; (S) Bill Savoy; (L) Ellen Gould; (MD) Roger Grodsky
Laura, Vera Caspary and George Sklar; (D) Thomas Oullette; (S) Richard Russell; (L) Penny L. Remsen
Blood Summit, Marc P. Smith; (D) Marc P. Smith; (S) Bill Savoy
Nunsense, book, music and lyrics: Dan Goggin; (D) and (CH) Jim L'Ecuyer; (S) Don Ricklin

Yale Repertory Theatre

STAN WOJEWODSKI, JR.
Artistic Director

VICTORIA NOLAN
Managing Director

Box 1903A Yale Station
222 York St.
New Haven, CT 06520
(203) 432-1515 (bus.)
(203) 432-1234 (b.o.)
(203) 432-1550 (fax)

FOUNDED 1966
Robert Brustein

SEASON
Oct.-May

FACILITIES
Yale Repertory Theatre
Seating Capacity: 489
Stage: thrust

University Theatre
Seating Capacity: 656
Stage: proscenium

FINANCES
July, 1991-June 30, 1992
Expenses: $3,177,040

CONTRACTS
AEA LORT (C)

As the artistic director/dean of the Yale Repertory Theatre/Yale School of Drama, I strive to guarantee that the rhythm of artistry becomes the dominant influence on cycles of planning and production. This requires a theatre always teeming with ideas, the ripest and readiest of which can then be born to the public view as their own internal logic dictates. Such a vision mandates that the institution become, in fact, a patron of the individual artist. Seasons are shaped in response to a wide range of artistic impulses which arise out of the identification and support of a diverse community of associate artists. In the consortium of theatre and school at Yale, we have a tangible head start toward the realization of this ideal. The classical repertoire is juxtaposed, as stimulus and target for aspiration, with new writing for the stage to provide an environment in which theatre professionals and conservatory students become engaged in the exchange of ideas vital to the creation of new works of art.
—*Stan Wojewodski, Jr.*

PRODUCTIONS 1991-1992

On the Verge, Eric Overmyer; (D) Stan Wojewodski, Jr.; (S) Matthew Moore; (L) Robert Wierzel; (C) Anna Oliver; (SD) Rob Gorton
My Children! My Africa!, Athol Fugard; (D) Elizabeth S. Margid; (S) Susan Branch; (L) Rick Martin; (C) Dennita Sewell; (SD) Mark D. Dingley
Fefu and Her Friends, Maria Irene Fornes; (D) Lisa Peterson; (S) Michael V. Sims; (L) Trui Malten; (C) Maggie Morgan; (SD) Jon Newstrom
The Death of the Last Black Man in the Whole Entire World, Suzan-Lori Parks; (D) Liz Diamond; (S) Riccardo Hernandez; (L) Glen Fasman; (C) Caryn Neman; (SD) Dan Schreier
Democracy in America, Colette Brooks; (D) Travis Preston; (S) Christopher Barreca; (L) Stephen Strawbridge; (C) Tom Broecker; (SD) David Budries
Edward the Second, Christopher Marlowe; (D) Stan Wojewodski, Jr.; (S) Michael Yeargan; (L) Jennifer Tipton; (C) Tom Broecker; (SD) Darren Clark
The Beauty Part, S.J. Perelman; (D) Walton Jones; (S) Nicholas Lundy; (L) Lynne Chase; (C) Susan Branch; (SD) Martin Desjardins

PRODUCTIONS 1992-1993

Hamlet, William Shakespeare; (D) Stan Wojewodski, Jr.; (S) Todd Rosenthal; (L) Robert Wierzel; (C) Katherine Roth
The Colored Museum, George C. Wolfe; (D) Donald Douglass; (S) Monica Raya; (L) Trui Malten; (C) Elizabeth Michal Fried; (SD) Mark D. Dingley
Children of Paradise: Shooting a Dream, adapt: Steven Epp, Felicity Jones, Dominique Serrand and Paul Walsh, from Marcel Carne and Jacques Prevert (co-produced by Theatre de la Jeune Lune) (D) Dominique Serrand; (S) Vincent Gracieux; (L) Frederic Desbois; (C) Trina Mrnak
Saint Joan of the Stockyards, Bertolt Brecht; trans: Paul Schmidt; (D) Liz Diamond; (S) Adam Scher; (L) Jennifer Tipton; (C) Lisa Tomczeszyn; (SD) Dan Moses Schreier
Escape from Happiness, George F. Walker (co-produced by Center Stage) (D) Irene Lewis; (S) Michael Yeargan; (L) Stephen Strawbridge; (C) Jess Goldstein; (SD) Janet Kalas
The Baltimore Waltz, Paula Vogel; (D) Stan Wojewodski, Jr.; (S) David Maxine; (L) Lynne Chase; (C) Denise Hudson; (SD) Martin Desjardins

Yale Repertory Theatre. *Saint Joan of the Stockyards*. Photo: T. Charles Erickson.

Young Playwrights Inc. James G. Macdonald and Seth Gilliam in *Man at His Best*. Photo: Tess Steinkolk.

Young Playwrights Inc.

(formerly Young Playwrights Festival)

SHERI M. GOLDHIRSCH
Artistic Director

BRETT W. REYNOLDS
Managing Director

ALFRED UHRY
Board President

321 West 44th St., #906
New York, NY 10036
(212) 307-1140
(212) 307-1454 (fax)

FOUNDED 1982
Stephen Sondheim, Ruth Goetz, Jules Feiffer, Eve Merriam, Murray Horwitz, Mary Rodgers, Richard Wesley

SEASON
Sept.-Oct.

FACILITIES
Playwrights Horizons Mainstage
Seating Capacity: 145
Stage: proscenium

FINANCES
Oct. 1, 1991-Sept. 30, 1992
Expenses: $607,000

CONTRACTS
AEA Off Broadway

Young Playwrights Inc. identifies and develops young American playwrights by involving them as active participants in professional productions of their plays. In the past 12 years, more than 8,500 writers aged 18 and younger have submitted their plays to the Young Playwrights Festival. YPI has produced the works of 65 of these writers in the Festival's annual Off-Broadway season. YPI is committed to making the arts an integral part of basic education nationwide by introducing students to playwriting and the experience of live theatre. The YPI Education Program includes in-school playwriting workshops; the Teacher Training Institute; the School Tour; and Take a Grownup to the Theater!, an intergenerational audience development program. Central to YPI's mission is its commitment to honoring multiculturalism. For YPI, cultural diversity extends beyond ethnicity to include age, gender, physical ability, sexual orientation and economic status. From the classroom to the audience to the boardroom to the stage, YPI considers it a responsibility to reflect and honor the diversity of the world in which we live.

—*Sheri M. Goldhirsch*

Note: During the 1991-92 and 1992-93 seasons, Nancy Quinn served as artistic director.

PRODUCTIONS 1991-1992

Young Playwrights Festival:
Sets by Allen Moyer, lighting by Pat Dignan, costumes by Elsa Ward and sound design by Janet Kalas.

Secrets to Square Dancing, Denise Maher; (D) Gloria Muzio
I'm Not Stupid, David E. Rodriguez; (D) Seret Scott
Donut World, Matthew Peterson; (D) Michael Mayer
Man at His Best, Carlotta Zimmerman; (D) Mark Brokaw
Hey Little Walter, Carla D. Alleyne; (D) Clinton Turner Davis

PRODUCTIONS 1992-1993

Young Playwrights Festival:
Sets by Loy Arcenas, lighting by Pat Dignan, costumes by Elsa Ward and sound design by Janet Kalas.

The P.C. Laundromat, Aurorae Khoo; (D) Richard Caliban
Taking Control, Terrance Jenkins; (D) Clinton Turner Davis
Mothers Have Nine Lives, Joanna Norland; (D) Gloria Muzio
Mrs. Neuberger's Dead, Robert Levy; (D) Michael Mayer
A Night With Doris, Stephanie Brown; (D) Brett W. Reynolds

Zachary Scott Theatre Center

ALICE WILSON
Producing Artistic Director

DAVE STEAKLEY
Managing Director

JOHN WHISENHUNT
Board President

1510 Toomey Road
Austin, TX 78704-1078
(512) 476-0594 (bus.)
(512) 476-0541 (b.o.)
(512) 476-0314 (fax)

FOUNDED 1933
ACT, Inc.

SEASON
Year-round

FACILITIES
Kleberg Stage
Seating Capacity: 200
Stage: thrust

Arena Stage
Seating Capacity: 130
Stage: arena

FINANCES
Sept. 1, 1992-Aug. 31, 1993
Expenses: $1,054,627

CONTRACTS
AEA SPT

Zachary Scott Theatre Center is a major voice for theatre in central Texas. Our season is an eclectic mix of contemporary, classic and international theatre works. Our goal is to produce theatre that speaks to the human spirit and offers new ideas, a fresh outlook and an opportunity to explore powerful emotional states. ZACH has a sustained commitment to social and cultural diversity. The programming and the intimate nature of our performance spaces ensure that at our theatre, art becomes part of a dialogue on issues of significance to the community. In addition to the mainstage season, ZACH looks to the development of future audiences and theatre artists by serving as an umbrella for a comprehensive performing arts school and a nationally acclaimed theatre-for-youth company, Project InterAct, which tours Texas. A rare blend of acknowledged artistry and commercial viability makes ZACH unique in our region.

—*Alice Wilson*

PRODUCTIONS 1991-1992

Sets and costumes by Stephen Wolf and lighting by Don Day unless otherwise noted.

Damn Yankees, book adapt: George Abbott and Douglass Wallop, from Douglass Wallop; music and lyrics: Richard Adler and Jerry Ross; (D) Ken Webster; (S) Richard J. Smith; (C) Amy Kuhn; (MD) Jim Fritzler; (CH) Christopher Boyd
Our Town, Thornton Wilder; (D) and (S) Jim Fritzler; (C) Big State Productions
A Christmas Carol, adapt: Alice Wilson, from Charles Dickens; (D) Alice Wilson; (S) Jim Caraccio; (C) Michael Raiford; (SD) John L. Williams
Six Women with Brain Death or Expiring Minds Want to Know, book: Cheryl Benge, Christy Brandt, Rosanna E. Coppedge, Valerie Fagan, Ross Freese, Mark Houston, Sandee Johnson and Peggy Pharr Wilson; music and lyrics: Mark Houston; (D) and (MD) Jim Fritzler; (L) Brenda Gray; (C) Sara Medina Pape; (CH) Judy Thompson Price

Shirley Valentine, Willy Russell; (D) Rod Caspers; (S) and (C) Michael Raiford; (SD) Lisa Byrd

Tartuffe, Moliere; trans: Ranjit Bolt; (D) Alice Wilson

Joe Turner's Come and Gone, August Wilson; (D) Boyd Vance; (S) John Harris; (L) Robert Whyburn; (SD) Lisa Byrd

Workin' Texas, Alice Wilson; (D) Jeff Frank

Nunsense, book, music and lyrics: Dan Goggin; (D) Ray Weikel; (MD) Neal Gibson; (CH) Greg Easely; (SD) Lisa Byrd

Sister Mary Ignatius Explains It All for You, Christopher Durang; (D) and (S) Ken Webster; (L) and (C) Subterranean Theatre Co.

PRODUCTIONS 1992-1993

Direction by Alice Wilson, lighting by Don Day, costumes by Michael Raiford and sound design by Lisa Byrd unless otherwise noted.

Shear Madness, Paul Porter; (S) Alice Wilson and Dave Steakley; (C) Alice Wilson; (SD) Cranberry Productions

Love Letters, A.R. Gurney, Jr.; (S) Alice Wilson and Dave Steakley; (C) Alice Wilson; (SD) Pat Fox

A Christmas Carol, adapt: Alice Wilson, from Charles Dickens; (D) Michael Cantrell; (S) Richard J. Smith

Beehive, book: Larry Gallagher; various composers and lyricists; (S) Tiffany Steakley; (L) Robert Whyburn; (MD) Gary Powell; (CH) Dave Steakley

Sex, Drugs, Rock & Roll, Eric Bogosian; (D) and (S) Jim Fritzler; (C) Ken Webster; (SD) Gunn Brothers

Mirandolina, Carlo Goldoni; adapt: Alice Wilson; (S) Michael Raiford

The Lady from Havana, Luis Santeiro; (D) Christina J. Moore; (S) John Harris; (C) Leslie Bonnell; (SD) Michael Crockett

Road to Nirvana, Arthur Kopit; (D), (S), (C) and (SD) Jim Fritzler; (L) Brenda Gray

I Hate Hamlet, Paul Rudnick; (S) John Harris; (C) Leslie Bonnell; (SD) Garland Thompson

Zachary Scott Theatre Center. Jeff Shaevel and Boyd Vance in *Shear Madness*. Photo: Paul Bardagjy.

THEATRE CHRONOLOGY

The following is a chronological list of founding dates for the theatres included in this book. Years refer to dates of the first public performance or, in a few cases, the company's formal incorporation.

1915
The Cleveland Play House

1925
Goodman Theatre

1928
Berkshire Theatre Festival

1933
Barter Theatre
Zachary Scott Theatre Center

1935
Oregon Shakespeare Festival

1937
Old Globe Theatre

1940
Cheltenham Center for the Arts

1942
Olney Theatre
Sacramento Theatre Company

1946
Stage One: The Louisville Children's Theatre

1947
Alley Theatre
Birmingham Children's Theatre
La Jolla Playhouse

1949
Emmy Gifford Children's Theater
New Dramatists

1950
Arena Stage

1954
Milwaukee Repertory Theater
New York Shakespeare Festival
TheatreVirginia

1955
Court Theatre
Honolulu Theatre for Youth
Williamstown Theatre Festival

1956
Academy Theatre
Philadelphia Drama Guild

1957
Detroit Repertory Theatre

1959
Dallas Theater Center
Society Hill Playhouse

1960
Asolo Center for the Performing Arts
Cincinnati Playhouse in the Park

1961
The Children's Theatre Company
La MaMa Experimental Theater Club
Theatreworks/USA
Utah Shakespearean Festival

1962
Great Lakes Theater Festival
Pioneer Theatre Company

1963
The Arkansas Arts Center Children's Theatre
Center Stage
Fulton Opera House
Goodspeed Opera House
The Guthrie Theater
New Jersey Shakespeare Festival
Seattle Repertory Theatre
Trinity Repertory Company

1964
Actors Theatre of Louisville
Hartford Stage Company
Mill Mountain Theatre
Missouri Repertory Theatre
O'Neill Theater Center
PCPA Theaterfest
South Coast Repertory

1965
A Contemporary Theatre
American Conservatory Theater
Cumberland County Playhouse
El Teatro Campesino
Long Wharf Theatre
Roundabout Theatre Company
Studio Arena Theatre

1966
INTAR Hispanic American Arts Center
Living Stage Theatre Company
Marin Theatre Company
New Stage Theatre
The Repertory Theatre of St. Louis
Yale Repertory Theatre

1967
Arizona Theatre Company
Classic Stage Company (CSC)
Magic Theatre
Mark Taper Forum
StageWest

1968
Alliance Theatre Company
Berkeley Repertory Theatre
Ford's Theatre
Omaha Magic Theatre
Ontological-Hysteric Theater
Playhouse on the Square
Repertorio Español

1969
Circle Repertory Company
Free Street Programs
Madison Repertory Theatre
Odyssey Theatre Ensemble
Organic Theater Company
The Shakespeare Theatre
Theatre X

1970
American Theatre Company
BoarsHead: Michigan Public Theater
The Empty Space Theatre
Mabou Mines
Manhattan Theatre Club
New Federal Theatre
The Salt Lake Acting Company
The Theater at Monmouth
TheatreWorks

1971
David Gordon/Pick Up Company
Dell'Arte Players Company
Jean Cocteau Repertory
Music-Theatre Group
The Playwrights' Center
Playwrights Horizons
Theater for the New City

1972
The Acting Company
Alabama Shakespeare Festival
GeVa Theatre
Indiana Repertory Theatre
Intiman Theatre Company
McCarter Theatre Center for the Performing Arts
New American Theater
The Open Eye: New Stagings

1973
Bilingual Foundation of the Arts
City Theatre Company
Florida Studio Theatre
Hippodrome State Theatre
Unicorn Theatre
The Wilma Theater

1974
CitiArts Theatre
Clarence Brown Theatre Company
George Street Playhouse
Germinal Stage Denver
Illusion Theater
The Independent Eye
Jewish Repertory Theatre

L. A. Theatre Works
Oakland Ensemble Theatre
The People's Light and Theatre
 Company
The Philadelphia Theatre Company
Portland Stage Company
Roadside Theater
Syracuse Stage
Victory Gardens Theater
Wisdom Bridge Theatre
Worcester Foothills Theatre
 Company

1975
American Stage Festival
The Colony Studio Theatre
Hangar Theatre
Milwaukee Chamber Theatre
Ping Chong and Company
Pittsburgh Public Theater
The Road Company
Seattle Children's Theatre
Theatre IV
The Wooster Group

1976
Addison Center Theatre
Arkansas Repertory Theatre
ArtReach Touring Theatre
California Theatre Center
Illinois Theatre Center
Mixed Blood Theatre Company
Nebraska Theatre Caravan
New York State Theatre Institute
The Penumbra Theatre Company
PlayMakers Repertory Company
San Diego Repertory Theatre
Steppenwolf Theatre Company
St. Louis Black Repertory Company
Theatrical Outfit

1977
Childsplay, Inc.
Coconut Grove Playhouse

Horse Cave Theatre
Pan Asian Repertory Theatre
Pennsylvania Stage Company
Source Theatre Company
Thalia Spanish Theatre

1978
A Traveling Jewish Theatre
Bloomsburg Theatre Ensemble
Crossroads Theatre Company
Great American History Theatre
The Group: Seattle's MultiCultural
 Theatre
Jomandi Productions, Inc.
Mad River Theater Works
Round House Theatre
Shakespeare & Company
The Studio Theatre
Tacoma Actors Guild
Theatre de la Jeune Lune
Women's Project & Productions

1979
American Repertory Theatre
Child's Play Touring Theatre
The Coterie
Delaware Theatre Company
Merrimack Repertory Theatre
New York Theatre Workshop
Perseverance Theatre
Remains Theatre
Second Stage Theatre
The Shakespeare Tavern
7 Stages
Stage West
Theatre for a New Audience
Virginia Stage Company

1980
Antenna Theater
The Bathhouse Theatre
Capital Repertory Company
Denver Center Theatre Company
Portland Repertory Theater

San Jose Repertory Theatre
Woolly Mammoth Theatre
 Company

1981
Philadelphia Festival Theatre for
 New Plays
Touchstone Theatre
Vineyard Theatre

1982
Bailiwick Repertory
Blackfriars Theatre
Huntington Theatre Company
Live Oak Theatre
Shakespeare Santa Cruz
Theater Emory
Theatre in the Square
West Coast Ensemble
Young Playwrights Festival

1983
Cleveland Public Theatre
Horizon Theatre Company
Irondale Ensemble Project
New Mexico Repertory Theatre
The Walnut Street Theatre
 Company

1984
Alice B. Theatre
American Music Theater Festival
Center Theater
New Repertory Theatre
Theater at Lime Kiln

1985
Ensemble Theatre of Cincinnati
Lincoln Center Theater
Riverside Theatre
Tennessee Repertory Theatre

1986
Cornerstone Theater Company
En Garde Arts
National Jewish Theater

1987
Bristol Riverside Theatre
First Stage Milwaukee
The Pollard Theatre
Pope Theatre Company
Shakespeare Repertory

1988
Actor's Express
Arden Theatre Company
The Phoenix Theatre Company
Stamford Theatre Works
White River Theatre Festival

1989
American Inside Theatre
Novel Stages

1991
The Purple Rose Theatre Company

1992
Bay Street Theatre Festival

REGIONAL INDEX

ALABAMA
Alabama Shakespeare Festival
Birmingham Children's Theatre

ALASKA
Perseverance Theatre

ARIZONA
Arizona Theatre Company
Childsplay, Inc.

ARKANSAS
The Arkansas Arts Center
   Children's Theatre
Arkansas Repertory Theatre

CALIFORNIA
American Conservatory Theater
Antenna Theater
A Traveling Jewish Theatre
Berkeley Repertory Theatre
Bilingual Foundation of the Arts
Blackfriars Theatre
California Theatre Center
CitiArts Theatre
The Colony Studio Theatre
Cornerstone Theater Company
Dell'Arte Players Company
El Teatro Campesino
La Jolla Playhouse
L. A. Theatre Works
Magic Theatre
Marin Theatre Company
Mark Taper Forum
Oakland Ensemble Theatre
Odyssey Theatre Ensemble
Old Globe Theatre
PCPA Theaterfest
Sacramento Theatre Company
San Diego Repertory Theatre
San Jose Repertory Theatre
Shakespeare Santa Cruz
South Coast Repertory
TheatreWorks
West Coast Ensemble

COLORADO
Denver Center Theatre Company
Germinal Stage Denver

CONNECTICUT
Goodspeed Opera House
Hartford Stage Company
Long Wharf Theatre
O'Neill Theater Center
Stamford Theatre Works
Yale Repertory Theatre

DELAWARE
Delaware Theatre Company

DISTRICT OF COLUMBIA
Arena Stage
Ford's Theatre
Living Stage Theatre Company
The Shakespeare Theatre
Source Theatre Company
The Studio Theatre
Woolly Mammoth Theatre
   Company

FLORIDA
Asolo Theatre Company
Coconut Grove Playhouse
Florida Studio Theatre
Hippodrome State Theatre
Pope Theatre Company
Riverside Theatre

GEORGIA
Academy Theatre
Actor's Express
Alliance Theatre Company
Horizon Theatre Company
Jomandi Productions, Inc.
7 Stages
The Shakespeare Tavern
Theater Emory
Theatre in the Square
Theatrical Outfit

HAWAII
Honolulu Theatre for Youth

ILLINOIS
Bailiwick Repertory
Center Theater
Child's Play Touring Theatre
Court Theatre
Free Street Programs
Goodman Theatre
Illinois Theatre Center
National Jewish Theater
New American Theater
Organic Theater Company
Remains Theatre
Shakespeare Repertory
Steppenwolf Theatre Company
Victory Gardens Theater
Wisdom Bridge Theatre

INDIANA
Indiana Repertory Theatre

KENTUCKY
Actors Theatre of Louisville
Horse Cave Theatre
Roadside Theater
Stage One: The Louisville
   Children's Theatre

MAINE
Portland Stage Company
The Theater at Monmouth

MARYLAND
Center Stage
Olney Theatre
Round House Theatre

MASSACHUSETTS
American Repertory Theatre
Berkshire Theatre Festival
Huntington Theatre Company
Merrimack Repertory Theatre
Music-Theatre Group
New Repertory Theatre
Shakespeare & Company
StageWest
Williamstown Theatre Festival
Worcester Foothills Theatre
   Company

MICHIGAN
BoarsHead: Michigan Public
   Theater
Detroit Repertory Theatre
The Purple Rose Theatre Company

MINNESOTA
The Children's Theatre Company
Great American History Theatre
The Guthrie Theater
Illusion Theater
Mixed Blood Theatre Company
Penumbra Theatre Company
The Playwrights' Center
Theatre de la Jeune Lune

MISSISSIPPI
New Stage Theatre

MISSOURI
The Coterie
Missouri Repertory Theatre
The Repertory Theatre of St. Louis
St. Louis Black Repertory Company
Unicorn Theatre

NEBRASKA
Emmy Gifford Children's Theater
Nebraska Theatre Caravan
Omaha Magic Theatre

NEW HAMPSHIRE
American Stage Festival

NEW JERSEY
Crossroads Theatre Company
George Street Playhouse
McCarter Theatre Center for the
   Performing Arts
New Jersey Shakespeare Festival

NEW MEXICO
New Mexico Repertory Theatre

NEW YORK
The Acting Company
Bay Street Theatre Festival
Capital Repertory Company
Circle Repertory Company
Classic Stage Company (CSC)
David Gordon/Pick Up Company
En Garde Arts
GeVa Theatre
Hangar Theatre
INTAR Hispanic American Arts
   Center
Irondale Ensemble Project
Jean Cocteau Repertory
Jewish Repertory Theatre
La MaMa Experimental Theater
   Club

Lincoln Center Theater
Mabou Mines
Manhattan Theatre Club
Music-Theatre Group
New Dramatists
New Federal Theatre
New York Shakespeare Festival
New York State Theatre Institute
New York Theatre Workshop
O'Neill Theater Center
Ontological-Hysteric Theater
The Open Eye: New Stagings
Pan Asian Repertory Theatre
The Phoenix Theatre Company
Ping Chong and Company
Playwrights Horizons
Repertorio Español
Roundabout Theatre Company
Second Stage Theatre
Studio Arena Theatre
Syracuse Stage
Thalia Spanish Theatre
Theatre for a New Audience
Theater for the New City
Theatreworks/USA
Vineyard Theatre
Women's Project & Productions
The Wooster Group
Young Playwrights Inc.

NORTH CAROLINA

PlayMakers Repertory Company

OHIO

ArtReach Touring Theatre
Cincinnati Playhouse in the Park
The Cleveland Play House
Cleveland Public Theatre
Ensemble Theatre of Cincinnati
Great Lakes Theater Festival
Mad River Theater Works

OKLAHOMA

American Theatre Company
The Pollard Theatre

OREGON

Oregon Shakespeare Festival
Portland Repertory Theater

PENNSYLVANIA

American Music Theater Festival
Arden Theatre Company
Bloomsburg Theatre Ensemble
Bristol Riverside Theatre
Cheltenham Center for the Arts
City Theatre Company
Fulton Theatre Company
The Independent Eye
Novel Stages
Pennsylvania Stage Company
The People's Light and Theatre Company
Philadelphia Drama Guild
Philadelphia Festival Theatre for New Plays
The Philadelphia Theatre Company
Pittsburgh Public Theater
Society Hill Playhouse
Touchstone Theatre
The Walnut Street Theatre Company
The Wilma Theater

RHODE ISLAND

Trinity Repertory Company

TENNESSEE

Clarence Brown Theatre Company
Cumberland County Playhouse
Playhouse on the Square
The Road Company
Tennessee Repertory Theatre

TEXAS

Addison Centre Theatre
Alley Theatre
Dallas Theater Center
Live Oak Theatre
Stage West
Zachary Scott Theatre Center

UTAH

Pioneer Theatre Company
The Salt Lake Acting Company
Utah Shakespearean Festival

VERMONT

White River Theatre Festival

VIRGINIA

Barter Theatre
Mill Mountain Theatre
Theater at Lime Kiln
Theatre IV
TheatreVirginia
Virginia Stage Company

WASHINGTON

A Contemporary Theatre
Alice B. Theatre
The Bathhouse Theatre
The Empty Space Theatre
The Group: Seattle's MultiCultural Theatre
Intiman Theatre Company
Seattle Children's Theatre
Seattle Repertory Theatre
Tacoma Actors Guild

WISCONSIN

American Inside Theatre
First Stage Milwaukee
Madison Repertory Theatre
Milwaukee Chamber Theatre
Milwaukee Repertory Theater
Theatre X

INDEX OF NAMES

A

Aanes, Kirk, 107
Aaron, Jules, 43, 98, 117, 169
Abady, Josephine R., 40
Abatemarco, Tony, 104
Abbitt, Jerry, 169
Abbott, Charles, 168
Abbott, George, 58, 105, 176
Abernathy, Chris, 148
Abrams, A., 156
Abuba, Ernest, 111
Accardo, Jon R., 83, 95
Ackamoor, Idris, 78
Acker, Deborah, 139
Ackermann, Joan, 4, 58
Ackerman, Robert Allan, 87
Acosta, Nanette, 20, 44, 139
Acosta, Vince, 43
Adam, Pamie, 17
Adams, Abigail, 114
Adams, Betsy, 12, 59, 101
Adams, David, 79, 157
Adams, Donna M., 148
Adams, Fred C., 165
Adams, Jeanne, 168
Adams, Lee, 61
Adamson, Eve, 74, 75
Adams, Randy, 160
Adams, Robert K., 161
Adams, Wayne, 70
Adler, Jeff, 68
Adler, Lisa, 68
Adler, Marion, 37
Adler, Richard, 105, 176
Adler, Sherri, 171
Adler, Warren, 75
Adrine-Robinson, Andika, 41
Adrine-Robinson, Kenyette, 41
Adshead, Patricia, 113
Aeschylus, 64
Agosto, Julie-Ann, 25
Agular, Siegfrido, 102
Aherns, Lynn, 80
Ahlberg, Allen, 67
Ahn, Michael, 54
Ahrens, Lynn, 9, 160
Ahronheim, Adele, 107
Aibel, Douglas, 166, 167
Aidman, Charles, 67
Aiken, Charlotte, 130
Aiken, George, 134
Aitken, Maria, 167
Akaji, Ada, 67
Akalaitis, JoAnne, 82, 100
Akerlind, Christopher, 9, 11, 36,
47, 61, 66, 78, 82, 86, 88, 102, 125
Akers, Janice, 155
Akers, Wesley Jay, 68
Akins, Rebecca, 34, 35
Alan-Williams, Gregory, 62
Albee, Edward, 7, 16, 42, 54, 55,
66, 88, 121, 138, 167
Albergini, Jim, 175
Albers, Kenneth, 91, 110
Albert, Michael P., 38
Alberts, K.L., 119
Albert, Stephen J., 66
Albrezzi, Steven D., 4, 79, 143
Alden, Christopher, 11
Aldous, Brian, 54, 75, 167
Aldredge, Theoni V., 46, 86
Aldrich, David, 169
Aldridge, Amanda, 12, 22, 89
Aleichem, Sholom, 28, 81
Alejandro, Lolly, 156, 157
Alexander, Bill, 141
Alexander, E.A., 168
Alexander, Jason Michael, 104
Alexander, Meredith, 165
Alexander, Robert, 134
Alexander, Robert A., 81
Alfaro, Luis, 122
Alford, Noel, 80
Allard, Dru P., 113
Allardice, Bruce, 118
Allen, Claudia, 21, 124, 145, 166
Allen, Faye, 137
Allen, Heath, 163
Allen, Janet, 71, 72
Allen, Jesse, 96
Allen, June, 132
Allen, Mark, 124
Allen, Michael, 86
Allen, Nancy, 158
Allen, Nancy Welch, 124
Allen, Philip G., 42
Allen, Ralph G., 38
Alley, Michael, 53
Alleyne, Carla D., 176
Allison, Richard, 158, 159
All Music, 25
Allyn, Angela, 21
Alonso, Francisco, 152
Alpaugh, Robert, 16
Alter, Steven E., 151
Altman, Peter, 69
Alvarez, Chana, 152
Alvarez, Lynne, 96, 128, 129
Alyoshin, Samuil, 113, 160
Ambrosi, Dario Di, 78, 79
Ambrosone, John, 11, 89
Ambush, Benny Sato, 6, 9, 105, 109

Ames, Craig, 124
Ames, Roger, 66
Amico, Michael, 165
Amis, Jeanne E., 43
Amis, Kingsley, 168
Amster, Peter, 72, 91
Anady, Mike, 153
Anania, Michael, 88
Andersen, Hans Christian, 17, 26,
30, 34, 55, 144, 154, 170
Anderson, Barbara, 119, 120
Anderson, Barry, 95
Anderson, Bradley D., 16, 17
Anderson, Cletus, 38
Anderson, Eric, 71
Anderson, Jane, 135, 171
Anderson, Laurie, 11
Anderson, Mark, 162
Anderson, Maxwell, 61
Anderson, Ron, 55
Anderson, Sarah Pia, 141
Anderson, Stephanie, 52
Anderson, Sue, 66
Anderson, Susan, 143, 173
Anderson, Timothy J., 25
Anderson, Valetta, 76
Andonyadis, Nephelie, 27, 28
Andrew, Mark, 33
Andrews, Dwight, 8, 47, 60
Andrews, Jessica L., 141
Andrus, Dolores, 51
Andrus, T. O., 51
Anduss, Mark, 142, 143
Angel, Anthony, 156, 157
Angelos, Maureen, 102
Angel, Sabina, 1
Annable, James E., 60
Annis, Eric, 143
Anouilh, Jean, 49, 74, 132
Ansky, S., 134
Ansley, Greg, 159
Anthony, 7
Antomarchi, Josette, 71
Aoki, Brenda Wong, 134
Appelt, Joseph, 92
Appel, Libby, 8, 71, 72, 91, 119,
128, 135, 143
Apperson, Richard, 142
Appino, Nikki, 7
Applebaum, Jeff, 21
Applegate, Steven, 43
Aprill, Arnold, 94, 156
Apt, Joan, 119
Aquilina, Corrine, 60
Araiza, Albert Antonio, 6
Araiza, Beto, 7
Arcenas, Loy, 7, 15, 23, 24, 36, 37,
60, 61, 66, 85, 87, 122, 137, 176
Archibald, William, 135
Archway Scenic, 70
Arditti, Paul, 80
A-Re, Celeste, 138
Arecco, Diana, 78, 102
Arellano, Leticia, 51, 52
Arjona, Ramon, IV, 67
Arlen, Harold, 19, 25, 77, 88, 101,
112, 149
Armenante, Jillian, 7
Armendizo, Eduardo, 37
Armour, Norman, 155
Armstrong, Alan, 6, 98, 128, 129
Armstrong, Paul, 58
Arne, Kira, 157
Arney, Randall, 147
Arnold, Jeanne, 2, 151
Arnold, Joseph, 113
Arnold, Nancy Ann, 143
Arnold, Phillip, 37
Arnone, John, 64, 69, 77, 100, 122,
131, 147
Aronson, Frances, 9, 11, 39, 77,
100, 105, 119, 137, 141, 156
Aronson, Henry, 66, 105
Aronstein, Martin, 87
Arrick, Larry, 40, 104
Arrieta, German, 127, 128
Arthur, Robin, 158
Asbury, Charlotte, 99
Aschenbrenner, John, 8, 106
Asch, Sholem, 75
Asher, Sandra Fenichel, 52, 55, 109
Ashley, Christopher, 36, 100, 117,
139, 161
Ashman, Howard, 12, 13, 120
Askew, Sidney N. Jr., 167
Askin, Peter, 61
Assaf, Michele, 61
Asse, Carlos Francisco, 66, 67
Ast, Mary Beth Gangler, 62
Atchak, Earl, 115
Atha-Harrod, Pam, 46
Atkin, Flora B., 13
Atkinson, Linda, 36
Atkinson, Susan D., 28, 29
Attea, Laurie, 21
Attebury, Rod, 92
Atwater, Florence, 34
Atwater, Richard, 34
Atwell, William L., 147
Aubrey, John, 4
Auerbach, Bruce, 97, 98
Augins, Charles, 57
Auletta, Robert, 8
Aural Fixation, 80, 118, 122, 137

INDEX OF NAMES

Austin, Lee J., 168
Austin, Lyn, 93
Autry, Charles, 114
Auwen, Ted, 13
Avalos, Steven, 169
Avecinna, 41
Averill, Richard, 13
Avery, Ramsey, 169
Averyt, Bennet, 6, 113, 152
Avian, Bob, 86
Avila, Alina, 73
Avila, Sergio, 135
Avni, Ran, 75
Ayckbourn, Alan, 2, 9, 31, 40, 47, 59, 74, 82, 85, 87, 89, 98, 109, 125, 129, 136, 143, 144, 145, 146, 159, 168, 171
Ayers, Josephine, 159
Ayvazian, Leslie, 124
Azar, Michelle, 78
Azenberg, Karen, 99
Azuela, Mariano, 25

B

Babb, Roger, 47
Babe, Thomas, 144
Babula, William, 169
Back, Maribeth, 11, 119
Backlund, Dan, 46
Badger, Mary M., 94
Badham, John, 171
Badrak, Jim, 11
Baer, Perry, 57
Baffa-Brill, Diana, 59, 159
Bagg, Robert, 27, 78
Bagsby, David, 13
Bagshow-Reasoner, Nancy, 33
Baierlein, Ed, 59
Bailey, Alan, 18, 36, 50
Bailey, Carol, 157
Bailey, Dennis, 79
Baird, Campbell, 73
Baisch, Jon, 28
Baitz, Jon Robin, 19, 23, 31, 37, 42, 47, 68, 80, 85, 87, 122, 125, 137
Baizley, Doris, 2, 79
Baker, Christopher, 7
Baker, Cliff Fannin, 17, 18, 29, 37
Baker, Don, 131, 153
Baker, Dylan, 97, 98
Baker, Ed, 139
Baker, Joseph, 168
Baker, Keith Alan, 29, 149, 150
Baker, Paul, 47
Baker, Peter-Tolin, 30, 37
Baker, R.C., 38
Baker, Tom, 171
Baldassari, Michael J., 36, 76
Balderston, John L., 139
Baldwin, Joseph, 22
Bale, Amy, 158
Balfior, Joseph, 101
Ballard, Barth, 105
Ballard, Doc, 104, 143
Ballard, Laurence, 2
Ballif, Ariel, 119
Ballmann, Greg, 111
Ball, Steve, 138, 139

Ball, Tina, 171
Ball, William, 9
Balph, Judith, 129
Baltz, Ellen Baker, 112
Bamman, Gerry, 24, 115, 125
Banda, Victor Hugo Rascon, 25
Banks, Susan, 83, 84
Banks, Whitney, 155
Banno, Joe, 142, 143
Baptist, Sarah, 113
Baraka, Amiri, 27, 114
Barbaley, Jim, 169
Barbarash, Ernie, 73, 96
Barber, Debi, 76
Barber, Philip, 85
Barbour, Frederick, 112
Barbour, Karen, 112
Barcelo, Randy, 8, 73, 88, 127, 128
Barclay, Shelley, 86, 98
Barclay, William, 47, 117, 167
Bardawil, Nancy, 7, 41
Barie, Gary, 129
Barker, Clive, 111
Barker, David, 35
Barker, Howard, 87
Barker, Rochelle, 8, 155, 159, 163
Barker, Steve, 79
Barker, Tommy, 156
Barkla, Jack, 34, 64, 91
Barkley, Lynnette, 124
Barlett, Glynn, 7
Barnard, Michael, 34, 35
Barnes, Anne, 55
Barnes, Antonitta, 148
Barnes, Gregg, 25
Barnes, Paul, 112, 165
Barnes, Peter, 2, 150
Barnes, Theo, 156
Barnes, Tom, 161
Barnett, Bob, 59, 60, 150
Barnett, Nancy, 123
Barnett, Robert, 36
Barnett, Ron, 158
Barnhart, Kent, 164, 165
Baron, Biff, 89
Baron, Neal, 164
Barranger, Milly S., 121
Barreca, Christopher, 31, 32, 47, 57, 66, 72, 131, 175
Barrett, Michael, 80
Barrett, Steve, 7
Barrett, William, 84
Barrett, William E., 37
Barrier, Andrea, 114
Barrie, James M., 5, 44, 74, 114, 120, 160
Barringer, Norman E., 86
Barringer, Scott, 86
Barrish, Seth, 78
Barroga, Jeannie, 160
Barron, Rob, 150, 170
Barry, B.H., 138, 159
Barry, Daniel, 78
Barry, Lynda, 57, 68, 136, 164
Barry, Paul, 97
Barry, Philip, 10, 40, 143
Barry, P.J., 70, 79
Barry, Raymond J., 127
Bartelt, William, 166
Bartenieff, George, 156

Barthelme, Jane, 68
Bartlett, Neil, 6, 15, 40, 47, 60
Bartlett, Paul, 93
Barton, Max II, 41
Barton, Todd, 2
Barto, Michael, 21
Bart, Lionel, 129
Baruti, Osayande, 134
Bassett, Nancy, 50
Bassi, Leo, 102
Bassuk, David, 102, 103
Bastian, Jon, 143
Bates, Edward, 118
Bates, Sandy, 152
Baton, Maisha, 45
Battle, Richard W., 160
Baudry, Michelle, 7
Bauer, Bartley H., 126
Bauer, Beaver, 9, 85, 140
Bauer, Jason, 78, 79
Bauer, Jeff, 44, 45, 127, 166, 172
Bauer, Zonnie, 104
Baum, L. Frank, 34, 101, 112
Baur, Stuart R., 169
Bayeza, Ifa, 46
Bazaldua, Charles, 25
Bazewicz, James, 27, 28
B., Diana, 91
Beach, Gail Stewart, 106
Beaird, David, 171
Beal, Melody, 97, 173
Beason, Janet, 54, 55
Beattie, Kurt, 53
Beatty, Eric, 163
Beatty, John Lee, 4, 37, 61, 80, 82, 85, 86, 87, 100, 105, 116, 119, 131, 136
Beaumont, Doug, 126
Beausoleil, Loyan, 78
Beautyman, Bill, 93
Beber, Neena, 54, 85
Beccio, Barbara, 33
Becker, Alma, 96
Becker, David, 97
Becker, Victor A., 35, 91, 101, 124, 150, 170
Beckett, Samuel, 5, 28, 38, 39, 41, 75, 83, 100, 138, 140, 144, 154, 155
Beckett, Terry, 139
Beckley, Barbara, 42
Beckman, Julie, 19
Beck, Carl, 94, 95
Beck, Emily J., 171
Beck, G., 157
Beck, Susan Baer, 95
Becvar, William, 151
Beecham, Jahnna, 128, 129
Beechwood, Jeanne, 164
Beesley, Christopher, 34
Behan, Brendan, 23, 28, 74
Behn, Aphra, 141
Behrman, S.N., 70, 118
Beier, Bridgett, 3
Belden, Ursula, 36, 40
Belew, Bill, 86
Belgrader, Andrei, 11, 39
Belknap, Allen R., 85
Bellamy, Lou, 113, 114, 122
Bellamy, Terry, 64

Bell, Barbara A., 22
Bell, David H., 9, 57
Bell, Neal, 24, 122, 171
Belov, Yuri, 157
Belver, Carla, 114
Belville, Lance S., 62
Belzer, Rick, 57
Bemelmans, Ludwig, 17
Benabid, Nadia, 88
Benedict, Gail, 89
Benedict, Paul, 105
Benemann, Linda, 130
Benett, Peter, 129
Benet, Stephen Vincent, 114
Benge, Cheryl, 18, 67, 121, 164, 165, 176
Bengford, Jeff, 160
Bengston, Brian, 107
Benitz, Monica, 156
Benitz, M. Dewayne, 156
Benjamin, Randy, 137
Benkovich, Gregg, 44, 92, 164, 165
Benner, Vikki, 115
Bennett, Brian, 29, 30
Bennet, Joel Faye, 98
Bennett, Mark, 24, 31, 32, 86, 88, 100, 102, 120, 137, 173
Bennett, Matthew, 171
Bennett, Patty, 14
Bennett, Peter, 12, 22, 119, 124, 129
Bennett, Robert J., 150
Bennett, Steve, 64
Bennett, Suzanne, 96
Benning, Janice, 77
Bensinger, Lenore, 44
Benson, Margaret Shyne, 113
Benson, Martin, 143
Bensussen, Melia, 96, 100, 116, 122
Bentley, Eric, 3, 63, 115
Benton, Robert, 61
Berc, Shelley, 11, 39
Berebitsky, Jerry, 114
Berend, Robert W., 74
Berezin, Tanya, 36
Bergeron, George, 113
Berger, Thomas H., 62
Bergman, Bernard S., 32
Bergman, Ingmar, 16, 19, 59, 116, 159, 171
Bergner, Bruce, 21, 95, 129
Bergstein. David, 100
Berg, Carole B., 23
Berg, Deanna, 171
Berg, Eric, 111
Berg, Paula, 21
Berg, Stephen, 171
Berigan, Charles, 96
Berkman, Howard, 110
Berkoff, Steven, 85, 103, 173
Berkowitz, Dan, 108
Berky, Robert, 93
Berliner, Charles, 91, 110
Berliner Ensemble, The, 4
Berlin, Irving, 86, 94
Berlin, Isaiah, 82
Berlin, Pamela, 19, 31, 58, 86, 146
Berman, Elaine, 31
Berman, Elliott, 1, 138
Berman, Irene B., 24, 115, 125

INDEX OF NAMES

Berman, Mat, 93
Berman, Paul Schiff, 108
Berman, Sabina, 109
Bermel, Albert, 102, 105
Bernard, Michael, 112
Bernhardt, Melvin, 25
Bernstein, Leonard, 43, 44, 66, 112, 170, 175
Bernstein, Mark D., 128
Berry, Brenda, 2, 52, 134, 136
Berry, Gabriel, 11, 24, 39, 47, 60, 66, 83, 87, 100, 102, 156
Berry, Matthew, 133
Berry, Stephanie, 47
Bertol, Gaetane, 126
Bertoncin, Jarrett, 92
Bessolo, Robert, 5
Best-Bova, Mary, 89
Besterman, Douglas, 19
Bethel, Shari, 160
Bethel, Tamara A., 174
Bettis, John, 19
Betti, Ugo, 31
Betts, Nancy, 49
Beudert, Peter, 126
Bevans, April, 28
Bevans, Loren, 156
Bevans, Steve, 27
Bevenger, Robert Jr., 168
Beverage, Sam, 29
Beverly, R.L., 163
Beville, Matthew, 169
Bewbom, Kristin, 7
Bhuwana, I Wayan Mardika, 83
Bialon, Jana, 171
Biancamano, Pip III, 89
Biasetti, Robert D., 33, 116
Bieganski, Ron, 57
Bielecki, Bob, 93
Bielefeldt, Fumiko, 85, 160
Bigelow, Dennis, 16, 109, 133
Big State Productions, 176
Bilder, Erica, 79, 118
Billig, Etel, 69, 70
Billig, Steve S., 69, 70
Billings, Glenn, 62, 76
Billings, Jim, 145
Billington, Ken, 42, 87, 171
Billone, Joseph, 61
Bim, David, 78
Bingham, Mark, 134
Bingham, Sallie, 89
Binkley, Howell, 7, 11, 12, 19, 25, 77, 78, 88, 93, 141
Birarelli, Rob, 147
Bird, Louis, 129
Birnbaum, Nathan, 87, 144
Birn, David, 65
Birt, Christine, 172
Birturk, Ricia, 34
Bishop, Andre, 80
Bishop, Conrad, 71, 128, 157, 161
Bishop, Cynthia, 53
Bishop, David, 141
Bishop, John, 37
Bishop, Linda, 161
Bitterman, Shem, 59, 122
Bixby, Jonathan, 75
Bixler, Larry, 89
Black, Bill, 39, 152, 165, 166

Blackburn, Annie, 76
Blackburn, April, 81
Blacker, Robert, 76
Black, George, 159
Black, Malcolm, 168
Blackman, Robert, 9, 50, 87
Blackmon, Michele, 64
Blackwell, Vera, 75
Blahnik, Jeremy, 79
Blair, D. Bartlett, 36
Blair, Randy, 13
Blair, Tom, 146
Blake, Elizabeth, 58
Blake, Jeanne, 55, 96
Blake, Paul, 9
Blake, Scott, 120
Blakesley, Todd, 27
Blankenship, Michael, 19, 55
Blasor, Denise, 104
Blatch-Geib, Inda, 41
Blattner, Robert A., 40
Blau, Eric, 12
Blecher, Hilary, 173
Bledsoe, Eddie, 104
Bledsoe, Tommy, 131
Blessing, Lee, 2, 28, 55, 83, 86, 95, 96, 120, 121, 147, 159, 165, 168
Blitgen, Carol, 165
Blitzstein, Marc, 167, 170
Block, Dick, 161
Block, Richard, 3
Blodgette, Kristen, 107
Bloeser, Jack, 142
Blong, Jenni, 150
Bloodgood, William, 6, 16, 72, 109, 110
Bloolips, 7
Bloom, Claire, 63
Bloom, Mark R., 168
Bloom, Michael, 85, 137, 143, 144, 170, 171
Bloomquist, Russ, 107
Bloom, Sidney S., 115
Blu, 78
Bluestein, Martin, 84
Bluh, Bonnie, 96
Bluhm, Richard D., 43
Blume, Judy, 46, 145
Blumenfeld, Mara, 21
Blumenthal, Hilarie, 74, 163
Blunt, John, 27
Bly, Robert, 52
Blythe, Joanna, 44
Bob-Drake, Luigi, 41
Bobo, Randy, 10
Bock, Jerry, 28, 29, 81, 131
Boddy, Claudia, 61, 122, 166, 172
Bodeen, Michael, 32, 61, 95, 111, 127, 139, 172
Boeke, Elisabeth, 78
Boesing, Martha, 20
Boesky, William, 78, 79
Boffey, Barnes, 89
Bogardus, Janet, 161
Bogart, Anne, 4, 7, 37, 54, 83, 96, 100, 134
Bogosian, Eric, 177
Bohart, Phebe, 20
Bohem, Hefi, 78
Bohmler, Craig, 34, 37

Bohr, Jimmy, 97
Boisvert, Alexandra U., 135
Bo-Kyoung, Choi, 78
Bolden, Frank A., 45
Bolinger, Don, 18, 36
Bolin, Cynthia, 77
Bolt, Jonathan, 161
Bolton, Guy, 59, 159
Bolton, Marian, 159
Bolt, Ranjit, 64, 153, 177
Bolt, Robert, 8, 39
Bommer, Lawrence, 111
Bond, Christopher, 14, 160
Bond, Edward, 109
Bond, Tim, 63, 64, 91, 136
Bones, Pamela Gray, 160
Bongo-Jerie, 34
Bonini, Robert J., 18
Bonnard, Raymond, 148
Bonnell, Leslie, 177
Bonney, Julia, 65
Bono, Ray, 101
Bontumasti, David, 21
Booker, Margaret, 19, 59, 73, 107
Bookman, Kirk, 19, 33, 34, 35, 36, 59, 60, 61, 66, 98, 136
Bookstein, Edith Leavis, 126
Bookwalter, Martyn, 135
Boomer, Diane, 134
Booth, Debra, 66, 100, 125, 126, 168
Boothe, Power, 156
Booth, Ken, 43
Booth, Phil, 7
Booth, Susan V., 38
Borden, Theresa, 170
Borden, William, 41
Borders, Marc, 156
Borgia, Carmen, 140
Boris, Russell, 43
Bornstein, Daryl, 69, 98
Bornstein, Rocky, 47
Borski, Russ, 47
Bosh, Robert, 78
Boswell, John, 161
Boswell, William, 51
Both, Andrei, 77, 137
Bottari, Michael, 76
Bottazzi, Pierluigi, 78
Bottrell, David, 37, 120, 137
Bouchard, Bruce, 30, 31, 146
Boughton, Andrew Wood, 15, 136, 137
Bourne, Bette, 7, 157
Bova, Jeff, 100
Bovender, Jack O. Jr., 151
Bowen, Gaye, 80
Bowen, Ken, 61
Bowers, Jill C., 160
Bowles, Patrick, 28
Bowling, Nick, 143
Bowman, Rob, 106, 107, 150
Bowmer, Angus, 109
Bowne, Alan, 157
Bowns, Kate, 115
Boyce, Jinkie Lee, 49
Boyd, Ann, 111
Boyd, Christopher, 176
Boyd, Greg D., 120
Boyd, Gregory, 7, 8, 19

Boyd, Jason, 54
Boyd, Julianne, 18, 19, 24, 25, 64, 77, 88, 93, 105, 123, 137, 149, 150, 151
Boyd, Kate, 37
Boyd, Kirk, 110
Boyd, Thomas, 62
Boyer, Michael, 168
Boyer, Tom, 43
Boylen, Dan, 49
Boynes, Corbiere, 62, 76
Boynton, Brad, 158
Boyter, James E., Jr., 69
Bradbury, Ray, 33, 95, 112
Bradley, Frank, 148
Bradley, Scott, 61, 98, 116
Brady, Darren, 43
Brady, John E., 161
Brady, Michael, 111
Brady, Patrick S., 93, 168
Brady, Roger, 173
Brainin, Risa, 71, 93
Bramble, Mark, 89
Brame, Loren, 43
Brancato, Joe, 99
Branch, Marilyn, 122
Branch, Susan, 98, 175
Brande, Angela, 169, 170
Brand, Linda Ade, 44
Brandt, Christy, 18, 67, 121, 176
Brandt, Daniel, 91
Branson, Allen, 133
Brassard, Gail, 25, 57, 72, 146, 149, 167
Brastow, Charles, 33, 114
Braverman, Carole, 173
Bray, Barbara, 74
Bread & Puppet Theater, 157
Brecht, Bertolt, 3, 21, 60, 63, 74, 75, 83, 100, 104, 115, 123, 141, 155, 170, 175
Brecht, Mary, 100
Breier, Margot, 173
Brel, Jacques, 12
Bremer, Mary, 126
Brennan, Allison, 26
Brenner, Donald, 129
Brenton, Howard, 5
Breseke, Nancy, 166
Bresnick, Robert, 156
Breuer, Lee, 82, 83
Brewer, Bill, 119
Brewi, Jimi, 17
Bricusse, Leslie, 30
Bridges, Suzette, 124, 129
Bridwell, Tom, 46
Brigden, Tracy, 96
Briggs-Graves, Anasa, 27
Briggs, John, 22, 88, 111, 124, 152, 159
Briggs, Patricia, 29
Brill, Robert, 77, 87, 109, 110, 134
Bringelson, Mark, 104
Brink, David, 107
Brinkley, Bonnie, 118
Brinkley, Susann, 23
Brito, Silvia, 152
Britt, Chuck, 120, 121
Broadhurst, Alan, 145
Broadhurst, Kent, 114

Broad, Jay, 19, 107, 108
Brock, Ed, Jr., 1
Brockley, Mark, 101
Brockway, Adrienne J., 108, 109
Brockway, Amie, 108, 109
Brody, Alan, 99
Brody, J. Raoul, 85
Broecker, Tom, 66, 98, 126, 175
Brogger, Erik, 121, 160
Brokaw, Mark, 57, 86, 96, 107, 116, 122, 136, 176
Bronson, James Graham, 45, 114, 132
Bronte, Emily, 106
Brookfield, Kathie, 18
Brookhouse, Cynthia Ann Orr, 65
Brooks, Colette, 175
Brooks, Donald, 78
Brooks, Jerry, 81
Brooks, Jim, 134
Brooks, John Hancock Jr., 166
Brooks, Mel, 32
Brooks, Susie, 129
Brooks, Teresa, 75
Broome, John, 138
Brosius, Peter, 104
Brosseau, Jim, 11
Brossier, Justin, 67
Brothers, Deborah A., 138
Brourman, Michael, 40, 62
Brourman, Michelle, 56
Brovarney, Dan, 90
Brown, Arvin, 81, 82
Brown, Carlyle, 15, 122
Brown, Christopher L., 146, 150
Brown, Claudia, 54
Brown, Dave, 89
Brown, David, 12
Browne, Alan, 18
Browne, Donna, 102
Browner, Richard, 58
Browning, Barry, 34, 71, 92
Brown, Jamie, 31, 60, 150
Brown, Jeanette, 80
Brown, John, 75
Brown, John Russell, 53
Brown, Kate, 157
Brown, K.C., 23
Brown, Kim, 38
Brownless, Steve, 84
Brown, Lewis, 141
Brown, Logan, 22
Brown, L. Russel, 75
Brown, Michael Henry, 82, 96, 114, 126
Brown, Michael Newton, 150
Brown, Paul, 113, 114
Brown, Sean, 157
Brown, Stan, 38
Brown, Stephanie, 176
Brown, Susan, 125
Brown, Tom, 169
Brown, Uzee, 97
Brown, Zack, 15
Bruce, Alex Allesandri, 120
Bruck, Therese A., 122, 171
Bruffee, Matthew B., 23
Bruice, Ann, 98, 117, 143, 144
Brumley, Keith, 165
Brumlik, Fran, 93

Brumm, Beverly, 21
Bruneau, Ainslie, 7, 8
Bruneaux, Debra, 109, 110, 133
Brune, Eva, 72
Brustein, Robert, 11, 175
Bryant, John, 104
Bryant, Lori, 13
Brys, Carol, 157
Buchanan, Linda, 8, 61, 69, 100, 122, 164
Buchanan, Sarah, 46
Buchman, Nanrose, 2
Buchner, Georg, 8, 100
Buch, Rene, 90, 105, 127, 128
Buck, Gene Davis, 2, 34
Buckley, Gail, 11, 12, 89, 99
Buckley, Kathleen, 139
Buckley, Peter, 49
Buckner, Clay, 153
Budbill, David, 18
Budin, Rachel, 72, 110, 146, 149
Budries, David, 8, 47, 58, 66, 77, 83, 86, 91, 100, 122, 125, 175
Buffett, Susie, 52
Buffington, Ray, 142
Bulgakov, Mikhail, 11, 61, 157
Bullard, Tom, 29, 103, 170
Bull, Karen E., 41
Bullock, Michael, 109
Bumblauskas, Thom, 32
Burbridge, Edward, 109
Burckhardt, Jacob, 83, 100
Burden, Michael, 114
Burdick, Susan Glass, 136
Buresh, Keith, 5
Burge, Gregg, 57, 61
Burgess, Alyne S., 158
Burgess, Anthony, 63, 112
Burgess, Granville, 57, 61, 168
Burgess, Linda, 138
Burgess, Melanie, 136
Burke, John, 141
Burkell, Scott, 56
Burke, Mary-Claire, 22
Burkhardt, Tom, 83
Burkhart, Laura, 44
Burleson, Kathryn, 133
Burnes, Brett, 37
Burnett, Frances Hodgson, 17, 30, 52, 67, 101, 161
Burns, Molly, 21
Burns, Tim, 156
Burr, Charles, 26
Burris, Michael Jon, 32
Burrows, Abe, 133, 151
Burrows, Allyn, 139
Burton, Rahn, 93
Burwinkel, James, 148
Busbee, Howard, 159
Busby, Barbara, 51
Busby, Gerald, 37
Busch, Charles, 143, 156, 157
Busche, Jeff, 89
Bush, Barbara, 50, 110
Bush, Max, 52, 53
Bushor, Geoffrey, 94, 95
Bussert, Victoria, 47, 63, 108
Bussey, Liz, 69
Butler, Bruce, 161
Butler, Lydia, 43

Butsch, Tom, 34
Buttenwieser, Paul A., 11
Butterfield, Catherine, 86
Butterfield, John, 37
Button, Jeanne, 5, 6, 63, 170
Bybee, Blair, 70
Byer, Marta, 89
Byerrum, Eliot, 143
Byers, Polly, 31, 146
Bynum, Brenda, 155
Byrd, David, 62
Byrd, Lisa, 177

C

Cabus, Mark, 46
Cackovich, Jim, 103
Cady, Joanne, 95
Caffey, Marion J., 67
Cain, Bill, 3
Cain, Candice, 36, 77, 109, 110, 125, 167
Caird, John, 89
Cairns, James, 164
Calandra, Dale, 32
Calandra, Denis, 32
Calder, Jim, 102, 163
Calder, John, 163
Calderon, George, 11
Caldwell, Charles, 5, 6
Caldwell, David, 89
Caldwell, Hugh, 173
Caldwell, Lauren, 66, 67
Caldwell, Scott, 63
Cale, David, 100
Cale, Kateri M., 5
Caliban, Richard, 79, 176
Calin, Angela, 104, 169
Calin, Maggie Belle, 34
Calitsis, Vasilios, 78
Callahan, Matt, 21
Callahan, Shelly, 121
Call, Edward Payson, 16, 74, 105
Cambridge, Edmund, 114
Cameron-Webb, Gavin, 72, 148, 149
Camoletti, Marc, 42
Campanella, Philip, 131
Campbell, Bob, 67
Campbell, Jane, 67
Campbell, Joseph, 108
Campbell, Mark, 93
Campbell, Mrs. Patrick, 56
Campbell, Norman, 46
Campbell, Sande, 173
Campbell, Sharon S.Q., 28, 71, 121
Campbell, Thomas, 71
Campers, The, 7
Camp, Karma, 132, 141
Camus, Albert, 155
Candelaria, Juan, 51
Candelaria, Maria, 51
Canter, Nina, 78
Cantrell, Michael, 177
Capenos, James, 119, 165
Capone, Steven, 99
Capote, Truman, 38, 125, 146, 162, 163
Capwell, Sara, 163

Caraccio, Jim, 176
Cardillo, Rimer, 73
Cardinalli, Joseph, 51, 52
Carey, Alison, 43
Carey, William D., 95
Care, Ross, 34
Carino, Glenda, 115
Carleton, Rex, 64
Carlile, John, 62
Carlisle, Barbara, 130
Carlis, Patricia, 112
Carlos, Laurie, 46, 54, 114
Carlsen, Allan, 49, 95
Carlson, Jenifer McClauchlan, 135
Carlson, M. George, 153
Carne, Marcel, 77, 155, 175
Carney, Kim, 51, 126
Carns, Stephen R., 28
Carpenter, Cassandra, 160
Carpenter, Chris, 129
Carpenter, Larry, 61, 69
Carpenter, Mel, 71
Carpenter-Simmons, Colleen, 64
Carreno, 152
Carrillo, Juliette, 4
Carroll, Baikida, 19, 46
Carroll, Brad, 112
Carroll, Lewis, 28, 30, 34, 103
Carroll, Nancy, 22
Carroll, Richard, 45
Carroll, Tim, 52
Carr, E.K., 157
Carr, Jack, 142
Carr, Laurence, 149
Carruthers, Tony, 157
Carsel, Gary, 96
Carson, Heather, 45, 83, 100, 102, 173
Carson, Jo, 27, 130, 132, 165
Carson, Steve, 21
Carter, Don, 89
Carter, Steve, 114, 166
Cartier, Jacques, 66, 69
Cartmill, Christopher, 21
Cartwright, Jim, 18
Carucci, Frank, 77
Cary, Richard, 104
Casazza, Jeff, 21
Casement, Barbara, 115
Case, Ronald, 76
Casey, Ariana, 7
Casey, Lawrence, 63
Casey, Warren, 7, 37, 142, 152, 166
Cash, Darla, 84
Cashion, Susan V., 160
Caspary, Vera, 175
Caspers, Rod, 81, 177
Castaneda, David, 99
Castanera, Rafael Colon, 133
Castellino, Bill, 40, 56, 61, 62, 103
Castilla, Sergio, 96
Castro, Alfredo, 73, 163
Cathcart, Carter, 126
Cather, Willa, 119, 160
Cattani, Loretta, 21
Cavallaro, Nicholas, 133
Cave, Jim, 84, 85, 160
Cavello, Carmen, 152
Cawthon, Dan, 37
Cazan, Ken, 90

Cecsarini, David, 90
Cedeno, Adrienne, 169, 170
Celli, Joe, 168
Centazzo, Andrea, 104
Cermak, Terry, 6, 159, 167
Cernovitch, Nicholas, 69, 82, 120
Cerqua, Joe, 32, 45, 172
Cerullo, Jonathan, 29
Cesario, Michael J., 119
Cevoli, Cathy, 41
Chafee, Claire, 85
Chaikin, Joseph, 100, 138
Chalcroft, Rory, 143
Chalenor, Fred, 91
Chamberlain, Anne, 153
Chamberlain, Marisha, 34, 122
Chambers, David, 96, 143, 144
Chambers, Jan, 170
Champa, Russell H., 5, 47, 78, 164
Chance, William, 125
Chandler, Terry, 148, 163
Chang, Kyung Won, 111
Chang, Tisa, 111
Channing, Carissa, 43
Chapin, Harry, 49, 129
Chaplin, Victoria, 7
Chapman, Alan, 115
Chapman, Linda, 96, 102
Chappelle, Eric, 23
Charlap, Mark, 5, 120, 160
Charles, David, 118, 131
Charlet, Allan, 156
Charnas, Fran, 16, 18, 152
Charney, Tina, 111
Charnin, Martin, 13, 29
Chase, Everett, 112
Chase, Lynne, 175
Chase, Mary, 129, 135, 159
Chase, Susan, 163
Chasse, Maurice, 111
Chatreux, Bernard, 54
Cheadle, Don, 93
Cheechoo, Shirley, 41
Chekhov, Anton, 11, 15, 51, 59, 63, 64, 75, 88, 89, 97, 103, 117, 119, 120, 125, 155, 160, 164, 174
Cheney, Mark, 168
Chen, H.T., 111
Chen, Tina, 111
Chepulis, Kyle, 54, 78
Cherney, Christopher, 156, 157
Chernin, Kim, 94
Chernomordik, Vlada, 89
Chertok-Tripolsky, Alla, 86
Chestek, Jeff, 117
Chevine, Theresa, 143
Chiang, Dawn, 34, 42
Chic Street Man, 24, 40, 47, 61, 72, 76, 87, 110, 116, 134, 137, 150
Child, Julia, 9, 39
Childs, Gale Fury, 112
Chiment, Marie Anne, 129
Chin, Jeff, 111
Chipman, Jerry, 120
Chlakishvili, Ilya, 107
Chong, Ping, 64, 71, 78, 118
Christen, Robert, 44, 60, 61, 100, 122, 147
Christensen, Tracy, 65
Christie, Agatha, 23, 28, 95

Christoffel, Fred, 123
Christopher, Roy, 42
Christopher, Sybil, 23
Christy, James J., 116, 117, 165, 166
Chumley, Daniel, 41, 134
Churchill, Caryl, 3, 24, 53, 79, 86, 102, 110, 120, 150
Church, Jeff, 43, 44, 164
Church, Joseph, 77
Chybowski, Michael, 11, 73, 173
Cibula-Jenkins, Nan, 60, 139, 147
Cilento, Wayne, 77
Cinque, Chris, 122
Ciolino, Joseph, 75
Cisek, Tony, 65, 143
Ciulei, Liviu, 15
Claiborne, Herbert III, 157
Clancy, Elizabeth Hope, 36, 39
Clark, B. Burgess, 34, 35, 92, 136, 165
Clark, Casey, 4
Clark, Danny, 148
Clark, Darren, 175
Clark, David, 21
Clarke, Bill, 11, 36, 86, 100, 121, 136, 137, 149, 167, 173
Clarke, Hope, 19, 24, 25, 77, 87, 88, 137, 173
Clark, Gerardine, 150
Clark, G. Thomas, 137
Clark, James A., 150
Clark, Jeff, 164
Clarkson, Janet, 158
Clark, Ted, 26
Clark, Tobin, 115
Clark, Tom, 9
Clark, Winston, 12, 22
Clarvoe, Anthony, 5, 50, 129, 144
Claussen, Diane, 58
Clayburgh, Jim, 173, 174
Clay, Diskin, 171
Claymore, Cindy, 49
Cleage, Pearl, 8, 97, 173
Cleary, Beverly, 34, 136
Clements, Freddie, 159
Clements, Jill Jane, 159
Clendenning, Bonnie, 98
Cless, Downing, 41
Cleveland, Carles, 161
Cleveland, Janet, 14
Cleveland, Rick, 107
Clifford, John, 110
Clifton, John, 26
Clinger, Will, 91
Clipper, Craig, 36, 72
Close, Del, 127
Cloud, Darrah, 96, 115, 119, 160
Clough, Peter, 30
Clyman, Evelyn, 75
Clyman, Robert, 43
Coale, Jessica, 1, 138
Coates, Doug, 168
Cobey, Patricia, 107, 156
Coble, McKay, 121
Coburn, D.L., 91
Cochren, Felix E., 11, 59, 97, 116, 149
Cocke, Dudley, 130, 131
Cocteau, Jean, 11
Codom, Fred, 54

Cody, Lisa, 89
Coffey, Denise, 90
Cofrin, David H., 162
Cohan, George M., 106
Cohen, Andy, 84
Cohen, Darren R., 76
Cohen, Douglas J., 108, 124, 125, 160, 161
Cohen, Edward M., 75, 76
Cohen, Gale, 79
Cohen, Jason Steven, 100
Cohen, Michael, 101
Cohen, Robert, 165
Cohen, Robert Elliot, 149
Cohen, Samuel D., 161
Cohn, Marya, 96
Cokor, Flora, 162
Colavecchia, Franco, 168
Colby, Michael, 42
Coleman, Ava T., 59
Coleman, Chris, 3, 8
Coleman, Rahn, 42
Coleman, RJ, 32
Coleman, Steve, 86
Cole, Ida S., 73
Cole, Jan, 72
Cole, Jonathan, 94, 95
Cole, Mark, 161
Coles, Michael H., 85
Colley-Lee, Myrna, 45, 46, 109, 113
Collins, Jeanmarie, 26
Collins, John, 78, 83, 157
Collins, Kathleen A., 57, 58, 67
Collins, Laurie, 84
Collins, Pat, 11, 31, 32, 66, 80, 82, 87, 88, 122, 131
Collins, Robert O., Jr., 3
Collins, Stephen, 118
Collodi, Carlo, 6, 17, 101
Colorado, Hortensia, 156
Colorado, Vira, 156
Colton, Jacque Lynn, 78
Columbus, Curt, 166
Colvin, Michele, 47
Colvin, Neil, 138
Colwin, Tom, 55
Coman, Sherry, 79
Comer, Amanda J., 12
Commons, Milt, 52
Compton, Steffani, 7, 8
Conant, Ralph, 153
Concklin, Eric, 79
Condon, Frank, 79, 104, 127
Cone, Jeff, 8
Conely, James, 6
Cone, Tom, 11, 32, 66
Confino, Ofra, 75
Congdon, Constance, 34, 129, 145
Congreve, William, 15, 69
Conklin, John, 4, 8, 31, 32, 64, 66, 87, 100, 170
Conklin, JR, 31, 32
Conlin, Kathleen F., 165, 166
Conlon, John, 171
Connally, C. Ellen, 40
Connor, Allison, 85, 160
Conn, Rogue, 136
Conrad, Gail, 156
Conroy, Pat, 57, 61
Constantine, Deborah, 111

Conti, Bill, 168
Conway, Dan, 67, 150
Conway, Dennis E., 163
Conway, Tommy, 153
Cook, Chris, 92, 93
Cook, Douglas N., 165
Cook, Dwight, 45
Cooke, Thomas P., 38, 39
Cook, Jeffra, 30
Cook, John Wayne, 134
Cook, Jon Paul, 49
Cook, Michael, 29, 30
Cook, Patrick, 57
Cook, Peter, 56
Cook, Stoney, 163
Cooper-Hecht, Gail, 75, 113, 168
Cooper, Giles, 54
Cooper, Judith, 34
Cooper, Martha Harris, 152
Cooper, Melissa, 134
Cooper, Seth, 19
Cooper, Susan, 26, 58, 89
Cooprider-Bernstein, Betsy, 72
Coppedge, Rosanna E., 18, 67, 121, 176
Coppick, Stephen C., 98
Coppock, Ada, 117
Corbett, Bill, 122
Corbett, Nancy, 67
Corbett, Sam C., 144
Cordes, Lisa, 44, 164
Cordova, Richard, 93, 167
Corley, Elisabeth Lewis, 140
Corley, Richard, 66, 85
Corneille, Pierre, 2, 5, 64, 110
Cornelison, Gayle, 29, 30
Cornelison, Holly, 29, 30
Cornelius, Robert, 166
Cornell, Allen D., 124, 129
Cornett, Ewel, 3, 26
Cornielle, Pierre, 153
Cornish, Anthony, 19
Cornwell, Bruce, 66
Corrado, Danielle, 142
Corson, Dan, 7
Cortese, Alda, 114
Cortez, Leo, 112
Corti, James, 94
Corti, Jim, 172
Corvinus, Dede, 121
Corwin, Walter, 156, 157
Corzatte, Clayton, 67
Cosier, E. David, Jr., 9, 47, 91, 137, 167, 170
Cossa, Roberto, 128
Costa, Jose De Ancieta, 100
Costigan, Ken, 22
Costin, James D., 91
Cothran, Robert, 39, 149, 152
Cotten, Kelly, 4, 5
Cotter, Gary E., 125
Cotter, Kevin, 170
Courts, Randy, 58, 72
Cousins, Craig, 76
Cousin, Tome, 38
Covault, James, 145
Covey, Elizabeth, 35, 113
Covington, Ron, 27
Cowan, Edie, 50, 152, 161
Coward, Noel, 6, 24, 25, 49, 50, 95,

119, 125, 135, 144, 165
Cox, Billie, 99
Cox, Douglas, 27
Cox, Randall, 76
Cox, Vivian, 142
Coyle, Bruce W., 113
Crabtree, Abigail, 46, 47
Crabtree, Ann, 46, 47
Crabtree, Jim, 46, 47
Crabtree, Mary, 46, 47
Crabtree, Paul, 46
Crain, Gene, 120
Cram, Lynette, 159, 163
Cranberry Productions, 177
Crandall, David, 142
Crane, David, 61, 161
Crane, Stephen, 44, 72
Crank, David, 6, 36, 98, 128, 159
Cranney, Jon, 33, 34
Craun, Charles D., 34, 92
Cravath, Paul, 67
Craver, Mike, 18, 56, 120, 129, 134
Crawford, Brett, 163
Creamer, Tom, 60, 61
Crenshaw, Jackie, 76
Crimp, Martin, 5
Crinkley, Richmond, 141
Crisp, Tom, 95
Cristofer, Michael, 105
Crockett, Michael, 177
Croghan, Robert, 89
Cromer, David, 94
Cronin, Pauline, 104
Cronwall, Eric O., 112
Cronyn, Hume, 26, 58, 89
Crooks, Rich, 157
Croswell, Anne, 57, 61
Croswell, Michael, 83
Crouse, Russel, 59, 159
Crouse, Steven, 129
Crowell, Richard, 124
Crow, Laura, 2, 16, 19, 37, 105, 116, 119, 136
Crowther, Elea, 70
Croy, Jonathan, 139
Cruse, Carol, 142
Cruz, Migdalia, 43, 54, 96, 173
Cryer, Mark, 71
Cuddy, Mark, 132, 133
Cuellar, Victor, 73
Culbert, Bobby, 16
Culbert, John, 44, 45
Cullen, Judith, 23
Cullinan, Francis, 165
Culman, Peter W., 31
Cumella, Thomas, 37
Cummings, Conrad, 78
Cumming, Richard, 47, 164
Cunningham, Laura, 96, 127
Cuomo, Douglas J., 131
Curchack, Fred, 5
Curiel, Tony, 52, 60, 77
Curi, Jorge, 105
Curley, Bill, 50
Curran, Chris, 1
Currens, Stephen, 169
Curreri, Alan, 134
Currin, Allyson, 143
Curry, Michael, 66
Curtis, Carl, 13

Curtis, Pam, 13
Custer, John F., 164
Custer, Marianne, 18, 38, 39
Cutarella, Bob, 79
Cuthbert, David Lee, 112
Cuthbertson, Jennifer, 41
Cuthrell, Elizabeth, 102
Cutler-Volz, Jeri, 158
Czogalla, Beate M., 130
Czoka, Lawrence, 27, 134

D

Dafoe, Willem, 173
Dahdah, Robert, 156, 157
Dahlgren, Kate, 55
Dahl, Kirsten, 79
Dahl, Roald, 52
Dahlstrom, Robert, 19, 64, 105
Daily, Carol, 99
Daines, John, 125
Daisical, Laka, 7
Daitsman, Judith, 27
Daley, Donna, 124
Dallas, L.B., 83, 100
Dallas, Walter, 116
Dallin, Howard, 35, 36
Dalton, Mark, 31
Daly, Jonathan Gillard, 112
D'Altilia, Tracy E., 14, 168
Dalzell, Karen, 53
Damashek, Barbara, 22, 85, 86, 109, 110
DaMata-Geiger, Darice, 21
D'Ambrosi, Dario, 41
Damiano, Joe, 104
Dana, F. Mitchell, 58, 59, 159
Dance Noise, 7
Dancy, Virginia, 4
Danforth, Roger T., 40
Dangerfield, Cory, 133, 134
Dang, Tim, 115
Daniel, Ana, 23
Daniele, Graciela, 57, 66
Daniel, Richard H., 119
Daniels, James, 138
Daniels, Jeff, 126
Danielson, Carl, 135
Danielson, Darcy, 18
Daniels, Patricia, 138
Daniels, Ron, 11, 12, 119
Dansky, Peter, 2
Dardenne, James, 166
Darion, Joe, 32, 65
Darnutzer, Don, 2, 16, 34, 50, 74
Darrow, Jason, 126
D'Augusta, Al, 58
Daum, Gary, 106
Davey, Babs, 102
Davidson, Gordon, 87
Davidson, Jeannie, 50, 109
Davidson, John, 114
Davidson, Micki, 45
Davidson, Robert, 23, 73, 74
Davidson, Sraa, 55, 127, 166, 172
Davidson, Suzanne Schwartz, 137
Davies, Sue, 141
Davis, Anthony, 11
Davis, Bill C., 30, 58

Davis, Bob, 85
Davis, Chris, 17
Davis, Clinton Turner, 4, 15, 96, 99, 110, 138, 164, 176
Davis, Dean, 120
Davis, Dee, 130
Davis, Guy, 97
Davis, Jeff, 40, 92, 132, 145
Davis, Jeffrey B., 132
Davis, Jennie L., 129
Davis, John Henry, 49, 117, 161
Davis, Jordan, 41
Davis, Kate, 120
Davis, Lindsay W., 4, 42, 61, 69, 85, 86, 88
Davis, Montgomery, 90
Davis, Nancy, 126
Davis, Ossie, 148
Davis, Rick, 8, 31
Davis, Ronald M., 14
Davis, Russell, 1, 129
Davis, Ted, 125
Davis, Tom, 129
Dawn, Karalee, 12, 90
Dawson, Taylor, 5
Day, Don, 176, 177
Day, Kingsley, 94
Deal, Jennifer, 168
Deane, J.A., 85
Dean, Jeffrey W., 56
Dean, Phillip Hayes, 63, 125
Deardorff, Charlotte, 28
Dearing, Judy, 8, 19, 40, 64, 66, 91, 93, 97, 116, 117, 122, 149
Dear, Nick, 104, 142, 155
Debassige, Blake, 41
de Beaumarchais, Pierre-Augustine, 16
de Beaumont, Mme. Le Prince, 30, 34, 101, 154
de Berry, David, 16, 109, 133
DeBerry, David, 155
DeBerry, Teresa, 68
de Brito, Davi, 128
de Cervantes, Miguel, 65
Deckel, Larry, 4, 91
Decker, Gary, 126
Decker, Pat, 70
Decker, Steven, 20
Decker, Tina, 89
Decker, William, 28
DeCuir, L.J., 39
DeDoes, Steve, 126
Deegan, John Michael, 59
Deer, Jennifer, 3
Deer, Sandra, 8, 9, 101
Dee, Ruby, 45, 46
Degan, Diane, 107
Degiez, S., 156
DeGrace, Lisa, 146
Degtjar, Yuri, 64
de Hartog, Jan, 31
Deiss, Paul, 158
de Jongh, James, 76, 161
DeJong, Jeanette, 72, 126, 171
de la Barca, Pedro Calderon, 127
de Laclos, Choderlos, 38, 160
Delaney, Dennis, 113
Delaney, John, 78
de la Parra, Marco Antonio, 163

Delattre, Susan, 71
DeLaurier, Peter, 48, 114
DeLaurier, Roger, 112
Delavan, Nelson, 65
del Castillo, Gonzalez, 152
Del Conte, Andrea, 152
Deleo, Bernie, 106
Delgado, Judith, 42
DeLillo, Don, 127
Delinger, Benton, 135
Delinger, Larry, 50, 74
del Rio, J. Sanchez, 127, 128
Demansky, Barry, 28
de Marivaux, Pierre Carlet, 88
Dembrow, Jon, 53
De Monaco, John W., 51
de Mora, Robert, 173
Dempsey, John, 62
de Musset, Alfred, 64
Dennison, Monty G., 53
Dennis, Rick, 31, 161
Dennis, Ronald, 164
Denson, Cheryl, 5
Denvil, Alasdair, 158
Denzer, Ralph, 79
De Paola, Paolo, 96
de Paola, Tomie, 34
DePoy, Phillip, 162, 163
DePoy, Scott, 163
Depta, Victor M., 1
de Pury, Marianne, 106, 107
Dereszynski, John, 162
de Rojas, Fernando, 25
de Rosa, Richard, 65
DeRoux, Dan, 115
DeRue, Cheryll, 56
de Saint Exupery, Antoine, 155
Desbois, Barbra Berlovitz, 154
Desbois, Frederic, 71, 77, 154, 155, 175
Desena, Fred, 42
DeShields, Andre, 78
Desjardins, Martin, 171, 175
DesRosiers, Anne B., 62
DeTurk, Scott, 9
de Vega, Lope, 25, 79
Devine, Michael, 143, 144
DeVinney, Gordon, 129
Devin, Richard, 40, 149
Devlin, Joan, 90
Devlin, John, 91
De Volder, Max, 128, 129
Dewell, Michael, 25, 90
Dewhurst, Keith, 11
Dewitt, Bobby, 21
Dewitt, Dawn, 21, 32, 157
Dew, Jonathan, 163
Diamond, Amanda, 42
Diamond, Liz, 47, 96, 173, 175
Diamond, Mark, 55
Diamond, Sallie, 59
Dibbell, Dominique, 102
Dickens, Charles, 2, 4, 7, 8, 9, 13, 26, 27, 29, 35, 36, 44, 47, 50, 57, 58, 59, 60, 61, 62, 63, 64, 66, 67, 69, 84, 88, 89, 91, 92, 94, 95, 99, 112, 114, 121, 123, 125, 129, 133, 134, 143, 144, 145, 149, 150, 151, 152, 162, 164, 170, 171, 176, 177
Dick, Ming, 144

Dicks, Goldie, 72, 76
Di Donna, Eddie, 156, 157
Diekmann, Nancy Kassak, 101
Diess, Paul, 158
Dietz, Steven, 2, 18, 61, 78, 86, 104, 120, 126, 133, 171
DiFonzo, Michael, 124
DiGabriele, Linda, 19
Dignan, Pat, 47, 102, 137, 168, 176
Dillard, Rob, 4
Dillen, Frederick G., 107
Dilliard, Marcus, 4, 34, 64, 121
Dillingham, Charles, 87
Dillingham, Howard, 65
Dillon, David, 21
Dillon, John, 90, 91
DiMenna, Stephen, 62
Dimock, George E. Jr., 64
Dingley, Mark D., 175
DiNicola, Donald, 11, 139
Dinkel, Jay, 12
DiNovelli, Donna, 143
DiPaolo, Elvira J., 38
DiPinto, John, 150
Dirie, Gerardo, 72
DiScala, Nick, 37
Dixcy, Marcia, 4
Dixon, Michael Bigelow, 72
Dmitriev, Alex, 33, 49
Dobbins, Ray, 157
Dobeck, Rey, 91
Dobrusky, Pavel, 50, 90, 115
Dodd, Joseph D., 24, 67, 136
Dodge, Marcia Milgrom, 15, 25, 60, 118, 167, 168
Dodge, Mary Maples, 55
Dodson, Colleen, 151
Doepner, Susan, 85
Doherty, Clayton, 29, 30
Doherty, Delia, 156
Dolan, Judith Anne, 8
Dolan, Shirley, 46
Dombroski, Joseph K., 48
Donaghy, Tom, 61, 164
Donahue, Alan, 21
Donahue, John Clark, 17, 34, 93
Donahue, Michael, 120, 121
Donahue, Nancy L., 88
Donahue, Thomas F., 106, 132
Donarski, Therese, 55
Dondlinger, Mary Jo, 40, 47, 62, 63
Done, Abil, 7
Donnelly, Candice, 24, 25, 32, 36, 39, 66, 82, 87, 100, 137, 141, 143
Donnelly, Jessica, 21
Donnelly, Kyle, 15, 69
Donovan, Derek, 99
Donovan, Diane, 99
Donovan, Jeremy, 99
Dooley, Ray, 121
Dorfman, Ariel, 8, 116, 134, 147
Dorlag, Arthur, 19
Dorr, Nicholas, 133
Dorsey, Kent, 8, 9, 16, 24, 105, 135
Dorton, Moses, 46
Dorwart, David, 170
Dostoevski, Fyodor, 14, 75
Doty, Pat, 90, 91
Dougherty, Christine, 9, 24, 103, 135

Dougherty, Eileen H., 78
Dougherty, Joseph, 80
Doughty, Bix, 26
Douglass, Donald, 46, 61, 95, 175
Douglass, Frederick, 103
Douglas, Steven C., 46
Doust, Paul, 167
Dowd, A. Elizabeth, 28
Dowd, Jayne, 56
Dower, David, 85
Dowling, Joe, 2
Dowling, Kevin, 58, 75, 122
Dowling, Sarah T., 163
Dowling, Vincent, 124
Downey, Roger, 16; 64
Doxsee, Lenore, 78, 79, 101, 139
Doyle, John, 103
Doyle, Julie, 161
Doyle, Ted, 46, 47
Drachman, Ted, 120
Draghici, Marina, 15, 24, 86, 100, 102, 120, 156
Drake, Gillian, 132
Drake, Ginger, 160
Drake, William F., 114
Draper, David, 9, 140
Draper, Ruth, 9, 39
Draud, Rocky, 66, 67
Dresser, Richard, 23
Dretsch, Curtis, 73, 113, 163
Dretzu, Jon, 125
Drexler, Rosalyn, 156, 157
Driscoll, Christopher, 15
Drobny, Christopher, 96, 170
Drotos, Ron, 161
Drown, Debra, 67
Drury, Chuck, 166
Dryden, Deborah M., 16, 24, 72, 109, 110, 135
Du Plantis, Daniel, 51
Du Rand, Le Clanche, 150
Duarte, Derek, 9, 24, 91, 110, 135
Duarte, Myrna, 156, 157
Dubay, Brenda Joyce, 52
Dubin, Al, 89
Dubin, Kitty S., 126
DuBois, Barbara, 160
Dubois, Shirley, 143
DuBose, Bruce, 5
DuBrock, Neal, 148
Duclos, Janice, 164
Dudley, Ray, 159
Dudley, Richard Shawn, 171
Dudzick, Tom, 56
Duea, Brian, 53
Duffin, Shay, 104
Duff, James, 40
Duffy, Gordon, 115
Dugan, Dennis, 41
Duke, Stuart, 57, 61, 62, 72, 117, 147
Dulack, Tom, 58, 104
Dumaresq, William, 160, 169
Dumas, Alexander, 21
Dumas, Charles, 113
Dumas, Debra, 73
DuMaurier, George, 19
Dumont, Cynthia, 97
Dunayer, Kevin, 7, 00
Duncan, A. Clark, 98

Duncan, Danny, 86, 160
Duncan, Emily, 103
Duncan, William B., 8
Dunkelberger, Beth, 58
Dunlap, Richard, 25
Dunlap, Shirley Basfield, 67
Dunn, Glenn, 129, 148
Dunn, John, 99
Dunn, Michelle, 7
Dunn, SK, 79
Dunn, Thomas G., 121
Durang, Christopher, 11, 21, 177
DuRante, Ed, 157
Durbin, Andrew, 18
Durbin, Holly Poe, 98, 128
Durfee, Duke, 147
Durling, Roger Arturo, 96
Durrenmatt, Friedrich, 15, 28, 59, 131, 170
Durrwachter, Jay, 156
Dutch Theater Exchange Program, 157
Duthie, G. Andrew, 150
Dwellingham, Herschel, 9
Dwyer, Terrence, 76
Dye, Billy, 158

E

Eader, Kathryn, 118
Earick, Rhonda, 144
Earle, Susan, 29
Easely, Greg, 177
Eastland, Wally, 46
Eastman, Donald, 9, 31, 32, 39, 82, 83, 100, 141, 168
Eastman, P.D., 53
Eaton, Vanessa, 81
Ebb, Fred, 91, 123
Eckard, Vicki, 134
Eckhart, Gary, 145, 149
Eck, Marsha Lovis, 101
Eddy, Carson M., 41, 99
Eddy, L. Stacy, 99, 174, 175
Edelman, David, 48
Edelman, Richard, 29
Edelstein, Barry, 152
Edelstein, Gordon, 25, 81, 82, 96, 131
Eden, Evert, 107
Edmiston, Scott, 113
Edmondson, James, 110
Edmunds, Kate, 9, 24, 32, 69, 87, 91, 135
Edouard, 76
Edwards, Ben, 122, 131
Edwards, Bill, 5
Edwards, David, 144
Edwards, Dex, 8, 91, 159
Edwards, Jack, 64
Edwards, Jason, 168
Edwards, Michael, 140
Edwards, Paul, 172
Edwards, Peter, 52
Edwards, Rod, 12
Edwards, Scott W., 33, 34, 93
Edwards, Sian, 38
Edwards, Stephen, 80
Edwards, Vaughan, 40

Efremoff, Andrei W., 171
Egan, Kathleen, 28
Egan, Robert, 87
Egelund, Kevin, 93
Egloff, Elizabeth, 10, 50, 77, 79, 96, 128, 165
Ehlinger, Mary, 56
Ehn, Erik, 53, 96
Ehrhart, Kevin, 52
Ehrlich, Jon, 161
Eich, Stephen, 147
Eigsti, Karl, 69
Eilenberg, Larry, 84
Einhorn, Ed, 96
Eisenhauer, Peggy, 57, 66
Eisenstein, Linda, 41
Eis, Joel, 86, 103
Eister, Karen, 11
Ekstrom, Peter, 4, 113
Elam, Harry J., 160
Elder, Eldon, 19, 57
Elhai, Robert, 161
Elias, Ralph, 26, 27
Elie, Matt, 101
Elisha, Ron, 147
Elkin, Michael, 168
Elkins, Doug, 15
Ellefson, Merry, 115
Ellington, Duke, 91
Ellington, Mercedes, 91, 113
Elliot, Diane, 71
Elliott, David K.H., 24, 136
Elliott, Kenneth, 11, 40, 156, 157
Elliott, Liz, 155
Elliott, Lynn, 89
Elliott, Marianna, 87, 120
Elliott, Mark, 32
Elliott, Richard H., 37
Ellison, David, 41
Ellison, Michael, 62
Ellis, Richard, 13
Ellis, Scott, 88, 131
Ellman, Bruce, 85, 86, 122, 150, 167
Ellzey, Brantley, 120
Elmore, Aaron J., 115
Emberton, David, 38, 39
Emerson, Pamela, 121, 129, 165
Emery, Drew, 7
Emmes, David, 143, 144
Emmons, Beverly, 40, 58, 88, 100
Emory, Randy, 153
Enderle, Curt, 110
Engelgau, Fred, 28
Engelhardt, Janice, 99
Engelsma, Shelly, 70
Engerman, John, 53
Engler, Michael, 85, 143
English, Gary, 12, 22, 89, 119, 129
Enloe, Mrs. Robert Ted, III, 47
Ennen, Thea, 71
Enos, Jerald, 135
Enters, Warren, 76, 149
Eppel, David, 146
Epperson, Dirk, 85
Epperson, John, 102
Epperson, Skip, 140
Epping, Cheri, 20
Epp, Richard, 35
Epps, Christian, 76, 148

Epps, Sheldon, 18, 40, 42, 64, 105
Epp, Steven, 77, 154, 155, 175
Epstein, Jonathan, 89
Epstein, Sabin, 9
Epsten, Chip, 138
Erdman, Jean, 108
Erickson, Ron, 151
Ernotte, Andre, 61, 107, 167
Ertl, Fritz, 96
Erven, Charles, 10, 55
Ervin, Denise, 95
Ervin, John, 153, 154
Ervin, Mike, 106, 115
Erwin, Gail, 52
Esbjornson, David, 39, 167
Escalante, Leopoldo, 152
Escalante, Rosa Maria, 52
Escudero, Guillermo, 152
Escudero, Laura, 152
Escudero, Pedro, 152
Eskey, Lee, 106
Eskin, Otho, 143
Esparza, Phillip, 51
Espenshade, John W., 57
Espinoza, Gabriel, 25
Esposito, Vickie, 116, 117
Essad, Michael, 30
Essen, B.J., 51
Essig, Linda, 91, 165
Esst, Garrison, 50
Esty, William P., 154
Etherege, Sir George, 19
Etheridge, Jack, 38
Etter, Gregory, 68, 69
Ettinger, Daniel, 22
Eucker, John, 156
Euripides, 27, 46, 54, 64, 78, 104, 146
Eustis, Oskar, 4, 87
Evans, Abigail, 36
Evans, Carol North, 35
Evans, Craig, 31
Evans, David, 161
Evans, Donna, 156
Evans, Jim, 123
Evans, Paul, III, 76
Everett, Claudia, 109, 110
Everett, William H., 170
Evers, Elizabeth, 78, 79
Eyen, Tom, 79
Ezell, John, 36, 45, 46, 63, 92, 128, 129

F

Fagal, Peter, 122
Fagan, Valerie, 18, 67, 121, 176
Fails, Connie, 18
Fairbanks, Evelyn, 62
Fairbanks, Richard, 98, 99
Faison, George, 32, 46, 88
Fajans, Michael, 47
Falabella, John, 25, 42, 61, 69, 167
Falcone, Vincent, 42
Falk, S.D., 142
Fallon, Daniel B., 119
Fallon, Richard G., 19
Falls, Gregory A., 1, 2
Falls, Robert, 60, 100

Fanning, Tony, 61
Fannon, Cecilia, 79
Farenwald, Stephanie, 28
Fargnoli, Margie, 71
Faria, Arthur, 8, 16
Farlow, Lesley, 39, 89
Farmer, Bill, 107
Farmer, Daniel, 53
Farquhar, George, 4, 83
Farrell, Chris, 111
Farrell, Christine, 124
Farrell, John, 163
Farrow, Mary, 30
Farrow, Mary Kathryn, 30
Farthing, Ann, 169
Fasbender, Bart, 173
Fasman, Glen, 175
Fassbinder, Rainer Werner, 32
Faulcon, Patrice, 142
Faulkner, Cliff, 105, 109, 143
Faulkner, William, 102
Fauss, M. Michael, 8, 9, 149
Faust, Nick, 146
Fay, Thomas, 11, 82
Fazia, Gaetano, 157
Fearnley, John, 129
Federico, Robert Weber, 105, 127, 128
Fedorcha, Ayun, 143
Feffer, Steve, 94
Feibleman, Peter, 12
Feiffer, Jules, 176
Feiner, Harry A., 149
Feingold, Michael, 104
Feist, Gene, 131
Fejer, Cordis, 166
Feldman, Eric Drew, 24
Feldsher, Scott, 134
Feldshuh, David, 6, 7, 9, 38, 47, 51, 58, 60, 72, 117, 128, 149
Fellini, Federico, 81, 133
Felton, Hilton C. Jr., 57
Fenhagen, James, 59, 85
Fenichell, Susan, 53, 73, 74, 98
Ferber, Edna, 9, 165
Ferdinand, Dave, 78
Ferencz, George, 73, 79
Ferguson, Carol Mignoni, 28
Ferguson, Margaret, 38
Ferguson, Michael, 135
Fernandez, Celena Mayo, 44
Fernandez, Evelina, 52
Ferra, Max, 42, 72, 73
Ferrante, Frank, 168
Ferreira, Ted, 43
Ferrell, Stephanie, 111
Ferrieri, Tony, 38
Fetterly, Ralph, 133
Feves, Angene, 9
Feydeau, Georges, 7, 69, 92, 110
Fey, Jerry, 43
Fey, Lorenne, 1
Fichandler, Thomas C., 14
Fichandler, Zelda, 2, 14, 15
Fichter, David, 41
Field, Barbara, 58, 64, 92, 94, 121, 143
Field, Chris, 157
Field, Christine E., 124
Field, Crystal, 156, 157

Fields, Michael, 49
Fife, Stephen, 75, 156
Figtree, Craig, 21
Figueroa-Story, Diana, 5
Filho, Antunes, 128
Filler, Deb, 78, 102
Fillo, Liz, 87
Finch, Carl, 4, 38
Findley, Mark, 7
Fingerhut, Arden, 80, 82, 87, 116, 170
Finkelstein, Richard, 101
Finnegan, Kish, 16
Finnell, Jan, 35, 118, 144, 145
Finney, Jack, 108
Finney, Shirley Jo, 45, 46, 71
Finn, William, 66, 105, 128, 150, 165, 172
Finque, Susan, 6, 7
Finstein, Arthur, 175
Finston, Betsy, 75, 170, 171
Fiori, Rick, 143
Fire, Richard, 110
Fischer, Corey, 19, 20, 23
Fishelson, David, 75
Fisher, John, 43
Fisher, Jules, 57, 80
Fisher, Linda, 32, 40
Fisher, Robert, 168
Fishman, Carol, 137
Fish, Maureen, 89, 170
Fish, Mike, 110
Fisk, Marcus J., 158
Fitch, Stona J., 35
Fitzgerald, Ed, 85
Fitzgerald, F. Scott, 62
FitzGerald, Jim, 91
Fitzgerald, Peter, 57, 105
Fitzhugh, Ellen, 11, 66
Fitzpatrick, Jane P., 24
Fitzpatrick, Lynn, 65
Five Lesbian Brothers, The, 7
Flad, David, 104
Flaharty, Chris, 165
Flaherty, Stephen, 9, 80, 160
Flake, Linda, 165
Flamand, Didier, 54
Flanders, John, 86
Flank, Jane Williams, 68
Flannery, James W., 155
Flax, John, 165
Fleigel, Janie, 22
Fleischer, Yolanda, 51
Fleischman, Deborah, 26
Fleming, Jawn, 71
Fleming, Rudd, 132
Fleming, Sam, 2, 90, 91
Fleming, Tom, 21, 32
Fletcher, John C., 9, 85
Fletcher, Robert, 9
Flint, Drew, 125
Flint, Peter H., 48
Flippin, Marianne, 85
Flood, Julia, 27
Floor, Callie, 9, 103
Flores, Cecelia, 5
Flores, Ralph, 21
Flower, Edward, 93
Flowers, Michael, 26
Floyd, Carlisle, 46

Floyd, Gary, 104
Fluty, Rex, 124
Flying Karamazov Brothers, The, 2
Fo, Dario, 9, 139
Foeller, William, 65
Fogelson, Georgia, 126
Foglia, Leonard, 78, 164
Folden, Lewis, 29, 49, 159, 173
Foley, John, 46, 59, 89, 98, 113, 150, 151, 168
Fontaine, Joel, 9, 72, 105, 128, 129, 135, 160
Forbes, Barbara, 58, 147, 168
Forbes, Jeff, 125
Forbes, Kathryn, 46
Forcade, Mary, 84
Ford, Alison, 89
Ford, Carolyn, 42
Ford, David, 85
Ford, Frank, 4
Ford, Georgia, 5
Ford, John, 100
Ford, Kim O., 15
Ford, Steven, 11
Foreman, Richard, 108
Forest, Dabney, 94
Fornes, Maria Irene, 85, 134, 157, 175
Forrest, Donald, 49
Forrester, Bill, 2, 67, 136, 151
Forrester, Sean David, 104
Forsberg, Carl, 21
Forster, John, 161
Forsyth, Jerold R., 117, 171
Forsyth, Stephen, 121
Fort, Beje, 47
Foscato, Kim, 84, 85
Foster, Jimi, 161
Foster, Michael, 49
Foster, Paul, 111
Foster, Sharon, 19
Foster, Stephen C., 134
Fotopoulos, Dionyssis, 78
Four Big Girls, 7
Fournier, Jack, 56
Fowler, Fred, 164
Fox and Perla, Ltd., 58, 73
Fox, David Michael, 89
Fox, Jennifer, 96
Fox, Meg, 7, 23, 73, 74, 104, 137
Fox, Pat, 177
Foy, Ken, 19, 25, 77, 88
Frabotta, Fred, 170
Fracher, Drew, 55
Franca, Veronica, 79
Francis, Kevin, 103
Franco, Cris, 134
Frank, Anne, 101
Frank, David, 149
Frankel, Gene, 42, 85
Frankel, Kenneth, 40
Frankel, Robert M., 38
Frankel, Scott, 86
Frank, Jeff, 177
Franklin, James F., 89
Franklin, J.E., 97
Fraser, John, 50
Frates, Vince, 133
Fratti, Mario, 81, 133
Frayn, Michael, 63, 79, 112

INDEX OF NAMES

Frazier, Grenoldo, 97
Frazier, Kermit, 19
Frazier, Ron, 76
Frederick, Rebecca G., 33, 49
Freed, Donald, 150
Freedman, Gerald, 62, 63, 92
Freed, Randy, 23
Freeman, Aaron, 44
Freeman, Thom, 68, 138
Freericks, Charles Avakian, 169
Freese, Ross, 18, 67, 92, 121, 176
Freiberg, Eric, 107
Freitas, Roslyn, 67
Frellick, Paul, 111
French, Erica, 159
Freyer, Frederick, 57
Frey, Matthew, 156
Frey, Tim, 163
Fried, Elizabeth Michal, 175
Fried, Lawrence, 93
Friedman, Allen Jay, 158
Friedman, Brad, 79, 156
Friedman, Gary William, 148
Friedman, Gene Emerson, 63, 92
Friedman, Mark, 25, 134
Friedman, Michael, 170
Friedman, Steve, 85
Friel, Brian, 67, 69, 74, 81, 114, 123
Frisch, Max, 109
Fritzler, Jim, 176, 177
Frkonja, Jeff, 23, 151
Fromer, Robert, 25
Fromholz, Steven, 81
Frost, Charles Lynn, 134
Frost, Judy, 111
Frost, Rebecca, 71
Frost, Sue, 61
Fruchter, Danny S., 114
Fruchter, Margaret E., 114
Frye, Andrea, 76, 112
Fry, Christopher, 90
Fry, Ray, 4
Fsakos, Karen, 156
Fuecker, Robert, 92
Fugard, Athol, 2, 8, 15, 31, 36, 44, 51, 72, 74, 77, 85, 86, 90, 98, 99, 114, 123, 125, 138, 146, 150, 155, 172, 175
Fui-Kyung, Kim, 78
Fulghum, Robert, 89
Fulginiti-Shakar, George, 132, 141
Fuller, Barry, 121
Fuller, Charles, 148
Fuller, Elizabeth, 71, 128, 157
Fuller, Susie, 147
Fulton, James, 89
Fulton, Kurt, 78
Funderburg, Barry, 12
Funicello, Ralph, 9, 87, 105, 143, 144
Furr, Connie, 145
Fusco, Thomas, 170
Futterman, Enid, 101

G

Gable, H. Lee, 150
Gaffney, Mo, 134
Gagliano, Frank, 96

Gail, Mary, 96
Gaines, Barbara, 139
Gaines, Frederick, 34
Galantiere, Lewis, 49, 132
Galati, Frank, 46, 50, 60, 61, 92, 106, 115, 119
Galban, Margarita, 25
Gale, Brian, 137, 144
Gale, Gregory, 75
Galik, Tannis, 169
Gallagher, Larry, 151, 177
Gallagher, Mary, 96
Gallardo, Edward, 25
Gallegos, Tina, 159
Galli, Allen, 23
Galligan, Carol, 105
Gallo, David, 31, 113, 136, 161
Galloway, Terry, 7
Gallu, Samuel, 4, 42
Galser, Sherry, 42
Gambara, Griselda, 169
Ganio, Michael, 50, 98, 109, 110, 129
Gann, Kyle, 28
Gantt, Cora Dick, 106
Garbi, Avner, 169
Garcia, Lisa, 49
Garcia, Oscar, 72
Garcia, Risa Bramon, 86
Gardener, Alan, 114
Gardiner, Robert A., 136
Gardner, Elizabeth, 41
Gardner, Grover, 173
Gardner, Herb, 38, 70, 92, 145
Gardner, Josie, 151
Gardner, Lee Mikeska, 173
Gardner, Tom, 167, 168
Gardner, William T., 119
Gardner, Worth, 19, 107
Garfias, Ruben, 25
Garland, Patrick, 4
Garlin, Jeff, 127
Garman, Rick, 43
Garnett, Constance, 119
Garonzik, Sara, 117
Garrett, Dave, 155
Garrett-Groag, Lillian, 110
Garrett, Renee, 46, 47
Garrity, Paul, 104
Gaskill, William, 141, 156
Gates, Sarah Nash, 109, 110
Gault, Jane, 94
Gavin, Patrick, 49
Gazzo, Michael, 10
GeBauer, Judy, 116
Geboe, Ben, 156
Geerdes, Sherri, 52
Gee, Shirley, 74
Geffen, Susan, 139
Gegenhuber, Paul, 10
Gehring, Kristen, 21
Geiger, Mary Louise, 4, 8, 28, 39, 60, 73, 98, 116, 119, 121, 156, 167
Geiser, Janie, 96
Geist, Gretel, 28
Geither, Mike, 41
Gelbart, Larry, 22, 79, 129, 175
Geld, Gary, 148
Geley, Linda, 161
Geller, Keith, 27

Gellman, Michael J., 111
Gelman, Alexander, 53
Gelzer, Terri, 41
Genet, Jean, 41
Gennaro, Liza, 61, 66, 80, 105, 159
Gennaro, Michael, 56
Gentry, Jon, 34, 35
Gentry, Judith L., 28
Geoghan, Jim, 104, 105, 172
George, Bridget, 163
George, George W., 129
George, Hal, 76
George, Richard R., 52
George, William, 163
Gerbhardt, Michael, 129
Gerckens, Stephanie R., 127
Gerety, Peter, 164
Gergel, John, 95
Gershman, Caryl, 101
Gershwin, George, 15, 28, 40, 86, 127
Gershwin, Ira, 15, 28, 40, 86, 127
Gerson, Elliot F., 66
Gersten, Alexandra, 147
Gersten, Bernard, 80
Geseck, Rosemary, 163
Gesner, Clark, 46
Gessler, Phyllis, 168
Getty, Robert, 29
Getz, S. Michael, 146
Giaimo, Kathryn M., 152
Giammona, Ted C., 43
Giancarlo, James, 142
Gianfrancesco, Edward, 31
Giannelli, Christina, 7, 8, 47
Giannitti, Michael, 58, 97, 98, 164
Giannunzio, Mitch, 124
Giardina, Anthony, 96
Gibboney, Mary, 29
Gibbs, Andrea, 75
Gibson, Anne, 165, 166
Gibson, John J., 109
Gibson, Neal, 177
Gibson, William, 13, 22, 28, 30, 65, 85, 106
Gifford, Emmy, 52
Giguere, Edi, 75
Gilbert, Christephor, 145
Gilbert, Edward, 69, 82, 119, 120
Gilbert, Ilsa, 157
Gilbert, Ronnie, 24, 91
Gilbert, Willie, 133, 149
Gilbert, W.S., 118
Gilb, Melinda, 4
Gildan, Laurie, 123
Gildin, Leon, 96
Gilleland, Beth, 71
Gillespie, John K., 111
Gillette, Greg, 126
Gilliam, Michael, 98
Gillig, Kathleen B., 110
Gilman, David, 147
Gilman, Mark S., 91
Gilmer, Robert N., 106, 107
Gilpin, Thomas, 156
Gilroy, Frank D., 108
Ginsberg, Jeff, 93, 94
Ginsberg, Marsha, 78, 85
Ginty, James, 10
Giomi, Rita, 53, 64, 115, 136

Giordano, Tony, 42, 124, 164
Giovanni, Greg, 168
Gipson, David, 83, 166
Girardi, Guido, 43
Giraudoux, Jean, 171
Giron, Arthur, 86
Gisondi, John, 12
Gisselman, Gary, 2, 33, 34, 71
Gjelsteen, Karen, 7, 53, 74
Gladden, Dean R., 40
Gladwell, Tom, 157
Glaser, John, 40, 156
Glasser, D. Scott, 83, 90
Glass, Joanna M., 43, 171
Glassman, Seth, 91
Glass, Philip, 11, 48, 82
Glass, Ted, 173
Glaze, Chris, 44
Glazer, Amy, 160
Glazer, Julie, 57
Glazer, Peter, 24, 61, 89, 135, 150
Glazier, Peter, 59
Glenn, Gregory, 97
Glenn, John, 158
Glenny, Michael, 113, 160
Glick, Donna, 98
Glover, Frederic, 107
Glowacki, Janusz, 15
Goecke, Tim, 143
Goethe, 79
Goetsch, David, 147
Goetzinger, Laurel Eldredge, 72
Goetz, Ruth, 176
Goetz, Sariva, 58
Goezler, Carolyn, 71
Goggin, Dan, 22, 37, 66, 81, 83, 99, 133, 142, 175, 177
Goheen, Douglas-Scott, 41
Going, John, 106, 119, 128, 129, 149, 150, 171
Goldberg, Gary, 156, 157
Goldberg, Jonathan, 174
Goldberg, Marc S., 33
Goldberg, Moses, 26, 144, 145
Golden, Andre, 99
Golden, John, 95
Goldhirsch, Sheri M., 176
Goldman, Alan I., 74
Goldman, A.E.O., 169
Goldman, James, 43, 99, 141, 168
Goldman, William, 124, 125
Goldoni, Carlo, 11, 32, 67, 134, 177
Goldray, Martin, 11
Goldsmith, Oliver, 16
Goldstein, David, 167
Goldstein, David Ira, 2, 16
Goldstein, Jess, 15, 23, 25, 32, 37, 40, 61, 66, 80, 82, 85, 87, 116, 117, 122, 131, 170, 175
Goldstein, Kenneth F., 33
Goldstein, Robert, 30
Goldstone, Bob, 161
Goldstone, Patricia, 107
Gold, Ezra, 71
Golub, Peter, 11
Gombrowicz, Witold, 104
Gomez, Marga, 100
Gomez, Marta, 152
Gonzales, Manuel B., 128
Gonzales, Michael, 105

Gonzalez, Amy, 52, 160
Gonzalez, Gloria, 128
Gonzalez-Jaen, Antonio, 72
Gonzalez, Jose Cruz, 25
Gonzalez, Joseph Julian, 52
Gooch, Bruce, 171
Goodchild, Tim, 57
Goode, James, 28
Goodhart, Peter, 139
Goodman, Jane, 145
Goodman, Mark R., 59
Goodman, Rob, 55
Goodman, Robyn, 137
Goodrich, Bruce, 142
Goodrich, Joe, 142
Good, Rick, 84
Goodwin, Rick, 135
Gordon, David, 48
Gordon, David P., 33, 117
Gordon, Laura, 10, 90
Gordon, Liz, 164
Gordon, Marvin, 161
Gordon, Michael, 96
Gordon, Michael-David, 161
Gordon, Ricky Ian, 11
Gordon, Seth, 156
Gordon, Stuart, 110, 166
Gordon, Troy, 7
Gorey, Edward, 11, 169
Gorman, Anna, 83
Gorman, Michael, 153
Gorostiza, Felipe, 127, 128
Gorton, Rob, 45, 46, 125, 175
Gorzelnik, Christopher, 49
Gorzycki, Anthony, 114
Goss, Bick, 135
Goss, Clay, 142
Gosse, Edmund, 11
Gossman, Kathleen, 94
Goss, Pamela, 120
Gottlieb, Jon, 25, 87
Gottlieb, Peter, 44, 95
Gott, Rick, 133
Gottschalk, Emily, 116
Gould, Ellen, 175
Gould, Erica, 65
Gould, Tom, 19, 31, 147
Gould, Valerie Zisser, 169
Goulet, Bill, 153
Gozzi, Carlo, 102
Grabowski, Christopher, 102
Grace, Charles, 121
Grace, Jessica, 39
Gracieux, Vincent, 77, 154, 155, 175
Graczyk, Ed, 62
Graese, Judy, 59
Graham, Bill, Jr., 105, 106
Graham, Billy, 157
Graham, Bruce, 16, 116, 117, 124
Grahame, Kenneth, 8, 22, 26, 30, 34, 67, 158
Graham, Ellen, 134
Graham, John D., 168
Graham, R.H., 162
Graham, Stephen, 101
Graham, William H., 105
Granata, Dona, 87, 105, 168
Graneto, Phillip A., 14, 114, 116
Granger, Christopher A., 147
Grant, Adam, 102

Grant, Bill, 45
Grant, Byron, 128
Grant, David Marshall, 127
Grantham, Ken, 8
Grant, Mitch, 134
Grant, William H., III, 6, 90, 91, 117, 149, 150
Gratch, Susan, 43
Gratz, Chib, 58, 72
Graver, Steven F., 75
Gray, Acia, 81
Gray, Amlin, 31, 91, 95, 96, 149
Gray, Brenda, 176, 177
Gray, Gordon, 98
Gray, Janet, 99
Gray, John, 8, 36, 129, 143
Gray, Kathy, 17
Gray, Richard, 64, 151
Gray, Simon, 4, 25, 66
Grayson, Vicki, 41
Gray, Spalding, 173
Greanier, Mary-Ann, 43
Green, Allen, 138
Green, Benny, 135
Greenberg, Albert, 19, 20
Greenberg, Charles, 167
Greenberg, Richard, 69, 85, 86, 143, 150, 164
Greenberg, Rob, 78, 125
Greenberg, Sue, 72
Greenblatt, Richard, 41
Green, Dennis, 75
Greene, Fred, 113
Greene, Gordon C., 54
Greene, Mildred, 163
Greenfield, Elana, 95, 96
Greenfield, Haze, 75
Green, Frank, 41
Greenhill, Mitchell, 98, 126, 171
Greenman, Stuart, 11
Greenspan, David, 100
Greenwald, Robert, 79
Greenwood, Jane, 80, 82, 86, 87, 122, 131, 159, 171
Gregg, Susan, 128, 129
Gregg, William, 159
Gregory, Dawna, 29, 83, 90, 91
Gregory, Helen, 60
Greif, Michael, 5, 32, 66, 77, 100, 137, 171
Greiss, Terry, 74
Gress, Jeff, 36, 54, 55
Gribbin, Michael, 112
Griffeth, Wm. T., 94
Griffin, Brent, 101
Griffin, Carmen, 97
Griffin, Donald, 72
Griffin, Sue, 159
Griffin, Tom, 47, 69, 93, 129
Griffith, Charles, 12, 13, 120
Griffith, Linda, 171
Griffiths, Trevor, 44
Grimaldi, Dennis, 76
Grimm, The Brothers, 26, 29, 30, 52, 53, 154, 161
Grissom, Doug, 143
Griswold, Christine, 5
Griswold, Mary, 8, 44, 45, 94
Grodin, Charles, 167
Grodsky, Roger, 175

Grody, Jeremy, 32, 122
Gromada, John, 7, 25, 32, 37, 49, 54, 77, 82, 100, 102, 116, 117, 122
Gronk, 134
Grooms, Red, 48
Grose, Andrew, 65
Grossman, Deborah, 143
Grossman, Larry, 42
Gross, Marilyn, 140
Gross, Patricia Dolan, 42
Grote, Susan Archibald, 160
Grove, Barry, 85
Grube, Mike, 144, 145
Gruenewald, Thomas, 113
Grumbly, Frances, 156
Grumer, Michael, 76
Grusby, Marty, 124
Grynheim, Joel, 72
Gryska, Edward J., 133, 134
Gsell, Guy, 156
Guaraldi, Mary G., 92, 129, 165
Guare, John, 31, 36, 40, 45, 80, 81, 129
Guarna, Ray, 79
Gudahl, Kevin, 139
Gudenius, Carl F., 106
Guenther, Jim, 34
Guerrera, Ana Martinez, 52
Guess, Andi, 18
Guisinger, Nathan, 83, 157
Gulyas, Shawn, 130
Gunderson, Steve, 4
Gunn Brothers, 177
Guptill, Chris, 37
Guralnick, Judi, 168
Gural, Ron, 161
Gurisik, Selcuk, 78
Gurney, A.R., Jr., 6, 9, 12, 19, 22, 25, 36, 37, 49, 58, 65, 69, 72, 92, 95, 98, 99, 105, 112, 113, 118, 119, 120, 122, 123, 134, 146, 149, 150, 151, 177
Guthrie, Ron, 6, 95
Guthrie, Tyrone, 64
Guthrie, Woody, 24, 61, 89, 135
Gutierrez, Carole, 32
Gutierrez, Gerald, 61, 80, 131
Gutierrez, Raymond, 49
Gutwillig, Stephen, 43
Guyer, Murphy, 114
Guy, Rosa, 45, 46, 160
Guzik, Jeff, 97, 114, 138, 150, 163
Gwinup, Martin B., 114

H

Haaga, Kathy, 120
Haas, Karl E., 4
Haas, Kate, 151
Haatainen, Christina, 77, 105
Habeger, Tim, 3, 159
Haben, Andy, 110
Haber, Bob, 37
Hackady, Hal, 37
Hacker, Linda, 40, 61, 62
Hacker, Seymour, 156
Hacking, Wes, 142, 168
Hackler, Karen Yamamoto, 67

Hadden, John, 139
Haddow, Jeffrey, 51
Hagar, David M., 132
Hager, Mark, 140
Hahn, Jessica, 94
Hailey, Elizabeth Forsythe, 168
Hailey, John Carter, 159
Haile, Evans, 40
Haimes, Todd, 131
Haines, Julia, 157
Hale, Pamela, 22
Hallas, Brian, 71, 78, 118, 167
Halleck, Dan, 26
Halley, Ben Jr., 143
Halligan-Donahue, Ann, 18
Hall, Adrian, 8, 11, 47, 100, 137, 164
Hall, Andrew, 65
Hall, Bernard, 148
Hall, Bob, 4, 95, 123
Hall, Carol, 62, 80, 123
Hall, Charlene, 2, 53
Hall, Daniel C., 65
Hall, Davis, 37, 126
Hall, Jeffrey A., 152
Hall, Michael, 66
Hall, Oakley, III, 30
Hall, Peter, 55, 80
Hall, Randy, 18, 29, 37
Hall, Tom, 104
Hall, Wilton E., Jr., 106
Hally, Martha, 31, 47, 92, 125, 161
Halman, Talat, 78
Hamburger, Anne, 53, 54
Hamburger, Richard, 47, 125
Hamer, Tom, 83
Hamilton, Del, 137, 138, 163
Hamilton, Edie, 123
Hamilton, Lionel, 68
Hamilton, Rob, 32, 172
Hamilton, Stephen, 23
Hamilton, Virginia, 103
Hamilton, William, 105
Hamlin, Michael, 129
Hammack, Warren, 68, 69
Hammerstein, James, 82
Hammerstein, Oscar, II, 5, 9, 37, 46, 47, 86, 95, 112, 120, 129, 158
Hammer, Joel, 76
Hammer, W.J.E., 114
Hammond, David, 121
Hammond, Paul, 143
Hammond, Thomas W., 158
Hammond, Wendy, 96
Hampton, Christopher, 4, 38, 47, 78, 82, 160
Hampton, Mark, 23
Hamrick, Hugh, 79, 156
Hanak, Christine, 168
Hancock, Andrew, 97
Handel, Beatrice, 47
Handel, Rob, 41
Handler, Evan, 137
Handley, Mark, 58
Handman, Wynn, 57, 148, 163
Hanes, Mary, 79
Haney, Anthony J., 160
Haney, Michael, 43
Hanff, Helene, 90
Hankin, Michael, 81

INDEX OF NAMES

Hanley, William, 45, 101
Hanna, Christopher, 167
Hannah, Jeroy, 159, 163
Hannah, Michael, 9
Hanreddy, Joseph, 83, 90, 91
Hansberry, Lorraine, 6, 91, 114, 133
Hansen, Hugh, 143
Hansen, Mary Ann, 172
Hansen, Thomas E., 86
Hanson, Bruce J., 115
Hanson, David, 96
Hanson, Hugh, 67
Hanson, Jeff, 160
Hanson, Kim, 168
Hanson, Les, 169
Hanzak, Hamsa, 71
Harburg, E.Y., 101, 112
Harding, Jerry, 157
Hardison, O.B., 141
Hardman, Chris, 13, 14
Hardstark, Michael, 75
Hardwick, Mark, 18, 46, 56, 59, 89, 98, 120, 129, 134, 150, 151, 168
Hardy, John, 22
Hardy, Peter, 107
Hard, Randi Collins, 32
Hare, David, 104
Harelik, Mark, 36, 49, 105, 112, 113, 123, 133, 149, 150, 159, 168
Hare, Mary Alyce, 17
Hargis, David, 123
Haring-Smith, Tori, 164
Harkey, Jerry, 16
Harley, Margot, 2
Harling, Robert, 46, 95, 174
Harman, Barry, 70, 99
Harman, Leonard, 46, 47
Harmon, Joan, 163
Harmon, Peggy, 37, 125
Harmon, Richard, 12, 97
Harness, Theo, 3
Harnick, Jay, 160, 161
Harnick, Sheldon, 15, 28, 29, 81, 89, 131, 152
Harper, Sherry, 158
Harper, William, 93
Harps, Sam, 156
Harriday, Sonja, 154
Harrington, Laura, 54, 66, 96
Harrington, Margaret, 156
Harris, Albert, 129
Harris, Albert J., 38, 39
Harris, Ann, 78, 79
Harris, Aurand, 6, 22, 72
Harris, Bill, 97, 148
Harris, Frederic, 78
Harris, Gary, 73
Harris, James Berton, 165
Harris, Jeanette, 125
Harris, Jed Allen, 38
Harris, Joel Chandler, 30
Harris, John, 76, 177
Harris, Laird, 63
Harris, Lee, 115
Harris, Mark, 79
Harris, Mary Lou, 78
Harris, Michael Walter, 78
Harris, Nick, 21, 95
Harrison, Christopher, 6

Harrison, Jean, 117
Harrison, Llewellyn, 18
Harrison, Margaret Keyes, 46
Harrison, Peter, 36, 45, 46, 49, 72, 117, 119, 129, 149, 161, 170, 171
Harrison, Tony, 116
Harris Sisters, The, 79
Harris, Patdro, 76
Harris, Richard, 149
Harrod, Amy, 165
Harron, Donald, 46
Harrsch, Anna, 152
Harsini, Manucher, 157
Hart, Chris, 169
Hart, Dan, 134
Hart, Lorenz, 69, 129
Hartman, Lynne M., 158
Hart, Marya, 62
Hart, Moss, 28, 29, 40, 63, 64, 69, 95, 143, 169
Hartswick, Maxine, 171
Hartwell, Peter, 141, 147
Hartzell, Linda, 135, 136
Harvey, Cameron, 165
Harvey, Peter C., 168
Harwood, Ronald, 47, 160
Hase, Michael K., 67
Hase, Thomas C., 8, 78, 83, 91, 95, 118
Haskell, Molly, 173
Hassen, John, 109
Hass, Karl, 119
Hasson, Albert, 84
Hastings, Edward, 9
Hastings, John, 42, 61
Hatcher, Chuck, 65
Hatcher, Jeffrey, 36, 50, 107
Hatcher, Samuel J., 145
Hauptman, William, 6, 46, 112, 152
Haupt, Paulette, 107
Hausch, Mary, 66, 67
Havard, Bernard, 168
Havard, Celine, 168
Havel, Vaclav, 38, 75
Havens, Anduin R., 171
Haviland, Sophie, 108
Hawdon, Robin, 42, 168
Hawk, Camilla, 139
Hawker, Paul William, 104
Hawkins, A. James, 30
Hawley, David, 62
Hawthorne, Nathaniel, 139
Hayashi, Marc, 160
Hayes, Elliott, 51, 70
Haynes, Carol, 141, 159
Haynes, C.E., 37
Hay, Richard L., 50, 105, 109, 110
Hays, Stephen E., 146
Hayter, Pearl, 21
Hazlett, Laura, 84, 86
Head, David, 162
Head, Edith, 127
Healey, Peg, 102
Healy, Bart, 18, 29
Hearne, Jan, 130
Heath, Robin, 15, 142, 143
Hebert, Julie, 134, 138
Hebert-Slater, Marilee, 3
Hecht, Ben, 8, 43
Hedges, John, 55

Hedley, Robert, 117
Hedstrom, Cynthia, 173
Heelan, Kevin, 164
Heeley, Desmond, 34
Heffernan, Maureen, 58, 119
Heibert, Frank, 138
Heijermans, Herman, 64
Heijermans-Houwink, Caroline, 64
Heimer, Tony, 49
Heine, Kate, 29
Heisler, Richie, 157
Heitman, Patricia, 102
Heligas, Kelly, 32
Heller, Annie, 43
Hellesen, Richard, 124, 133
Hellman, Lillian, 6, 12, 69, 109, 112, 121, 135
Hellyer, Paul, 85
Helton, Ingrid, 134
Hempel, Cynthia, 41
Hench, Richard, 169
Henderson, Criss, 139
Henderson, David, 12
Henderson-Holmes, Safiya, 97
Henderson, Kate, 91
Henderson, Rodger, 27
Henderson, Stephen McKinley, 148
Henderson, William, 5
Henery, Keith, 31, 146
Henion, Reid, 89
Henkel, Clare, 27, 105
Henley, Beth, 10, 12, 27, 32, 99, 133, 151, 158
Hennessey, Keith, 7
Henry, Chad, 7, 50, 136, 151
Henry, Markas, 78
Henry, O., 4, 58, 72, 80, 113
Henry, Patrick, 57
Henry, Ruth Ammons, 26
Hensley, Charlie, 18, 167, 168
Hensley, Nancy Turner, 173
Hensley, Todd, 94, 95, 166
Henson, Lance, 84
Henson, Richard, 109
Henton, Donnell A., 28
Herbert, Lettie, 57
Herbert, Ned, 51
Herbert, Victor, 158
Herman, Danny, 82
Herman, Ian, 137
Herman, Nate, 110, 111
Hernandez, Fran, 51
Hernandez, Riccardo, 11, 47, 73, 175
Herochik, John, 58
Herrick, Jack, 153
Herring, J. Daniel, 145
Herring, Linda, 96
Herrington, Phil L., 16
Herrmann, Keith, 70, 99
Herschler, Andrea, 62
Herskovits, David, 78
Hess, Ivan, 49
Hessler, John, 113
Hewitt, Frankie, 56
Hewitt, Kenneth R. Jr., 51
Heydenburg, Patrick, 75
Hickey, Michael, 29
Hicklin, Walker, 7, 37, 117, 143,

144
Hickman, Steve, 91
Hickok, Molly, 74
Hickox, A.C., 27, 167
Hickox, Phillip Jay, 21, 95
Hicks, Israel, 50
Hicks, Munson, 99
Hicks, Paul Def., 117
Hicks, Yslan, 18, 61
Higgins, Frank, 170
Higgins, H. Scott, 100
Higgins, Joel, 58
Higgins, Paul, 146
Hightower, Tina, 3
Highway, Tomson, 115
Hildebrant, Rick, 13
Hilferty, Susan, 8, 24, 31, 60, 61, 64, 77, 85, 86, 137
Hill, Cindy, 163
Hill, Eric, 146
Hill, Gary Leon, 85
Hillgartner, Malcolm, 128, 129
Hill, Greg, 52
Hilliard, Vickie, 84
Hill, Jane, 49
Hill, Jeff, 146
Hill, Kelly, 142, 143
Hill, Tamara, 163
Hillyard, Sylvia, 159
Hilton, Wayne, 22
Himes, Ronald J., 148, 150
Hinchcliffe, Stephen F. Jr., 87
Hines, Kim, 71, 103
Hines, Melissa, 53
Hinton, S.E., 55
Hiraki, Hisako, 78
Hirschl, Barbara, 85
Hirson, David, 109, 143
Hitchcock, Jane Stanton, 139
Hitler, Adolf, 7
Hochhauser, Jeff, 76
Hochoy, David, 72
Hochstedler, Darren, 67
Hochstine, Dan, 45
Hodgin, Jere Lee, 89
Hoeflich, Randye, 143
Hoeger, Mark, 52
Hoehler, Richard, 157
Hoelscher, Erica, 111
Hoepner, Cara, 104
Hoey, John Stephen, 14, 168
Hoffman, Constance, 79, 97
Hoffman, David J., 135
Hoffman, E.T.A., 121, 128
Hoffmann, David, 140
Hoffman, S. Mark, 138
Hofsiss, Jack, 40, 58, 86, 88
Hogan, Abby, 112
Hogan, Tim, 112
Hogle, Richard, 2, 23
Hogya, Giles, 75
Hohanshelt, Laura, 17
Hoiby, Lee, 9, 39, 47, 50
Holcombe, Michael, 109, 110
Holden, Joan, 9, 24, 41
Holden, Sarah J., 127
Holden, Vicki, 19
Holder, Donald, 19, 24, 25, 47, 57, 58, 72, 82, 85, 87, 113, 119, 122, 136, 137, 150, 167

Holder, Laurence, 57, 148, 157, 163
Holdgrive, David, 31, 36, 161
Holgate, Danny, 25, 77, 88
Hollaender, Friedrich, 104
Hollaender, Melodie, 104
Holland, Dr. Endesha Ida Mae, 8, 13, 35, 67, 71, 74, 105, 168
Hollis, Stephen, 6, 36, 99
Hollman, Ray, 45
Holloman, Fredrick, 155
Hollywood, Danielle, 161
Holmes, Bob, 76
Holmes, David, 140
Holmes, Emmelle, 134
Holmes, Rupert, 59, 66, 94
Holmes, Vance, 34
Holm, John Cecil, 58
Holmond, Charles, 55
Holms, John Pynchon, 31, 96, 125
Holten, Michael, 67, 136, 137
Holt, Will, 148
Holtz, Andrew F., 37
Holtzman, Jonathan, 58
Holtzman, Willy, 96
Holzman, Dean, 71
Homer, 109, 163, 171
Hook, Cora, 157
Hooker, Brian, 9, 128, 165
Hooper, Jeff, 4, 83, 84
Hooper, Ruth, 18
Hoover, Richard, 31, 105, 122
Hoover, Ted, 107
Hopkins, John, 79
Hopkins, Mark, 133
Hopkins, Richard, 56, 160
Hopper, Elizabeth Weiss, 158
Hopper, Gary C., 158
Hormann, Nicholas, 72
Horne, Michael, 158, 159
Horner, John, 38, 39, 46
Horner, Paul, 86
Horovitz, Israel, 79, 160
Horowitz, Jeffrey, 155, 156
Horsley, Michael, 30, 37
Horst, Amy, 55
Horvath, Odon von, 4
Horvitz, Wayne, 64
Horwith, Shirley, 114
Horwitz, Murray, 8, 13, 16, 25, 36, 78, 112, 113, 167, 176
Hoskins, Jim, 60
Hotchner, Kathy, 13
Hotchner, Steve, 13
Hough, Lawrence A., 141
Houghton, Ruth, 65
Hould-Ward, Ann, 57, 66, 105, 156
Houseman, John, 2
House, Ron, 104
Housman, Arthur L., 121
Houston, Dianne, 76
Houston, Mark, 18, 67, 121, 165, 176
Houston, Velina Hasu, 126, 150
Houvardas, Yannis, 78
Howard, Andrew, 75, 159
Howard, Ed, 13, 29, 91, 123, 134
Howard, Elizabeth, 120
Howard, Mel, 42
Howard, Richard, 64
Howe, James, 44

Howell, Greg, 42
Howe, Tina, 137
Howland, Gerard, 9, 144
Hoyes, R. Stephen, 87
Hoyle, Geoff, 24
Hsieh, Jerry, 157
Huang, Helen Q., 106, 150
Hubbard, Alison, 161
Hubert, Jerry, 97
Huckaby, William, 15
Huddle, Elizabeth, 73, 74
Huddleston, Will, 29, 30
Hudson, Bill, 115
Hudson, Clarissa, 115
Hudson, Denise, 175
Hudson, Ken, 81
Hudson, Richard, 60
Hudson, Roy R., 26
Huff, Keith, 173
Huffman, Eric, 32, 147
Huff, Walter, 3
Hughes, Allen Lee, 2, 15, 64, 66, 74, 87, 115, 129, 137
Hughes, Douglas, 50, 64, 72, 77, 122, 136, 137
Hughes, Dusty, 147
Hughes, Langston, 100, 114
Hughes, Mark, 17, 18, 59, 159
Hugill, J. Randall, 62
Hull, Charles, 160
Hume, Michael J., 31
Humperdinck, Engelbert, 161
Hundley, C.L., 39, 40, 150
Hunkins, Lee, 109
Hunt, Catherine Meacham, 134, 136
Hunter, Deborah, 3
Hunter, Ed, 160
Hunter, Harold J., 130
Hunter, Timothy, 88
Hunt, Gordon, 75, 171
Huntington, Burr, 51
Hunt, Jeff, 85, 86, 133
Hunt, Kathy, 64
Hunt, Mame, 84, 85
Hunt, Margaret, 166
Hunt, Pamela, 42, 91, 119, 128, 129
Hunt, Peter, 170, 171
Hunt, Sam, 68, 69
Huppe, Alex, 169
Hupp, Robert, 74, 75
Hurlbut, Bruce, 52
Hurley, Barbara, 156
Hurst, Gregory S., 58
Hurston, Zora Neale, 24, 40, 47, 61, 72, 76, 87, 110, 116, 134, 137, 150
Hurt, Morrigan, 9, 10
Hurwitz, Nathan, 38, 119
Huszti, Douglas, 171
Hutchinson, T. Kay, 150
Hutchins, Jonathan R., 152
Hutchins, Ron J., 18
Hutchison, Patrick, 3, 21
Hwang, David Henry, 4, 16, 65, 66, 67, 91, 120, 123, 129, 136, 159, 160, 172
Hwong, Lucia, 123
Hyde, William York, 106
Hyung-O, Choi, 78

I

Iacovelli, John, 47, 105, 117, 143, 144
Iams, Sarah, 168, 171
Iazzetti, Marcello, 41
Ibsen, Henrik, 8, 11, 16, 19, 24, 31, 47, 50, 59, 82, 98, 105, 111, 115, 116, 125, 130, 135, 136, 140, 171
Iddings, Kyle, 63
Imani, 97, 173
Imburgia, John, 166
Inasy, J. Kent, 43
Inawat, Ebenezer, 111
Ingalls, James F., 9, 11, 24, 32, 47, 60, 61, 64, 80, 147, 164, 168
Inge, William, 4, 113, 114, 164
Ingham, Rosemary, 165, 173
Ingram, David, 114
Ingram, Martha Rivers, 151
Ing, Wendell, 67
Insull, Sigrid, 16, 104
Intraub, Neil, 91
Introna, Nino D., 30
Ionesco, Eugene, 29, 162
Irvine, Kate, 84
Irvine, Perry, 160
Irving Productions, 13
Irving, Washington, 18, 95
Irvin, Charles, 46
Irwin, Bill, 5
Irwin, Tom, 147
Isaacs, Jerry, 107
Isackes, Richard, 6, 80, 165
Isbell, Anthony, 120, 121
Isham, Christine D., 38
Isherwood, Christopher, 123
Israel, Robert, 11
Ito, Genji, 78, 79
Ivanov, Alexander, 30
Ivey, Rachel V., 15
Iwasaki, Hiroshi, 14, 139, 171

J

Jablonski, Carl, 36
Jack, Angel, 78
Jacker, Corinne, 119
Jack, John, 13
Jackness, Andrew, 36, 137, 141, 173
Jackoway, Jon, 121
Jackson, Brian Keith, 156, 157
Jackson, C. Bernard, 25
Jackson, Judith Alexa, 79
Jackson, Lyle, 71
Jackson, Marsha A., 76
Jackson, Nagle, 4, 50, 136, 149
Jackson, Randal, 1
Jackson-Smith, Caroline, 41
Jackson, Suzanne, 103, 104, 160
Jacob, Abe, 88
Jacob, Lou, 75
Jacobs, Douglas, 134
Jacobs, Jim, 7, 37, 142, 152
Jacobs, Liz, 139
Jacobson, Kenneth, 76, 106
Jacques, David Martin, 47
Jaffee, Claudia, 169

Jaffery, Jason, 41
Jagim, Jay Michael, 7, 8
Jakes, John, 99
James, Henry, 135, 138, 139
James, Julie, 67
James, Michael, 123
James, Toni-Leslie, 4, 11, 24, 32, 36, 45, 46, 69, 87, 100
Jampolis, Neil Peter, 8, 42, 47, 61, 105
Janas, Mark, 18, 66
Janick, Lynn, 98
Jankell, Alice, 96, 171
Janklow, Linda Leroy, 80
Janosko, Linda, 28
Jared, Robert, 91, 110, 119
Jarrett, G. Jane, 144
Jarrett, Jack, 111
Jarrett, Stephen, 143
Jarvis, Brett, 13
Jarvis, Martin, 79
Jarvis, Michelle, 72
Jasien, Deborah, 58
Jay, Isla, 78
Jeffcoat, A. E., 85
Jeffe, Douglas, 79
Jeffreys, Stephen, 121, 170
Jeffries, Chris, 7
Jeffries, Lynn, 43
Jelavich, Peter, 38, 39
Jemilo, Donna, 69
Jendresen, Erik, 12
Jenkin, Len, 34, 39, 136, 162
Jenkins, Alice A., 145
Jenkins, Bill, 158
Jenkins, David, 40, 58, 59, 80, 88, 131, 168, 173
Jenkins, Elizabeth, 132
Jenkins-Evans, Hollis, 4
Jenkins, Martin, 79
Jenkins, Paulie, 24, 98, 143
Jenkins, Richard, 163, 164
Jenkins, Ron, 139
Jenkins, Terrance, 176
Jenkins, Thom, 68
Jenks, Barbara, 150
Jennings, Eric, 138
Jennings, James, 156
Jennings, Katherine, 15
Jennings, Richard, 38
Jensen, Howard, 165
Jensen, John, 92, 128
Jensen, Julie, 89, 143
Jenson, Katie, 115
Jenyon, Elizabeth, 174
Jessup, Molly, 44, 92
Jesurun, John, 78, 79
Jevnikar, Jana, 95
Jewel-Ann Creations, 70
Jewkes, Richard, 133, 134
Jheri, 86
Jiler, John, 107, 122
John, Mary, 90
Johns, Ernest, 109
Johns, Janet, 52
Johnson, Alan, 48, 86
Johnson, Art, 76
Johnson, Bill, 99
Johnson, Chris, 62
Johnson, Cindy Lou, 86, 98, 168

INDEX OF NAMES

Johnson, Crockett, 161
Johnson, Douglas, 8
Johnson, Grey, 89
Johnson-Hood, Susan, 34
Johnson, Jack, 171
Johnson, James, 174
Johnson, Jan, 161
Johnson, Jillian, 66
Johnson, Joanne, 126
Johnson, Ken, 81, 90
Johnson, Kendra, 38
Johnson, Kenneth, 45
Johnson, Mark, 99
Johnson, Marsha, 106
Johnson, Michael, 133
Johnson, Monica, 11
Johnson, Myron, 34, 71
Johnson, Orville, 52
Johnson, Sandee, 18, 67, 121, 176
Johnson, Servalia, 52
Johnson, Shellie K., 152
Johnson, Stacie, 98
Johnson, Stephanie, 103, 109, 160, 173
Johnson, Terry, 150
Johnson, Tom, 120
Johnson, Virgil C., 53
Johnson, Virginia, 46
Johnston, Bob, 76
Johnston, Brian, 8, 31
Johre, Gro, 35
Johson, Robert, 97
Joiner, Burnham, 27
Jones, Andrew, 30
Jones, Barney, 84, 85
Jones, Bernard, 123
Jones, Bob Devin, 114, 120
Jones, Brian, 134
Jones, B.J., 94
Jones, Charles, 94, 95, 170
Jones, Christine, 11, 66, 100, 111, 171
Jones, Dawn Renee, 45
Jones, Don, 62, 152
Jones, Douglas, 158
Jones, Eleanor Brodie, 95
Jones, Ellen, 166
Jones, Elroyce, 107
Jones, Felicity, 77, 154, 155, 175
Jones, Frank, 21
Jones, Jeff A.R., 120, 121
Jones, Jeffrey M., 38, 96
Jones, Jessie, 37, 120, 137
Jones, LeRoi, 27, 114
Jones, Martin, 159
Jones, Nathan, 97
Jones, Paul, 38
Jones, Rhodessa, 78
Jones, Richard, 11, 100
Jones, Robert A., 151
Jones, Seitu Ken, 114
Jones, Stephen Mack, 51
Jones, Steve, 120
Jones, Suzanne Clement, 124
Jones, Syl, 93, 114
Jones, Thomas Cadwaleder, 145
Jones, Thomas W., II, 72, 76, 97, 114, 134, 150, 163
Jones, Tom, 31, 43, 89, 92, 119
Jones, Walton, 46, 119, 128, 135, 159, 175
Jonson, Ben, 24
Jordan, Arthur D., 148
Jordan, Clarence, 49, 129
Jordan, Dale F., 22, 128, 129
Jordan, Louis, 57
Jorgenson, Mary Ann, 62
Jorissen, Robert, 34
Jory, Jon, 3, 4, 81
Joselovitz, Ernest, 143
Joseph, Chief (Nez Perce), 7
Joseph, Stephen, 148
Joslin, Steve, 163
Jost, Lawrence J., 96
Journey, Edward, 26
Joyce, Brian, 102, 103
Joyce, Robert, 153
Joyce, Tom, 139
Joy, James Leonard, 25, 35, 36, 40, 61, 64, 69
Joy, Judy E., 162
Jozefiak, Susan, 67
Jucha, Brian, 4
Juengling, Dietrich F., 104
Julien, Ryan, 62
Jung, Philipp, 24, 49, 61, 117, 135, 143
Jurglanis, Marla, 14, 33, 48, 49, 58, 114, 159
Justesen, Gary, 134
Justice, John B., 129
Justice, Vicki, 111
Justin, David, 10

K

Kacir, Marylynn, 51
Kaczorowski, Peter, 31, 32, 37, 40, 66, 69, 82, 85, 86, 88, 100, 131, 149
Kading, Charles, 6
Kaelin, Stephen A., 28
Kafka, Franz, 103
Kahn, Michael, 88, 141
Kahn, Si, 24, 62, 91
Kaikkonen, Gus, 28
Kaiserman, Ron, 10
Kaiser, Charles R., 17
Kaiser, Jim, 50
Kaiser, Robert, 7
Kakuno, Kyle, 67
Kalan, Sandy, 46, 47
Kalas, Janet, 31, 32, 46, 47, 57, 86, 122, 136, 175, 176
Kalbfleisch, Jon, 141
Kalcheim, Lee, 147
Kaletta, Andrew, 41
Kalfin, Robert, 42
Kalinski, Richard, 21
Kallok, Peter, 146
Kalmar, Bert, 61
Kammer, Karen, 101
Kander, John, 91, 123
Kanegson, Andras, 157
Kane, John, 101, 112
Kanin, Garson, 4, 86
Kanshansky, Larry, 119
Kapilow, Robert, 11, 173
Kaplan, Howard Tsvi, 19, 22, 152, 159
Kaplan, Steve, 161
Kaplan, Warren, 21
Karanth, Prema, 78
Kareishi, Hanif, 141
Karimah, 46
Karimi-Hakak, M., 156
Karkosh, Clayton, 98
Karoff, Jeffrey, 150
Karp, Steve, 146, 147
Karuschak, Sandra, 44
Karvonides-Dushenko, Chrisi, 61
Kasbaum, Scott, 145
Kase, Judith Baker, 22
Kaskel, Stephanie, 8, 155
Kassinoir, Chico, 78
Kat, Huseyn, 78
Katims, Jason, 33
Katkowsky, Robert, 27, 28, 51
Kattelman, Beth, 106
Katz, Gail, 22
Katz, Jonathan Ned, 21
Katz, Leon, 5
Katz, Natasha, 8, 11, 19, 45, 66, 85, 86, 100, 131, 137, 164
Katz, Nicole, 79
Katz, Paul, 42
Kauffman, Carlotta, 67
Kauffman, John, 67
Kauffman, Marta, 61, 161
Kaufman, George S., 9, 15, 28, 29, 40, 61, 63, 64, 69, 95, 127, 143, 165, 171
Kaufman, Mark, 88
Kaufmann, Lynne, 4
Kaufmann, Mark D., 50
Kausen, Roland, 129
Kaushansky, Larry, 52
Kavee, Elliot, 134
Kawaoka, Gerald, 67
Kaye, Deena, 29
Kaye, Doug, 159
Kay, Robert J., 83
Kayser, Chris, 163
Kazanoff, Ted, 89
Kearney, Kristine, 6
Kearns, Michael, 142, 143
Keathley, George, 91, 92
Keatley, Charlotte, 69
Keck, Michael, 71, 131
Keech, Pamela, 41
Keehbaugh, Ann, 92
Keeler, Richard L., 114
Keenan, Cecilie, 21
Keen, Elizabeth, 161
Keever, Stephen, 142, 168
Keim, Carolyn, 2, 16
Keith, Edward, 29
Keith, Warren David, 79
Kelin, Daniel A. II, 67
Keller, Frederick King, 149
Keller, James, 30, 109
Keller, John-David, 143, 144
Keller, Neel, 126, 127, 171
Keller, Ron, 46
Keller, Thomas L., 37
Kelley, Robert, 160
Kelley, Samuel, 66
Kellner, Peggy, 16
Kellogg, Marjorie Bradley, 6, 8, 33, 40, 66, 136
Kelly, Alexa, 168
Kelly, Brian P., 161
Kelly, Bridget, 37
Kelly, Colleen, 89
Kelly, George, 131
Kelly, John, 78, 93
Kelly, Patrick, 5
Kempinski, Tom, 36, 58, 138, 139
Kemp, Kevin, 3
Kendrick, D. Polly, 57, 163
Keneally, Thomas, 2, 36, 38, 68, 70, 83, 120, 144, 154, 170
Kenmore, Linda, 104
Kennan, George F., 162
Kennedy, Adrienne, 41, 63
Kennedy, Ashley York, 2, 8, 105, 121, 134, 135, 137
Kennedy, Margaret, 85
Kennedy, Patrick, 143
Kennedy, Steve, 77
Kennedy, Steven, 34
Kenney, Francis, 64
Kennon, Skip, 11
Kennon, Walter Edgar, 66, 108
Kennon, William, 100
Kenny, Frances, 53, 74, 87, 104, 109, 151
Kenny, Francis, 16
Kent, Art, 44, 164, 165
Kent, David G., 88, 89
Kent, Steven, 20, 131
Kenyon, Neal, 37
Keosheyan, Robert A., 50
Kern, Dan, 169
Kerner, Ian, 107
Kerner, Susan, 36, 58
Kern, Jerome, 86
Kerwin, Patrick, 166
Kesey, Ken, 8
Keskin, Erol, 78
Kesselman, Wendy, 40, 145
Kesselring, Joseph, 37, 50, 123, 169, 175
Kessler, Ann, 28
Kessler, Lyle, 151
Kessler, Michael, 161
Kessler, Stephen Burns, 129
Ketchum, Blake, 41
Ketchum, Perry, 121
Ketter, Sari, 64, 93
Kettler, Brian, 8
Key, Mirielle Lellouche, 142, 143
Key, Tom, 49, 129
Khabie, Fifi, 156
Khan, Ricardo, 9, 45, 46
Kholomanian, Sonia, 94
Khoo, Aurorae, 176
Kiamco, Rich, 78
Kidd, Linda K., 12
Kidd, Ronald, 107
Kilgore, John, 39, 69, 85, 86
Kilkelly, Ann, 130
Killian, Philip, 45, 72, 109, 165
Kilty, Jerome, 56
Kimberlain, Sora, 106, 107
Kime, Jeffrey, 54
Kim, Ja Kyoung, 78
Kim, Kyoon, 78
Kim, Randall Duk, 67

Kim, Willa, 80
Kinard, Jeff, 145
Kindlon, Peter M., 155
King, Cindy, 150
King, Kelly L., 150
King, Larry L., 80, 81, 123
King, Lloyd Broadnax, 139
King, Ramona, 169
King, Terry Lee, 157
King, Woodie, Jr., 59, 96, 97
Kinley, Kevin, 99, 132
Kinnard, Charles, 47
Kinney, Michelle, 79
Kinney, Terry, 147
Kipling, Rudyard, 17, 30, 34, 57, 67, 95, 128
Kirkup, James, 59
Kirk, Patricia Van, 7
Kirkwood, Neal, 79
Kirsch, Jan, 43
Kischer, Wayne, 67
Kiseljov, Boris, 30
Kiselov, Mladen, 4, 38
Kiser, Anthony C.M., 137
Kisor, David, 55
Kissel, David, 57
Kissin, Mike, 93
Kissman, Katha, 132
Kizziah, Casey, 75
Klaers, Michael, 93
Klassen, Magrita, 37
Kleiman, David H., 71
Kleiman, Harlan, 81
Klein, Jon, 32, 49
Klein, Jonathan, 116
Kleinmann, James A., 19
Klein, Randall E., 31, 60, 150
Kleinsinger, George, 32
Kleintop, Michael, 142
Klein, Steven M., 2, 7, 15, 16, 53, 63, 64, 73, 74, 136, 137, 165, 166
Kletter, Debra J., 37, 100, 122
Klima, Michael D., 18, 46
Klimchak, 1, 138
Kline, Linda B., 161
Klingelhoefer, Robert, 19, 58, 111
Kling, Kevin, 4, 5, 61, 142
Kloth, Kenneth, 83, 91
Klousia, Ivan, 5
Kluge, Marilyn, 52
Knapp, Rick, 28
Knee, Allan, 75, 124
Kneubuhl, Victoria Nalani, 67
Knight, Darwin, 6, 149
Knight, Dudley, 79
Knight, Marvette, 34, 93, 114
Knighton, Maurine D., 113
Knott, Frederick, 158
Knox 3, Kerro, 65
Knox, Wendy, 122
Knuth, Robert A., 21
Koch, David, 7, 64
Koch, David Hunter, 2, 137, 151
Koch, Lisa, 7
Kodner, Eric, 64
Koenig, Claus, 32
Koenig, Jeanne G., 31
Koerner, Michael, 154
Koernig, Wilton, 134
Koff, Chris, 98

Kogan, Deen, 141, 142
Kogan, Jay, 141, 142
Koger, Jeffrey, 157, 170
Kohan, Buz, 42
Kohl, Katherine, 62
Kohn, Barry, 132
Kohout, Alfred, 63
Kolb, Norbert, 19
Kolmanovsky, Alex, 169
Kolo, Fred, 113
Komar, Kathleen L., 38, 39
Kondoleon, Harry, 84, 157
Konecky, Isobel Robins, 95
Konopka, Albin, 61
Kopischke, Karin Simonson, 44, 55, 86, 91, 147
Kopit, Arthur, 61, 81, 88, 93, 100, 133, 147, 152, 177
Korf, Geoff, 27, 28, 43, 61, 165, 166
Kornbluth, Josh, 137
Kornfield, Larry, 156
Kornhauser, Barry, 58
Korogodsky, Danila, 55
Kortum, Chris, 77
Kosarin, Michael, 108
Kossup-Kennedy, Deborah, 55
Koste, V. Glasgow, 52
Koszyn, Jayme, 170
Kotlowitz, Dan, 48, 61, 91, 100, 126
Koue, Scott, 24, 136
Koutoukas, H.M., 157
Kovac, Kim Peter, 26, 173
Kowal, James, 57
Kozak, Ellen, 55, 91, 162
Kozak, Stan, 63, 92
Kracklauer, Beth, 96
Kraemer, Martin, 138
Krahnke, Steve, 91
Krajec, Debra, 90
Krajniak, Paul, 71
Krakower, Bob, 4
Kral, Brian, 30
Kramer, George, 36
Kramer, Larry, 37
Kramer, Milton, 2, 114, 145
Kramer, Randall, 149
Kramer, Sherry, 89, 96
Kramer, Stephen R., 59
Krane, David, 42
Krass, Michael, 6, 25, 36, 65, 90, 105, 116, 122, 161
Krausnick, Dennis, 138, 139
Kravitz, Barbra, 19, 69, 113, 141
Krebs, Eric, 58
Kreider, William, 113
Kreitler, John Henry, 55
Krejci, Marina S., 55
Krenz, Frank, 131
Krenz, Karen, 40
Kress, Donna M., 7, 47, 125
Kress, Phyllis, 133
Kretzu, Jon, 10, 55
Kriebs, David, 106, 142
Krieger, Barbara Zinn, 166
Krieger, Henry, 79
Krielkamp, Ben, 71
Kring, T. Newell, 126
Kriz, Zdenek, 156
Kroeger, Perry Arthur, 58, 157
Kroetz, Franz Xaver, 32, 79

Krohn, Chesley, 8
Kron, David J., 126
Kron, Lisa, 102
Kronzer, James, 106, 132, 143, 150, 173
Kross, Ed, 70
Krouse, Ian, 25
Kruck, Stefan, 104
Kruger, Robert J., 5
Krug, Monika, 117
Kruse, Mahlon, 83
Kruse, Paul J., 27
Kryah, Nicholas, 128, 129
Kuchar, Daniel, 79
Kuhn, Amy, 176
Kuhn, Hans Peter, 64
Kuipers, Kristen R., 5, 6, 124
Kulick, Brian, 85
Kunibe, Betsy, 115
Kuramoto, Soh, 78
Kurland, Rachel, 170
Kuroda, Kati, 111
Kurta, Kay, 40, 150
Kurtz, Howard Vincent, 173
Kurtz, Kathryn, 115
Kurtz, Kenneth N., 168
Kurtz, Marcia Jean, 137
Kushner, Tony, 2, 5, 87, 110
Kutner, Sheila, 14
Kutos, David, 73, 163
Kwallek, Lynda J., 7
Kwaloff, Peter, 79
Kyle, Barry, 156
Kyle, Christopher, 169
Kyte, Mary, 60, 132, 145

L

Labenz, Craig, 7, 73, 74
Labiche, Eugene, 50
La Boissere, Mary, 103
LaChiusa, Michael John, 11, 122
Lack, John A., 36
Laczko, Brian J., 62, 151, 152
Ladman, Jeff, 8, 69, 77, 80, 105, 134
Laev, James, 108
Laffey, Diane, 21
Lagomarsino, Ron, 80
Laing, Stewart, 100
LaJoye, Gale, 158
La Marshe, David, 108
Lambert, Jane, 29, 30
Lambert, Stephen, 42
Lambie, Lauren K., 149
Lamee, Maggie, 98
Lamont, Alonzo D., Jr., 55, , 103, 138
LaMorte, Dan, 32
Lamos, Mark, 65, 66, 122
LaMotte, Jane, 8, 105, 134
Lampkin, Pamela, 135, 160
Lamude, Terence, 19, 101, 147
Lancaster, Samuel, 50
Lancet, Carolyn, 133
Landau, Bob, 157
Landau, Tina, 7, 11, 54, 77
Landesman, Heidi, 137
Landis, Dave, 120

Landis, Lynn, 122
Landisman, Kurt, 9, 30, 84, 85, 86, 160
Landsburg, Valerie, 79
Landwehr, Hugh, 8, 25, 39, 64, 69, 82, 124, 136, 170, 171
Lane, Larry, 98, 99
Lane, Linda, 166
Lane, William, 164
Lang, David, 39
Lange, Ed., 101
Langham, Michael, 66, 156
Langley, Jeff, 24
Langley, Robert A., 136
Lang, Patsy, 41
Langsner, Jacobo, 127, 128
Langston-Perkins, Garrett, 133
Langworthy, Douglas, 78
Lansbury, Edgar, 2
Lansdale, Jennifer, 99
Lapham, Ken, 49, 159
Lapidus, Deborah R., 50
LaPierre, Robert, 45
Lapine, James, 18, 66, 77, 95, 105, 112, 128, 150, 160, 165, 168, 172
La Ponsie, Steven, 134
Lardner, Ring, 171
Large, Richard J., 169
Larice, Lisa, 51, 52
Larke, Paula, 130
Larkin, Gary, 120
Larsen, David, 5
Larsen, Jeffrey, 86
Larsen, Rick, 52
Larson, Becky, 92
Larson, James, 52, 53
Larson, Larry, 53, 124
Larson, Mary, 134
Larson, Rebecca S., 164, 165
Larson, Roberta, 52, 53
Larsson, Stig, 83
Lasdun, Gary, 157
Laskin, Arthur, 90
Lastufka, Marta Ann, 115
Laszlo, Miklos, 131
Latham, Susan, 108
Lathrop, Craig, 62, 150
Lathrop, Mary, 53
Lathrop, Patrick, 27
LaTouche, John, 43, 44, 170
Latta, Richard, 27, 28
Lattimore, Richard, 78
Laughton, Charles, 75, 123
Lauren, Ellen, 146
Laurents, Arthur, 66, 112
Lau, Christopher T., 159
Lauro, Shirley, 85
Lavery, Byrony, 21
Lavine, Michael, 124
Lavrakas, Paul, 26
Law, Alma H., 75
Law, Darren, 3
Lawless, Sue, 60, 173
Lawrence, Donna, 145
Lawrence, Jeremy, 38, 39
Lawrence, Jerome, 120
Lawson, Daniel L., 63
Lawson, Kevin J., 15
Laws, Holly, 78
Lawton, Chris, 147

Laywood, John, 119
Lazarev, Eugene, 155
Lazarus, Frank, 119
Lazarus, Paul, 25, 161
Lea, Allen, 34, 35
Leach, William, 165
Leaming, Greg, 125, 126
Leathers, Scott, 152
Leavengood, Wm. S., 60, 107
Leaver, Harold, 3
Leayman, Charles, 34
Lebhar, Dione, 105
Lebow, Barbara, 1, 86, 99, 117, 121, 138, 158
LeBrecht, James, 77
L'Ecuyer, Jim, 175
LeCompte, Elizabeth, 173, 174
Ledger, Karen, 67, 151
Lee, Angie, 59
Lee, Cherylene, 107
Leeds, Michael, 102, 161
Lee, Eddie Levi, 53, 124, 163
Lee, Eugene, 8, 15, 100, 124, 137, 164
Lee, Franne, 100
Lee, Gordon D., 43
Lee, Guinevere W., 168
Lee, Harper, 46, 50, 101
Lee, Hyunyup, 78
Lee, Jeff, 168
Lee, Jennifer, 7
Lee, Leslie, 18, 70, 148
Lee, Liz, 6, 8, 78, 159
Lee, Ming Cho, 4, 86, 116
Lee, Robert E., 120
Lees, C. Lowell, 118
Lee, Vicky, 43
Lee, V. Joy, 53
Lee, Yvonne, 8, 68
LeFebvre, Matthew, 62
Legawiec, Stephen, 169, 170
Legere, Phoebe, 156
LeGrand, Stephen, 9, 24, 69, 135
Leguizamo, John, 61
Lehan, Carole Graham, 106
Lehne, John, 169
Lehrer, Jim, 171
Lehrer, Lucy Tom, 142
Lehrer, Scott, 36, 37, 80, 85, 86, 87
Lehrer, Tom, 43
Lehr, Wendy, 33, 34
Leibert, Michael W., 23
Leibfried, Rich, 49
Leicht, John, 91
Leigh, Carolyn, 5, 120, 160
Leigh, Mitch, 65
Leishman, Gina, 15, 49
Lelbach, Bill, 126
LeMaster, Liane, 111
L'Engle, Madeleine, 33
Leo, Jamie, 102, 156
Leonard, Hugh, 114
Leonard, James Jr., 145
Leonard, Phil, 130
Leonard, Robert H., 130
Leone, Vivien, 11
Leon, Kenneth, 8, 60, 76, 91, 114, 150, 163
Leon, Steven, 169, 170
Lerner, Alan Jay, 61, 119, 129

Leroux, Gaston, 152
Leschin, Luisa, 133, 134
Leshner, Lori, 99
Leslee, Ray, 107, 122
Leslie, F. Andrew, 37
Lesnichaja, Vera, 30
Lesser, Sally, 73, 79, 173
Levans, Daniel, 11
Leveaux, David, 131
Levenson, Eric, 99
Leveque, Linda, 20
Levey, Alan, 115
Levin, Cheryl Anne, 111
Levin, Cynthia, 164, 165
Levine, Andrew, 95
Levin, James A., 40, 41
Levin, Maurice C., 103
Levitow, Roberta, 98, 100, 122, 125, 133
Levowitz, Adam, 12
Levy, Jacques, 160
Levy, Robert, 176
Levy, Sharon, 162
Levy, Stephen, 75
Lewine, Richard, 129
Lewis, Bram, 117, 118
Lewis, Carter W., 79
Lewis, Colleen Troy, 29, 30
Lewis, C.S., 22, 99, 120
Lewis, Garry, 114
Lewis, Irene, 31, 32, 175
Lewis, Jeff, 127
Lewis, J. Barry, 124
Lewis, Kenneth J., 99
Lewis, Kristin, 160
Lewis, Matthew G., 91
Lewis, Terri, 125
Lewton, Christopher V., 15, 143
Libaek, Lita B., 160
Liberman, Adam, 86
Libertella, Jose, 42
Lickteig, Regina, 86
Liddy, Richard A., 128
Lieberman, Joyce, 171
Lieberman, Sali, 86
Lieber, Jeffrey, 111
Liebhauser, Robert, 90
Liebman, Steve, 55
Lienke, Henrietta, 157
Liepins, Renee Starr, 111
Life, Regge, 161
Liljestrand, Eric, 11, 54, 100, 173
Lilly, Judlyne A., 142
Limauro, Cindy, 38
Limber, Chris, 55
Lim, Genny, 169
Lim, Karen, 37, 160
Limosner, Pilar, 100, 173
Lincoln, Michael, 23, 72, 122
Lindblade, Tom, 160
Linden, Jessica R., 68
Lindfors, Viveca, 156
Lindley, Jon, 106
Lindsay, Howard, 59, 95, 159
Linfante, Michele, 49
Linke, Paul, 102, 168
Linklater, Kristin, 138
Linklater, Tom, 115
Link, Ron, 7
Linnerson, Beth, 33

Linney, Romulus, 5, 51, 91, 96, 104, 110, 125, 132, 157, 170
Lino, Christopher, 118
Lion, John, 84
Lipkin, Joan, 21
Lippa, Louis, 114
Lipschulz, Carole Harris, 70
Lipsky, Jon, 89
Lipton, Michael, 72
Liquori, Mary, 97
Liscow, Wendy, 58
Lisenby, Jeff, 152
Lisz, Gary, 58, 88
Littethun, Abby, 56
Littleford, Laura, 71
Littleway, Lorna, 148
Lively, David, 145
Livingston, Lamar, 5, 47
Livingston, Robert, 148
Llewellyn, Carol, 163
Llewellyn, Don, 104
Loadholt, Tony, 68, 76, 163
Lobel, Adrianne, 15, 77
Lockwood, Connie, 14, 116, 117, 168
Lockwood, Debra Garcia, 43
Lock, Keven, 59, 159
Loeffler-Bell, Chester, 90
Loesser, Frank, 61, 80, 133, 151
Loewe, Frederick, 61
Loewenberg, Susan Albert, 79
Loewith, Jason, 104
Loflin, Jon M., 124
Lofting, Hugh, 136
Loftin, Steve, 152
Logan, John, 60, 166, 172
Logan, Joshua, 46, 70, 129
Lohman, Mark, 95
Lohr, Lynn, 62
Lombardo, Francesca, 73, 163
London, Chuck, 37, 105, 116, 136
London, Daniel, 67
Loney, Andrea, 45
Long, Kathryn, 121, 149
Long, Meredith J., 7
Long, Naomi, 67
Long, Quincy, 171
Long, William Ivey, 131
Look, Phyllis S.K., 24, 85, 136
Loomer, Lisa, 35, 96, 171
Lopez, Benjamin, 72
Lopez-Castillo, Miguel, 78, 118
Lopez, Chip, 167
Lopez, Jose, 77, 98, 134
Lopez, Josefina, 19, 52, 64
Lopez, Juan, 110
Loquasto, Santo, 85, 86, 137
Lorca, Federico Garcia, 15, 25, 72, 90, 100, 127, 128
Lorden, Terry C., 12
Lord, Mark, 14
Loree, Lori, 17
Lott, Bob, 139
Loud, David, 131
Louey, Paul Chi-Ming, 53, 136
Loughridge, Gregg, 104, 151
Loui, Amy, 148
Loveless, David, 75
Lovett, Winston, 157
Love, Edith H., 8

Low, Dana, 166
Lowe, Frederick, 119
Lowe, Harrison, 84
Lowe, Leslie, 79
Lowell, Robert, 64
Lowe, Malcolm, 142
Lowy, Craig, 96
Lozano, Rosario, 127
Lubar, Kathryn, 98
Lubin, Shellen, 169
Lucas, Bob, 4, 38, 84
Lucas, Charles, 133
Lucas, Craig, 4, 18, 33, 37, 56, 58, 66, 67, 68, 81, 106, 117, 120, 121, 123, 145, 160, 164
Lucas, Greg, 2, 16, 34, 35
Lucero, Amarante L., 35
Luce, Clare Boothe, 3, 86, 134, 149
Luce, William, 124, 129
Ludel, William, 143, 144
Ludlam, Charles, 4, 22, 28, 95, 98, 115, 119, 123, 126, 129, 145, 159
Ludwick, Patricia, 44
Ludwig, Amy, 166
Ludwig, Ken, 6, 18, 22, 29, 59, 66, 81, 86, 89, 106, 112, 113, 118, 119, 125, 129, 145, 146, 149, 150, 151, 159, 164, 168, 170
Luft, Andrew, 31
Luigs, Jim, 4
Luisi, Jere, 35
Luke, Jayne, 119
Lundeberg, Karl, 104
Lunden, Jeffrey, 61, 100, 161
Lundy, Nicholas, 175
Lundy, Richard, 127
Lupton, Jennifer, 136, 151
Lutvak, Steven, 128
Lutwak, Mark, 64, 96
Lutz, Douglass, 142
Lutz, John David, 72
Lwanga, Namu, 173
Lyall, Susan, 137
Lyden, James E., 17
Lynch, Patty, 122
Lynch, Sharon, 122, 161
Lynch, Thomas, 15, 60, 80, 88, 131, 147
Lynge, Stephanie, 46
Lyon, Sherry, 23, 53

M

Maar, Paul, 34
MacArthur, Charles, 8, 43
MacDermot, Galt, 169
MacDevitt, Brian, 31, 37, 39, 65, 116, 122, 168
MacDonald, Ann-Marie, 39, 120
MacDonald, Antony, 11
MacDonald, Betty, 136
MacDonald, Bob, 98
MacDonald, Karen, 139
Macdonald, Richard, 87
MacDonald, Robert David, 75
Macdonald, Sharman, 149, 168
MacDonald, William E. III, 62
Mace, Mimi, 49
MacFetrich, Noel, 157

INDEX OF NAMES

Macgregor, Robin, 71
Machado, Eduardo, 82, 96
Machiavelli, Niccolo, 125
MacIntyre, Dianne, 45
MacIvor, Daniel, 150
Mackay, Harper, 9
MacKay, Zoe, 157
Mack, Carol, 96, 114
Mackender, Greg, 44
Mackender, Stephana, 164
MacKenzie-Wood, Barbara, 74
MacLaughlin, Whit, 27
MacLean, Ross, 4
MacLeod, Charles R., 50
MacLeod, Doug, 70
MacLeod, Joan, 70, 115
MacLeod, Wendy, 59, 96, 132
MacNamee, Jay, 12
Macks, Adam, 33
Macut, Debra, 145
Madeira, Marcia, 69, 168
Madsen, Gayla A., 28
Madsen, Wade, 7
Maeda, Jun, 78, 79
Magaldi-Unger, Karin, 140
Magee, Rusty, 11, 39
Maggio, Frances, 44, 45, 94, 127, 147, 166
Maggio, Michael, 32, 60, 61, 100, 172
Magid, Paul, 15, 77, 137
Magnuson, Ann, 100, 173
Magnuson, Marty, 52
Maguire, Kate, 146
Maguire, Matthew, 96
Maguire, Roberta, 166
Magune, Jack, 174
Maher, Denise, 176
Mahone, Ozella, 13
Maier, David, 9, 10
Maifeld, Kevin K., 49
Majewski, David, 158
Maki, Kathleen, 53, 63, 64
Malcolm, Debbie, 41
Maleczech, Ruth, 82, 83, 157
Maleitzky, Peter, 37
Maler, Steve, 11
Malleson, Miles, 123
Malone, Mike, 150
Malone, Sheila, 52
Maloney, Rachel, 164
Malpede, Karen, 157
Maltby, David, 109
Maltby, Richard, Jr., 8, 13, 16, 25, 36, 37, 83, 93, 112, 113, 120, 152, 158, 164, 167
Malten, Trui, 175
Mamet, David, 3, 11, 24, 32, 33, 35, 65, 67, 75, 83, 89, 91, 114, 115, 125, 133, 138
Manassee, Jackie, 31, 35, 36, 45, 46, 63, 69, 92, 146, 173
Mandell, Alan, 4, 120
Mandel, Ellen, 75
Manet, Eduardo, 142
Manganaro, Eileen, 32
Mangione, Jerre, 60
Mangum, Edward, 14
Manheimer, John, 22
Manheimer, Josh C., 126

Manheim, Ralph, 74, 104, 155, 170
Manley, Frank, 155
Manners, J. Hartley, 22
Manning, Jerry, 143
Mannshardt, Steven B., 160
Mann, Emily, 46, 56, 87, 88
Mann, Harry, 79
Mann, Jeremy, 112
Manoff, Arnold, 79
Manoff, Dinah, 79
Mansfield, Karl, 125
Mans, Lorenzo, 73
Mantello, Joe, 23, 36, 37
Maradudin, Peter, 2, 9, 24, 72, 74, 77, 87, 91, 105, 109, 120, 135, 136, 137, 143, 144
Mara, Pamela A., 124
Marasco, Robert, 126
Marcais, Lorenza Elena, 41
Marcante, Mark, 156, 157
Marchbanks, Greg, 80
Marcus, Frank, 27, 170
Marcus, Jim, 111
Marcus, Paul, 143
Marcus, Tony, 24
Mardikes, Tom, 63, 92, 128, 165
Margid, Elizabeth S., 175
Margolin, Deb, 7
Margulies, Donald, 85, 129, 143
Mariano, Michael, 156
Maria, Soraya, 128
Marini, Ken, 32, 33, 114
Marker, Frederick J., 16, 19, 59, 116, 171
Marker, Lise-Lone, 19, 59, 116, 171
Marki, Csilla, 87
Marks, Debra, 27
Marley, Donovan, 49, 50, 112
Marlowe, Christopher, 175
Marold, Dennis, 41
Maronek, Jim, 6, 146, 149
Marowitz, Charles, 29, 101
Marquez, Gabriel Garcia, 127, 128
Marquis, Don, 32
Marquis, Melissa, 120
Marrero, Maria, 59, 149, 150, 159
Marron, Barry, 142
Marr, Doug, 53, 106
Marshall, Catherine, 47
Marshall, Don, 38
Marshall, Dorothy L., 92, 128, 129
Marshall, LaRue, 43
Marshall, Maynard, 150
Marshall, Rob, 105, 128, 131
Marshall, Vikki, 92
Marshall, William McNeil, 114
Marsh, Frazier W., 4
Marsillach, Adolfo, 128
Martenson, Edward A., 64
Martin, Christopher, 39, 72
Martin, Diane, 115
Martin, Jane, 4, 56, 60, 121, 164
Martin, Janis, 89
Martin, Jennifer, 61
Martin, Joe, 83
Martin, John, 77, 134
Martin, Judith, 52
Martin, Manuel, Jr., 127, 128
Martin, Nicholas, 122
Martin, Ricardo, 14

Martin, Rick, 175
Martin, Robert, 166
Martinson, Leslie, 160
Martin, Steven David, 6
Martin, Tom, 128, 129
Martin, Vincent L., 90
Martis, Robert, 153
Marton, Laszlo, 4
Martorella, Drew, 98
Martus, Darien, 142
Marvin, Mel, 34, 60, 132, 145
Marx, Arthur, 168
Masarik, Rich, 41
Mashburn, Robert, 39
Maslon, Laurence, 15, 132, 159
Mason, Bruce, 46, 145
Mason, Cecelia, 10, 91
Mason, Marshall W., 36, 37, 105, 116, 119, 136
Mason, Rich, 158
Mason, Richard, 12
Mason, Timothy, 17, 34, 36, 121
Maso, Michael, 69
Massimo, Donna, 149
Masteroff, Joe, 123, 131
Masters, Edgar Lee, 67
Masterson, Marc, 38
Masterson, Peter, 80, 123
Mastrosimone, William, 124
Mast, Edward, 44, 95, 111
Matalon, Vivian, 47
Mathers, Albert C., 124
Mathews, Marguerite, 12
Mathieu, Patty, 7, 136, 151
Matson, Jim, 162
Matson, Robert, 123
Matsushita, MJ, 67
Mattei, Peter, 84, 96
Matthews, Jeffrey, 129
Matthiessen, Peter, 23
Mattox, Cameron, 29
Mattox, David, 159
Mattson, Kathrine, 23
Matura, Mustapha, 15, 64, 80, 91, 169
Maugham, Somerset, 99
Mau, Michael, 67
Maurer, Laura, 91
Maurette, Marcelle, 159
Maxem, Mimi, 60
Maxfield, Dennis, 41
Maxine, David, 175
Maxmen, Mimi, 31, 40, 85
Maxwell, George, 119
Mayer, Andrew, 34
Mayer, Michael, 65, 96, 161, 176
Mayes, Kevin D., 78
Mayo, Lisa, 41
May, Donna, 99
May, Jonathan, 46
Mays, Ben, 131
Mazer, Sharon, 96
Mazzone-Clementi, Carlo, 49
Mazzonelli, Joan, 35
McAden, Marshal, 153
McAlexander, JR, 46
McAllister, Jamie, 43
McAnuff, Des, 76, 77
McBride, James, 11
McBroom, Amanda, 40, 56, 61

McCabe, Terry, 166, 172
McCallion, Michael, 114
McCallum, Kim, 26
McCall, Kit, 104
McCants, Laurie, 27, 28
McCarry, Charles, 38, 73, 119
McCarthy, Eugene, 44
McCarthy, Jim, 92
McCartney, Ellen, 57, 86, 122, 136, 137, 174
McCauley, Ann, 50
McCauley, Gilbert, 61, 103
McCauley, Robbie, 114
McCaw, Ken, 47
McClain, Kenneth B., 45
McClatchy, Eleanor, 132
McClay, Hollie, 106
McClellan, Cathie, 168
McClennahan, Charles, 11, 15, 116, 148, 157
McClinton, Marion Isaac, 32, 64, 66, 71, 93, 96, 113, 114, 126
McCloskey, Robert, 19
McCluggage, John, 135
McClure, Rory, 81
McCoin, Mark, 31
McComb, Chris, 29
McConnell, Steve, 89
McCormick, Leonard, 145
McCormick, Megan, 133
McCourt, Frank, 62
McCoy, Hal, 163
McCoy, Horace, 50
McCracken, Bob, 114
McCracken, Rich, 160
McCray, Maria, 57
McCroom, Darren, 64, 71, 136
McCullers, Carson, 59
McCulley, Johnston, 55
McCulloh, Barbara, 29
McCullough, Mark, 73, 102
McCulough, Ken, 18, 120, 121
McCutchen, Heather, 37, 96
McDaniel, John, 19
McDaniel, William Foster, 19
McDermid, Ed, 69
McDermott, Kevin, 68
McDermott, Robert, 44
McDevitt, Brian, 119
McDevitt, Mary, 71
McDonald, Antony, 119
McDonald, Betsy, 171
McDonald, Heather, 24, 173
McDonald, Peggy, 53, 63, 151
McDonough, Glen, 158
McDonough, Joseph, 55, 159
McDonough, Tim, 155
McDowell, B. Christine, 97
McDowell, W. Stuart, 29
McDuffee, Colleen, 158
McElhaney, Susan, 95
McElvain, Richard, 89, 163
McFadden, Neil, 106, 132, 143, 173
McGarty, Michael, 78, 157, 164
McGeachy, Martin, 17
McGeehon, Bart, 153
McGee, Lindsay, 126
McGhee-Anderson, Kathleen, 45, 46
McGillicuddy, Dennis, 56

McGillivray, David, 43
McGinnes, Mac, 166
McGough, Roger, 158
McGovern, Christopher, 161
McGrail, J. Patrick, 174
McGrath, Bob, 78, 79
McGrath, John, 82
McGravie, Anne, 110
McGruder, Jasper, 157
McGuire, Dorothy, 77
McGuire, Judy, 71
McIlrath, Patricia, 91
McIlroy, Andrew, 155
McIntyre, Dennis, 117, 126
McIntyre, Robin W., 62
McIsaac, Paul, 79
McKay, Gardner, 16, 146, 174
McKay, W. Colin, 117
McKeaney, Grace, 114
McKechnie, Donna, 86
McKelvey, Duncan, 159
McKenney, Kerry, 66
McKenzie, Julia, 86
McKie, Jack, 37
McKinney, John, 60
McKneely, Joey, 15, 47, 167
McKnight, Jack, 59
McLain, John, 19, 42, 101
McLane, Derek, 7, 11, 23, 31, 37, 88, 100, 102, 122, 141
McLaughlin, Ellen, 167
McLaughlin, Suzi, 145
McLean, Jamison, 115
McLeish, Kenneth, 64
McLeod, Bruce, 160
McLeod, Kevin R., 4
McLure, James, 18
McNally, Terrence, 8, 19, 21, 22, 31, 42, 65, 67, 86, 87, 99, 110, 117, 133, 136, 137, 150, 158, 159, 164, 165
McNaughton, Robert, 111
McNeal, Sandy, 99
McNicholas, John, 6
McPherson, Fillmore, 21
McPherson, Scott, 61, 67, 68, 69, 122, 137
McSherry, Frances Nelson, 99
McSweeny, William F., 56
McVay, Marcelle, 166
McVay, Robert, 5
Meaden, Wendy, 72
Meade, Michelle, 129
Meadows, Marianne, 150
Meadow, Lynne, 85
Mecyssne, Victor, 46
Medak, Susan, 23
Mederios, Michael, 22
Medioli, Joanna, 138
Medley, David, 148
Medoff, Mark, 145
Mee, Charles L., Jr., 54
Meehan, Thomas, 13
Meeker, Roger, 69
Megee, Ron, 44
Meier, Todd, 43
Mejia, Al, 25
Melcori, Frank, 110
Melero, Antonio Perez, 152
Melia, Paul, 171

Melissas, Jackie, 21
Melloy, Linda, 147, 165
Melvin, Ken, 66
Menchell, Ivan, 70, 113
Mendelson, Evan, 19
Mendel, D.J., 157
Mendenhall, Jennifer, 173
Mendoza, Carlos A., 105
Menken, Alan, 12, 13, 120
Menke, Rick, 146, 149
Mennone, Kate, 157
Menotti, Gian Carlo, 46
Meola, Tony, 131
Mercer, Bryan, 68, 159
Mercer, Sally, 168
Mercier, G.W., 19, 31, 35, 72, 85, 125, 146, 149, 167
Mercier, Skip, 156
Merkey, Ryland, 69
Merkin, Lewis, 7
Merriam, Eve, 176
Merrick, Jack, 153
Merrill, Bob, 95
Merrill, Bruce, 30
Merritt, Michael, 11, 139, 147
Mertes, Brian, 96
Merwin, W.S., 15, 64
Meschter, David, 48
Meshejian, Paul, 33, 114
Mesmer, R., 124
Mesney, Barbara, 9, 86, 133
Metheny, Russell, 47, 72, 106, 141, 148, 149, 150
Methot, Christien, 65
Metropulos, Penny, 109, 110
Metzger, Teresa, 151
Meyer, Marlane, 171
Meyer, Meleanna, 67
Meyer, Michael, 98
Meyers, Andrew, 10, 90, 110, 162
Meyers, Larry John, 38
Meyers, Patrick, 10
Meyer, Tom, 173
Micelli, Mark, 16
Michaelian, Michael, 16
Michel, Marc, 50
Michener, James A., 46, 129
Michener, John, 62
Michilinda, Douglas, 105
Mickelsen, David Kay, 16, 34, 109, 110, 152
Mickey, Susan E., 6, 8, 35, 59, 60, 98
Middleton, Lisa Rose, 142, 143
Miers, David, 29
Miguel, Gloria, 41
Miguel, Muriel, 41
Mikhailov, Alexander, 30
Milbauer, Mark, 97, 98
Milburn, Rob, 47, 60, 61, 95, 147, 164
Miles, Cindy, 67
Miles, Julia, 172
Miles, William A., Jr., 106
Militello, Anne, 134
Millan, Bruce E., 51
Millburn, Rob, 100
Miller, Allan, 104
Miller, Arthur, 29, 33, 49, 55, 64, 65, 69, 81, 82, 83, 86, 91, 92, 94,
120, 125, 128, 131, 133, 159
Miller, Barry I., 18
Miller, Bruce, 157, 158
Miller, Celeste, 138
Miller, Craig, 61, 69, 80, 131
Miller, David, 158
Miller, Drew, 27
Miller, Frank, 159
Miller, Jim Wayne, 69
Miller, John E., 115
Miller, JP, 40
Miller, Kathryn Schultz, 18, 129
Miller, Lawrence, 40
Miller, Mary, 103
Miller, Michael, 16
Miller, Milo, 72
Miller, M.L., 52
Miller, Nan, 146
Miller, Pat, 155
Miller, Rebecca, 55
Miller-Rickel, Aime, 64
Miller, Robert, 145
Miller, Roger, 6, 46, 112, 152
Miller, R. Michael, 19, 25, 150
Miller, Scott, 5
Miller-Stephany, John, 2
Miller, Walter, 21
Millman, Howard J., 49, 59, 60, 149, 150, 159, 165
Mills, David A., 103
Mills, Patsy, 138
Milne, A.A., 44, 55, 145, 158
Milton, James, 167
Minerd, Douglas E., 158
Mines, Barry, 153
Minetor, Nic, 59, 60
Minjares, Joe, 93, 105
Minton, David, 4, 5
Miranda, Miguel, 163
Mitchell, Adrian, 55, 64, 79, 81, 127
Mitchell, Aldora B., 169
Mitchell, Bunny, 27
Mitchell, David, 46, 152, 171
Mitchell, Gary, 138, 139
Mitchell, Gary C., 160
Mitchell, H. Maurice, 17
Mitchell, Kabby, III, 7
Mitchell-Leon, Carol, 163
Mitchell, Margaret, 145
Mitchell, Mark, 23, 61, 136
Mitchell, Ron, 30, 37
Mittelman, Arnold, 41, 42
Miyagawa, Chiori, 111
Mocahbee, Mark, 55
Mochel, Ned, 111
Mockus, Jeff, 112
Modern, B., 133, 140
Moffett, D.W., 126
Mofsie, Louis, 156, 157
Mogavero, Richard, 23
Mohanshelt, Laura, 34
Moher, Frank, 19, 144
Mohl, Larry, 21
Mokeiev, Mikhail, 45
Moliere, 6, 9, 15, 23, 32, 34, 39, 40, 47, 49, 50, 66, 69, 72, 76, 82, 105, 106, 116, 120, 121, 123, 144, 155, 163, 165, 177
Molina, Armando, 133, 134
Molnar, Ferenc, 27, 92, 109, 170,
171
Molyneux, Lisa, 36
Monat, Phil, 31, 47, 59, 60, 61, 92, 119, 120, 122, 149, 150, 159, 167
Moncada, Raul, 105, 128
Moncada, Santiago, 152
Monderer, Jack, 43
Monette, Trudy, 52
Monios, Melanie, 78
Monk, Debra, 46, 56, 59, 89, 98, 120, 129, 134, 150, 151, 168
Monroe, Michael, 3, 159
Montalvo, Lina, 25
Monteith, John, 151
Monte, Bonnie J., 97, 98
Montford, Charles, 130
Montgomerie, Jeffrey, 40
Montgomery, L.M., 44, 46, 145
Montgomery, M. Michael, 33, 114, 117
Montgomery, Reggie, 47
Montoya, Richard, 77
Moody, Michael R., 86, 97
Mooney, Ken, 171
Moon, Gerald, 13
Moon, John, 158
Moore, Benjamin, 136
Moore, Christina J., 177
Moore, Christopher, 21
Moore, David, Jr., 121
Moore, Diane, 70
Moore, Dudley, 56
Moore, Edward J., 37
Moore, Kenneth, 127
Moore, Kevin, 134
Moore, Matthew, 175
Moore, Randy, 47
Moore, Richard, 5
Moore, Sanford, 93
Moore, Stephanie, 81
Moore, Stephen, 70
Moore, Tom, 87, 156, 171
Moore, William, 155
Mooy, Brad, 18
Morace, John, 78
Moran, Jim, 38, 39
Moran, John, 78, 79
Moran, Lisa, 112
Mordecai, Benjamin, 71
Moreland, David, 28
Moreland, Ken, 168
Morettini, Margaret, 166
Morey, Charles, 118, 119, 129
Morgan, Cass, 46, 59, 89, 98, 150, 151, 168
Morgan, Charles, 12, 22, 89, 175
Morgan, Edward, 91, 132
Morgan, James, 19, 40, 62
Morgan, Joseph D., 163
Morgan, Maggie, 98, 175
Morgan, Marlo, 44
Morgan, Robert, 9, 105
Morgan, Roger, 11, 131
Moritz, Susan Trapnell, 1
Moriyasu, Atsushi, 111
Morizono, Lesli-Jo, 107
Morrison, Charles, 99
Morrison, James, 133, 134
Morrison, Malcolm, 47
Morris, Bonnie, 70, 71

Morris, Cleveland, 48, 49
Morriss, Bruce K., 48
Morris, William S., 150
Morse, Tom, 100
Mortilla, Michael, 104
Mortimer, John, 92, 110
Morton, Frederick, 29
Morton, Joe, 122
Mosby, Gary, 164, 165
Moscou, Jacqueline, 64, 74, 137
Mosely, Eva, 154
Moses, Ken, 163
Moses, Laurie Lee, 21
Mosse, Spencer, 55, 174
Moss, Robert, 65, 122
Moss, Spencer, 75, 109
Mostel, Joshua, 137
Most, Steve, 49
Motherwell, Phil, 156
Mouawad, Jerry, 91
Moulds, Steven P., 135
Mountain, Martha, 106, 173
Mountain, Vincent, 8
Mount, Lisa, 137
Moyer, Allen, 116, 122, 137, 167, 176
Moynihan, Leslie, 41
Moynihan, Michael, 55
Mrazek, Roger, 157
Mrnak, Trina, 77, 155, 175
Mtonga, Mapopa, 28, 130
Mudd, Patricia A., 29, 30
Mueller, Carl R., 104
Mueller, Lavonne, 165
Muhammad, Exavier, 157
Muirhead, Janice, 81
Muirhead, Jayne, 151
Muller, Chris, 79, 97
Mullins, Carol, 54
Mullins, Robin, 153
Mund, Dr. Rene Serge, 4
Mundell, Anne, 119, 120
Munger, Robyn, 52
Muratova, Olga, 30
Murbach, John, 172
Murdoch, Christine, 134
Murdock, Andy, 85
Murdock, Christine, 130
Murfitt, Mary, 56, 120, 129, 134
Murillo, Carlos A., 54
Murin, David, 25, 35, 36, 69, 82, 117, 137
Murnane, Michael, 34
Murphy, Amy L., 14
Murphy, Kevin, 55
Murphy, Michael, 64
Murphy, Robert, 92, 128, 129
Murphy, Russell, 111
Murphy, Tom, 44
Murphy, Vincent, 6, 8, 155
Murray, Brian, 131
Murray, Christine, 13
Murray, Criswell, 103
Murray, Steve, 155
Murray-Walsh, Merrily, 66, 170
Murray, William, 114
Murrell, John, 43, 115, 120
Muscha, Colleen, 165
Musial, John, 44, 127
Musky, Jane, 58

Musser, Tharon, 82, 86
Musumeci, Joseph B., Jr., 99, 132
Muzio, Gloria, 4, 23, 131, 137, 173, 176
Myers, Andrew, 130
Myers, Larry, 156, 157
Myers, Lynda K., 44
Myers, Mary, 22, 54, 122, 157
Myers, Michael E., 110
Myhre, Keven, 133, 134
Myler, Randal, 50, 105

N

Nabokov, Vladimir, 127
Nachtmann, Rita, 124
Nadoolman, Deborah, 9
Nagy, Phyllis, 96
Najera, Rick, 133
Najimy, Kathy, 134
Nakagawa, Jon, 166
Nakahara, Ron, 4, 58, 67
Napier, Mick, 127
Narun, John, 21
Nash, Jeff, 78, 79
Nash, N. Richard, 89, 158
Nason, Brian, 75, 76, 86
Naso, R.C., 41
Natinsky, David, 5, 47
Naunton, David, 60, 61, 111
Nause, Allen, 125
Navarro, Paul Anthony, 43
Navarro, Tina Cantu, 19, 98, 116
Ndlovu, Duma, 11
Neal, Jeff, 110, 111
Neal, Robert F., 61
Neal, Rome, 157
Neal, Vicki, 163
Near, Holly, 87
Near, Timothy, 24, 87, 135
Neary, Julia, 111
Nebozenko, Jan, 42
Negin, Mark, 82, 120
Nehring, Karl-Heinz, 4
Neipris, Janet, 116
Nellhaus, Gerhard, 83, 100
Nelson, Jennifer, 114, 132, 142, 143
Nelson, J.D., 84
Nelson, Karen E., 163
Nelson, Margaret L., 110, 111
Nelson, Michael Price, 26
Nelson, M. Elizabeth, 160
Nelson, Novella, 4
Nelson, Richard, 80, 88, 121, 137
Nelson, Tim Blake, 137
Neman, Caryn, 15, 137, 175
Nemeth, Sally, 166
Nessen, Julie, 126
Netherland, Mark, 21
Neuhaus, Robert, 44, 45, 94, 139
Neu, Jim, 79
Neumann, Frederick, 82, 83
Neville-Andrews, John, 104, 165
Nevin, Stan, 111
Newberger, Charlotte, 93
Newbom, Kristin, 7
Newcomb, Don, 149, 161
Newcott, Rosemary, 8, 68
Newell, Carol, 43

Newell, Charles, 6
Newhauser, Tina M., 120
Newkirk, Ricky Green, 13
Newley, Anthony, 30
Newlin, Jon, 91
Newman, David, 61
Newman, Molly, 22
Newman, Naomi, 19, 20
Newnam, Luetta, 34, 35
Newstrom, Jon, 175
Ney, Rick, 55
Ngema, Mbongeni, 11
Ngor, Haing S., 89
Nicholas, Anna, 79
Nichols, Alex, 85
Nichols, Daniel, 157
Nichols, Heather, 46
Nichols, Jackie, 120
Nichols, Mike, 18, 120
Nicholson, Brett A., 17
Nicholson, William, 2, 6, 106, 120, 123, 125, 144
Nichols, Peter, 3, 132
Nicola, James B., 18, 174
Nicola, James C., 101, 102
Nidi, Alessandro, 78
Niederer, Barbara, 35
Niederkorn, Tom, 65
Nielsen, Todd, 43
Nieminski, Joseph, 44, 45, 60, 61, 92
Niesen, Jim, 74, 163
Niesen, Toby, 83, 157
Nigro, Don, 114
Nimoy, Leonard, 90
9th Street Theater, 156, 157
Nissen, James Christian, 126
Noble, Merry-Beth, 104
Noe, Jennifer, 68, 69
Noel, Craig, 104, 105
Noel, Normi, 139
Nolan, Philip, 21
Nolan, Victoria, 175
Nolen, Terrence J., 14
Noling, David, 61
Nolte, Charles, 147
Nonas, Richard, 83, 157
Noonan, John Ford, 147
Noone, James, 25, 31, 59, 60, 61, 86, 122, 126, 137, 150, 161, 167
No-Ra, Prince, 132, 142
Norberg, Douglas E., 1
Norberry, Jeff, 15
Norgren, Catherine F., 72
Norland, Joanna, 176
Norman, Marsha, 4, 58
Norris, Bruce, 127
Norris, Frank, 24
Norris, Jennifer, 85
Norwood, Richard, 38
Nottbusch, Kaye, 147
Nova Lizard Project, The, 41
Novak, David Alan, 126
Novak, Elizabeth, 6, 72, 110, 119
Novak, Jan, 75
Nova, Barbara, 169
Novelli, Stephen, 114
Nowicki, Rob, 163
Nunemaker, David, 79
Nunnelley, Pamela J., 58, 167, 168

Nussbaum, Mike, 127
Nussbaum, Susan, 106, 115, 127

O

Oates, Joyce Carol, 79, 171
Oathaut, Kim, 22
Obispo, Fabian V., Jr., 15
O'Brien, Edna, 139
O'Brien, Jack, 69, 80, 104, 105
O'Brien, Justin, 155
O'Brien, Linda, 12, 99
O'Brien, Marianne, 64
O'Brien, Mary Claire Lowy, 71
O'Brien, Michael, 145
O'Brien, Michael P., 20
O'Callahan, Jay, 163
O'Casey, Sean, 167
Occhiogrosso, Anne, 67
Ocel, Tim, 133, 155
O'Connell, Paul, 63
O'Conner, Ricarda, 75
O'Connor, Sara, 27, 90, 91, 121, 170
O'Connor, Sean, 157
Odets, Clifford, 12, 29, 147, 150
O'Dierno, Angelo, 119
Odishaw, Tracy, 16
Oditz, Carol, 91
Odland, Bruce, 9, 43, 122
Odle, Dwight Richard, 143, 144
Odle, Robert L., 13
O'Donnell, Mimi, 14
O'Donnell, William, 38
O'Donohue, Kathi, 104
Odorisio, Rob, 12, 75, 97, 98, 119, 122, 125, 126, 137, 168
Oerlting, Candace, 89
O'Farrell, Stephen, 41
O'Flaherty, Michael, 61, 62
O'Hara, David, 56
O'Hara, John, 69
O'Hara, Michaela, 95
O'Horgan, Tom, 58, 78, 157
Oien, Tim, 62, 76
Okun, Alexander, 19, 59
Oler, Kim, 161
Olesker, Lizzie, 157
Olich, Michael, 2, 9, 60, 74, 87, 104, 110, 136, 137, 151
Olinder, Lauri, 78, 79
Olive, John, 4, 38, 106, 151
Oliver, Anna, 86, 140, 175
Oliver, Arthur, 138, 139
Oliver, Cynthia, 120
Oliver, Edgar, 78, 79
Oliver, Helen, 78, 79
Olmos, Carlos, 128
Olson, Marcus, 161
Olson, Thomas W., 17, 34, 44, 55, 62, 72, 101
O'Malley, Judy, 21
Omni Tech, 101
Ondaatje, Michael, 115
O'Neal, Cecil, 166
O'Neal, John, 20
One Dream, 78, 93
O'Neill, Eugene, 32, 36, 58, 59, 69, 77, 82, 89, 116, 118, 119, 131, 174
O'Neill, John, 58

O'Neill, Raymond, 40
O'Neill, Robert K., 28
Ong, Han, 11, 85
Orchard, Robert J., 11
Ordover, Andrew, 163
O'Reagan, Terry, 44
O'Reilly, Robert, 43
O'Reilly, Terry, 82, 83, 157
Orendorf, Bruce, 111
Orfinger, Alex P., 137
Ornyece, 97, 173
Orrick, Katy, 156
Orth, Jennifer S., 152
Ortiz, Gladys, 72
Ortmann, Jeffrey, 172
Orton, Joe, 77
Orwell, George, 55, 106
Osborn, Agda, 65
Osborne, John, 15
Osborne, Will, 150
Osborn, Paul, 105, 118
Osgood, Steve, 74
Osherow, Michele, 14, 114
Oshiro, Kiyono, 133
Oshry, Joseph, 56, 99
O'Slynne, Timothy, 127
Osofisan, Femi, 155
Ossorguine, Serge, 80
Ostermann, Curt, 92
Osterman, Marilyn, 52
Oster, Michael, 12, 174, 175
Ostling, Daniel, 21, 32
Ostrovsky, Alexander, 155
Ostrowski, Andrew David, 119
Oswalt, Lynda, 52
Ota, Dean, 163
Othuse, James, 52, 95
Otis, Emmanuel J., 33
O'Toole, Maureen A., 26
Ott, Lori, 171
Otto, Lyndall L., 50
Ott, Sharon, 23, 24, 69
Oullette, Thomas, 174, 175
Ouyoung, Juliet, 111
Ovadia, Moni, 78
Overly, Wendy, 89
Overmyer, Eric, 53, 122, 125, 175
Overton, Paul Preston, 135
Ovington, John, 99
Owen, Bobbi, 121
Owen, Ellen, 33
Owen, Paul, 4
Owens, Catherine L., 133
Owens, Elizabeth, 131
Owens, Ellen M., 14
Owens, Matthew, 7
Owens, Robert, 106
Owens, Rochelle, 78
Owerko, Carrie, 74
OyamO, 45, 96

P

Pabst, Joseph, 158
Pace, Atkin, 58
Pace, Lynne A., 29, 30
Pace, Robert, 78
Pace, Roberto, 93
Packard, Stephen, 95

Packer, Tina, 138, 139
Padova, Kathleen J., 168
Padveen, Susan, 93, 94
Pagano, Duane, 120
Page, Alex, 34
Page, Anita, 34
Pagnol, Marcel, 70
Paine, Don, 67
Painter, Devon, 80, 129, 148
Painter, Walter, 42
Pair, Stephen, 121
Pakledinaz, Martin, 61, 77, 88, 131, 141
Palacios, Monica, 6
Palas, Lisa, 145
Palka, Joe, 143
Palmer, Charly, 55
Palmer, Lee, 55
Palmer, Tim, 54
Panaiotis, 83
Pankhurst, Patrick, 169
Paoletti, John, 8, 44, 72, 95
Pape, Ralph, 33
Pape, Sara Medina, 176
Pappas, Ted, 40, 161
Pappas, Victor, 74
Pardee, Rosemary, 106, 132, 173
Pardess, Yael, 7, 87
Pareiras, Manuel, 157
Parekh, Shafi, 4
Parent, Matthew, 12
Parichy, Dennis, 7, 8, 36, 37, 40, 49, 77, 82, 85, 86, 105, 116, 117, 120, 131, 136, 149
Parich, Mitchell, 129
Parker, Evan, 140
Parker-Jones, Jill, 81
Parker, Matthew, 46
Parker, Stewart, 132
Park, Hwa K.C., 97, 156
Parkins, Zeena, 96, 102
Parkman, Russell, 98, 121, 125
Parks-Satterfield, Deb, 7
Parks, Suzan-Lori, 4, 15, 47, 96, 104, 175
Parnell, Peter, 122
Parra, Marco Antonio de la, 73
Parris-Bailey, Linda, 103
Parr, Larry, 160
Parrott, Robert C., 38
Parry, Chris, 77, 144
Parry, Raphael, 5
Parsley, Jett, 107
Parsons, David, 93
Parsons, Elaine, 55
Parsons, Estelle, 79
Parson, Annie-B, 74
Partha, I Ketut, 83
Partington, Rex, 22
Partington, Tony, 22
Partlan, William, 91, 107
Partridge-Nedds, Laura, 52
Partyka, John, 46
Pascal, David, 7, 53, 64, 74, 78, 136, 137
Paschke, Ed, 162
Pasquesi, David, 127
Pastko, Earl, 126
Patch, Jerry, 110, 111
Patel, Neil, 32, 104, 134

Paterson, Katherine, 55
Patinkin, Sheldon, 60, 94, 147
Paton, Alan, 61
Patricca, Nicholas A., 21
Patrick, John, 22
Patterson, Anne C., 171
Patterson, Billy "Spaceman", 45
Patterson, Howard, 15, 77
Patterson, Kelly James, 81
Patterson, Laura, 4
Patterson, Vaughn, 91, 161
Patton, Joseph, 65
Patton, Nancy Linn, 149
Patton, Pat, 110, 125
Patton, Patti, 107
Patton, William W., 109
Paulin, David C., 40, 72, 119
Paulsen, Cris, 134
Paulsen, Rick, 2, 16, 53, 74, 136, 137
Paul, David, 157
Paul, Kent, 118
Paul-Thompson, Mayme, 7
Pax, Stephen, 18
Payne, Brian, 71
Payne, Darwin Reid, 26
Payne, Jim, 25
Pazik, Liz, 21
Pazos, Juan, 166
Peak, Danny, 49
Peakes, John, 28
Pearcy, Benjamin, 171
Pearle, Gary, 60, 132, 145
Pearl, Precious, 7
Pearson, Barbara, 163
Pearson, David, 20
Pearson, Sybille, 83, 87, 152
Peaslee, Richard, 55, 64, 78, 93
Pechar, Thomas, 135
Peck, Andre, 76
Peck, Gregory, 77
Peck, James, 65
Peck, Sabrina, 43
Pederson, Rose, 2, 16, 24, 136, 137
Pedito, Paul, 79
Pedota, Julio, 21
Peebles, Kay, 134
Peery, Reiner, 133
Pelletier, Carol Ann, 78, 79, 118
Pellicciaro, Elena, 74, 163
Pelster, Joette M., 43
Peluso, Ron, 10, 62
Pelzig, Daniel, 61
Pence, Ann-Carol, 40, 62
Pendleton, Austin, 16, 82, 171
Peniston, Pamela, 84, 103
Penn, Matthew, 58
Pennoyer, John, 138, 139
Pen, Polly, 37, 107, 125, 167
Penrod, Jacqueline, 21, 94, 172
Penrod, Richard, 21, 94, 172
Peperone, Jerry, 81
Pepper, Pam, 113
Peraino, Christopher, 29
Percy, Pamela, 161
Perdick, Bob, 14, 33, 114
Pereira, George, 37
Perelman, S.J., 175
Peretz, Deborah, 14, 33, 114
Pergolizzi, Mark, 120

Perkins, DW Phineas, 72
Perkins, Kathy, 72, 92, 148, 166
Perlman, Arthur, 61, 100, 161
Perloff, Carey, 9, 39
Perna, Daniele, 170
Perrault, Charles, 17, 26, 47, 55, 101, 112, 128, 158
Perry, Alvin, 6, 9, 86
Perry, Charles D. Jr., 26
Perry, Doug, 167
Perry, Jeff, 92, 147
Perry, Karen, 122
Perry, Steven, 149
Perry, William, 158
Peryon, Lynne, 104
Petersen, Christian, 127
Peterson, Brian, 16
Peterson, Eric, 8, 36, 129, 143
Peterson, Hannibal, 93
Peterson, Kevin, 21
Peterson, Lisa, 31, 32, 66, 77, 96, 102, 122, 175
Peterson, Matthew, 176
Peterson, Michael A., 112
Peterson, Rick, 16
Peterson, Robert, 8, 16, 60, 72, 91, 105, 109, 110, 128
Peterson, Tonja, 130
Peterson, Wade, 140
Peters, Clarke, 57
Peters, Phil, 22
Peters, Scott, 93
Peters, Wes, 72
Petosa, Jim, 105, 106
Petrarca, David, 47, 61, 100, 122, 164
Petrovich, Victoria, 52, 60, 77, 97, 134, 135
Petty, Stephen, 3, 8
Pewitt, Betty, 26
Pfuderer, Bil, 80, 81
Pharr, Peggy, 67
Phelan, Ceal, 114
Phelan, Jane Schloss, 106, 173
Phelan, Tony, 161
Phetteplace, Gordon R., 28
Philadelphia Anti-Grafitti Network, 103
Philippi, Michael S., 44, 45, 60, 95, 127, 139
Phillips, Bob, Jr., 40
Phillips, Chris, 32, 94, 166, 172
Phillips, J.H., 163
Phillips, R. Scott, 165
Phippin, Jackson, 31, 32, 47
Phipps, Wanda, 78, 79
Picinich, Susan, 126
Pickering, Steve, 110, 111
Pick, John C., 95
Pickle, Cecelia, 120, 121
Pickover, Stephen, 96
Pielmeier, John, 2, 16, 129
Pierce, Eddie, 158
Pierce, Jean, 26
Pietraszek, Rita, 44, 45, 61, 69, 94, 127, 139
Pietri, Pedro, 96
Pifer, Drury, 173
Pilar, Susan, 9
Pilbrow, Richard, 42, 80

Pilcher, Paul, 89
Pinkney, Leon, 156
Pinkney, Scott, 29
Pinn, Irene, 42
Pino, Joe, 7
Pintauro, Joe, 23
Pinter, Harold, 9, 59, 75, 91, 109, 131, 143, 169
Pirandello, Luigi, 15, 114
Pirkle, Mac, 62, 151, 152
Pirolo, Mark, 124
PiRoman, John, 19
Pittman, Mike, 17
Pittman, Robert W., 100
Pitts, Barbara, 102
Pitts-Wiley, Ricardo, 139
Pizzaro, Raymond, 156
Placido, Stephen, Jr., 124
Platt, Martin L., 5, 59, 60, 98, 121, 128
Platt, Peggy, 7
Plaxton, James, 41
Plimpton, George, 23
Ploof, Katrina, 129
Plummer, Joe, 166
Pockriss, Lee, 57, 61
Podagrosi, June, 35
Podagrosi, Victor, 35
Poertner, Tim, 81
Poe, Edgar Allan, 35, 67
Poggi, Gregory, 71
Pogrebin, Robin, 161
Polak, Roman, 139
Polen, Patricia, 133
Poleszak, Andrew, 12
Poleszak, Andrew J., 175
Poling, Chan, 154
Polk, Gregory, 18
Polk, Julie, 157
Polyansky, Nikita, 157
Pomo Afro Homos, 7
Poole, Chris, 24
Poole, Laura, 12
Poole, Stanley, 159
Poole, Tom, 34, 154
Pope, Barbara, 56
Pope. L, William, 163
Popkin, Adina Kaufman, 109
Poplyk, Gregory A., 29
Porter, Brenda, 163
Porter, Cole, 36, 59, 135, 159
Porterfield, Donna, 130
Porterfield, Robert, 21
Porter, Kim, 85
Porter, Lynne, 68
Porter, Paul, 177
Porter, Regina M., 122
Posante, Jim, 126
Posner, Aaron, 14, 114
Posner, Adrienne, 101
Posner, Kenneth, 25, 31, 66, 100, 113, 122, 126, 136, 137, 167
Posse, Carl A., 115
Post, Douglas, 147, 166
Postel, Steve, 78
Poster, June, 48
Pothier, Kevin, 22, 89
Potok, Chaim, 94, 116
Potter, Lynn T., 129
Potter, Nicole, 74

Pottlitzer, Joanne, 73, 163
Potts, David, 19, 36, 40
Pound, Ezra, 132
Pound, Janet, 51
Powell, Anthony, 50
Powell, Barbara, 120
Powell, Donna Vidas, 10
Powell, Gary, 177
Powell, J. Dakota, 107
Powell, Mary Ann, 149
Powell-Pa, Marianne, 109
Power, Harriet, 33
Powers, Dennis, 9, 47, 50
Powers, P.J., 16, 17
Powers, Terrie, 158
Preminger, David, 82
Prendergast, Shirley, 45, 46, 57, 59, 63, 116
Pressgrove, Larry, 128, 129
Preston, Scott, 163
Preston, Travis, 72, 96, 175
Prevert, Jacques, 77, 155, 175
Prewitt, Tom, 120, 125, 132
Preziosi, Thomas, 153
Price, Bill, 150
Price, Bob, 5
Price, Jane E., 136
Price, Judy Thompson, 176
Price, Lonny, 47, 57, 61, 167
Price, Michael P., 61
Price, Reynolds, 68, 169
Price, William A. III, 142, 143
Prida, Dolores, 127, 128
Priestley, J.B., 136, 171
Prieto, Jorge, 152
Prigmore, James, 119
Primeau, Soni Moreno, 156
Prince, Charles, 37
Prischepenko, Elena, 78
Proctor, 70
Proctor, Nina, 80
Proett, Daniel, 45, 46, 57
Provenza, Rosario, 98, 126, 133
Provonsha, Carol, 124
Pruitt, Dan, 3, 21
Pryor, Bryn, 34
Psacharopoulos, Nikos, 170
Puff, Michael, 160
Pulliam, Rence, 37
Purcell, Luann, 3
Purdy, Claude, 7, 40, 47, 92, 119
Purdy-Gordon, Carolyn, 110
Purdy, James, 156
Purdy, Stephen, 46
Purry, Lester, 71
Push, Vernon, 26
Puszh, David, 32
Putch, Jean, 9, 39
Putch, Pamela, 169
Pyles, Cathy Susan, 95
Pyne, James F., Jr., 14, 114
Pyskacek, June, 166

Q

Quan, Dori, 134
Quayle, Anthony, 38
Queary, Charles, 14
Queen, Jim, 13

Quick, Bobbie, 104
Quigley, Erin, 69, 147
Quill, Barbara J., 41
Quinn, Don, 22
Quinn, Stephen, 34
Quinones, Ramon Mendez, 128
Quintero, Joaquin, 171
Quintero, Jose, 8
Quintero, Serafin, 171
Quinton, Everett, 134, 171

R

Rabb, Ellis, 98, 118
Rabe, David, 12, 59
Rabun, Joe, 163
Radisch, Neil, 167
Radosh, Steve, 169
Radzinsky, Edvard, 75
Rae, Stacey, 27
Rafter, Michael, 76
Ragey, Joe, 120, 140, 160
Ragland, Jim, 2, 7, 64, 73, 74, 137
Rahman, Aishah, 114
Raiford, Michael, 176, 177
Raiselis, Robert M., 170
Raitt, James, 8, 42, 105
Rajeckas, Paul, 91
Ramay, Steven, 56
Ramey, Nayna, 62, 93
Ramont, Mark, 28
Ramos, Richard Russell, 72, 98, 119
Rampino, Lewis D., 4
Ramsaur, Michael F., 160
Ramsey, Galen G., 21, 110, 166
Randall, Bob, 40
Randolph-Wright, Charles, 39
Rankin, John, 113, 120
Rankin, Rick, 6, 7
Ranney, Don, 67
Ranson, Edward, 111
Raphael, Jay E., 35, 113
Raphael-Schirmer, Nanalee, 172
Raposo, Joe, 15, 89, 152
Rappaport, Stephen, 20
Rasche, David, 166
Raskin, Kenny, 155
Rasmussen, Rick, 10, 55, 90, 91
Rasmussen, Steve, 133, 134
Rater, Joan, 157
Rathke, Kathryn, 23, 53
Rathman, John G., 160
Rauch, Bill, 43, 54
Ravicchio, Giacomo, 30
Rawicz, Karl, 37, 85, 86
Rawls, Keith, 76
Rawn, Debbie Wools, 18
Raya, Monica, 175
Ray, Constance, 18, 36, 37, 113, 159
Raye, Jillian, 5
Ray, Gregory O., 114
Ray, Reggie, 150
Raywood, Maggie, 111
Razymovskaya, Ludmilla, 64
Reagan, Randall, 120
Ream, James, 145
Rea, Oliver, 64
Reaves, Sandra, 9, 46
Rebeck, Theresa, 137

Reber, James P., 135
Recht, Ray, 75, 76, 119, 120
Reddin, Keith, 32, 61, 86, 172, 173
Redd, Randy, 99
Redman, John, 134
Redmond, Barbara, 59, 60
Redwood, John, 46
Redwood, Lillie-Marie, 46
Reeder, Barbara, 172
Reeds, Allison, 61, 147
Reed, Brian, 44
Reed, Brian Alan, 104
Reed, Charles, 163
Reed, Molly Welch, 135
Reese, Kevin, 30
Reese, Mike, 53
Reeves, Kelly, 103
Rehm, Rush, 160
Reid, Graham, 19, 31
Reid, Hazel, 41
Reid, Nick, 105
Reid-Petty, Jane, 99
Reiffel, David, 43
Reinert, Matthew J., 4
Reinking, Ann, 170
Rein, Mercedes, 105
Reiser, Robert, 8
Reiser, Steve, 71
Reish, Michelle, 157
Reisman, Jane, 8, 42, 105
Reiter, Tom, 76
Reith, Jeanne, 169
Reitman, Deborah, 47
Rejsa, Reid, 34
Remsen, Penny L., 174, 175
Renard, Jules, 70
Renner, Daniel, 74
Rennie, Bruce, 158
Reno, 61
Repole, Charles, 61
Retallack, John, 141
Reuler, Jack, 92, 93
Reyes, Carlos Jose, 127, 128
Reynolds, Brett W., 176
Reynolds, David, 171
Reynolds, Michael, 159
Reynolds, Sally, 62
Rheam, Carol, 27
Rhone, Trevor, 166
Ribant, Alan, 126
Ribman, Ronald, 11
Ricca, Bobbi, 49
Ricci, Anthony PM, 164
Ricciardi, Gene, 100
Rice, Elmer, 171
Rice, Ric Thomas, 149, 150
Rice, Ross, 120
Rice, Susan, 62
Rice, Tim, 46, 65, 112, 119, 168, 170
Richard, Ellen, 131
Richards, Lloyd, 9, 61, 107, 137
Richardson, Bruce, 5
Richardson, Gary, 67
Richardson, Harry, 170
Richardson, Karl, 19
Richardson, Katryn, 168
Richardson, L. Kenneth, 45
Richardson, Paul, 14, 168
Richardson, Stanley, 139

Richards, Stephen, 14
Richmond, David, 4, 55, 95, 123
Richmond, Jeff, 35
Richter, Charles, 112, 113
Rickel, David, 13
Rickel, Larry, 64
Ricket, David, 13
Ricklin, Don, 174, 175
Rickman, Pam, 120
Rickman, Victor, 133
Rider, Ivan, 99
Ridley, Arthur, 72, 128
Rieck, Margaret, 119
Rieling, Dale, 167
Riford, Lloyd S., III, 67, 101
Rigdon, Kevin, 8, 11, 32, 91, 117, 147, 172
Rigdon, Lisa, 26
Riggs, Lynn, 5, 46, 112, 120, 153
Riggs, P. Dudley, 115
Riggs, Rita, 9, 39
Rigler, Lou, 80, 81
Riley, Donna, 37, 82, 97, 98
Riley, Eric, 152
Riley, Stacy, 22
Rincon, Jennifer McCray, 50
Rinehart, Delmar L. Jr., 36
Rinne, Kelly A., 28
Rintels, David, 170
Ripa, Augustine, 163
Riske, Marc, 34, 35
Rita, Rui, 170, 171
Rivela, Francisco, 157
Rivera, Jose, 4, 66, 77, 100, 145
Rivera, Jose M., 113, 168
Rivera-Resto, John, 41
Rivers, Keena, 1
Roach, Dan, 59
Roach, Jim, 126
Roach, Kevin J., 83
Roark, Jonathan, 70
Robbins, Carrie, 171
Robbins, Jeff, 67
Robbins, Jerome, 28
Robbins, Polly Allen, 125
Robbins, Tim, 79
Robelen, Elizabeth, 142, 143
Roberson, Jerome, 76
Roberts, Chapman, 107, 122
Roberts, Garth, 31
Roberts, Jimmy, 161
Roberts, Jordon, 133
Roberts, Kitty, 12
Roberts, Marianne Claire, 136
Robertson, Allen, 81
Robertson, Jimmy, 99
Robertson, Lanie, 21, 32, 36, 47, 60, 64, 86, 91, 92, 99, 145, 171
Robertson, Toby, 168
Robertson, Will, 4
Roberts, Rhoda, 76, 106
Roberts, Steven, 38
Roberts, Tony, 167
Robinette, Joseph, 30, 52, 99, 136
Robins, Michael, 70, 71
Robinson, Barbara, 26, 55
Robinson, Daniel, 128
Robinson, Donald Nathaniel, 27
Robinson, Dorothy Marie, 22
Robinson, Greg, 85

Robinson, Jeff, 44
Robinson, Mary B., 115, 116
Robinson, Maureen, 104
Robinson, Nelson, 5, 145
Robinson, Rob, 160
Robinson, Robert, 79
Robinson, R.T., 66
Robinson, Sharon, 101
Robinson, Tim, 159
Robins, Robert, 66, 67
Robison, Richard, 159
Robles, Elsa Ortiz, 72
Robles, Frank, 72
Rocamora, Carol, 116, 117
Roche, Nancy K., 31
Rock, Christopher, 153, 154
Rodale, Anna, 112
Rodgers, Bruce E., 19, 124, 149
Rodgers, Mary, 93, 161, 175, 176
Rodgers, Richard, 5, 9, 29, 37, 46, 47, 69, 91, 95, 112, 120, 129, 158, 175
Rodrieguez, Yolanda, 157
Rodriguez, David E., 176
Rodriguez, Diane, 133, 134
Rodriguez, Marcia, 112
Rodriguez, Pancho, 52
Rodriguez, Paul Bonin, 7
Rodriguez, Robert Xavier, 173
Roehrman, Todd, 73, 74, 144
Rogan, Heather, 173
Rogers, Jennifer, 147
Rogers, Roxanne, 122
Rogers, Theodore C., 155
Rohrer, Sue Ellen, 58
Rohr, Sandy, 104
Rojo, Jerry, 104, 147, 171
Roland, Lori, 115
Rolf, Wendy, 78
Romance, Paul D., 56
Roman, Munoz, 152
Rome, Atif, 164, 165
Rome, Harold, 70
Romero, Christopher, 83
Romero, Constanza, 9, 72, 74, 91, 137
Romersberger, Sara, 96
Rominger, Brett, 150
Rooney, Deborah, 114, 161
Roose-Evans, Janes, 90
Root, Melina, 11, 37, 66, 100
Rose, David, 43
Rose, Howard, 46, 47, 69
Rose, Louisa, 73
Rosenblatt, Jana, 161
Rosenblum, Joshua, 122
Rosenblum, M. Edgar, 81
Rosenbush, Marc, 32
Rosendaul, Christina, 142
Rosenfeld, Amy, 157
Rosenfeld, Hillary, 58
Rosenkranz, Ian, 172
Rosen, Louis, 141
Rosen, Robert, 154, 155
Rosen, Steven, 89, 97, 98, 99, 174
Rosenthal, Sandy, 16
Rosenthal, Todd, 146, 175
Rose, Philip, 148
Rose, Richard, 12, 21, 22, 66, 67, 89, 175

Rose, Stella, 169
Roslevich, John, Jr., 128, 129, 148
Rossen, Howard, 113
Rossett, CaCa, 100
Rossetti, Christina, 37, 125
Ross, Aden, 133, 134
Ross, Barbara Hauben, 74
Ross, Carolyn L., 128, 129, 165
Rossi, Al, 104
Rossi, Richard, 86
Rossing, Peter, 125
Ross, Jerry, 105, 176
Ross, Katherine, 44
Ross, Kevin E., 168
Ross, Monica Long, 34, 35
Ross, Pamela, 42
Ross, Sharlene, 76
Ross, Stuart, 8, 42, 61, 105, 161
Rostand, Edmond, 9, 43, 63, 92, 112, 128, 165
Rotch, Arthur, 115
Rothchild, Kennon, 74, 163
Rothenberger, Ronna, 97
Roth, Ann, 11, 37, 85, 168, 173
Roth, James A., 27
Roth, Katherine, 140, 175
Rothman, Carole, 137
Rothman, Stephan, 59
Roth, Michael, 77, 85, 133, 134, 137, 143, 144
Roth, Robert Jess, 161
Rotondo, David A., 164
Rouco, Jose-Antonio, 157
Roudebush, William, 168
Rough, William, 153
Rourke, Michael, 6, 166, 172
Rousseau, Brenda, 76
Rousselet, Didier, 163
Rowe, Gregory T., 114
Rowlings, Jeff, 37, 84, 85
Rowny, Stefan, 53
Rowser, Bertin, 11
Royal, Reginald, 167
Royce, James, 53
Rozovsky, Mark, 78
Ruben, Anne, 93, 113, 114, 154
Ruben, Martin, 114
Rubenstein, Kim, 113
Rubin, Adelle S., 49
Rubin, Jeff, 142
Rubin, Judith O., 122
Rubinstein, Madelyn, 167
Rubin, Steven, 9, 69, 90
Rubio, Jose Lopez, 152
Ruby, Harry, 61
Ruch, Alan, 34, 35
Rucker, Mark, 140, 144
Rudall, Nicholas, 44, 45, 105, 130
Rudman, Michael, 100
Rudnick, Paul, 6, 10, 18, 42, 47, 58, 83, 99, 106, 151, 175, 177
Ruebsaat, Norbert, 32
Rueff, Roger, 143, 144, 166
Ruhl, Malcolm, 61, 163
Runyan, Jim, 13
Runyon, Damon, 151
Rupel, Bill M., 29, 30
Rupnik, Kevin, 149, 150, 159
Rupp, Kimberly J., 67
Rush, David, 59

Russell, Cindy, 152
Russell, C. David, 171
Russell, Gail, 86
Russell, Jerry, 145
Russell, John C., 96
Russell, Mark, 57
Russell, Norman, 38
Russell, Richard, 174, 175
Russell, Roberta, 53
Russell, Willy, 12, 13, 28, 31, 36, 65, 72, 89, 90, 95, 105, 113, 138, 146, 158, 168, 175, 177
Ruth, Anita, 34, 71
Rutherford, Carolyn, 94, 95
Rutherford, Stanley, 173
Ruyle, Leigh Ann, 70
Ruzika, Donna, 143, 144
Ruzika, Tom, 143
Ryack, Rita, 86
Ryan, James C., 158
Ryan, Kate Moira, 96
Rybolt, Peter, 110, 111
Rye, James W., 26
Ryerson, Judith A., 112
Ryskind, Morrie, 15, 28, 40, 61, 127

S

Saar, David, 34, 35
Sabatini, Rafael, 159
Sabido, Miguel, 25
Sabinson, Mara, 49, 170
Sabourin, Marcel, 67
Saccomandi, Gigi, 78
Sachs, Ann, 124
Sachs, Buckley, 145
SADHAPPY, 137
Saez, Isabel, 109
Safan, Craig, 40, 56
Sagal, Peter, 43
Sage, Jefferson, 6, 9
Sahlins, Bernard, 44, 45
Saidpour, Massoud, 41
Sailer, John, 89
Saimo, Dan, 7
Saint, David, 119, 122, 136, 137, 171
Sakren, Jared, 6
Salas, Tomas, 51
Saldivar, Norma, 91
Sale, James, 19, 109, 110
Salen, James, 71
Salerni, Lou, 47, 122
Salerno, Chip, 18
Salett, Peter, 115
Salinas, Ric, 77
Salinger, Michael, 41
Salomon, Wayne, 148
Salovey, Todd, 134
Salowich, David, 165
Salsbury, Lynda L., 22, 31
Saltz, Amy, 36, 72, 107
Salzberg, Marc, 8
Salzer, Beeb, 27
Salzman, Eric, 10
Sames, Barry, 116
Samoff, Marjorie, 10, 11
Sampson, Edward, 53
Sams, Milton, 3

Samuels, Mark, 23
Sanchez, Edwin, 21
Sanchez-Scott, Milcha, 116
Sandberg, Lynn, 32, 172
Sandberg, R.N., 136, 145
Sandefur, James D., 7, 47, 66, 92
Sandelin, Sandy, 67
Sanders, Kerry, 150
Sanders, Kim, 120
Sanders, Naila, 169
Sanderson, Kirsten, 37, 122
Sanders, Ty, 111
Sanders, Wes, 41
Sandler, Susan, 37
Sandoval, Mari, 25
Sandra-Christine, 168
Sandvik, Mel, 115
Sandys, Nick, 145
Sanford, Suzi, 51
Sankiavicus, Tim, 139
Sankowich, Lee, 86, 119, 120
Santana, Rodolfo, 166
Santa Vicca, Edmund, 41
Santeiro, Luis, 42, 73, 98, 160, 177
Sanville, Guy, 126
Sapienza, Christopher, 103
Sarazin, Archie, 55
Sargent, Peter E., 128, 129
Sarnoff, Rosita, 93
Saroyan, William, 15, 160, 169
Sarring, Goran, 30
Sartre, Jean-Paul, 163
Sarver, Linda, 119
Sass, Joel, 155
Saternow, Tim, 7, 53, 118, 136
Sater, Steven, 36
Saucedo, Jose Guadalupe, 98
Sauerbrey, William J. III, 22
Saunders, Lilian, 64
Savage, Linda, 120
Savage, Stanley D., 136
Saver, Jeffrey, 15
Savick, Wesley, 162
Saviola, Camille, 167
Savoy, Bill, 12, 175
Sawaryn, David, 122
Sawyer, Cathey Crowell, 129
Sawyer, Ruth, 54, 55
Scarborough, Fred, 18
Scardino, Don, 122
Scarlata, Estela, 25
Scarritt, Hunt, 107
Scassellati, Vincent, 92
Scatuorchio, Tee, 11, 37
Schachter, Beth, 36, 96, 137
Schachter, Richard, 78
Schaechter, Ben, 107
Schaeffer, Eric, 48, 49
Schave, Ellsworth, 80
Schay, Daniel, 22
Schechner, Richard, 79
Schechter, David, 128, 159
Scheder, Jo, 67
Scheer, William, 169
Scheie, Danny, 140
Schein, David, 57
Schein, Gideon Y., 31
Schellenbaum, Tim, 78, 79, 93
Schell, Maureen, 156, 171
Schembri, Julian, 53

Schenkar, Joan, 96
Schenkkan, Robert, 87
Scheper, Lori, 55
Schermer, Phil C., 1, 2
Schermer, Shelley Henze, 2, 136
Schertler, Nancy, 15, 36, 136, 137, 141, 149, 167
Scher, Adam, 175
Schickele, David, 13
Schierman, Linda, 7
Schifter, Peter Mark, 40
Schildkraut, Leonora, 142
Schiller, Friedrich, 75
Schilling, Sandra, 150
Schimmel, John, 46, 59, 89, 98, 150, 151, 168
Schirle, Joan, 49
Schirmer, Tim, 32, 172
Schisgal, Murray, 94
Schlesinger, Sarah, 161
Schlitz, Laura Amy, 144, 145
Schmidman, Jo Ann, 106, 107
Schmidt, Amy, 94
Schmidt, Chuck, 144, 145
Schmidt, Douglas W., 69, 105
Schmidt, Ed, 105
Schmidt, Harvey, 31, 43, 89, 92, 119
Schmidt, Henry J., 100
Schmidt, John, 102
Schmidt, Paul, 174, 175
Schmidt, Robert N., 8
Schmidt, William, 65
Schmidt, W.F., 125
Schmidt, Zoltan, 64
Schmiedl, Eric, 55
Schmiel, William F., 129
Schmink, Joanna, 3, 68, 138
Schmitt, Ed, 47
Schneeberger, Frank, 83
Schneggenburger, Marie, 150
Schneider, Jeffrey D., 72, 104
Schneider, John, 161, 162
Schnick, Dana, 115
Schnitzler, Arthur, 27, 69, 70, 91, 96
Schnormeier, Kimberly, 170
Schoenfeld, Pat, 172
Scholey, Arthur, 69
Schons, Alain, 49
Schooler, Luan, 115
Schrader, Dan, 132, 173
Schreiber, Terry, 25
Schreier, Dan, 16, 19, 31, 39, 141, 173, 175
Schreier, Tom, 145
Schreiner, Don, 164
Schroder, William, 33, 34
Schubert, Barbara, 44
Schudson, Ruth, 90
Schuette, James, 11, 54, 102
Schuler, Duane M., 34
Schulfer, Roche, 60
Schulman, Charlie, 85
Schulman, Susan H., 116
Schultz, Gloria Jones, 161
Schultz, Joanne, 156
Schulz, Gretchen, 140
Schulz, Karen, 104
Schuman, Craig E., 135
Schuster, Heather, 96
Schwartz, Delmore, 160

Schwartz-Hartley, Steven, 98
Schwartz, Robert Joel, 22, 75
Schwartz, Stephen, 18, 43, 89, 120
Schwarz, Dahn, 18, 19
Schwarz, Willy, 84
Schweikhard, Jon, 5
Schweizer, David, 100, 171, 173
Scofield, Pamela, 4, 59, 60, 106, 150
Scott, Barry, 152
Scott, Bryan, 4
Scott, Campbell, 127
Scott, Christopher, 161
Scott, Douglas, 49, 59, 113, 117
Scott, Dred, 134
Scott, Harold, 45, 46, 63
Scott, James, 31, 63, 92, 116, 118
Scott, Mary, 49
Scott, Oz, 19, 35, 93, 107
Scott, Seret, 8, 9, 45, 72, 96, 105, 168, 176
Scott, Stephen P., 123
Scott, Steve, 21, 60, 61, 111
Scott, Sue, 71
Scott, Terry, 120
Scuder, Domenick, 142
Scully, Patrick, 71
Scully, Sunny Jung, 173
Seago, Howie, 7
Sears, Gretchen, 54, 55
Sears, Joe, 13, 29, 91, 123, 134
Sears, Marnie, 133, 134
Seawell, Donald R., 49
Sebastian, Ellen, 85
Sedaris, David, 79, 156
Sedlachek, Buffy, 122
See, Cynthia, 67
Segall, Scott, 43
Segal, David F., 66, 69, 105, 137
Segal, Gilles, 27, 91, 170
Seger, Richard, 9, 50, 105
Seibert, John, 126
Seidel, George, 138
Seiden, Serge, 150
Seifter, Harvey, 84, 85
Seigler, Ben, 96
Seine, Curt, 114
Sekon, R.P., 126
Selden, Cynthia Mason, 59
Selden, William, 59
Sellers, Barbara E., 49
Selman, Matthew, 129
Selskaya, Fagilla, 136
Seltzer, Daniel, 87
Semmelhack, Henry P., 148
Senelick, Laurence, 38, 39
Senie, Curt, 14, 49, 116
Senske, Rebecca, 55
Sepesy, Michael, 41
Seppi, Lisa, 41
Serdiuk, Tanya, 157
Sergel, Christopher, 46, 50, 55, 101
Sergel, Kristen, 44, 55, 158
Serrand, Dominique, 77, 154, 155, 175
Serrano, Jose, 152
Serroni, J.C., 128
Server, Darren, 169
Seton, Mimi, 104
Seuss, Dr., 34
Sevilla, 152

Sevy, Bruce K., 50, 151
Sewell, Dennita, 175
Sewell, Richard, 153, 154
Seyda, Barbara, 163
Seyd, Richard, 9, 86, 109
Shaffer, Amanda, 40, 41
Shaffer, Anthony, 69, 170
Shaffer, E. Scott, 143
Shaffer, Peter, 4, 13, 48, 66, 89, 90, 99, 119, 123, 125, 131, 159, 160, 169, 170
Shaffer, Tanya, 41
Shaiman, Marc, 78
Shakespeare, Robert A., 165
Shakespeare, William, 2, 4, 5, 6, 8, 11, 14, 22, 23, 26, 27, 30, 31, 43, 44, 47, 50, 54, 60, 63, 64, 66, 69, 72, 73, 75, 77, 78, 79, 80, 87, 88, 89, 90, 91, 92, 97, 98, 100, 102, 105, 106, 109, 110, 116, 118, 119, 121, 131, 133, 136, 137, 138, 139, 140, 141, 143, 146, 152, 153, 154, 155, 156, 158, 159, 163, 164, 165, 166, 169, 170, 171, 175
Shaktman, Ben, 119
Shalwitz, Howard, 173
Shamash, Beba, 61
Shamas, Laura, 117
Shanahan, Patrick, 44
Shange, Ntozake, 45, 46
Shankman, Scott, 155
Shanks, Joyce, 13
Shank, Terrance, 42
Shanley, John Patrick, 3, 85
Shannon, Peggy, 79, 97, 135
Shapiro, Diane E., 104
Shapiro, Herb, 148
Shapiro, Leo, 78, 157
Shapiro, Steve, 42
Sharif, Bina, 156, 157
Sharp, Kurt, 32, 139, 147
Sharp, Michael, 23
Shattuck, Scott, 74
Shaver, Diane, 169
Shaw, Barnett, 69
Shaw, Brad, 44
Shaw, Deborah, 40
Shaw, George Bernard, 6, 11, 14, 21, 24, 28, 30, 32, 39, 50, 56, 59, 65, 66, 69, 72, 75, 77, 83, 86, 90, 98, 99, 113, 119, 129, 131, 137, 141, 143, 145, 150, 154, 167
Shaw, Guillermo Fernandez, 128
Shaw, Man, 171
Shawn, Wallace, 125, 130
Shaw, Paul, 7
Shaw, Peggy, 7, 78
Shaw, Richard, 101
Shaw, Ron, 18, 54, 55
Shaw, Stephen, 46
Shea, Andrew, 98
Shearer, Steve, 80
Shearman, Alan, 104
Sheck, Kenneth E., 153
Sheehy, Pat Murphy, 142
Sheffield, Ann, 57, 61, 72
Shelley, Percy Bysshe, 75
Shelley, Steven L., 125
Shell, Martin, 28

Shepard, Jane Merlin, 161
Shepard, Joan, 26
Shepard, Sam, 3, 10, 27, 43, 99, 125, 138
Shepherd, Elizabeth, 32
Sheppard, Cherie, 153
Sheppard, Mark, 53
Sher, Bartlett, 64
Sherer, Carrol Russell, 57
Sheridan, Peter, 81
Sheridan, Richard Brinsley, 55
Sheridan, Rossa, 81
Sherin, Edwin, 131
Sherin, Mimi Jordan, 4, 100, 125
Sher, Jonathan, 14, 171
Sherman, Charley, 111
Sherman, Geoffrey, 124, 125
Sherman, Guy, 80, 118, 122, 137
Sherman, James, 42, 113, 142, 166
Sherman, Jonathan Marc, 122
Sherman, Kim D., 160
Sherman, Loren, 12, 37, 58, 82, 86, 117, 119
Sherman, Margo Lee, 156, 157
Sherman, Martin, 171
Sherman, Stuart, 157
Sherman, Susan, 78
Sherman, Ted, 120
Sherrin, Ned, 175
Shevelove, Burt, 22, 129, 175
Shields, Robert, 42
Shields, Timothy J., 59
Shiffrin, David E., 81
Shilhanek, Todd, 89
Shilling, A. Gary, 97
Shimizu, Kunio, 111
Shimosato, Kiko, 134
Shimp, Chris, 41
Shinner, Sandy, 166
Shinn, P. Hamilton, 8
Shinn, Rob, 132
Shin, Sung, 81
Shippee, Deborah L., 72
Shire, David, 37, 83, 120, 152, 158, 164
Shireman, Ellen, 37, 86
Shirky, Clay, 21, 174
Shissler, Mary, 10
Shockley, Ed, 11, 136
Shoemaker, Laurel, 95
Shohet, Jeffrey M., 134
Shook, Robert, 61, 94, 139, 147, 166
Shook, Warner, 9, 73, 74, 87
Shorter, Alan, 34
Short, Ron, 131
Shortt, Paul, 19
Shotwell, Judith, 1
Shouse, Carolyn, 112
Shouse, Jack, 111, 112
Shouse, Rebecca, 69, 145
Shriver, Chris, 59, 150
Shue, Larry, 8, 46, 91, 95
Shulgasser, Mark, 9, 39
Shultz, Sherrie, 145
Shuman, Mort, 12
Shumann, Peter, 157
Shuman, Patricia, 151
Shvartz, Yevgeny, 14
Shyre, Paul, 57
Sibilia, Michelle, 157

Sicangco, Eduardo, 36, 37, 88
Sickels, Q. Brian, 149
Sidner, Syd, 171
Siefert, Lynn, 122
Siegel, Betty, 15
Siegle, Peggy, 125
Sienna, James, 78
Sierra, Ruben, 63, 64
Sie, James, 44
Siklos, Csanad Z., 50, 136
Silbert, Peter, 53
Siler, Michele, 129
Sillen, Richard J., Jr., 17
Silva, Alfred J.S., 67
Silva, David, 52
Silven, Diane, 160
Silver, Joan Micklin, 18, 64, 93, 105, 123, 137, 149, 151
Silverman, Stanley, 93
Silver, Nicky, 85, 167, 173
Silversher, Michael, 55
Silvestri, Martin, 58, 169
Simard, Sherrol A., 160
Simmons, Bill, 58, 111
Simmons, Gary, 104
Simms, Laura, 156, 157
Simo, Ana Maria, 96, 102
Simone, Denise, 158
Simon, Barney, 44
Simon, Eli, 165
Simon, Mayo, 4, 120, 147
Simon, Neil, 10, 12, 31, 58, 89, 92, 135, 145, 151, 160, 167, 168, 174
Simon, Roger Hendricks, 174
Simonson, Eric, 44, 79, 147
Simpson, Jim, 54, 96
Simpson, Mark, 9, 10
Simpson, Tanya, 18
Sims, Michael V., 97, 98, 175
Singer, Connie, 170
Singer, Gammy L., 169
Singer, Isaac Bashevis, 94
Singer, Nora, 98
Sinise, Gary, 147
Sinkkonen, Eric, 37, 133
Sinnott, Christine, 157
Sinsheimer, Karen, 140
Siquenza, Herbert, 77
Sirikh, Natalia, 136
Sirlin, Jerome, 19
Sisley, Todd, 9
Sissons, Norelle, 152
Sjoblomv, Paula, 156
Skaggs, Calvin, 37, 96
Skelton, Geoffrey, 64
Skelton, Thomas, 63, 168
Skeoch, Skipper, 133
Skipitares, Theodora, 78, 79, 156
Sklar, George, 175
Skloff, Michael, 61, 161
Skoczek, Carri, 162
Skorstad, Deborah, 23
Skratthult, Olle, 62
Skupin, Rebecca, 123
Slabe, Ron, 41
Slade, Michael, 161
Slaiman, Marjorie, 15
Slater, Sindy, 104
Slavin, Kenda, 52, 106, 107
Slawson, Carla, 90

Slee, Paul, 95
Slick, Kahlei A., 83
Slisky, C.E., 8
Sloan, Hilary, 21
Sloan, Larry, 127
Slovic, David, 14
Slowiak, James, 41
Small, Vicky, 56
Smart, Richard, 25
Smart, Roger, 21
Smeal, Dennis Raymond, 14
Smeltzer, Steven, 129
Smith, Alan Keith, 17
Smith, Amy, 61, 72
Smith, Anna Deavere, 45, 87, 100
Smith, Baker S., 61, 92
Smith, Brandon, 71
Smith, Buzz, 165
Smith, Charles, 96, 166
Smith, Christopher A., 23
Smith, Chuck, 62, 76
Smith, David, 19, 27, 35, 36
Smith-Dawson, Beverly, 34
Smith, Deborah, 115
Smith, Doug, 13
Smith, Douglas D., 42
Smith, Edward G., 6, 148, 149
Smith, Elaine, 96
Smith, Felton, 99, 142
Smith, Gary, 42
Smithheimer, Eileen, 69
Smith, James, 145
Smith, Jennifer Q., 72
Smith, John Dale, 28
Smith, Kendall, 12, 22, 89
Smith, Lindsey, 156
Smith, Lisa, 55
Smith, Louise, 71
Smith, Marc P., 174, 175
Smith, Matt, 53
Smith, Mavis, 161
Smith, Michael, 71
Smith, Michael C., 8, 72, 76, 91, 109, 110
Smith, Molly D., 115
Smith, Nancy Jo, 49
Smith, Novella T., 86
Smith, Paul, 52
Smith, Peter, 27
Smith, Peyton, 173
Smith, Ray, 164
Smith, Richard J., 51, 176, 177
Smith, Rob, 171
Smith, Robert G., 111
Smith, Robin Lynn, 137
Smith, Roger Guenveur, 103
Smith, Rusty, 57, 136
Smith, Scott, 168
Smith, Stephen G., 88
Smith, Steven Scott, 37, 120, 158, 164
Smith, Susan Arnout, 107
Smith, Susan Harris, 106
Smith, Turner P., 39
Smith, Valerie, 120
Smith, Vicki, 2, 34, 50, 91, 109, 119
Smoot, Gary, 7, 53
Smoots, Jonathan, 90
Smulyan, Jane, 161
Smythe, Robert, 33

Snider, Clay, 61
Snider-Stein, Teresa, 39, 75, 98, 125, 157, 167, 170
Snodderly, Ed, 130
Snodgrass, Brett A., 32
Snowden, Susan, 24, 135
Snow, Kevin, 127
Snow, Tom, 40, 56, 62
Snyder, Huck, 78, 93
Snyder, Patricia Di Benedetto, 101
Sobczak, Leonard, 161
Sobel, Shepard, 22
Sod, Ted, 136
Soetaert, Susan, 45, 75
Soileau, Randall, 80, 81
Solano, Bernardo, 107
Solger, Christine A., 147
Solis, Meme, 73
Solis, Octavio, 52
Solly, Billy, 174
Solotaire, Benjamin A., 20
Soltanoff, Phil, 96
Somerfield, Mark, 11, 33
Sommers, Michael, 4
Somogyc, Anne, 111
Somsen, Pennell, 143
Sondheim, Stephen, 14, 18, 22, 43, 44, 66, 86, 95, 112, 121, 129, 159, 160, 168, 170, 175, 176
Sonnichsen, Ingrid, 99, 175
Soon-Bok, You, 78
Sophocles, 9, 45, 49, 64, 74, 132, 133, 153, 163, 171
Sorce, Tom, 85
Sorensen, Per-Olav, 115
Soriano, Rowena, 152
Sorkin, Aaron, 90
Sossi, Ron, 103, 104, 127
Soule, Robert D., 164
Southwick, Kathleen, 22
Souza, Katrina, 112
Souza, Ryk, 112
Soyinka, Wole, 148
Spadaccini, Daryl, 136
Spain, Craig, 120, 152
Sparks, Amy, 41
Speare, Elizabeth George, 17
Spear, Katherine, 1
Spector, Estelle, 94
Speer, Alexander, 3
Spelman, Jon, 56
Spelvin, M., 13
Spencer, Gerard L., 85
Spencer, Norm, 112
Spencer, Sara, 144
Spencer-Stark, Cherry, 158
Spencer, Tommy, 153
Sperling, Fran, 157
Sperling, Ted, 7, 69, 80
Sperry, Adam, 59
Spewack, Bella, 5, 19
Spewack, Samuel, 5, 19
Spiderwoman Theatre, 41
Spiese, Stephen, 58
Spiller, Tom, 53
Spiro, Matthew, 24
Spiteri, Carmela, 41
Spitler, Brian, 129
Split Britches, 7
Spock, Tom, 1, 138

Sprague, Carl, 93
Sprague, Sharon, 23
Sprayberry, Robert, 50
Spring, Dawn, 157
Spyri, Johanna, 17, 55, 161
Stabile, Bill, 73, 101
Stables, Audrey, 113
Stacklin, Andy, 49
Stacy, Steve, 52
Stafford, Kate, 102
Stafford, Richard, 89
Stage Right, 1
Stairs, Stanley T., 72
Stancari, Lou, 173
Staniunas, John, 37, 83
Stankowski, Marq, 9
Stanley, Audrey, 140
Stanley, Mark, 82
Stanton, Elizabeth Cady, 7
Stapleton, Tim, 28
Stark, Wendy, 95
Starmer, John, 162
Starr, Bruce, 163
Stauffer, Janice, 166
Stauffer, Scott, 76
Stazo, Luis, 42
St. David, Wayne, 142
Steakley, Dave, 176, 177
Steakley, Tiffany, 177
Stebbins, Marie, 146
Stecker, Robert D., Sr., 47
Steefel, Jeffrey, 43
Steele, Jevetta, 93
Steele, Lezley, 168
Steele, Willy, 166
Stefanek, Lore, 138
Stefanowicz, Janus, 116, 117
Stefan, Craig, 62
Stegmeir, Johann, 46, 89, 152
Stein, Alan L., 9
Steinbeck, Bob, 38
Steinbeck, John, 46, 50, 60, 92, 106, 115, 119
Steinberg, Paul, 11
Stein, Daniel, 163
Stein, Debra, 8, 42, 105, 161
Stein, Douglas, 2, 7, 15, 63, 64, 66, 77, 105, 156
Stein, Gertrude, 93
Stein, Jane Alois, 12, 89, 175
Stein, Joseph, 28, 43, 81, 167
Stein, Mark, 21, 79
Steinmetz, Lynn, 173
Stein, Paule Sandoval, 163
Steitzer, Jeff, 1, 2, 125
Stella, Tim, 61, 80
Stenborg, Derek, 128
Stephens, Claudia, 73, 171
Stephens, C.Y., 105
Stephens, John, 8, 159, 163
Stephens, Kent, 35, 122
Stephenson, Vera, 120
Stephens, Phillip, 90
Stephens, Thomas W., 107
Stepowany, Michael, 142, 143
Steppe, Steven, 27
Sterling, Mary K., 16
Sterling, Pamela, 55, 67, 136
Sternbach, Gerald, 40, 56, 62, 79
Stern, Daniel, 11

Stern, Edward, 35, 36, 71, 92, 128, 129
Sterner, Jerry, 7, 8, 13, 22, 28, 50, 51, 58, 59, 83, 91, 95, 128, 146, 149, 159
Stern, Marcus, 4, 85
Stetson, Jeff, 44, 62, 76, 115, 148
Stetzel, Dan, 21
Stevens, Anna, 83
Stevens, David, 31, 56, 60, 119, 124, 150, 168
Stevens, Debra K., 35
Stevens, John, 8, 51
Stevens, Keith, 88
Stevenson, Robert Louis, 34, 129, 161
Stevens, Tony, 42, 61
Stewart, Anita, 11, 39, 47, 64, 66, 102, 121, 125, 136, 173
Stewart, Christopher, 102
Stewart, Ellen, 77, 78, 79
Stewart, Gary, 55
Stewart, Jaye, 166
Stewart, Lindsay, 104
Stewart, Louis, 111
Stewart, Michael, 89, 95
Stewart, Vicki, 83
Stewart, William, 170
St. Germain, Mark, 25, 58, 72
Sticco, Dan, 125
Stidfole, Arthur, 171
Stiefel, Kaye, 91
Still, Chuck, 24
Stillings, Cynthia, 63
Still, James, 52, 72, 161
Still, Peter, 64
St. James, Ann, 41
Stockdale, Muriel, 167
Stockdale, Sheri-Kurk, 133
Stocker, Margarita, 25
Stockley, Travis, 44
Stoddard, Roger, 164, 165
Stodola, Jana Beard, 18
Stoker, Bram, 4, 8, 22, 30, 95, 123, 126, 129
Stokes, Simon, 147
Stoklos, Denise, 78, 79
Stollmack, Noele, 8
Stoltzfus, Helen, 19, 20, 23
Stone, Daryl, 21
Stone, Peter, 29
Stone, Rebecca, 78
Stoner, Leroy, 90
Stone, Sarah, 170
Stoppard, Tom, 32, 59, 63, 69, 92, 131, 150
Storch, Arthur, 59, 150
Story, John, 90, 91
Story, Ted, 153
Stotts, Michael, 97
Stout, Liz, 171
Stout, Stephen, 121
Stovern, Debra, 115
Stowe, Harriet Beecher, 134
Stowell, Jim, 71
Strachman, Alan, 135
Straiges, Tony, 12, 31, 40, 42, 47, 168
Strand, John, 173
Strand, Richard, 166

Strane, Robert, 19
Strang, David A., 12, 31, 146
Strange, Aralee, 55
Strann, Sandra J., 90
Stratmann, Erich, 125
Stratton, Stephen, 118
Strauss, John, 71
Strawbridge, Stephen, 4, 8, 31, 32, 39, 47, 66, 69, 72, 86, 175
Streeter, James E., 29
Street, Kent, 174
Streicher, Ron, 79
Strell, Meghan, 111
Stretch, Kevin, 13
Stribling, Laura, 115
Strickland, Robert, 155
Strimbeck, Leigh, 27
Strindberg, August, 9, 15, 39, 88, 162
Stroman, Jeff, 91
Stropnicky, Gerard, 27, 28, 163
Strouse, Charles, 13, 43, 61
Struckman, Jeffrey, 9, 85, 129, 133, 135, 140, 160
Stryk, Lydia, 50
Stuart, Sebastian, 156
Studler, Brian, 135
Sturchio, Mal, 119
Sturges, Preston, 116
Sturge, Tom, 31, 32, 76, 113
Sturiale, Grant, 70, 167
Sturm, Jason, 90
Stutts, Will, 49, 168
Styne, Jule, 175
Styn, Ronald L., 26
Subterranean Theatre Co., 177
Sucke, Greer, 13
Sudraka, King, 43
Suggs, Charles C., II, 122, 123
Sullivan, Arthur, 118
Sullivan, Barbara, 6
Sullivan, Daniel, 15, 23, 28, 80, 87, 119, 136, 137, 147
Sullivan, Greg, 9, 74, 137
Sullivan, Jenny, 171
Sullivan, John Carver, 19, 59, 61, 110, 128, 129, 148
Sullivan, J.R., 83, 95
Sullivan, Maureen, 84
Sullivan, Michael, 123
Sullivan, Sarah, 146
Sullivan-Wothman, Lori, 114
Summers, Alison, 78, 102
Summers, J. Bruce, 128, 129
Sumption, Christine, 151
Sunde, Karen, 171
Sundstedt, Bern, 95
Sun-Hi, Shin, 78
Surface, Mary Hall, 29, 30, 34, 44, 67, 132, 158
Surrey, Kit, 141
Suttell, V. Jane, 19
Sutter, Bart, 62
Sutter, Ross, 62
Sutton, Joe, 96
Sutton, Mary, 19
Sutton, Thomas C., 143
Svich, Caridad, 73, 122
Swackhamer, Leslie, 40, 122
Swados, Elizabeth, 44, 85, 103, 156

Swanbeck, John, 166
Swanson, Henry, 120
Swanson, Patrick, 138
Swartz, Eric, 152
Swenson, Janet, 165
Swerling, Jo, 151
Swiderski, Dawn, 30
Swift, Jonathan, 111
Swiggum, Randy, 162
Swindler, Billy, 78
Swindley, Ted, 124, 134
Swonger, Jim, 58
Syer, Fontaine, 12, 109, 110
Symczak, Mark, 157
Synge, John Millington, 80, 109, 114, 154, 160, 163, 169
Szabo, Jessica, 163
Szadek, Max, 85
Szentgyorgyi, Tom, 122

T

Tabori, George, 85
Taccone, Anthony, 23, 24, 87
Taggart, Jack, 134
Tait, Shevra, 85, 86
Tait, Tony, 105
Takanashi, Mikiko, 78
Takazauckas, Albert, 9, 30, 84, 86
Talcott, Randy, 20
Talking Band, The, 157
Tally, Ted, 113
Tambella, Mark, 78
Tandet, A. Joseph, 85
Taneri, Matthew, 156
Tanji, Lydia, 24, 136
Tanner, John, 55, 91
Tanner, Tony, 169
Tan, Victor En Yu, 11, 19, 36, 46, 101, 126, 149, 150
Tarbox, Catherine, 18
Tarses, Jay, 122
Tasca, Jules, 120
Taschetta, Sal, 43
Tate, Gregory R., 41, 134
Tate, Neal, 25
Tauser, Carol, 157
Taxi, Fortuna, 45
Tayler, Mildred D., 136
Taylor, Bert, 19
Taylor, Clifton, 6, 9, 12, 22, 89, 124
Taylor-Corbett, Lynn, 58, 76, 167
Taylor, C.P., 9, 72, 99
Taylor, Darren J., 86
Taylor, David, 113
Taylor, David M., 67
Taylor, Dominic, 46
Taylor, Don, 46
Taylor, Giva, 5
Taylor, Karen, 6
Taylor, Leslie, 6, 8, 89, 155, 159
Taylor, Noel, 8
Taylor, Patricia, 39
Taylor, Regina, 4
Taylor, Susan, 125
Tazewell, Paul, 2, 6, 15, 32, 40, 66, 80, 92, 119, 137, 171
Tchoupitoulous, Faboo, 107
Tebelak, John Michael, 18, 120

INDEX OF NAMES

Teguns, Neal San, 104
Teirstein, Andy, 84
Teixeira, Raul, 128
Temple, Riley K., 14
Templeton, Fiona, 96
TenEyck, Karen, 36, 49, 116, 117, 171
Tennenbaum, Debra, 11
Ter Meulen, Annette, 79
Terrell, Stephen, 136, 151
Terrill, Ken, 145
Terry, Megan, 106, 107
Tes, Sam-Oeun, 111
Tesich, Steve, 60, 100, 139
Teti, Tom, 114
Teverino, Robert, 163
Thaler, Martin, 145
Thatcher, Kristine, 28, 83, 139
Thayer, David, 77
Thayer, Robert, 60
Theatre Grottesco, 172
Theatre Sound, 11, 173
Thedford, Dello, 148
Theisen, William, 55
Therriault, Daniel, 96
Thierree, Jean-Baptiste, 7
Thies, Howard, 41, 78, 118
Thies, Tracy, 52
Thigpen, John, 68, 159
Thirkield, Robert, 36
Thomas, Alex, 62
Thomas, Birch, 37
Thomas, Biyi Bandele, 96
Thomas, Brandon, 9, 25, 72, 169
Thomas, Colin, 21, 55
Thomas, Dylan, 75, 81, 82
Thomas, Eberle, 19, 35, 59, 60, 67
Thomas, Evelyn, 149
Thomas, Francine, 99
Thomas, Freyda, 9
Thomas-Jones, Linda, 41
Thomas, Joyce Carol, 38
Thomas, L.B., 94
Thomas, Michael, 35
Thomas, Ted, 121
Thomas, Todd, 157
Thomas, Tonis, 27
Thomley, Sandy, 28
Thompson, Anne, 38
Thompson, Blanche, 1
Thompson, Bob, 84
Thompson, Bruce, 114
Thompson, Carol Delk, 5, 6
Thompson, David, 88
Thompson, Evan, 26
Thompson, Garland, 177
Thompson, Gil, 88, 141, 149, 150
Thompson, Kent, 5, 6, 146, 149
Thompson, Raymond, 134
Thompson, Richard D., 34, 114
Thompson, Robert, 123
Thompson, Ron Stacker, 103
Thompson, Scott, 28
Thompson, Steven, 171
Thompson, Tazewell, 2, 15, 40, 137, 150
Thompson, Timothy, 106
Thompson, Tommy, 129
Thompson, Walter, 74, 163
Thomsen, Barbara Channer, 28
Thomsen, Richard, 28
Thomson, Jeff, 16, 34
Thomson, Lynn M., 33, 117
Thomson, Virgil, 93
Thorne, Creon, 60
Thorne, Erika, 71
Thorne, Joan Vail, 173
Thornton, Carey W., 34
Thorpe, Robert A., 29
Thulin, Richard E., 163
Thuna, Leonora, 40, 76, 106
Thunderbird Dancers, 156
Thurston, Jim, 153
Tichenor, Austin, 46
Tidwell, David, 52
Tierney, Thomas, 30, 120
Tilford, Joseph P., 35, 36, 40, 150
Tilley, Terry, 113, 114
Tillinger, John, 81, 82, 86, 87, 131
Tillman, Ellis, 42
Tilton, James, 42, 98, 118, 168
Tindall, Don, 22
Tine, Hal, 161
Tingle, Jennifer, 99
Tinsley, Dana Harnish, 59, 60
Tipton, Jennifer, 32, 64, 66, 73, 174, 175
Tiscornia, Nelly Fernandez, 25
Titus, Hiram, 34
Tkachenko, Irina, 30
Tkacz, Virlana, 78, 79
Tobey, Elisabeth, 153, 154
Toce, Thomas, 161
Todhunter, Jeffrey, 26
Toewe, Anne M., 89
Tofteland, Curt L., 145
Tolan, Kathleen, 173
Tolan, Stephanie, 55
Toles, Bill, 97, 173
Tolley, David, 62
Toma, Dan, 101
Tomarrow, Todd, 157
Tomboulian, Lee, 84
Tomczeszyn, Lisa, 175
Tomei, Paula, 143
Tomkins, Steve, 7, 16, 18, 53, 151
Tomlinson, Neil, 142
Toner, Don, 80, 81
Toner, Irlyn, 81
Toney, Kevin, 36
Tophman, Verl R., 165
Torgersen, David, 14, 24
Torgov, Morley, 160
Toroba, Federico Moreno, 128
Torres, Edward F., 166
Torres, Joan, 15
Torroba, Federico Moreno, 128
Toser, David, 61
Toth, Melissa, 31
Towers, Charles, 6, 36, 69, 110, 146, 167
Townes, Tad, 13
Townley, Jason, 7
Townsend, Christopher, 15, 132, 173
Townsend, Clista, 102, 103
Townshend, Pete, 77
Trach, Edward, 106
Trachtenberg, Amy, 84
Tracy, William, 86
Trader, Beverly, 97
Traister, Andrew J., 16, 105
Trammell, Brent, 8
Tramparullo, Silvia, 41
Trapani, Paul, 168
Trauger, Shirley M., 32
Travis, Mark W., 102
Traylor, David, 168
Traylor, Mary, 44, 164, 165
Treibs, Karl, 53
Tremonte, Michael, 88
Trethewey, Alan, 41
Trettenero, Patrick, 21
Trevethan, Laurie, 148
Treyz, Russell, 49, 109, 129
Triana, Jorge Ali, 127, 128
Trifonov, Yuri, 79
Trimble, David, 124
Tripp, Loren, 37, 133, 160
Tromovitch, Lisa A., 5
Trowbridge, Staci, 158
True, Jim, 147
Truss, Tori, 14
Truth, Sojourner, 7
Tsappas, Giorgus, 150
Tsuji, Yukio, 78
Tsurdinis, George, 78
Tsu, Susan, 6, 8, 19, 110
Tsypin, George, 9, 24, 60
Tuama, Aodh Og O, 160
Tubert, Susana, 64
Tucker, Carole, 129
Tucker, Margaret S., 1
Tucker, Sarah, 110, 111
Tucker, Stan, 62, 152
Tullidge, Thomas Jr., 157
Tumminello, Jay, 26
Turgenev, Ivan, 82
Turlish, Susan, 142
Turner, Chris, 164
Turner, Clinton Davis, 15
Turner, Evan, 41
Turner, Jerry, 109, 110, 135
Turner, Lynette, 115
Turner, Ret, 42
Turner, Tom, 168
Tuscher-Ancede, Diane, 32
Tutor, Rick, 151
Tuttle, Jane, 140
Tuttle, John, 37
Tuttleman, Steven, 102
Tveit, Tanya, 3
Twain, Mark, 6, 30, 46, 50, 71, 72, 112, 121, 152, 161
Tynes, Antoinette, 97, 148, 163
Tyranny, 'Blue' Gene, 47
Tyrell, Kathy, 66
Tyrrell, Louis, 123, 124

U

Udell, Peter, 148
Uematsu, Yuriko, 64
Ueno, Watoku, 78, 79, 118
Uhry, Alfred, 4, 39, 176
Ulben, Deniz, 141
Ullman, Jeffrey L., 104
Ulmer, John, 56
Umfrid, Thomas C., 165
Underground Railway Theatre, 41
Underhill, Kate, 65
Underwood, Joel, 50
Unsoeld, Willi, 2, 16
Uribe, Nicolas, 128
Urich, Michael, 130
Urrutia, David, 102
Ursano, Ron, 106, 150, 173
Uselman, Carol, 91
Usher, Teal, 31
U-Tate, 21
Utterback, Tom, 151

V

Vaccaro, John, 157
Valdez, Anahuac, 51
Valdez, Kinan, 51
Valdez, Luis, 51, 52
Valdez, Mino, 52
Valdez, Patssi, 134
Valdez, Socorro, 52
Valency, Maurice, 15, 131, 170, 171
Valente, Barbara, 160
Valenzuela, Jose Luis, 134
Valk, Kate, 173
Valla, David, 13
Valle-Inclan, Ramon del, 73
Vallerga, Paul G., 29, 30, 160
Valone, Ginger, 59
van Bergen, James, 102, 111, 120, 126, 156
Van Burek, John, 67
Vance, Boyd, 177
Vance, Nina, 7
Van Deest, Bill, 52
Vandenbroucke, Russell, 38, 125, 146, 163
Vanderlaan, Willard P., 76
van der Wege, Gary, 80, 81
Van Druten, John, 46, 174
Van Halteren, Marjorie, 96
Van Horne, Elly, 28
van Itallie, Jean-Claude, 64, 97, 157
Vanlandingham, Kathy, 46
Van Landingham, Michael, 30
VanNoy, Rick, 133
Vann, Marc, 32
Van Woerden, Ron, 133, 134
Van Zyl, Antony, 110
Varbalow, Jennifer, 37
Vardiel, Claire, 23
Varga, Joseph, 46, 83
Varner, Gary, 123
Vassil, Peter, 141
Vaughan, Barbara, 148
Vaughn, Gary, 7
Vawter, Ron, 173
Vazquez, Adolfo, 128
Vazquez, Michael, 157
Velasco, Dorothy, 142
Velasco, Javier, 4
Velasco, Joseph, 51
Velikovsky, Alexander, 107
Venberg, Lorraine, 38
Venne, William,
Venzke, William Jay, 90
Vercoutere, Maurice, 86, 133, 140, 160

Verdery, Jim, 64
Verheyen, Mariann, 36, 69
Vermilye, Peter, 69
Vernier, Stephan, 49
Versteegt, Michael, 175
Vesco, Angela M., 38
Vetere, Richard, 58
Vicente, Danny, 43
Vidal, Sergio, 152
Vienhage, Rocco, 169
Viertel, Jack, 108
Vieth, Bradley, 61, 81, 100
Vig, Joel, 161
Vilanch, Bruce, 42
Villar, Braulio, 127, 128
Villarreal, Edit, 25, 79, 91, 135
Villegas, Lilliana, 127, 128
Vincent, Irving, 97
Vincent, Steven, 123
Vinkler, Greg, 139
Virchis, William A., 105
Vissman, John W., 54
Vitali, Michael, 162
Vitarelli, Steven, 21
Vladimer, Meryl, 77
Vogel, David, 71
Vogele, Chrissy, 27
Vogel, Paula, 7, 23, 32, 37, 38, 61, 85, 103, 110, 126, 175
Vogt, Gerard P., 149
Volkov, Youri, 108
Vollack, Lia, 149
Vollrath, Lisa A., 8, 167, 168
Volonte, D. Silvio, 43
Voltaire, 39, 43, 44, 163, 170
von Brandenstein, Patrizia, 101
Von Drehle, Courtney, 91
von Hausch, Gregory, 66
von Mayrhauser, Jennifer, 88, 122
Von Waldenburg, Raina, 97
Vosburgh, Dick, 119
Voss, Gayla, 44
Voyce, Kaye, 65
Voyt, Harriet, 11
Vreeland, Diana, 23
Vreeland, Martin E., 7
Vrtol, Stephen F. III, 95

W

Waack, Katherine, 83
Wadbrook, Russell, 102, 103
Wade, Stephen, 2, 114, 145
Wadler, Michael, 42, 43
Wadsworth, Stephen, 88
Wagenhurst, Georgia, 5
Wager, Douglas C., 14, 15
Wagner, Daniel MacLean, 106, 141, 149, 150, 173
Wagner, Dee, 159
Wagner, Doug, 96
Wagner, Gladys, 32
Wagner, Jane, 53, 89, 123
Wagner, Robin, 86
Waite, Ralph, 164
Waites, Luigi, 106, 107
Walch, Gay, 108
Walcott, Derek, 45
Walden, Stanley, 160

Walden, Wanda, 64, 110
Waldhart, Mary, 83
Waldie, John, 14
Waldrop, Mark, 36
Walker, Chris, 74
Walker, Daniel C., 126
Walker, Daron, 71
Walker, Fred E., 81
Walker, George F., 32, 120, 132, 175
Walker, Jewel, 38
Walker, John P., 166
Walker, Joseph, 45
Walker, Katrina, 155
Walker, M. Burke, 53, 74
Walker, Natalie, 54
Walker, Paul, 93
Walker, Sarah Huff, 30
Walker, Sheafe, 54
Wallace, Bradford, 56
Wallace, Peter, 15
Wallach, Eric, 27
Wallach, Jeffrey, 156
Wall-Asse, Marilyn, 66, 67
Waller, Fats, 8, 13, 16, 25, 36, 112, 113, 167
Wallize, Pamela, 6
Walloch, Greg, 7
Wallop, Douglass, 105, 176
Walsh, Paul, 9, 39, 77, 155, 175
Walsh, Robert, 12, 89, 98, 99, 175
Walsh, Sheila, 114
Walsh, Thommie, 69, 80
Walters, Cory, 7
Walton, Ella, 23
Walton, Emma, 23
Walton, Sharon, 103
Walton, Tony, 23, 80, 131
Wangen, Mike, 113, 114
Wang, Yu, 7
Wann, Jim, 46, 59, 89, 98, 150, 151, 168
Wanstreet, David, 119
Warburg, Joan M., 2
Ward, Buzz, 35
Ward, Donald, 174
Ward, Elsa, 100, 126, 137, 173, 176
Ward, Kirk, 51
Ward, Mark, 79
Ward, Ramona, 121
Ward, Randy, 130
Waring, James, 106
Warner, Michael, 89
Warner, Roger, 89
Warrender, Scott, 7, 50
Warren, David, 69, 167
Warren, Harry, 89
Warren, Joel B., 117
Warren, kj, 41
Warren, Mary Mease, 6, 45
Warren, Skelly, 90
Warrilow, David, 82
Washington, Kenneth, 119, 133
Wasserman, Dale, 8, 65
Wasserstein, Wendy, 4, 16, 40, 58, 65, 68, 80, 94, 120, 133, 164, 165
Watanabe, Susan, 169
Waterman, Carole, 53
Waters, Les, 11
Watkins, Jeffrey, 140, 141

Watling, E.F., 133
Watson, Bill, 80, 81
Watson, Judy, 134
Weatherly, T. Gary, 26
Weaver, Lois, 7, 78
Weaver, Ves, 169
Webb, Elmon, 4
Webber, Andrew Lloyd, 46, 65, 112, 119, 168, 170
Webber, Julian, 96
Webber, Robert, 71
Webb, Gavin Cameron, 6
Webb, Jeff, 166
Webb, Robert, 37
Weber, Debbie, 17
Webster, C.J., 4
Webster, Eric, 16
Webster, Gary, 163
Webster, John, 9, 110
Webster, Ken, 176, 177
Wechsberg, Orin, 66
Wedepohl, William F., 90
Wedin, David, 130
Wegener, Eric, 69, 110
Weiant, Ted, 98
Weidman, John, 121
Weidner, Paul, 66, 131
Weikel, Ray, 177
Weill, Kurt, 61, 170
Weil, Tim, 9, 47, 50, 57, 61
Weiner, William P., 28
Weinger, Don, 84
Weinstein, Evan, 43
Weinstein, Linda Cornell, 59
Weinstock, Jack, 133, 149
Weisberg, Steve, 79
Weisheit, Eric, 18, 19
Weisheit, Shelley, 18
Weisman, Jael, 49, 134
Weisman, Jim, 125
Weiss, Elliot, 161
Weiss, Julie, 40, 58
Weiss, Marc B., 40, 131, 150, 159
Weiss, Peter, 64
Welch, Anna Morman, 80
Welch, John D., 19
Welch, Nancy D., 124
Weldin, Scott, 2, 137
Welk, Bob, 52
Wellborn, Michael, 53, 74, 136, 151
Welles, Parmalee, 22
Wellman, Mac, 54, 150, 162
Wells-Day, Carol, 119
Wells, H.G., 19, 107, 136, 167
Wells, Mary Robin, 121
Wells, Palmer D., 158
Welty, Eudora, 99
Weman, Golda, 134
Wendt, Angela, 47, 100, 152
Wenger, Jayne, 85
Wengrow, Arnold, 6
Wenick, Adam, 33
Wenman, Susan, 55
Wentworth, Scott, 37
Werch, Shifra, 21
Werner, Howard, 58, 124, 147
Werner, Ken, 171
Werner, Sharon, 139
Werner, Stewart, 37, 105, 116, 136
Werner, William, 49

Wernick, Adam, 141, 171
Wertenbaker, Timberlake, 2, 9, 36, 38, 68, 70, 83, 120, 144, 154, 170
Wesler, Ken, 168
Wesley, Richard, 45, 114, 142, 176
West, Cheryl L., 15, 40, 61, 76, 137, 148, 150, 160
West, Darron L., 121, 170
West, Dennis, 6, 155
Westerland, Jim, 7
Westfall, Greg, 164
West, Gweneth, 143
West, Nathanael, 77
West, Patty, 7
West, Peter, 93
West, Randal K., 160
West, Thomas Edward, 161
Wexler, Peter, 87
Wharton, Edith, 114, 138, 139
Wharton, John, 95
Wheeldon, Carole, 110
Wheeldon, Kathy, 94, 95
Wheeldon, Steven D., 52, 94, 95
Wheeler, David, 11, 164
Wheeler, Hugh, 14, 43, 44, 159, 160, 170
Wheetman, Dan, 105
Whelan, Peter, 150
Whiddon, Jerry, 132
Whip, Carmen, 45
Whisenhunt, John, 176
Whitehead, Graham, 30
Whitehill, Brian J., 11
Whitehill, B.T., 156, 157
Whiteley, Ben, 105
Whiteley, Rose Marie, 107
Whitelock, Patricia A., 50
Whiteman, Bart, 142
Whitemore, Guy, 47
Whitemore, Hugh, 7, 25, 89, 145
Whiteway, Philip, 157
White, Andrew, 79
White, Chester E., 165
White, Cynthia, 6, 109, 110, 122
White, Dana, 126
White, David A. III, 54, 55
White, Diz, 104
White, Edgar Nkosi, 79
White, E.B., 30, 52, 99, 136
White, George C., 107
White, Ken, 18, 46
White, Lisa D., 116
White, Marvin L., 99
White, Michael Franklin, 138
White, Mickey, 72
White, Molly, 173
White, Pamela, 68, 69
White, Richard E.T., 8, 9, 24
White, R.A., 85
White, Susan A., 40
White, Susan R., 2, 15, 137, 143, 150
White, Tanya, 21
White, T.H., 129
White, Wayne, 91
Whiting, John, 71
Whiting, Nancy, 71
Whitlock, Diedre, 62
Whitlock, Lewis, III, 114
Whitman, Karen, 124

Whitney, Walter, 49
Whitsett, Edie, 136
Whittlesey, Peregrine, 85
Who, The, 77
Whyburn, Robert, 80, 81, 177
Wicks, Debra, 110, 125
Wiegant, Kelly, 145
Wiener, Matthew, 16
Wierzel, Robert, 11, 19, 34, 72, 98, 121, 122, 126, 173, 175
Wieselman, Doug, 15
Wieting, Carl, 41
Wiggall, David, 31, 146
Wilbur, Richard, 32, 43, 44, 50, 66, 69, 82, 105, 120, 165, 170
Wilcock, T.J., 37, 160
Wilcox, Charles, 154
Wilcox, Clay, 133
Wilcox, Lola, 154
Wilcox, Patricia, 42
Wilde, Oscar, 24, 27, 34, 47, 59, 74, 97, 114, 172
Wilder, Kit, 30
Wilder, Matthew, 77
Wilder, Thornton, 6, 8, 15, 23, 34, 35, 49, 61, 75, 89, 90, 114, 140, 162, 165, 176
Wildhorn, Frank, 19
Wildman, James, 31, 59, 60, 150
Wilhelm, Michael, 52
Wilkerson, Tyrone, 13
Wilks, Talvin, 45, 46, 54, 64
Willard, Frederick, 65
Willardson, Peter, 119
Will, Geoff, 153
Williams, Brenda S., 123
Williams, Diane Ferry, 9
Williams, Emlyn, 22
Williams, Fred, 37, 51
Williams, F. Elaine, 28
Williams, Hank, 105
Williams, Jaston, 13, 29, 91, 123, 134
Williams, Jay, 67
Williams, Jerry R., 47
Williams, JoBeth, 79
Williams, John L., 176
Williams, Kappitola, 138
Williams, Kyle, 109
Williams, Linda, 153
Williams, Lori-Anne, 121
Williams, Mac, 80
Williams, Margery, 34, 35, 52, 89, 136, 161
Williams, Michael, 148
Williamson, Claire, 47
Williamson, Laird, 9, 47, 50, 64, 105
Williams, Rae, 76
Williams, Robin, 153
Williams, Samm-Art, 50
Williams, Sandy, 123
Williams, Tennessee, 5, 8, 9, 10, 15, 18, 21, 28, 31, 32, 40, 47, 50, 77, 83, 88, 98, 99, 110, 133, 146, 152, 164, 169
Williams, Tom, 160
Williams, Traci Halima, 81
Willinger, David, 156, 157
Willis, Brendan, 7
Willis, Sally, 104

Willson, Meredith, 61
Wilmott, Phil, 96
Wilson, Alice, 176, 177
Wilson, August, 8, 9, 19, 50, 61, 70, 89, 92, 95, 109, 110, 113, 114, 116, 119, 120, 125, 137, 145, 148, 149, 164, 177
Wilson, Cintra, 85
Wilson, Daniel, 7
Wilson, Erin Cressida, 85
Wilson, Jack Forbes, 83, 91
Wilson, Joan, 18
Wilson, John, 99
Wilson, John Bonard, 149, 160
Wilson, Jonathan, 36, 45
Wilson, Lanford, 14, 33, 36, 37, 88, 89, 98, 105, 114, 116, 133, 136, 164
Wilson, Mark P., 128
Wilson, Mary-Louise, 23
Wilson, Michael, 7, 8
Wilson, Peggy Pharr, 18, 121, 176
Wilson, Richard, 13
Wilson, Robert, 8
Wilson, Ron, 92
Wilson, Sherry, 134
Wilson, Tim, 115
Wilson, Tristan, 168
Wimer, Jo, 13
Winberg, Sarah, 53
Windsor, Valerie, 117
Windsor, William J., 39
Wines, Halo, 106
Wing-Davey, Mark, 24, 86, 102, 120
Winick, Eric, 143
Winkler, Richard, 40, 85, 119
Winn, Marie, 38
Winn, Robert, 5
Winograd, Judy, 8, 155
Winther, Barbara, 13
Wise Guise, The, 157
Wisely, Steve, 133
Wiseman, Elizabeth, 165
Wise, Birgit Rattenborg, 61, 100
Witten, Matthew, 147
Wittow, Frank, 1, 117, 138
Wittstein, Ed, 66
Wodehouse, P.G., 59, 159
Wojewodski, Robert, 47, 82, 105, 136, 137
Wojewodski, Stan, Jr., 175
Wojtas, Tom, 4
Wolcott, Judy, 23
Wolfe, Brett, 115
Wolfe, George C., 24, 40, 47, 61, 72, 76, 87, 100, 103, 110, 116, 134, 137, 150, 175
Wolf, Eugene, 130
Wolff, Art, 42
Wolford, Lisa, 41
Wolf, Stephen, 176
Wolk, James, 95, 106, 116, 117, 166, 171
Wollner, Donald, 96
Womack, David, 99
Womack, Ricky, 134
Wombwell, Judith, 120
Wondisford, Diane, 93
Wong, Anthony, 102
Wong, Carey, 64, 151

Wong, Elizabeth, 111, 166
Wong, Gilbert, 63
Wong, Nathan, 43
Wonsek, Paul, 6, 113, 117, 125, 149, 168
Woodall, Sandra, 9, 85
Woodard, Charlayne, 86
Woodard, W. Philip, 86
Wood, Bennett, 120
Wood, Bradford, 18, 29
Woodbury, Richard, 60, 61, 100, 127, 147
Wood, Carolyn, 133
Wood, Douglas, 44
Wooden, Rod, 147
Wood, Frank, Jr., 99
Woodhouse, Sam, 134
Wood, Karen S., 87
Woodman, William, 44, 121
Wood, Robert, 160
Woodruff, Don, 43
Woodruff, Herbie, 92, 93, 154
Woodruff, Joyce, 83
Woodruff, Pamela, 162
Woodruff, Robert, 9, 77, 96
Woods, Collier, 6, 7, 64, 110, 136
Woods, Steve, 46, 156
Wood, Stephen, 107
Woods, Terry, 72
Wood, Tom, 68
Woodward, Greer, 161
Woodward, Jeffrey, 87
Woolard, David C., 7, 8, 19, 25, 49, 64, 77, 88, 93, 105, 117, 137, 150
Wooldridge, Rebecca, 123
Woolf, Steven, 128, 129
Woolf, Virgina, 167
Worley, Lee, 41
Woronicz, Henry, 109, 110
Worth, Dawn B., 90
Worthman, Lori Sullivan, 2, 36, 71
Worts, Veronica, 22, 116
Wrangler, Jack, 37
Wren, James, 66, 67
Wrenn-Meleck, Peter, 113
Wren, Todd, 42
Wright, Ann-Marie, 83, 157, 161
Wright, Bagley, 136
Wright, Craig, 117
Wright, Fred, 142
Wright, Garland, 64
Wright, Judson, 83, 100
Wright, Nicholas, 15, 160, 168
Wright, Richard, 38
Wrightson, Ann G., 8, 40, 91, 101, 109, 119
Wright, Tamlyn, 145
Wright, Tony, 140, 141
Wurtele, Margaret, 64
Wurtzel, Stuart, 91
Wurzel, Nick, 99
Wutz, Darci Brown, 91
Wyatt, John Alan, 67
Wyatt, Larry, 20
Wycherley, William, 150
Wylie, John, 129
Wyne, Sheila, 115

X

Xenos, George, 75, 97, 102, 173

Y

Yaji, Shigeru, 109, 143
Yamada, Yoshiaki, 78
Yamaguchi, Eiko, 111
Yamamoto, Kayoko, 78
Yancey, Happy, 5
Yancey, Jacqueline, 38
Yanik, Don, 67, 136
Yankowitz, Susan, 96, 138
Yarmo, Leslie, 173
Yates, Chip, 172
Yazbek, David, 58
Yeager, Kenton, 168
Yeargan, Michael, 32, 61, 66, 82, 88, 175
Yeckel, Judith, 43
Yegen, Christian C. Jr., 131
Yellen, Sherman, 29
Yellow Robe, William S., Jr., 52, 67
Yelusich, Andrew V., 50, 64, 105
Yep, Laurence, 24, 111, 136
Yesselman, Robert, 47
Yeston, Maury, 81, 133, 152
Yetman, Charlotte M., 40, 57, 61, 62, 113, 149
Yew, Chay, 47
Yionoulis, Evan, 50, 61, 96, 121, 125, 150, 167
Yoder, Erica, 163
Yoder, Loretta, 72
Yokobosky, Matthew, 118
Yore, Tom, 111
York, Joe, 81
York, Y, 64, 96
Youmans, James, 85, 97, 100, 137, 150, 167
Youngblood, Shay, 5, 18, 46, 114, 143, 148, 160
Younger, Charles, 53
Young-Evans, Michael, 104
Young Goldstien Architects, 163
Young, Karen, 157
Young, Richard H., 8
Young, Sally, 78
Young, Susan, 7, 78, 79, 102
Young, Yoko, 160
Younts, Janet, 18, 152
Yourgrau, Tug, 147
Yulin, Harris, 104
Yungkurth, Kristin, 65
Yunker, Ken, 159
Yun-Taek, Lee, 78
Yurieff, Michael, 107
Yvetta, 41

Z

Zabriskie, Nan, 139
Zacek, Dennis, 166
Zaida, Chriss, 37
Zak, David, 20, 21
Zakowska, Donna, 9, 78, 93

Zaldivar, Gilberto, 127
Zambello, Francesca, 11
Zanotti, Judy, 155
Zapata, Carmen, 25, 90
Zarzyski, Paul, 62
Zaslove, Arne, 22, 23
Zax, Andrea, 138, 139
Zazofsky, Joanna, 99
Zdravkovic, Margo, 89, 170
Zeder, Susan, 22, 109
Zeh, Amy, 10
Zeisler, Peter, 64
Zelkowitz, Matt, 65
Zellner, Joe, 26
Zemke, Susan, 154
Zemmels, David R., 150, 173
Zenoni, Robert, 55, 90, 162
Zentiss, Robert W., 104
Zerbe, Anthony, 59, 60
Zerlin, David, 44, 45, 111
Zerlin, Walter Jr., 43
Ziegler, Tom, 153
Zielinski, Scott, 11, 16, 60, 64, 66, 97, 98, 125, 126
Zigler, Scott, 4
Zimmerman, Carlotta, 176
Zimmerman, Ken, 120
Zimmerman, Mary, 32, 61, 127
Zinger, Pablo, 128
Zink, Geoff, 113
Zinn, David, 65, 73, 74, 78, 157
Zinoman, Joy, 149, 150
Zipprodt, Patricia, 80
Zizka, Blanka, 171
Zizka, Jiri, 171
Znidarsic, John, 108
Zofrea, Thomas J., 160
Zola, Emile, 171
Zook, Cheryl, 150
Zorn, John, 83, 157
Zsamira, 156
Zuber, Catherine, 2, 11, 31, 32, 61, 64, 66, 136, 137, 141
Zublin, Catherine, 134
Zuckerman, Steve, 59
Zufall, Kristi, 37
Zulia, Ernest, 89
Zupanc, Victor, 33, 34
Zychal, Kietryn, 106

INDEX OF TITLES

A

Abingdon Square (La Plaza Chica), 134
Absent Forever, 79
Absurd Person Singular, 31, 82
Abundance, 27, 32, 99, 133
Accident, 156
Accident, The, 96
Accomplice, 59, 66
According to Coyote, 67
Achilles: A Kabuki Play, 171
Across a Crowded Room, 96
Acted Within Proper Departmental Procedure, 46
Act Without Words I and II, 38
Actor Retires, The, 127
Adventures in the Skin Trade, 82
Adventures of Tom Sawyer, The, 121
Aesop's Fables, 26
African Company Presents "Richard III", The, 15
African Tourist, 173
After the Dancing in Jericho, 70
After the Fall, 55
After the Heart Is Broken, 157
Afterthoughts, 157
Agamemnon, 64
Agape, 42
Agnes, 122
AIDS Show, 74
Ain't Got Long to Stay Here, 152
Ain't Misbehavin', 8, 13, 16, 25, 36, 112, 113, 167
Akin, 78, 93
Alabama Rain, 37, 96
Aladdin, 145
Aladdin and the Wonderful Lamp, 17
Alcalde de Zalamea, El, 127
Alchemy of Desire/Deadman's Blues, 122
Alfred and Victoria: A Life, 150
Alfred Stieglitz Loves O'Keeffe, 21, 64, 145
Alice in Concert, 103
Alice in Wonderland, 30
Alice's Adventures in Wonderland, 28
All I Really Need To Know I Learned In Kindergarten, 89
All My Sons, 33, 133
All Night Strut, The, 16, 18, 152
All's Well That Ends Well, 66, 100, 105, 109

All the Tricks but One, 91
All You Can Eat, 14
Almost Asleep, 138
Almost September, 128
Alone at the Beach, 23
Alone Together: Betty Buckley in Concert, 171
Along the Susquehanna, 27
Always...Patsy Cline, 124, 134
Ama and the White Crane, 26
Amadeus, 48, 89, 170
Amahl and the Night Visitors, 46
Ambrosio, 91
Amelia Earhart, 19
American Buffalo, 83, 115
American Century, The, 114
American Gothic, 118
American Nervousness, 162
American Plan, The, 150
American Vaudeville, 7
America Play, The, 15, 47, 96
Amigo's Blue Guitar, 70, 115
Among Our Own, 71
Amphibians, 173
Amphigorey, 11
Analysis of Mineral #4, The, 145
Anansi, 13
Anarchy in the OK, 96
Anastasia, 159
Anatomy of Suicide, 96
Ancients, The, 41
And a Nightingale Sang, 72, 99
And Baby Makes Seven, 37
Andrea Del Conte and the American Spanish Dance Theater, 152
Androcles and the Lion, 22, 150
And the World Laughs, 46
And We Were Left Darkling, 89
Angel Fragments, 138
Angel From Montgomery, 79
Angelina's Pizzeria, 156
Angel of Death, 85
Angels, 163
Angels in America, 87
Angel Works, 138
Animal Crackers, 61
Animal Farm, 55
Animal Tales and Dinosaur Scales, 35
Anna, 156
Anna Christie, 58, 131
Anne of Green Gables, 44, 46, 145
Annie, 13
Annie Oakley & Buffalo Bill, 26
Annual Pow Wow & Dance Concert, 157

Another Columbus, 58
Another Kind of Hero, 168
Another Person is a Foreign Country, 54
Another Time, 47
Anthesis, 169
Antigone, 9, 49, 74, 132, 163
Antigone in New York, 15
Antony and Cleopatra, 4, 110
Any Place But Here, 73
Anything Goes, 59, 159
Apocalyptic Butterflies, 132
Appalachian Christmas, 163
Appalachian Voices, 91
Appearance of Civilization, The, 14
Apple Dreams, 153
Approximating Mother, 173
archy & mehitabel, 32
Arden of Faversham, 53
Are You My Mother?, 53
Arms and the Man, 6, 30, 32, 69, 77, 83, 86, 98, 99, 167
Arsenic and Old Lace, 37, 50, 123, 169, 175
Art of Success, The, 104, 142
Art of Waiting, The, 132
Arthur and Leila, 107
Arthur: The Musical, 61
As You Like It, 22, 100, 106, 110, 141, 159, 171
Assassins, 121
At Long Last Leo, 21, 79
At the Still Point, 133
At Wit's End, 56
Attack of the Capitol Hill Nazis, 143
August Snow, 169
Avenue X, 107, 122
Avner the Eccentric, 15
Awake, 96
Awake and Sing!, 147, 150
A...My Name is Alice, 18, 123
A...My Name is Still Alice, 64, 93, 105, 137, 149, 151

B

Babes in Toyland, 96, 158
Baby, 83, 152
Baby Dance, The, 135
Baby, Fourteen Clowns and Xylophone, 78
Babylon Gardens, 36
Bacchae, The, 104
Back Way Back, 84
Bad Axe, 79
Balcony, The, 41

Ballad of the Blacksmith, 105
Ballroom, The, 154
Baltimore Waltz, The, 7, 32, 37, 38, 61, 85, 103, 110, 126, 175
Bang the Drum Slowly, 79
Banjo Dancing, 2, 145
Barbeque in 29 Palms, 59
Bargains, 105
Barriers—Soft and Hard, 107
Basement, 78
Basic Needs, 1
Basketball Jones, 169
Bathtub, 96
B/C Historia, 25
Bear Facts, The, 130
Beatrix Potter's Christmas, 34
Beau Jest, 42, 113, 142
Beauty and the Beast, 30, 34, 101, 154
Beauty Part, The, 175
Beaux' Stratagem, The, 4
Bed, 18
Beehive, 151, 177
Before Eva, 169
Before It Hits Home, 137
Beggars in the House of Plenty, 85
Beirut, 18
Belches on Couches, 107
Bell, Book, and Candle, 174
Belle of Amherst, The, 124, 129
Belle Reprieve, 7
Benefits of Doubt, The, 96
Benny Kozo, 96
Berkeley Square, 139
Bessie's Blues, 76
Best Christmas Pageant Ever, The, 26, 55
Best Little Whorehouse in Texas, The, 80, 123
Bete, La, 109, 143
Betrayal, 9, 91, 109
Betsey Brown, 46
Better Him Than Me, 96
Between East and West, 88
Bible Belt, 7
Big Butt Girls/Hard Headed Women, 78
Big Numbers, The, 117
Big River, 6, 46, 112, 152
Billy Bishop Goes to War, 8, 36, 129, 143
Billy Nobody, 173
Bite the String Snake, 130
Bitter Cane, 169
Bitter Homes and Gardens, 122
Black, 79, 171
Black Belts, 93

INDEX OF TITLES

Black Comedy, 131
Black Eagles, 148
Black Forest, 96
Black Hats, 84
Black Nativity, 114
Black Orpheus, 45
Black Snow, 11, 61
Blackwater, 107
Blazing the Outback, 44
Blind Date, 169
Blind Sight, 79
Blithe Spirit, 6, 25, 165
Blonde Like You, 20
Blood Knot, 2, 15, 98
Blood Orgy of the Bermuda Triangle Zombie Assassins, 53
Blood Summit, 175
Blood Wedding, 100
Blowin Smoke, 49
Blue Corridor, 104
Blue Heaven, 157
Blues in the Night, 18, 42
Blue Sky is a Curse, 157
B-Movie, The Play, 68
Bobby, Can You Hear Me?, 116
Bobby Gould in Hell, 32
Bobos, 11
Bocon!, 35
Bodas de Sangre, 128
Body Leaks, 106, 107
Boesman and Lena, 85
Bombing the Cradle, 156
Bon Appetit!, 9, 39
Bondage, 4
Bon Voyage, 50
Book of Lamb, The, 107
Booth is Back, 82
Borders of Loyalty, 96, 126
Born Yesterday, 4, 86
Bosque County, Texas, 81
Botanica, 127, 128
Boundary Waters, 143
Boy Meets Girl, 5
Boys Next Door, The, 47, 69, 93, 129
Brace Up!, 174
Braille Garden, 96
Brave Little Tailor, The, 145
Brave New Smiles, 7
Brave Smiles...Another Lesbian Tragedy, 102
Break, 122
Breakfast with Les and Bess, 147
Breaking the Code, 7, 25, 145
Breaking Up, 105
Break, The, 12
Brewster Papers, The, 175
Bribe, The, 83, 157
Bricklayers, 38
Bridge to Terabithia, 55
Brief But Exemplary Life of the Living Goddess, The, 85
Brief Lives, 4
Bright and Bold Design, The, 150
Brighton Beach Memoirs, 174
Brilliant Traces, 98, 168
Broadway Bound, 10, 12, 31, 92, 167
Broken Bough, The, 67
Brooklyn Trojan Women, The, 173

Brothers Booth!, The, 29
Brothers Karamazov, The, 15
Brothers K, The, 14
Buffalo Hair, 122
Buk: The Life and Times of Charles Bukowski, 79
Bundle Man, The, 157
Bunnicula, 44
Bunny & Doris, 156
Burn This, 98, 164
Burning Hope, 105
Business of Murder, The, 149
Bus Riley's Back in Town, 114
Bus Stop, 113
Butcher's Daughter, The, 40

C

Cabaret, 123
Cabaret Verboten, 38, 39
Cacodemon King, 54
Cafe con Leche, 128
Cakewalk, 12
California Cowboy, 143
Caligula, 155
Calliope Jam, 7
Cambodia Agonistes, 111
Camelot, 129
Camping with Henry and Tom, 25
Candida, 50, 65, 113, 131
Candida Erendira, La, 127, 128
Candide, 39, 43, 44, 163, 170
Canterville Ghost, The, 34
Captains Courageous, 57
Carbon que ha Sido Brasa, El, 127, 128
Caretaker, The, 75, 143
Carmen Kittel, 138
Carnival, 95
Carousel, 120
Carreno, 42
Carrott Carrot and Other Proclivities, The, 21
Carving of Mount Rushmore, The, 4
Casa de Bernarda Alba, La, 127, 128
Cat on a Hot Tin Roof, 9, 31, 88, 146, 152
Catch!, 33
Catch Me If You Can, 149
Catherine: Concerning the Fateful Origins of Her Grandeur, with Diverse Musical Interludes, Three Elephants and No Ballet, 73
Cat's-Paw, 124
Caucasian Chalk Circle, The, 3, 115, 170
Caveat Emptor! Buyer Beware!, 14
C. Colombo Inc. Export/Import, Genoa, 102
Celestina, La, 25
Celos Del Aire, 152
Cementville, 121
Cemetery Club, The, 70
Cemetery Man, The, 96
Cena Para Dos, 152
Cenci, The, 75
Centerburg Tales, 19

CEO, 83
Chain, 97, 173
Champagne Charlie Stakes, The, 116
Change Partners & Dance, 14
Changin' Lanes, 165
Chaos, 96
Chapel of Perpetual Desire Presents A Liturgical Circus of Religious Fervor and Live Sex on Stage, The, 41
Charley's Aunt, 9, 25, 72, 169
Charlie and the Chocolate Factory, 52
Charlie's Wedding Day, 107
Charlotte's Web, 30, 52, 99, 136
Cheek to Cheek, 79
Cherry Orchard, The, 103
Chicago Conspiracy Trial, The, 127
Chicks, 114
Child Is Born, A, 111
Children of Eden, 89
Children of Paradise: Shooting a Dream, 77, 155, 175
Children's Hour, The, 12
Child's Christmas in Wales, A, 81
Chocolate Ambassador, The, 167
Christchild, 97
Christina Alberta's Father, 107, 167
Christmas Carol, A, 2, 4, 7, 8, 9, 13, 26, 27, 29, 35, 36, 47, 50, 57, 59, 60, 61, 63, 64, 66, 67, 69, 84, 88, 89, 91, 92, 95, 99, 114, 125, 133, 134, 143, 144, 149, 150, 151, 152, 164, 170, 176, 177
Christmas Carol—The Gospel According to Dickens, A, 134
Christmas Memory, A, 162
Christmas that Almost Wasn't, The, 35
Christopher Columbus, 29
Christopher Columbus Follies, The, 41
Christopher Columbus! Or, Business as Usual, 157
Christopher's Shirt, 71
Christy, 46
Chronicles of Plague, The, 55
Cigarettes and Moby Dick, 96
Cincinnati Man, 93
Cinderella, 26, 47, 55, 112, 158
Circle, The, 99
Cirque Invisibles, Les, 7
City Called Forest, A, 78
Clarence Darrow, 170
Class Clown, 161
Claveles, Los, 152
Clearance Sale at the Five and Dime, 96
Closer Than Ever, 37, 120, 158, 164
Closer, The, 96
Club Magic, 8
Cobb, 86, 120, 147
Cockburn Rituals, The, 173
Cocktail Hour, The, 9, 22, 25, 36, 49, 72, 92, 99, 113, 119, 120, 146
Cole, 135
Collected Works of Billy the Kid, The, 115
Color Blind, 157

Colored Museum, The, 76, 103, 175
Columbus, 161
Come Back, Little Sheba, 164
Comedians, 44
Comedy of Errors, The, 6, 30, 98, 100, 141, 153, 156
Comedy On a Grand Scale, 7
Come Up and See Me Sometime, 170
Coming Back, 111
Company of Angels, The, 99
Comrades and Lovers, 21
Confessions, 71
Connecticut Yankee in King Arthur's Court, A, 50
Connections of the Heart, 21
Conrack, 57, 61
Contents Under Pressure, 7
Contrabando, 25
Control Freaks, 32
Convict's Return, The, 24
Cooking the World, 93
Coriolanus, 141
Corn is Green, The, 22
Corpse, 13
Cotton Patch Gospel, 49, 129
Couch Piece, 111
Council, The, 52, 67
Counsellor-at-Law, 171
Count of Monte Cristo, The, 21
Country Christmas Carol, A, 62
Country Girl, The, 12
Country Wife, The, 150
Cover of Life, The, 66
Covers, 71
Cowboy Colors, 62
Coyote Road, 84
Cradle of Maybe, The, 108
Creditors, 9, 39
Crib, The, 157
Cries in the Night, 168
Crimes of the Heart, 10, 12, 158
Criminal Hearts, 60
Criminals in Love, 132
Crimson Thread, The, 79
Cross-Dressing in the Depression, 85
Crossing Delancey, 37
Crossing the Broken Bridge, 20
Crucible, The, 69, 81, 83
Cruising Close to Crazy, 96
Crushed Tomatoes, 143
Crusoe, Friday, and the Island of Hope, 154
Crying to Laugh, 67
Cry of the Americas, 84
Cry, the Beloved Country, 61
Cuban Swimmer, The, 116
Curious Tale, A, 157
Custer Rides, 138
Custom of the Country, The, 139
Cut on the Bias, 71
Cymbeline, 69, 110
Cyrano, 128
Cyrano de Bergerac, 9, 63, 112, 165

D

Daddy, Daddy Go Away! I Don't

INDEX OF TITLES

Like the Games You Play, 81
Daedalus in the Belly of the Beast, 73, 163
Damn Yankees, 105, 176
Dance and the Railroad, The, 67
Dance of Exile, 20
Dancing at Lughnasa, 67, 69, 81, 123
Dancing Spider, The, 52
Dancing to the River, 142
Dancing With Ourselves, 143
Dandelion, 52
Dandelion Wine, 112
Danny and the Deep Blue Sea, 3
Dante and Virgil Go Dancing, 96
Danton's Death, 8
Dark Cowgirls & Prairie Queens, 103
Dark Fruit, 7
Dark Rapture, 53
David's Mother, 40
Day God Died, The, 96
Day in Hollywood/A Night in the Ukraine, A, 119
Day in the Death of Joe Egg, A, 132
Day Mary Shelley Met Charlotte Bronte, The, 142
Day Room, The, 127
Days of Rondo, 62
Days of Wine and Roses, 40
Daystar, 21
Day the Bronx Died, The, 82, 96
Daytrips, 27, 132, 165
D. Boone, 4
Dead Book, The, 122
Deadly Virtues, 4
Deadweight, 106
Deal, The, 147
Dear Liar, 56
Dearly Departed, 37, 120, 137
Dear Miss Elena Sergeyevna, 64
Death and the Maiden, 8, 116, 134, 147
Death and Life of Sherlock Holmes, The, 109
Death Catches the Hunter, 96
Death of a Salesman, 64, 91, 92, 120, 159
Death of the Last Black Man in the Whole Entire World, The, 175
Death of Zukasky, The, 166
December, 71
Deep in a Dream of You, 100
Delire D'Interpretations, 96
Deloatch Suite, The, 7
Democracy in America, 175
Der Golem, 78
Desdemona, 23
Deshima, 78, 118
Dessert at Waffle House, Breakfast Anytime, 169
Destiny of Me, The, 37
Detroit Stories, 51
Deungsinbul, 78
Devils, The, 96
Devotees in the Garden of Love, 4
Diary of an African American, 93
Dickens Christmas Carol Show, The, 69
Different, 107

Dining Room, The, 149
Dinner at Eight, 9
Dinosaur Play, The, 13
Dinosaurus, 44
Dirt, 171
Dirty Work at the Crossroads, 99
Disappearance, The, 45, 46
Disappeared, 96
Distant Mirror, A, 33
Dividing Lines, 71
Diviners, The, 145
Doctor Dolittle in the Moon, 136
Dog Lady, 116
Doll House, A, 31, 47, 111, 140
Do Lord Remember Me, 76
Don Juan, 115
Don Juan & the Non Don Juan, The, 167
Do Not Pass Go, 71
Don't Dress for Dinner, 42
Don't Sleep Under the Mapou Tree, 13
Donut World, 176
Do the Write Thing!, 35
Down The Road, 168
Down the Shore, 61
Downtown Psychobroads, 156
Downwinder Dance, 55
Do You See What I'm Saying, 107
Dracula, 22, 30, 129
Dracula, A Musical Nightmare, 8
Dragon, The, 14
Dragonwings, 24, 136
Dream, 45
Dream Catchers, 56
Dreamers of the Absolute, 156
Dream House, 96
Dream of a Common Language, 24, 173
Dream of Aladdin, The, 30
Dream of the Red Spider, 11
Dream of Wealth, A, 86
Dressing Room, The, 111
Driving Miss Daisy, 4, 39
Dr. Terror's 3-D House of Theatre, 53
Duchess of Malfi, The, 9
Duet for One, 138, 139
Duke's Place, 91
Dumas, 6
Dust, 156
Dutchman, 27, 114
Dybbuk, The, 134

E

Eagle or Sun, 109
Early Dismissal, 96
Early One Evening at the Rainbow Bar and Grill, 124
Earth and Sky, 166
Eastern Standard, 164
East Texas Hot Links, 15
Easy Living, 156
Echoes & Postcards, 130
Echoes of the Jazz Age, 14
Eclipse, El, 128
Eddie, 96
Eden, 99

Edna Earle, 99
Educating Rita, 13
Edward the Second, 175
Effie's Burning, 117
Egypt, 78
8 Miles from New York, 169
84 Charing Cross Road, 90
Elaine's Daughter, 147
Electra, 45, 64, 133
Eleemosynary, 2, 28, 83, 121
Elektra, 132
Elephant Memories, 118
11th Festival of New Plays, 41
Ellen Universe Joins the Band, 59
Elves and the Shoemaker, The, 29, 30
Emiliano, 52
Empathy, Inc., 107
Emperor's New Clothes, The, 22, 26
Emperor's Nightingale, The, 144
Empty Hearts, 37
Endgame, 5, 75
End of Summer, 118
End of the Day, The, 122
Enemy of the People, An, 82
Engagement, The, 58, 155
Enlightenments, 96
Enlightenments on an Enchanted Island, 71
Enough, 155
Entries, 107
Equus, 169
Escape from Happiness, 32, 175
Esperando la Carroza, 127, 128
Etiquette of the Undercaste, 14
Etta Jenks, 171
Eulogy, 107
Eulogy for Mister Hamm, 122
Evelyn and the Polka King, 4, 38
Evening of Mamet, Gray and Linney, An, 91
Everybody Loves Opal, 22
Every Day Newt Burman, 79
Everyone Knows What a Dragon Looks Like, 67
Everything in the Garden, 54
Evil Little Thoughts, 50
Evita, 65, 119, 170
Exchange, 79
Execution of Justice, 56
Executive Leverage, 143
Expense of Spirit, The, 21
Explorers Club, The, 125
Explosions, 78
Extended Forecast, 79
Extra Man, The, 85, 143
Eye of God, 137
Eye of the Beholder, The, 114
Eye To Eye, 14

F

Fairy Bones, 111
Faith Healer, 74, 114
Fallen Angel, 78
Falling in Love Again, a holiday cabaret with Craig Figtree and Steve Carson, 21
Falsa Cronica de Juana la Loca, La, 25

Falsettoland, 66, 128, 150, 165, 172
Falsettos, 105
Families, 1
Family Affair, A, 45, 155
Family Man, A, 122
Family Rhyme-Time, 1
Family Secrets, 42
Fanny, 70
Fantasio, 64
Fantasticks, The, 43, 92
Far Fetched Fables, 90
Farndale Avenue Housing Estate Townswomen's Guild Dramatic Society Murder Mystery, The, 43
Fast!, 169
Father, The, 15
Fat Men in Skirts, 85
Faust/Gastronome, 79
Fear of Falling, 49
Fefu and Her Friends, 175
Felicia, 156
Fences, 19, 70, 109, 113, 119, 120, 145, 149, 164
Fertility Rights, 16
Fever, The, 130
Few Good Men, A, 90
Few Simple Truths, A, 110
FF: The Brontes, 134
Fiddler on the Roof, 28, 81
Fields of Ambrosia, The, 58
Fifteen Minute Christmas Carol, The, 162
Fifteen Minute Hamlet, The, 131
Fifth of July, 133
Film Society, The, 68
Fin del Mundo, El, 52
Firebird, The, 136
Firebugs, The, 109
Fire in the Rain/Singer in the Storm, 87
Fire or Ice, 129
Fires in the Mirror, 100
Fisherman, The, 76
Fishmas, 115
Fish Story—Part 1, 174
Fish Story—Part 2, 174
Five Guys Named Moe, 57
500 Hats of Bartholomew Cubbins, The, 34
500 Years–A Fax from Denise Stoklos to Christopher Columbus, 79
Five in the Killing Zone, 165
Flaubert's Latest, 122
Flea in Her Ear, A, 7, 110
Flesh and Blood, 21
Flight of Chung Sop Lee, 78
Floating Milkpods, 107
Flood, The, 156
Flower Therapy, 67
Flying Doctor, The, 105
Flying Karamazov Brothers in The Brothers Karamazov, The, 137
Flyin' West, 8
Fool for Love, 3, 125
Foreigners: A Play of Cristoforo Colombo, 145
Foreigner, The, 46, 91
Forever Plaid, 8, 42, 105

40 Deuce, 157
42nd Street, 89
Four Baboons Adoring the Sun, 80
Four Part Harmony, 158
Fourplay, 171
14 Years in One Night: A Retrospective, 20
Foxfire, 26, 58, 89
Fran & Brian, 18
Frankie and Johnny in the Clair de Lune, 22, 158
Frauleins in Underwear, 104
Freaky Friday, 161
Frederick Douglass Now, 103
Freedom Bound, 84
Freedom is My Middle Name, 109
Freedom Train, 161
Freefall, 96, 166
Freemen and Lunatics, 55
Free Will & Wanton Lust, 173
Frida, 173
Frog Prince, The, 30
From Sea to Shining Sea, 161
From the Mississippi Delta, 8, 13, 35, 67, 71, 74, 105, 168
Front Page, The, 8, 43
Frozen in Time, 96
Fuente Ovejuna, 25, 79
Fugue, 40
Full Gallop: An Evening with Diana Vreeland, 23
Full Moon, 68
Funny Thing Happened on the Way to the Forum, A, 22, 129, 175
Fur, 96
Futz, 78

G

Galileo, 75
Gamblers, The, 120
Generations of the Dead in the Abyss of Coney Island Madness, 114
Genesis, 115
Geneva, 75
George and Elba, 96
Get Hur, 157
Getting Around, 27
Getting Married, 59
Ghost in the Machine, 147
Ghost—Live From Gallillee, 79
Ghosts, 8, 98, 105, 130
Giant's Baby, 67
Giants: Myths and Legends, 17
Gift of the Magi, The, 4, 113
Gifts of the Magi, The, 58, 72
Gigli Concert, The, 44
Gig, The, 108
Gin Game, The, 91
Girl Bar, 96
Girl's Guide to Chaos, A, 41
Give 'Em Hell, Harry!, 4, 42
Glass Menagerie, The, 5, 10, 18, 28, 77, 98, 99, 110, 133, 164
Glengarry Glen Ross, 3, 114
Goblin Market, 37, 125
God of Vengeance, 75

God's Country, 18, 78, 104, 133
God's Hands, 160
Godspell, 18, 120
Gold, 71
Golden Shadows Old West Museum, The, 81
Golem, The, 23
Golf with Alan Shepard, 79
Golliwhoppers, 13
Good, 9
Good Doctor, The, 160
Good Evening, 56
Good Hope, The, 64
Good Person of Setzuan, The, 60, 155
Good Sports, 62
Good Times Are Killing Me, The, 57, 68, 136, 164
Goodnight Desdemona (Good Morning Juliet), 39, 120
Goose and Tomtom, 59
Gorey Stories, 169
Grande de Coca-Cola, El, 104
Grapes of Wrath, The, 46, 50, 92, 106, 115, 119
Gravity of Honey, The, 124
Grease, 7, 37, 142, 152
Great American Backstage Musical, The, 174
Great Day in the Morning, 144
Greater Good, 96
Greater Good, The, 91
Greater Tuna, 13, 29, 91, 123, 134
Great Expectations, 58, 94, 112
Great Gatsby, The, 62
Great War of Rikki-Tikki-Tavi, The, 30
Greek, 85
Green Bird, The, 102
Greetings, 56
Groucho: A Life in Revue, 168
Groundhog, 85
Grover, 37
Guardsman, The, 27, 109, 170
Guest House, 1
Gulf War, 79
Gulliver's Last Travels, 111
Gun, A Book, A Photograph, A Name, A, 96
Gunmetal Blues, 37
Guys and Dolls, 151

H

Haarlem Nocturne, 78
Habana: Antologia Musical, 128
Hadley's Mistake, 96
Hairy Ape, The, 77
Halcyon Days, 2, 171
Hamlet, 11, 72, 89, 119, 121, 131, 141, 146, 158, 175
Handy Dandy, 28
Hanna, 96
Hannah Davis, 18
Hannah Free, 21
Hans Brinker or the Silver Skates, 55
Hansel and Gretel, 26, 52, 53, 161
Hapgood, 32

Happy Journey, The, 114
Happy Prince, The, 96
Hard Times, 121, 170
Harold and the Purple Crayon, 161
Harvey, 129, 135, 159
Harvey Milk Show, The, 3, 21
Hatful of Rain, A, 10
Haunted House, 78
Hauptmann, 166
Hay Fever, 125, 135, 144
Heartbeats, 40, 56, 61
Heartbreak House, 6, 11, 66, 137, 143, 145
Hearts Beating Faster, 33
Heat, 7
Heathen Valley, 110
Hedda Gabler, 11, 50, 115, 125, 136
Heidi, 17, 55, 161
Heidi Chronicles, The, 4, 16, 40, 58, 65, 68, 94, 120, 133, 164, 165
Helen of Athens, 122
Heliotrope Bouquet by Scott Joplin & Louis Chauvin, The, 122
Hello and Goodbye, 155
Hello, Mrs. President, 156
Hell on Wheels, 53
Henceforward, 87, 125, 168
Henry IV, Part 1, 6, 97, 141
Henry IV, Part 2, 6
Henry V, 119, 156
Henry VI Chronicles, The, 139
Henry VI, Parts 1-3, 5
Henry VI, Part 3, 110
Her Aching Heart, 21
Here's Love, 61
Hero At Last, 107
Herringbone, 11, 66
Hey Little Walter, 176
Hey Love, 93
Hibiscus Story, 78
H.I.D., 5
Hidden History, 7
Hidden Laughter, 66
Higher Powers, 156
Hi-Hat Hattie!, 160
Him, Her & You, 42
Hippolytos, 78
His First, Best Country, 69
Ho Ho Ho the Christmas Show, 113
Holiday, 10
Holiday Evening With Friends, A, 130
Holiday Memories, 38, 125, 146, 163
Holiday Survival Game Show, The, 7
Hollywood Canteen, 92
Holy Ghosts, 5
Home, 50
Home and Away, 61
Homecoming, The, 131
Homer Gee and the Raphsodies, 46
Home Show Pieces, The, 100
Homeward Bound, 51, 70
Honor Song For Crazy Horse, 96
Hope for Breakfast, 122
Hope Zone, The, 164
Hospitality Suite, 143, 166
Hostage, The, 23, 28, 74
Hotel Oubliette, 171

Hot Fudge, 150
Hot 'n Cole, 36
Houseguests, The, 157
House of Bernarda Alba, The, 90
House of Blue Leaves, The, 31, 36, 40, 45, 81
How Else Am I Supposed To Know I'm Still Alive, 52
How I Got That Story, 31, 91
How the Other Half Loves, 74
How to Succeed in Business Without Really Trying, 133
Huck Finn's Story, 72
Huipil II, 156
Hula Hoop Sha-Boop, 91
Human Comedy, The, 160, 169
Humpty Dumpty, 52
Hunchback of Harlem, The, 157
Hunger, 84
Hunters of the Soul, 96
Hurricane Dreams: The Voyages of Christopher Columbus, 17
Hyaena, 4
Hysterics, 150

I

I Ain't Yo' Uncle, 134
I Can Fit My Fist in My Mouth, 43
I Can't Pay the Rent, 43
Ice Fishing Play, The, 4
Iceman Cometh, The, 59
Ichabod!, 95
Idioglossia, 58
Idiot, The, 75
I Do! I Do!, 31, 119
I Don't Want to Go to Bed, 30
If We Are Women, 171
If We Never Meet Again, 71
I Hate Hamlet, 6, 10, 18, 42, 47, 58, 83, 99, 106, 151, 175, 177
I Have Often Dreamed of Arriving Alone in a Strange Country..., 107
Illegal Motion, 106
Illusion, The, 2, 5, 64, 110
Images of Addiction, 1
Imaginary Invalid, The, 23, 123
Imagine, 30
Imagine Drowning, 150
Imago: The Theatre Mask Ensemble, 91
Immigrants, 114
Immigrant, The, 36, 49, 112, 113, 123, 133, 149, 150, 159, 168
I'm Not Rappaport, 38, 70, 92, 145
I'm Not Stupid, 176
Imperceptible Mutabilities in the Third Kingdom, 104
Importance of Being Earnest, The, 24, 27, 47, 59, 74, 97, 114
Importance of Being Irish, The, 104
Impossible Dreams, 67
Incommunicado, 104
Incunabula, Incunabulorum, 79
Independence, 120
Indians, 88
India Plays, 106
Inherit the Wind, 120

In My Father's Court, 94
In My Mother's House, 94
Inner House, 138
Innocents' Crusade, The, 86
Innocents, The, 135
Inside George, 32
Inspecting Carol, 23, 28, 119, 136, 137, 147
Inspector Calls, An, 171
Interior Decoration, 105
Interpreters, 160
Interrogation, The, 107
In the Flesh, 111
In the Jungle of Cities, 83, 100
In the Land of Giants, 96
In the Presence, 89
In the White Harvest: The Importance of Road Construction, 71
Intimate Exchanges, 74, 144
Into the Woods, 18, 112, 160, 168
Intrigue at Ah-Pah, 49
In Two Worlds, 115
Invisible Friends, 136
Invisible Man, The, 136
I Ought To Be in Pictures, 58
Iphigenia at Aulis, 64
Iphigenia in Tauris, 78
I Remember Mama, 46
Irish Reunion, An, 91
Irish Stew, 62
Iron Lung, 78
It Is It Is Not, 157
It's a Bird, It's a Plane, It's Superman, 61
It's A Wonderful Life, 10
It's Only A Play, 164
It's the Truth (If You Think it Is), 15
Ivona, Princess of Burgundia, 104
Ivory Alphabet, The, 165
I Want Someone to Eat Cheese With, 127
I Witness, 103

J

Jack and the Beanstalk, 55, 145, 158
Jack Frost, 17
Jacques Brel is Alive and Well and Living in Pari, 12
Jamboree, 156
Jamie 22, 30
Japango, 35
Jar the Floor, 15, 40, 76, 148, 150, 160
Jax and the Graviteers, 8
Jekyll & Hyde, 161
Jemima Boone: Daughter of Kentucky, 145
Jennine's Diary, 4
Jenny Keeps Talking, 86
Jesus Christ Superstar, 46, 112, 168
Jibaros Progresistas, Los, 128
Jigsaws, 147
Joanna's Husband, David's Wife, 168
Job, The, 122
Joe Turner's Come and Gone, 110, 116, 177

John Brown's Body, 114
Joined at the Head, 86
Joseph and His Amazing Technicolor Dreamcoat, 112
Judevine, 18
Julie Johnson, 96
Julius Caesar, 50, 69, 137, 138, 139, 141, 165
Junebug Jack, 131
Jungalbook, 95
Jungle Book: Tales from Peace Rock, The, 17
Jungle Book, The, 17, 34
Juno, 167
Just So Stories, 67

K

Kafka, Father & Son, 78
Kanashibetsu, 78
Karmic Games, The, 41
Kate's Sister, 45
Kathy & Mo Show: Parallel Lives, The, 134
Katzelmacher, 32
Keely and Du, 4
Kentucky Cycle, The, 87
Kerfol: A Ghost Story, 139
Kiddie Pool, The, 7
Kids for President!, 35
Kill, 156
Killing Jazz, 107
Kimchee and Chitlins, 166
Kind Ness, 64, 71, 118
Kind of Arden, A, 5
Kingdom of Earth, 32
King Lear, 6, 92, 105, 109, 139, 153, 165
King of Carpets, The, 76
King of Coons, 114
King of the Kosher Grocers, The, 93, 105
Kitchen Table U, 41
Kitty-Kitty, 53
K-Mille, 133
Knights of the Round Table, The, 18
Knockin' Em Dead at the Limbo Lounge, 7
Korbel, 49
Koulaba, 45
Krapp's Last Tape, 39
Kringle's Window, 145
K2, 10
Kuru, 22, 126
Kvetch, 173

L

Ladder, The, 163
Ladies of the Camellias, The, 110
Lady Bracknell's Confinement, 167
Lady Chieftains, 96
Lady Day at Emerson's Bar and Grill, 32, 36, 47, 86, 91, 92, 99, 171
Lady from Havana, The, 42, 73, 177
Lady from Maxim's, The, 92
Lady from the Sea, The, 24

Lady in Red, The, 58
Lady-Like, 117
Lady Lou Revue, The, 115
Lady's Not For Burning, The, 90
Lake Street Extension, 55, 96
Lamb on Fire, 163
Landscape Painter, The, 139
Language of Love, 7
L.A. Plays, The, 11
Lardo Weeping, 7
Last Fairytale, The, 8
Last Laugh, The, 75
Last Minstrel Show, The, 114
Last Supper, 53
Last Total Eclipse, 122
Last Yankee, The, 86
Late Bus to Mecca, 97, 173
Late Great Ladies of Blues & Jazz, The, 9, 46
Later Life, 122
Latins Anonymous, 133
Latins Anonymous Lifetime Achievement Awards, The, 134
Laughing Wild, 21
Laughter in the Dark, 127
Laura, 175
Law/Order, 32
Leandras, Las, 152
Learned Ladies, The, 9
Lear Project, The, 155
Leaving Egypt, 131
Legacies, 19
Legend of Sleepy Hollow, The, 18
Legend of St. Nickolas, A, 23
Lend Me a Tenor, 6, 18, 22, 29, 59, 66, 81, 86, 89, 106, 112, 113, 119, 125, 129, 145, 146, 149, 150, 151, 159, 164, 168, 170
Lesbians Who Kill, 78
Let Me Sing and I'm Happy, 86
Letters to a Student Revolutionary, 111
Lettice and Lovage, 4, 13, 66, 90, 99, 119, 123, 125, 159
Let's Play Two, 144
Liaisons Dangereuses, Les, 38, 160
Liar, The, 153
Liberace, The Magic of Believing, 162
Library Love, 156
Life and Times of Deacon A.L. Wiley, The, 62
Life During Wartime, 32, 172, 173
Life in the Lost Track, 93
Life in the Theatre, A, 33, 65, 75, 138
Life of a Worm, The, 41
Life of Galileo, The, 123
Life's Too Short to Cry, 157
Light in Love, 21
Light in the Heart of the Dragon, 21
Light Inside, The, 41
Light in the Village, 110
Light Sensitive, 105
Light Up the Sky, 169
Lilies of the Field, The, 37
Lion in Winter, The, 43, 99, 141, 168
Lion, the Witch and the Wardrobe, The, 22, 99, 120

Lips Together, Teeth Apart, 8, 19, 31, 42, 65, 67, 87, 110, 117, 137, 159, 164, 165
Lisbon Traviata, The, 21, 99, 133, 136, 150, 164
Listen to the Lions, 147
Little Egypt, 122
Little Footsteps, 113
Little Foxes, The, 6, 69, 112, 121, 135
Little Lord Fauntleroy, 52
Little Match Girl, The, 34
Little Night Music, A, 159
Little Princess, A, 30
Little Prince, The, 155
Little Red Riding Hood, 26
Little Shop of Horrors, 12, 13, 120
Living in Exile, 89
Living, The, 50
Lloyd's Prayer, 142
Locked Doors and Lightning Bugs, 107
Long Christmas Dinner, The, 162
Long Day's Journey into Night, 69, 118
Long Journey Home, 156
Loose Knit, 137
Lorca: Child of the Moon, 25
Los de Abajo, 25
Lost Electra, 19, 124, 149
Lost Highway, 105
Lost in Yonkers, 145
Lotus Hooks, 55
Louisiana Purchase, 7
Love and Revolution, A Brecht Cabaret, 4
Love Diatribe, 84
Love Letters, 6, 12, 19, 37, 65, 95, 98, 112, 123, 134, 146, 149, 150, 151, 177
Loveplay, 71
Love's Labour's Lost, 23, 30, 156
Love Space Demands, The, 45
Love Suicide at Schofield Barracks, 104
Luck, Pluck & Virtue, 77
Lucky Nurse, 122
Luisa Fernanda, 128
Lust and Pity, 21
L-Word, The, 157
Lynched Hopes and Unsung Songs, 81
Lypsinka! A Day in the Life, 102

M

Macbeth, 8, 73, 97, 116, 139, 140, 154, 164
Macbett, 29
Machines Cry Wolf, 96
Made in Lanus, 25
Madeline and the Gypsies, 17
Mad Forest, 24, 53, 86, 102, 110, 120
Madwoman of Chaillot, The, 171
Magical Adventures of Pretty Pearl, The, 103
Magic Fish, The, 1
Maisie, 138

INDEX OF TITLES

Major Barbara, 24, 72
Make and Break, 79
Make Me Pele for a Day, 136
Make We Merry, 163
Malasangre, La, 169
Malice Aforethought, 12
Malpractice or Love's the Best Doctor, 49
Mama Drama, 124
Man and Superman, 39
Man at His Best, 176
Mandrake, The, 125
Man For All Seasons, A, 8, 39
Man in His Underwear, 122
Manners and More, 139
Man of La Mancha, 65
Man of Mode, The, 19
Man of the Moment, 40
Man that Corrupted Hadleyburg, The, 71
Man Who Came to Dinner, The, 64, 143
Man Who Lived Underground, The, 38
Man Who Wrote Peter Pan, The, 50
Man with the Flower in His Mouth, The, 114
Man, Woman, Dinosaur, 122
Map of My Mother, 41
Map of the World, A, 104
Ma Rainey's Black Bottom, 92, 119
Marathon Dancing, 54
March of the Falsettos, 66, 128
Marina, 108
Marisol, 4, 66, 77, 100
Marks in the Water, 102
Marriage Play, 7, 42, 88
Martha War, The, 67
Martian Chronicles, The, 95
Martin Guerre, 66
Marvin's Room, 61, 67, 68, 69, 122, 137
Mary Stuart, 75
Masks, 1
Mask, The, 173
Mass Appeal, 30
Master and Margarita, The, 157
Master Builder, The, 135
Mastergate, 79
"Master Harold"...and the boys, 36, 74, 123, 150
Matchmaker, The, 49
Maximum Tumescence: A Triptych of the Geometry of Love, 41
Mayhem: The Invasion, 79
M. Butterfly, 16, 65, 66, 91, 120, 123, 129, 136, 159, 160, 172
McTeague: A Tale of San Francisco, 24
Me, a Scientist?, 35
Measure for Measure, 44, 98, 100, 140, 141
Meat My Beat/Latin Lezbo Comic, 6
Medea, 157
Media Amok, 11
Medicine Show, The, 170
Meetings, 64, 91
Meeting, The, 44, 62, 76, 115, 148
Member of the Wedding, The, 59
Memory of Splendor, A, 139

Memory Tricks, 100
Me Nobody Knows, The, 148
Men's Lives, 23
Merchant of Venice, The, 165
Merchant of Venus, The, 163
Merry Christmas, Strega Nona, 34
Merry Wives of Windsor, The, 141, 165
Metamorphosis, 103
Mexico Romantico, 128
Miami Lights, 160
Micropolis, 156
Middle Ages, The, 58
Midsummer Night's Dream, A, 2, 6, 30, 43, 47, 80, 92, 110, 139, 140, 154, 166, 170, 171
Mighty Gents, The, 114
Millionairess, The, 90
Mind King, The, 108
Minor Demons, 16
Minotaur, The, 170
Miracle at Graceland, 142
Miracle Man, 159
Miracle Worker, The, 13, 22, 30, 65, 106
Mirandolina, 134, 177
Misalliance, 11, 90
Misanthrope, The, 6, 32, 40, 47, 82, 116
Miser, The, 34, 72, 144
Mishuganismo, 127
Miss Evers' Boys, 6, 7, 9, 38, 47, 51, 58, 60, 72, 117, 128, 149
Mission of Jane/A Love Story, The, 138
Miss Julie, 88
Mission, The, 77
Mojo and the Sayso, The, 114
Molly and James, 114
Monk 'n Bud, 157
Montana Molly and the Peppermint Kid, 34, 35
Monte Carlo, 50
Month in the Country, A, 82
Moon for the Misbegotten, A, 32, 36, 89, 116, 119
Moon Over the Brewery, 124
Moonshadow, 124
Moot, 91
More Fun Than Bowling, 120, 126
more intimacies, 142
More of the Laughing Buddha Wholistik Radio Theatre, 27
Mormons in Malibu, 96
Morning Dew with Trellis, 58
Morning's at Seven, 105, 118
Mosquito Succulence, 79
Most Happy Fella, The, 61, 80
Most Valuable Player, 30, 34, 44
Motel Blue 19, 78
Mother Clap's Molly House, 96
Mother Courage, 63
Mother Courage and Her Children, 141
Mother Jones: The Most Dangerous Woman in America, 24, 91
Mother of Us All, The, 93
Mothers, 45, 46
Mothers and Daughters, 139
Mothers Have Nine Lives, 176

Mother's Work, 41
Mountain, 49, 59, 113, 117
Mountain Tales and Music, 131
Mount Allegro, 60
Mouse Esquire, The, 67
Mousetrap, The, 23, 28, 95
Mr. Popper's Penguins, 34
Mr. Raccoon & His Friends, 44
Mr. Rickey Calls A Meeting, 105
Mrs. Klein, 15, 160, 168
Mrs. Neuberger's Dead, 176
Mrs. Warren's Profession, 28
Much Ado About Nothing, 8, 75, 77, 88, 97, 119, 139, 141
Much Ado Musical, The, 169
Mud People, 173
Muerte y La Doncella, La, 134
Munci Meg, 153
Murder as a Fine Art, 143
Murdering Green Meadows, 147
Murder of Crows, A, 162
Murrow, 29
Musicians of Bremen, 154
My Ancestors' House, 157
My Chekov Light, 96
My Children! My Africa!, 2, 31, 44, 51, 90, 99, 114, 125, 138, 146, 172, 175
My Fair Lady, 119
My Favorite Year, 80
My Mother Said I Never Should, 69
My Son the Lawyer is Drowning, 70
Mysteries and What's So Funny?, The, 48
Mysterious Connections, 107
Mystery Cycle: Creation, The, 44, 45
Mystery Cycle: Passion, The, 45
Mystery of Edwin Drood, The, 94
Mystery of Irma Vep, The, 4, 22, 28, 95, 98, 115, 119, 123, 126, 129, 145, 159
Mystic Voices, 84
My Thing of Love, 147
My Three Angels, 19
My Visits with MGM, 25, 79, 91, 135

N

Nacre, 96
Nagasaki Dust, 117
Name for the Moon, A, 107
Nancy and Plum, 136
National Anthems, 117, 126
Nativity, 157
Near the End of the Century, 58
Necessities, 126
Nerd, The, 95
Neuro Sisters, 157
Neverland, 44
New Americans, The, 156
New Business, 160
New Jersey/New York, 157
New Voices, 35
New York Profiles, 79
Nightingale, The, 34, 154
Night, Night Max, 41
Night of the Iguana, The, 40

Night Sky, 138
Night With Doris, A, 176
Nine, 81, 133
1940's Radio Hour, The, 46, 119, 128, 135, 159
1984, 106
1993 Holiday Survival Game Show, The, 7
Nixon: Live! The Future is Now, 110
Noah Johnson Had a Whore, 143
Nobody Here But Us Chickens, 150
Noche Antillana, 128
Noel Coward at the Cafe de Paris, 49
No Exit, 163
Noises Off, 112
Nonna, La, 128
Noodle Doodle Box, 34
Nooner, 126
Nora, 16, 19, 59, 116, 171
Normal Life, A, 160
Northeast Local, 164
Nosferatu, 78, 118
Nostalgia Tropical, 73
Nothing Sacred, 120
Nova Velha Estoria, 128
No Way to Treat a Lady, 124, 125
Nunsense, 22, 37, 66, 81, 83, 99, 133, 142, 175, 177
Nutcracker and the Mouse King, The, 128
Nutcracker: A Play, The, 121

O

Oak and Ivy, 45
Obake!, 134
Objects in the Mirror are Closer than They Appear, 71
Occasional Grace, 54
Odd Jobs, 19, 144
Odyssey, The, 109
Oedipus, 153
Oedipus The King, 171
Of Mice and Men, 46, 60
Of One Blood, 79
Of Thee I Sing, 15, 28, 40, 127
O. Henry Christmas, An, 80
Oh, Holy Allen Ginsberg: Oh, Holy Shit Sweet Jesus Tantric Buddha Dharma Road, 21
Ohio State Murders, The, 63
Oil City Symphony, 56, 120, 129, 134
Okiboji, 128
Oklahoma!, 5, 46, 112, 120
Old Actress in the Role of Dostoevsky's Wife, An, 75
Old Boy, The, 105, 118
Old Devils, The, 168
Old Lady's Guide to Survival, The, 4, 120
Old Times, 59, 169
Oleanna, 11
Oliver, 129
Oliver Twist, 44
Olle from Laughtersville, 62
Olympus On My Mind, 70

INDEX OF TITLES

Onafhankelijk Toneel, 157
Once In Doubt, 127
Once on This Island, 9, 160
Once Removed, 82, 96
One Crazy Day or The Marriage of Figaro, 16
One Flew Over the Cuckoo's Nest, 8
One for the Money, 164
110 in the Shade, 89
One Inch Fellow, 154
One of the All-Time Greats, 167
One Shoe Off, 137
One Thousand Cranes, 55
1,000 Hours of Love, 157
One Tit, a Dyke & Gin, 143
Only Kidding!, 104
On the Bum, 122
On the Open Road, 60, 100, 139
On the Verge, 125, 175
On the Way Home, 114
On the Wings of the Hummingbird: Tales of Trinidad, 34
O, Pioneers!, 119, 160
Opium War, 102
Opium Wars, The, 96
Oracle Mountain, 71
Orestes, 54
Oriki of a Grasshopper, The, 155
Orphans, 151
Orphee, 11
Orpheus in Love, 37
Oscar and Bertha, 85
Othello, 44, 63, 98, 109
Other People's Money, 7, 8, 13, 22, 28, 50, 51, 58, 59, 83, 91, 95, 128, 146, 149, 159
Our Country's Good, 2, 36, 38, 68, 70, 83, 120, 144, 154, 170
Our Lady of the Alley, 114
Our Lady of the Tortilla, 73, 98, 160
Our Town, 6, 8, 34, 35, 89, 90, 114, 140, 165, 176
Out of Purgatory, 105
Outsiders, The, 55
Owners, 102
Oxford's Will, 43

P

Pacific Ocean, 96
Pack of Lies, A, 89
Pain of the Macho, 133
Paint Your Wagon, 61
Pal Joey, 69
Palm Court, 93
Panic in Paris, 69
Pantomine, 45
Parenteen Theater, 57
Park Your Car in Harvard Yard, 79
Partial Objects, 89
Party, 21
Party, The, 167
Passion, 3
Passion of Dracula, The, 4, 95, 123
Past Times, 74
Pastorela, La, 52
Pastorela '92: A Shepherds' Play, 105
Path With No Moccasins, 41

Patio/Porch, 18
Paul Robeson, 63, 125
P.C. Laundromat, The, 176
Peacetime, 31
Pearl, The, 142
Pecong, 114
Peephole, 59
Peg of My Heart, 22
Penny for the Guy, A, 60
Penny Serenade, 70
Pension para Senoritas, 128
Pentecost, 132
Perfect Balance, A, 30
Perfect For You, Doll, 36
Perfect Ganesh, A, 86
Pericles, 100, 139
Pericles, Prince of Tyre, 31, 79
Permanent Signal, A, 96
Persecution and Assassination of Jean-Paul Marat as Performed by the Inmates of the Asylum of Charenton Under the Direction of the Marquis de Sade, The, 64
Peter Pan, 5, 74, 114, 120, 160
Petomane, Le, 77
Phantom, 152
Philadelphia Story, The, 40, 143
Philanthropist, The, 82
Phoebe Joins the Circus, 35
Photo Op, 78
Piano Lesson, The, 8, 9, 50, 70, 89, 95, 114, 125, 137, 148
Pick Up Ax, 5
Picnic, 4
Picture of Dorian Gray, The, 172
Piece of My Heart, A, 85
Pilgrims of the Night, 162
Pill Hill, 66
Pill Hill Stories, The, 163
Pineapple Face, 157
Pinocchio, 6, 17, 101
Planet of the Mutagens, 96
Play, 41
Playboy of the West Indies, 80, 169
Playboy of the Western World, The, 109, 114, 154, 163
Playland, 8, 77, 86
Play of Lights, The, 116
Play Strindberg, 59
Play to Win, 161
Play With Repeats, 5
Pleasant Dreams, 162
Plucky and Spunky Show, The, 106, 115
Point of Debarkation, 79
Police Boys, 32
Popcorn and Peanut Butter, 67
Pope and the Witch, The, 9
Porcelain, 47
Pornographic Man, The, 111
Portraits in Shame, 67
Possessed—The Dracula Musical, 126
Postcards, 114
Power Pipes, 41
Powwow, 156
Praying For Laughter, 51
Preliminary Inquiry Into the Methods Used to Create and Maintain a Segregated Society, A, 21
Prelude to a Kiss, 4, 56, 67, 68, 81, 106, 117, 120, 121, 123, 145, 160, 164
Pretty Fire, 86
Pretty Polly, 131
Price, The, 29, 49, 86, 94, 125, 131
Prince of Madness, The, 41, 79
Princess and the Pea, The, 17, 26
Private Lives, 24, 95, 119
Pro Game, 106
Promise, The, 145
Prospect, 52
Psycho Beach Party, 143
Pterodactyls, 167
Puddin 'n Pete, 61
Puerto Rico: Encanto y Cancion, 128
Pump Boys and Dinettes, 46, 59, 89, 98, 150, 151, 168
Punch!, 49
Punch Me in the Stomach, 78, 102
Puntila and Matti, 104
Puppetmaster of Lodz, The, 27, 170
Purlie, 148
Purple Hearts, 92
Putana: A Romance, La, 114
Putting Flesh Back on the Bones, 51
Putting It Together, 86
Puttin' on the Ritz, 94
Pygmalion, 129

Q

Quarks, 41
Quarrel of Sparrows, A, 40
Quartermaine's Terms, 4, 25
Queen and the Rebels, The, 31
Queen's Garden, The, 134
Queer Thinking, 71
Quiet Little Wedding, A, 50
Quilters, 22
Quilting Circle, The, 96
Quorum, 162

R

Rabbit Foot, The, 70
Radio Gals, 18
Rags, 43
Rain Always Falls, The, 157
Rainbow Gave You Birth, The, 1
Rainmaker, The, 158
Raisin in the Sun, A, 6, 91, 114, 133
Rajeckas & Intraub, 91
Ramona Quimby, 34, 136
Rapunzel, 161
Rash Acts, 71, 157
Rat's Mass, A, 41
Rats!! The Pied Piper of Hamlin, 129
Real Inspector Hound, The, 131
Realists, The, 114
Reality: Friend or Foe?, 71
Real Life, 96
Real Women Have Curves, 19, 64
Reasons to Live, 85
Recital of the Bird, The, 41

Reckless, 18, 33, 58, 66, 121
Recruiting Officer, The, 83
Red Badge of Courage, The, 44, 72
Red Diaper Baby, 137
Red Fox and Second Hangin', 131
Red Scare on Sunset, 143
Red She Said, 143
Red Sneaks, The, 44
Redwood Curtain, 37, 105, 116, 136
Redwood Curtain: The Scar Tissue Mystery Trilogy, 49
Rehearsal for the Apocalypse, 127
Reincarnation of Jamie Brown, The, 96
Reluctant Dragon, The, 30, 34, 67, 158
Remember or Repeat, 135
Remembrance, 19, 31
Reno Once Removed, 61
Restoration, 109
Resurrections in the Season of the Longest Drought, 96
Return of Kate Shelley, The, 84
Return of the Raven and Other Stories, The, 157
Revenge of Space Pandas, 67
Revengers' Comedies, Parts I & II, The, 2
Rev. Tartuffe: A Divine Musical, 163
Rez Sisters, The, 115
Rhinoceros, 162
Richard II, 6, 87, 139, 166
Richard III, 110
Richest Dead Man Alive, The, 172
Rikki Tikki Tavi, 128
Ring Around the Rosie..., 93
Ripe Conditions, 124, 145, 166
Rising Sun, Falling Star, 157
Rivalry of Dolls, 156
Riverboatin', 84
River Book, The, 96
River's Edge, 71
Riverview, 60
Road Not Taken, The, 49
Roadside, 153
Road to Mecca, The, 72
Road to Nirvana, 93, 147, 177
Robert Johnson: Trick the Devil, 97
Roca, La, 157
Rock, 143
Rock 'N' Roles From William Shakespeare, 4
Rocky and Bullwinkle, 52
Rodgers and..., 91
Rodgers & Hart, 129
Role Play, 111
Roll of Thunder, Hear My Cry, 136
Roman Fever, 114
Romance Concerto, 96
Romance/Romance, 70, 99
Romeo and Juliet, 23, 26, 30, 92, 102, 106, 141
Romeo and Juliet and Julius Caesar...Nice Play, Shakespeare, 139
Rosa Parks and the Montgomery Bus Boycott, 72
Rosen by Any Other Name, A, 160
Rosencrantz and Guildenstern Are

Dead, 150
Rose Quartet, The, 37
Rose Tattoo, The, 21, 50
Rothschilds, The, 29
Rough Crossing, 63, 92
Round and Round the Garden, 89
Rover, The, 141
Royal Family, The, 165
Royal Hunt of the Sun, The, 160
Rubber Heat, 157
Ruby's Bucket of Blood, 134
Rumors, 89, 135, 151, 168
Rumpelstiltskin, 52, 145
Running for Blood No. 3, 96
Rushing Waters, 43, 96

S

Sabina, 96
Sacred Rhythms, 96
Safe Place, A, 142
Saga of the Famous Mrs. Grimes, The, 96
Saint Joan, 14, 21, 141, 154
Saint Joan of the Stockyards, 21, 74, 175
Salt Lake Salt Lake, 134
Samuel's Major Problems, 108
Sanctuary, 96
Sandbox, The, 138
Sand Mountain, 132
Santa's Adventure in the Merrywood Mega Mall, 26
Santa's Secret, 29
Sarah and Abraham, 58
Savages, 129
Say Zebra, 79
Scalding Steam & Lonesome Rails, 153
Scapin, 39, 155
Scaramouche, 159
Scarlet Letters, The, 41
Scarlet Letter, The, 139
Scars and Stripes, 145
Scenes From an Execution, 87
School Alley, 163
School for Husbands, The, 105
School for Scandal, The, 55
School for Wives, The, 15, 120
Scotland Road, 36, 107
Scott and Zelda: The Beautiful Fools, 62
Scrub, The, 122
Scully and Royce, 51
Scum City, 62
Seagull, The, 11, 64, 97, 117, 164
Sea Horse, The, 37
Sea Marks, 16, 146, 174
Search for Signs of Intelligent Life in the Universe, The, 53, 89, 123
Seascape, 55
Seasons Greetings, 109
Secret Garden, The, 17, 67, 101, 161
Secret History of the Future, The, 72
Secrets to Square Dancing, 176
Separation, 36, 58
Serenading Louie, 33
Serious Money, 79

Servant of Two Masters, The, 11, 32, 67
17 Black, 107
17 Days, 43
Seventy Scenes of Halloween, 38
Sex, Drugs, Rock & Roll, 177
Shadowlands, 2, 6, 106, 120, 123, 125, 144
Shakespeare Circle, The, 169
Shakespeare's Greatest Hits, 139
Shakin' the Mess Outta Misery, 5, 18, 114, 143, 148, 160
Shatterhand Massecree, 78
Shayna Maidel, A, 86, 99, 121, 158
Shear Madness, 177
Sheila's Day, 11
She'll Find Her Way Home, 76
She Loves Me, 131
Sherlock's Last Case, 101
She Stoops to Conquer, 16
Shine!, 114
Shirley Valentine, 12, 28, 31, 36, 65, 72, 89, 90, 95, 105, 113, 138, 146, 158, 168, 175, 177
Shmulnik's Waltz, 75, 124
Shoeman, 96
Shooting Simone, 4
Shooting Star, 84
Show and Tell, 129
Showbiz, 172
Show Host, The, 166
Show Me Where the Good Times Are, 76, 106
Show-off, The, 131
Sicilian Wife, The, 114
Side by Side by Sondheim, 175
Sight Retrieved, 96
Sight Unseen, 85, 129, 143
Silence, Cunning, Exile, 11
Simpatico, 47
Simply Maria, 52
Sin, 96
Sincerity Forever, 150
Sing For Your Supper, 37
Sins of the Father, 94
Sirens, The, 96
Sister Mary Ignatius Explains It All for You, 177
Sisters, 76
Sisters Rosensweig, The, 80
Sisters, Wives and Daughters, 63
Six Degrees of Separation, 129
Six Women with Brain Death or Expiring Minds Want to Know, 18, 67, 121, 176
Skin of Our Teeth, The, 15, 23, 61, 75
Skirting the Issues, 173
Slapstick, 49
Sleeping Beauty, 17, 29, 101
Sleuth, 69, 170
Slip of the Tongue, A, 147
Slow Dance on the Killing Ground, 45, 101
Small Delegation, A, 116
Small Domestic Acts, 21
Smaller Place, A, 124
Small Family Business, A, 85
Smalltown Gals, 157
Small Town Triumphs, 62

Small World, A, 15
Smile Orange, 166
Smiling Through, 113
Smoke on the Mountain, 18, 36, 37, 113, 159
Snakebit, 127
Snake Talk, 20
Snow Ball, The, 69
Snowflake, 158
Snowflake Avalanche, The, 64
Snow Queen, The, 30, 170
Soap Scum, 107
Social Work: An Election Year Fantasy, 41
Soldier's Play, A, 148
Solemn Oaths and Looney Tunes, 57
So Long On Lonely Street, 9
So Many Words, 144
Some Americans Abroad, 121
Some Enchanted Evening, 9
Some Sweet Day, 62
Some Things You Need to Know Before the World Ends (A Final Evening with the Illuminati), 53, 124
Sometimes We Need a Story More Than Food, 20, 23
Song of Grendelyn, The, 1
Song of Jacob Zulu, The, 147
Songs Lucifer Sang, 157
Songs of War, The, 94
Sonic Disturbance, 41
Son of Fire, 21
Sons of Don Juan, 19
Sophistry, 122
Sound and the Fury, The, 102
Sound Fields, 106
South of the Mountain, 131
South Pacific, 46, 129
Spain, 157
Speed-the-Plow, 24, 35, 125, 133
Spic-O-Rama, 61
Spiele '36 or the Fourth Medal, 166
Spike Heels, 137
Spine, 58
Spinning Into Blue, 166
Spinning Top, The, 107
Spirit Warrior's Dream, The, 139
Spoon River Anthology, 67
Spunk, 24, 40, 47, 61, 72, 76, 87, 110, 116, 134, 137, 150
Squaring the Circle, 156
Stand-Up Tragedy, 3
Stanton's Garage, 4
Stardust, 129
Starting Out Small, 84
Statements After an Arrest Under the Immorality Act, 155
State of the Art Heart, 27
State Prisoners, 1
States of Independence, 11
Steal Away, 169
Stealing the Scene, 96
Steel Magnolias, 46, 95, 174
Step on a Crack, 22
Still Life, 76
Stonewall Country, 153
Stop the World—I Want to Get Off, 30

Stories About the Old Days, 148
Stories from the Nerve Bible, 11
Straight Arrows, 151
Straight Man, 107
Strange Feet, 54
Streetcar Named Desire, A, 8, 47, 83
Strength and Indifference of the Snow, The, 162
Strictly Dishonorable, 116
Strindberg In Hollywood, 173
Stronger, The, 15
Stuart Sherman's 18th Spectacle, 157
Stuffed Puppet, 157
Stump the Host, 79
Stupid Kids, 96
S2, 111
Sub Rosa, 7
Substance of Fire, The, 19, 31, 42, 47, 80, 85, 87, 125, 137
Succulence, 96
Suddenly Last Summer, 169
Suds, 4
Sullivan and Gilbert, 118
Sum of Us, The, 31, 56, 60, 119, 124, 150, 168
Summer and Smoke, 15
Summer Remembered, A, 147
Sunday in the Park with George, 95
Sunset Gang, The, 75
Sunsets and Glories, 2
Sunshine Playlot, 46
Survivor: A Cambodian Odyssey, The, 89
Svengali, 19
Swan, The, 10, 77, 79, 128, 165
Sweeney Todd, 14, 160
Sweet & Hot, 19, 25, 77, 88
Sweet By 'n' By, The, 170
Sweet Justice, 42
Sweet 'N' Hot in Harlem, 149
Sword in the Stone, The, 18, 19

T

Take to the Bed, 157
Taking Control, 176
Taking Steps, 9, 47, 145, 146, 159
Talented Tenth, The, 45, 142
Tale of a Tiger, The, 139
Tale of Cymbeline, 153
Tale of Two Cities, A, 134, 145, 171
Tales From Hollywood, 78
Tales from the Arabian Nights, 72
Tales From the Vienna Woods, 4
Tales of a Fourth Grade Nothing, 46, 145
Tales of Brer Rabbit, 30
Tales of the Grotesque, 35, 67
Tales of the Lost Formicans, 145
Tales of Tinseltown, 42
Talking Bones, 46
Talking With, 56
Talk-Story, 160
Tall and the Short of It, The, 91
Talley's Folly, 14, 89, 114
Tall Tales and Small People, 67
Taming of the Shrew, The, 27, 30, 97, 98, 139, 140

INDEX OF TITLES

Tango & Folklore Argentino 1992, 152
Tango & Folklore Argentino 1993, 152
Tango Pasion, 42
Tania, 11
Tapdancer, 71
Tartuffe, 50, 66, 69, 121, 165, 177
Tatterhood, 52
Tavern, The, 106
T Bone N Weasel, 32, 49
Tea, 150
Tears of Rage, 2, 79
Teen Street, 57
Telegram from Heaven, A, 79
Tempest, The, 14, 64, 69, 91
Temptation, 38
10th Festival of New Plays, 41
Territorial Christmas Carol, A, 123
Testimony, 97
Texas Romance, A, 80
Texts for Nothing, 100
That Serious He-Man Ball, 55, 103
Theatre Grottesco, 165
Theatre of the Air, 2
Theda Bara and the Frontier Rabbi, 76
Theme and Variations, 113, 160
Therese Raquin, 171
They Shoot Horses, Don't They?, 50
Thimble of Smoke, A, 107
Thin Air, 96
Things That Break, 96
This Old Man Came Rolling Home, 166
Those Sweet Caresses, 142
Those the River Keeps, 12
Thousand Cranes, A, 129
Three Card Monte and The Royal Flush, 51
Three Cuckolds, The, 5
3 Drops of Blood, 153
Three Hotels, 23, 37
Three Little Pigs, 26, 158
Three Little Sisters, The, 156
Three Men on a Horse, 58
Threepenny Opera, The, 170
Three Sisters, The, 59, 88, 119
Through the Leaves, 32
Through the Looking Glass, 34
Through the Wheat, 62
Thunder: Perfect Mind, 157
Ties That Bind, 126
Time and Again, 108
Time Flies When You're Alive, 102
Time Machine, The, 19
Time of your Life, The, 15
Time on Fire, 137
Times Square Angel, 156, 157
Timon of Athens, 90, 165
Tintypes, 60, 132, 145
Tiny Tim is Dead, 1, 117, 138
'Tis Pity She's a Whore, 100
Toby Show, A, 6
Today, 76
To Distraction, 79
Tod, the Boy, Tod, 64
Tofa Samoa, 67
To Grandmother's House We Go, 43

Toilet, The, 27
To Kill a Mockingbird, 46, 50, 101
Tomfoolery, 43
Tom Sawyer, 30, 161
To My Chagrin, 96
Too Short to be a Rockette, 42
Tortoise and the Hare, The, 145
Touch of the Poet, A, 82
Tough Call, 107
Tough Love, 33
Toute Une Nuit, 162
Toymaker's Apprentice, The, 17
Toys in the Attic, 109
Toy Theater Festival, 157
Toy Truck, The, 43
Trafficking in Broken Hearts, 21
Trail of Tears, 18, 19
Traps, 3, 102
Trap, The, 155
Travelling Jekyll and Hyde Show, The, 129
Travesties, 59
Treasure Island, 34
Trials of Brother Jero, The, 148
Trinidad Sisters, 15
Triple Exposure, 172
Triumph of Love, The, 88
Troilus and Cressida, 139, 141
Trojan Women, The, 146
Tropical Pickle, The, 126
Trouble, 85
True West, 10, 43, 99
Truly Remarkable Turkey Drive of 1912, The, 49
Trust, 2
Truus Bronkhorst, 157
Tuesday, 38
Twelfth Night, 60, 72, 89, 110, 118, 121, 133, 136, 139, 143, 152, 164, 170
21A, 5
Twilight: Los Angeles, 1992, 87
2, 170
Two, 147
2 X 5 X 4, 91
Two by Two, 29
Two Gentlemen of Verona, 105, 139
Two Men on a Roof, 30
Two Rooms, 165
Two Shakespearean Actors, 80
2-2-Tango, 150
Two Trains Running, 61

U

Ugly Duckling, The, 17, 30, 55
Ulysses, 163
Uncertainty, 50
Unchanging Love, 51, 125
Uncle Vanya, 63, 89, 119, 120
Under African Skies, 28
Underground, 78
Under Milk Wood, 75
Undesirable Elements, 118
Undiscovered Country, 69
Unexpected Universe, 58
Unfinished Stories, 87
Universal Wolf, The, 96
Unquestioned Integrity: The Hill/

Thomas Hearings, 85
Unseen Hand, The, 27
Upward Path to Ignorance, The, 157

V

Valentine Touch, The, 37
Valley of the Human Spirit, The, 107
Vanek Plays, The, 75
Van Gogh Gallery, The, 155
Vanquished by Voodoo, 54
Velveteen Rabbit, The, 34, 35, 52, 89, 136, 161
Venetian Fever, 157
Very Nice Neighborhood, A, 117
Victims, 110
View from the Bridge, A, 65, 92, 128
Villains, 92
Vincent, 90
Virgen del Tedeyac, La, 52
Virginia, 139
Virgin Molly, The, 171
Virtus, 104, 151
Visit, The, 15, 28, 131, 170
Vital Signs, 164
Vivisections From the Blown Mind, 138
Voice of the Prairie, The, 106, 151
Voices of Christmas, 64
Voir Dire, 96
Volare, 41, 78
Volpone, 24
Voodoo Nickel, 107
Voyage of Mary C, The, 149
Voyage of the Red Hat, The, 129
Vulture Speaks, The, 163

W

Waiting for Godot, 28, 83, 138, 140, 144, 154
Waiting for the Parade, 43, 115
Waiting Room, The, 171
Wait Until Dark, 158
Walk Around the Block, 156
Walk in the Woods, A, 95, 159
Walt Whitman, 168
War and Peace, 156
Warhol In Hell, 157
War in Heaven, The, 138
Warrior, 74
Warrior Ant, Part 7C, The Ma Ha Bhar Ant A, The, 83
Wasteland, 1
Watch Your Back, 85
Watermelon Rinds, 4
Watermotions, 156
Way of the World, The, 15, 69
We All Fall Down, 163
Weather Report, 156
Weldon Rising, 96
Wenceslas Square, 8
West Memphis Mojo, 159
West Side Story, 66, 112
What a Man Weighs, 96
What Fools These Mortals Be, 5

What is Art?, 60
What Part Will I Play, 29
What the Butler Saw, 77
What to Say, 122
What You Will, 146
When I Was A Girl, I Used to Scream and Shout, 149, 168
When Night is Near, 96
When She Danced, 171
When the Bough Breaks, 43
When the Nightingale Sings, 38
When We Are Married, 136
When You're Smiling, 162
Whick Wack, 84
Whispers of the Olde World, 22
Whistling Girls & Crowing Hens, 71
White as Snow, Red as Blood, 52
White Devil, The, 110
White Disabled Talent, 7
White Liars, 131
White Money, 89, 143
White Oak, 107
White Sails, Dark Seas: The Voyages of Columbus, 26
White Whore and The Bit Player, The, 79
Who Causes the Darkness, 64
Who Collects the Pain?, 157
Who's Afraid of Virginia Woolf?, 16, 66, 121, 167
Whosis, 163
Who's Tommy, The, 77
Why We Have a Body, 85
Widow's Best Friend, The, 18, 29
Wild Swans, The, 107
Wiley and the Hairy Man, 22
Will and Bart Show, The, 171
Willi, 2, 16
Willie and Esther, 45, 114, 132
Will Power on Tour, 139
Will Rogers' U.S.A., 57
Will Stutts' Tallulah!, 168
Will, The, 96
Wind in the Willows, The, 8, 22, 26, 158
Windshook, 96
Wings, 61, 100
Winnie the Pooh, 44, 55, 145, 158
Winter's Tale: An Interstate Adventure, The, 43
Winter's Tale, The, 64, 105
Wise Men of Chelm, The, 109
Wishbone, 71
Witch of Blackbird Pond, The, 17
Wizard of Hip, The, 76, 114, 150, 163
Wizard of Oz, The, 101, 112
Wizards of Quiz, The, 94
Wolf at the Door, 53
Wolf Child: The Correction of Joseph, 44
Wolf-Man, 50
Woman Called Truth, A, 52, 55, 109
Woman in Mind, 59, 98, 129, 143
WOMBmanWARs, 79
Women of Bakkhos, 27
Women of Troy, The, 46
Women of Will, 138
Women, The, 3, 86, 134, 149

Women Without Men, 25
Wonderful Ice Cream Suit, The, 33
Wonderful Life, A, 15, 89, 152
Wonderful World of Oz, The, 34
Woodman and the Goblins, The, 114
Woody Guthrie's American Song, 24, 61, 89, 135
Words and Works of Dr. Martin Luther King, Jr., 1
Words Divine, 73
Working Magic, 166
Workin' Texas, 177
World of Mother Goose, The, 17
Woyzeck, 100
Wreck of the Good Ship "Humboldt", The, 49
Wrinkle in Time, A, 33
Writing Is...Child's Play, 35
Wrong Mistake, The, 79
Wuthering Heights, 106

X

XXX Love Act, 85

Y

Year of My Mothers Birth, The, 96
Year of Pilgrimage, 143
Years, The, 86
Yellow Boat, The, 35
Yerma, 15, 72
Yo Me Bajo en la Prozima. Y Usted?, 128
You Can't Take It With You, 28, 29, 40, 63, 69, 95
You Could Be Home By Now, 100, 173
Young Cherokee, 18, 19
Young Rube, 129
Your Children: The Testimony of Charles Manson, 155
Your Home in the West, 147
Yours, Anne, 101
You Send Me, 107
You, The Night & The Music, 3
You're a Good Man, Charlie Brown, 46
Yunus, 78
Y York: No Props, 96

Z

Zara Spook and Other Lures, 58
Zion, 97
Zora Neale Hurston, 57, 148, 163
Zorro, 55

ABOUT TCG

Theatre Communications Group is the national organization for the American theatre. Since its founding in 1961, TCG has provided a national forum and communications network for a field that is as aesthetically diverse as it is geographically widespread, developing a unique and comprehensive support system that addresses the artistic, management and governance concerns of the theatre companies and individual artists that collectively represent our "national theatre."

TCG's mission is to celebrate and inspire excellence in the artistry of theatre in America. To carry out this mission, TCG serves theatre artists and nonprofit professional theatre organizations by: recognizing and encouraging artistic diversity; providing a forum for the open and critical examination of issues, standards and values; fostering interaction among theatre professionals; collecting, analyzing and disseminating information within the profession and to others interested in, and influential to, the health of the field; and serving as the principal advocate for America's nonprofit professional theatre.

TCG's centralized services facilitate the work of thousands of actors, artistic and managing directors, playwrights, literary managers, directors, designers, trustees and administrative personnel, as well as a constituency of more than 300 theatre institutions across the country that present performances to a combined annual attendance of more than 16 million. TCG's chief programs include grants, fellowships and awards to theatre artists and institutions; conferences, workshops and roundtables; government affairs; surveys and research; a national arts employment bulletin; and a publications program that produces a line of books and periodicals, including plays and anthologies, resource and reference books, works of theory and criticism, and the monthly magazine, *American Theatre*.

THEATRE COMMUNICATIONS GROUP, INC.

Peter Zeisler, Executive Director
Lindy Zesch, Deputy Director

Board of Directors

Zelda Fichandler, *President*
Ricardo Khan, Vice *President*
William P. Wingate, *Treasurer*
Jaan W. Whitehead, *Secretary*

Steven J. Albert, *Managing Director*
    Hartford Stage Company, Hartford, Conn.
Benny Sato Ambush, *Associate Artistic Director*
    American Conservatory Theater, San Francisco, Calif.
André Bishop, *Artistic Director*
    Lincoln Center Theater, New York, N.Y.
Tim Bond, *Artistic Director*
    The Group: Seattle's MultiCultural Theatre, Seattle, Wash.
Zelda Fichandler, *Artistic Director*
    The Acting Company, New York, N.Y.
Philip Kan Gotanda, *Playwright*
Amlin Gray, *Playwright/Translator*
Gregory A. Hicks, *Trustee*
    Intiman Theatre Company, Seattle, Wash.
Allen Lee Hughes, *Lighting Designer*
Dana Ivey, *Actor*
Marsha Jackson, *Co-Artistic/Managing Director*
    Jomandi Productions, Atlanta, Ga.
Ricardo Khan, *Artistic Director*
    Crossroads Theatre Company, New Brunswick, N.J.
Heidi Landesman, *Scenic Designer/Producer*
Eduardo Machado, *Playwright*
Ruth Mayleas, *Advisor, International Culture Programs*
    Ford Foundation, New York, N.Y.
Timothy J. McClimon, *Vice President, International Programs*
    AT&T Foundation, New York, N.Y.
Charles L. Mee, Jr., *Playwright/Historian*
Victoria Nolan, *Managing Director*
    Yale Repertory Theatre, New Haven, Conn.
Bill Rauch, *Artistic Director*
    Cornerstone Theater Company, Los Angeles, Calif.
Christopher Reeve, *Actor*
Roche Schulfer, *Producing Director*
    Goodman Theatre, Chicago, Ill.
Anna Deavere Smith, *Actor/Playwright*
Molly Smith, *Artistic Director*
    Perseverance Theatre, Douglas, Ala.
Jeff Steitzer, *Artistic Director*
    A Contemporary Theatre, Seattle, Wash.
Jose Luis Valenzuela, *Director, Latino Theatre Initiative*
    Mark Taper Forum, Los Angeles, Calif.
Jaan W. Whitehead, *Trustee*
    The Acting Company, New York, N.Y.
William P. Wingate, *Vice President*
    National Arts Stabilization Fund, New York, N.Y.
Peter Zeisler, *Executive Director*
    Theatre Communications Group